SALES MANAGEMENT

Robert F. Hartley
CLEVELAND STATE UNIVERSITY

Merrill Publishing Company
A Bell & Howell Information Company
Columbus • Toronto • London • Melbourne

Published by Merrill Publishing Company
A Bell & Howell Information Company
Columbus, Ohio 43216

This book was set in Meridien.

Administrative Editor: Pamela B. Kusma
Production Coordinator: Molly Kyle
Cover Designer: Brian Deep
Text Designer: Connie Young

A previous edition of this book was published by Houghton Mifflin.

Library of Congress Catalog Card Number: 88-60719
International Standard Book Number: 0-675-20747-9
Printed in the United States of America
1 2 3 4 5 6 7 8 9—92 91 90 89

Preface

Sales management is an exciting subject—a pleasure to teach and intriguing and satisfying to study. Sales management is real, it is vital, and something that students can easily relate to. In the general field of marketing, selling and sales management are, after all, where the action is.

This book covers the traditional topics of sales management as well as areas of emerging importance. It is career-oriented, with a strong commitment to stimulating the reader's personal involvement. Numerous examples and exercises, within and at ends of chapters, invite the reader to place himself or herself in a particular situation, analyze it, arrive at a decision, and assess the probable consequences—in other words, to be both critical and creative. In addition, we describe the more important tools of sales management and offer the student the opportunity to get involved with them. After just a few years, most sales representatives make the important next step into sales management. Many will be able to put these tools to use quickly and may also want to refer back to them months and years later.

During the many years I have taught sales management, I have also stressed the real need to go beyond analytical and quantitative tools. Successful managers must be people-oriented, attuned to people problems and challenges. The mark of any successful manager is how much one can accomplish through people; the more successful managers do a better job of supervising, motivating, and even inspiring. While such things cannot really be learned from a textbook, we can at least discuss people problems and how to resolve them. In addition to the people problems, the real-life cases at the ends of chapters have been classroom tested. They provoke lively discussion, and the questions are useful both in class and as homework assignments.

Selling and sales management are evolving in several directions, and we have tried to take this fully into account. In particular, we are seeing more and more women successfully enter sales and sales management. Some specifics are described in Chapter 1. (Throughout the book, the term *salesperson* is used far more than the traditional *salesman*, and *sales manager* should be understood to be either male or female.) More sophisticated tools and techniques of planning and control are being used today, because of both the availability of the computer, which offers prompt and voluminous data feedback, and the fact that better educated and highly trained people are assuming leadership positions in this field. Finally, in today's social and governmental environment, we must give more attention to legal and ethical considerations than ever before.

Since virtually all students will reach sales management through success as sales representatives, the first three chapters deal with the personal selling function and effective selling techniques. Not the least of the topics in this section is that of time management—how to free up the most time for face-to-face selling. And while telemarketing is becoming widely used, most important sales are still closed by personal contacts, with individual customers or buying committees.

The rest of the book is organized by traditional management functions: planning sales efforts, organizing and staffing, directing sales efforts, and controlling sales efforts. Although every manager is involved with these functions, sales management embraces them in some distinctive ways. That many sales forces are geographically scattered, for example, makes the jobs of planning, directing, and controlling much more challenging than where face-to-face interaction with colleagues and subordinates is the rule.

Particularly valuable to the manager-to-be is the chapter on supervision, which reflects my conviction of the importance of good personal interaction for effective management. Disciplining, motivating, and delegating deserve special attention.

Chapter 15, Implementing Effective Distributor–Customer Relations, addresses a growing problem. Busy organizations are often tempted to give short shrift to customer service and satisfaction because of supposedly more important concerns. As a recent *Wall Street Journal* article notes:

> The quality of much service today, like the quality of many manufactured goods 15 years ago, stinks. When you do encounter the rare, high-quality service, the experience stands in stark and lonely contrast to the undifferentiated mass of miserable service.*

This situation makes for great vulnerability to competition—and great opportunity. It is time that we expose managers-to-be to the primary importance of customer relations and how to enhance this attitude throughout their organizations.

During my fourteen years in business, many individuals and firms have provided practical and relevant materials for this text, but my greatest debt is to my students, who have made my classes a mutual learning experience. Academic colleagues have also made important suggestions for the book. In particular, I want to acknowledge the help of Donald W. Scotton, my esteemed former colleague at Cleveland State University, and to Ram Rao and Jan

---

*Robert E. Kelley, "Poorly Served Employees Serve Customers Just as Poorly," *Wall Street Journal*, October 12, 1987, p. 18.

Muczyk, also at CSU. I appreciate the suggestions of Paul Cretien at Baylor, especially regarding the quantitative material, and his intriguing simulation. I am also grateful to Gene Holland, Columbia Basin College; Joyce Graham, University of Wisconsin-Eau Claire; Dr. Jim Moore, Southern Illinois University; Malcolm Morris, University of Oklahoma; Kerry Gatlin, Henderson State University; Lynn Loudenback, New Mexico State University; Joe Bellizzi, Kansas State University; H. Reed Muller, Salisbury State College; Richard Bennington, High Point College; and Neil Ford, University of Wisconsin-Madison, for their detailed and thoughtful analyses of the manuscript at various stages of its development. And to my editors at Merrill, Pam Kusma and Tim McEwen, thank you for your kind suggestions and your confidence.

R. F. H.

Contents

PART I
PERSONAL SELLING   1

Chapter 1
Introduction to Selling and Sales Management   2

How Personal Selling Relates to Marketing   4
How Important Is Personal Selling?   5
What Sales Management Is All About   8
Career Opportunities in Selling and Sales Management   11
What It Takes to be a Sales Manager   15
Women in Sales and Sales Management   17

Chapter 2
Fundamentals of Selling   20

Types of Selling Jobs   22
What Salespeople Do Besides Selling   25
What Makes for Success in Sales?   27
Trends in Selling   30
Making the Transition from Selling to Managing   34

Chapter 3
Effective Selling Techniques   42

The Steps to Effective Selling   44
Applying the Behavioral Sciences to the Sales Process   53
How to Develop and Maintain Good Customer Relations   55
Toward Better Time Management   57

PART II
PLANNING SALES EFFORTS   65

Chapter 4
The Planning Process and Strategic Planning   66

The Concept of Planning   68
Types of Planning   70
Why Plan?   71
Strategic Planning and the Planning Process   71
Translating Plans into Operations   78
Planning at the Sales Manager Level   80
The Need for Market Information in Planning   84

Chapter 5
Analyzing the Market: Assessing Potential   92

Why Determine Market Potential?   94
Relationship of Market Potential to Other Planning Factors   94
How to Assess Market and Sales Potential   96
Sources of Data   100
Using Market Potential Measures   109
Constraints on Realizing Full Potential   116

Chapter 6
Forecasting Sales   122

Importance of Forecasting   124
Factors Affecting Sales   124
Procedure for Forecasting   127
Forecasting Techniques   128
Evaluation of Forecasting Techniques   140
Coping with Forecasting Uncertainties for New Products or Changing
      Conditions   145
Criteria for Effective Forecasting   146

Chapter 7
Budgeting the Sales Efforts   156

Reasons for Budgets   158
Types of Budgets   160
Procedure of Budgeting   162
Requirements for Successful Budgeting   168
Cautions in Budgeting   171

PART III
ORGANIZING AND STAFFING 179

Chapter 8
Organizing the Sales Efforts 180

Essentials of Organizing 182
Transition of Organizations 183
Issues in Organizing Sales 185
Variations in Organizational Structure 194
Organization of Field Sales 199
The Individual in the Organization 200

Chapter 9
Assembling the Staff: Recruiting and Selecting 210

Role and Importance of Staffing 212
Determining Specific Requirements for the Sales Force 212
Recruiting 222
Selection of the Sales Force 227

Chapter 10
Deploying the Staff Through Time and Territorial Assignments 250

Reasons for Establishing Sales Territories 252
Guidelines for Territory Decisions 253
Procedure for Dividing Territories 256
Revising Sales Territories 270
Cautions in Administering Territories 272
Time Management—Routing and Scheduling 273

Chapter 11
Deploying the Staff Through Quotas 284

Definition of a Quota 286
Uses of Quotas 286
Types of Quotas 287
Characteristics of a Good Quota 290
Developing the Quota 291
Administering the Quota 297

PART IV
IMPLEMENTING SALES EFFORTS   305

Chapter 12
Training for Selling Effectiveness   306

Types of Sales Training   308
Benefits of Training   308
Determining the Scope of the Training   311
Selecting Topics   313
Methods and Procedures   317
Administering the Training Program   320
Cautions in Planning and Executing Training Programs   328

Chapter 13
Directing and Motivating Through Compensation   336

Morale and Motivation   338
Characteristics of a Good Compensation Plan   340
Should the Present Plan Be Revised?   343
Developing a Compensation Plan   344
Types of Compensation Plans   348
Fringe Benefits   355
Compensation Problems   356
Selling Expenses   359

Chapter 14
Directing and Motivating Through Supervision   372

Ingredients of Supervision   374
How Closely Should You Supervise?   383
Methods of Supervision   384
Problems in Supervision   389
Use of Incentives   394

Chapter 15
Implementing Effective Distributor–Customer
Relations   408

Channel Conflict   410
Building Loyalty   410
Developing Dealer Push   415
Cementing Customer Relations with Good Customer Service   421
Measuring Customer Satisfaction   429
Abuses of Service   431

PART V
CONTROLLING SALES EFFORTS **441**

Chapter 16
Controlling Through Analyzing Overall Sales Performance **442**

Nature of Control   444
Measures of Overall Marketing Performance   446
Sales Analysis   447
Market Share Analysis   454

Chapter 17
Controlling Through Analyzing Marketing Costs and by the Marketing Audit **468**

Nature of a Marketing Cost Analysis   470
Procedure for Analyzing Marketing Costs   472
Problems Involved in Analyzing Marketing Costs   476
Areas for Corrective Action   479
The Marketing Audit   484

Chapter 18
Controlling Through Evaluating Individual Performance **494**

Benefits of Individual Performance Evaluation   496
Problems in Evaluating Performance   498
How Complex Should the Evaluation Procedure Be?   500
Supervisory Guidelines for Evaluating Personnel   501
Procedure for Evaluating Performance   503
Management by Objectives   521

Chapter 19
Handling Legal and Ethical Considerations **534**

Government Regulation   536
Ethical Considerations   541
Incentives for Questionable Practices   544
Ethical Issues Facing Sales Managers   545
A Sales Manager's Code of Conduct   548

INDEX   557

PART I
PERSONAL SELLING

CHAPTER 1
Introduction to Selling and Sales Management

CHAPTER 2
Fundamentals of Selling

CHAPTER 3
Effective Selling Techniques

CHAPTER 1
Introduction to Selling and Sales Management

CHAPTER PERSPECTIVE

Sales management by its very nature is career oriented. We will be talking about real-world action, not theories or vague concepts. You will learn tools and techniques—estimating market and sales potentials, planning strategic moves, evaluating performance—to help you do a better job and, we hope, to advance quickly in your career path.

After all, sales provides most of the entry opportunities found in business, or any other career field. Millions of young people start out in sales and from there move into a wide variety of management and staff positions. So, as you develop your selling skills, you can look forward to different challenges and accomplishments as they lead you into management.

Sales management offers a frequently used route to upper-level executive positions. Furthermore, it permits both men and women more freedom, more room for initiative, and greater financial rewards than almost any other career field. Why? Because

selling is paramount to any firm. Without the revenues generated by sales, there is no need for other activities and other employees—without earnings, a business cannot exist. It is only reasonable that the most vital aspect of a business will attract the most attention, provide the greatest opportunities, and pay the highest rewards.

In teaching you about sales management, I want to go beyond merely examining analytical and evaluative tools. We will be looking also at the human side of business, the importance of the manager's personality, and the crucial ability of a manager to deal effectively with people at all levels. A manager's success relates directly to how much he can accomplish through subordinates—individuals with different drives, needs, and motivations. Subordinates should never be considered merely pins on a map of sales territories. Therein lies at once the great challenge and opportunity of management.

CHAPTER OBJECTIVES

☐ Know how personal selling relates to the complete marketing function.
☐ Realize the importance of personal selling to business.
☐ Understand the role of the sales manager and how management principles apply to the job.
☐ Recognize and appreciate how sales management differs from other management positions.
☐ Become aware of the different levels of sales managers and the hierarchical progression in responsibilities.
☐ Become apprised of the significant career opportunities in selling and sales management, as well as the inevitable drawbacks.
☐ Know what it takes to be a successful sales manager.
☐ Finally, achieve a better understanding of the opportunities for women and minorities in selling and sales management.

HOW PERSONAL SELLING RELATES TO MARKETING

Personal selling is part of the marketing function of a business and constitutes one of those activities that together are commonly called the *marketing mix.* The components of the marketing mix are

Products and product features

Prices

Distribution channels

Promotion

Personal selling is part of "promotion" and is complemented by advertising and sales promotion. Figure 1.1 depicts the relationship of personal selling to promotion and thereby to marketing.

Advertising is nonpersonal communication and is transmitted by one or more kinds of media, such as direct mail, billboards, broadcast media (TV and radio), or print (newspapers and magazines). Through advertising to vast or small audiences, selective market segments can be reached. Whereas some firms spend hundreds of millions of dollars for mass media advertising, small firms and individuals may spend under $10 for an ad in the classified section of a newspaper. In general, advertising is not as persuasive as other components of the mix, particularly personal selling.

Sales promotion covers a wide range of techniques that provide an extra short-term incentive or inducement to patronize a store or buy a product. Techniques include demonstrations and exhibitions, samples, premiums, cou-

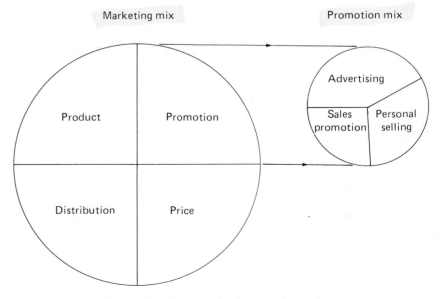

FIGURE 1.1 Relationship of personal selling to the marketing mix.

4

pons and cents-off deals, games and contests, trading stamps, displays, store and window signs, and package inserts. Sales promotion reinforces the other parts of the promotion mix and improves their short-term effectiveness.

Personal selling is the personal communication between a salesperson and a potential customer or group of customers. The communication may be highly persuasive, or it may be mostly informative. Although the audience of personal selling efforts is smaller than with mass media advertising, the interpersonal contacts can make it the most effective element of the promotion mix. For some products, such as industrial products and goods of high-unit value, personal selling is essential; advertising may help with brand and product recognition, but it will not close the sale.

Not only the various elements of the promotion mix but also those of the marketing mix are closely related. You can imagine how difficult selling can be if the products are of poor or inconsistent quality, if prices are out of line with competition, or if advertising is used ineffectively. Similarly, if the sales force fails to do its part, the other elements of the marketing mix cannot compensate for this lack.

Much has been written about the *marketing concept.*[1] This term describes attitudes toward marketing activities, thoughts that have evolved in most business firms in recent decades. Essentially, it means that the marketing function has assumed new importance and new responsibilities within a firm. Along with upgrading the entire marketing function has come a philosophy that we call "customer orientation," that all aspects of the firm's operation should be directed to better satisfying its customers.

The sales function has two ways of implementing the customer orientation of the marketing concept: (1) by its selling contact with the customer and the way in which this is carried out; (2) through market feedback or market sensors. Simply pushing goods onto customers is not the way to stay competitive in business today. Customers are likely to buy and then to give repeat business only if their needs and wants have been correctly ascertained and if products and services do in fact satisfy these needs and wants. The sales department also provides market feedback, which in turn influences product development, pricing, and policies regarding promotions and dealer relations. The sales manager is responsible for guiding the sales force in the direction of an effective customer orientation.

HOW IMPORTANT IS PERSONAL SELLING?

Magnitude of Selling Costs

Table 1.1 shows average sales force costs in selected major industries. For example sales force expenses for durable consumer goods manufacturers average 6 percent of sales; for prescription drug firms, 6.9 percent. Although sales force costs for industrial goods manufacturers average somewhat less,

TABLE 1.1 Sales force costs as a percentage of sales in selected industries (1985).

Industry	Percentage of Sales
Consumer goods	
Durable goods	6.3
Ethical pharmaceuticals	6.9
Major household items	5.8
Industrial goods	
Automotive parts and accessories	2.1
Computers	2.9
Electronics	4.2
Fabrics and apparel	4.5
Machinery (heavy)	5.8
Machinery (light)	8.5
Office and educational equipment	10.4
Printing and publishing	7.0
Rubber, plastics, and leather	4.3

Note: Costs include total compensation, travel, and entertainment expenses for salespeople and sales management.

Source: "1986 Survey of Selling Costs," *Sales & Marketing Management* (17 Feb. 1986): 57.

they still range from 4 to 10 percent of sales for many industries. The expenses shown in Table 1.1 include only the compensation, travel, and entertainment expenses of salespeople. When we add the additional costs of sales management, staffs, branch offices, and miscellaneous selling costs, we are talking about a substantial expense category, one that may reach 10 to 15 percent of sales for many companies.

Another way of looking at the importance of the sales function is to consider the costs of making a business-to-business sales call. This cost reached $229.70 in 1985.[2] At the same time it may cost less than a penny to reach a reader or listener through a magazine advertisement or TV commercial. Why use costly salespeople, then? (You know.) A salesperson is far more likely to reach interested people and persuade them to buy; the mass media can reach thousands and millions, but most are uninterested, bored, and need more than a fleeting advertising message to be induced to buy.

Perhaps the best way to consider the importance of personal selling is to compare how executives rate its importance relative to other promotional tools. Table 1.2 shows such a rating based on a survey of almost 500 top executives. As you can see, personal selling is rated well above the other promotional alternatives.

The expense of selling, of course, attests to the importance of the personal selling function. Such costs would hardly be long tolerated if they were not deemed worthwhile and essential.

TABLE 1.2 Executive ratings of the relative importances of the various elements of the promotional mix.

	Percentage of Total Promotional Budget		
	Industrial Goods Manufacturers	Consumer Durables Manufacturers	Consumer Nondurables Manufacturers
Advertising	13.4	26.8	35.7
Personal selling	69.2	47.6	38.1
Packaging	4.5	9.5	9.8
Miscellaneous promotional activities	12.9	16.1	16.4

Note: Later study had similar results; evidently executive perceptions of the importance of the personal selling function had not changed. (Clyde E. Harris, Jr., Richard R. Still, and Melvin R. Crask, "Stability or Change in Marketing Methods," *Business Horizons* [October 1978]: 35).

Source: Jon G. Udell, *Successful Marketing Strategies in American Marketing* (Madison, Wis.: Mimir Publishers, 1972), 47.

Revenue Generation

Selling is the basis of a firm's revenue generation (and often, the only contributor). Without revenues all other business functions and activities become meaningless. For of what use is production? It is a major cost to the firm in facilities required, and in materials and labor needed to manufacture goods. These goods generate no revenue for the firm, however, until (and unless!) they are sold. Staff activities such as personnel, accounting, computer services, and legal counsel cannot exist without sales to support them.

Few businesses escape the need for a sales force. Although a firm may spend a lot for advertising, it needs salespeople to follow up on the advertising and actually close the sale; advertising can pave the way for salespeople, but it can seldom replace them. Still other firms spurn advertising and rely mostly on their sales force; this method characterizes many industrial firms. Other firms are small and cannot afford the high costs of mass media advertising. In businesses where customers are limited in number and are geographically concentrated, personal selling is usually more advantageous. (And it is an essential strategy when technical information must be supplied.)

Public Countenance

The salesperson is the public countenance, or persona, of the company. The sales representative may be the only person in the firm with whom a customer has any direct contact. Employees in production, engineering, or accounting are seldom visible to outsiders. Thus the honesty, knowledge, personalities, and effectiveness of the sales representatives can convey a good impression of the company, or a mediocre, "blah," or negative image. The sales representative may be the key factor to having a satisfied and loyal customer rather than a lost customer.

WHAT SALES MANAGEMENT IS ALL ABOUT

Sales management concerns directing or managing the personal selling aspect of an organization's marketing operation. Sales managers have three main areas of responsibilities:

1. Involvement in strategy considerations such as planning and directing the marketing program as it applies to the district or region
2. Responsibility for personnel relations, ranging from recruiting, training, and motivating the sales staff, to evaluating their performance and determining corrective action when needed
3. Analyzing overall results; targeting areas for improvement and areas of potential opportunity

Sales management is a special form of management, and as such it fully involves the usual functions of management—planning, organizing, staffing, directing, and controlling. Figure 1.2 depicts how sales management relates to these common management functions and also shows the major characteristics that distinguish it from other types of management. This book is organized according to these general management functions, which are also briefly described in the following section.

General Functions of Management

Management is the direction of efforts of individuals toward a common goal. In doing so, the manager:

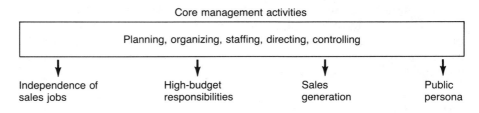

FIGURE 1.2   Unique characteristics of sales management in addition to its basic management functions.

Plans—Determines objectives, sets policies, and establishes programs, campaigns, and specific procedures and schedules

Organizes—Groups activities necessary to carry out the plans and defines personnel relationships

Hires staff—Selects and trains the people required for the job to be done

Directs—Guides and supervises subordinates

Controls—Sees that results conform to plans and takes corrective action where needed

Additional, Unique Functions

Managing the sales force has some unique and particularly challenging aspects. Most colleges and universities therefore have separate sales management courses in addition to the more general "principles of management" or "theory of administration" courses.

Sales generation.   The manager of the personal selling is responsible for sales generation. No other executive, line or staff, is quite as crucial to the firm's viability, because all other activities of the firm cannot be funded without successful sales.

Public persona.   As noted, the sales staff represents the firm to the public. They convey the image of the firm and cement satisfactory and durable customer relations. Selecting and supervising worthy representatives is highly challenging.

Independence of sales jobs.   Selling can be intriguing and highly stimulating. The salesperson operates with considerable independence compared with colleagues who are "chained" to a factory, store, or office. Substantial traveling often is required; thus face-to-face supervision of sales staff may be impossible for long periods of time. The sales representative, within certain budget constraints, is free to disperse company funds for entertaining clients as well as for his own travel expenses. However, as a sales manager of an industrial coatings firm notes:

> The sales job can be lonely and discouraging. It often involves contacting persons who are not interested. When a potential customer says "no" to the request for an order, this can be most discouraging, especially if the salesperson has invested considerable time with the account. Adding to this sense of failure may be that it has to be endured in lonely isolation from supporting colleagues. These factors make the job of managing the sales force most challenging. We need to encourage, to build up ego strength, to motivate . . . to seek the proper mix of supervision and control without stifling the employee's motivation, initiative, and creativity.

The sales manager constantly faces the challenge of finding ways to stimulate salespeople to greater efforts; encouraging them when they are discouraged; building up those who are weak; and using firm, disciplinary measures on those taking advantage of the freedom from close supervision.

High-budget responsibilities.   The sheer cost of selling gives it importance to a firm. Selling costs can run from 10 to 20 percent of sales, far more than advertising, research and development, marketing research, office expenses, and most other aspects of the business. Consequently, sales executives have bigger budget responsibilities than executives at comparable management levels.

Levels of Sales Management

Sales management involves executives at many levels in a company. The top sales job usually is "vice president, sales." However, in some companies the president is also directly involved in sales, especially when it comes to contacting the most important customers. Below the vice-presidential level may be several layers of sales managers, depending on the size of firm. Figure 1.3 depicts four different levels of sales management, with the number of executives typical in a large firm.

The first step into sales management is usually as a field sales manager (such as a district sales manager), responsible for the activities of perhaps six to ten sales representatives in a particular geographic sales district. This person usually is hired from the sales representative staff, where he gained first-hand exposure to customers, performed well and indicated an interest in a man-

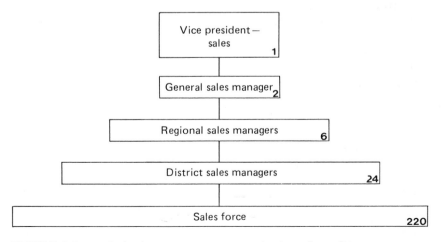

FIGURE 1.3   Typical sales management organization—large firm.

agement career path. The next step is regional sales manager, followed by sales executive.

CAREER OPPORTUNITIES IN SELLING AND SALES MANAGEMENT

Selling has suffered from a poor public image. In the early years of the United States, in the small towns and sparsely populated hinterland, the smooth-talking Eastern salesman sometimes hoodwinked a barely literate populace, even though more often he performed a sorely needed service of providing access to goods not otherwise available. *Huckster* was a derogatory term used to describe all salespersons; almost as derogatory were *peddler* and *hawker*. The implication was that these people could not be trusted; they were flimflam artists, snake-oil purveyors. But the early peddler's life was far from easy: "At the onset they walked. Those of more stature rode horseback and the even more prosperous rode in wagons and carriages. . . . The peddler's life was strenuous, lonely, and hazardous."[3]

The Yankee peddler has long gone, the predecessor of the retail stores in the remote places of our country. There is little room for the snake-oil charmer and the artist of high pressure in today's environment of skeptical and de-manding customers. Today, success in selling is built on establishing and preserving long-term relationships with customers, and this bond results from a thorough understanding of a customer's needs and a reputation for honest and dependable business dealings.

Unfortunately, students' attitudes toward careers in selling have been far more negative than positive.[4] While this negativity has changed significantly in the last 10 to 15 years, misperceptions still remain. For example, a recent study compared the perceptions of students with those of people actually engaged in sales. These experienced salespeople rated their sales jobs consid-erably more positively than students did in regard to status and prestige, security, contributions to society, financial rewards, professionalism, and feel-ings of accomplishment.[5]

Today's sales positions are interesting, well-paid, and offer such bonuses as company cars, liberal entertainment allowances, and travel to exotic places for sales meetings and conventions (or as rewards for excellent performance). In addition, sales offers challenge, stimulation, and sometimes lasting friend-ships with customers. Let us now look specifically at entry into management, compensation, and advancement opportunities.

Entry into Management

Selling is the gateway to a myriad of other executive positions, from sales manager right up to company president. The abilities developed in selling a

People Management

Directing and managing people can be a heady experience for a new manager. It will remain a continual challenge. A manager's success is directly related to how much he or she can accomplish *through people;* the success of the sales manager is measured by the success of the sales force.

Being a sales manager provides an excellent opportunity to practice leadership (that is, to get people to do what you want them to do). In sales there is more direct involvement with people than in most other middle-management jobs. The responsibility for a group of salespeople involves their selection, training, supervision, motivation, evaluation, and discipline. Furthermore, there is the challenge of managing a group of persons who daily confront a variety of changing and nonroutine situations. In such a position you can gain excellent experience in how to respond to change, how to seek productive alternatives, and how to deal with crises. These experiences can be stimulating and psychologically rewarding.

company and its products and in achieving good and lasting customer relations can be of benefit throughout one's entire career, because training in selling is transferable; in later years it may be used to persuade the executive committee or the board of directors toward a particular course of action.

In the first level of sales management, the district sales manager, one has the opportunity to demonstrate managerial abilities and to develop these skills as quickly and effectively as possible. Immediately all the basics of management must be mastered: planning, organizing, staffing, directing, and controlling. These are evident at all management levels. Of course, a top executive may spend more time planning and controlling than directing (compared with lower-level executives), but the functions are still inherent in all managerial jobs.

Compensation

Some successful sales representatives may receive a higher total compensation package (salary and commission) than executives several echelons higher. Salary will reflect the worth of the position. Thus national sales managers will make upward of $100,000. Regional sales managers will earn $70,000 to $90,000; district sales managers, $50,000 to $60,000.

In addition the compensation package usually has considerable indirect monetary benefits or "executive perks." These perks include company-paid insurance plans, pensions systems, stock options, and even country club memberships. A company car and use of a company airplane may be furnished the sales manager to ease his travels. And, of course, liberal expense accounts are usually taken for granted because the sales executive is expected to entertain important clients. Such benefits and perks are seldom available to other executives of the same level in the organization (e.g., the production manager) but rather reflect the unique requirements of the sales manager's role in furthering the company's image and representing it to clients and customers.

Indicative of the relatively high level of compensation found in a sales career is its being singled out as one of the top money-making careers of the 1980s. Furthermore, strong demand exists for people in international sales.[6]

Advancement Opportunities

A successful career in sales can lead to a number of career options (Figure 1.4). A person may decide to stay in professional sales, reaping high income and strong job satisfaction, while spurning the responsibilities of line management. Alternatively, one may opt for a career path geared to such staff assignments as marketing research, brand management, or advertising and sales promotion management. For our purposes let us assume that the desired career path embraces line management (sales management leading to higher managerial possibilities).

Successful sales managers often climb the path of advancement quickly— and go far. Perhaps the ultimate example of this is Lee Iacocca.

Why the fast track in sales?   Three factors account for faster career advancement in sales than in other areas of the firm.

First, a sales manager has direct responsibility for accomplishing the firm's objectives. In contrast, accounting, personnel, purchasing, research, data processing, and engineering exist to *help* accomplish the objectives. Line executives advance more quickly because their jobs are more crucial to the success of a firm.

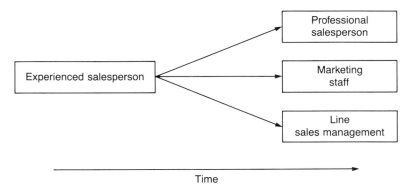

FIGURE 1.4   Career options for salespeople. (*Source*: Adapted from David L. Kurtz, H. Robert Dodge, and Jay E. Klompmaker, *Professional Selling*, 4th Ed., Plano, Texas: Business Publications, Inc. 1985, 47.)

Lee Iacocca—From Engineer to Salesman

In November 1978 Lee A. Iacocca became president of Chrysler, an ailing auto maker. Many doubted that he could save the company; indeed, that anything could. But of course we know that he did and went on to become the highest-paid executive in the United States, with over $20 million in compensation in 1986.

Iacocca embodied the great American success story. The son of an Italian immigrant, he saw education as the route to success. He attended Lehigh University and then Princeton for a master's degree in engineering. "In my day you went to college . . . to embark on a career that paid you more money than the guy who didn't go," said Iacocca.

He started with the Ford Motor Company as an engineering trainee in 1946. But he found that engineering held little interest for him; he wanted to be where the action was, in sales. Eventually, he talked a district manager into giving him a low-level desk job in fleet sales, mostly telephone work. By 1949 he got out from behind the telephone and was made a zone manager.

As he moved upward through the Ford organization, Iacocca was responsible for introducing in 1964 the trend-setting Mustang, and followed up with the Maverick, Pinto, and Fiesta. By 1977 he was president of Ford; a falling out with Henry Ford II eventually brought him to Chrysler and international fame.

"Executive Pay: Who Got What in '86," *Business Week* (14 May 1987): 50–51.

Second, the performance and effectiveness of salespeople and sales managers are readily and directly measurable. Sales and profit performance of the territory, district, division, or region provide objective data on accomplishment. Contrast such objective measures of performance with the dilemma of the outstanding accountant, personnel manager, and research director. How is their performance to be measured objectively? It usually cannot be. Subjective appraisals by superiors and reliance on such intangible character factors as enthusiasm, loyalty, ambition, conscientiousness, and thoroughness must be substituted for dollars-and-cents indicators of performance.

Third, the sales "personality" is most in demand for top executive positions. The chief executive of a business often is called on to "sell" the

Key Challenge and Opportunity of the Sales Manager

Those in sales face a major career opportunity. But they also confront daily pressure and frustration. The less able, the careless, and the lazy simply cannot cope. What characteristics inherent in the sales job make it so unique?

Performance and effectiveness are easily measured in sales, more so than in most other jobs. The combination of sales volume and selling expenses that determine profit performance enables a person to prove his worth to an employer. When direct comparison is made with sales and profit performance of other territories and divisions, the better achievers are quickly identified—as are the poorer performers. Promotions often quickly follow such proven performance.

company and its policies to major customers, suppliers, government officials, stockholders, creditors, the general public, and the company employees. The chief executive plays a key role in stimulating the entire organization to achieve new and more ambitious goals. Many firms view the sales personality as so crucial to their highest executive positions that they pass over production, finance, and staff executives to fill these jobs.

Drawbacks

Not everyone is suited to sales—or wants it! What are the major drawbacks of careers in sales management? Many of the negative aspects of the job of the sales manager are the same as those for top management positions.

First, recognize that *drawbacks* to some people will always be *attractions* to others—for example, travel. The amount of travel in sales jobs can vary considerably, depending on such factors as the size of the company and the geographic distribution of its customers. The average sales manager spends about 1 week per month traveling to sales meetings, conventions, the sales branches, or certain key customers. So the typical sales manager is not chained to a desk.

Because sales performance is so easily measured, superiors become immediately aware when results do not meet expectations. That means pressure! Promotions and pay raises depend on dollars-and-cents performance. Furthermore, most sales managers' compensation plans include some incentive bonus and commission arrangements; coupled with family and personal obligations, such plans create pressure *always* to produce to the maximum. One sales manager commented,

> I have always thrived on pressure—it brings out the best in me. Maybe this developed when I was a kid trying out for the varsity. Pressure gives zest and challenge to any job. But let's face it—pressure gives some people ulcers and heart attacks. With my salespeople I try to be careful how much I pressurize them. Some bloom and others wilt under pressure.

There are people who would not like being responsible for their staff's performance. If a salesperson loses a customer account or fails to make a quota, the sales manager cannot escape accountability. But the best efforts of subordinates can be more assured by selecting staff wisely and carefully, thoroughly training and working with them, and continually monitoring their performance and taking corrective action when needed.

WHAT IT TAKES TO BE A SALES MANAGER

There are valid reasons for selling as the entry position for sales management. The manager must understand the problems as well as the opportunities of the salespeople to understand, guide, train, and motivate them. This knowledge is best gained by experiencing the selling situation at first hand. Furthermore, just as a baseball or football team looks up to the coach who in younger days was a successful player, so the selling team has more respect and confidence in the leader who was also a successful sales representative.

The salesperson who would be manager need not (and should not) spend years in selling before making the move into management. One or two years may be sufficient. However, these should be fruitful years, a time in which the skills and personal qualities that can be used in later, more responsible jobs can be developed—persuasiveness, enthusiasm, perception of customers' needs, and talent for public speaking and demonstrating before groups.

Must the future sales manager be the best salesperson? Not necessarily. In fact, the best salesperson often does not make the best sales manager. He may be too geared to making customer contacts, too wedded to the independent life and travel of the typical salesperson to feel comfortable sitting behind a desk, involved with the planning and budgetary aspects of a manager's job. The star salesperson often abhors paperwork, seeing it as an impediment to selling, rather than as a communication and control device needed for the best-functioning sales organization. Generally, the person who would make sales manager should be an effective seller, but not necessarily the best.

Almost 30 years ago the following characteristics were proposed for "the salesman who will make manager"—they hardly differ today, except that they apply to both men and women:

1. He works endlessly on his sales presentation. He is always prepared to meet the objections of his prospect and varies his presentation to meet the situation.
2. He sells across the board. He knows which items carry the best margin and pushes them, though not neglecting the remainder of the line.
3. He has a nose for new customers. He never stops building the clientele.
4. He follows a definite pattern of territory coverage, thereby minimizing the time spent en route to calls.
5. He apportions the contact time between accounts in proportion to the potential business available from them.
6. He knows the value of reports and does not neglect this aspect of his job.
7. He services his customers' customers. He does not stop working once the order is in his pocket.
8. He works cooperatively with the credit department. He knows that it is useless to sell goods if they are not paid for at the proper time.
9. He is an intelligence agent in the field for his company, continually on the alert for competitive developments, new products, new merchandising ideas, new uses for the product, and trade gossip.[7]

For some sales jobs, a college degree is not required; for most high-level jobs, it is. The person who completes the rigor of a college program usually has shown some ability to organize time, plan and accomplish objectives, see a wider perspective, and achieve reasonable facility with words, both spoken and written. Such a person is far more likely to better represent the company to important customers. A salesperson must be prepared to talk with people who have college degrees, perhaps even advanced degrees. Not being college-trained puts most persons at a psychological disadvantage in such situations, despite any self-education they may have gained in practical business matters. Furthermore, to be considered for promotion to sales manager, a college degree is a must. The days of the old-time sales representative or sales manager who achieved their success on personality and a gift for words are over. Professional, college-trained men and women represent the new wave.

WOMEN IN SALES AND SALES MANAGEMENT

Traditionally personal selling and sales management, excluding retail sales, have been male-oriented; but this situation is changing rapidly. For example, Brown & Bigelow, a manufacturer of advertising specialty items, had almost no saleswomen in 1978; by 1985, 25 percent of its salespeople were women. The salesforce of Johnson & Johnson, a marketer of medical and pharmaceutical supplies and consumer products, employed 17.6 percent women in 1978; by 1984, it was composed of 31 percent women.[8] Even in industrial equipment, long a bastion of male dominance, women are making strong inroads and are proving that they can be as knowledgeable as any man.

Undoubtedly, women sales managers face some difficulties, especially when placed in a situation with older, skeptical salesmen. There may be problems in gaining acceptance and cooperation. Women may have to work harder to prove themselves to subordinates and superiors alike and are more likely to be in the spotlight as the firm's "first women" sales managers. Under such scrutiny, any mistakes or uncertainties may be painfully visible. Women managers also tend to face communications problems of two kinds. (1) Male associates feel they have to watch their language when a woman is present. (2) Women are often not included in the informal communications network that operates over lunch, on the golf course, and in neighborhood pubs. These communication issues are rather superficial difficulties.

The entry of women into sales and sales management seems bound to increase.[9] Spurring such inroads are Title VII of the 1964 Civil Rights Act, which prohibits sex discrimination in hiring, promotions, and compensation; and Revised Order No. 4 of the Office of Federal Contract Compliance, which requires firms doing business with the federal government to develop written affirmative action programs.

Without legal prodding, more and more firms—Del Monte, General Tire, Philip Morris, 3M, RCA, and R.J. Reynolds, to name a few—are finding that women are highly competent and successful sales managers.[10] In recognition of this emerging trend, in this book the terms *sales manager* and *salesperson* are used to apply equally to men and women.

In the past, blacks and other minority groups also were often excluded from the higher-level sales positions. But this situation has also changed greatly in recent years. Excellent employment opportunities now can be found in selling and in the career progression to sales management.

SUMMARY

Sales is the stepping stone to sales management and then to the highest executive positions. The reasons for this progression reflect the key importance of selling as the firm's revenue generator and public countenance.

Although sales managers are involved with the same management tasks as other managers (i.e., planning, organizing, staffing, directing, and controlling), they have extra tasks that make it both a more challenging and more rewarding job. The career opportunities in selling and sales management are many, but the selling position is the entry level. Effectiveness at the entry level paves the way for greater responsibilities, and opportunities for women and minorities have never been better in the field of sales.

QUESTIONS

1. Why are personal selling and advertising complementary rather than substitutes for each other?

2. How would you respond to the idea that the star performer of the sales force should always be promoted to sales manager?

3. What types of individuals do you think are best suited for a career in sales management? Least suited? Why?

4. Selling is the entry for many high executive positions. How do you account for this fact?

5. How would you assess the opportunity for women in sales and sales management today?

6. Describe specifically how the sales manager is involved in each of the five general functions of management.

**CAREER-
PLANNING
PROJECT**

It is beneficial to set goals for what you want to accomplish in 5, 10, and more years down the road. Several advantages come from such career mapping. First, with planned, reasonable expectations, you are not like the wood-chip in the stream, buffeted by an uncaring current; you can direct your fate and make strategic moves as opportunities open up (or are not realized). Second, many company recruiters ask such questions of job seekers as indicators of their planning and organizational capabilities. I invite you also to ponder what you see as your strengths and weaknesses—these, too, are common interviewing questions. But be aware that some weaknesses ought not be revealed to an interviewer. These faults include "hate to take responsibility," "not well-organized," "don't like taking orders," "lack self-confidence," and the like. Rather, quietly work on these problems in order to improve.

1. List your specific career objectives 5 years after graduation.
2. Write your objectives 10 years after graduation.
3. Write your ultimate career objectives.
4. Why do you think these objectives are reasonable?
5. How do you plan to get there?
6. What are your strengths?
7. Your weaknesses?

NOTES

1. For recent articles, see Roger C. Bennett and Robert G. Cooper, "The Misuse of Marketing: An American Tragedy," *Business Horizons* (November–December 1981): 51–61; and A. Parasuraman, "Hang on to the Marketing Concept!" *Business Horizons* (September–October 1981): 38–40.
2. "Survey: Business Sales Calls Costing $229.70," *Marketing News* (1 August 1986): 1.
3. From Tom Mahoney and Leonard Sloane, *The Great Merchants*. New York: Harper & Row, 1966, p. 5.
4. For example, see "Selling Is a Dirty Word," *Sales Management* (5 October 1962): 44–47; Gordon W. Paul and Parker Worthing, "A Student Assessment of Selling," *Southern Journal of Business* (July 1970): 57–65.
5. Alan J. Dubinsky, "Perceptions of the Sales Job: How Students Compare with Industrial Salespeople," *Journal of the Academy of Marketing Science* (Fall 1981): 352–367.
6. Steven S. Ross, "The 12 Top Money-Making Careers in the 1980s," *Business Week's Guide to Careers* (Spring 1983): 7–9.
7. From William C. Dorr, "The Salesman Who Will Make Manager," *Sales Management* (20 May 1960): 47–48. Reprinted by permission from *Sales & Marketing* Magazine. Copyright © 1960.
8. Rayna Skolnik, "A Woman's Place Is on the Sales Force," *Sales & Marketing Management* (1 April 1985): 34.
9. See Robert W. Cook and Timothy Hartman, "Female College Student Interest in a Sales Career: A Comparison," *Journal of Personal Selling & Sales Management* (May 1986).
10. For other articles dealing with women in sales management, see Robert N. Carter and Milton R. Bryant, "Women as Industrial Sales Representatives," *Industrial Marketing Management* (February 1980): 23–26; Douglas W. Naffziger, "The Smooth Transition," *Training and Development Journal* (April 1986): 63–65; Alex Taylor III, "Managing," *Fortune* (18 August 1986): 17–23; and Warren Boeker, Rebecca Blair, Frances M. Van Loo, and Karlene Roberts, "Are Expectations of Women Managers Being Met?" *California Management Review* (Spring 1985): 148–157.

CHAPTER 2
Fundamentals of Selling

CHAPTER PERSPECTIVE

In this chapter we take a broad look at personal selling. We discuss the diversity of selling jobs, which range from relatively simple to exceedingly complex, requiring great skill and training. We examine the traits that seem to characterize the most successful individual salespeople as well as the best sales organizations. We take a close look at the newest trends in selling, such as systems selling, major account management, telemarketing, and the growing use of the personal computer in selling. Finally, we consider the important career step from selling to managing.

CHAPTER OBJECTIVES

□ Know the various type of selling jobs and their differing degrees of difficulty and creativity.

□ Identify the traits of the most successful salespeople that differentiate them from the less successful.

□ Recognize the newest trends in selling, and understand how these may affect your career.

□ Attain a better perspective of the role that the personal computer will likely play in your selling career.

□ Become aware of the characteristics of America's best sales forces and which firms are the best in their industries.

□ Achieve a better understanding of the transition from sales to management.

TYPES OF SELLING JOBS

Sales jobs carry many different titles, reflecting their managerial and technical nature and increased prestige. The term *salesperson* can mean the inexperienced, low-paid retail clerk and the Good Humor ice cream vendor, as well as the highly trained, well-paid account executive of an advertising firm and the sales engineer of a high-technology firm.

The number of persons engaged in selling in the United States is about 6 million, about 30 times more than are employed in advertising. The following list shows some of the variety in selling job titles[1]:

Sales engineer

Account executive

Communications consultant

Sales consultant

Area manager

Industrial representative

Industrial account manager

Marketing representative

Customer service representative

Key account supervisor

General agent

Executive representative

Territory manager

Field representative

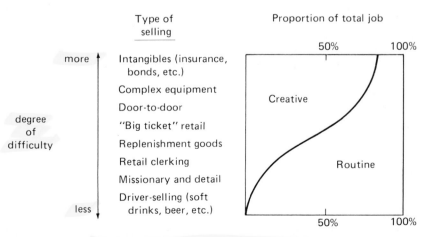

FIGURE 2.1 Sales jobs displayed by degree of difficulty and creativity involved.

Figure 2.1 shows various types of selling ranked by degree of difficulty and the proportion of creative selling to routine efforts involved. Degree of creativity required and the prestige and compensation of the job are highly correlated. Low pay and low prestige accompany the more routine jobs, which characteristically require less training, education, experience, and competence (performance is often rigidly specified—even to routing and scheduling calls) than the higher-level, more creative type of selling.

Classified by Selling Situations

Sales jobs may involve (1) sales originating, (2) order taking, and (3) supporting. Many salespeople participate in all three, although the emphasis may vary considerably.

Sales originating involves developing new business.* It is the hardest kind of selling but also the most fascinating. Creative skills are called into play here, as the salesperson seeks the best way to adapt products and presentation to the customer's needs. The best-paid and most successful professionals predominate. Such creative selling can deal with tangible products, such as vacuum cleaners, computers, and industrial equipment. Intangibles, such as insurance, mutual funds, and advertising also require creative selling, and this often is the most difficult kind of selling because there is no tangible product for demonstration.

In *order taking* the salesperson simply performs the mechanics of the transaction; for example, the retail clerk takes the merchandise from the customer, packages it, and records the sale. The customer in this case has already decided to buy, and the salesperson may suggest a few additional items or a higher-priced article, but opportunities to do more than this are limited. Sometimes the order-taking salesperson's job is primarily delivery of the product, any selling responsibilities being secondary. An example here is the driver-salesperson for soft drinks, beer, milk, and bread. Obviously, such order taking is far easier than originating sales. Salespeople who are primarily order takers are typically lower paid and less experienced. However, order taking should be the goal of all salespeople, even those of the highest level. Sales origination, if successful, can lead to order taking. This should be the goal of any type of selling—to cement relations with customers through service and satisfaction of their needs so that customer loyalty develops, resulting in repeat business. Although such transactions then become relatively routine and repetitive, selling efficiency can be greatly increased because such customers are virtually presold in the atmosphere of trust and customer satisfaction.

Supporting salespeople do not try to secure orders; their job rather is to provide specialized services and create goodwill. We find two general types,

---

*Some authors refer to this as *order getting;* however, this term often leads to confusion with *order taking,* the less creative type of selling.

missionaries and *technical specialists*. Missionaries are employed by such manufacturers as Procter & Gamble and General Foods to work with dealers, perhaps to develop point-of-purchase displays, train dealer salespeople to do a better job of selling the product, provide better communication and rapport between distributor and manufacturer, and in general, aggressively promote the brand. *Detailers* are used in the drug industry to call on doctors and other professionals; they are a type of missionary. They leave samples and explain applications and research information about new products, thereby hoping to encourage prescriptions for their brand.

Technical specialists who are engineers and scientists assist regular salespeople. Sometimes certain products require a higher degree of technical expertise than a regular salesperson can be expected to provide, or a certain piece of equipment may require tailoring to the particular requirements of the customer.

Classified by Employers and Customers

Sales personnel can also be classified by whom they sell for and to. Table 2.1 presents these classifications with the most common characteristics of each type. The manufacturer's salesperson selling to other industrial users often represents the highest-quality salesperson. Months of preparation and discussion with top executives may be necessary to achieve a single sale, such as a new computer system or a major piece of factory equipment.[2] Selling to dealers (wholesalers and retailers) may require a fairly high-level person, but the work tends to be more routine and less creative. Missionary salespeople usually are involved in work that is not creative or particularly rewarding; often turnover is high, although some firms use the missionary jobs as part of the management-training program.

Manufacturers' salespeople who sell directly to consumers—door-to-door—are involved in the most difficult type of selling, especially when the product is relatively high priced, such as encyclopedias. Often the caliber of salesperson is low, training is minimal, and pay is straight commission (if nothing is sold, there is no pay). Under such conditions the marginal workers are quickly eliminated, and only the more able (which often translates to those more aggressive and high pressure) are likely to survive, and they may do quite well.

Selling for wholesalers and retailers usually is low-level and noncreative work. Wholesalers' sales forces, for example, sell mostly from catalogs and are order takers. Retail selling typically requires little skill or experience and is the first job for many young people, but there are exceptions. Retail selling for such high-priced items as cars, appliances, expensive clothing, and the like may require high-caliber salespeople and can be highly creative and rewarding. A direct relationship often exists between the price of an item and the competence of the salesperson involved. Consider, for example, the Fuller

TABLE 2.1   Selling jobs classified by employer and by customer.

Employer	Customer	Caliber of Salesperson	Type of Selling
Manufacturer	Industrial users	High	Creative; order getting
Manufacturer	Wholesalers	Reasonably high	Some creativity, but also routine order taking and servicing accounts
Manufacturer	Retailers	Reasonably high; may also be less high-caliber if missionaries	Similar to selling to wholesalers; may be missionary
Manufacturer	Consumers (door to door)	Usually low	Creative sometimes, but may use canned (memorized) presentation; often very difficult
Wholesaler	Retailers and/or manufacturers	Not particularly high	Primarily order taking and selling from catalogs and price lists
Retailer	Consumers	Generally low, but may be high-caliber for big-ticket items such as automobiles, appliances, carpeting, men's clothing	Most often order taking; can be more creative for big-ticket items

Brush salesperson versus the successful encyclopedia salesperson; the cleaning supplies salesperson versus the computer sales representative; the variety store clerk versus the furniture salesperson.

WHAT SALESPEOPLE DO BESIDES SELLING

Salespeople are not involved strictly with selling, although sales generation may be the most important component of the sales job. Sales force tasks can be categorized as follows[3]:

Joe Girard, Super Auto Salesman

The *Guinness Book of World Records* lists Joe Girard's feat of selling 1,425 cars and trucks for Merollis Chevrolet of East Detroit in 1 year as the all-time auto-selling record. His commissions that year totaled $189,000, and he has sold more cars than anyone else in the world almost every year since 1966. Yet, just 3 years before 1966, he had lost all his money in the construction business.

Joe's secret? He sells service to his customers, so much so that 65 percent of the business he does now is in resales to customers satisfied with his efforts to ensure them proper service for their cars. He also uses an elaborate filing system in which everyone who has ever shopped with Girard receives greeting cards for birthdays, holidays, and on special occasions. He also sends his customers "bird-dogging kits," which are lists of prospective customers, and a stack of his business cards; if a bird dog sends Girard a customer, she wins $25.

Now Joe Girard is only selling cars part-time. He has developed a sales technique film series and a sales training program. But his most successful venture is a book, *How to Sell Anything to Anyone*, which has hit the best-seller lists.

Joe Girard, *How to Sell Anything to Anyone* (New York: Warner, 1978).

- ☐ Prospecting—finding new customers
- ☐ Communicating—conveying information about the company's products and services
- ☐ Selling—actually generating orders
- ☐ Servicing—providing assistance to customers in various ways, not only regarding technical product assistance and customizing, but also such diverse aspects as consulting on customers' problems, arranging financing, expediting delivery, as well as handling any unexpected customers' problems in the client relationship
- ☐ Information gathering—providing the company with diverse feedback from the field
- ☐ Allocating—prioritizing shipments and servicing according to customers' needs, especially during times of product shortages

Some firms designate priorities. For example one firm may designate 80 percent of a salesperson's time for servicing and getting orders from existing customers with 20 percent for prospecting. Missionary salespeople typically spend more of their time on communicating, servicing, and information gathering.

Many companies have found that servicing is increasingly important to maximize customer satisfaction and ward off competitors. Gillette's Safety Razor Division, for example, has directed its salespeople not merely to push products, but to "talk to buyers about pricing, distribution, promotion, and display."[4] Xerox even ties customer service and satisfaction to the compensation plan, surveying its accounts from four standpoints: service, customer ratings of Xerox products, the salesperson's professionalism and attentiveness, and Xerox's administrative support.[5]

Some firms are increasing emphasis on information gathering, as sales executives realize that systematic feedback from the field can enable them to detect competitive and environmental market changes more quickly and be prepared either to react or to take aggressive action aimed at new opportunities. Information gathering does not often require any new report forms. But it does require that salespeople understand the importance of their field reports and that management actively use the information, which will demonstrate its usefulness to the salesforce. We will discuss the use of sales reports in much more detail in Chapter 18.

WHAT MAKES FOR SUCCESS IN SALES?

As with most questions dealing with success and failure—whether in athletics, business, or personal lives—the answers concerning success or failure in business are complex. Insights into any identifiable patterns for success and failure are crucial in helping both organizations and individuals to achieve more. We will examine this question from the twin perspectives of the sales organization and the individual salesperson.

What Makes for America's Best Sales Forces?

Sales & Marketing Management magazine each year surveys executives, asking them to rate the firms in their industry by the quality of their sales forces. The characteristics by which they evaluated themselves were also rated. Table 2.2 shows the ranking of the various characteristics involved in determining this "quality."

TABLE 2.2   Characteristics of a Quality Sales Force

Characteristics	*Percentage Saying "Extremely Important"*
Reputation among customers	66
Holding old accounts	62
Opening new accounts	47
Ability to keep salespeople	45
Innovation	35
Product/technical knowledge	34

Source: Based on a survey of 1,000 sales executives. "America's Best Sales Forces," *Sales & Marketing Management* (June 1987): 45.

Who were the winners? Following are the top sales forces in each of their industries[6]:

Apparel	Liz Claiborne
Chemicals	Du Pont
Computers and office equipment	IBM
Electronics	AT&T
Food and beverages	Coca-Cola
Forest products	Kimberly-Clark
Industrial and farm equipment	Black & Decker
Life insurance	Northwestern Mutual
Metal products	Gillette
Pharmaceuticals	Merck
Scientific and photographic equipment	Xerox
Wholesale distribution	Bergen Brunswig
Textiles	Armstrong World Industries

Liz Claiborne, the New York city maker of working women's apparel, was the overall winner, receiving one of the highest grades in six of the seven categories in the Best Sales Force balloting. The intensity of the competition to be best, however, shows up in the 1987 survey results, in which only two defending sales force champions—IBM and Du Pont—managed to retain their titles.[7]

Traits of High-Performance Salespeople

You should have a keen interest in what it takes to be a success in selling; your career depends on this, whether you choose to remain in selling or move into management. Later, as a manager, you will also be vitally concerned with the characteristics of success because these will increase the productivity of your operation.

Numerous studies (see following discussion) have focused on what makes one person successful and another not. Many of these studies have been contradictory, so that the job of selecting the best prospects is still uncertain, as we will discuss in much more detail in Chapter 9. However, certain differences can be identified. Some interesting distinctions are shown in Figure 2.2. The successful salespeople are better listeners than talkers; they do a better job of planning and following company policies, and they show more managerial talent. They are interested in others, and they feel more socially satisfied. The successful salespeople also prefer to work on commission, rather than straight salary; you can make a lot more money on straight commission than you can on straight salary, *if* you are a good salesperson. Most of the factors shown in Figure 2.2 involve personality traits. Now let us examine some success elements in the selling process itself.

Success factors in the selling process.   The steps in the selling process, which are described in the next chapter, are well-known and usually are

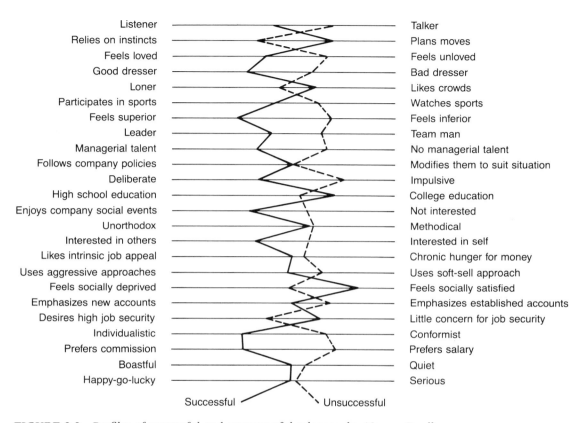

Listener		Talker
Relies on instincts		Plans moves
Feels loved		Feels unloved
Good dresser		Bad dresser
Loner		Likes crowds
Participates in sports		Watches sports
Feels superior		Feels inferior
Leader		Team man
Managerial talent		No managerial talent
Follows company policies		Modifies them to suit situation
Deliberate		Impulsive
High school education		College education
Enjoys company social events		Not interested
Unorthodox		Methodical
Interested in others		Interested in self
Likes intrinsic job appeal		Chronic hunger for money
Uses aggressive approaches		Uses soft-sell approach
Feels socially deprived		Feels socially satisfied
Emphasizes new accounts		Emphasizes established accounts
Desires high job security		Little concern for job security
Individualistic		Conformist
Prefers commission		Prefers salary
Boastful		Quiet
Happy-go-lucky		Serious

Successful — Unsuccessful

FIGURE 2.2 Profiles of successful and unsuccessful salespeople. (*Source*: Bradley D. Lockeman and John H. Hallaq, "Who Are Your Successful Salespeople?" *Journal of the Academy of Marketing Science* (Fall 1982): 466.)

incorporated in every sales training program as well as most books on selling. But the skills and orientations of outstanding performers discussed here are more subtle.

Highly successful sales representatives earn a strong trusting relationship with their clients as well as inside their own organizations. They tend to share information internally to a greater degree than do moderate producers, and they tend to involve others and solicit opinions.[8] With their customers the sales task is more an exchange of information than a product pitch.[9] They may even forego a sales opportunity when they feel that the customer's needs might better be served by another product or at another time. They recognize the importance of understanding customers' needs, in addition to presenting product benefits, which helps promote a trusting relationship with the customer, who is seen as a cherished client. Successful salespeople embody personal integrity. They strive to make the best use of customers' time and to

Are Good Salespeople Born or Made?

A traditional controversy concerns the sales personality. For decades it was assumed that salespeople had personality traits that ensured their success. They were essentially born with glibness, an extroverted personality, a hearty enthusiasm, some kind of personal mystique that transmitted itself into dominance over their peers. Lacking this personality, the old notion went, there was no use even trying to sell. Very much akin to this notion of the born seller was the idea that leaders were also born not made. Without such god-given talents—and experts disagreed as to what, specifically, these magical talents were—one was doomed to be a follower.

Today we know that leadership abilities can be developed, sales prowess can be nurtured, and "born" leaders and salespersons *are made not born.* We now recognize that product knowledge, customer knowledge, and customer service are more important than any magnetic sales personality who tries to compensate for lack of product and customer knowledge. Training and motivation have become the ingredients of successful sales performance.

convey needed information objectively and without bias and exaggeration. They develop advisory relationships, are problem solvers, customer advocates, deal makers, and in some cases, delivery or repair expediters; they willingly accept servicing responsibilities. High performers do not abdicate responsibility for installation, implementation, and service to technical support staff. They continue to maintain a close relationship with their clients after the sale and are a source of information and support for their customers in the event of problems.

Does this mean that hard sell is not a characteristic of these successful sales representatives? It does indeed! Treating the customer as a respected and valued client summarizes the notably successful. Transcending short-term selfish concerns for an order builds durable customer relations that result in steadfast, repeat business. The good salesperson wants a satisfied and loyal customer. The mark of the great salesperson is better customer satisfaction than offered by competing sales representatives.

TRENDS IN SELLING

Because businesses are becoming larger and more complex, a new kind of selling situation has developed. Sales of equipment worth millions of dollars and affecting many parts of a customer's company (e.g., computers, machinery, pollution-control systems) may take several years to consummate, which changes the role of sales. This type of sale usually involves many levels of buying decision makers rather than a single purchasing agent or buyer, as discussed earlier in this chapter. Various executives may be involved, including top executives, production people, staff and consulting engineers, and the purchasing department. Each level brings a different set of concerns and interests that the salesperson must deal with throughout the selling process. The salesperson may have to contact each level personally or may have to give the presentation before a committee. In such an environment, systems selling has come into prominence, and major account management has received greater attention.

Systems Selling

The federal government introduced the idea of purchasing total systems in its buying of major weapons and communications systems. Essentially, this required one seller or contractor to package all the components of a system, often coordinating the work of many subcontractors. For any large customer, systems selling can provide better service, although it certainly increases the responsibility of the major seller or contractor of such a package or system.[10] Two components have been identified for such system selling: (1) the design of well-integrated groups of interlocking products (which is likely to involve participation with other subcontractors or original equipment manufacturers) and (2) the implementation of a system of production, inventory control, distribution, and other services to meet a major customer's needs for a smooth-running operation.[11]

Major Account Management

Recognizing the importance of major customers has come belatedly to some sellers. These very large customers often represent a major part of a firm's total sales volume, and satisfying them in an increasingly competitive environment requires special treatment. "Major account management" philosophy stresses both sales and developing long-term relationships with such customers.[12] (Actually, the idea of developing good long-term relations should be fostered with all customers.) Service becomes increasingly stressed as a way to better satisfy and cement relations.

The trend among these large customers toward decision by committee for major purchases has also led to team selling. With this type of selling, the sales representatives can call on the services of additional personnel and experts. The salesperson's own research, engineering, marketing, and upper management are interlocked with those of the customers, so that the salesperson becomes a kind of committee chairman within her company.

As far as the salesforce is concerned, such account management is resulting in changes in many sales organizations. Many firms are changing their compensation plans from straight commission, which encourages sales but not service, to salary plus bonus, which is far more compatible with developmental "partnerships" with customers. Separate sales forces are being developed, with one being a force of "account managers," who devote all their time to one or a few major customers, while the other sales force calls on smaller customers in the normal fashion.

Telemarketing

Improved communications technology has produced a new sales tool, telemarketing. This is simply selling by telephone. Its one tremendous advantage over regular selling is that it is much more cost effective. The cost of each regular sale call averaged over $229 in 1986,[13] but even the most sophisticated and complicated telephone contact costs less than $35.[14] And many more contacts can be made in any given time frame. As an example of how telemarketing can be effective, consider TechTel Communications (see Application 2.1).

In general, telemarketing can (1) help in prospecting, qualifying, and servicing accounts so that salespeople can concentrate on closing sales; (2) handle small, marginal, or geographically remote accounts that cannot be covered efficiently in person; (3) obtain faster account coverage for new developments, such as new products and special sales programs.[15]

For most products and services, however, telemarketing is not a substitute or replacement for a regular sales force. Rather, it can complement and supplement such efforts so that overall selling efficiency can be improved.

Other Trends

Computer use in selling.[16]   We are seeing greatly increased use of computers in selling as in all areas of business. With the advent of the relatively inexpensive and portable personal computers (PCs) and easy-to-use software, training to use can be relatively simple, and sales force and sales management acceptance typically very good.

These personal computers are becoming lighter and less expensive, while providing better quality features. So-called *portable computers,* or PCs (also

---

APPLICATION 2.1   Telemarketing

TechTel primarily markets technical products to medical professionals. "When we introduced telemarketing to the medical profession the conventional thinking was that doctors would never buy anything as specialized and costly as diagnostic equipment by telephone. . . . But, they appreciated not being bothered by personal visits and getting correct information by telephone. Our phone calls were a fast way for them to get information and request literature to help them decide without a lot of pressure."

"Automated Telemarketing Lowers Costs of Selling to Professionals," *Marketing News* (14 March 1986): 44.

known as laptops, kneetops, or briefcase size), are beginning to replace the larger desktop models. The portables weigh only 9 to 10 pounds, have good display quality, can be upgraded as needed, have greatly increasing software availability, and now have a battery life as long as 10 hours; some are priced even less than $1,000, while the higher prices are falling. With their easy accessibility and portability, they are increasingly helpful for salespeople in prospecting; doing call reports; and providing quick information on inventory situations, delivery target dates, as well as other market information. Sales managers are using PCs for sales analysis, promotional budgeting, sales territory designations, and routing of sales personnel. For example one firm uses computers to assist salespeople and managers in (1) ranking sales leads according to their potential, (2) providing salespeople with information needed for following up, and (3) giving management information useful for evaluating individual sales representative performance.[17] Another firm has used its computer technology to provide (1) an analysis of coverage of the more important leads; (2) trace movement of leads through the pipeline, indicating potential bottlenecks and whether enough leads are being generated; and (3) a review of potential future sales and resources needed to cope with these expectations.[18] A simple example of how a PC can help with a particular problem is given in Application 2.2.

Computer use by customers is also impacting on the sales representative's job. Retailers' and wholesalers' use of computerized buying is increasing for routine reordering of regularly carried goods and supplies. Rather than waiting and relying on a salesperson for replenishment orders, these customers depend on computers to maintain inventory control by identifying reorder points and even writing fill-in orders for basic stock items. In such a situation the salesperson's role is changed from regular servicing of accounts on a frequently scheduled basis to less-routine selling. Such nonroutine activities might involve new product introductions, special promotions, and the handling of

---

APPLICATION 2.2 Example of One Use of a PC

Problem: You are charged to increase your monthly sales from $45,000 to $55,000. You need to develop a plan to accomplish this.

Solution: You need to use an appropriate software program, one that gives weekly and monthly summaries of your activities, including appointments made, cold calls, demonstrations, orders, and revenues. Input of past relationships between appointments, demonstrations, and orders received would also be desirable. At this point with the PC, you can develop a spreadsheet of your past performance, but with the revenue figure changed from $45,000 to $55,000. The software program would automatically show how your appointments, calls, and demonstrations would have to change if you are to meet your new sales goal.

For more details on this problem and other problems that can be solved using a PC, see "Find Your PC IQ: A Hands-on Test," *Sales & Marketing Management* (December 1986): 83–90.

any unusual problems or servicing requirements not normally encountered in routine sales calls.

New insights into profits.   Firms now are recognizing that sales profitability is more important than mere sales volume. Consequently, the sales emphasis is shifting from volume to profits in developing sales objectives and in evaluating sales performance. The typical firm has a wide range of products, and these may carry many different markups, due to competitive as well as other factors. Sales managers are beginning to realize that the person who pushes those items carrying the higher gross margin is making a greater contribution to the company than one who emphasizes easier-to-sell, low-margin and sale items. Firms therefore are beginning to pay bonuses and commissions on gross margin of sales rather than strictly on sales volume.

MAKING THE TRANSITION FROM SELLING TO MANAGING

As discussed earlier in this chapter, certain low-level selling jobs have rigidly prescribed duties. Routes may be carefully laid out and customer calls specified. The selling message may be canned or memorized, its words determined by the home office. In this situation there is little room for initiative or for personal management by the salesperson, and transition to management is difficult.

Importance of Time Management

The more common selling situation finds the salesperson with wide latitude. True, the territory often is prescribed, and potential customers in the territory may be identified somewhat. But supervision is indirect, because salespersons' reports and empirical sales results provide the primary data for superiors' direction and follow-up. And these superiors may be hundreds of miles away in a district or regional sales office. In these circumstances the successful sales representative must exercise considerable management ability in doing the job as effectively as possible. She must budget her time to produce the most sales possible.[19] Time spent in waiting rooms and lobbies can be costly. Time spent calling on accounts who are already giving as much business as possible is time not spent with more lucrative potential customers. Time spent with people who cannot make the buying decision or are not the major decision makers likewise is misused. And time spent stuck in heavy traffic, or backtracking because of inefficient routing, is simply wasted. We will discuss time management in more detail in Chapter 3.

Relationship of Planning and Territory Management

To budget time as effectively as possible, and to correctly ascertain customer needs so that a better sales presentation can be given, considerable planning is needed. Of course, customer visits should be scheduled as efficiently as possible. But effective planning also includes determining who will be seen, the preparation needed for the particular sales call, the most effective presentation for the customer's needs and problems as well as the personalities of the potential buyers. When mistakes are made and a lost sale or lost customer results, corrective action that might repair the situation should be planned.

The good sales manager develops in salespeople the sense of "managing" a territory in order to strengthen their selling effectiveness. Without the managing emphasis, many salespeople under the pressure of sales quotas and directives tend to forget about managing and concentrate solely on making sales calls, however inefficient and ill planned.

The job of selling can be great training ground for higher positions if the idea of territory management is conscientiously applied. As the salesperson progresses to sales management, responsibilities shift to planning, directing, and controlling the efforts of others. But the skills required are very different from those developed in managing one's own efforts.

Differing Perspectives Must Be Overcome

The fledgling sales manager will be aware that certain differences exist between sales and managing skills. Some merely are in one's perspective, but managers coming from the ranks may find them difficult to surmount. For example, a new sales manager must change her perspective from a self-centered orientation to focusing on the development of teamwork. Primary concern therefore must switch from developing customer accounts in the territory to developing subordinates, to guide them to do a better job.

No longer is our new sales manager "one of the boys." Now he is a member of management, is in command, needs a broader perspective, may have to act in a manner contrary to the desires of former associates, and may even have to avoid close relations with former buddies to avoid any semblance of favoritism. If the new sales manager is a woman, she knows that greater attention is focused on her performance and that she may have to assume the sometimes uncomfortable role of trailblazer.

Another requirement of the transition from selling to managing is the assumption of more diverse responsibilities. These will include coping with a host of personnel matters and problems, running a branch office, dealing with certain key accounts, developing and analyzing reports, handling correspondence, and working with other departments, such as advertising, engineering, credit, and production scheduling.

Despite the differences, the transition from selling to managing can be relatively easy. The successful salesperson should be able to approach the job of managing with confidence, recognizing it as an intriguing new challenge.

SUMMARY

In general, sales jobs can be classified as sales originating, order taking, and supporting. Sales originating normally carries the most prestige, challenge, and compensation, whereas order taking is usually the least difficult and least creative.

The activities in which salespeople are typically involved often include more than simply selling. For example servicing and information gathering are important salesperson's activities in many firms.

What makes a great sales force and what makes a successful salesperson are intriguing questions. The "born-to-sell" personality is a myth; a strong and honest commitment to customers seems to differentiate the more successful from the less successful.

The most recent trends in selling are systems selling, major account management, telemarketing, the use of PCs by salespeople and sales managers, and the growing recognition that profits are more important than sales and good profit performance ought to be rewarded. The growing use of PCs in particular suggests that future sales representatives should be prepared to use this useful tool.

Finally, the important transition from selling to managing requires particular skills and abilities. Time management and planning as well as territory management are important. Making the transition to management also requires a shift in perspective from a self-centered orientation to focusing on the development of teamwork.

QUESTIONS

1. Differentiate between creative and service selling.
2. What rationale can you give for some companies' requiring management trainees to serve a stint as missionary salespersons?
3. What is the difference between missionaries and detailers?
4. Discuss the advantages and limitations of telemarketing.
5. What advantages do PCs offer field salespeople?
6. What traits differentiate the more successful salespeople from the less successful?
7. What are the characteristics of America's best sales forces?

8. What is systems selling? How does it differ from major account management?

9. How would you assess the different attributes and perspectives needed in making the shift from sales to management? Is such a shift likely to be easy or difficult? Why?

At the end of many chapters we will have a multiple-choice question such as the following. Evaluate each of the alternative answers in arriving at the one that seems best to you. For example why do you like or not like alternatives 1 and 2? The solution requires good judgment as well as an understanding of the topic and problem involved, rather than simply rote memory. A manager's success is largely determined by her people interactions, how well people problems and challenges are handled. Here is your chance to deal with rather common people problems, to reflect on them, and to come up with reasoned solutions. At the same time it's important to recognize that there may not be any absolutely right or wrong approach, but only a more right or less likely to be right approach.

EXERCISE IN HANDLING PEOPLE PROBLEMS

You have just been promoted to sales manager in your district, jumping over several older and more experienced salespeople in the process. Now you suddenly find that some of your former buddies are acting cold toward you, while others seem to be trying to butter you up. How would you handle this transition from selling to managing?

PEOPLE PROBLEM— PROMOTION FROM THE RANKS

1. Avoid any close relations with your former buddies.

2. Attempt to regain your former close association by showing them that you are still one of them.

3. Firmly show them that you are the boss, even if some will resent this.

4. Explain to them that you are still on their side.

5. Try to ignore any initial resentment or attempts at favoritism; these should go away with time.

---

1. For a report on a study of how job titles can affect job prestige, see Robert T. Adkins and John E. Swan, ''Increase Salespeople's Prestige with a New Title,'' *Industrial Marketing Management* (February 1980): 1–9.

2. Related to this, see Robert E. Hite and Joseph A. Bellizzi, ''Differences in the Importance of Selling Techniques Between Consumers and Industrial Salespeople,'' *Journal of Personal Selling & Sales Management* (November 1985).

NOTES

3. Philip Kotler, *Marketing Management,* 5th Ed. (Englewood Cliffs, N.J.: Prentice-Hall, 1984), 678.

4. "Gillette Hones Salespower to a Fine Edge," *Sales & Marketing Management* (June 1987): 59.

5. "Xerox's Makeover," *Sales & Marketing Management* (June 1987): 68.

6. "America's Best Sales Forces," *Sales & Marketing Management* (May–June 1987): 41–68.

7. *Ibid,* 42–45.

8. For more discussion, see "Survey Identifies Traits of High-Performing Sales Reps," *Marketing News* (16 September 1983): 14.

9. Related to this, see Camille P. Schuster and Jeffrey D. Danes, "Asking Questions: Some Characteristics of Successful Sales Encounters," *Journal of Personal Selling & Sales Management* (May 1986).

10. For a relevant strategy see Dan T. Dunne, Jr., and Claude A. Thomas, "Strategy for Systems Sellers: A Grid Approach," *Journal of Personal Selling & Sales Management* (August 1986).

11. Philip Kotler, *Marketing Management: Analysis, Planning and Control* 5th ed. (Englewood Cliffs, N.J.: Prentice-Hall, 1984), 165–166.

12. Arthur J. Bragg, "National Account Managers to the Rescue," *Sales & Marketing Management* (10 August 1982): 30–34.

13. "Survey: Business Sales Calls Costing $229.70," *Marketing News* (1 August 1986): 1.

14. "Reps' Fear of Telemarketing Present Management Hurdle," *Marketing News* (25 April 1986): 8.

15. William C. Moncrief, Charles W. Lamb, Jr., and Terry Dielman, "Developing Telemarketing Support Systems," *Journal of Personal Selling & Sales Management* (August 1986), and Jeffrey Pope, "Ringing up Industrial Sales by Phone," *Sales & Marketing Management* (12 October 1981): 50.

16. For a sampling of articles dealing with the use of computers in sales, see Bob Woods, "The Sales Force Gets a Helping Hand," *Sales & Marketing Management* (6 December 1982): 50ff.; G. David Hughes, "Computerized Sales Management," *Harvard Business Review* (March–April 1983): 101–104; Richard Plank and Norman Heinle, "Business, University Foster Computer Use in Selling," *Marketing News* (14 March 1986): 48; "Special Section: Computers in Sales and Marketing," *Sales & Marketing Management* (December 1986): 75–113.

17. Thayer C. Taylor, "Giving Sales Leads a Leading Edge," *Sales & Marketing Management* (14 Sept. 1981): 35–37.

18. "Scitex Meets Its Matchmakers," *Sales & Marketing Management* (December 1986): 78.

19. A number of articles have noted that out of a 40-hour work week, only 12 to 15 hours are spent in the buyer's office, resulting in a tremendous amount of nonproductive time. For example, see Ralph Bascarello, "Zero in on Productive Selling," *Industry Distribution* (February 1977): 46–47.

cases

2.1   Designing a Program Leading to Sales Management

You are a newly hired salesperson for the Kincaid Industrial Supplies Company. With your brand-new college degree in business administration, you had hoped to land a job in management, but had to settle for a selling job that hopefully will lead eventually to management and a fast career path.

In your interview with the Kincaid Company, you had expressed this desire for management, but were given only a vague promise, "If you work out well, there will be management opportunities."

The sales job involves selling various cleaning and janitorial compounds to industrial and com-mercial users. Your territory covers the southern part of Ohio. For the most part the other sales-people in Ohio are older and more experienced than you are. You suspect that most of them are not interested in management. Indeed, one of them, Sam Williams, told you, "Why do you want to go into management, with all its headaches? We sales-men have a good life. They pay us well, we don't work as hard as Ed [the sales manager] does, and we don't have all that responsibility."

QUESTION

How would you design a plan for yourself to become a sales manager? Be as specific as you can.

2.2   The Weinberg Corporation: Selecting a Sales Manager

Ben Cardullo frowned as he shuffled the papers on his desk. He had to make a decision soon re-garding a sales manager for the West Coast. Paul Gabriel, the previous sales manager, had really dealt him a low blow, Ben reflected, suddenly leav-ing to go with a competing firm. To make matters worse, Paul had never groomed a replacement—something Ben had always encouraged his man-agers to do.

Ben is the vice president of sales of the Weinberg Corporation, a manufacturer of women's dresses. Weinberg is a medium-size firm, with sales ap-proaching $30 million in its good years, and head-quartered in New York City, as are most dress manufacturers. Because of the fickleness of fash-ions, sales tend to be erratic. Since becoming vice president 4 years before, Ben had worked diligently to solidify relations with the major customers so that there was some continuity of business, thus minimizing the extremes of sales fluctuations. He had also expanded the sales organization to four regions: the West Coast, the Midwest, the South and Southeast, and the East.

The West Coast region is the third largest in sales. Six salespeople cover it, and all are fairly new. Although Ben did not consider this to be a problem sales region, still he had never thought it was op-erating at full potential. The problem could be the relative inexperience of the salespeople. Gabriel had believed in recruiting from college campuses rather than looking for older, experienced salespeople. This was OK, Ben thought, but only if good training and coaching were given such "green" people. And he had never been satisfied with Gabriel's alleged commitment to training.

Again he picked up the folder of Joe Willett and paged through it. Joe is one of the two candidates for the job. On the surface he seems a shoo-in. He is the top sales producer in the Midwest region and usually the top in the whole company. He is 45 years old and has been with Weinberg for almost 20 years. He probably knows more about the garment business than anyone else in the sales organization, Ben mused, even though he was not sure that Joe had even completed high school. Ben had talked with Joe earlier today and as always was impressed with the easy banter of the man, a personality that customers obviously found compatible.

Ben had asked, "Why after all these years, Joe, do you want to get into management? You know you'll probably make less money, at least at first, than you do now. And do you really want to relocate?"

"I'm getting tired of being on the road 5 days of almost every week. While I like and expect some travel, the life of a traveling salesman is just getting too much—both for me and my family. Besides," he had said with a grin, "we're getting tired of the cold winters in Chicago."

The only other candidate from within the company is Donna Hammer, and she is almost the direct opposite of Joe. Ben flicked open her folder again. She is just 26 years old and has been with the company for only 3 years. She has a marketing degree from NYU and had joined Weinberg after working a year and a half as a buyer trainee at Macy's. "I just wanted to have more independence and room for initiative than you have working in a store," she had said. Ben hired her and had been pleased with his judgment, as Donna proved to be conscientious, hard working, and creative. Although she was not yet the top salesperson in the East, she was above average, which was a considerable achievement for her 3 years because strong customer ties seemed to require some years to develop.

She was also ambitious, Ben thought, smiling wryly as he recalled her statement to him yesterday as they discussed this possible promotion. "I want to get into management in the worst way," she had said. "You know, I just might want your job someday."

Ben tapped his pencil absently as he thought of the other alternative to filling this position. He could go outside the firm and try to find an experienced sales manager. He shuddered a little thinking of this, for it could be a time-consuming process. And then you never could be sure how such an outsider would really fit into the organization. He swiveled his chair around and looked out at the gray overcast shrouding the skyline. It would be so much easier picking either Joe or Donna, he thought. But was either one capable to do the management job out west, 3,000 miles from himself and company headquarters?

QUESTIONS

1. List and evaluate all the pros and cons you can think of for each of the three alternatives facing Ben. On balance, which do you recommend?

2. Ideally, what further information should he have before making a decision?

CHAPTER 3
Effective Selling Techniques

CHAPTER PERSPECTIVE

A sales manager must know effective selling techniques. Unless one is an above-average salesperson, the odds are against reaching the position of sales manager. And in training and supervising, the sales manager must be able to show salespeople how to maximize their abilities and opportunities. This chapter presents an overview of the selling process, focusing on practical sales techniques. Like most "how-to" approaches to selling, this chapter describes various steps or hurdles involved in leading or guiding the prospective customer to a buying decision. The process leading to a sale, however, is more of a flow than a series of discrete steps. Customer relations and time management, introduced in Chapter 2, are expanded on here, stressing their practical applications.

As you read this chapter, reflect on how you might best respond when a buyer tells you that he does not have much time to listen to your sales presentation.

CHAPTER OBJECTIVES

□ Know the steps or activities involved in the selling process.
□ Be able to identify the best sources for finding prospects.
□ Become familiar with effective ways to handle leads.
□ Become aware of the differences between canned and custom-tailored presentations for effective selling.
□ Understand the type of objections likely to be encountered and how best to handle them.
□ Know various closing techniques.
□ Become acquainted with the applications and promise of psychological and behavioral sciences to selling.
□ Be able to develop and maintain good customer relations, and know what to do about lost customers.
□ Gain some practical techniques of improving time management of individual salespeople.

THE STEPS TO EFFECTIVE SELLING

Millions of copies of books dealing with selling are marketed every year, bearing intriguing titles such as *The Power of Enthusiastic Selling, 1,000 Ways a Salesman Can Increase His Sales,* and *The Magic of Thinking Big.* Selling is still an art and not a science, although necessary skills can be increased by analysis and training. The intangibles of face-to-face interaction do not lend themselves to complete systematizing and planning; the challenge remains. But there are identifiable steps in the selling process, and their mastery can help one do a better job of selling.

Figure 3.1 depicts the processes or steps usually involved in persuading the prospect to make the purchase commitment. Each of these steps or stages can gradually blend into the next, sometimes with barely recognizable sequence. For example beginning the sale and making the presentation may be smooth and free flowing; objections and sales resistance can occur at any time or not at all; closing the sale may be a natural and comfortable finale with the issue not in much doubt or a last desperate effort with a reluctant customer. Some steps may be short, whereas others may require considerable time. The insurance salesperson, for example, can find prospecting very time-consuming indeed.

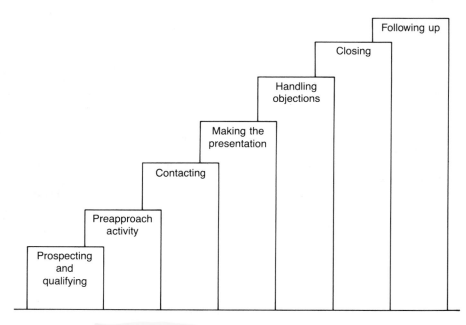

FIGURE 3.1   The steps in making a sale.

Prospecting and Qualifying

In prospecting as a sales representative, you seek to identify prospective customers.[1] The company may help with this task for commercial and industrial products by turning over leads from advertising inquiries, and assigning existing accounts within the specified sales territory. Furthermore, the types of companies that represent potential customers should be known. The sales representative, in addition to servicing present customers, is expected to track down and contact potential customers. For services such as insurance, door-to-door sales, and products of generally wide appeal, salespeople are often given more responsibility for finding potential customers, perhaps within their formally assigned territories. For some types of selling, such as insurance sales and some financial services, good prospecting is essential for sales success.[2]

Some of the best sources and techniques for finding prospects follow:

Present and past customers

Directories, such as city directories, state industrial directories; *Thomas Register of American Manufacturers; Dun & Bradstreet; Moody's Industrial Manual; Standard & Poor's Register of Corporations, Directors, and Executives,* vol. 2; membership directories of trade associations, professional societies, and civic and social organizations

Mailing lists[3]

Prospecting services, such as *Sales Prospector,* a monthly publication of Prospector Research Services, Inc.

Trade shows and exhibits[4]

Advertisements that attract mail and phone inquiries[5]

Various miscellaneous sources, such as acquaintances, other salespeople, suppliers, nonsales employees in the firm, and the like

Once potential customers have been identified, they should be *qualified,* which is the process of determining a prospect's validity. A prospect usually is valid when three specific factors are present. The prospect should have (1) the financial ability to buy, (2) the authority to make the purchase decision, and (3) a present or latent need for the product or service. Time spent on potential customers who do not meet these requirements is wasted.

Handling leads.   A frequent complaint of sales managers is that their salespeople do not follow up on the leads or inquiries generated by direct mail, print advertising, trade shows, and unsolicited inquiries. Usually, such lack of sales force responsiveness is a result of bad previous experiences with leads that usually turned out to be poorly qualified prospects. Robert Hood suggests that inquiries be followed up before the lead is sent to the field. This can be done by phone to those inquiring—sometimes called *telequalifying*—to determine the extent of the interest. Each inquiry then can be categorized as follows:

Hot lead—intends to buy within 3 months

Warm lead—intends to buy in 3 to 12 months

Long-term prospect—no purchase intent in the next 12 months, but is a definite prospect

No potential—has no application for the product or is not a decision maker or influencer

Unusable—not a business, no longer in business, or the like[6]

Such prequalified leads can be a real morale booster for the sales force because they should represent good potential business.

Preapproach Activity: Preparing for an Effective Sales Call

Preapproach activity can be likened to informal marketing research. As the sales representative, you normally will do this on your own, and the subject is the single prospective customer. To better meet this customer's needs, you simply want to find out as much as you can about him.

You will have obtained considerable information in the prospecting and qualifying steps. Now you should surpass that information to enrich your initial presentation, to make it stand out from competing sales calls, and to increase the likelihood of a sale now or in the near future.

Of course, you will want, and probably already will have, specific information as to name, title, address, and phone number of the person you want to contact. In addition the following types of information are useful, and sometimes essential, for the most effective sales contact:

- ☐ The decision maker and influencers
- ☐ The customer's needs
- ☐ Present and potential competitors
- ☐ The firm's standing in the industry and any likely changes
- ☐ Personal information about the customer that might be relevant

Buying decision makers and influencers. In many firms the purchasing agent, the obvious person to contact for a major expenditure, is not the decision maker. A committee of executives or the technically oriented engineering staff may make large equipment decisions, whereas the purchasing agent handles only the paperwork. Researchers have grouped the participants in the buying process into five categories: (1) users, (2) influencers, (3) gatekeepers, (4) buyers, and (5) deciders.[7]

Users work with the product or service and may or may not be significant influencers on such purchase decisions. Users often are below the executive level but have first-hand experience into problems and needs in their work. *Influencers* are usually technical experts whose knowledge is valued in making decisions about sophisticated equipment. *Gatekeepers* control the flow of information to other people involved in the purchasing process and include purchasing agents and suppliers' salespeople. *Buyers* are purchasing agents who usually are directly involved in making contacts and negotiating purchases. Their range of discretion varies among organizations and with the importance of the decisions; it is more constrained with extraordinary and costly purchases. The *decider* is the person (or committee) who has the final authority to make a purchase decision. With important purchases, even the top executive may be directly involved.

For nonroutine purchases the sales representative faces a significant challenge to determine the roles played by the various parties to a buying decision.[8] If the organization is large, identifying the key decision makers may be particularly difficult. So you need to obtain answers to several questions: Who will actually make the purchase decision? Who will influence the decision? With whom are long-lasting favorable relationships most desirable?

Customer's needs.   A purchase is made when the customer feels that a particular product and/or service will satisfy specific needs. The salesperson who can appeal to a customer's dominant buying needs is far more likely to close a sale and have a satisfied customer. Information such as the following is helpful:

> What are the limitations of my product as they apply to the prospect?
>
> What particular benefits do my product and service afford?
>
> What are the prospect's requirements in terms of quantity desired and time of delivery?
>
> What does my product offer a customer in reducing costs and saving money?
>
> Is the prospect bargain conscious?
>
> What procedures does the prospect prefer regarding follow-up calls?
>
> How secure is the prospect in his present position?

Knowing the prospect's job security status is useful because an insecure buyer will be reluctant to take a chance with a new supplier or may allow emotion to influence purchasing decisions.

Other information.   Personal information about the prospect may enhance rapport. Knowing the prospect's family background, hobbies, memberships, and any special interests may be helpful. Company and competitive information is helpful also:

Is the company an innovator and leader in its industry, or is it more of a follower?

Are the fortunes of the company trending upward?

Who are the competitors for our type of products, and how strong are they in such things as product improvements, quality, and service?

Is our competition for this prospect's business primarily based on price? If not, what other factors may be more important?

Knowing any restrictions in calling on this prospect also is important, including preferred days or time of day, desired length or frequency of sales call, and perhaps even formality or informality preferences.

Where can you obtain preapproach information?   Sometimes you can get relevant information through secondary information sources and other data obtained before the sales call. Standard sources follow:

Standard & Poor's Register of Corporations, Directors, and Executives explains the prospect's business affiliations, position in the company, and membership in organizations.

Dun & Bradstreet provides credit ratings and an appraisal of the business.

Moody's Industrial Manual gives data on company size, names of executives, and financial data.

Thomas Register of American Manufacturers includes information about the company and its products.

Various trade journals (e.g., *Modern Packaging, Iron and Steel Age,* and *Drug Topics*) give data on industry conditions.

You can also get more qualitative information from other customers, perhaps your fellow salespeople, people in the community, as well as your company records. As you develop your own detailed and up-to-date records, you will have ready sources of information.

Buying needs and motives may be more difficult to identify in advance. You will need to develop your skill in listening and asking questions during the sales interview to uncover some of this information, or at least to confirm your prior suppositions.

A *customer file* can be a vital tool for making more effective sales calls. You should start the file during the preapproach period and add to it with each sales call, then review it before the next call. It is not unusual for a successful sales representative to beat out the competition primarily because of more complete and specific information about many facets of the customer and his operation.

Defining the objectives and developing the strategy. Although the ultimate goal of the sales call is to get an order, attaining some intermediate goals may be necessary:

- ☐ Make a courtesy and get-acquainted call; perhaps also leave some samples and brochures.
- ☐ Obtain more information about the prospect.
- ☐ Lay the groundwork for a formal and more lengthy presentation and/ or demonstration at some later time.
- ☐ Introduce a new product or a new promotional campaign.
- ☐ Handle a particular problem of the buyer, perhaps in maintenance, operational efficiency, or staff's inadequate product knowledge.

With the objective(s) of the sales call defined, you need to plan how best to accomplish them and conduct the presentation or visit. Now carefully prepare your presentation and any visual aids, rehearsing if necessary, reviewing all information you have about the prospect, and anticipating objections and how you can best respond to them.

Contacting and Beginning the Sale

Approaching prospective customers may be a long and tedious procedure. For many types of industrial and commercial selling, you may need to make a number of calls before you will be permitted to make a formal presentation. As discussed in the last section, you should try to know as much as possible about the potential customer's business, then the initial ice-breaking call(s) should be geared to gaining rapport and making the customer receptive at least to hear your sales presentation.

Need for creativity. At this point all your creativity may be needed, because many customers' needs and wants are already adequately covered by existing suppliers. Wedging in, for the new salesperson and firm, may require a special service, sales personality compatible with the customer, or some unique and outstanding product feature (which is more difficult to find in an increasingly competitive environment).

The importance of the first impression. A poor first impression may be difficult to overcome. Some experts maintain that a sales representative's first impression is crucial to the success of the sales call. One author has gained best-seller stature with his suggestions on the importance of clothing in business.[9] Certainly, the total impression that the sales representative gives, whether highly professional, sloppy, or something in between, can be a powerful influence. For example a grimy business card suggests that you're careless and not professional or "first class." A shopworn sample or a wrinkled flyer or brochure also creates a poor image. Taking a prospect to lunch in a messy car suggests a lack of consideration for your client as well as a lack of pride in yourself. A good first impression can be destroyed by a late confirmation letter full of misspellings and other errors.

Making the Presentation

Although the eventual goal of any sales presentation is to make a sale, expecting this always to be the result is naive. As noted, a call may be made simply to cultivate a customer, to pave the way for a successful future relationship. A complex product may require a number of calls to make a complete presentation. Some of the barriers sales representatives must face in making the first sale are shown in Figure 3.2.

A sales presentation may take two directions. It may primarily demonstrate product or service benefits. Or it may be used to sharpen the seller's determination of customer needs, as most sales training experts advocate.[10]

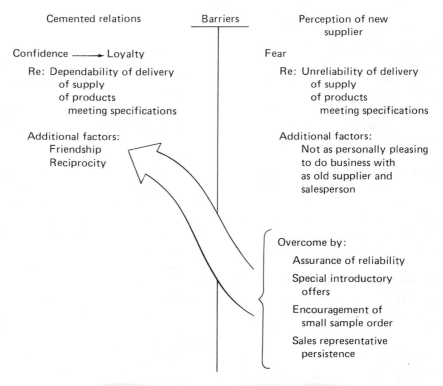

FIGURE 3.2   Barriers to be overcome in making the first sale.

Canned Versus Custom-Tailored Sales Presentations

The sales presentation varies from canned to custom tailored. Canned presentations are memorized messages designed to present all the information the customer needs to make a buying decision and are couched in the most persuasive language—often as determined by home office personnel. Canned approaches give the beginning salesperson some confidence, but unfortunately, they tend to be flawed. A memorized sales message *sounds* memorized and permits neither the flexibility nor the special tailoring to customer needs that many sales necessitate.

Consequently, most successful salespeople now use a more custom-tailored approach to fit the particular situation and customer requirements. This approach may require exploration of customer needs and will require the salesperson to gain sufficient knowledge about the company and the purchase decision makers. When the sales presentation is not canned, the salesperson is better able to adjust to the prospects' reactions.

The first approach with a standardized presentation is more useful for salespeople who contact a large number of prospects and do not have time to assess each as carefully as should a salesperson trying to develop a long-lasting relationship. Emphasis on product features rather than customer needs is used more often in selling automobiles, clothing, and encyclopedias or in any situation in which the objective is immediate sales. The extreme of such a standardized or "shotgun" sales presentation is the "canned" presentation.

Making an effective demonstration. Demonstrations can be a particularly effective selling tool because they direct all the prospect's senses to what is being sold. Demonstrations permit showmanship. They also can nicely involve the prospect in an active role by encouraging touching, handling, or operating the product. Demonstrations require careful planning and practice to ensure a smooth performance.

Visual aids increase the impact. These include booklets, flip charts and easels, cassettes, catalogs and other literature, films or slides, and swatches and samples. Written testimonials from satisfied customers can be particularly effective, especially if these customers are reasonably similar to the prospect.

Several cautions apply to demonstrations and visual aids. They should be personalized to the customer whenever possible and should not be general, memorized material. Any visuals should be ready to use and not require tedious assembly and dismantling which distract the customer and interrupt the presentation. Demonstrations and visuals should not consume so much time that they irritate an impatient prospect.

Handling Objections and Sales Resistance

Objections can occur at any time during the presentation. The salesperson should be prepared for and welcome them, for they usually indicate some initial interest and also offer the opportunity to present additional selling points in the process of answering them. Common objections concern price, satisfaction with the present supplier, reluctance to make a decision at the time, no immediate need for the product or service, negative or neutral feelings about the salesperson's firm, and insistence on unacceptable special deals and offerings. The salesperson must anticipate such objections and plan to respond.

Discussing the selling process in much depth is beyond the scope of this book. Handling objections, in particular, could be treated in much more detail, and there are a number of specific techniques used by experienced salespeople.[11] An example of one is the so-called *boomerang method,* which is quite widely used by life insurance agents in particular, and converts an objection into a reason for buying. A young father wryly admits the need for a life insurance policy, "But I can't possibly afford one now. I have all I can do to barely make ends meet." To which the insurance agent responds, "Joe, that's all the more reason for you to buy life insurance. Just think what would happen to your family if you were not here."

Closing the Sale

The culmination of the selling process, of course, is the closing of the sale. Here the seller asks the prospect for the order; few prospects actually volunteer to buy, so they need to be led to this point by the seller. Customers emit clues or signals that they are ready to close (a purchasing agent may ask, "What kind of a delivery date could I get?" or "Does your company have a warehouse for spare parts in this city?"). Techniques for closing the sale vary. For example the seller may act as though the major buying question is settled and ask questions concerning details, "How do you want this shipped?" or "What financing will you want?"[12] Experts cite body language and physical actions as providing valuable clues for closing the sale.[13]

Invariably, some salespeople are better closers than others. The sales manager may need to help those who too often carry the sales presentation up to the culmination and then muff it through inadequate timing of their closing moves or, more likely, show timidity in asking for the order.

For some kinds of selling, such as insurance, the closure is the time to ask for leads, the names of acquaintances who might also be interested in the particular product or service.

Handling a nonsale.   Not every contact results in a sale. The *batting average* (the ratio of sales made to sales calls) may vary from 1:3 to 1:20 or more. A nonsale may result in a sale later, and your reaction to the refusal may determine the likelihood of a future sale. A resentful or surly attitude will probably destroy any future chances, but complacency does not characterize the good salesperson. Rather, a careful self-analysis of the lost sale and the presentation can increase one's batting average.

In its training manual Addressograph-Multigraph Corporation suggests that every salesperson ask the following questions after an unsuccessful sales call:

1. Did I contact the right person?
2. Was my approach effective?
3. Was I confident during my approach?
4. Did I talk too much or too fast?
5. Did my prospect understand my story?
6. Did I talk the prospect's language, or did I use technical and trade terms not understandable to the prospect?
7. Did I lack poise during my approach and thereby detract from the effectiveness of my reasoning?
8. Was my explanation and presentation of proof effective?
9. How did I handle the objections raised? Were my answers reasonable, logical, and effective?
10. Did I offend my prospect by discourtesy?
11. Did I argue rather than sell?
12. Did I make my bid for an order at the proper time?[14]

Following up

In an increasingly competitive environment, the follow-up is more important than ever. Most firms recognize that their continued successful operation depends on satisfied customers who are repeat buyers. Cemented buyer–seller relations suggest that you should perform at least the following:

- ☐ Reassure the customer of the widsom of the purchase.
- ☐ Handle the order and delivery as efficiently as possible.
- ☐ Check back to see that the product is performing satisfactorily.
- ☐ Be prepared to handle any problems quickly and expedite replacement of any parts.

The term *customer manager* has been used to describe a salesperson's involvement in the complaint handling of his customers.[15] The importance of follow-up for good customer relations and the ultimate in follow-up, relationship management are elaborated on later in this chapter.

APPLYING THE BEHAVIORAL SCIENCES TO THE SALES PROCESS

Both sales researchers and practitioners are devoting considerable attention to the behavioral sciences, particularly psychology and sociology, to understand and better adjust to the many factors involved in the purchase decision. Concepts of communication, perception, learning, goals, life-style, role conflict and ambiguity, social influences, and many other aspects of consumer behavior are relevant to sales. The complexity of behavioral science should dispel any notion that effective selling can be done by simple formulas.

The Dyadic Relationship

We are now recognizing the importance of the buyer–seller interaction, a *dyadic interaction*. A successful transaction depends on the nature of the interaction and on the roles played by both seller and customer in a particular encounter.[16] An interesting avenue of research in this area suggests that effective salespeople have characteristics similar to their customers in age, size, and other demographic and social variables.[17] This idea has some profound implications for sales managers. For example selecting and hiring sales applicants who are likely to be more successful might require a careful study of the characteristics of the customers of the firm.

The individual salesperson can reinforce the salesperson–customer similarity by specific techniques. For example the salesperson may seek a common ground to establish mutual interests, such as similar reference groups (family, community), leisure activities, and so on. Another tactic is to refrain from actions that might be incompatible with the customer's tastes. If there is no evidence that the customer smokes, the wise sales representative would refrain. Or if the customer is soft spoken and serious, a loud, joking personality might be ineffective in fostering a smooth interaction. Another reinforcer is to be supportive of the customer, such as voicing agreement or giving praise (such as, "I hadn't thought of that").[18]

Identifying Social Style as an Aid to Interaction

Social styles represent customer's general behavior. Figure 3.3 presents a matrix of four commonly defined types of social style among executives in their role as customers. Once a salesperson has identified the prospect's category, then supposedly the selling message can be adapted. For example if the social style is a "driver," who is strongly result oriented and very thorough and demanding, then the sales representative is more likely to achieve success with a short and dynamic presentation, talking facts and bottom-line results. The advice is also to go through the closing quickly.[19]

The psychological aspects of selling can provide worthwhile insights for some situations and customers. However, there is no magic formula guaranteeing sales success. Generalizations about customers' characteristics reveal many exceptions. Still, the dyadic interaction needs improvement, and psychology and the other behavioral disciplines can provide intriguing ideas.

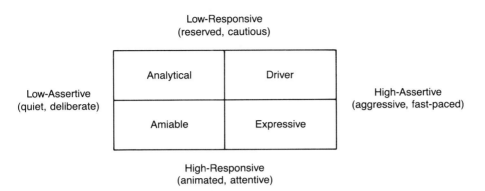

FIGURE 3.3   Matrix of social styles. (*Source*: Adapted from Wilson Learning Corporation, as described and illustrated in Ronald D. Balsley and E. Patricia Birsner, *Selling: Marketing Personified*. New York: Dryden Press, 1987, 90–99.)

HOW TO DEVELOP AND MAINTAIN GOOD CUSTOMER RELATIONS

Customer satisfaction and good customer relations are basic to virtually all kinds of selling (excluding the few that have no repeat business, such as sales of recreational land or home improvements). As stressed before (and later), good customer relations lead to repeat business, which usually requires much less selling time and effort than for the initial sale. Satisfied customers are more likely to give good word-of-mouth publicity for a company and its products. They can also be a good source of information about the marketplace and can alert a firm to emerging problems and opportunities that might have escaped detection.

Impediments to Good Relations

Rapport gained during the initial selling contact obviously helps. However, despite compatible personalities between seller and buyer, if service promises are not fulfilled or the product is defective and fails to meet customer expectations, then good relations are threatened. Some sales representatives succumb to the temptation to load their customers with goods—more than they reasonably can use in the near future. This practice results in higher immediate commissions but jeopardizes future trust and confidence.

Occasionally, a salesperson encounters difficulties in long-term contacts with customers. Although the *threshold appearance* (the impression made by the seller on the first call and/or the first sale) may have been satisfactory, the ongoing impression may not be. Some salespeople do not wear well; unless their firm has given them something new to sell or a customer problem must be solved, they find it difficult to provide the call with a sense of purpose that makes the customer pleased to see them. Just dropping in to say hello and tell a story or two becomes trite and may annoy a busy buyer.

Keeping Customers Satisfied

Even if customers are reasonably satisfied with the delivery time, the product, and any special tailoring or installation, you may still need to devote effort to maintaining good relationships. Keep in touch with customers and call on them regularly to emphasize your interest in them and any problems they might have. Large, important customers generally are called on more frequently than small accounts; otherwise, the selling costs in dealing with the smaller customers may become uneconomical. Contact can be maintained with small accounts periodically by phone or mail.

"Keeping in-touch" contacts are most productive and appreciated when the salesperson solves any problem the customer may have with the goods. The contact may also serve to improve the product knowledge of the customer's employees, return defective goods, or obtain an extra part. With smaller customers the salesperson may suggest a better display or different use of the product. Any customer complaints should be dealt with promptly and fairly. Although these calls may generate some additional business, that should not be considered the sole criterion of their effectiveness.

Relationship management. Philip Kotler has used the term "relationship management" to denote the importance of a close, continuing association with customers, especially the larger key accounts:

> [Sales representatives] must do more than call when they think customers might be ready to place orders. They should call or visit at other times, taking customers to dinner, making useful suggestions about their business, and so on. They should follow the fortunes of their key accounts, know their problems and opportunities, and be ready to serve them in a number of ways.[20]

Relationship management becomes the fullest extension of customer relations and keeping customers satisfied. Often the relationship will include not only sales representatives and their sales managers interacting with these customers but higher company executives as well.

What to Do About Lost Customers

Invariably, some customers will be lost. Their needs may change, or they may become dissatisfied with matters beyond the salesperson's control, such as slow deliveries or lack of repair parts. A more persuasive competitor or one with better merchandise or better prices may have succeeded in obtaining

The Power of Positive Listening

Many salespeople could do a much better job of selling if they spent more time listening. They are so bound up in persuading the customer of product benefits and how these should meet all customers' needs that they fail to listen. Several factors contribute to this subordination of listening:

☐ Listening is passive rather than aggressive, and passivity is not seen as compatible with selling.

☐ The salesperson may be inclined to show off the product and his technical knowledge.

☐ Salespeople often feel that to sell we need to persuade and to persuade we need to talk.

☐ The salesperson may be impatient to make the next sales call.

☐ The salesperson may anticipate objections rather than waiting for them.

Good "listenership" is necessary to uncover the specific customer's needs, buying motives, and relevant product and service benefits. Listening is needed to develop the rapport that is so important for repeat business and loyal customers.

The sales call should consist of interaction and mutual communication not merely persuasion. Good listeners encourage a customer's comments by active and interested listening and thoughtful questions.

their business. Can you, as a salesperson, do anything in these circumstances? The loss of customers should not dissuade you from continuing personal contacts and efforts to win them back.

Sometimes you must face it: The blame for the lost account must rest firmly on your shoulders. Perhaps you yielded to the temptation to exaggerate a bit or made false promises to swing the sale; perhaps you were careless in service; maybe a brief lapse in courtesy or a personality defect—such as being too cocky or overbearing—became offensive to the customer. If you are indeed the major contributor to losing the customer, this should be a learning experience, enabling you to better guard against future lapses or temptations.

Regardless of the reasons, real or assumed, for the lost customer, recording all the details is advisable. This information can help in determining corrective action and precautions to minimize the loss of other customers.

TOWARD BETTER TIME MANAGEMENT

Time management is particularly important in selling because the hours available for productive face-to-face interaction with customers are limited. You want to accomplish as much as you can in this available time, and not waste it in traffic jams, inefficient routing and travel, waiting rooms, or writing reports, letters, and other nonselling activities. If you can free up enough time to make one more customer call a day, the chances are your sales would be impressively increased.

Planning is the key to successful time management. To do a better job of planning, a detailed log should be kept of daily activities. This can help you analyze each segment of time. The log may indicate that too much time is spent with smaller accounts. Although the relationship may be pleasant, the potential to increase sales with these customers may be limited. Time spent on accounts should be based on potential contribution; thus, bigger accounts are worth more time than smaller ones.

Waiting time can be reduced by making appointments in advance, and calling just before the visit to confirm that the customer is free and expecting you. Some waiting is usually unavoidable, but it can be used to handle reports and other paperwork.

Travel time may be lessened by planning routes carefully, ensuring that calls are not made in a zigzag pattern requiring backtracking. Planning may also help you avoid rush-hour traffic congestion.

Some customers' time for sales calls may be restricted to certain hours. For example some retailers are particularly busy when opening and on weekends. And special sales events may leave little time for listening to sales presentations. Querying your customers regarding time constraints is a good practice.

In the quest to make the best use of your time, one expert suggests,

> You may have two or more customers in the same area who are early risers and like to have you make calls on them first thing in the morning. Get them together for breakfast. The result will be two calls at once.[21]

As with any plans some flexibility is needed in dealing with the unexpected, such as an appointment broken without notice, a customer calling to say that you are needed right away, or an unexpected sales meeting. Planning can help minimize the impact of such unforeseen demands on your time.

Common Time-Drain Problems

Time-drain situations, which eat into your productive selling time, often can be anticipated and helped by planning. For example when you encounter unexpected waiting time, you can catch up on some report writing, or use the time for job-related reading. You can hardly ignore the customer who "needs you now," but time planning can help you identify priorities and tasks that can be postponed if time is inadequate. Another common time drain is individual sales calls taking too much time. Calls should be planned according to goals. Unplanned calls invariably consume more time. Finally, you may find that you are simply wasting time. Valuable time can be drained from your day if you are uncertain what to do after concluding a particular sales call. Planning should give you a reasonable sequence of activities.[22]

Tips for Developing a Time-Management Plan

After analyzing your past activities with a log, which should help you identify common and recurring time drains, you are ready to plan your work. Planning is simple:

1. List the activities you want to do each day. These may not all be work activities but may also involve personal things including recreation. (You may want to plan further ahead and do this for each week rather than each day.)

2. Establish priorities. Consider which activities are most important, and must be accomplished, and which are of lower priority, and if necessary may be postponed.

3. Earnestly pursue your planned goals but modify as necessary.

4. Make daily or weekly activities plans and goals a habit.

Managing time is within your control, and it is worth the effort![23]

SUMMARY

At the beginning of this chapter I asked you to think of the rather common selling situation where the prospective customer tells you that he doesn't have much time to listen to your sales presentation. If you recognized that this problem is more common with cold calls (calls made without appointments), good! Making an appointment generally is best, perhaps by phone or letter. Scheduling an appointment may not be practical, however, when approaching a new prospect who might be reluctant to plan a meeting with an unknown salesperson and company, or when the salesperson unexpectedly has time to make a call. When confronted with the prospect's statement of limited time, the salesperson must decide whether to give an abbreviated presentation, ask for an appointment, or consider the prospect's lack of time as a condition that could change if he becomes interested during the presentation.

The topic of basic selling activities paves the way for the sales management topics of the rest of the book, because success in selling is generally a prerequisite for sales management.

The steps involved in the personal selling process begin with prospecting—identifying prospective customers—and qualifying them—determining if they are valid prospects who have the money, the authority, and the need for the product or service.

Preparing for an effective sales call requires preapproach planning—investigating as much as possible about the customer and his needs, defining the objectives of the call, and determining the strategy.

In the approach and presentation, the sales representative tries to build rapport and interest. A presentation tailored to the specific customer and his situation usually is more effective than a canned or memorized message used for all customers. Visual aids and demonstration skills can be effective.

Objections should be expected at any time during the presentation. Most objectives can be anticipated and categorized (such as about price, no immediate need, reluctance to make a decision now), and the sales representative should have planned how best to respond.

In the closing the salesperson asks the prospect for the order. Alertness is needed for clues that suggest the prospect is ready to close, but above all the salesperson should not be timid about asking for the order. If the sales call does not result in a sale, a careful self-analysis may help future sales.

The follow-up is important to ensure that customers are satisfied and thus are likely to be repeat buyers.

Certain behavioral science concepts can be applied to the sales situation, in particular, the dyadic relationship and social style of the prospect.

Developing and maintaining good customer relations are important. The ultimate in customer relations is relationship management, which is characterized by a close, continuing association with customers.

Affecting each step of the sales process, time management can be improved through planning, thus freeing up more time for productive sales efforts.

QUESTIONS

1. Compare and contrast the sales presentation made to a major buyer with that made to a group of buyers.

2. In a large organization, identifying the proper person to be contacted can be a problem. How would you recommend that a salesperson make such an identification?

3. What would you suggest a salesperson do about an important customer who was recently lost to a competitor?

4. Give some suggestions for achieving a good "threshold" appearance when visiting an industrial purchasing agent. Would these suggestions differ for a salesperson selling mutual funds via referrals? A person selling encyclopedias door-to-door?

5. Under what circumstances would you recommend using a canned presentation? Why?

6. What are the steps in the selling process? Which would you see as most crucial for an insurance salesperson? A manufacturer of machine tools? Why?

7. What are information sources for finding prospects?

8. What suggestions and caveats do you have for making effective demonstrations?

9. What are some implications of a dyadic relationship?

10. How would you develop a time-management plan?

11. Discuss the idea of relationship management. Does this really differ from the idea of a customer manager?

Select a product or service and the type of buyer or buyers you wish to sell it to, such as a purchasing agent, a retail store buyer, or a final consumer. Taking the role of salesperson and asking one or more of your classmates to act as customer(s), make a sales presentation before the rest of the class. The class should be prepared to criticize the presentation constructively.

ROLE-PLAYING EXERCISE

NOTES

1. For a time-effective approach to identifying and reaching prospects, see Marvin A. Jolson, "Prospecting by Telephone Prenotification: An Application of the Foot-in-the-Door Technique," *Journal of Personal Selling & Sales Management* (August 1986).

2. "A Refresher Course for Salespeople: Prospecting for Fun and Profit," *Sales Manager's Bulletin* (15 January 1980): 5–7.

3. For help in using direct mail lists for prospecting, see John Chapman, "Get Your Sales Leads by Mail: Here's How," *Marketing Times* (July/August 1979): 12–13.

4. Robert B. Konikow, "Spotlight Your New Product Via Tradeshows," *Marketing Times* (July/August 1981): 22; "Trade Shows: Where Prospects Call on You: A Special Report," *Sales & Marketing Management* (28 August 1979).

5. Sally Scanlon, "Striking It Rich with Industrial Ads," *Sales & Marketing Management* (18 June 1979): 39–44.

6. Robert Hood, "Increase Sales by Decreasing Number of Bad Leads," *Marketing News* (23 May 1986): 18.

7. Frederick E. Webster and Yoram Wind, *Organizational Buying Behavior* (Englewood Cliffs, N.J.: Prentice-Hall, 1972), .

8. Joseph A. Bellizzi, "Organizational Size and Buying Influences," *Industrial Marketing Management* (October 1981): 17–21.

9. John T. Molloy, *Dress for Success* (New York: Peter H. Wayden, 1975). And John T. Molloy, *The Woman's Dress for Success* (Chicago: Follett, 1977). Also see Mortimer Levitt, "Clothes: The Executive Look and How to Get It," *Marketing Times*

(September/October 1980): 18–22; and Ron Kolgraf, "Salesman in the Gray Flannel Suit," *Industrial Distribution* (April 1981): 103.

10. For example see James Lorenzen, "Needs Analysis Replacing Product Presentation," *Marketing News* (25 April 1986): 8.

11. Any book on salesmanship goes into the topic of handling objections in great detail. Recent articles dealing with this subject include Daniel K. Weadcock, "Your Troops Can Keep Control and Close the Sale—by Anticipating Objections," *Sales & Marketing Management* (17 March 1980): 101–104; and Dan Weadcock, "Saying Yes . . . But Is Really No Way to Overcome a Buyer's Objections," *Sales & Marketing Management* (15 October 1979): 94–96.

12. For examples of closing techniques, see Charles E. Bergman, "Secrets of the Industrial Close," in "Closing the Sale: A Special Report," *Sales & Marketing Management* 1977.

13. For examples of the role of body language in closing the sale, see Julius Fast, *Body Language* (New York: Evans, 1970); and Gerhard Gaschwandtner, "How To Read Your Prospect's Body Language," *Industrial Marketing* (July 1981): 55–59.

14. The questions salespersons might ask themselves after a sale are adapted from a list in Charles Atkinson Kirkpatrick, *Salesmanship*, 5th ed. (Cincinnati: South-Western, 1971), 396–397.

15. Hartmut Kimstadt, "Sales Reps of Future To Be Customer-Managers," *Marketing News* (25 April 1986): 6.

16. For example, see Barry J. Hersker, "The Ecology of Personal Selling," *Southern Journal of Business* (July 1970): 41–46; Barton A. Weitz, "Effectiveness in Sales Interactions: A Contingency Framework," *Journal of Marketing* (Winter 1981): 85–102.

17. F. B. Evans, "Selling as a Dyadic Relationship," *The American Behavioral Scientist* (May 1963): 76–79; A. Parasuraman, "Assigning Salesmen to Sales Territories: Some Practical Guidelines," *Industrial Marketing Management* (December 1975): 335–344.

18. Adapted from Ronald D. Balsley and E. Patricia Birsner, *Selling: Marketing Personified* (New York: Dryden Press, 1987), 87.

19. *Ibid.*, 96.

20. Philip Kotler, *Marketing Management*, 5th ed. (Englewood Cliffs, N.J.: Prentice-Hall, 1984), 712.

21. Richard D. Nordstrom, *Introduction to Selling* (New York: Macmillan Co., 1981), 70.

22. Adapted from Nordstrom, *Introduction to Selling*, 71–73.

23. For more details on time management, see Nordstrom, *Introduction to Selling*, Chap. 6; and Alan Lakein, *How to Get Control of Your Time and Your Life* (New York: Signet Books, 1973).

cases

3.1 Persuading a Tough Customer

James McDowell has been in sales with the Skirig Company, a rental company for cars and trucks, for the last 2 years. Although his ultimate objective is to enter management, he realizes that his sales experience is invaluable as preparation for management and yields a satisfactory standard of living. He faces a tough customer in Carol Buchanan, but the challenge of trying to win this account is intriguing. The particular problem with this company is that Carol has an inordinate pride in her fleet of trucks, all colorfully painted with the green and white logo of her company.

"This is the best publicity I could ever hope to achieve," Carol has reiterated several times to James. "People see these trucks and they immediately think of our stores. That is why we take great pains to keep them freshly painted, clean, and no more than 2 years old. This visibility is worth thousands of dollars of advertising."

James, faced with this pride of ownership, has carefully compiled figures to show that Carol could save about $50,000 a year if she switched from owning to leasing trucks. But the salesman faces the dual problem of first counteracting a customer's strong commitment to her present way of doing business and, second, proving the desirability of his particular product and service in better meeting the customer's needs.

James rather hesitantly broached the subject of the cost savings.

"I know you mean well, young fellow," was the quick customer response. "I appreciate the time you've spent in compiling these data. And I'm sure you'll go far. But you are not going to convince me to change what I'm doing now."

Recognizing an obdurate customer, James was prepared to give up. However, his boss called to say, "You have to develop a better argument to *prove* that Carol Buchanan needs our service. You have to do a better job of stressing the dollars-and-cents savings to her. James, you need to develop a hard-hitting pitch that will convince her."

QUESTIONS

1. How would James give a convincing presentation? Develop a step-by-step presentation.
2. What should be the primary focus of the presentation? Develop a few key selling sentences for James.

3.2 Donnelley Co.: Can We Improve the Effective Selling Time of Our Salespeople?

Susan Wain, sales manager for the Donnelley Co., a marketer of telephone answering services to small businesses and professionals, was pondering one of the perennial problems facing a sales force: the large proportion of unproductive time consumed daily. She had recently read an article in a business journal that summarized a survey of how industrial salespeople spend their time:

Industrial salesmen spend only 39% of their time—or about 3¾ hours a day—in face-to-face selling. . . . A typical salesman spends most of his day driving to interviews, making reports, attending meetings, and making service calls. . . . A similar survey in 1978 showed that salesmen then spent 23 minutes more in face-to-face selling situations.

Susan doubted that her sales force spent its time much more effectively than that. Indeed, there was probably more wasted time because many of the professionals who were called on—physicians, lawyers, engineers, architects, accountants—were so solidly booked with appointments that a sales representative could be wedged in only periodically and then given only limited time.

The next day, Susan called in Tom Spero, one of the older sales representatives, for a discussion of this problem. Susan believed in coming quickly to the point, "How many hours a day, Tom, do you think you spend in productive, face-to-face selling?"

Tom cleared his throat nervously. "I've never really thought about it, but I suppose only about half the day is spent in such selling. Of course, I often take a customer or prospect out to lunch, and we probably talk about business part of that time. . . ." His voice trailed off. "I guess I can't really give you a definite answer."

"Tom, I'm going to ask you and the other sales reps to keep a detailed log of each day's activities. Will you do this for me? We'll keep it quite simple, so it won't take much time. We won't use these as a basis for criticism or anything like that, so there'll be no sense in fudging or padding. And suppose we do this for, shall we say, 2 weeks, and then see what we have?"

At the end of 2 weeks, the logs were turned in, and Susan's assistant compiled the data. The results were as follows:

Percentage of Sales Representatives	Hours per Day of Face-to-Face Selling
12%	4−4.5
26	3.5−4
32	3−3.5
18	2.5−3
8	2−2.5
4	less than 2

Susan was shocked at the results, not only because there was such a wide spread from the most effective to the least effective people, but because the median itself was not much more than 3 hours.

She recognized that there were some differences in territories and in customer mixes, which would make certain representatives show more productivity than others. But this could hardly account for a range of less than 2 hours to 4½ hours a day.

She decided to talk with the four salespeople reporting less than 2 hours per day of face-to-face selling. Several complained that their territories' customers were too scattered to be handled more efficiently.

Chuck Nagy, however, had a different rationale, "I am keenly aware of the importance of my customers' time. I don't want to waste any with idle chatter. So I get right down to the point with each visit. I bet if you check, you'll find I make as many sales calls as anybody."

"Maybe you're not spending enough time with your customers," Susan said.

But Chuck was adamant, "My customers want it this way. I'll bet you'd find some of those reps who report the most face-to-face time don't have nearly as good a sales as I do."

"Chuck, I'm going to look into this. But I still think you could be more efficient in your scheduling and in making appointments," Susan said as she showed Chuck to the door.

Chuck's remarks bothered her during the next several days. She finally took her assistant from another assignment and asked him to determine the relationship between reported hours of face-to-face selling and sales productivity.

A few days later he brought in the results. "It's kind of a mixed-up relationship," he explained. "We seem to have good and poor producers in both categories. Oh, there are slightly more who show up poorly both in sales and in face-to-face selling time. But not as many as we expected."

"Thanks, Jerry. How do you assess this time-management situation?"

"I think they all could do a better job of managing their time. I think you should schedule a series of training sessions on time management."

QUESTIONS

1. What do you think Susan should do at this point?
2. Do you think the logs were likely to be valid? Why or why not?
3. Design a program for increasing the productive use of selling time for such a firm.

PART II
PLANNING SALES EFFORTS

CHAPTER 4
The Planning Process and Strategic Planning

CHAPTER 5
Analyzing the Market: Assessing Potential

CHAPTER 6
Forecasting Sales

CHAPTER 7
Budgeting the Sales Efforts

CHAPTER 4
The Planning Process and Strategic Planning

CHAPTER PERSPECTIVE

Planning is important at all organizational levels to grasp opportunities, to avoid "decisions by crisis," and to create order. This chapter examines planning first from the corporate level, and this leads to the strategic planning concept, which is long-range environmental-sensitive systematic planning and has become the vogue in recent years. Planning at the sales manager level follows, with consideration of the procedures involved in translating company objectives and planned strategies into district goals and then into individual sales representatives' goals and plans for action.

CHAPTER OBJECTIVES

□ Understand the planning concept and the reasons for planning.

□ Become familiar with the types of planning, and in particular the strategic planning concept.

□ Know the steps involved in the planning process and how they are related.

□ Become acquainted with those goals of the sales department that are sometimes incompatible with those of various other organizational units, and understand how these goals can be reconciled.

□ Familiarize yourself with planning at the sales manager level and its relationship to company plans and objectives.

□ Understand the importance of market information in planning and the sales department's role in providing this information.

THE CONCEPT OF PLANNING

Simply stated, planning is deciding now what to do later—what courses of action to take. Accordingly, planning requires anticipating the consequences of decisions as well as external factors. Planning directs company efforts and resources toward common objectives so that divisions, departments, and employees do not work at cross purposes.

Planning can vary widely in extent and formality. Some large firms have planning staffs and committees, prepare formal written documents, and include executives and employees at all levels. At the other extreme is the firm that makes no plans other than the financial and accounting budgets and addresses only daily problems and operations, which often results in "decision by crisis" and "firefighting."

Planning is a tool that should be used at all levels in an organization, from general management down to the greenest sales recruit. But as with all tools, planning does not guarantee success; it may be misused, or unforeseen events may shatter the best-laid plans. Following are some specific examples of breakdowns in planning.

Planning Mistakes

A classic example. In 13 years, Boise Cascade grew from a $35 million lumber operation to a $1.8 billion conglomerate. The secret was an aggressive plan of growth through acquisitions. In 1966 Boise entered the recreational land-development field. This seemed the great growth arena of the coming decades because consumer leisure time and per capita income was increasing. By 1968 Boise's sales of recreational land was $90 million; in 1969 this spurted to $165 million.

In the rush to acquire firms active in recreational land development, Boise also obtained their executives and salespeople. These acquisitions were permitted to run themselves with only hazy and uncoordinated objectives and planning. These land developers tended to be of the old school, concerned with quick sales, not customer satisfaction. Their attitude toward land was also selfish, "Cut it up, develop it, sell it, and get out." But public attitudes were rapidly changing, and Boise neither anticipated such environmental changes nor planned any effective strategy to cope. Boise eventually had to spend $60 million to settle lawsuits charging misrepresentation. And ecologists were mobilizing public opinion for more open spaces, underground utilities, and full sewage-treatment facilities.

Profits plummeted in 1970. But the ax fell in 1971, with a staggering $85.1 million loss. Plagued by deficits and lawsuits, Boise eventually worked its way out of the land business, taking some $300 million in losses and write-offs.

Analysis.   Boise exemplifies the disaster that can occur with faulty planning. Boise lacked definitive plans and policies for the recreational land acquisitions. The acquisitions operated autonomously, with only such vague goals as "increase sales." Policy modifications to adapt to changing environmental pressures were not made in time. Finally, control is an essential ingredient of sound planning that Boise lacked. Performance must be monitored at key points to assure that operations are meeting policies and objectives. Boise was negligent, first, in monitoring operations sufficiently to know that problems existed and, second, in correcting them quickly. For example Boise desperately needed to monitor the field sales force and curb their high-pressure techniques.

Recent examples.   A pattern of unwise diversification—overdiversification—has continued to plague U.S. firms. They evidently learned nothing from the Boise debacle and others in the 1960s and 1970s. The siren call for growth distorted sound planning and judgment. Such diversifications often suffer from the same flaws noted with Boise: no clear sense of direction (except to expand), failure to recognize a changing environment, and loose controls. For example see Application 4.1.

APPLICATION 4.1   Overdiversification

Greyhound Corporation has been criticized for its diversifications into car rentals, computer leasing, institutional feeding, soap manufacturing, insurance, and travelers checks, in addition to its basic transportation services—a hodgepodge of unrelated businesses. Eventually, it found an urgent need to slim down, and sold off 15 of its subsidiary companies.*

Household International (formerly Household Finance) has had a similar pattern of unrelated acquisitions: Coast-to-Coast Hardware stores; discount, grocery, and furniture retailers; an Alaskan airline; a dredging company; a rental car company; banks; and factories making such things as vacuum jugs, barbecues, ice coolers, plumbing fixtures, fireplace inserts, turbochargers, and gears.

Household International grew, with revenues in 1983 of $8.3 billion. But "we never had a game plan," admitted a former officer, and profitability was spotty. By 1987 Household International had pared down to a $2.3 billion company. "One wonders what all the buying and selling accomplished except to make the investment bankers rich," one executive pondered.**

---

*Steven Greenhouse, "The Reshaping of Greyhound," *New York Times,* 5 November 1983, Midwest edition.
**"Happy Endings," *Forbes,* 10 August 1987, 73.

TYPES OF PLANNING

Planning can be categorized by time frame, scope, and formality (see Figure 4.1).

By time frame, planning can be categorized as strategic, annual, and short-term. Strategic planning is usually done at the highest level, as top management and their staffs make the decisions that will guide the firm's growth, development, and acquisition strategy over the long run. Annual planning should be compatible with the longer-range strategic objectives, but it involves more specific goals, plans, and forecasts for the immediate future. Obviously, the accuracy of planning varies inversely with the length of the planning period: The shorter the period, the more accurate the plans. When the focus is over several years, planning becomes more tenuous, although it still can provide guidelines for long-term decisions. More detailed planning must generally be limited to the short term.

Plans can further be designated as *standing plans* (plans that are used repeatedly) and *single-use plans.* General policies and standard operating procedures constitute standing plans. Examples that apply to the sales department are policies regarding credit, supply requisitions, and sales compensation. Single-use plans can guide special projects, such as introducing a new product, capturing a new market, or increasing market share in an existing territory.

The planning procedure can be formal and comprehensive, involving many people from a variety of disciplines, or it can be informal and limited only to the most essential financial and accounting budgets, involving a few specialized staff departments.

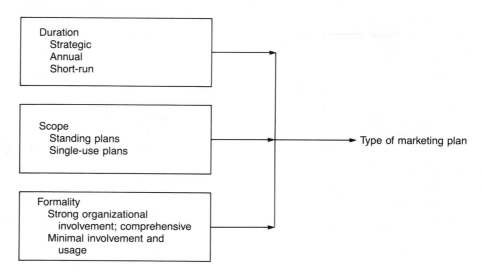

FIGURE 4.1   Categorizing marketing plans.

WHY PLAN?

Planning entails certain disadvantages. Executive time and effort that could be directed to other matters must be involved to some extent, depending on the detail and formality of the planning process. Of course, the planning and forecasting accuracy can be suspect, especially with longer-range plans and those made during periods of major economic, technological, and social uncertainty. Furthermore, the plan's policies and procedures may lead to such rigidity that unforeseen opportunities are missed, with initiative and creativity thwarted.

Some of these alleged problems (particularly those of rigidity and non-adaptation to changing conditions) can be lessened with good strategic planning, which theoretically focuses attention on the environment, both in reacting to it and acting to influence it. In any case the advantages of planning outweigh any inherent disadvantages, because careful planning is likely to reduce the potential for crises and mistakes. Anticipating problems avoids firefighting, as Boise Cascade learned the hard way. Planning can ensure more consistent and integrated action. Planning often results in economies of operation because time can be taken to consider the best approaches to decisions and the most effective alternatives. When standing plans are involved, the executive can delegate to subordinates with reasonable assurance that the work will be performed within the established guidelines.

Perhaps the greatest benefit of planning is that it furnishes the basis for control by providing standards for measuring performance. Any deviations from plan are readily evident, signaling the need for corrective action. For example if a salesperson does not reach the planned sales figures for a certain time period, she may need additional coaching or sales training, her territorial potential may need reassessing, or she may need to be replaced. Similarly, if expenses are out of line with budgeted figures, the salesperson can be cautioned to be more conservative in spending and entertaining.

STRATEGIC PLANNING AND THE PLANNING PROCESS

The Boise case demonstrates how a changing environment (changing public attitudes toward high-pressure selling techniques as well as ecological concerns) forced changes in previously accepted business methods. Strategic planning should help an organization better adapt, adjust, and take advantage of the environmental changes that invariably arise to disrupt the status quo.

Strategic planning is the managerial process of planning to cope with an ever-changing environment over the long run. Strategic planning is very much forward looking. One manager described it as "an eager seizing of opportunities." This type of planning should permeate an organization and not be limited to top executive suites and headquarter's "ivory towers." A hierarchy of plans should be involved, from corporate strategic plans, to strategic business unit plans, and programs for individual organizational entities.

Corporate strategic planning involves the broad mission statement and overall goals and objectives. It may include such major moves as acquisitions and divestitures, as well as the general allocation of company resources among the various facets of the business.

A strategic business unit, or SBU, is any organizational unit that has both a defined business strategy and a manager with sales and profit responsibility.[1] *Profit center* is a good term for SBUs, because their performance is easily measured in tangible operating results against other similar SBUs in the organization. Each SBU should have its own specified mission and objectives, with well-laid plans for accomplishing the desired objectives.

In programs for individual organizational entities, the broader corporate plans are filtered down to specific plans and objectives for SBUs. These in turn must be filtered down or translated into the individual functions or entities in the organization. In the sales organization this means filtering the plans down to the sales staff and individual sales representatives. Specific goals and plans for reaching them must be communicated to all facets of the organization.

The entire planning process involves more than simply laying out objectives and broad strategies for the overall corporation and the various definable units. The nitty-gritty of a definitive sales forecast, and setting budgets accordingly, also must permeate all units of the organization. The specific plans of action must be designed and broken down as finely as possible, even to the individual sales representative. Finally, all these plans must be implemented and controlled. Although the specifics of the strategic planning process are beyond the scope of this book, it is important to recognize that sales planning, both in total and by smaller unit breakdowns, should operate within the environment created by strategic planning.[2]

The Steps Involved in Planning

Figure 4.2 shows the steps involved in planning and the relationship of planning to the general management functions. As the diagram shows at the corporate level, the first steps in planning—the strategic planning role—involve determining the company mission and setting overall corporate objectives. However, the objectives must be tempered by assessing market potential and relevant environmental factors. The sales forecast is derived from the analysis of market potential and future demand, but it should also account for major changes contemplated in the plan of action, such as increased advertising expenditures or an expanded sales force, or introducing a new and exciting product (see the two-way arrows in Figure 4.2). In conjunction with the sales forecast, expense and operating budgets are developed, which the plan of action also should affect. Designing a specific plan of action is the final step in the direct planning process. The management functions of organizing, staffing, and directing the organization serve to implement the plan.

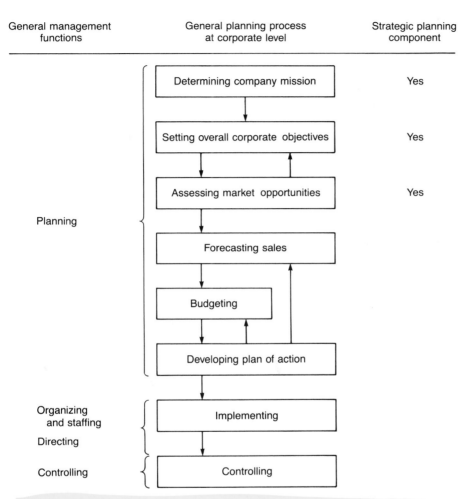

General management functions	General planning process at corporate level	Strategic planning component

Determining company mission — Yes

Setting overall corporate objectives — Yes

Assessing market opportunities — Yes

Planning {

Forecasting sales

Budgeting

Developing plan of action

Organizing and staffing — Implementing

Directing

Controlling — Controlling

FIGURE 4.2   The planning process as it relates to strategic planning and the general functions of management.

Finally, results are compared with the planned goals and standards of performance, and any deviations are noted for corrective action.

The strategic planning component is primarily involved with the first three steps of the planning process, where longer-range opportunities and strategies are developed.

Company Mission

Strategic planning begins with the determination of the company's fundamental mission. Usually, this involves deciding "What business should we be in?" Which may or may not be the same as "What business are we presently in?" A mission determination should involve the following three factors:

1. Assessing the environment and how it is changing or is expected to change
2. Appraising competitive factors and how these may be changing
3. Weighing the particular strengths and weaknesses of the company— what it does best and where it has been deficient

For example one company (ITT Barton, a subsidiary of ITT) developed this mission statement:

> The mission is to serve the industry and government with quality instruments used for the primary measurement, analysis, and local control of fluid flow, level, pressure, temperature, and fluid properties. This instrumentation includes flow meters, electronic readouts, indicators, switches. . . . Markets served include instrumentation for oil and gas production, gas transportation, chemical and petrochemical processing, cryogenics, power generation, aerospace, Government and marine, as well as other instrument and equipment manufacturers.[3]

Mission statements can be too broad—"to make a profit"—or too narrow, focusing on a particular product or service that may become obsolete as technology and customer requirements change. Three decades ago Theodore Levitt cautioned against too narrow a definition of business mission or purpose, and he advised railroads to think of themselves as being in the transportation business and not just the railroad business; petroleum firms, the energy business; and motion picture companies, the entertainment business.[4] Narrow definitions restrict perspectives and the grasping of different opportunities, just as too broad a definition is useless as a guide for definitive action.

Determining Objectives

After the company mission has been determined, objectives or performance goals should be established. Again, as with the mission statement, a goal of "to make a profit" is an oversimplication and not specific enough to aid planning.

Firms may have multiple goals, although in many, especially smaller firms, these may be implicit or ill-defined. Goals may be stated too vaguely or smack of the flavor of public relations. Nevertheless, there are important benefits of stating goals and objectives in explicit language and in order of priority, because some may conflict. Goals that are well communicated and understood by all departments of the organization can provide criteria for making policy decisions and introduce consistency into decision making. The following are typical goals:

- ☐ Growth of the firm, a division, a product line, or a product
- ☐ Short-term profit maximization

- ☐ Profit maximization over the long run
- ☐ Service to customers
- ☐ Enlargement of size of market
- ☐ Increase in share of market
- ☐ Achievement of industry leadership

A firm that does not have well-defined and current objectives and policies is vulnerable to competitors. For example Wrigley in gum, Hershey in candy, and Mennen in men's toiletries are family-owned firms that had no clear plans for growth. None of these introduced a new product for decades. As a result they eventually faced aggressive competitors who took advantage of their vulnerability and complacency.

Reconciling strategic business unit goals. Often, the sales department's attempts to mobilize company resources to maximize customer satisfaction are basically incompatible with other departments' attempts to maintain efficient performance. For example the two departments, sales and production, would have the following incompatible goals:

Sales	Production
Short production lead time	Long production lead time
Short runs with many models	Long runs with few models
Frequent model changes	No model changes
Custom orders	Standard orders
Aesthetic appearance	Ease of fabrication
Tight quality control	Average quality control

Similar differences of perspective exist between sales and such departments as engineering, purchasing, inventory, servicing, physical distribution, finance and accounting, and credit:

Sales	Credit
Extending the range of customers by	Minimizing bad debts by
Easy credit terms	Tough credit terms
Liberal risks	Accepting only good credit risks

Sales	Installation and Servicing
Prompt and dependable installations and/or providing of repair parts	Cost containment by gearing the operation to a "normal" level of demand

If installations must be made or servicing and repair parts are an important part of the product package, obviously, the efforts of the sales force will be seriously jeopardized by any inefficiencies or ill-considered economies in these areas. Servicing should be closely coordinated with the sales function to back it up as smoothly and efficiently as possible. However, the sales staff can constantly deluge the service departments with unreasonable demands. Compromises may need to be made, but care must be taken to prevent major problems or insufficient support.

Sales	*Physical Distribution*
Fast delivery with complete warehouse stocks	Hold down costs by
Good packing and order filling	Lean warehouse inventories
	Minimal labor costs

As with servicing, these activities can help cement a sale and gain a loyal and satisfied customer, or they can help lose a sale and a customer. Offering faster delivery than competitors can be a strong sales inducement. However, some trade-offs may be necessary. For fastest delivery the ordered items must be in stock in nearby warehouses. Depending on such variables as level of demand, evenness of orders, and resources of the company, maintenance of sufficient stocks of all goods at nearby location may be too costly. Again, a compromise may be needed.

Toward a balanced role for the sales department. The sales department is fundamentally important to the firm because it develops the firm's revenues, but it may need to be restrained. Peak sales probably would result from special modifications of products; reduced prices; unusually speedy delivery; easy credit terms; a heavy, maintained inventory; and broad product lines with many models. But the firm's profitability might be jeopardized. Therefore, any additional costs should be weighed against the resulting increase in customer satisfaction and sales.

Assessing Market Opportunity

The final step of the strategic planning process is to assess market opportunity or potential, which should be guided by the more generally stated objectives and goals of the firm. The firm's present business is the starting point for this assessment, commonly called *portfolio analysis*. The analysis may use a product–market opportunity matrix (other approaches are the Boston Consulting Group matrix, Profit Impact of Market Strategy [PIMS], and the Porter generic strategy model) (see Figure 4.3), which presents four alternatives for grasping growth:

1. Market penetration. Sales are increased to present customers with present products.
2. Market development. New markets are sought for present products.
3. Product development. New products are developed to appeal to the present market.
4. Diversification. New products are aimed at new markets.[5]

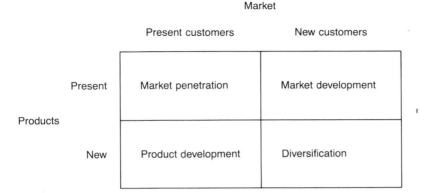

FIGURE 4.3   The product–market opportunity matrix. (*Source*: Adapted from H. Igor Ansoff, "Strategies for Diversification," *Harvard Business Review*, September–October 1957:113–124.)

In conducting a portfolio analysis, present customers should be identified and their characteristics specifically determined, such as their size, location, and industry group. Then other potential customers should be considered and perhaps verified as offering potential opportunity as a result of previous business with them, similarity of their operations to those of present customers, intriguing growth possibilities, or simply that competitors are disregarding them or seem vulnerable.

A strategic window.   Sometimes defining the business mission and assessing opportunities, developing a new product idea, or simply being alert to environmental changes, may reveal a strategic window. A *strategic window* is a market opportunity not presently well tapped by competitors that fits well with the firm's competencies. Strategic windows often exist only briefly. Application 4.2 includes two examples of strategic windows. In the first example ROLM successfully maintained its technological advantage with a high-tech product. In the second the smaller rental car companies found that the "Big Four" had opened a window.

Sales representatives and sales managers can sometimes find strategic windows in the geographical areas they serve. They may detect a competitor's vulnerability in not meeting customers' needs and see an advantage their firm can offer, perhaps in better servicing, product modification, or a better price. Alertness to opportunities characterizes the more successful persons and organizations.

―――――――――――
―――――――――――

APPLICATION 4.2   The Strategic Window

ROLM Corporation. In 1975 ROLM was a small $4 million manufacturer of military computers, when its engineers developed an electronic private branch exchange (PBX) suitable for the telecommunication industry. PBX was a computer-controlled system with the capacity to handle from 100 to 800 telephone exchanges. Behemoths were already in this growing market, which included IBM, AT&T, ITT, Northern Electric, Philips, and Nippon Electric. But ROLM's system was technologically more advanced and yet was priced competitively. It filled a strong market need for simplified voice and data communication. ROLM had found a strategic window and moved rapidly to exploit it. By 1979 sales had rocketed to $86 million, by 1983 to $500 million. In 1986 IBM bought the company for over $1 billion.

''Small Fry'' Auto Rental Firms. After years of vicious price competition, the big rental car companies began raising prices by more than 10 percent in 1987 over 1986. Their profits soared. Industry leader Hertz's profits rose 268 percent in a year; Budget's jumped 178 percent in only 6 months. This opened the door for Alamo, Dollar, Thrifty, and General Rent-a-Car. These firms traditionally were limited to tourist business, while the Big Four cashed in on the most lucrative market, the corporate customer. These small firms have a lower cost structure, partly because they shuttle air travelers to rental counters outside airports, thus avoiding high airport fees. Now with rates 30 percent under Hertz and the other majors, corporate customers are being wooed.

For more detail see ''Small Fry Start Nipping At the Whales of Auto Rental,'' *Business Week*, 31 August 1987, 81.

TRANSLATING PLANS INTO OPERATIONS

The longer-range guidelines developed by strategic planning require translating into operational plans and strategies. The starting point is the sales forecast.

The Need for Accurate Sales Forecasts

Planning is based on a whole set of assumptions about future conditions. The state of the economy, the efforts of competitors, the subtle change in buyers' optimism, the effects of a price change or a promotional campaign, the popularity of a new product feature or new style, the effectiveness of the sales force—all are factors that will affect future sales and operating. Obviously, if the estimates or forecasts of future conditions are greatly inaccurate, then the planning will be of limited use and perhaps detrimental.

An accurate sales forecast is vital to successful planning, because almost every aspect of the operation is based on sales. Although the sales manager is concerned primarily with the sales forecast's accuracy as it affects the sales staff, their number, and their budgets, an inaccurate forecast also affects other aspects of the operation that at least indirectly will affect the performance and effectiveness of the sales force. For example inventory levels, raw material purchases, and production planning are all geared to expected sales. The advertising budget is often planned as a certain percentage of estimated sales. If a firm forecasts a much higher sales figure than is actually achieved, inventories may be seriously out of line and advertising and selling costs may be too high. Too conservative a sales forecast, however, may result in production and inventory insufficient to meet customer demand, as well as insufficient advertising expenditures and an inadequate sales staff to capitalize on the potential demand. The sales department will likely be faced with customer ill will and may even lose customers because of chronic late deliveries and out-of-stock merchandise. Table 4.1 depicts the probable consequences of significantly inaccurate sales forecasts.

In efforts to make sales forecasts more reliable, firms are becoming more sophisticated in gathering and analyzing economic and market data. Methods of forecasting may involve complex mathematical models and computers. Usually, the sales department provides some input (perhaps news of market

TABLE 4.1   Effects of Inaccurate Sales Forecasts

	Too High	*Too Low*
Production planning	Overstock of material and perhaps underutilization of plant and equipment	Insufficient material and production capability
Inventory	Overstock	Understock
Advertising	Advertising costs too high	Insufficient advertising to realize potential
Customer relations	Probably no negative effect	Jeopardized because of late deliveries and out-of-stocks
Sales force	Too many salespeople, resulting in high selling costs	Insufficient numbers of trained salespeople to tap the market adequately
Profits	Expenses out of line with sales; profit probably drastically reduced	Net profit percentage may be acceptable, but total profit dollars will be far below what could have been achieved

condition changes or drastically revised marketing plans), but specialized staff departments primarily may be responsible for the sales forecast.

Despite the most sophisticated and costly forecasting techniques, the future still remains uncertain. A surprise oil embargo, for example, can invalidate forecasting and planning efforts. In the mid 1970s the auto industry was seriously whipsawed in its prediction of demand for small and large cars. Forecasting a major shift in demand toward the smaller economy cars, whole factories were reoriented to expanding production of Pintos, Vegas, Pacers, and Sunbirds. Inventories of these small cars mounted to 120-day supplies, and production lines shut down. All the while the fickle consumer was eagerly buying the bigger cars that now, alas, were in short supply.

More recently, even a "star" such as Federal Express seriously miscalculated on one of its new products, the Courier Pak, an overnight document delivery service. The need seemed obvious, the strategic window existed, but sales faltered far below expectations. Federal Express had expected to sell 6,000 Courier Paks per day within 6 months. Only 1,100 per day were sold the first year and 2,600 the second year, but sales improved. By the third year sales had climbed to 6,800 per day, and then they leaped to 14,100 per day.

Need for flexibility.   If fairly accurate forecasts could be guaranteed, adjusting in "midstream" would not be necessary. Accuracy, as we have seen, may not always be attainable. Planning and budgeting therefore must be flexible, which may require developing alternative sales and budget figures to update the forecast as events transpire. Budgets can be reviewed continually so that if sales figures are not met or are significantly exceeded, they can be quickly revised, and the expense budget can be changed accordingly.

Budgeting

After the sales forecast is determined and allocated to the various departments and divisions of a firm, expense budgets can be specified. As noted in the last section, much of operational planning depends on the sales forecast. Advertising, purchasing, selling expenses, and numerous other expense categories (or lines) budgets are based on the sales forecast. Budgets for particular expenses may be influenced by previous years' figures, but they usually are determined more by current expectations.

PLANNING AT THE SALES MANAGER LEVEL   – 2nd plan

Figure 4.4 shows the planning steps that usually directly involve the sales manager. Total company mission designation, objectives, sales forecasts, and budget plans must be adapted to individual areas of responsibility, which are primarily the sales force. Operational planning must be done within the constraints and guidelines of corporate plans. The sales manager breaks down

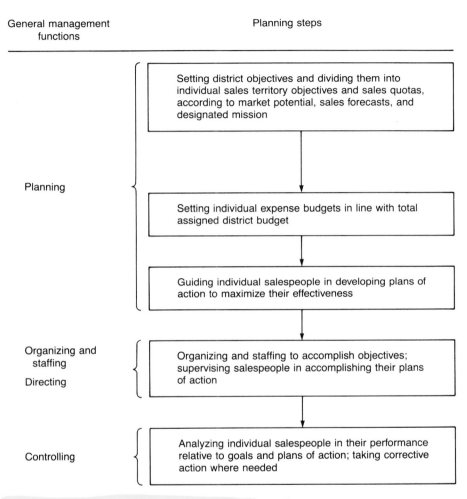

General management
functions

Planning steps

Planning

Setting district objectives and dividing them into
individual sales territory objectives and sales quotas,
according to market potential, sales forecasts, and
designated mission

Setting individual expense budgets in line with total
assigned district budget

Guiding individual salespeople in developing plans of
action to maximize their effectiveness

Organizing and
staffing

Directing

Organizing and staffing to accomplish objectives;
supervising salespeople in accomplishing their plans
of action

Controlling

Analyzing individual salespeople in their performance
relative to goals and plans of action; taking corrective
action where needed

FIGURE 4.4   Planning steps for the sales manager.

corporate plans into individual assignments, quotas, and standards of performance and is responsible for the achievement of the goals assigned to each district or territory.[6]

Developing a Plan of Action

After allocating specific sales and profit figures to divisions and sales territories, the sales manager must develop concrete plans to realize these objectives. *Strategy* is the general plan of action to achieve the specified objectives. *Tactics* are the details involved in engineering the strategy. Application 4.3 clarifies the difference between strategy and tactics.

APPLICATION 4.3   Strategy Versus Tactics

A consumer goods manufacturer decided to change its promotional strategy. It previously had relied mostly on mass-media advertising to "presell" its brands. But it was having difficulty matching the promotional expenditures of its larger competitors. The firm decided to reduce expenditures for mass-media advertising and directed the sales force to push more vigorously for more shelf space and dealer participation in company-sponsored trade promotions.

Unfortunately, the sales force proved inadequate to switch from order taking to more direct selling. The change in strategy proved ineffective. In response the firm devised tactics to reassess the sales representatives' abilities and to retrain the competent.

In this action stage of the planning process, the sales manager must formulate specifics for achieving the territorial or divisional goals. This requires working with the sales force so that individual planned efforts will be compatible with those of the district and will contribute to the total objective. For numerous expense categories, such as travel, telephone, and entertainment, the budget figures may need to be changed to reflect the change in district objectives.

Translating a company objective into an operational plan.   Hanover Company executives were concerned about several periods of declining profits, despite acceptable sales gains. Consequently, SBUs (profit centers) were ordered to increase profits. For the sales division this was a rather ambiguous objective that required more specific operating plans (see Figure 4.5). Profit goals were set for each territory. As Figure 4.5 shows, this involved increasing the gross profit on sales—selling items carrying a higher profit margin. The budget for selling expenses also was reduced. The sales manager clearly communicated each products' profitability to the salesforce and instructed them to concentrate on the larger, potentially more profitable accounts. The sales manager then established specific guidelines and clarified answers to the following questions:

- What constitutes a large or key account?
- For what size of customer would personal visits be eliminated?
- How often will the larger accounts be visited?
- What level of customer or executive can be taken to lunch?
- How much can be spent for lunch and for other entertainment?
- Are smaller accounts to be contacted occasionally by telephone in lieu of personal visits, and if so, how often?
- Will we continue to provide dealer display aids, and if so, how can we be more careful in distributing them?

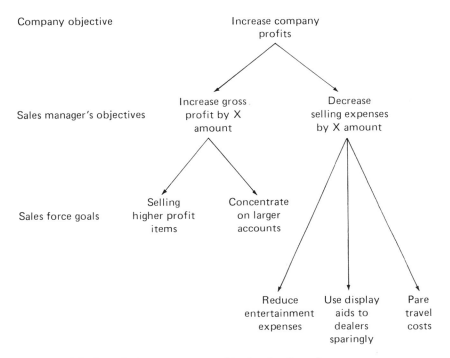

FIGURE 4.5   Translating a company objective by the sales manager.

Even this incomplete listing of specific decision issues shows that the planning process can be complex and time-consuming. Decisions on certain plan components will not be easy and may require considering various alternatives. Alternatives may be discussed with the interested parties—the sales people, the sales manager's superiors, and certain staff members who could estimate cost of various proposals. Some customers might be queried to determine their needs and reactions to cutbacks in service.

Implementing the Plan

Three management aspects are involved in any implementation: (1) organizing resources to facilitate accomplishing the planned objective(s), (2) ensuring sufficient staff to do so, and (3) supervising staff to guide their compliance with the strategy and achievement of planned objectives. The present staff and organization may be sufficient, or some changes may be required, especially if the objective and strategy are new. Communication is vital to effective supervision, and the approved plan of action must be well communicated to the sales force, who will act on the plans. Many managers involve subordinates in planning and budgeting because judgment is likely to be sounder with additional inputs and subordinates are more likely to accept and adhere to plans and budgets when they have contributed and may feel a personal stake in the outcome.

As noted, a plan or budget should not be so rigid that it cannot be changed or modified. Plans are based on predictions that are affected by external variables such as competition, the economy, even the weather; plans usually are not exactly on target. Furthermore, suggestions for improving existing plans may become evident shortly after implementation. For example a plan to concentrate selling efforts on the larger accounts to the extent of eliminating all calls on smaller customers may reveal that some calls on larger accounts can be eliminated. Thus, smaller accounts may still be visited occasionally. Sales managers should welcome suggestions for improvements and, if feasible and desirable, incorporate them. The alert and aggressive sales manager usually can find a wide latitude of appropriate actions or tactics that will be compatible with overall departmental and company goals and strategies.

Controlling

Culminating the planning and implementation process is the follow-up, measuring actual performance against the plans. Invariably, deviations occur, with some aspects of performance exceeding expectations and others falling short. The manager exercising sound control promptly detects deviations from plans at strategic points and then takes corrective action. For example profitability of sales (the gross margin on products sold) may fall considerably short of expectations in two territories. Under a good control system, profitability information readily appears on periodic sales analyses. The sales manager, alerted to such underperformance, is then able to determine the problem's cause and to take action to correct or improve the situation. Corrective action might involve stepped-up training, increased motivation, job rotation, or more promotional activities. An investigation of the problem may reveal that because of the particular customer mix in the two territories, or unusually aggressive competitive activities and price cutting, the original profit plan is not attainable and should be modified.

THE NEED FOR MARKET INFORMATION IN PLANNING

For effective sales planning, market information is important. In particular the sales manager needs answers to the following questions:

- □ How big is the present market for the product(s)?
- □ How is that market divided geographically?
- □ What is the company's present market share of the entire industry?
- □ How does this market share vary among the territories?

□ What changes are occurring in the market regarding competitive activities, economic conditions, laws and regulations, and technology?

The sales manager should both receive and supply market information. The sales department, which is in close contact with customers and market conditions, can provide feedback from the field—in particular, about buyer expectations and changing environmental and competitive conditions—more promptly than any other source. Sales department feedback can be an important component of a firm's *marketing information system.*

The focus of a marketing information system is on broad, centralized, and timely processing of information to help management in decision making. In the quest for such data, however, firms run the risk of being deluged with too much unassimilated materials. Therefore, in addition to providing wide-ranging data, a marketing information system must incorporate screening and order.

Sources of Market Information for Planning

Figure 4.6 shows the three major sources of market information: internal accounting data, market intelligence data, and marketing research findings. Internal information about sales, inventory levels, and customers is often not detailed or current enough for fast reaction, especially under changing competitive conditions, unless special efforts are made to provide better tools for planning and control. Desirable information covers past and present sales trends by products, customers, and territories, as well as such customer data as size and industry.

Market intelligence gathering can be systematized to quickly transmit marketplace changes to those executives who need the information. Salespeople often are the first to hear of rumors and changes and should be encouraged to listen carefully and pass on such information. A *market log* can be a practical way to gather market information systematically and thoroughly.

Other information can be obtained from such public sources as trade journals, business-oriented periodicals, dealers, and trade shows. The major problem is not finding the information but systematizing the collection pro-

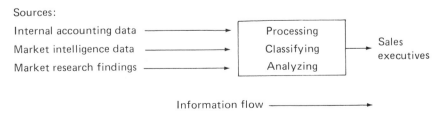

FIGURE 4.6   A marketing information system.

A Market Log

A market log is simply a form for systematically recording all developments in industrial markets that have some bearing on the firm's sales experience and future prospects. It may be as informal as a notebook kept by a salesperson and periodically reviewed with the sales manager, or it may be a more formal record keeping forwarded either to the marketing research department or another corporate office.

The log would include information about changes in the company's own prices and/or special offers that were made and the responses to those offers; reports on changes in competitors' prices; statements by customers and noncustomers to salespeople; and information on the amount and form of competitors' sales efforts, including copies of their advertisements, indications of additions to their sales forces, and new sales programs. The purpose of the market log is to assemble all the information affecting changes in a firm's sales and thus to ensure against basing conclusions on vague general impressions.

The idea of a market log perhaps originated with Alfred R. Oxenfeldt, *Executive Action in Marketing* (Belmont, Calif.: Wadsworth Publishing, 1966), 284.

----

cess, classifying the data, and ensuring that relevant material reaches the attention of the proper people.

Marketing research in a general information system refers to planning, conducting, and analyzing the special studies needed. Studies may include an evaluation of the market potential for a new product, a study of advertising effectiveness, or a design for a new point-of-purchase display to be furnished dealers—the nonroutine type of information.

Important to all market studies and data gathering is trend information, which includes changes such as which types of customers are being won or lost and which products are gaining or losing market share. Studies and analyses that are conducted once or only sporadically may allow a slowly deteriorating situation to go unnoticed and uncorrected. The information system should provide *sensors* of marketplace conditions and changes. When such information is not gained in a timely manner, or when it is not heeded by responsible executives, loss of competitive position may result.

Role of the Field Sales Manager in Providing Marketing Intelligence

Market intelligence should represent the most important sales department input to the marketing information system. The field sales manager should be a focal point for this information feedback from the market. The problem is that the sales force does not always pass on field information, and even when it does, the sales manager and other executives may ignore the information. As one sales manager noted:

> Systematically gathering and transmitting information takes time. When it comes to giving us feedback, some of our best sales reps are also the worst in actually produc-

ing sales. The feedback sometimes becomes a vehicle for providing excuses for not doing a better job. And as such, I and my boss tend not always to trust it.

The sales force will quickly neglect its information-gathering role without active encouragement and insistence on comprehensive and accurate reporting. The ability of a firm to identify insidious problems and to exploit emerging opportunities may depend on prompt, complete, and accurate information coming from the field.

Planning is deciding now what to do in the future. Plans vary as to their duration, scope, and formality. Planning takes management time, sometimes leads to rigid operations, and is not always as accurate as necessary. But its advantages far outweigh the drawbacks in helping avoid crises, integrating actions, and providing a basis for control.

Strategic planning is a long-range focus on opportunities and challenges in an evolving environment that particularly involves determining company mission, setting overall objectives, and assessing market opportunities. Portfolio analysis (evaluating the firm's present businesses) and strategic windows (market opportunities that fit the firm's competency) relate to strategic planning. Incompatible SBU (strategic business units) goals, such as between the sales department and production and credit departments, must be reconciled or balanced for the greater good of the corporation in pursuing its mission and objectives.

The operational components of the planning process are the sales forecast, budgets, plan of action, implementation, and control. The sales manager, who is usually involved with the other aspects of the planning process, is particularly responsible for the latter three components. These involve translating company objectives and planned strategies to the district and individual sales territory levels.

The sales department can provide important input for a firm's market information system in its feedback from the field.

SUMMARY

---

1. Why is formal planning desirable? Are there any disadvantages to this procedure?

2. Name as many specific sales department goals as you can. Given an average firm (one not facing any extraordinary problems), what priorities would you recommend for these goals? Are any incompatible? How would you handle incompatible goals?

3. Why would an overly optimistic sales forecast result in heavy inventory? How would customer relations likely be affected by a high sales forecast? Would you expect sales force recruiting efforts to be adversely affected by inaccurate sales forecasts?

QUESTIONS

4. Would you recommend that all sizes and types of firms use formal planning? Why or why not?

5. What incentives would you establish to ensure better market feedback from your sales force?

6. One of the alleged advantages of planning is to avoid firefighting, or constantly having to cope with unexpected circumstances. Can planning ensure that nothing unexpected will occur? How do planners account for the unexpected?

7. Discuss the relationship between planning, forecasting, and budgeting.

PEOPLE PROBLEM— PLANNING HOW TO EXECUTE A TOP-LEVEL DIRECTIVE

Please evaluate the desirability of each of the alternatives.

As sales manager you have been directed to obtain a better gross margin in your district this coming year. How would you go about planning for this with your salespeople?

1. Simply instruct them to sell more higher-profit items.

2. See that every salesperson has a convenient listing of the profitability of each item in the line, and inform them that a major part of the performance evaluation will be based on the profit they obtain.

3. Change the commission structure for your district so that commissions are paid on gross profit obtained from sales, rather than on net sales.

4. Stress the theme of an improved gross margin in all sales meetings throughout the year; strive to develop an enthusiastic team geared to this objective.

5. Require each salesperson to submit a report to you each week on the gross margin for each order as well as explanations of all sales made of low-margin goods.

NOTES

1. David A. Aaker, *Strategic Market Management* (New York: Wiley, 1984), 8.

2. Books dealing with the totality of the strategic planning process include David A. Aaker, *Strategic Market Management* (New York: Wiley, 1984), and Lester A. Neidell, *Strategic Marketing Management* (Tulsa: PennWell, 1983).

3. John A. Pearce II, "The Company Mission As a Strategic Tool," *Sloan Management Review* (Spring 1982): 17.

4. Theodore Levitt, "Marketing Myopia," *Harvard Business Review* (July–August 1960): 45–56.

5. H. Igor Ansoff, "Strategies for Diversification," *Harvard Business Review* (September–October 1957): 113–124.

6. Related to the sales managers role in operational and corporate planning, see William Strahle and Rosann L. Spiro, "Linking Market Share Strategies to Salesforce Objectives, Activities, and Compensation Policies," *Journal of Personal Selling & Sales Management* (August 1986).

cases

4.1 Coping with a Conservative Sales Forecast

As sales manager, you have reason to believe that the corporate forecast for your division is much too low. Although in theory you were supposed to provide input for this forecast, in reality the corporate controller, a conservative man, had the most influence. At this point you cannot raise the sales forecast (later, of course, if sales are significantly higher than forecasted, you can expect some adjustments).

QUESTION

What, if anything, can you do to compensate for too conservative a forecast and without jeopardizing your sales potential?

4.2 Coping with Poorly Supported Plans

Paul Jamison is sales manager for the northcentral district of the Everett Murphy Company, a wholesaler/distributor for notions and housewares sold to discount stores. The firm has sales of about $100,000,000 and distributes to all the United States except the West Coast and Rocky Mountain states.

Paul's district comprises the three states of Illinois, Wisconsin, and Minnesota, and he has 17 salespeople working under him, most of whom are concentrated in the Chicago, Milwaukee, and Minneapolis/St. Paul metropolitan areas. In his 5 years with the company, Paul has seen his district become number 1 in sales growth percentage in 2 of the last 3 years. He was justifiably proud of this, but lately had become concerned about new aggressiveness by competitors, especially in the Chicago area. Usually, the agressiveness consisted of undercutting Everett Murphy in prices. Paul several times had expressed his concern to company headquarters, but apparently with little result, until now.

The summons came on Sunday afternoon to fly into New York for a Monday morning meeting with Andrea Witkowski, the marketing vice president. Before flying out Paul had armed himself with concrete evidence of the price competition taking place in Chicago. He hoped to persuade headquarters to allow more discounts to meet direct price competition. He also hoped to convince the company to stock some lower-priced items in certain product categories.

The marketing vice president seemed to have other ideas, however. Paul was hurriedly ushered into the vice president's office to be told: "Paul, our board of directors has just stipulated that we take increased service to our customers for our corporate objective this coming year. They think this may indirectly enable us to increase our share of the market in your part of the country without getting involved in cut-throat price competition. I would like you to give me a proposal for providing such improved service by this time next week."

"Chief, will I be allowed any increase in sales force to achieve such improved customer service?"

"The board didn't address this. I think you should plan, however, for a small increase—1 or 2 percent, no more—in the sales budget."

"But that won't even be enough to hire one additional person," Paul protested.

"No, but you can increase your telephone and travel expense lines a bit. But let's talk more about this after you have fleshed out the bones of this general company objective."

QUESTION

What specifics for improving customer service, without increasing the sales force, should Paul recommend?

4.3 The Hawiian Candy Company—Planning for Growth

For a number of years, the Hawaiian Candy Company in Honolulu had been operated as a family enterprise. The Japanese–American owner and his wife handled the management of the company and had six employees who were candy dippers. Although the company was small, its candy was well accepted within its small market, and it had a deservedly good reputation for quality. This was partly due to the good ingredients used, and it also reflected the expert work of the dippers who were dedicated workers despite their relatively low salaries.

Honolulu had a number of other candy manufacturers, but most specialized in candy types other than chocolates, such as coconut, macadamia nuts, and passion fruit. Two other firms specialized in chocolate candies: Alice and Don's Candies and Ice Cream Company and Kay's Candies. Alice and Don's sold high-quality chocolates both by the box and as wrapped bars. They distributed through their own stores and also through hotels, department stores, and drugstores. This company was the market leader of Hawaiian candy makers. Kay's Candies was a small operation of no competitive significance. The market share and competitive efforts of all three companies were static, with none attempting to step up production or promotional efforts to obtain a larger share of the market.

The death of John Say, owner of the Hawaiian Candy Company, brought changes. His widow tried to continue operating the company, but found it beyond her ability. A friend of her husband persuaded her to hire Bernice Meyer, a young college graduate who had majored in marketing and who was aggressive and ambitious.

"A business cannot long exist without growing," she told Mrs. Say. "You have to develop some new ideas, perhaps put in some more money, and be prepared to grow, if the business is to survive. Otherwise, your competitors will take over the market, or perhaps some new firms from the mainland will find this an attractive market."

Mrs. Say hired Bernice as manager, and with her forceful manner, she soon took over the entire operation of the company. She was determined to make it the industry leader in Hawaii. Accordingly, she set out to learn all she could about the candy industry and candy production. She visited candy makers on the West Coast and inspected their processes and equipment. She learned that one of the major companies was using flash freezing to maintain freshness in storage for more than a year without loss of quality.

Bernice's analysis of her current production facilities showed that under peak production periods, 135 pounds of hand-dipped chocolates could be produced by the work force in an hour. This was far below the capacity of Alice and Don's larger and more modern machinery. Because training hand dippers was a lengthy process and few sought such employment, the transition from hand dipping to machine production or a combination of the two seemed the best course of action.

Based on her analysis and study, Bernice presented Mrs. Say the following plan of action. (1) Lease a larger facility, (2) install new equipment to expand production, and (3) market the candy under a new name, "Aloha Candies," packaged in a striking new box with the cover designed by Bernice. Mrs. Say consented to the expansion and withdrew money from her savings to help finance it.

A former roller skating rink was leased to provide more floor space for the new production layout. While waiting for the new machinery to arrive, production at the old facility was kept at a peak level. Workers were given a pay raise, the first in a long time, which proved an excellent incentive and spurred them on to greater efforts. Bernice began worker production records, and each tried to outdo the others.

With production on the verge of being substantially increased, Bernice turned her attention to sales. "We have to aggressively go out and get business," she told Mrs. Say. "We can no longer be content just to passively wait for customers, and stand in line behind Alice and Don's." Mrs. Say looked at her wonderingly.

Bernice found Walter Kenyon, a retired food broker who was rather bored and more than willing to get back into selling. "If business expands as I'm sure it will, you'll soon be the company sales manager. So keep your eyes open for good prospective sales reps who want in on the ground floor of a growing company. Tell them that before long we'll be expanding to the mainland." Bernice paid Kenyon 10% on all sales he produced. She also hired an attractive young woman to pass out candy samples in shopping centers. These efforts resulted in the largest discount chain on the islands taking on the products. As a further move to increase market share, especially at the expense of Alice and Don's, Bernice reduced prices. Demand quickly outstripped production, but Bernice assured her customers that the new machinery soon to arrive would be more than ample for the near term. "Of course, when we expand to the mainland, we'll have to increase production facilities again."

Bernice also saw a bonus potential in the flash-freezing process. She thought it could well be used for mainland shipping of highly perishable fish and tropical fruit that now could not be shipped fresh.

Another possible project that seemed promising involved macadamia nuts, which were used in much of the candy. The company's expanded nut requirements apparently could be more cheaply met from company-owned groves. Bernice therefore began negotiations to acquire 430 acres of nut trees on the island of Hawaii. Because both the nuts and the fish (to be flash-frozen) would have to be transported from the island of Hawaii to Oahu, acquiring one or two cargo aircraft appeared logical. Again she began acquisition negotiations.

With so many projects developing, Bernice found the demands on her time almost overwhelming. She could not delegate any planning or supervision, because Mrs. Say had retreated to an uneasy retirement. Machinery began to arrive for installation in the new facilities. The flash-freezing project reached the development stage requiring cash investment. The nut grove and aircraft negotiations both also required funds.

"I have great news for you," Bernice told Mrs. Say. "We are all set to become a multimillion dollar business. In fact I'm estimating that we'll hit two this year. Only a moderate amount of additional investment by you will make this all possible."

"I . . . I don't have any more money to invest in the business," Mrs. Say hesitatingly replied. "You have used it all up."

"But you have to have," she insisted. "At least you must give me enough to install the machinery?"

But Mrs. Say sadly shook her head.

QUESTIONS

1. What recommendations do you have for Bernice at this point?
2. What specific mistakes were made?
3. Design an expansion plan that would have avoided this dilemma.

CHAPTER 5
Analyzing the Market: Assessing Potential

CHAPTER PERSPECTIVE

As noted in the last chapter, analyzing market opportunity or potential is an important part of the planning process. Market potential is the measure of the total amount of business available in the market—the expected sales for a particular product or service category for the entire industry at the present time.

Chapter 5 describes methods of calculating potential and the major data sources. The use of mar-

ket potential calculations is discussed, as well as their importance for particular decisions and allocations and in identifying opportunities for better market penetration. Finally, certain limitations that a firm might face in reaching its full potential are considered.

CHAPTER OBJECTIVES

☐ Gain a perspective of the impact of market potential on other operational planning functions, such as sales forecasts and quotas.

☐ Become acquainted with the mathematics of deriving multiple factor measures of potentials, both for consumer goods and industrial products.

☐ Understand methods of determining the potential for new products with no sales history.

☐ Know the most common sources of statistics for market potential measures.

☐ Become acquainted with the important uses of market potential measures.

☐ Become familiar with application of these tools to identify major opportunities that would otherwise remain untapped.

WHY DETERMINE MARKET POTENTIAL?

Unless a firm is in a secure monopolistic position, it obviously cannot reasonably expect to achieve a sales volume equal to the market potential, because competitors are also in the market. Why then should a firm bother trying to determine the market potential for its products and/or services? The answer lies in the two perspectives that one should have of the market—*absolute* and *relative*. By knowing the absolute dimensions of a market, a firm can plot its marketing strategy accordingly. The market's total size—and whether it likely will increase through normal business transactions or only through additional marketing efforts—and the market share that the firm is most likely to achieve in view of competitive efforts should be major influences on strategy. For example if the market potential is thought to be large, with perhaps considerable untapped business, a firm may want to increase advertising and selling efforts to reach this unclaimed potential more effectively. Conversely, if the total market potential is deemed small and limited, a firm may better direct its major efforts elsewhere. Limited market potential is not always unsatisfactory. A small and limited market may insulate an established firm against the entry of competitors.

Assessing market potential enables a firm to ascertain relative differences in total sales to be achieved in its various geographical markets. Naturally, some geographic areas, because of heavy population or concentration of customers, will afford more market opportunity than other areas. For example consider the contrasting potentials of metropolitan New York City with the plains states of the Dakotas and Montana. As another example an analysis of market potential might indicate that Denver, Colorado, has four times the potential of Cheyenne, Wyoming, and may deserve four times the sales efforts given to Cheyenne.

RELATIONSHIP OF MARKET POTENTIAL TO OTHER PLANNING FACTORS

Market potential is the highest possible expected industry sales of a particular product or service in a given time period. *Sales potential* is the share of the market potential that a firm can expect to achieve. The *sales forecast* is the prediction of sales for a given time period and considers the marketing efforts. The *sales quota* is the assigned sales goal used for managing sales efforts.

Figure 5.1 shows the relationship between market potential, sales potential, the sales forecast, and a sales quota. You can see that a firm's sales potential will generally be less than the market potential, because of the presence of competitors in the industry. The sales forecast is usually somewhat less than the sales potential, whereas the sales quota is slightly less than the sales forecast.

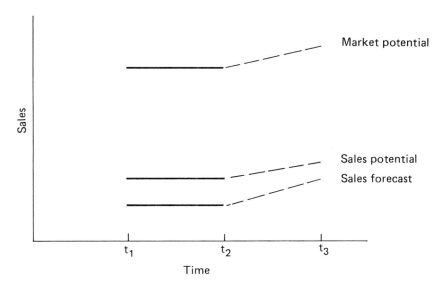

FIGURE 5.1   Relationships of market potential, sales potential, the sales forecast, and the sales quota.

Figure 5.1 shows that the market or industry potential is nearly static from t_1 to t_2. However, in this example estimates for t_3 show that industry sales will increase. The firm's sales potential at both t_1 and t_2 was estimated at about one-third the potential of the entire industry. As the market potential is expected to rise in t_3, so does the estimate of sales potential. The sales forecast for t_1 and t_2 is somewhat less than the sales potential. Many firms prefer to set their sales forecasts conservatively, at a figure less than their estimate of sales potential. The sales potential estimate may be a goal or inspirational target, whereas the sales forecast is the more realistic and prudent expectation based on planned marketing efforts. In Figure 5.1 the firm has planned to allot proportionately more expenditures for advertising and selling efforts in t_3 than in t_1 and t_2. Consequently, in this example the sales forecast for t_3 is estimated to become closer to the sales potential. The sales quota could be set as equivalent to the sales forecast. However, many firms prefer to keep the sales quota a bit below expected sales. This gives the sales force more chance of surpassing the quota and thereby earning some commission on the sales over quota, as well as more opportunity to achieve sales goals and feel successful.

Table 5.1 shows the relationships of the forecasting factors in a somewhat different light, by giving concrete examples of how each of the factors might be applied in a particular situation.

TABLE 5.1 Forecasting factors.

Factor	Definition	Use
Market potential	Highest-possible expected industry sales of a product or service in a given time period	Estimated sales of snow tires in Great Lakes states during the coming winter
Sales potential	Share of the market potential that can be expected to achieve	Expected sales of Sears' brand of snow tires
Sales forecast	Actual prediction of sales for the time period	Actual prediction of sales for Sears' snow tires— 1,000,000 tires
Sales quota	Assigned sales goal used for managerial purposes	Quota for Ohio—90,000 snow tires

HOW TO ASSESS MARKET AND SALES POTENTIAL

In market potential analyses a commonly used term is *market factor*. A market factor is some variable or aspect of the market that causes or determines demand for a product or service; it correlates with demand. For example recent births are a market factor for many kinds of infants' furniture, playthings, food, and apparel. Birth announcements in newspapers often trigger efforts of life insurance agents, focusing on the new family's need for more insurance, and of photographers, capitalizing on new parents' desires for baby pictures.

For some products a single market factor may be a good determinant of demand. For example registration data on Ford cars in each sales territory could be used as a single-factor index to estimate potential for Ford parts. More often a firm will find that the sales of its products correspond with a number of factors in the market. The firm can then develop complex multiple-factor indexes to account for the varying influences on sales. Tailoring a multiple-factor index to a firm's particular products and experience may provide a better measure of market potential.

Development of a Single-Factor or Multiple-Factor Market Index

Much of a firm's success in estimating market potential depends on how well it identifies and measures those factors that affect demand for its products. Elaborate market research studies and statistical analyses may be used and hundreds of possible factors may be analyzed to determine those that correlate best with sales.

Correlation analysis often is used to identify market factors. To pinpoint the most meaningful market factors, the correlation of variations in factors with variations in demand for the product must be computed mathematically. A correlation analysis requires a sales history and therefore is not usable with relatively new products or older products that have been significantly modified, remarketed to appeal to different sectors of the market, or given new uses. Correlation analysis assumes that previous conditions and influences will continue without change. The belief that the past indicates future may sometimes be suspect, especially for an industry of rapidly changing technology or in an economy at a turning point.

As an alternative to sophisticated analytical techniques, a firm may rely primarily on *subjective judgments,* which various managers and/or salespersons can make about factors that best relate to potential product demand. These judgments, which tend to be intuitive and unvalidated, may be fairly accurate, especially if they are based on seasoned experience; however, more often they are not and are merely unsubstantiated guesses.

The preceding discussion concerned measuring market potential on an absolute basis, in terms of the total market. To be of most use, the absolute potential must be converted to relative potentials of the various geographic markets.

Developing a multiple-factor market index. Hanson Corporation is a manufacturer of hardboard and related products used in the building industry as decorative interior paneling, exterior siding, and roofing, as well as doors and other products. It sells primarily to builders and contractors and to large hardware stores and lumber dealers who, in turn, sell both to consumers (do-it-yourselfers) and to smaller builders.

To better allocate sales efforts, forecast demand, and evaluate the performance of its sales representatives and distributors, management decided to develop a market index. Further, they hoped to ascertain the potential of various geographic areas. Accordingly, the vice president of sales, in informal consultation with several of his sales managers and larger dealers, concluded that the following six factors affected sales:

- □ Retail sales
- □ Population
- □ Residential building permits (total floor space)
- □ Commercial and industrial building contracts (total floor space)
- □ Personal income
- □ Marriage licenses issued

Both residential permits and commercial and industrial building contracts were accorded twice the weight of the other factors. An index was then computed for each state. First, each state's percentage of the U.S. total was computed for each factor. Then the weighted average of the six factors was calculated. For example the Arizona index of potential is shown in Table 5.2.

Arizona was determined to have 2.5 percent of the national market potential, and therefore approximately this percentage of the company's marketing efforts would be applied in that state. In Exercise 5.1 you are asked to take a critical look at Hanson's method of calculating its market potential.

EXERCISE 5.1

1. Critique the Hanson firm's method of deriving its market index.
2. Are there different factors (and weightings) that you would recommend for computing potential for this firm?

Market Potential for New Products

For new products without a sales history, real problems are encountered in determining market potential, and the validity of the results often is questionable. For a product significantly different from anything presently on the market, sales potential is equivalent to market potential, because, at least in the beginning, there is no direct competition. Accordingly, for new products, the terms *market potential* and *sales potential* can be used interchangeably.

Lacking past sales that can be correlated with various market factors, one is tempted to ask prospective customers how much they would buy, even

TABLE 5.2 Arizona index of potential.

	Column 1 Percentage of U.S. Total	Column 2 Weight	Column 3 Weighted Total (Col. 1 × Col. 2)
Retail sales	2.1	1	2.1
Population	1.8	1	1.8
Residential building permits (total floor space)	3.6	2	7.2
Commercial and industrial building contracts (total floor space)	2.8	2	5.6
Personal income	2.0	1	2.0
Marriage licenses issued	1.5	1	1.5
Total		8	20.2
	20.2 ÷ 8 = 2.5%		

though they have no product experience on which to base their opinions. Usually, a valid measure of market potential can be obtained only when at least part of the market has had some experience with the product, perhaps through a test market or other early market experience. Then sales results can be extrapolated to the entire market, as follows:

$$X_U = \frac{n}{a}$$

where,

X_U = total market potential in units

n = number of units sold in test area

a = proportion of total national market
that the test area represents

As an example suppose that South Carolina has 2.5 percent of the U.S. population, and the market potential of the product is believed to be directly related to population. If the product is test marketed in South Carolina with annualized sales of 7,800 units, the extrapolation of national sales would be the following:

$$X_U = \frac{7,800}{0.025} = 312,000 \text{ units}$$

The potential expressed in dollars rather than units is easily obtained with the addition of the following formula:

$$X = \frac{np}{a}$$

where,

X = total market potential in dollars

P = revenue per unit

If the manufacturer's revenue per unit is $30, the dollar market potential is the following:

$$X = \frac{7,800 \ (\$30)}{0.025} = \$9,360,000$$

Determining the Sales Potential

As defined earlier the sales potential is the firm's expected market share of total industry demand. The temptation is to equate sales potential with present market share. For example if a beer manufacturer has 15 percent of all beer sales in a given area, then he can estimate that his sales potential is about 15 percent of the market potential in that area. But this is a simplistic and often unrealistic judgment, because it assumes that sales equal sales potential and is based on a questionable assumption, that all territories are cultivated to their maximum. This is seldom the case, as data later in this chapter will prove. Potential demand is a better basis for ascertaining sales potential than past sales, although determining demand is more difficult than identifying the market share of the preceding periods. The next section examines data sources useful in deriving market potential and sales potential figures.

If market share is used to estimate sales potential, several additional cautions should be noted: (1) trend of market share, (2) any major competitive changes, and (3) market segments being appealed to. Regarding trend of market share, take again the example of the beer manufacturer. If over the last several years aggressive competitors have forced his market share to drop from 18 to 15 percent, then, unless there are good reasons to think that market share has stabilized or that the trend has been reversed, the realities of the situation should be recognized, namely that the market share in the coming year is likely to be lower than 15 percent unless major countermoves are made to reverse the decline. Similarly, the addition of a new competitor, or the loss of a major competitor, should affect market share and sales potential. A firm's particular brand may appeal to a slightly different market or consumer segment than the rest of the industry. Computations of industry potential consequently might not correlate well with the firm's individual sales potential. When this is the case, fluctuations in the particular brand's sales may little resemble the fluctuations of industry sales, and the task of calculating the sales potential becomes much more difficult.

SOURCES OF DATA

As in any research study, two general sources of information usually exist, primary and secondary. *Primary data* sources are gathered specifically for the study, in this case the assessment of potentials. *Secondary data* sources are already available and have been collected for other purposes, usually by a second party.

Primary Data

The three major ways of obtaining primary data for estimates of market and sales potentials are market surveys, test markets, and sales force estimates. Each has limitations regarding validity and use.

Market surveys are more useful for industrial goods, which have limited customers and potential customers in contrast to most consumer goods. If the probable market consists of only a few users who are relatively well-known, a questionnaire can be sent to each, asking them to estimate their purchases in advance. More often, even for industrial goods, the market is sufficiently large that only a sample of users and prospective users can be surveyed. The sampling questionnaire must ask each respondent the amount they will purchase and how they will use the product. The questionnaire will be used to determine the relationship between the number of employees in the plant (or the value added by manufacturing) and the rate of product use. With such a *use rate* established by size of plant, the dimensions of the total market can be estimated through secondary information of industry statistics.

For consumer goods the problem is complicated by the market's sheer size and, for most products, the difficulty of isolating significant segments of consumers for sampling purposes. But sampling is feasible for specialized consumer sectors. Again the sample's use rate is projected to the entire market.

Sample surveys are inappropriate for new products, because as noted previously, potential users' (industrial or consumer) lack of experience with the new product renders them unable to judge how well it will substitute for existing products or meet present needs.[1]

The *test market* gives a more realistic appraisal of demand for a new product, because sales occur in the market area(s) being tested. Commonly used with consumer packaged goods, the test market introduces the new product (or advertising, or price, or whatever is being tested) into one or more test areas, which should be as comparable and representative as possible. The sales results in these markets can then be extrapolated to indicate probable sales potential for the entire United States, as described earlier in this chapter.

The test market approach has some limitations, however. It is costly; expenses may exceed $1 million for a single product. The expense might be tolerable if test market results guaranteed success, but products sometimes fail even after test marketing suggested sufficient potential. Test marketing takes considerable time, and it may delay introducing the product or the market innovation, enabling competitors to do so first. For most industrial goods a market test is not possible because of the great costs of developing prototypes and, often, the concentration of potential customers in only a few market areas.

A *company's sales force* can also be used to gather primary data. Being in close contact with customers and the market, salespeople can obtain purchase estimates from purchasing agents and other customer executives. They can observe changes in facilities and strengths and weaknesses of competition in their territories. They can be alert to government contract awards, keep attuned to information on new companies entering their territories, and in general provide good sensors of market conditions—market changes and how to exploit these. The sales force can exercise the market intelligence function described in Chapter 3; the estimate of total market potential can be *built up*, or aggregated, from the individual territory estimates.

Of course, relying on sales force estimates assumes that all salespeople are objective and equally knowledgeable and conscientious about obtaining relevant information to make an estimate of potential. A salesperson usually is more motivated to underestimate territorial potential, because sales look better in a territory of limited potential than in one of much higher estimated potential.

Secondary Data

Secondary data are used primarily to implement the market factor approach described earlier in this chapter. Sources of relevant secondary data for determining sales and market potentials are many and varied and include internal company records, governmental agency reports, trade and business associations, universities, private firms, and advertising media.

Most industries provide specialized publications and statistics that enable a member firm to assess the size of its potential market. Certain widely used general sources should be familiar to most marketers. The following sections briefly describe five sources: (1) Standard Industrial Classification System (SIC codes), (2) U.S. censuses, (3) certain other government publications, (4) trade associations, and (5) media.

Standard Industrial Classification System.   The SIC system is a widely used identification of manufacturers by product and type of operation. Twenty major industrial groups are classified by two-digit numbers and then further divided into three- and four-digit groups. For example, all apparel manufacturers are identified under #23. For a more detailed classification, #2394 denotes apparel manufacturers dealing primarily with canvas products.

Some problems are encountered with the SIC codes, chiefly with those establishments that manufacture a wide variety of products and for which it therefore is difficult to determine the most appropriate SIC code. But this system provides a uniform classification of many manufacturing-related statistics.

The U.S. censuses.   The U.S. Bureau of Census develops eight censuses. These data sources are particularly useful in forecasting sales, developing market potentials, and making various store and plant location decisions. The censuses cover population, business, manufacturers, housing, mineral industries, agriculture, transportation, and governments. The following three censuses are of most interest to sales:

The Census of Population is taken every 10 years and gives a population count by state, county, city, metropolitan area, and *census tracts*. The tracts are fixed areas of about 4,000 persons in the larger cities. Census tracts tend to be homogeneous in character and are particularly useful for marketing research surveys. The population is further broken down by age, sex, education, family size, occupation, and income.

The Census of Business is taken every 5 years, in the years ending in 2 and 7. This census provides statistics on the retail trade, wholesale trade, and selected services. It supplies data on total sales, number of employees, payrolls, and number of establishments for each principal type of business, with this information broken down by state, county, metropolitan area, and city.

The Census of Manufacturers is conducted simultaneously with the Census of Business and gives data on the number and size of establishments for about 430 industries, supplying payroll size, sales by customer class, inventories, capital expenditures, and selected costs. It is a valuable data source for industrial market potentials because it estimates the number of potential customers in various industries and locations.

The principal shortcoming of these censuses is the time lag between data collection and publication, which may exceed 2 years. In dynamic market conditions such a delay may reduce the data's value. A further limitation results from the prohibition about releasing data that would identify individual firms; in a small market area, where one or a few firms dominate, the data may therefore be inadequate.

Other government publications.   Other government publications, particularly registration data, can be of value. Statistics on births, deaths, marriages, school enrollments, automobile registrations, organizations' membership lists, income tax payments, and many other items are available through local, state, and federal governmental agencies. In general these data are more difficult to locate than census data because of the sheer variety both of data and of sources.

The monthly *Survey of Current Business* is widely available and provides statistics on 2,500 business and economic indicators, including the national income accounts. Although less detailed, the annual *Statistical Abstract of the United States,* containing data on virtually all aspects of the economy, is available in most libraries.

The Census Bureau's annual *County Business Patterns,* which provides industrial employment data on a county basis, has been widely used by industrial marketers. However, this is far from an ideal guide because, depending on the industry and technology level, employment does not relate very well to plant output level. For example some types of production are labor intensive. The apparel industries typically are low in labor productivity, and the petroleum industry, which is highly automated, ranks high in output per employee.

Local chambers of commerce often provide the following data:

Major retail facilities in the metropolitan area

Inventory of parking facilities

Principal firms and their approximate employment

Census tract maps showing the racial breakdown, number of households, median income for families, and approximate total income

Growth in various economic indexes, such as total payroll, annual earnings per worker, employment, total retail sales, and bank deposits

Trade associations.   Over 2,000 trade associations are in the United States. A trade association is a group of firms with common business interests who share problems as well as operating and market information. Each member reports on its own operation, and these reports are compiled into statistics for the entire industry. Such trade associations can range from the National Lubricating Grease Institute to the formidable Association of American Railroads. The statistics compiled can be invaluable for market analyses of many highly specialized industries. However, the quality of trade association statistics depends on the cooperation of the member firms in providing data and on the uniformity of methods used to develop the statistics. Furthermore, not all firms of an industry may belong to the trade association, so any assessment of market potential may require estimating nonmember operating results as well.

Media.   Newspapers and magazines often compile information on the markets they serve. For example since 1945 the *St. Paul Dispatch-Pioneer Press* has conducted yearly surveys of St. Paul, Minnesota, families regarding consumer preferences for leading brands of many product categories; family characteristics, such as income group, occupation, age of children, education level, and dwelling-unit characteristics; patronage factors, such as stores and shopping centers visited for purchases of various categories of goods; and "favorite store" breakdowns by consumers' area, income, and age.

Sales & Marketing Management surveys.   One of the best-known sources of market potential information is provided by *Sales & Marketing Management* magazine. Each year it publishes four survey issues that provide comprehensive statistics for both consumer and industrial marketers. *Survey of Buying Power*, published in July, includes the current estimates of the demographic and socioeconomic factors of states, metropolitan markets, leading counties, and others. *Survey of Buying Power, Part II*, published in October, rearranges the basic *Survey* data in terms of TV and newspaper markets, so that markets can be evaluated in media terms. It also gives a 5-year projection of metropolitan markets. *Survey of Selling Costs*, published in February, includes detailed information on the basic selling costs of the leading metropolitan markets in the United States and Canada, plus data on such marketing-related expenses as sales training, sales meetings, car rentals, and salespersons' compensation. *Survey of Industrial and Commercial Buying Power*, published in April, provides data on total manufacturing activity at the county level as well as local market information on 454 customer industries that buy goods and services from consumer and industrial products manufacturers.

Figure 5.2 shows sample items from the *Survey of Buying Power* for the District of Columbia and contiguous counties of metropolitan Washington, D.C., while Figure 5.3 gives a representative page from the *Survey of Industrial and Commercial Buying Power*. The *Survey of Selling Costs* will be examined in

DISTRICT OF COLUMBIA

D.C. S&MM ESTIMATES — METRO AREA / County / City	Total Population (Thousands)	% Of U.S.	Median Age of Pop.	% of Population by Age Group 18–24 Years	25–34 Years	35–49 Years	50 & Over	Households (Thousands)	Total Retail Sales ($000)	Food ($000)	Eating & Drinking Places ($000)	General Mdse. ($000)	Furniture/Furnish./Appliance ($000)	Automotive ($000)	Drug ($000)
WASHINGTON	3,544.0	1.4573	31.8	11.3	20.5	22.9	20.5	1,317.4	26,757,621	4,839,527	2,738,363	3,141,396	1,789,270	6,680,074	960,383
District of Columbia	620.0	.2550	33.1	13.2	20.5	19.4	26.6	252.9	3,392,998	591,240	746,449	312,719	212,707	196,095	171,265
• Washington	620.0	.2550	33.1	13.2	20.5	19.4	26.6	252.9	3,392,998	591,240	746,449	312,719	212,707	196,095	171,265
Calvert, Md.	43.6	.0179	30.9	8.7	18.6	21.2	21.2	14.2	107,384	32,754	14,551	7,032	2,180	16,466	4,247
Charles, Md.	89.5	.0368	29.1	9.9	18.4	23.6	15.5	27.5	318,420	85,140	25,130	11,752	10,849	70,809	41,392
Frederick, Md.	134.6	.0554	31.4	10.5	19.3	21.4	21.6	45.4	771,251	169,330	65,187	94,546	31,197	193,505	16,936
• Frederick	33.9	.0139	32.2	12.9	20.5	16.1	28.1	13.3	537,027	135,372	41,490	77,803	21,673	128,751	12,152
Montgomery, Md.	653.1	.2685	33.9	9.5	18.5	23.7	24.4	245.7	6,053,328	1,051,753	445,041	743,198	481,239	1,684,030	183,700
Rockville	48.0	.0197	31.9	10.3	19.0	24.3	19.8	16.6	755,074	130,193	62,990	43,564	90,560	233,998	15,085
Prince George's, Md.	679.1	.2792	29.7	13.5	20.7	22.1	17.0	240.2	5,253,177	1,024,023	430,933	644,207	289,198	1,436,192	157,501
Alexandria city, Va.	111.8	.0459	32.7	11.5	28.4	20.5	23.1	55.2	1,121,025	135,013	121,688	168,578	65,040	405,961	31,109
Alexandria	111.8	.0459	32.7	11.5	28.4	20.5	23.1	55.1	1,121,025	135,013	121,688	168,578	65,040	405,961	31,109
Arlington, Va.	156.4	.0643	33.6	13.2	25.9	20.0	26.4	74.3	1,244,048	198,949	164,719	92,229	81,406	447,544	66,236
• Arlington	156.4	.0643	33.6	13.2	25.9	20.0	26.4	74.2	1,244,048	198,949	164,719	92,229	81,406	447,544	66,236
Fairfax, Va.	701.5	.2885	32.1	9.5	20.0	26.8	17.3	250.8	5,456,029	1,000,177	481,729	710,331	441,480	1,310,337	189,155
Fairfax city, Va.	20.1	.0082	31.8	13.1	20.1	23.0	20.5	7.3	829,472	86,912	69,025	158,791	66,591	275,182	29,576
Fairfax	20.1	.0082	31.8	13.1	20.1	23.0	20.5	7.3	829,472	86,912	69,025	158,791	66,591	275,182	29,576
Falls Church city, Va.	9.4	.0039	37.1	8.6	21.0	21.9	31.5	4.4	301,183	29,042	17,902	60,223	12,097	123,353	8,534
Falls Church	9.4	.0039	37.1	8.6	21.0	21.9	31.5	4.3	301,183	29,042	17,902	60,223	12,097	123,353	8,534
Loudoun, Va.	71.0	.0292	31.1	8.2	20.0	25.3	16.9	23.6	371,334	118,817	22,587	16,672	21,161	68,603	20,141
Manassas city, Va.	19.4	.0080	28.8	10.6	24.1	20.6	14.5	6.6	304,518	55,509	19,761	16,092	8,007	137,878	5,476
Manassas	19.4	.0080	28.8	10.6	24.1	20.6	14.5	6.6	304,518	55,509	19,761	16,092	8,007	137,878	5,476
Manassas Park city, Va.	7.2	.0030	25.9	12.5	21.3	19.8	10.8	2.2	16,602	8,380	1,365		826	3,069	1,488
Manassas Park	7.2	.0030	25.9	12.5	21.3	19.8	10.8	2.2	16,602	8,380	1,365		826	3,069	1,488
Prince William, Va.	174.2	.0716	27.9	10.9	21.9	25.2	9.2	51.1	1,024,301	187,265	92,474	92,037	63,910	276,741	32,452
Stafford, Va.	53.1	.0219	29.9	10.3	19.2	24.0	16.3	16.0	192,551	65,223	19,822	12,989	1,382	34,309	1,175
SUBURBAN TOTAL	2,733.7	1.1241	31.4	10.7	20.2	24.0	18.7	977.0	21,583,548	3,913,946	1,785,705	2,658,645	1,473,484	5,907,684	710,730
TOTAL METRO COUNTIES	620.0	.2550	33.1	13.2	20.5	19.4	26.6	252.9	3,392,998	591,240	746,449	312,719	212,707	196,095	171,265
TOTAL STATE	620.0	.2550	33.1	13.2	20.5	19.4	26.6	252.9	3,392,998	591,240	746,449	312,719	212,707	196,095	171,265

D.C. S&MM ESTIMATES — EFFECTIVE BUYING INCOME 1986 — METRO AREA / County / City	Total EBI ($000)	Median Hsld. EBI	% of Hslds. by EBI Group (A) $10,000–$19,999	(B) $20,000–$34,999	(C) $35,000–$49,999	(D) $50,000 & Over	Buying Power Index
WASHINGTON	61,476,304	37,209	14.3	23.3	19.1	34.1	1.8662
District of Columbia	9,998,993	24,753	21.5	24.5	14.2	20.4	.2876
• Washington	9,998,993	24,753	21.5	24.5	14.2	20.4	.2876
Calvert, Md.	493,276	30,517	17.7	28.4	21.2	19.4	.0139
Charles, Md.	1,010,139	33,106	15.1	27.3	25.7	20.6	.0308
Frederick, Md.	1,638,120	30,697	18.6	28.2	21.8	19.8	.0543
• Frederick	424,922	25,924	21.9	29.3	19.0	14.2	.0208
Montgomery, Md.	13,121,366	44,874	11.3	20.4	18.4	43.8	.3967
Rockville	833,270	43,866	10.7	19.5	20.3	41.8	.0333
Prince George's, Md.	10,273,670	35,944	14.7	26.3	21.0	30.5	.3350
Alexandria city, Va.	2,511,778	35,322	14.3	26.8	18.9	31.7	.0740
Alexandria	2,511,778	35,322	14.5	26.7	18.8	31.7	.0740
Arlington, Va.	3,612,500	37,619	14.3	24.6	17.3	36.2	.0988
• Arlington	3,612,500	37,619	14.4	24.5	17.3	36.2	.0988
Fairfax, Va.	13,873,600	48,324	9.2	18.9	19.6	40.2	.4012
Fairfax city, Va.	398,557	46,063	10.1	20.7	18.8	45.6	.0252
Fairfax	398,557	46,063	10.1	20.7	18.8	45.6	.0252
Falls Church city, Va.	224,852	41,469	12.3	22.1	19.8	40.8	.0107
Falls Church	224,852	41,469	12.3	22.1	19.7	40.8	.0107
Loudoun, Va.	1,009,260	36,083	13.7	25.0	23.0	28.9	.0303
Manassas city, Va.	279,257	37,791	13.5	24.7	27.5	27.5	.0125
Manassas	279,257	37,791	13.5	24.7	27.5	27.5	.0125
Manassas Park city, Va.	68,510	28,311	15.6	45.3	21.6	7.9	.0021
Manassas Park	68,510	28,311	15.6	45.3	21.6	7.9	.0021
Prince William, Va.	2,321,162	40,231	11.3	23.6	26.7	33.1	.0741
Stafford, Va.	641,256	33,670	16.6	27.5	24.0	23.3	.0190
SUBURBAN TOTAL	47,439,889	40,555	12.3	22.8	20.6	37.7	1.4590
TOTAL METRO COUNTIES	9,998,993	24,753	21.5	24.5	14.2	20.4	.2876
TOTAL STATE	9,998,993	24,753	21.5	24.5	14.2	20.4	.2876

FIGURE 5.2 Representative page of *Survey of Buying Power*. (*Source:* Reprinted from 1987 S&MM *Survey of Buying Power*, July 27, 1987, p. C40.)

1986 **S&MM** Est.

County SIC — Industry	Establishments Total	Large	Shipments/Receipts ($ Mil.)	% Of U.S. Ship./Recpt.	% In Large Estab.
VIRGINIA					
Accomack All mfg.	18	8	319.9	.0148	88
2016 *Poultry-dressing plants*	2	2	121.2	1.7897	100
Albemarle All mfg.	16	7	315.3	.0146	89
2037 *Frozen fruits & vegetables*	1	1	82.9	1.1048	100
Alexandria city All mfg.	40	9	353.7	.0164	68
8062 *General medical & surgical hospitals*	3	3	98.6	.0546	100
Alleghany All mfg.	1	1	5.4	.0003	100
Amelia All mfg.	6	1	20.9	.0010	44
Amherst All mfg.	9	2	98.0	.0045	56
Appomattox All mfg.	5	3	60.4	.0028	90
Arlington All mfg.	30	7	254.2	.0118	56
7011 *Hotels, motels, & tourist courts*	17	8	102.1	.3286	71
7372 *Computer programming & software*	7	4	123.5	1.0806	88
8062 *General medical & surgical hospitals*	3	3	126.9	.0702	100
Augusta All mfg.	23	10	337.5	.0157	77
Bath All mfg.	2	1	8.2	.0004	65
Bedford All mfg.	5	1	79.8	.0037	64
Bedford city All mfg.	14	6	171.1	.0079	71
Bland All mfg.	2	2	18.7	.0009	100
Botetourt All mfg.	11	5	116.0	.0054	73
Bristol city All mfg.	39	26	712.9	.0331	94
Brunswick All mfg.	14	5	96.4	.0045	54
Buchanan All mfg.	3	1	94.6	.0044	94
1211 *Bituminous-coal & lignite mining*	20	7	465.9	2.8673	77
Buckingham All mfg.	3	1	15.5	.0007	56
Buena Vista city All mfg.	11	6	102.4	.0047	84
Campbell All mfg.	17	13	494.5	.0229	97
2511 *Wood household furniture*	2	2	141.2	1.9496	100
Caroline All mfg.	10	1	41.6	.0019	8
Carroll All mfg.	10	4	67.1	.0031	80
Charlotte All mfg.	10	3	54.4	.0025	48
Charlottesville city All mfg.	27	12	426.6	.0198	86
3661 *Telephone & telegraph apparatus*	3	3	117.9	.6195	100
3662 *Radio & TV communication equipment*	1	1	38.7	.1147	100
8062 *General medical & surgical hospitals*	2	2	141.8	.0785	100
Chesapeake city All mfg.	36	10	354.3	.0164	56
Chesterfield All mfg.	16	8	650.9	.0302	94
2869 *Industrial organic chemicals n.e.c.*	1	1	317.9	.9967	100
Clarke All mfg.	3	3	64.9	.0030	100
Clifton Forge city All mfg.	1		6.8	.0003	0
Colonial Heights city All mfg.	6	3	46.8	.0022	81
Covington city All mfg.	8	5	499.7	.0232	98
2631 *Paperboard mills*	1	1	232.7	2.8699	100
2819 *Industrial inorganic chemicals n.e.c.*	2	1	233.7	1.3718	98
Craig All mfg.	1	1	4.5	.0002	100
Culpeper All mfg.	13	6	132.0	.0061	67
Danville city All mfg.	32	14	857.9	.0398	89
2211 *Cotton-weaving mills*	1	1	130.0	2.6643	100
2261 *Cotton-finishing plants*	1	1	153.2	10.8123	100
3524 *Lawn & garden equipment*	1	1	66.1	3.8107	100
8062 *General medical & surgical hospitals*	1	1	60.2	.0333	100
Dickenson All mfg.	2	1	13.3	.0006	71
1211 *Bituminous-coal & lignite mining*	7	2	87.2	.5367	69
Dinwiddie All mfg.	18	6	202.1	.0094	58
8062 *General medical & surgical hospitals*	2	2	129.6	.0717	100
Grayson All mfg.	11	5	87.4	.0041	77
Halifax All mfg.	3	3	49.0	.0023	100
Hampton city All mfg.	42	10	426.7	.0198	63
8062 *General medical & surgical hospitals*	3	3	141.9	.0785	100
Hanover All mfg.	33	4	192.7	.0089	40
Harrisonburg city All mfg.	37	17	397.0	.0184	72
8062 *General medical & surgical hospitals*	1	1	55.0	.0304	100
Henrico All mfg.	13	2	113.6	.0053	51
Henry All mfg.	16	10	411.5	.0191	95
2211 *Cotton-weaving mills*	1	1	26.6	.5452	100
2511 *Wood household furniture*	4	3	317.1	4.3783	99
Highland All mfg.	1		2.5	.0001	0
Hopewell city All mfg.	13	7	993.8	.0461	97
2821 *Plastics materials & synthetic resins*	2	2	266.5	1.2509	100
2824 *Noncellulosic synthetic organic fibers*	2	2	247.1	3.5199	100
2869 *Industrial organic chemicals n.e.c.*	2	2	389.9	1.2224	100
Isle of Wight All mfg.	5	3	501.1	.0232	99
2011 *Meat-packing plants*	2	2	482.2	1.0798	100
James City All mfg.	4	2	64.5	.0030	90
King and Queen All mfg.	4	1	27.9	.0013	74
King George All mfg.	6	2	104.8	.0049	82
King William All mfg.	3	1	31.4	.0015	56
Lancaster All mfg.	14		63.2	.0029	0
Lee All mfg.	4	2	26.0	.0012	76
Lexington city All mfg.	4	1	31.3	.0015	46
Loudoun All mfg.	23	8	235.3	.0109	58
Louisa All mfg.	7	4	54.8	.0025	89
Lunenburg All mfg.	15	8	134.3	.0062	56
Lynchburg city All mfg.	76	38	1,375.4	.0638	78
2819 *Industrial inorganic chemicals n.e.c.*	1	1	57.6	.3381	100
3662 *Radio & TV communication equipment*	1	1	208.5	.6177	100
Madison All mfg.	5	1	23.3	.0011	36
Manassas city All mfg.	2		7.5	.0003	0
Martinsville city All mfg.	31	20	1,067.7	.0495	96
2253 *Knit-outerwear mills*	3	3	222.5	5.8738	100
2321 *Men's & boys' shirts & nightwear*	1	1	54.4	1.5173	100
2511 *Wood household furniture*	5	5	139.3	1.9233	100
2824 *Noncellulosic synthetic organic fibers*	1	1	481.5	6.8589	100
Mathews All mfg.	1	1	5.9	.0003	100
Mecklenburg All mfg.	21	14	223.3	.0104	89
Middlesex All mfg.	7		23.3	.0011	0
Montgomery All mfg.	18	10	231.3	.0107	83
Nelson All mfg.	5	2	42.7	.0020	80
New Kent All mfg.	4		14.5	.0007	0
Newport News city All mfg.	38	21	1,627.2	.0755	96
3731 *Ship building & repairing*	2	2	1,123.6	14.2995	100
8062 *General medical & surgical hospitals*	4	4	122.4	.0677	100
Norfolk city All mfg.	98	29	1,495.8	.0694	75
2711 *Newspapers*	3	2	83.7	.3787	98
3079 *Miscellaneous plastics products*	1	1	63.4	.2661	100
3711 *Motor vehicles & passenger-car bodies*	1	1	393.9	.4106	100
3731 *Ship building & repairing*	9	6	176.0	2.2399	95
4011 *Line-haul-operating railroads*	2	1	203.7	.8234	98
6025 *National banks, federal reserve system*	3	2	445.1	.3225	99
7011 *Hotels, motels, & tourist courts*	13	4	42.7	.1374	75
8062 *General medical & surgical hospitals*	6	6	334.7	.1852	100
8221 *Colleges & universities n.e.c.*	3	3	80.2	.3005	100

FIGURE 5.3 Representative page of *Survey of Industrial and Commercial Buying Power.* (*Source:* Reprinted from 1987 S&MM *Survey of Industrial and Commercial Buying Power,* April 27, 1987, p. 89.)

some detail in Chapter 13. Now let us examine specifically the use of these surveys for determining relative market potentials for both consumer and industrial goods.

Allocating sales efforts according to the relative market potential—using the *Survey of Buying Power.*

Assume that you are a sales manager for a firm distributing a premium-priced line of dog food. You want to determine how much local promotional efforts to put into various markets. You have a $500,000 national budget for local sales promotional efforts. From Figure 5.2 you pull the following statistics:

	Total Effective Buying Income ($ Hundreds)	Percentage of U.S. Population	Buying Power Index
District of Columbia	$ 9,998,993	0.2550	.2876
Montgomery, Md.	13,121,366	0.2685	.3967
Prince Georges, Md.	10,273,670	0.2792	.3350

However, you are uncertain as to which statistics are most relevant for allocating selling efforts to the District of Columbia and these two adjacent counties. Having a higher-priced product suggests that income is important, but population should also be considered. You note that Montgomery County has considerably more total buying income than Washington, D.C., and also more than the larger Prince Georges County. But Montgomery County is one of the wealthiest counties in the entire nation. The buying power index interests you. It is a multiple-factor index derived from the following formula:

$$BPI_a = .5i_a + .3s_a + .2p_a$$

where,

BPI_a = percentage of total national buying power found in area a

i_a = percentage of national effective buying income in area a

s_a = percentage of national retail sales in area a

p_a = percentage of national population found in area a

Because income is weighted the highest, you decide to use this buying power index in allocating your sales efforts, and you assign these budgets:

District of Columbia	$500,000 × .2876 = $1,438
Montgomery, Md.	$500,000 × .3967 = $1,984
Prince Georges, Md.	$500,000 × .3350 = $1,675

Now complete Exercise 5.2.

1. What other data from Figure 5.2 warrant consideration in this allocation?
2. What criticisms, if any, do you have of the method of allocation used?
3. From the statistics in Figure 5.2, construct a different weighted index and calculate new sales promotion budgets for these three territories. Defend your reasoning.
4. What other data not available from the *Survey of Buying Power* do you think would be appropriate for this measurement of relative market potential?

Allocating sales efforts according to the relative market potential—Using the *Survey of Industrial and Commercial Buying Power.* Assume that you are the general sales manager of a small firm manufacturing a specialized machine component and distributing it in Indiana, Michigan, and Ohio. Your customers are in three industries: SIC #3522, farm machinery; #3531, construction machinery; and #3537, industrial trucks and tractors. You need to determine the relative market potential for these states in order to allocate your sales efforts most effectively and assign sales quotas to your sales representatives as equitably as possible.

To determine the relative market potentials, you turn to the *Survey of Industrial and Commercial Buying Power* and find the value of shipments (in millions) for the three SIC industries in the three states to be as follows:

Indiana			Michigan		
#3522	#3531	#3537	#3522	#3531	#3537
$177.5	$107.8	—	—	$34.1	$111.7

Ohio		
#3522	#3531	#3537
$127.7	$313.2	$131.7

State totals	
Indiana	$ 285.3
Michigan	$ 145.8
Ohio	$ 572.6
Grand total	$1,003.7

The market potential of each state follows:

Indiana $\dfrac{285.3}{1,003.7}$ = about 29 percent

Michigan $\dfrac{145.8}{1,003.7}$ = about 14 percent

Ohio $\dfrac{572.6}{1,003.7}$ = about 57 percent

Complete Exercise 5.3 using the preceding analysis.

1. Do you see any limitations or contaminating factors in the analysis of relative market potential?	**EXERCISE 5.3**

1. Do you see any limitations or contaminating factors in the analysis of relative market potential?
2. If you have seven salespeople, how would you allocate them by states? Would you need other information to make such an allocation?
3. If your sales plan is $42 million, how would you assign quotas by state?

USING MARKET POTENTIAL MEASURES

This chapter has presented several uses of market potential analyses. This section elaborates on these uses and examines in detail the use of a customer analysis as an adjunct in identifying industrial market potential to achieve a better market penetration.

Defining Sales Territories

Salespeople should have enough sales potential in their territories to use their time effectively; too much potential cannot all be handled and sales are lost. Potential demand is a better basis for defining sales territories than past sales. Past sales, unfortunately, may bear little relationship to potential; one territory's potential may be fully tapped, while another requires two or three times the selling efforts. For example consider the following four sales territories and the results of an analysis of relative market potentials:

		Territory		
	A	B	C	D
Percentage of total U.S. market potential in territory	10.5	8.5	10.0	16.0

Although all territories will not have precisely the same potential, the disproportion in territory D deserves attention and, perhaps, realignment. If we assume that each territory is handled by one salesperson, then the job in territory D appears far easier than in the other three. Of course, geographical factors such as size of territory, transportation conditions, and concentration of accounts should be considered. But if one assumes that these conditions are relatively similar, then the salesperson in D has a definite advantage. Potential sales are probably being sacrificed in D because the territory is too big for one person to handle adequately. As a consequence it is probably being *skimmed*, that is, only the easiest business is being sought by the sales representative.

Setting Sales Quotas

Sales quotas are best set after market potentials have been established. Relative differences in competition in various sales territories, of course, must be considered. Because the quota is a performance standard for judging the salesperson and is often part of the compensation plan, the sales quota therefore is more equitable, more easily defended by management, and a better measure of selling effectiveness when it is used in conjunction with the relative market potentials of respective territories. Returning to the previous example of four territories, the actual sales produced in each territory follow:

	Territory			
	A	B	C	D
Percentage of market potential	10.5	8.5	10.0	16.0
Sales last year	$210,000	$300,000	$265,000	$310,000

Which territory had the highest level of sales performance? Territory D achieved the highest actual sales, but when sales are compared with sales potential, performance is found wanting. Territory B, with roughly half the sales potential of D, achieved almost the same sales volume. At this rate the salesperson in territory B would have achieved almost $600,000 in territory D.

Because of inequities in territorial potentials, sales quotas are better for evaluating sales performance. If all factors excluding market potentials are approximately equivalent in the four territories, then sales quotas based on such potentials would be as follows:

	Regional total	Territory			
		A	B	C	D
Sales last year	$1,085,000	$210,000	$300,000	$265,000	$310,000
Percentage of market potential	45.0	10.5	8.5	10.0	16.0
Regional sales forecast this year	$1,500,000				

Quota, at 80% of forecast: $1,200,000

$$\text{Territory A:} \quad \frac{10.5}{45.0} \times 1,200,000 = \$280,000$$

$$\text{Territory B:} \quad \frac{8.5}{45.0} \times 1,200,000 = \$226,667$$

$$\text{Territory C:} \quad \frac{10.0}{45.0} \times 1,200,000 = \$266,667$$

$$\text{Territory D:} \quad \frac{16.0}{45.0} \times 1,200,000 = \$426,667$$

Although sales quotas should reflect differences in territorial potentials, other factors that should also be considered in determining potential include the salesperson's experience and ability, past sales performance, relevant exogenous factors (i.e., competition), and differing economic conditions (such as a depressed industry in one territory). Sales quotas are examined in much more detail in a later chapter.

Allocating Sales Efforts

Allocating local advertising and sales promotion efforts to particular territories is usually best based on relative market potentials. In the preceding examples if realignment is impractical, then territory D would receive more local advertising dollars than any of the other territories and might also justify some additional sales help, such as one or more training positions. Of course, the number, strength, and vulnerability of competitors should be considered, as well as the availability of suitable local media and the ability to follow up on the promotional efforts.

   Do Exercise 5.4, a review problem on calculating and using market potential.

It has been determined that sales of a particular appliance are related to retail sales, weighted 2; population, weighted 1; residential building permits, weighted 4; personal income, weighted 3; and marriage licenses issued, weighted 2.

EXERCISE 5.4

1. Calculate the market potential for Ohio, if Ohio's percentages of the U.S. total for these factors are 5.5, 4.1, 6.5, 7.4, and 6 percent, respectively.
2. If estimated national sales are $200 million, what should we expect for Ohio?
3. Of a national sales force of 40, how many should be assigned to Ohio?
4. If the quotas are computed at 90% of sales, what is Ohio's quota?
5. If $12 million are budgeted for local advertising and promotions, what is Ohio's share?

Identifying Opportunities for Better Market Penetration

The previous three examples showed direct uses of measures of potential. An indirect use is made when the measures convince a firm that it is not realizing an adequate share of its estimated market potential. The company may then consider making a careful analysis of present and potential customers to improve market penetration. In this section customer analysis is approached from the perspective of a small industrial goods manufacturer who seeks to expand.

Customer analysis. A customer analysis is a systematic identification of present customers. Answers to questions such as the following are desired in a customer analysis:

☐ Where is volume concentrated—among what types of customers?

☐ Who are the major customers?

☐ How profitable is the business with specific types of customers?

☐ What is the trend of business with each customer?

A customer analysis can identify certain patterns of a firm's business. The firm can pinpoint the kinds of customers it is attracting and whether it is gaining or losing ground with them. Perhaps an even more important use for a customer analysis is identifying gaps in coverage. For example a firm may do considerable business with several plumbing fitting customers, SIC #3432, but may not do business with a number of other firms in the same industry group. The firm can then investigate whether such potential customers have been contacted or why they have not bought the product or service despite its success with similar firms. In addition a firm can identify former customers and can question why these were lost.

Customer analysis method. A customer analysis need not be complex. In its simplest form the analysis lists customers and tabulates billings. Space should be left for remarks or feedback from salespeople, customers, or others for each account. Table 5.3 is an example of a simple form of customer analysis for a small nonferrous foundry. Note that the SIC codes of the customers are listed, as well as the sales trend over several years. This information will be useful for the following analysis.

Most firms find that a minority of customers contribute most of the sales volume. This is called the *80/20 rule*—80 percent of a firm's business is done with only 20 percent of its customers. Of course, this percentage varies, but it is often surprisingly close to 80/20. These customers are *key accounts,* and great care should be given to assure their satisfaction and keep them. The key accounts are so important that a firm should learn as much as possible about them.

For the industrial firm with relatively few customers, the easiest way to obtain customer information is simply to contact these customers and explain that marketing research is being conducted to serve them better. As noted earlier in this chapter, if the market is sufficiently large, the survey need include only a sample of customers, and the customer analysis may have to be limited to the more important customers.

Identifying potential customers. The first step in identifying potential customers is to determine the characteristics of present customers. An industrial goods firm should know the SICs of present customers to identify the

TABLE 5.3 Customer analysis for a nonferrous foundry.

Customer	SIC Code	Shipments ($ thousands)				Remarks
		1984	1985	1986	1987	
A	3561	210	140	116	101	???
B	3562	140	121	108	106	Old, loyal customer, but slipping in their industry
C	3586	22	30	40	57	New product lines; good growth prospects; small, but like us
D	3562	—	—	65	120	Beat out competition on basis of quicker deliveries
E	3586	110	160	106	125	Erratic, not very profitable business, hard to satisfy
F	3586	95	40	—	—	Difficult engineering problems, not profitable enough

The foundry described in Table 5.3 exhibits a grievous deficiency, as evident from the data. Look at Customer A, formerly one of the major customers, which should be a key account. Sales have dropped steadily so that now they are less than half those of 4 years before. *And this firm does not even know the reason for the drastic decline in business.* A problem that might have been corrected apparently was overlooked for far too long.

industries in which its business is concentrated. The dollar value of orders in the various SIC categories should be tabulated. Table 5.4 shows one version of such an analysis of customers, again for a nonferrous foundry.

By tabulating sales over several years, a firm gains important trend information. For example in Table 5.4, the data for one industry category, #3561, show a decline in sales, not only to a single customer, but for the entire industry. These sales data spotlight a trouble area. By recognizing a problem, the firm can focus attention on taking corrective action.

Profit analysis also is desired and should indicate which SICs are more profitable. Although profitability will vary somewhat among firms, especially by customer size, often certain industry groups are less profitable customers than other groups. Profitability should guide a firm's thinking in choosing the SICs on which to concentrate its marketing efforts.

Market penetration alternatives. In seeking additional business three penetration approaches are possible: (1) Expand in the present market with other firms of the same SICs as present customers. (2) Expand beyond the present geographic area into adjoining counties or states. (3) Expand into

TABLE 5.4   Sales analysis ($ thousands) for a nonferrous foundry.

Customers	3561 1985	3561 1986	3561 1987	3562 1985	3562 1986	3562 1987	3586 1985	3586 1986	3586 1987	Others 1985	Others 1986	Others 1987
A	140	116	101									
B				121	106	105						
C							30	40	57			
D					65	120						
E							160	105	125			
F							40					
Etc.												
Totals	600	500	450	650	800	900	700	500	800	15 (3585)	10 (3585)	15 (3589)

Grand Totals, all SICS: 1985   1,965
                         1986   1,900
                         1987   2,300

Present customers												
Total		19			2			15			2	
Large firms		3			2			4			0	

other SICs and find new types of customers. Of course, a firm's resources, capabilities, and preferences influence the type of market penetration attempted. But market potential should also weigh heavily on the decision. For example if the market statistics of certain other SICs suggest good market potential, further investigation might be desirable, and additional investment might even be considered in order to tap such prospective business. Furthermore, the competition's vulnerability must be assessed when considering expansion.

Expansion within the present market. The *Survey of Industrial and Commercial Buying Power* is a highly useful tool for all of these market analyses dealing with industrial goods. For example the nonferrous foundry is doing business in two northern Ohio industrial counties, Cuyahoga and Summit. Its business is primarily with firms in SICs #3561 (pumps and compressors), #3562 (ball and roller bearings), and #3586 (measuring and dispensing pumps). From the *Survey of Industrial and Commercial Buying Power*, the firm obtains the total number of plants in the various SICs in each county (not included are those small firms with under twenty employees), as well as the number of large plants (those with one hundred or more employees). Table

TABLE 5.5   Total market and share of market held by nonferrous foundry.

| | Number of Plants | | | | | |
| | SIC #3561 | | SIC #3562 | | SIC #3586 | |
	Total	Large	Total	Large	Total	Large
Cuyahoga County	55	14	6	3	72	6
Summit County	8	4	2	2	33	7
Total market	63	18	8	5	105	13
Present customers	19	3	2	2	15	4

5.4 provides the number of present customers of the foundry. The total market and the foundry's share of this market are tabulated in Table 5.5.

With the information in Table 5.5, the sales manager should investigate how many other firms bearing the same SICs as present customers have been contacted by sales representatives. Obviously, not all firms in a given SIC are likely to be customers. But some of these businesses may not even have been approached and informed about products and services. Locating these other firms usually is not difficult. Lists are available through mailing list companies, directories such as the *Thomas Register,* chambers of commerce, and reference books of Dun & Bradstreet. Even telephone directories can be useful.

Geographic expansion.   Another alternative is expansion of the firm's geographic market area. The foundry could well attempt to approach customers beyond its two-county area, moving into nearby counties in northern Ohio. Again, the firm can turn to the *Survey of Industrial and Commercial Buying Power* and look for counties that show a good concentration of plants in these same SICs. Likewise, the firm can use the survey as a guideline for expanding into other states, because the survey also shows the SIC concentration by state.

Expansion into other SICs.   The third possibility for expansion is in finding new markets and new types of customers—SICs not represented by present customers. In the foundry's case, Table 5.4 shows a very small amount of business with SICs #3585 and #3589. Expanding or penetrating these markets might be investigated. Executives and salespeople may have ideas for other types of customers for which the firm's products and services might be competitive. The firm can hold exploratory talks with representative firms in the prospective SIC groups to ascertain their needs, their interest in finding another supplier, and the business potential with them.

CONSTRAINTS ON REALIZING FULL POTENTIAL

Market potential suggests available opportunities. In assessing market opportunity the aggressive and confident firm with sufficient managerial and financial resources may see the way to wedge out competitors. However, most firms today face some constraints in maximizing their portion of the total market potential. Both internal and external factors may induce a company to settle for less than the maximum market share. For example a company may be operating at near capacity, and the capture of much more business might necessitate expensive new plant additions and/or might lead to industry overcapacity, resulting in falling prices and profits throughout the industry. A firm may not be fully equipped to mass-distribute its products and may elect to settle for less.

For large firms the threat of governmental intervention and regulation may inhibit aggressive expansion and seizure of maximum market potential. Antitrust laws and the threat of breakup if its market share increased have been credited for General Motors' hesitancy in attaining a larger market share, which its size and resources probably would have enabled, before the incursion of foreign imports.

A firm may also have to handle competitive reactions and retaliations if it aggressively attempts to seek a greater market potential share. Especially in oligopolistic industries (industries composed of only a few dominant firms), fear of competitive reactions and counterstrategies induce firms not to move too aggressively.

Most firms, however, are best geared to growth. A growth orientation motivates an organization and makes it sufficiently aggressive. When most firms in an industry actively seek growth, products and services tend to be maximized to the customers' betterment. Unless rivalry degenerates into unethical and dishonest practices, competition better hones marketing efforts and motivates a sales force to the fullest.

SUMMARY   Market potential is a measure of the total business available for that industry or market. Sales potential is the share of total market potential that a firm can expect to achieve. To be successful in estimating market potential, a firm must identify and measure those factors that affect demand for its products.

A variety of data sources, including both primary and secondary data, are helpful in developing measures of potential. Test markets can provide primary data, and secondary data sources are many and varied. In particular the *Survey of Buying Power* and the *Survey of Industrial and Commercial Buying Power* are useful for some consumer goods manufacturers and industrial goods manufacturers, respectively.

Market potential measures are particularly important in defining sales territories, setting sales quotas, allocating sales efforts such as advertising and local sales promotion to various geographical areas, and identifying opportunities for better market penetration.

Certain internal and external factors sometimes may induce a firm to settle for less than its full sales potential. A firm, for example, may not wish to incur the costs of more aggressive growth.

---

1. Discuss the relationship between sales forecasting, budgeting, sales potential, and market potential.

2. What is a market factor? What market factors would be relevant for a soft drink bottler?

3. How can the market potential for new products be determined?

4. Discuss the advantages and disadvantages of a test market. For which of the following products would you recommend this technique, assuming that competitive entry is not an immediate concern?
   a. A turbine automobile
   b. A new kind of dog food
   c. An advanced-design generator

5. What are the advantages and disadvantages of relying on sales force estimates of sales potential?

6. What is a major problem in using SIC codes? In using the government censuses?

7. What are the uses of a measure of market potential?

8. What are the major limitations on a firm's realizing its maximum sales potential? Do these necessarily apply to all firms?

9. What likely will be the impact, if any, of a major competitor in a particular territory being acquired by a large conglomerate? What action, if any, should a sales manager take?

PEOPLE PROBLEM: REACTING TO A NEW COMPETITOR

Please evaluate each of the alternatives.

You have just discovered that a major new competitor has moved into your district and is beginning to market aggressively. What action would you recommend?

1. You inform both top management and your sales force of this significant new development, and give top priority to improving customer service in the district.

2. You immediately notify top management of this new development and press for more promotional funds.

3. You immediately inform your sales force and direct them to be more aggressive in their sales efforts.

4. Reluctantly, you inform your company that the sales potential must be reduced in your district because of this major change in the environment.

5. At this point you adopt a "wait and see" attitude, before pushing the panic button.

NOTES

1. In a careful analysis of various screening techniques used in lieu of test marketing, Tauber found them all flawed in predicting success of new consumer products. He cogently says, "It is cheaper to have a lot of market failures than it is to avoid the loss and miss a big sales winner." Edward M. Tauber, "Forecasting Sales Prior to Test Market," *Journal of Marketing* (January 1977): 80–84.

cases

5.1 Problems with an Information Source for New Product Potential

Sam Rivera is a detail man for a major pharmaceutical concern. In the past his input about the sales and market potential of new drug products—based largely on his effective communication with physicians in his territory—had been very accurate. Lately, however, his estimates have been wrong, usually on the low side.

Janice Butler, who had compiled an outstanding sales record in another part of the company, was appointed Sam's district sales manager. She hoped there were no personal reasons for his recent poor judgment and useless field reports but suspected there might be. She called him in for an interview.

After preliminary small talk, Janice went to the point, "Sam, in the past your estimates of market potential for our new products have been some of the most reliable in the company. Lately they haven't been. Aren't you communicating well with your physicians now, or what?"

Sam became visibly defensive, despite Janice's efforts to minimize the blame. "I don't know. I guess with all the new drugs coming out, the MDs are confused. I can only report to you what they tell me."

QUESTION

In light of this inconclusive conversation with Sam, what would you recommend that Janice do?

5.2 Stairway to Heaven: What Is Our Market Potential?

Dave Ranalli was tossing sleeplessly in bed again. He was unable to rid his mind of problems down at work. "Perhaps that is the penalty of a new business for which you have put yourself deeply in debt," he thought.

Dave had a good product, and the enterprise was not totally new but rather an expanded operation of a small mom-and-pop curved-stair–making operation. Still, a considerable investment had been made in expanding—maybe they had overexpanded. Dave wondered if there was enough potential business to warrant the ambitious expansion and to meet the now-heavy financial obligations. The decision seemed right at the time, with upscale housing in evergrowing demand. But now that the plant capacity was 1,500 stairs a year, Dave wondered if that sales volume was achievable. He realized now that he needed a better mea-

sure of market potential, sales estimates, and the market potential concentration. He realized now that this information should have been solidly established before expanding. But he was ambitious, and his enthusiasm had been contagious to his venture-capitalist backers.

Stairway to Heaven was located in a small town in rural Ohio that had low labor costs, close proximity to lumber sources and transportation, and satisfactory shipping facilities. Customers chose the design and material they wanted and provided size specifications. A job order was then prepared for each staircase, raw materials were collected from the inventory, and the staircase was designed according to the customer's specifications. The crafted staircase was then shipped to the customer and installed by local workmen. Prices ranged from $6,000 to over $15,000 without installation.

Stairway to Heaven's customized products allowed installation of curved staircases in private residences, multilevel business offices or buildings, institutions, country clubs, condominiums, apartments, as well as historical restorations. To date, however, almost all the installations had been in new residential construction. The price normally limited installation to more expensive constructions.

Marketing strategy. Stairway to Heaven planned to market nationwide, although initial efforts would be more concentrated east of the Mississippi. The present sales force consisted of one salesperson and three manufacturers' representatives. The representatives were independents who sold the products of various noncompeting manufacturers and received a 5 percent commission on all sales. By selling through manufacturers' representatives, Stairway to Heaven expanded its distribution without employing and training a larger sales force.

The salesperson, Sherry Knox, worked out of the factory. She acted as sales manager with the manufacturers' representatives and recruited them and communicated with them, in addition to soliciting business. She spent considerable time on the telephone, giving estimates and recording job orders from both customers and manufacturers' representatives. Occasionally, she made on-site visits. She also planned to attend trade shows to acquaint builders with Stairway to Heaven and to solicit business.

Stairway to Heaven used print advertising, although Dave was not sure that it had directly resulted in sales. He had contracted for a year of advertising in two trade magazines. The monthly *Builder* (the official magazine of the National Association of Home Builders) had a circulation of 220,500 primarily in the South and West Coast to builders, developers, contractors, remodelers, and special trade contractors. The annual cost for a monthly, one-page, four-color advertisement was $9,585. The *Professional Builder* had a circulation of 138,968 primarily in the North Central, New England, and the Middle and South Atlantic states. The annual cost for a similar ad was $8,795.

Early results. The expansion had been completed 3 months before, so production should have been approaching full capacity. Unfortunately, orders were 40 percent below expectation, and the trend was not encouraging. Dave's worried financial backers were phoning. One backer had told him, "Dave, you just have to get out there and find out where your market potential is—and then go after it. I don't think you really know your market for sure, do you?"

The next day, Dave sat down with Sherry Knox, his salesperson, to address this problem and to determine the direction of sales efforts. Dave and Sherry analyzed the sales results by region. The representative in the upper midwest had sold four small staircases; the representative in New England, eight small to medium; and the representative in the southeast had sold twelve including one large commercial order. The majority of the sales had been in the three nearest states, Ohio, Indiana, and Kentucky.

"Sherry, do you know much about our customers? Most of our sales have been for personal residences, haven't they?"

"Almost all have been, although we should increase sales to condominium developers and maybe some offices."

"What price of home have we sold to?"

"I don't know for sure. I would guess though that most are over $200,000."

"Couldn't we sell our lower priced units in homes down to $150,000?"

"I suppose so. Sure," Sherry conceded.

As they further attempted to identify their target market and market potential, Dave realized how little they really knew about their market, but he began to know it better. Looking at the U.S. Census of Housing for 1980, he found that 2.76% of all homes were valued at over $150,000. This figure of almost 3% was consistent with data from the Census of 1970, after accounting for inflation. With 8 years of further appreciation since the 1980 Census, he felt safe in concluding that 3 to 5 percent of the homes built annually were worth over $150,000. When a conservative estimate of 3 percent was applied to the number of private residential homes built during 1988, the result was that about 7,856 of such homes were worth over $150,000. In addition various trade associations reported a current trend in housing toward high-value features such as curved stairways and for homes and condominium apartments of more than one floor. All this information seemed to indicate a positive future for Stairway to Heaven, Dave thought. In addition renovators and developers of offices and other structures were an unknown and practically untapped demand. He concluded that the market existed for Stairway to Heaven. But he still needed more specific information on how best to tap it. Competition, Dave felt, would not be a major impeding factor. He firmly felt that no other large-scale producer of curved staircases could match his company's customized, high-quality products.

QUESTIONS

1. Do you agree with Dave's assumptions? Do you think others should be added?

2. Using data in your library, calculate the market potential for your metropolitan area. Make any assumptions needed from the available data, but be prepared to defend these assumptions.

3. How would you advise Dave to gain more information about his customers?

4. What approach should Dave and his sales department take to reach and convince the potential market of the merits of Stairway to Heaven curved staircases? Be as specific as you can.

CHAPTER 6
Forecasting Sales

CHAPTER PERSPECTIVE

Chapter 5 analyzed the market in terms of current demand. This chapter is concerned with the techniques to estimate future demand. *Sales forecasting* is predicting sales for a given period of time. The most common period for forecasting is the short term, up to 1 year. Unfortunately, predicting sales is almost akin to picking the winning horse or the great growth stock of the coming year. Despite sophisticated analyses, one author pessimistically suggests, "Forecasting is like trying to drive a car blindfolded and following directions given by a person who is looking out the back window."[1] Although problems and inaccuracies abound, the quest for more valid forecasting techniques is worthwhile and deserves our attention.

As you read this chapter, consider one of the most difficult forecasting problems—predicting sales for a new product with no sales experience. What forecasting techniques would you recommend and why?

CHAPTER OBJECTIVES

☐ Be able to assess the factors affecting sales, both the controllable and uncontrollable, which can lead to active versus passive approaches to forecasting.
☐ Understand the steps used in developing a sales forecast.
☐ Become acquainted with the various forecasting techniques, how they are derived, and their usefulness.
☐ Gain a perspective of the general limitations to forecasting.
☐ Recognize the particular forecasting problems for new products and changing conditions.
☐ Know the criteria for most effective forecasting.

IMPORTANCE OF FORECASTING

As noted in Chapter 4, the sales forecast guides the firm's operations, because the sales estimate determines commitments ranging from production planning (procuring raw materials, labor, and capital equipment) to marketing (advertising, sales force buildup, and inventory requirements). You may want to review Table 4.1 in Chapter 4 for a listing of the consequences of inaccurate sales forecasts.

A major problem with forecasting is that it is so dependent on prior sales. The assumption is that the past indicates the future, and it is true that projected sales may be accurate for years in stable industries. But firms that rely on forecasts sometimes find themselves in dire straits (see Application 6.1); the importance of accurate forecasting is indisputable.

FACTORS AFFECTING SALES

We can categorize forecasts as either *passive* or *active*. Many sales forecasts are passive, involving estimates of possible external influences on sales and predictions of the resulting sales volume if the firm continues on its present course. Sales forecasting is thus regarded as being imposed on the company and beyond its control.

This passivity can be questioned. Sales are a result not only of external economic and competitive conditions but also of the firm's own actions. Sales thus will vary as a function of advertising, price policy, product changes, and

---

APPLICATION 6.1   The Consequences of Faulty Forecasting

In the early 1970s, AT&T experienced a service crisis of monumental proportions in New York City. The number of serious complaints of delayed dial tones and circuit-busy signals grew to more than 4,000 in the first 8 months, more than three times the total for all of the previous year. Pay phones were broken or vandalized and remained unfixed; telephone installation required 2 to 3 months of lead time. The strategic importance of New York City as a communication center made the service breakdown all the more serious.

What caused this unexpected situation? A number of factors contributed, particularly faulty forecasting and trend analysis. For example the New York Telephone Company erroneously had expected the gross national product growth curve to flatten out and accordingly cut its construction budget. Meanwhile, a stock market trading boom developed, increasing telephone traffic unexpectedly. Unpredicted changes in calling patterns also developed in residential areas. For example, New York City began to pay for welfare clients' telephones, resulting in a huge use increase between formerly light-traffic areas. AT&T's reliance on historical trend-line planning proved inadequate.

other marketing efforts. Alternative strategies can be considered. This concept is not new; more than three decades ago it was called "manipulating demand."[2]

It is useful to classify the various factors affecting (or influencing) sales volume as *controllable* and *uncontrollable*. Controllable factors are elements of the internal business environment and planning activities over which the firm has control, subject perhaps to certain constraints regarding resource availability. Examples are plant and equipment capability, personnel strength, executive competence and preferences, financial resources, and business objectives. Uncontrollable factors are elements of the environment over which the firm has little or no control in the short run. Examples are cultural, demographic, political, and economic factors, as well as the competitive climate and the dynamics of technology.

The sales forecast links the evaluation of external factors affecting the operation with the internal resources and objectives that management controls. As forecasts cover a longer period of time, the external climate becomes more important, because it sets overall constraints that affect company growth.

Figure 6.1 shows the theoretical contrasts between active and passive approaches to forecasting. In the passive approach the environmental and competitive uncontrollable factors are estimated as to their effects on company fortunes, and the sales forecast is made accordingly. In the active approach such uncontrollable factors or influencers are considered, but planned changes in strategic inputs are also considered. Strategic factors may be given more weight than environmental and competitive factors, depending on how sweeping and effective changes are expected to be. The active sales forecast is a composite of uncontrollable and controllable predicted inputs. The model shown in Figure 6.1 of the active approach to forecasting can be given more power by weighting the various uncontrollable and controllable factors as to their probable importance in affecting future sales. Weighting usually represents the expert judgment of the key executives involved. In Figure 6.1 the weightings reflect the estimated relative importances of the various factors:

Environmental uncontrollable factors, weighted .1

Competitive uncontrollable factors, weighted .2

All the controllable inputs, weighted .7

The model in Figure 6.1 does not give a specific forecast. Rather, it represents the basis for forecasting, giving a systematic evaluation of the factors expected to influence future sales. However, even though a business identifies environmental conditions and strategic actions that will probably affect sales in the immediate period, the effects often can be only approximated. Forecasting is still an inexact science.

Competition, in particular, can complicate the outcome, because competitors' actions and any countermoves may be unexpected. Competition must

Passive Approach

Influences of Sales

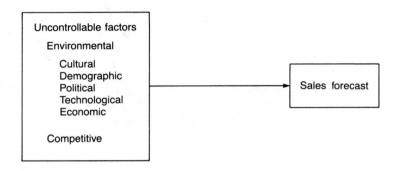

Active Approach

Influences of Sales

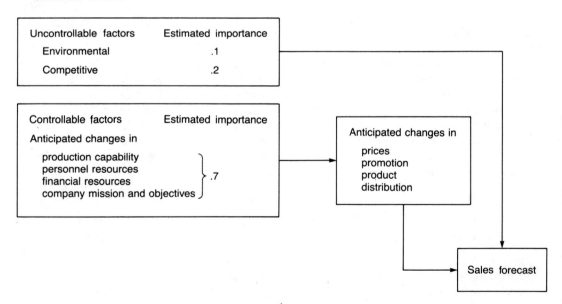

FIGURE 6.1   Contrasts of active and passive approaches to forecasting.

be further classified to better understand and cope with it. In particular inter-industry competition must be differentiated from intra-industry competition.

Interindustry competition involves actions taken to induce consumers and other users to procure products of one industry rather than those of another. This competition extends beyond the parameters of a single, obvious industry. An example is the competition between aluminum and steel, each of which can be readily substituted for the other in some products. In the consumer sphere competition for leisure dollars can cover a multitude of industries, from backpacking equipment to yachts.

Intra-industry competition is the common notion of competition. If com-petitive conditions within an industry change, either through a variation in the number of firms competing or a change in their activities regarding ad-vertising, selling, or product design, then future sales volume will be affected. Any changes in price strategies of competitors may have a major effect.

PROCEDURE FOR FORECASTING

With the growing complexity of forecasting, many companies now assign the task to specialists. Forecasters may work in the sales department, but when the company has a marketing research department or an economist, the function is often placed there. Some companies are wholly or partially de-pendent on outside advisers.

What is the sales manager's role in forecasting? While guided by the sales forecast, is the sales manager involved in determining it? Most firms give the sales manager some input, ranging from direct submission of sales estimates to a more or less tacit approval of a staff-developed forecast. Field sales managers often are requested to submit their own forecasts, which are then reviewed and reworked into a final form acceptable to top management. This is usually called a *bottom-up* forecasting procedure. Generally, developing a sales forecast involves the five following steps:

1. Gather the forecasting information. The noncontrollable factors in the business environment, such as increased competition, economic slowdown, expected shortage of materials, should be recognized. Information should also be gathered about the controllable factors if an active approach is used. If planned marketing efforts are significantly different from past efforts, their effect on future sales cannot be disregarded.

2. Apply forecasting techniques. Specific forecasting techniques, for eval-uating data and projecting sales, are described in the next section.

3. Translate the sales forecast operationally. Through the budgeting pro-cess, which is discussed in Chapter 7, the forecasted sales are broken down into various expense lines and profit control units, such as product lines, and departmental and geographical units. Specific targets are translated into op-

erational programs, such as marketing programs, production schedules, purchasing plans, financial requirements, personnel needs, and inventory levels.

4. Audit the forecast. During the forecast period and at its end, actual and forecast sales are compared, and discrepancies are analyzed. This major aspect of controlling is described in Chapter 16.

5. Refine the forecast. When serious discrepancies occur between actual and forecast performance, the forecast and forecasting procedures may need to be modified, projections and adjusting techniques reevaluated. The aim here is twofold, first, to make any necessary operational adjustments in light of a changed sales picture and, second, to develop more accurate sales forecasting in the future.

FORECASTING TECHNIQUES

Forecasting techniques can be classified as *quantitative* and *qualitative*. Many firms use elaborate statistical techniques in forecasting. Sometimes these techniques produce accurate sales forecasts, and indeed, the sophisticated use of numbers and complex mathematical formulations is satisfying. Unfortunately, their accuracy is not guaranteed, as the AT&T example demonstrated earlier in this chapter. At the other extreme are subjective "guesstimates" and forecasts by intuition, which also usually leave something to be desired. But subjective or qualitative estimates should not always be repudiated; at times they are superior to the statistical analyses. Even "gut feel" may be appropriate in forecasting (see Application 6.2).

Qualitative Methods

Qualitative or subjective techniques involve judgment, opinion, or hunch of an individual or a group. The results can range from fairly good to very poor.

Executive opinion.   Executive opinion represents an individual's opinion or combines the views of numerous executives, possibly top executives or regional sales managers, as Aegis used. Some of these opinions may be supported by considerable factual material or may be based on one or several other forecasting methods; others may depend on observation and hunch only. The major advantage of using executive opinion is that it is easily and quickly obtained. For firms in industries where styles change rapidly and capriciously, such as parts of the garment or toy industries, experienced judgment may be the best method available. The disadvantages are numerous, although these primarily result from lack of thoroughness among the executives. At its worst executive opinion may be little more than group guessing. Furthermore, many executives, such as the production manager, have no way of knowing the field situation. If basic economic and market statistics are not

---

APPLICATION 6.2   Intuition or "Gut Feeling" in Forecasting

Despite computer technology and sophisticated techniques, forecasting may involve sufficient unknown and undecipherable factors to merit using gut feelings.

In September 1986 Aegis Corp. was developing its 1987 forecasts. The marketing department performed the sales forecasts and needed to decide whether to include sales data for the first 9 months of 1986 or to exclude first-quarter results because they were lower than projected by historical sales data. Were the first quarter results atypical, or did they indicate a changing trend?

Data used in Aegis forecasts included general economic information, industry sales figures, and factory shipment figures; additional inputs were the subjective opinions of the fourteen regional sales managers. The sales force also contributed, although members did not make formal forecasts. Despite considerable quantitative data laced with the qualitative inputs of expert judgment, the marketing department encountered particular difficulty in calculating the effect on sales and profits of factors such as (1) increased distribution (i.e., a greater number of outlets in the period ahead); (2) change in spending for advertising and promotion; (3) price–volume tradeoffs (i.e., price elasticity); (4) new product activity; and (5) competitive activity.

Difficulties were encountered regarding new products, not only in predicting their sales volume but also in determining whether they would lead to incremental sales or would steal sales from other products in the line. Competitors, of course, could confound forecasts by introducing a different and exciting product or changing their marketing strategy, especially regarding pricing and advertising. Although past actions would indicate some likely competitive behavior, the competition could change as its executives change.

With all these variables and unknowns, Aegis was ready to adjust its forecasts if conditions changed or if early results were inaccurate. Said one company official, "If we can come within 5 percent we've been pretty accurate." They decided to ignore possibly atypical early-year results in projecting the next year's sales. Management substituted the first-quarter data with an estimate (a gut feeling) of more typical results. The sales results were reasonably close to expectations.

---

used in compiling the estimate, any breakdown of sales by products, customers, and so on for operating and controlling purposes is difficult.

Sales force composite.   In the sales force composite method, each salesperson estimates future sales of various products in her territory. These individual territorial estimates are then compiled to derive the total sales forecast. The advantages of this method follow:

1. It uses the specialized knowledge of the people closest to the market.

2. Those who must produce the results perform the forecast.

3. The sales force has greater confidence in the quotas developed from forecasts.

4. Results have greater stability and accuracy because of the number of contributors.

5. Product, territory, customer, and salesperson breakdowns are easily developed.

The most commonly encountered arguments against using salespeople in forecasting are the following:

1. They are poor estimators, being either too optimistic or too pessimistic.

2. If estimates are used as a basis for setting quotas, salespeople are inclined to understate the demand to make their goals easier to achieve.

3. Salespeople are often unaware of broad economic patterns that shape future sales; furthermore, they may not be aware of new products that are not yet in the marketplace or of contemplated changes in marketing efforts.

4. Forecasting requires considerable time, which the sales force might better spend in contacting customers.

Opinion survey of "experts" or "people who know." Knowledgeable people include jobbers, wholesalers, and retailers, who may be polled on the theory that they have an intimate "feel" of the market. Although this is an informal approach, it may be the best available for some companies. It is best suited to industrial equipment forecasting, which involves specialized middlemen and buyers. The experts' sentiments can change quickly, however, and the experts' basis for forecasting is hard to identify. Experts may mostly use hunch and impulse under pressure of inquiry.

Opinion sampling of customers. Customer opinion sampling uses market research. Individual firms perform customer opinion samples, and the Survey Research Center of the University of Michigan regularly samples customer opinion to measure willingness to buy durable goods (autos, appliances, etc.). Other surveys, less well-known, have been developed (e.g., by Sindlinger and Co., The Conference Board, Inc., and the Commercial Credit Corporation) to measure consumer confidence, intentions to buy, and anticipated purchases of new cars and other appliances.

The obvious argument for this method of forecasting is that the customer actually determines the sales results. Why not, therefore, go directly to the source, whether industrial purchaser or consumer? But the disadvantages of this technique should not be viewed lightly. Professed intentions to buy are notoriously poor predictors and often are not confirmed by a sale. The prevailing state of business heavily influences buying plans, so buying intentions can change rapidly. This method therefore is primarily useful for only short-term forecasting, from 3 to 6 months ahead. Another difficulty is that unless customers surveys are conducted carefully by highly qualified people, they tend to be biased and not sufficiently representative.

Delphi method.   A more sophisticated and often effective variation of the expert opinion forecast is the Delphi method, developed by a senior mathematician at the Rand Corporation. Although the Delphi method was first applied to technological forecasting, it is relevant to business, especially during conditions of relative uncertainty, or when forthcoming major innovations or improvements will affect the firm or the industry.

In the Delphi technique experts in the investigation area are questioned; the survey results are distributed to the participating experts, and they are questioned again, thereby allowing changes in opinion and predictions based on feedback. This technique is a process of successive feedback and reevaluation of expectations. See Figure 6.2 for a graphic model of the Delphi technique. If the questions and experts are well chosen (and if circumstances favor the honest opinions of a range of knowledgeable people, which may not be possible under severe competitive circumstances), the Delphi method may result in valid predictions.

Quantitative Methods

The use of statistical methods is increasing. These quantitative forecasting techniques range from very simple trend projections to sophisticated multiple-correlation analyses and mathematical models.

Projection of trends (trend analysis).   Trend projection is a common method of forecasting based on the assumption that past rates of change will continue into the future and, thus, that the relative impact of all factors affecting sales will continue to be the same. Trend projection often is fairly accurate, except at turning points and major shifts in growth rates. But these changes can provide the firm's biggest opportunities for success or failure. This method typically uses growth curves that are fitted to historical data and then extrapolated. Satisfactory extrapolation requires a sales history, usually from 2 to 5 years if seasonal elements are present. Trend projection therefore is not appropriate for new products.

Two common statistical techniques use trend analysis: moving averages and exponential smoothing. These are widely used, and a sales manager should be familiar with them.

Moving averages.   Moving averages are series of averages whose high and low values are cushioned and made less extreme. The number of data points chosen should be sufficient to eliminate the effects of seasonal variations or irregularity. Table 6.1 illustrates a 3-year moving average. Note that as each new year's sales are added to the averages, the oldest year's sales are dropped. In addition to eliminating the effects of irregularities, moving averages tone down the most recent sales results, thus leading to more conservative forecasts during times of increasing sales.

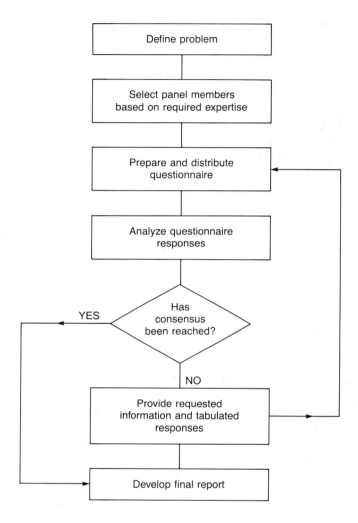

FIGURE 6.2 Model of the Delphi technique. (*Source*: Adapted from Raymond B. Taylor and L. Lynn Judd, ''Forecasting Environmental Trends in Tourism.'' Paper delivered at the Conference on Marketing of Tourism, Cleveland State University and the Academy of Marketing Science, Cleveland, 25 and 26 September 1986.)

The formula for the moving averages method follows:

$$F_{t+1} = \frac{S_t + S_{t-1} + \ldots + S_{t-n+1}}{n}$$

where,

F_{t+1} = forecast for the next period

S_t = sales in the current period

n = number of periods in the moving average

For example, in Table 6.1 the forecast for 1988 was derived as follows:

$$F_{t+1} \text{ (forecast for 1988)} = \frac{20,000 + 18,000 + 17,250}{3}$$

$$= 18,417$$

Figure 6.3 shows the data from Table 6.1, readily demonstrating the removal of cyclical, irregular, and random fluctuations—the peaks and valleys of sales. The more periods used for a moving average the smoother the curve. Consequently, a 5-year moving average would show less fluctuation than the 3-year; it would be less sensitive to change.

A drawback to the moving average is that all the time periods are weighted equally. Therefore, the moving average method is not a sensitive trend indicator, because it treats data from the oldest and the most recent periods with the same importance and weight. The exponential smoothing method corrects this deficiency of the moving average.

TABLE 6.1   Sales forecasts ($ hundreds) using a 3-year moving average.

Year	Sales*	Sales for 3-Year Period†	Three-Year Moving Average Forecast‡
1980	16,250	—	—
1981	17,000	—	—
1982	20,000	53,250	—
1983	16,000	53,000	17,750
1984	15,000	51,000	17,667
1985	17,250	48,250	17,000
1986	18,000	50,250	16,080
1987	20,000	55,250	16,750
1988	—	—	18,417

*S_t

†$S_t + S_{t-1} + S_{t-2}$

‡$F_{t+1} = \frac{S_t + S_{t-1} + S_{t-2}}{3}$

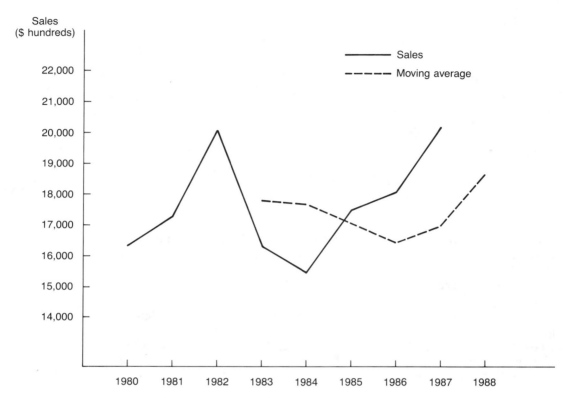

FIGURE 6.3 Sales and 3-year moving average forecasts depicted graphically.

Exponential smoothing. Exponential smoothing is designed to overcome the moving average's insufficient response to the most recent results. In this modification of the moving average, more recent observations or sales results can be given a heavier weight. The weight applied to the most recent sales figure, which represents the forecaster's estimate of its relative importance, is designated as α (alpha) and termed *the smoothing constant*. The α is given a value between 0.0 and 1.0. In equation form the exponentially smoothed average is expressed as follows:

$$F_{t+1} = \alpha\, S_t + (1 - \alpha)\, \overline{S}_t - n$$

where,

F_{t+1} = forecast for the next period $(t + 1)$

α = the smoothing constant

S_t = actual sales in period t

$\overline{S}_t - n$ = smoothed (averaged) forecast for period $t - 1$

The greater the weight given to the latest observation, the more important it will be in the new average and, thus, the less important prior data will be. When a lower figure is used (such as .2), the current results are deemed less important. As example of this calculation, return to Table 6.1, and calculate a new forecast for 1988. Using an α of .6 (to give more weight to most current sales figures), results in the following:

$$F_{t+1}(\text{forecast for 1988}) = .6\ (20,000) + \left(\frac{.4\ (18,000 + 17,250)}{2} \right)$$
$$= 12,000 + .4\ (17,625)$$
$$= 19,950$$

Now, how is the value of α determined? As a general guide if sales are relatively stable, historical sales patterns probably are more important, and less weight therefore would be given to the most current figures—hence a lower α. But when sales fluctuate considerably, current figures are probably more indicative of next year's performance and would be given a higher α value (such as .6 or .8). To determine the value of α more specifically, a firm can test a number of different values on past sales records and ascertain which α value would have led to the smallest forecasting error. This value could be used for future smoothing, although testing must be done periodically to determine if the same α value remains best or if a change would improve forecasting accuracy.

A particular advantage of exponential smoothing is the relative ease in calculation because only past sales data are used. However, managers often prefer to consider additional variables; correlation or regression analysis then may be advantageous.

Now complete Exercise 6.1 to help you gain a sufficient perspective of the exponential smoothing method.

---

1. In the previous example, if sales for 1988 were $22 million what would be the forecast for 1989 using the same α?
2. What would be the forecast for 1988 if α were designated as .2?
3. What might account for the assignment of a .2 weight to the current year's sales?

EXERCISE 6.1

Correlation analysis (regression equations). Correlation analysis is a quantitative technique relating sales to economic, competitive, or other internal or external variables that vary (correlate) to some degree with the firm's sales. Where a single economic or other factor shows such a correlation and where a linear or straight-line relationship is assumed, the formula is as follows:

$$Y = a + bX$$

where,

$Y =$ the dependent variable (sales)

$X =$ the independent variable (for example, changes in gross national product, GNP)

$a =$ the Y-intercept value (the value of Y when X equals zero)

$b =$ the average increment of sales change (the slope of the equation)

The statistical calculations for regression analyses are beyond the scope of this book.[3] However, we can note that equations are derived by finding an equation that best fits a trend line to historical data. The *least squares method* is commonly used where a single independent variable is used. This method minimizes the sum of the squares of all the errors between actual and predicted sales to find the coefficients, *a* and *b,* of the regression line. Thus, the equation, $Y = 55 + 2.1X$, indicates that sales are 55 plus a trend of 2.1 for every unit of time, such as each year.

A fuel oil supplier's experience demonstrates the relation of sales to other factors. Sales increased and decreased in rather close harmony with temperatures. Therefore, sales comprised the dependent variable and temperature was the independent variable; sales were dependent on temperature. Unfortunately, this correlation had little practical value because temperature prediction is an inexact science. A sales correlation with a factor like new housing starts is far better for forecasting because this type of factor can be estimated with more certainty and probably would be a leading indicator.

Leading indicators are series of data whose movements precede similar movements in the company's sales, perhaps by several months or even longer. A lead-lag relationship between sales and an economic or other statistical series enhances forecasting accuracy. Examples of leading indicators for certain firms are percentage change in GNP, industrial building contracts awarded, average hours worked, and new housing starts. Some companies have found that changes in personal income may lead sales of their products. For example a furniture manufacturer has found that a jump in personal income presages an increase in sales by a few months.

Unfortunately, although leading indicators are not uncommon and often are accurate, they are not infallible and can misdirect a forecast. Changes in economic conditions intervening in the lead-lag may cause great variations in the relationship between the leading indicators and sales. The search continues for additional factors and multiple correlations that will match with company sales as closely and consistently as possible.

Multiple regression analysis.   Most forecasting models involve more than a single independent variable and use multiple regression analysis with sales that are related to numerous variables. The general formula follows:

$$Y = a + b_1 X_1 + b_2 X_2 + \ldots b_n X_n$$

with $X_1 \ldots X_n$ representing the different independent variables.

Computers and readily available programs have made the use of regression analysis in forecasting easy by eliminating the complex computations of multiple correlations. The ease of determining possible associations of sales with other variables has led to a wide search for variables and extensive testing by many firms. The ideal sales–factor correlation is a perfect 1.0, but this is seldom achieved. Even if the correlation is not high, however, such predictors may warn of business turning points (see Application 6.3).

Computers enable the development of increasingly complex forecasting methods aimed at yielding more precise predictions. More complex causal models have been developed for forecasting, including econometric models and input–output models. The first Nobel Prize in economic science was awarded to two econometricians in 1968. Econometric models, however, for all their complexity and sophistication, have a crucial weakness. They are projections based on past experience and therefore do not consider unexpected changes, and the customer is not always sufficiently predictable. It is beyond the scope of this book to discuss these models in greater detail.

APPLICATION 6.3   Correlation Analysis Using a PC to Forecast Sales

The following example illustrates how sales correlation and forecasting may be assisted by a Lotus 1-2-3 spread-sheet program.

Betty Rizzo, the sales manager of a toy manufacturer, must forecast sales for a new territory. She is considering using correlation analysis for this territory that has a population of 5,250,000 with an average household income of $29,375. Analyzing her ten existing territories to correlate their sales with these two variables, she developed the data shown in Table 6.2.

TABLE 6.2   Data correlating sales with population and income.

Sales ($)	Population (Million)	Average Income ($)	Sales Forecast from Population ($)	Sales Forecast Based on Population and Average Income ($)
10,250	2.514	22,300	11,888	10,387
3,500	0.843	17,498	4,651	1,732
25,000	5.910	34,790	26,596	28,993
18,500	4.322	21,655	19,719	17,576
46,750	8.670	36,054	38,550	40,805
28,900	6.413	28,312	28,775	28,647
32,475	7.066	32,773	31,603	32,992
8,300	1.212	29,478	6,249	7,710
15,240	3.075	35,247	14,318	17,514
36,375	9.684	19,840	42,942	38,933

APPLICATION 6.3   *continued*

Betty first examined population alone and then population and average income to determine the higher correlation with past sales.

1. Sales forecast based on population as a single independent variable:

Regression Output

Constant		999.803
Standard error of Y estimated		3,940.737
R^2		0.927
No. of observations		10
Degrees of freedom		8
X coefficient(s)	4,331.046	
Standard error of coefficient	428.776	

Linear regression: using population to forecast sales

Sales = 999.803 + Pop. × 4,331.046

When population is 5,250
Sales forecast is $23,738

2. Sales forecast based on the two independent variables population and average income:

Regression Output

Constant		−8,248.342
Standard error of Y estimated		3,109.418
R^2		0.960
No. of observations		10
Degrees of freedom		7
X coefficient(s)	4,109.107	0.372
Standard error of coefficient	350.547	0.154

Sales forecast based on linear regression with population and average income:

Sales = −8,248.342 + Pop. × 4,109.107 + Average income × 0.372

Given population and average income figures, forecast sales by the linear regression equation with two independent variables:

Population = 5.250
Average income = $29,375
Sales forecast = $24,264

Using the Lotus 1-2-3 regression function, Betty calculated R^2 values of 0.927 and 0.960 for population-based and population and average income-based regressions, respectively. R^2 shows the percentage of explained variation in sales. By correlating sales with population, Betty explained 92.7 percent of sales variations. But she found that including average income added a small degree of predictability to the forecast, and she therefore made the forecast of $24,264.

For this example I am indebted to Professor Paul Cretien at Baylor University.

Commentary on regression analysis. The concept of correlation or regression analysis is shown in Figure 6.4. In the first example the scatter diagram of number of business failures and company sales shows no relationship. In example 2 when total amount of industry advertising is plotted with company sales, a negative relationship emerges, as sales tend to be lower during periods of heavy competitors' advertising. Example 3 depicts a relationship, though it is not a straight line. Sales for the particular firm (or product) appear to benefit from moderate rainfall but are hurt by too little or too much. Forecasters generally seek the type of relationship found in example 4, a positive straight-line correlation.

The advantages most often cited for correlation analysis in forecasting are that this method is more objective than many other commonly used forecasting methods and forces consideration of the major factors influencing

Example 1: No correlation

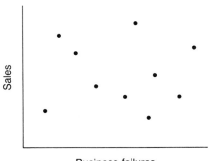

Example 2: Negative correlation

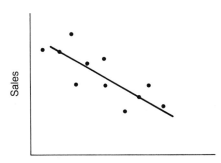

Example 3: Nonlinear correlation

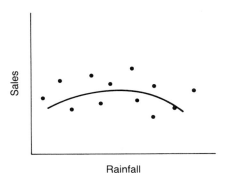

Example 4: Linear correlation

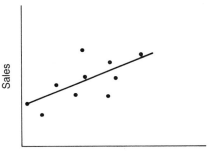

FIGURE 6.4 Correlation possibilities plotted.

sales and quantification of the assumptions underlying the estimates. It also indicates the degree of reliability that can be attached to such relationships. Correlation analysis benefits from the opinions of other forecasters if company sales correlate with well-known indicators. If good leading indicators exist, identification of turning points can be much improved over the time-series analyses and projection methods.

Correlation analysis, however, has inherent limitations. The sales forecast is tied to indicators that also must be forecast. Overreliance on sophisticated techniques is a danger, particularly if the result is a disregard for the feel of the market (as gleaned from qualitative techniques). Relationships can change unexpectedly or too subtly to be noticed and can result in inaccurate forecasts. Because the techniques are rather complex, some managers may react skeptically to the forecast results. Like trend projection methods, correlation analysis requires a history—usually a minimum of 2 years—which rules out its use with new companies and new products.[4]

EVALUATION OF FORECASTING TECHNIQUES

Quantitative Versus Qualitative

Quantitative methods, emphasizing careful analysis, mathematics, and statistics, seem best for most forecasting. These methods use complex and sophisticated tools, and their objectivity, compared with the less sophisticated qualitative techniques, is relatively high. But some of them, especially econometric models and input–output models, are very costly and time-consuming; and quantitative techniques cannot penetrate far into the future without relying on subjective judgments. For new products and new companies, which have no lengthy sales history, and those in rapidly changing environments, complexity of forecasting is no ensurance of predictive accuracy.

The qualitative techniques are particularly susceptible to criticism regarding their inconsistent caliber. Distinguishing between careful, shrewd judgments and hunches or guesses is not easy, especially when judgments of numerous persons are required.

What forecasting techniques do business firms use?   Table 6.3 shows the results of a survey that asked this question.[5] Note that the mathematical techniques, both the simpler trend projections and the more complex correlation and mathematical models, are used to only a modest extent. The techniques used most often are qualitative, such as executive opinion, sales force estimates, and survey of user intentions. Note also, however, that consumer goods manufacturers use sales force estimates and user intentions much less than do industrial goods manufacturers, which reflects a more scattered market for consumer goods.

TABLE 6.3 Company use of major forecasting techniques.

Forecasting Method	Percentage of Companies Reporting		
	Heavy Use	Moderate Use	Very Little or No Use
Industrial goods manufacturers			
Executive opinion	47	32	20
Sales force composite	50	36	13
Survey of users' intentions	22	37	41
Time-series projections	23	30	48
Mathematical models	12	20	69
Consumer goods manufacturers			
Executive opinion	53	24	23
Sales force composite	27	24	50
Survey of users' intentions	10	27	63
Time-series projections	29	29	43
Mathematical models	11	24	66

Source: Based on information from ninety-three industrial goods manufacturers and thirty-nine consumer goods manufacturers. Compiled by Stanley J. PoKempner and Earl L. Bailey, *Sales Forecasting Practices: An Appraisal*, Experiences in Marketing Management, no. 25 (New York: National Industrial Conference Board, 1970), 10.

The use of quantitative techniques may be increasing since the 1970 survey in Table 6.3. Another study in 1975 found that many executives believed that quantitative techniques produced forecasts more accurate than those of subjective methods. However, some believed that the organizational involvement in forecasting committees still made the subjective approaches more desirable.[6]

A number of "success stories" in the use of quantitative methods have been reported in the business press in recent years. For example Cessna Aircraft Company used a multiple regression model to predict its sales of private planes.[7] E. L. Wiegand Division of Emerson Electric has also found multiple regression forecasts to be effective in predicting sales of its industrial electric heating equipment for automotive product manufacturers.[8] The classic example of the use of quantitative forecasting techniques is that of Lydia Pinkham's Vegetable Compound. Five independent variables were found to account for 94 percent of the yearly variation in sales over more than 5 decades.[9] Inserting the figures for these in the forecasting equation should then produce rather accurate predictions, provided that the relationships did not change and that these five variables themselves could be accurately ascertained.

A multimethod approach, involving both quantitative and qualitative techniques, often is preferred. If the different techniques produce approximately the same results, then the findings generally are valid. If the results diverge widely, then the most credible must be selected. Analyzing the accuracy of past forecasts usually leads to better predictions.

Example of a multimethod approach.   Under a multimethod approach forecasting results may be disparate. For example a small electronics manufacturer with seven salesmen obtained the following sales estimates for the coming year:

Extrapolation of trend data	$4,200,000
Total of salesmen's territorial estimates	$3,600,000
Average of opinions of president, chief financial officer, and production manager	$4,600,000
Average of opinions of four major customers	$5,000,000

How would you use these data in producing your annual sales forecast? Is there any other information essential to making this forecast? These data, of course, have many uses in determining the annual sales forecast. All four unweighted data inputs simply could be averaged. A modification would be to throw out the high and the low and then to average the two remaining. Some weighting might be desirable, however, such as giving much importance to the extrapolation of trend data. Sales representatives tend toward lower sales estimates, especially if quotas and performance evaluation are tied to the forecast; customers tend to be overly optimistic; and the production manager's knowledge of the future may be questionable. The best course of action seems to be a weighted average, according to the accuracy of such forecasting inputs over the last several years. For example if sales force estimates have been the most accurate in the past, they deserve to be weighted heavier now.

Figure 6.5 shows the combination of quantitative and qualitative techniques that would seem best under certain conditions. With longer-range forecasts, newer products, and less staple or more fashionable products the need for qualitative techniques increases. For shorter-range forecasts (up to a year), more staple products, and more mature products (i.e., those with longer sales histories), a quantitative technique is likely to be more accurate.

General Limitations to Forecasting

Unreliability is usually a forecasting problem. All forecasts are subject to error, although, hopefully, it can be brought within tolerable limits. As noted earlier in this chapter, for Aegis a 5-percent error was entirely acceptable. Lack of care in formulating the forecast obviously will affect its reliability. Mere guesswork and unfounded hopes may have been relied on. Perhaps the underlying assumptions were unsupported by facts, reasonable estimates, or accurate reflection of policies and plans, especially when these are changing, as in the active approach to forecasting depicted in Figure 6.1. Even the most carefully

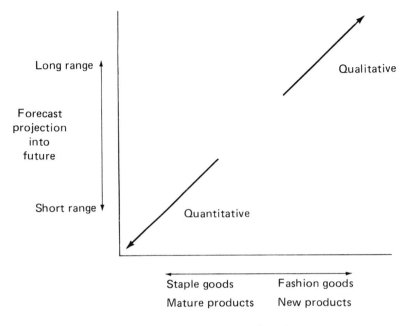

FIGURE 6.5   Guidelines for relative use of qualitative and quantitative forecasting techniques.

prepared forecast, however, may be rendered irrelevant by unforeseen actions by competitors and extraordinary events within or outside the company. Finally, the reliability of most forecasts diminishes rapidly as projections are made further into the future.

Time, money, and qualified personnel are needed to forecast properly, depending on the market's complexity and the forecasting method. The benefits of more accurate forecasts over the additional costs should be considered, especially for small- and medium-sized firms; the slightly more accurate forecasts derived from complex techniques may not be of sufficiently greater value.

In addition to the reliability problems previously described, special situations or factors sometimes may affect forecasting:

☐ Uncertain growth elements
☐ Lack of sales history
☐ Fashion
☐ Changing customer attitudes

Many firms are uncertain whether their present growth rate will continue or begin to level off. In particular new firms often experience a period of rapid growth that is difficult to maintain over the long term, and their major issue in forecasting is deciding whether growth will begin to level off in the current year. Forecasting for a new product or firm is hazardous because no past sales record exists as a benchmark. Estimating the market share that will be captured, or even the size of the total market, for the new product or firm is therefore difficult.

As discussed in Application 6.4, a fashion element in a firm's products always causes substantial risk in predictions, because sales depend on how well the market accepts the styles.

When demand for the product depends on unstable customer attitudes, forecasting becomes difficult. Measuring attitudes is uncertain at best and especially so when economic or social conditions cause instability. The classic example of vulnerability to undetected and changing consumers' attitudes was the Edsel. In 1957 Ford introduced this big and powerful automobile. But the Edsel was a monumental failure, costing the company hundreds of

---

APPLICATION 6.4   Prediction Risk Factor: Fashion

The toymaker Coleco introduced Pac-Man video games and Cabbage Patch Kids, two of the biggest hits in toy industry history. But most of Coleco's toys were fads that peaked and declined. Sales became a feast and famine situation, as shown in Figure 6.6, which includes Coleco's earnings over the last 10 years. Coleco was totally dependent on consumers' whims. In desperation it now is trying to broaden its product base, to seek more stability and to survive.

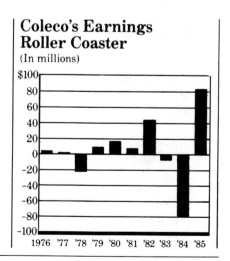

Coleco's Earnings Roller Coaster
(In millions)

FIGURE 6.6   The effects of fashion trends on Coleco's earnings.

For more details of Coleco's dilemma, see "Coleco Aims to Broaden Its Product Base," *Wall Street Journal,* 29 October 1986.

millions of dollars. Although extensive marketing research accompanied the Edsel's planning, some of this was flawed and most of it was dated, conducted several years before the Edsel entered the market. The research failed to detect changing consumer attitudes and increasing preferences for smaller, more economical cars.

As mentioned previously, the computerized analysis of data results in more sophisticated forecasts, but prediction remains uncertain. Inaccuracy generally increases as forecasting extrapolates from the national economy to industry sales, to company sales, and finally to territory and product sales.

COPING WITH FORECASTING UNCERTAINTIES FOR NEW PRODUCTS OR CHANGING CONDITIONS

With a new, substantially different product and/or when customer acceptance and the growth rate are substantially uncertain, the risks of forecasting are twofold. (1) The firm may be far too conservative in the forecasting. (2) The firm may be too bold, aggressive, or optimistic in its forecasting and resultant planning.

Overly Conservative

The overly conservative firm runs the risk of the new product becoming so successful that demand outstrips the firm's ability to meet it, at least in the near term. This invites competitors to fill the gap with hastily introduced similar products. Many products can be quickly matched; competitive entry is neither difficult nor time-consuming. Even patent protection seldom reduces the risk of competitors' introducing similar products, because a minor modification or feature can result in a new patent. Given the common situation of easy competitive entry, the firm that is timid about allocating strong resources to a promising new product may find that more aggressive competitors will grab much of the market share.

Overly Aggressive

If a firm enthusiastically plunges into the market with its promising new product, and gears up factory capability and other resources, demand may be far less or far slower to develop than expected. The financial resources of the firm may be strained, and under extreme conditions its viability can even be threatened. (Case 6.2 at the end of this chapter presents a concrete example of a firm's dilemma with a relatively new product, with an uncertain demand, and in an easy-entry industry.)

Faced with the twin risks of sales either far less or more than expected, the firm with a new product must very closely monitor sales against expec-

TABLE 6.4 Monthly monitoring of actual sales to estimated sales.

	Total for Year	January	February	March	April
Estimated sales					
Percentage of total year*	100	4.0	4.2	7.4	8.0
Unit breakdown ($)	50,000	2,000	2,100	3,700	4,000
Actual sales ($)					
Scenario #1	—	1,250	1,350	2,100	2,100
Scenario #2	—	2,800	2,800	4,500	5,500

*Based on company's seasonal experience with somewhat similar products.

tations. Sales monitoring is best done monthly, although with certain fast-growing products such as fad items, weekly or even daily monitoring may be preferred. Table 6.4 shows close monitoring of a product predicted to have seasonal sales.

In Table 6.4 monthly sales expectations are broken down by the normal monthly percentage of total yearly sales, which should be available from past sales records for related products. Scenario #1 shows actual sales falling considerably below monthly expectations; scenario #2 shows them substantially above expectations. Complete Exercise 6.2.

EXERCISE 6.2

1. In the two scenarios in Table 6.4, when would you change your original forecast of sales? At the end of 1 month? 2 months? 3 months? Later? Why?
2. In scenario #1, if April sales were 4,000 units, what adjustment if any would you make to your forecast? In scenario #2, if actual sales for March were 4,000 units, would you change your forecasted figures? Why or why not?

CRITERIA FOR EFFECTIVE FORECASTING

Effective forecasting depends on a number of factors, not the least of which is luck. However, certain criteria that lead to better forecasting can be identified.

Consideration of all key influences. Key influences in the growth of the industry should be determined and evaluated. Strengths and weaknesses of the company and of its competitors should be analyzed. The capacities of the different company functions to support the forecast and plan should be projected over a sufficient period.

Accuracy. Although accuracy is important, it should be weighed in terms of the marginal precision compared to cost. For example a consumer survey may be ruled out, because only imprecise results could be achieved at high cost.

Plausibility. The executives who use the forecast should trust the methodology. Most executives will be skeptical of elaborate techniques that only statisticians understand.

Durability. The underlying assumptions and relationships should be stable; the forecast model should not fall apart in a short time.

Flexibility. The variables should be adjusted occasionally to meet changing conditions, and future revisions should be planned. Forecasts should not be rigid and unbending but should be adjustable to changing conditions and mistaken estimates, as discussed in the previous section. To achieve flexibility most firms examine the sales forecast and budgets monthly or quarterly, revise if necessary, based on current conditions, and extend this update throughout the forecast. The forecast methods also can be audited and reviewed, by comparing actual and forecast sales and by analyzing any discrepancies. The methodology audit should determine reasons for deviations and improve future assumptions and techniques for more accurate sales forecasts.

Availability. The availability criterion applies mainly to correlation analysis. The various statistical indexes correlated with company sales are more useful if published weekly or monthly (such as the Federal Reserve Board production index, the Bureau of Labor Statistics wholesale price index) than only every five years (such as the census of manufacturers).

Organizational participation. All organizational levels and most functions should perform forecasting and planning. Direction and motivation, as well as breadth of judgment, are the results, providing a strong argument for involving the sales force in the forecasting routine. Sales management, at least, should be involved because the sales organization contributes directly to sales. Exclusion from the forecasting process may negatively affect the sales department's commitment to sales targets, and marketplace factors that could affect future sales may be overlooked. Staff departments that are divorced from the realities of selling in the field should not compile sales forecasts.

In preparing forecasts it is tempting to simplify everything to meeting or beating last year's figures. However, this approach does not account for future sales potential; a poor year's figures are easily met the following year, and an exceptionally good showing may be due to fortuitous circumstances and may be impossible to repeat. Therefore, the meet-or-beat approach not only can unfavorably affect all forecast-based planning but it also can have demoralizing consequences on employees whose competence is determined by the achievement of sales targets. Furthermore, in a period of inflation, meeting or beating the previous year's figures may lull an organization into thinking that it is progressing, when it may be losing ground to competitors.

SUMMARY

At the beginning of this chapter I asked you to think about how you would forecast sales for a new product. For new products without a sales history, forecasting depends more on guesswork and may require qualitative techniques, which may be little more than subjective estimates. After conducting one or more test markets, the sales results usually can be projected satisfactorily (unless competitors have "muddied the waters" with their own promotions in the test cities). With many new products the sales history of similar products may be relevant and may furnish a basis for forecasting.

Sales forecasting involves predicting sales. This estimate provides the basis for planning and budgeting for the period ahead and is vitally important because severe miscalculations can affect adversely all aspects of the operation.

Sales are not alone the result of external factors over which the firm has no control. An active approach to forecasting recognizes that a firm's own activities can affect its sales positively.

Developing a sales forecast generally involves gathering the forecasting information, applying forecasting techniques, adapting the forecast operationally through the budget process, auditing the forecast, and refining it when serious discrepancies occur between actual and forecast performance.

Forecasting techniques include such qualitative methods as executive opinion, sales force estimates, opinion surveys of experts and/or customers, and the Delphi method. Quantitative methods include trend projections (moving averages, and exponential smoothing), and correlation analyses involving either simple or multiple regressions. Each method has strengths and weaknesses; none is the panacea.

Forecasting problems concern reliability and the time and money required. Especially for new products with no sales history and for significantly changing conditions, forecasting often is inaccurate. The forecasting process can be improved, however, by observing certain criteria, such as flexibility for revisions, and organizational participation.

QUESTIONS

1. Should the sales manager be involved in sales forecasting? Why or why not?

2. Discuss the effect of interindustry and intra-industry competition on a firm's future sales. Which generally is more predictable and why?

3. Evaluate the use of customers as a major source of information for forecasting sales.

4. What forecasting techniques would you recommend for a small company with limited resources? For a large firm?

5. The problem of predicting turning points (i.e., turns in the economy, from good times to bad or from a recession to a resurgence) is not solved by most forecasts, not even the more complex techniques. Which forecasting techniques would you recommend using during periods of uncertainty?

6. What are a firm's defenses for coping with the possibility of an inaccurate sales forecast?

7. Discuss the importance and the limitations of long-range forecasting. On balance, what is its practical relevance?

PEOPLE PROBLEM: DISPUTING THE COMPANY FORECASTING PROCESS

Please evaluate each of the alternatives. You are the sales manager for a company whose sales forecasts have been accurate within ± 3 percent for the last 5 years, since the planning department initiated more sophisticated mathematical forecasting. In the last few years, the planning department has paid increasingly less attention to your forecasting input. The sales forecast for next year of a 15-percent gain disturbs you greatly. The feel of the market—you have gained this from talking with your customers, your sales representatives, and others in the field—suggests that next year there may be little or no percentage increase in sales. What should you do at this point?

1. Try to obtain corroboration from suppliers, other customers, friends in related industries, and so on before taking any further action.

2. Notify your boss of your suspicions, but also begin moderate retrenchment of your controllable budget items so that if your fears are justified, you will still show reasonable profitability.

3. Wait for at least 3 months to see if sales results confirm your suspicions.

4. Notify your boss and other levels of management of your suspicions and your rationale for them. Let higher management make the decision of retrenchment versus aggressive optimism.

5. Talk to the staff people in your firm who are involved in the forecast, explain your suspicions, and ask them either to modify their forecast or to make a contingency forecast.

NOTES

1. Philip Kotler, *Marketing Management*, 3rd ed. (Englewood Cliffs, N.J.: Prentice-Hall, 1976), 117.
2. Joel Dean, *Managerial Economics* (Englewood Cliffs, N.J.: Prentice-Hall, 1951), 142.
3. For more specifics of statistical calculations, see John E. Hanke and Arthur G. Reitsch, *Business Forecasting*, 2nd ed. (Boston: Allyn and Bacon, 1986), and G. David Hughes, *Demand Analysis for Marketing Decisions* (Homewood, Ill.: Irwin, 1973).
4. For more detailed comparisons of advantages and disadvantages of the various forecasting techniques, see Vithala R. Rao and James E. Cox, Jr., *Sales Forecasting Methods: A Survey of Recent Developments* (Cambridge, Mass.: Marketing Science Institute, 1978); and George C. Michael, *Sales Forecasting* (Chicago: American Marketing Assoc., 1979).
5. Stanley J. PoKemper and Earl L. Bailey, *Sales Forecasting Practices: An Appraisal*, Experiences in Marketing Management, no. 25 (New York: National Industrial Conference Board, 1970).
6. Douglas J. Dalrymple, "Sales Forecasting Methods and Accuracy," *Business Horizons* (December 1975): 69–73.
7. Conway L. Lachman, "A Forecasting Model for the Firm in the Private Aircraft Industry," *Industrial Management* (January–February 1980): 24–26.
8. Robert F. Soergel, "Probing the Past for the Future," *Sales & Marketing Management* (14 March 1983): 39–40, 42–43.
9. Kristian S. Palda, *The Measurement of Cumulative Advertising Effects* (Englewood Cliffs, N.J.: Prentice-Hall, 1964), 67–68.

cases

6.1 Coping with Forecasting Inaccuracies

Les Rizzo is the sales manager for a manufacturer of linens and bedding. He sells two lines to different types of retailers. The first line is high-quality, is relatively expensive, and has a well-known brand sold primarily through department stores. The other line is more moderately priced, carries a less well-known brand, and is geared to discount stores and other high-volume mass merchandisers.

Les has developed the sales forecasts, and in the past he has relied heavily on the judgments of the president, the vice president of finance, and the company's advertising agency. Sales have grown but erratically. Over the last 10 years, sales have increased from $24 million to $40 million, although some of the increase represents inflation rather than actual business growth.

In some years the forecasts have been fairly accurate but in others very inaccurate, causing seri-ous repercussions throughout the company. Les had not realized the extent and frequency of the forecasting deviations until he tabulated actual sales versus the sales forecasts over the last 10 years. He was shocked when he received the information shown in Table 6.5.

Les was especially puzzled by the erratic showing because the bedding industry was not highly fashionable. Also, the deviations showed no consistency, with some years far below, and other years far above, actual sales achieved. Although certain styles and patterns of linens and bedding seemed to have periodic waves of popularity, Les apparently did not anticipate these demand changes. Consequently, Les needed to develop more accurate forecasts.

QUESTION

What would you advise Les about this problem? Defend your recommendations.

TABLE 6.5 Actual sales versus sales forecasts.

Year	Sales Forecast ($ Millions)	Actual Sales ($ Millions)	Percentage Deviation
1979	26.1	24.1	− 7.7
1980	25.0	27.5	+10.0
1981	30.0	32.2	+ 7.3
1982	34.0	29.5	−13.2
1983	32.0	36.7	+14.7
1984	34.0	34.3	+ 0.9
1985	38.0	36.0	− 5.3
1986	38.0	33.7	−11.3
1987	37.0	40.2	+ 8.6
1988	43.0	37.5	−12.8

6.2   Trac Company: Sales Forecasting for a New Product

(Note: Although this case concerns a situation oc-curring more than a decade ago, I think it is the best illustration of the problems in forecasting for a new product in an uncertain environment. I strongly recommend studying this case.)

In 1977 a new fad appeared on the U.S. scene. The extent and longevity of this phenomenon was subject to considerable disagreement. Jogging ap-peared to be in a wild ascendancy, but how long would it last?

The Trac Company was a small manufacturer of track and running shoes. Its major competitors were Adidas, a German manufacturer and the dominant supplier among serious runners; New Balance, an American shoe company that was rap-idly overtaking Adidas with long-distance runners; Brooks; Etonic; Nike; Converse; Tiger; and a num-ber of other manufacturers, some of whom sold under dealers' private labels.

Jogging, or running (as the more serious par-ticipants insisted on calling it), experienced a tre-mendous surge of popularity by the mid-1970s. Many people became interested in physical fitness, and emerging medical studies strongly suggested that running 20 to 50 or more miles a week might greatly reduce the risk of cardiovascular problems, including heart attacks. Numerous local running organizations appeared, sponsoring races almost every weekend, which sometimes attracted crowds of thousands. For example a 13.1-mile race (a half-marathon) through Cleveland, Ohio, in 1977, at-tracted more than 2,100 men and women runners of all ages.

Trac's sales of its two models of running shoes rose from $265,000 in 1971 to $5,400,000 in 1977. Table 6.6 shows the dollar value of sales and the percentage increase over the preceding year.

Shoe sales showed considerable seasonality, with the most demand, as would be expected, in the months of best outside running conditions. The previous 5 years' sales of each month as a per-centage of total yearly sales are shown in Table 6.7.

Late in 1977 the sharp rise in the number of women runners led Trac to develop a running shoe styled for them.

Some of the other companies had made half-hearted efforts to design for women, but many still

TABLE 6.6   Sales and percentage of annual increase.

Years	Sales ($)	Percentage Increase
1973	265,000	
1974	540,000	104
1975	1,225,000	127
1976	2,870,000	126
1977	5,400,000	89

TABLE 6.7   Monthly percentage of annual sales, 5-year average.

Months	Percentage Total Year
January	3.2
February	3.3
March	7.8
April	10.4
May	12.5
June	11.2
July	8.6
August	8.3
September	11.4
October	9.6
November	6.7
December	7.0
Total	100.0

considered the men's smaller sizes adequate for women. Trac's shoe designer, Peggy Sellors, thought that women would be attracted to a shoe that was not a smaller version of a man's but was different in styling and color and available in narrower lasts. The Effem was the result. Aimed to sell for $32.95 by retailers, with a 40-percent markup (pricing that compared favorably with the better styles in men's shoes), it was successful in early tests with some of the better women runners. Other women who saw the shoe also gave many favorable comments. Sales manager Ken Abrams was impressed, as were his salespeople, who were in contact with running groups and stores that handled non-private-brand running shoes.

By 1977 Trac had six salespeople, one of whom was a woman. Since the company sold nationwide, the sales representatives spent most of their time on the road and covered multistate territories. A "pull" promotional strategy had been used rather successfully. The sales representatives appeared at the major racing events in their areas to display the shoes and to distribute literature describing the advantages of such shoes for serious runners. Several of the sales representatives had even helped conduct "fun runs," joining with either a retailer or a local running organization, and these events had helped publicize Trac shoes as "shoes for the serious runner."

The immediate problem facing Ken Abrams and Peggy Sellors was the sales forecast for the new women's shoe. Although they did not know the exact number of women runners, they knew that many women were starting every month; sports publications previously had estimated the total conservatively at well over a half-million. Of course, Ken and Peggy realized that not all the women were the type of serious runners who would be in the market for Trac's shoes. In addition other shoe manufacturers could be expected to quickly introduce their own women's shoes if demand was sufficient. The majority of women still were thought to be more likely to buy either smaller sizes of men's styles or the less sophisticated tennis shoes that were much lower priced.

Production facilities at Trac could accommodate almost any reasonable sales volume. Considerable lead time would be required, however, if orders proved heavier than expected. For example if sales were 50,000 pairs and only 20,000 had been forecasted, at least 3 to 4 months would probably be required to gear production to meet demand.

The first shoes were scheduled for distribution in late December, and a number of retailers had ordered trial shipments. Trac placed an initial advertisement in the January edition of *Runner's World*, the magazine of serious runners (to hit the newsstands in December).

There was no sales feedback to help in making the forecast. Comments from retailers and consumers showed disagreement. All of the women using the prototypes were enthusiastic. One even said, "It's about time you gave us women our own shoes, rather than men's castoffs. I predict in another year there will be no small sizes of men's shoes sold—unless some men have small feet." But several retailers questioned whether many women were serious enough about running to invest so much in an "athletic shoe." One retailer maintained, "For the type of jogging most women do, a cheap pair of tennis shoes will do it. And how many women do you think are going to stick with jogging and get all sweaty?" A nearby retailer whose judgment Ken and Peggy respected raised several questions and drew a product life-cycle curve to illustrate his concern (see Figure 6.7). "We just can't be sure where the running boom is on the curve. Are we at (1), with strong growth yet to come? Are we at (2), with the major growth behind us and sales beginning to level off? Are we at (3), on the brink of a major decline? And will the decline be gradual, as with (A), or abrupt at (B)? I just don't know."

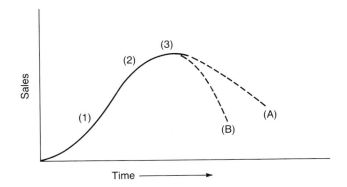

FIGURE 6.7 Product life-cycle curve.

Ken and Peggy were sober as they readied their forecast for 1978. "Peggy, I see risks for us if we're too conservative or too optimistic. But how can we forecast with any accuracy for a new product in such an uncertain future?"

QUESTIONS

1. What forecasting techniques would be most effective for this product?

2. What specific sales forecast would you make in December 1977 for the year 1978?

3. What contingencies would you establish to handle the situation in which sales were far below expectations and far above expectations?

4. If you assume that early 1978 sales results indicate a big winner with this shoe and that production can—given sufficient advance notice—handle almost any sales volume, how would you direct your selling and promotional efforts to maximize your sales opportunity with this new product?

CHAPTER 7
Budgeting the Sales Efforts

CHAPTER PERSPECTIVE

The budget is the culmination of planning and expresses an organization's goals and operational strategies in specific numerical terms. The operating budget accounts for not only anticipated revenues but also expenditures. Therefore, profit can be estimated, provided that the budget generally is followed. The converse of budgeting is ignorance of the operation until it is too late to take any remedial action for that period.

CHAPTER OBJECTIVES

☐ Understand the major reasons (advantages) for budgets.
☐ Know the different types of budgets and the two that most involve the sales manager—the sales budget and the sales expense budget.
☐ Become acquainted with the procedures for developing a budget.
☐ Know the two extremes of budgets, tight and loose.
☐ Grasp the different methods of budgeting marketing expenses.
☐ Understand the requirements for successful budgeting.
☐ Become aware of cautions about budgeting.

REASONS FOR BUDGETS

The process of developing a budget produces numerous benefits including improved planning, coordination, and communication; control and performance evaluation; psychological benefits; and most important, the avoidance of calamities. Some of these benefits result from planning, and the budget is an integral part of planning.

Improved Planning

Budgeting improves the quality of planning by adding specificity. It translates hazy and descriptive courses of action into concrete terms. Although the sales forecast gives a definitive revenue figure for the firm and its various units, the operating budget provides the specific guidelines for the various expense categories to translate plans and sales forecasts into profit expectations. Although the budgeting process does not ensure realization of profit expectations (as the sales forecast does not ensure sales achievement), estimating specific results for the budget period tends to improve the quality of planning.

Enhanced Coordination and Communication

Because budgeting involves the entire organization, balance and coordination are encouraged among interdependent entities. For example if production is not geared closely to the sale department's sales expectation, inventories will be either too heavy or so lean that orders cannot be filled and sales (and perhaps customers) may be lost. The personnel and training department also must be oriented to any planned expansion or contraction of the sales force. The budgeting process therefore can readily identify imbalances among or within departments. The budget states the plans of each department in specific and comparable terms, which aids coordination. Furthermore, unified planning encourages information exchange among departments, especially those dependent on each other. Interchange begun in the budgeting process may also extend to other matters.

Control and Performance Evaluation

Departments and their personnel cannot be held responsible for a level of accomplishment unless it is clarified in specific numerical terms. Of course, this level of accomplishment should include sales objectives, but it should also include expense objectives. Specific limits for expenses such as entertainment, travel, office supplies, and sales salaries facilitates expense control and reduces the likelihood that expense categories will exceed the budget unreasonably.

Clearly defined sales goals and cost responsibilities establish a *standard of performance.* A sales representative, a district sales manager, and the entire

---

APPLICATION 7.1 Dealing with Deviations from Expected Performance

Tom Zallocco, a sales manager for Spiro Corporation, a medium-size manufacturer of specialized dental equipment, was concerned with the latest operating results for his district. Sales goals had been achieved, but profit expectations were not. As he compared actual against budgeted expense lines, he noticed that entertainment and travel costs were over budget. He talked with several of his sales representatives to get their inputs and explanations. More judicious guidelines for entertaining customers needed to be established. But he decided to revise the budget upward for travel expenses, because gasoline and vehicle maintenance costs were higher than expected and showed no signs of declining.

---

sales department can be evaluated by comparing performance with budgeted goals. Deviations or variances from planned performance targets can be readily identified, the causes ascertained, and corrective action taken (see Application 7.1).

Corrective action may be an adjustment of an overly optimistic sales forecast. Certain expense category budgets may require adjustment, as in Application 7.1. Selling efforts may need reallocation, or careless and inefficient performance may indicate remedial or disciplinary action. Conversely, superior performance can also be identified. Control and performance evaluation are so important to sales management that Part V of this book is devoted to these subjects.

Psychological Benefits

With its emphasis on expenses and profits, budgeting encourages a profit awareness throughout the firm. Without the constraints of expense control, maximizing sales becomes the major concern. But pursuing the sales goal can erode profit when the firm seeks marginal customers, increases promotional efforts to a point of diminishing returns, and builds too large a sales force for most efficient sales productivity with disproportionate travel and entertainment expenses.

Systematic budgeting also helps reduce "crisis reactions." A firm without well-defined plans and budgets may resort to fire-fighting reacting to repeated problems and crises, without having time for the cool judgment that better anticipation can produce.

Avoiding a Catastrophe

Occasionally, a firm demonstrates an extreme lack of budgeting or imprudent budgeting, resulting in calamity, even the firm's demise. See Application 7.2, which describes Osborne Computer's budgeting disaster.

APPLICATION 7.2 Lack of Budgeting

New firms rarely experience a meteoric rise surpassing the most optimistic expectations of founders and investors. In the heady excitement anything seems possible and the enterprise appears invincible. Sometimes, however, this rare early success reverses. Perhaps the best example in modern business is the almost vertical rise and collapse of Osborne Computer Corporation. It was founded in 1981 when Adam Osborne detected an unfilled niche in the personal computer market. In barely 18 months the business boomed at $100 million. But by the spring and summer of 1983, unexpected and huge losses emerged and grew. Finally, on September 14, 1983, the business was in Chapter 11 of the Bankruptcy Code.

What went wrong? Lack of budgets and controls was the most obvious failing. Managers did not know their inventory, their expenses, or their required expenses. As a result, expenses ran rampant, and in the excitement of rapid growth, staff bought anything they wanted. By the spring of 1983, cash flow was reduced to a trickle. The firm initiated a cost-cutting program, but the action was too late.

TYPES OF BUDGETS

Most firms have some kind of budget, although the comprehensiveness can vary. We can categorize budgets as *operating,* which shows planned operations for the coming period; *capital,* which details planned changes in fixed assets; and *financial,* which deals with anticipated sources and uses of funds. The sales manager generally is not involved with capital or financial budgets. Consequently, we will focus on two subtypes of operating budgets that do concern the sales manager.

The Sales Budget

A sales budget is the starting point for all the other operating budgets. In addition to planning selling and marketing expenses, the sales budget determines production and financial budgets. Only after the firm estimates product sales can production gear planning and purchasing needs to meet expected sales. The finance department also depends on the sales budget to compute estimated revenues.

The Sales Expense Budget

The sales expense budget stipulates target figures for the sales expense categories. To achieve profit expectations based on estimated sales, the sales department must not exceed its budget. For most firms a partial listing of sales expenses includes the following "lines":

Salaries and bonuses paid to sales representatives

Travel and entertainment expenses of the sales force

Salaries and expenses of technical specialists

Training

Telephone and postage

Catalogs, brochures, and price lists

Samples and models

Conventions and trade shows

Cooperative advertising allowances

Customer clinics

Rent or depreciation on sales office and warehouse

Office and warehouse supplies

Utilities

Clerical salaries

Salaries paid to service and repair personnel

Carrying cost of parts inventory

In preparing these selling expense estimates for the coming period, the previous years' figures should serve as guidelines. However, conditions do change. Salaries, travel and entertainment expenses, postage, and utilities often will be higher than the preceding period due to inflation. If more vigorous efforts are planned for increasing sales, some expense categories may rise substantially.

The sales manager should recognize that some selling expenses vary with sales volume. Commissions and bonuses paid to salespeople obviously will increase as sales increase; costs of samples, catalogs, and cooperative advertising allowances may also rise. Other expenses, such as sales office and warehouse expenses, may increase with increased sales but not as directly. Costs such as utilities, rent, and depreciation are relatively stable and will not change with normal sales increases.

Another way of categorizing expenses is by stipulated, committed, and managed costs. *Stipulated costs* include utility costs, maintenance, rent, and depreciation and involve little disagreement on the proper budget figures. *Committed costs* include insurance costs and depreciation on facilities, which are previously contracted expenditures that therefore cannot change in the short term. Obviously, stipulated and committed costs require little discussion or decision making in budget preparation. *Managed costs* are discretionary. Management can control the amount spent without much scientific basis for judging the optimum level. Many selling expenses are managed costs, for example, costs for advertising, trade shows, conventions, brochures; and customer clinics. Entertainment costs also are discretionary, at least whether these should be liberal or conservative. Determining managed costs will be discussed later in this chapter.

PROCEDURE OF BUDGETING

Two general approaches to making the budget and assigning budget-making responsibility are a breakdown method and a buildup approach (see Figure 7.1). In the *breakdown method,* top management determines the budget level, and allocations are then made down the line. The budget also can be *built up* from lower management levels—even from the field sales representatives—to a total budget that top management reviews and possibly revises. The buildup method generally better reflects market conditions, whereas a breakdown approach is more compatible with the overall objectives and strategy of the firm, as well as any financial considerations.

The budget procedure usually is not conducted solely by the finance or accounting departments. Thus, the budget becomes a tool of management and not primarily an accounting device. The budget should reflect the functions for holding individual executives accountable by showing their controllable costs. Each manager should prepare budget requests for their activities and be prepared to support their requests. For example if a manager proposes an increase in training clinics for customers' employees, he should be ready to back up the request for a higher budget on the grounds of specific benefits—and the probable effects on sales and profits.

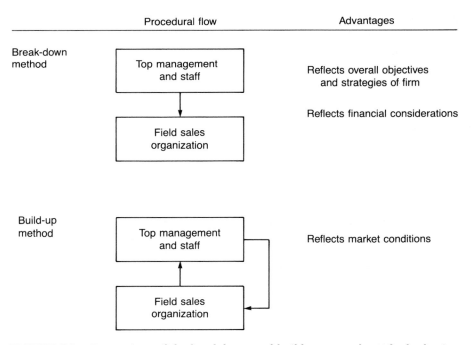

FIGURE 7.1   Comparison of the breakdown and build-up procedures for budgeting.

Figure 7.2 shows a representative form for a sales expense budget. In addition to designating the relevant expense categories, it identifies the amounts spent in several previous years. The form also permits quarterly revisions, if warranted.

Time Frame

Most budgets cover a period of 1 year and usually are broken down by months, which constitute the basic time period for comparing actual results with the budget. Sometimes the budget is reviewed and revised quarterly, as in Figure 7.2. In a quarterly review, the quarter just completed may be dropped, the figures for the remaining three quarters revised according to the more recent expectations, and an additional quarter added to the end, thus making an updated 12-month budget. This is called a *rolling budget* and will be described in more detail later in the chapter, along with several other alternatives that allow flexibility in budgeting.

Rigor of the Budget

Should the budget be tight or loose? The tight budget sets costs at the most efficient level. The goal is outstanding efficiency and the strongest incentive to reduce costs. An extreme penny-pinching philosophy, however, tends to inhibit sales maximization; it is incompatible with an aggressive sales effort. For example a phone call may be waived in favor of a letter, and a sale may be lost or an order not handled as punctually as necessary for customer satisfaction.

Classification	1986	1987	Original 1988 budget	April revision	July revision	October revision
Sales salaries						
General salaries						
Auto expense						
Entertainment						
Supplies						
Samples						
Telephone						

FIGURE 7.2 Sample sales expense budget form for 1988.

The loose budget sets expense goals at a more reasonable level that is easily attained with average efforts. Although it provides far more flexibility than the tight budget, some flaws are apparent here also. Personnel have less incentive to curb expenses, and only the more obvious inefficiencies probably will be noticed. The effect on net profit may be just as detrimental as a tight budget. Costs may be undercontrolled to the extent that more sales may not bring more profit dollars.

Some firms vascillate between these two extremes. After a good year of satisfactory sales and profits, a firm may loosen its budget. After a bad year a firm may call for belt-tightening and vigorously enforce tight budgets. A more moderate and consistent course is preferred.

How much detail?   Detail is another issue confronting the budget maker and extremes are as likely here as in budget rigor. One extreme is including only one budget item or line, such as ''selling expenses,'' thereby lumping the whole variety of such costs into one account. The other extreme is breaking down selling expenses into twenty-five or thirty different categories, which requires unnecessary distinctions, causes greatly increased budget and control efforts, and leads to frustration among sales representatives and sales managers. The extent of budget detail should depend on (1) the amount of salesperson and sales manager control, and (2) the significance of the expense category as a factor for either inducing sales or affecting profits.

Bad debt losses for many firms are a significant expense category. The sales force may argue that bad debts are not under their control and should not be included in their selling expense budgets. But strong counterarguments can be raised that the sales department is responsible for screening out the poorer credit risks, even if some sales are lost. In contrast, because the sales department has little control over warranty costs arising from manufacturing deficiencies, these should be excluded from selling budgets, even if the expense is significant.

Determining Budget Levels

As noted earlier in this chapter, certain budget categories are so-called *managed costs,* over which management has wide discretion. Increasing costs such as advertising, promotional material, and sales salaries (reflecting salesforce size) is assumed to stimulate sales. Generally this is true, but the dilemma is that the sales stimulation may not compensate for the increased costs.

Although many firms follow historical patterns in budgeting managed costs, the past budgets may not have been the best or more than marginally acceptable. However, no single technique can best resolve the twin problems of determining (1) the total sales budget and (2) the best allocation among the promotion categories.

Marketing is an inexact science, which does not optimize the promotional mix—that blend of personal selling efforts, advertising, and sales promotion techniques. If, by accident, an optimal allocation were made, the firm would hardly realize that such had been attained and, indeed, it would probably be a fleeting phenomenon, as competition and other elements of the environment continued to change.

There are four common methods of budgeting managed marketing costs including advertising funds and sales force costs.

Affordable method.   Some companies budget just enough to meet other expenses and then plow everything else into the promotional program. Such a method of budgeting seems arbitrary, yet it can be reasonably effective for the new company hoping to establish a market niche and needing as much short-term impact as possible. The amount a company can afford is subject to interpretation by differing executive viewpoints. Without some other rationale for setting the sales budget, it is likely that other efforts eventually will be undermined.

Percentage-of-sales method.   A widely used method of budgeting marketing efforts bases expenditures on a specified percentage of sales, either current or anticipated.[1] This method is easily computed and orders the budgeting process somewhat, but it has several crucial, if theoretical, weaknesses. In the sales-percentage method marketing efforts essentially are viewed as the *result* of sales, when they really *cause* sales. Use of this method often typifies the complacent firm, using historical spending patterns; a more aggressive approach or one tailored to product or territory expenditures is recommended. Furthermore, this method commits a firm to decrease the marketing budget when sales decline (due either to a recession or to other circumstances), but the preferred action might be maintaining or increasing sales activity until the sales decline is corrected.

Following competition.   A firm may follow a major firm in the industry or industry averages in order to maintain competitive parity of selling and advertising efforts. Following the competition is a weak method implying that other firms know better (when they probably do not) and that it is best to stabilize industry spending. Furthermore a firm's needs, goals, and resources may be quite different from those of its competitors.

Objective and task method.   By setting objectives and determining the tasks and costs involved in attaining them, a firm may develop a more logical approach to spending than under the previous three methods. Figure 7.3 shows the steps involved. This method is gaining popularity and is comparable with the strategic planning and better-defined objectives that are influencing management today.

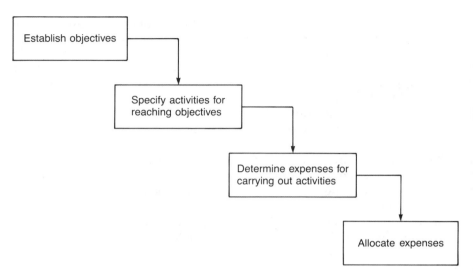

FIGURE 7.3   Steps involved in budgeting by objective and task.

A major flaw in the objective and task method is the difficulty of correctly estimating the amount and type of selling efforts needed to reach an objective. For example if brand preference should be increased by a certain percentage, determining the required expenditure is difficult (lacking any definitive measure of the relationship between sales cost and effects), and the answer will be affected by factors the firm cannot control, such as competitive actions. Despite these weaknesses the objective and task method is a substantial improvement, mostly because it builds up desired appropriations by products and by territories. But the difficulties remain in estimating payoffs of alternative sales budgets, so most firms continue to use the more simplistic approaches to budgeting sales and promotional expenses.

Other methods.   Sophisticated mathematical models may aid the budgeting process. *Simulation* shows perhaps the most promise as a practical tool and mathematically represents the firm's environment. Using a computer permits handling many variables and relationships simultaneously. The computer analyzes very complex systems of interactions, such as are encountered in the real world of marketing. Different strategies and selling expenses can be used to estimate effects on sales and profits.

The market simulator represents the company's best understanding of the market and business environment. Although some of the simulation data may be obtained from statistical surveys and analyses, other data usually come from management hunch or feel. So many intangibles and relationships are involved and are so complex that these computerized market models seldom provide definitive answers to such knotty questions as the amount to budget and how to allocate it.

Several other methods of deploying resources are worth brief mention. A bidding system is sometimes used, with the sales department competing with other functional areas, based on expected payoff of the allocated funds. A returns-oriented approach considers attractive alternative uses of capital and financial support for the selling function.

A returns on assets managed (ROAM) approach relates expansion opportunities such as additional sales territories to the incremental investment required.[2] The ROAM approach focuses attention on the profitability of any decision option, but it assumes that incremental investment and profit contribution can be estimated reasonably, although in reality any accurate estimate may be impossible.

Finally, *zero-based budgeting* disregards historical patterns and previous periods' budgets. Each period starts from scratch, and each amount requested must be fully justified. Each ongoing program is forced to prove its requirements before receiving funds. Although in theory divorcing the future from the past may seem advantageous, continually proving financial needs is a terrible waste of time.

The Budget Calculation

The overall budget format is very similar to the profit and loss statement or income statement of a firm or its entity. The key difference is that the budget deals with the future, not the recent past. You should be familiar with the form that such a complete budget takes. Let us work through the calculations for the budget of the following medium-size firm:

The Ray T. Jones Distributing Company forecast sales of $15.4 million for the coming year. The cost of goods sold was estimated at 80 percent of sales. The expense budget was as follows:

Sales force, 5 percent commission

Advertising, 3 percent of sales

Administrative overhead, $800,000

Sales office expenses, $385,000

Travel and entertainment expenses for ten salespeople, $360 per week per person, for 48 weeks

Inventory expenses, 8 percent of the inventory at cost, with a 60-day inventory maintained

Develop an expense budget for the year and the estimated income statement at the end of the year's operation.

Solution

Sales		$15,400,000
Cost of goods sold		$12,320,000
Gross margin		$3,080,000
Expenses		
Sales commissions	$770,000	
Advertising	$462,000	
Administrative overhead	$800,000	
Sales office expenses	$385,000	
Travel expenses	$172,800	
Inventory expenses		
(12,320,000 × 60/360 × .08)	$164,267	$2,754,067
Net profit		$325,933

Now, to gain a little more familiarity with the budget setup, complete Exercise 7.1.

EXERCISE 7.1   You must develop the budget for your sales district for the first quarter of 1989. In November 1988, which constitutes 14 percent of the year's sales volume, your sales were $66,000. January, February, and March should yield sales of 7, 5, and 9 percent, respectively, of total year's sales volume. Selling costs are planned at 6 percent of sales, branch office expenses are budgeted at $5,200 for the quarter, and travel and entertainment expenses are $200 per week for each of three salespeople. If the average markup is 25 percent of selling price, what is the budgeted profit contribution for the first quarter of 1989, assuming that sales will be at the same rate as last November? (For simplicity, you can assume that the first quarter has 12 weeks.)

REQUIREMENTS FOR SUCCESSFUL BUDGETING

Although the benefits of budgeting are significant, budgets must meet several requirements to avoid burdening salespeople and executives with useless additional paperwork or imposed sets of figures.

Organizational Involvement and Follow up

Operations people must participate in the budget preparation. The budget should reflect operations input and should be considered reasonable and attainable according to carefully formulated plans. Otherwise, staff likely will resist the budget and generally criticize it, especially when they feel the figures are not readily attainable or too restrictive.

Budget estimates—as they affect various departments—must be coordinated. Because most operations in a firm are interdependent, estimates must be well communicated and adjustments should be dovetailed. For example the sales manager who discovers that a product line's original sales estimate is seriously inaccurate must quickly communicate the error to the other departments concerned.

A major benefit of budgeting is control. Deviations from expectations are identified quickly, enabling corrective action and/or estimate adjustments. To realize the control benefit, management must follow up and act on budgets. The organization otherwise will quickly (and eagerly) conclude that budgeted figures need not be taken seriously.

Flexibility in Budgeting

Perhaps the most important requirement for budgets is flexibility. Seldom will conditions and results duplicate those assumed in preparing the budget. Sales may be higher or lower than planned; certain costs, especially during inflationary times, may soar; prices may likewise change during the budget period; some emergency may occur; or perhaps a nascent opportunity may develop and absorb additional marketing expenses. Viewing the budget as a harsh and unyielding taskmaster indicates dangerous rigidities in the budget structure.

An emergency fund may partially resolve unexpected demands during the budget period. Of more use in adjusting to overall changing conditions are alternative budgets, flexible budgets, and regular revisions.

A firm may prepare several budgets, perhaps one based on favorable business conditions, another on unfavorable circumstances, and a third on the presently anticipated conditions. Although a firm may use the middle-of-the-road budget initially, it can quickly shift to an alternative budget if the business environment improves or worsens. Most firms, however, find single budgets too time-consuming to prepare three or more separate budgets.

The flexible budget is similar to alternative budgets. Usually, a low-volume and a high-volume budget are prepared, and expense-acceptability levels are then interpolated between the two alternatives according to the actual achieved sales for the period. Although flexible budgets can be adjusted easily to different sales levels, they have several serious limitations. They are best used by a department or firm that makes only a single product, because the complexities of the interrelationships make them unwieldy. For example some products may post sales increases, while others show decreases. Furthermore, flexible budgets assume that a straight-line relationship exists between costs and sales. This may be true with sales commissions, but many other categories of costs do not vary with volume at a constant rate. The biggest drawback of flexible budgets is that the activity level is not known until the period's conclusion; then they can be used only in diagnosis, not planning.

Many firms rely on regular budget revisions, so-called *rolling budgets,* in securing desired flexibility. With a rolling budget, revisions are made regularly at the end of each month or each quarter. The last period is then dropped, the next period is revised according to latest results, and a new period is added to the end of the budget to make a 12-month budget. Table 7.1 illustrates in simplified form a department's rolling budget.

As Table 7.1 shows, first-quarter results fell below budget expectations, primarily because sales were substantially lower. Because selling expenses were geared to the higher sales plan, they were too high for the reduced sales,

TABLE 7.1 Simplified example of a rolling budget ($ thousands).

		Sales	*Selling Expense*
Quarter 1	Original budget	150	35
	Actual budget	140	34
Quarter 2	Original budget	170	38
	Revised, 4/1	162	36
	Actual results	165	36
Quarter 3	Original budget	200	42
	Revised, 7/1	195	41
	Actual results		
Quarter 4	Original budget	160	36
	Revised, 10/1		
	Actual results		
Original annual budget		680	151
Quarter 5	Original budget	145	34
	Revised, 1/1		
	Actual results		
New annual budget as of 4/1		667	148
Quarter 6	Original budget	170	38
	Revised, 4/1		
	Actual results		
New annual budget as of 7/1		670	149

Formulas for rolling budget:
    Or = original budget for quarter
    Rev = revised budget for quarter
    Quarters referred to as 1, 2, 3, 4, 5, and 6
Original annual budget = $Or_1 + Or_2 + Or_3 + Or_4$
Revised annual budget (at end of 1st quarter) = $Rev_2 + Or_3 + Or_4 + Or_5$
Revised annual budget (at end of 2nd quarter) = $Rev_3 + Or_4 + Or_5 + Or_6$
Calculations from Table 7.1:
    Original annual budget:
    Sales   = 150,000 + 170,000 + 200,000 + 160,000 = 680,000
    Expenses = 35,000 + 38,000 + 42,000 + 36,000 = 151,000
    Revised budget, 4/1:
    Sales   = 162,000 + 200,000 + 160,000 + 145,000 = 667,000
    Expenses = 36,000 + 42,000 + 36,000 + 34,000 = 148,000
    Revised budget, 7/1:
    Sales   = 195,000 + 160,000 + 145,000 + 170,000 = 670,000
    Expenses = 41,000 + 36,000 + 34,000 + 38,000 = 149,000

and profitability consequently was reduced. The results of this first quarter generally extend to the following period at least, suggesting that estimated sales for the second quarter are also too high. Here the budget can be revised. If the sales estimate for the second quarter is reduced, then selling expenses can be correspondingly reduced. As a result, profitability will not be as adversely affected as it would be if the sales forecast were unchanged and selling expenses were geared to a higher level of expectation. In the process of dropping the first quarter from the current budget, the first quarter of the next year would be picked up. Such a rolling annual budget would reflect the latest estimates of sales and expenses.

A judgment must be made, however, in revising a rolling budget. In this example, with low results in one quarter, the following decision must be made: Is the disappointing result due to unusual events, or does it indicate changing conditions? If the shortfall is deemed unusual and not a trend indicator, then the next period's budget probably would not be revised downward.

CAUTIONS IN BUDGETING

Despite the significant benefits, the budgeting process has limitations and flaws: it cannot project the course of future events; long-term commitments may suffer from short-term orientation; it is time-consuming; gaining acceptance may be difficult; and finally, waste may occur.

Inability to Project Course of Future Events

As the previous example demonstrated, we have problems in projecting with any certainty the course of future events. Does a missed budget figure presage worsening operating conditions, or is it an anomaly? For budgets to have any semblance of reality, the sales forecast must be reasonably accurate, because everything depends on it. The sales forecast structures the expenditures for a wide range of operations and finances. (At this point, you may want to review Table 4.1 in Chapter 4 on the consequences of inaccurate sales forecasts.)

Repudiation of the Long Term

The budget process negatively affects the long-term consequences of many selling expenditures. For example the costs of hiring and training the most able salespeople may result in current period expenses' exceeding budgeted figures. The full rewards of such expenditures will not appear until a later budget, which tends to discourage management from making such expenditures, especially during tight budgetary periods.

Time Involved

A thorough budget process, with all concerned staff participating, requires time. Some would argue that budgeting time is unproductive, that the time would be spent better on money-making activities. Such complaints sometimes are justified. A budgetary system may be too complicated. However, for most firms that conscientiously use budgeting, the benefits of better planning, coordination, and control far outweigh the time and effort involved.

Gaining Acceptance

The problem of gaining acceptance of budgets has been mentioned previously in this chapter but is worth repeating. The organization not involved in and accepting the budgeted figures likely will bicker and condemn the whole process as unrealistic and unnecessarily restrictive. Furthermore, unless upper management follows up on budget deviations, the rest of the organization will not be motivated to achieve the planned figures. When budgets are used as a management tool to evaluate performance and personnel (as the budget control function may be used), individuals will be tempted to overstate anticipated expenses while understating estimated sales because their performances will appear better. And this temptation leads us to the waste problem.

Waste

Budgeting waste seems present in all organizations, but is a particular cross in governmental and nonprofit organizations, simply because these are not guided by the same profit motives and profit-based performance evaluations as are business firms. Where budget requests are traditionally cut down, the temptation, and even the need, is to pad the budget—to ask for more than is really necessary in the expectation that the final, reduced budget figure can be lived with. Waste also occurs when a department does not require all of its budget for a given period but, fearing that this underspending will result in a lowered budget approval for the next period, spends the full amount unnecessarily and even frivolously.

What can be done about the budget waste? Some executives believe waste defies any answer or solution. But certain actions can curb the worst abuses. If budget requests are not always cut back, the necessity to pad may be removed. Carefully monitoring budget requests, rewarding the department that is under budget, will help. In business firms, if the individual organizational units are evaluated on their profit contribution, and rewarded accordingly, the motivation to manipulate the budget is greatly diminished. Unfortunately, governmental and nonprofit entities cannot incorporate a direct evaluation of profit contribution.

Despite all the budgeting criticisms and flaws, it remains of great value in planning. Without budgets to give anticipated results of operating plans, planning is only half done, and control and evaluation of performance for any desirable corrective action will be thwarted.

SUMMARY

Budgeting gives numbers to the planning process. It can improve planning, aid coordination and communication, permit control and performance evaluation, produce psychological benefits such as profit awareness and reduced crisis reactions. The primary reason for budgeting is to avoid a catastrophe induced by uncontrolled expenses and unexpected financial problems.

The sales department is primarily concerned with operating budgets, both sales and sales expense budgets. The two general approaches to making a budget are the breakdown method, in which top management determines the level of the budget, and the buildup method, in which the field sales organization gives the initial input, subject to top management's concurrence.

Budgeting issues concern how tight or loose budgets should be, how detailed, and how levels should be determined. The four most common methods of budgeting controllable marketing costs are (1) all that is affordable, (2) percentage of sales, (3) following competition, and (4) objective and task.

For successful budgeting, operations people should participate in the preparation. Also, budgets should be flexible to cope with changing conditions.

Budgets can be limited by problems in projecting future events, too much emphasis on the short term, time involved, gaining organizational acceptance, and waste.

QUESTIONS

1. Does every firm need to budget? Why or why not?
2. Differentiate between sales and sales expense budgets. Which is more important?
3. What are managed costs? How are these commonly budgeted?
4. Discuss the relative pros and cons of tight and loose budgets.
5. What is the major argument for involving operating people in the budget preparation?
6. Explain how budgets are essential for control purposes.
7. Can the problem of budgeting waste—particularly prevalent in governmental and nonprofit organizations—be minimized or eliminated? How?
8. Do you see any inherent dangers in budget flexibility?

PEOPLE PROBLEM: HANDLING WASTE IN BUDGETS

Please evaluate each of the following alternatives.

You are the general sales manager, with five district sales managers under you. You have become increasingly concerned about waste in the district budgets; each district manager is asking for more than is needed or expected in anticipation of cuts in budget requests. In addition, you are annoyed that every expense category in every district is always fully spent. You have talked to the district managers about this, but with no noticeable improvement. What, if anything, do you try now?

1. The situation is hopeless; even the President of the United States cannot do anything about bureaucratic waste in budgeting.

2. Inform the sales managers that next year's budgets will be cut 5 percent from this year's figures, unless and until higher budget figures in certain specific areas can be justified.

3. Decide that the budgeting will be done in less detail; give the sales managers a total dollar amount for their districts and let them decide how this money should be allocated.

4. Institute a system of rewards for those districts turning back some budgeted monies at the end of the year.

5. In stronger language than before, insist that accurate budget requests be turned in and do not cut any of those that seem reasonable.

NOTES

1. A. J. San Augustine and W. F. Foley, "How Large Advertisers Set Budgets," *Journal of Advertising Research* (October 1975): 11–16; N. K. Dhalla, "How to Set Advertising Budgets," *Journal of Advertising Research* (October 1977): 11–17.

2. J. S. Schiff and Michael Schiff, "New Sales Management Tool: ROAM," *Harvard Business Review* (July–August 1977): 59–66.

cases

7.1 Coping with Too Tight a Budget

You work for a firm that believes in tight budget control, allowing few, if any, deviations from budget. The budgets are finely detailed, and the budgeting process therefore is cumbersome and unduly time-consuming. You have complained several times to the controller (who is highly regarded by top management) that this situation deters flexibility and freedom of action needed in the sales division.

This year the matter has come to a head. The costs of maintaining your sales force have abruptly increased 30 percent due to increased gasoline, lodging, and meal costs necessitated by an unusual number of new accounts gained the year before. In desperation, you have instructed your salespeople to reduce their travel and to use the telephone more often to contact their customers. But now, even the telephone budget is almost gone.

QUESTION

Assuming that 4 months of this budget period still remain, draw up an action or persuasion plan aimed at freeing some necessary funds for your operation.

7.2 Wohlert Company: Manipulating the Budget

"Look what they're trying to do to me!" Bill Wohlert shouted to his secretary. "That new controller is determined to destroy the most successful sales region of the company!" Bill threw some papers disgustedly on his desk. "Jane, he sent back my entire budget. He said that every item on it was higher than the average of all the other regions, with some items the highest by far."

Bill swiveled his chair around and gazed soberly out the window. In a quieter voice he explained his concerns. "Headquarters wants me to substantiate almost every item, with proof of how much had been spent the preceding year, and how this coming year would compare. I don't think I can do that, Jane. But the real knife to the throat is this statement: 'No budget padding is to be tolerated. All requests must be reasonable and supportable. If they cannot be substantiated, the allowable expenditure in each budget category will be reduced to the lowest ratio of the six regions.' Jane, you know what this would do to us. We're a high-cost region—living costs are the highest in the nation. Our salespeople have much greater distances to cover than those in other regions. This decree means that we'll lose all of our best people.

The sales organization I've been so careful to build up will be destroyed. Darned if I know what to do now."

Bill was the West Coast sales director and was the son of the founder of the Wohlert Company, a manufacturer of plumbing fixtures and equipment. Twenty-one salespeople reported to him. There were two field warehouses, one in Los Angeles and the other in Portland, Oregon. Bill preferred living in San Francisco and maintained his regional sales office there, justifying this as being centrally located for his sprawling western region, which in addition to the three Pacific Coast states included Nevada, Idaho, and Arizona.

Although sales in Bill's region were usually the highest in the company (closely followed by the Midwest region), he traditionally has incurred a higher expense budget than any of the five other regions, and his expense/sales ratio was always the poorest. In 1987 the expense/sales ratio was particularly bad compared to the other regions, as shown in Table 7.2.

The budgeting process involved each regional director's submitting detailed estimates of expenses for the coming year. Usually these were closely

TABLE 7.2 Regional expense/sales ratio ($ hundreds).

Region	Sales	Expenses	Expense/Sales Ratio (%)
West	18,340	1,867.1	10.2
Midwest	18,210	1,530.0	8.4
Middle Atlantic	16,780	1,235.6	7.4
Southeast	15,900	1,120.5	7.0
South	13,115	1,176.3	8.9
Northeast	12,675	987.5	7.5

matched with the previous year's expenses, and a moderate increase was proposed, unless unusual circumstances, or a change in marketing strategy, necessitated a major revision.

Bill had always chafed at the detail demanded in these budgets. For example, in addition to salespersons' compensation, there were three selling expense budget categories: travel expenses, entertainment expenses, and lodging and meals. Bill thought that this breakdown was an unnecessary impediment and that the budget would be just as effective and less burdensome to his salespeople and himself if there was only one expense category: salespersons' expenses.

The budget for 1987 had been as follows:

Branch office salaries	$ 32,000
Office supplies	2,600
Office equipment	8,000
Warehouse salaries	82,000
Warehouse equipment	5,000
Sales force compensation	880,000
Travel expenses	214,000
Entertainment expenses	146,000
Lodging and meals	235,000
Administrative salaries	125,000
Advertising	60,000
Promotion	75,000
Miscellaneous	2,000
Total	$1,867,100

Bill found considerable advantages in being far removed from the New York home office. He had more freedom and was subjected to less headquarters supervision, or "snooping," as he liked to call it. Perhaps because of this distance from headquarters and the looseness of controls, he had grad-

ually begun to manipulate the budget, until now he was doing so with abandon. For example he shifted costs from one expense category to another that had more money left. In particular he liked to play with the promotion budget used for sales promotion efforts such as point-of-purchase displays, samples, and brochures.

Bill had also become a master at padding his budgets, requesting more money than he knew he needed. He felt free to request $5,000 for warehouse equipment when he knew that $2,000 would be ample. He always rationalized these inflated budget requests: "They will always cut down your budget requests. Therefore, the only way to get close to what you need is to ask for more than you need. When they pare the budget request, then you'll be about right." Bill never permitted any money to be left in a particular budget category at the end of the year. He always said, "If they see you didn't spend all the money this year, no way they are going to let you have as much next year."

Bill had always believed in paying his salespeople top dollar. He knew their compensation was well above those of any other region. One way he could get away with this in his budget was always to estimate more heavily than needed on travel and lodging expenses. Because of the distances traveled in these rather sparsely populated areas, until now the home office had never challenged this figure. Bill also manipulated selling expense budgets further by having the sales representatives bill some of their travel and entertainment expenses as promotional costs applied to the promotion budget line. Then through dummy vouchers he transferred moneys from the travel and entertainment expense accounts to the sales force as compensation.

He justified his actions on the grounds that salaries necessarily were higher on the West Coast; therefore, if he wished to attract the best people, he had to pay them well. If his company was penurious and rigid in its compensation policy, well, then he was forced to employ devious methods.

In June 1987 Bill's father retired from the board of directors. A new controller joined the New York office at about the same time. In September, budget requests for 1988 were due in New York. Bill dutifully completed his budget, generally requesting about 10 percent more than the previous year.

QUESTIONS

1. Evaluate Bill's actions based on the effectiveness of his region and that of the firm as a whole.

2. What factors lead to padding in many organizations?

3. Do you think the new controller is unreasonable in his actions?

4. Do you think that budgets should be as detailed as Wohlert's, or should they be more general for each region, thereby permitting the director to shift funds as he thinks best? Evaluate the policy of detailed versus general budgets.

5. Do you think sales force compensation should be uniform in all parts of the country?

PART III
ORGANIZING AND STAFFING

CHAPTER 8
Organizing the Sales Efforts

CHAPTER 9
Assembling the Staff: Recruiting and Selecting

CHAPTER 10
Deploying the Staff Through Time and Territorial Assignments

CHAPTER 11
Deploying the Staff Through Quotas

CHAPTER 8
Organizing the Sales Efforts

CHAPTER PERSPECTIVE

Organizing is the next important step after planning, as we follow the general functions of management. *Organizing* is establishing relationships among individuals and assigning activities in order to conduct the plans and objectives of the enterprise. Regardless of size, some organization is needed. Even a two-person venture must have an understanding of what each person should do. In this chapter we examine various types of organizations and organizational problems and issues. And we delve into such provocative topics as "the deadly parallel" and "weak" and "strong" branches.

As you read this chapter, think about why two firms of about the same size and in the same industry will most likely not have the same organizational structure. Does this reflect their strengths or weaknesses in the industry?

CHAPTER OBJECTIVES

□ Identify the essential elements of organizing.
□ Understand how organizations must change as they become larger.
□ Know the major issues in organizing sales, and the factors that should be considered in resolving them.
□ Be able to describe the various organizational structures and their appropriateness for various situations.
□ Become familiar with the arguments for strong and weak branch sales organizations.
□ Consider how various aspects of the organization affect individual job satisfaction and effectiveness.

ESSENTIALS OF ORGANIZING

To organize, a firm must: (1) identify similar activities and separate them from unrelated activities; (2) assign or delegate to specific individuals the authority and responsibility for specified activities; and (3) exercise some control over the activities.

✳Activities

Activities can be identified and separated, i.e., organized, according to the following categories:

- □ Functions, such as production, sales, advertising, personnel, and finance
- □ Products, for example, petroleum, coal, chemicals, and plastics
- □ Geographic areas, such as Northeast, Midwest, South, and Far West

Sometimes a major firm, especially in its sales organization, will have an additional breakdown by certain customer types, such as by position in the channel of distribution (e.g., retail chains and department stores, industrial distributors, and wholesalers). Most large firms must organize activities in various combinations of these categories.

Delegation

In delegating authority and responsibility for various activities, we would naturally expect selling to be separated from warehouse maintenance; in all but the smallest organizations, different individuals have authority and responsibility for these activities. Delegation is covered more extensively in Chapter 14, on supervision; let us note here an important principle of delegation. While the manager can delegate authority to subordinates and hold them responsible to her for their actions, she cannot escape ultimate responsibility for the performance of subordinates. This is true for a first-line supervisor, the president of a firm, or the President of the United States. President Harry Truman's classic comment expressing this fact is "The buck stops here."

Generally, the responsibility and authority delegated to any position should be equal. If a person is obligated to perform certain duties satisfactorily, she should have the permission or authority to take the actions necessary to perform these duties. (As discussed later in this chapter, however, one organizational structure involving product managers, violates this principle.) To aid the clarification of authority relationships, various lines of authority should be designated so that every employee knows the superior–subordinate relationships: who is responsible to whom, what each job is, and who supervises whom.

⚡ Control

Finally, we need some control over the activities. As discussed in previous chapters, *control* means seeing that operating results coincide as closely as possible with expectations and taking corrective action when they do not.

Organizations must be flexible and responsive to changing conditions. As a firm becomes larger, some organizational changes usually are needed. Even a change in objectives or a different planned strategy may lead to reorganizing certain activities to do a better job.

Many large firms use formal, written organization charts to define duties and lines of authority. These charts, however, fail to show informal relationships and communications flow, which affect the smooth functioning of any organization.

TRANSITION OF ORGANIZATIONS

In the smallest firm, the owner (perhaps with family members or part-time helpers) constitutes the organization. All activities necessarily fall on the owner. As the firm grows, one person can no longer handle all the activities. The firm hires new employees and delegates them duties such as selling, bookkeeping, and handling deliveries. As the firm grows larger, the owner must hire one or more managers to assist in planning and supervising. With increasing size, a natural organizational adjustment is to departmentalize.

Departmentalization

Departmentalizing is simply grouping various activities for the purpose of better administration. The sales manager may divide work into several sales territories, a customer service department, and an advertising department, and then assign these to subordinates.

Departmentalization affords two major advantages: specialization and control. By being responsible for one specific department, such as customer service or advertising, an employee can specialize in that activity. A better job should result. Control is needed if operations are to adhere as closely as possible to plans. Controlling operations is easier if records and performance can be measured by discrete groupings of activities, called either departments, divisions, bureaus, branches, offices, or units. If customer service is deficient, ascertaining the area requiring corrective action is simple.

The deadly parallel. A particularly effective departmental arrangement is the establishment of two or more operating units of comparable size and characteristics. In such a "deadly parallel," sales, expenses, and profit contributions can be compared readily, and strong as well as weak performances can be identified and actions taken accordingly. Besides providing control and performance evaluation, the deadly parallel fosters intrafirm competition, which can stimulate best efforts (see Application 8.1).

The deadly parallel organizational arrangement can be both a key to rapid advancement and positive recognition and a source of critical comparisons when performance slackens.

To use the deadly parallel effectively, the operating units or sales territories must be as equal as possible in sales potential and in ability to provide adequate coverage. If territories are inequitable either in potential or ease of coverage (such as one territory concentrated geographically in the Northeast and another widely scattered in the Dakotas and Wyoming), then the control and motivational device is being misused unless ample allowances are made for the differences. Territorial design and a related topic, sales quotas, will be discussed in Chapters 10 and 11.

Need for Staff Departments

As firms grow, they require numerous staff and service departments. Rather than operations departments, these are primarily advisory and provide expertise to help a line department, such as sales or production, to do a better job. Generally, staff people have no authority over line personnel, such as sales representatives, and they normally can only advise line executives such as the sales manager. There are exceptions to staff's advisory role. If the expertise involves legal counsel, auditing, technical knowledge, or a skill not possessed by other personnel, then the role is likely to evolve beyond strictly advising. This is especially likely when these staff executives or departments have made important contributions in the past, and so their judgment is respected. Examples of staff departments with which a sales manager is likely

---

APPLICATION 8.1   The Deadly Parallel in Operation

Julie Baxter, the sales manager of the Peoria, Illinois, district, was proud of having one of the top sales-producing districts in the Chicago region. She has always relished this intrafirm competition and knows that her effective handling of responsibilities has resulted in a fast career track. Indeed, as tangible evidence of her success, four of her sales representatives were promoted to district managers—more than any other district has produced. Julie is among the highest paid district sales managers in the company, despite her youth. And she knows she is the prime candidate for the next regional sales manager opening.

The last quarter, however, has caused Julie concern. Unexpectedly, and for unknown reasons, the Peoria district was second from the bottom in sales increases and new customers gained, among the eight districts of the Chicago region. Julie has just been called to Chicago to meet with Brian Sollito, the regional sales manager, to explain her district's poor showing. She is suddenly at a loss for words.

to be involved are personnel, credit, service, advertising, marketing research, and delivery. Public relations and customer relations are other departments of increasing importance, especially in large firms.

ISSUES IN ORGANIZING SALES

In the process of determining and structuring an effective sales organization, a number of issues must be confronted and resolved. The principal issues are (1) optimum grouping of activities, (2) span of supervision, (3) extent of centralization or decentralization, (4) staff's role, (5) handling of national and key accounts, (6) company sales force versus independent representatives. Each will be discussed in more detail in the following sections. In general, decisions concerning these issues depend on three factors: (1) amount of specialization needed; (2) amount of customer service desired (or necessary for competitive reasons); and (3) caliber of the sales force. Greater specialization encourages a finer breakdown of activities, more departments, and more staff assistance. It may require separate sales forces for different product categories and different types of customers—in general, a more complex organization. Likewise, if a high level of customer service is necessary, a firm must consider organizing a sales force along customer lines, expanding service and repair functions, and a strengthening commitment to quality control, as well as dependability of delivery. Finally, the sales force caliber, which should reflect the type of customer and the difficulty of selling the firm's products (i.e., the products' complexity and technical level, the amount of product information needed, and, perhaps, special tailoring to customer needs), will influence the organization's structure regarding span of supervision, extent of supervision, and backup technical support.

Optimum Grouping of Activities

Departments can be structured by function, such as sales, finance, or production; customer; territory; product; and by combinations of these factors. But problems frequently arise with coordination and specific lines of authority. For example sales efforts may be organized by types of customers or industry, but how should relevant activities such as credit, delivery, operating reports, and quality control be organized and to what executive level should they be assigned? Similarly, a warehouse may bring interdepartmental controversies regarding personnel recruitment, inventory levels, speed of order filling, and the like. So decisions on grouping of activities tend to be complex if authority–responsibility lines are specified in sufficient detail.

No formula exists for determining the optimum grouping of activities. The major operating factors and goals should influence the degree and characteristics of departmentalization. Later in this chapter we will examine more specifically the different organizational structures and their rationale and limitations.

Span of Supervision

The number of employees supervised by a single executive constitutes the span of supervision. This is intimately related to another aspect of organization, levels of supervision. Both are illustrated in Figure 8.1, which shows that the narrower the span (the fewer the number of subordinates supervised by or reporting to one manager) the more supervisory levels and the more executives (and their secretaries and staffs) required for the same number of employees. What is the ideal supervisory span and number of levels?

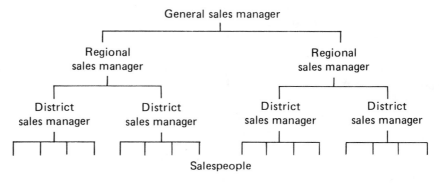

FIGURE 8.1 Span and levels of supervision.

APPLICATION 8.2   Supervisory Span and Levels

Sarah Lindstrom is having great difficulty with her job. She has been sales manager for the Dallas district of the Harriet Beame Cosmetic Company for 9 months. As sales manager she still has major accounts to service personally. Under her are eight salespeople, three of whom are experienced, but the others were recently hired by Sarah in anticipation of expanding sales in her district.

The sales buildup, however, continues to be disappointing. Sarah had thought that as the inexperienced salespeople gained job experience, their production would rise—but it is doing so quite slowly. Of even more concern is the inability of the older salespeople to make their quotas. Sarah is in a quandary. Servicing her own accounts takes much of her time, and yet much more personal supervision of her sales staff seems necessary.

In terms of costs only, a wide span is advantageous because fewer executives and their staffs must be paid. A wide span is conducive to decentralization. It contributes to the development of initiative and self-reliance in subordinates—simply because they cannot be so closely supervised. However, the number of subordinates one person can supervise adequately is limited. Many experts have studied organizations and concluded that higher management can supervise four to eight subordinates, whereas the span can be effectively increased to eight to fifteen or occasionally more at the lower levels. Obviously, with more experienced and able supervising executives (as well as the subordinates) and more stable operations, a wider supervision span can be handled adequately. See Application 8.2.

In addition to a higher executive payroll with a narrow span, more levels of supervision present several other drawbacks. With more executive levels involved, communication up and down the levels becomes increasingly difficult and less accurate; less flexibility and promptness of action also result, because more executives will be involved in any particular problem or decision. Morale also tends to be adversely affected in an organization with many levels, simply because the senior executive is further removed from the salespeople and has less direct personal influence. This leads to a sense of remoteness and reduced feelings of worth and recognition on the part of those executives and workers who are at some distance from this senior executive. Distance and remoteness entail feelings of detachment and the loss of the esprit de corps that can permeate youthful growth firms.

Extent of Centralization or Decentralization

The issue of centralization versus decentralization is directly related to the location of authority for detailed planning and decision making. In a centralized organization authority is retained at central headquarters and is limited mostly to the top executives and their staffs. When an organization is highly decentralized, executives close to operations are free to make most decisions (subject to certain policy and budgetary constraints, of course). Decentralization requires considerable delegation of authority by higher executives. Centralization versus decentralization can be viewed as a continuum:

complete centralization	_____ moderation _____	maximum amount of decentralization

Therefore, degrees of decentralization can exist, depending on the extent of power and authority delegated by higher executive levels.

Evaluation.   Generally, more able lower- and middle-level executives welcome a decentralized organization, because it gives them greater freedom of operation and scope for their initiative and creativity. Decentralization also tends to produce higher rewards in compensation and advancement, because executives take on more authority and responsibility and gain greater experience for higher-level positions. Decentralization requires capable subordinates, or the freedom given for increased decision making may result in serious mistakes due to inexperience or incompetence. It also requires highest-level executives to release some of their authority to subordinates (and they may be reluctant to because of a lack of confidence in subordinates or unwillingness to take a chance).

Centralization and decentralization, at the extreme points as shown on the continuum, pose some dangers. Application 8.3 presents a classic example of extreme centralization.

The Boise Cascade example in Chapter 4 showed how a firm also can be mistaken in choosing maximum decentralization (which in the extreme prac-

---

APPLICATION 8.3   Centralization: Korvette Discount Stores

At one time Korvette was the fastest-growing retailer in the United States. Its founder, Eugene Ferkauf, could not bring himself to decentralize, partly because Korvette was not getting high-caliber management people to run its stores, but also because he failed to recognize the need either for decentralization or for improved policies, budgets, and communications so that centralized management could function adequately.

During most of the growth years, Ferkauf ran the company with a group of thirty-eight men, almost all of whom were his Brooklyn high school pals. When there had been no more than a dozen outlets, Ferkauf, on "foot patrol," could give on-the-scene guidance. But as the firm grew to forty stores, his organization failed to provide any serious substitute for the diminishing face-to-face supervision of Ferkauf and his home office executives.

tically amounts to a hands-off policy), and permitting company reputation to be almost destroyed by an unsupervised and unscrupulous sales division.

Historically, there have been several swings in the general popularity of centralization and decentralization. A centralized, autocratic style of management was prevalent until after World War II, when management philosophy began shifting toward a more decentralized and democratic or participatory type of management. This style was seen as more compatible with management development and the requirements of larger organizations. In recent years, due to the advent of computers and centralized data banks—which permit a distant headquarters to keep informed about and in close control of diverse operations—a tendency toward centralization is again growing.

Hiring and firing authority.   An important question for the first-level sales manager is where the authority to hire and fire salespeople resides. As a general rule, when the sales force is relatively low paid, the district sales manager does the hiring. When higher-paid salespeople are involved (especially when the sales position is viewed as an entry and training ground for future management positions), the decision of hiring, firing, transferring, and promoting more often is made at higher levels. To some extent the higher-level authority may seem to dilute the sales manager's authority, but she still exercises power over subordinates by formal performance evaluations.

Role of Staff

Staff specialists can provide the executive with specialization and expertise to make the managerial job easier and more efficient. They sometimes handle tasks that the manager would rather not be involved with. For example the sales manager might wish to delegate nonsales functions, such as supervision of warehouse and clerical personnel, to staff assistants. Staff people can enable a manager to operate with a wider span of supervision and thereby eliminate the need for additional supervisory levels and more executives and their support people.

The use of staff, however, has some drawbacks. Staff positions add to costs without directly benefiting sales and profits, because they are not line positions. Perhaps the major disadvantage of heavy staff use is that it adds to the complexity of organizational relationships because the particular relationships of staff people to the rest of the organization sometimes are hard to define. For example they may issue instructions and check up on other members of the organization. But this may be resented because staff people have no formal authority. The issue of increasing delegation to operational personnel or staff specialists consequently confronts most organizations and can be difficult to reconcile.

Special Handling of National and Key Accounts

Know the differences of key accounts & the pros & cons of each one

In many firms a substantial part of the total business comes from just a few customers (as mentioned in Chapter 5 and discussed further in Chapter 17). These important customers are variously labeled as house accounts, corporate accounts, or national accounts. For consistency we refer to them as *key accounts* or *key customers*.

An 80/20 rule often characterizes key accounts. When 20 percent of clients provide 80 percent of the business, it follows that these 20 percent ought to have special attention to satisfy the needs of these large and important customers and maintain a favorable relationship.[1]

Key accounts undoubtedly deserve special treatment. Furthermore, if competitors are organized to do a better job of servicing key accounts, then improving service is a matter of competitive necessity. But the regular sales force may not be best suited to deal with these accounts, unless the key accounts are rather numerous and require large amounts of routine servicing.

The size of the selling firm is a factor in how these key customers are to be handled. If a manufacturer is small, its dealings with its few large customers will almost naturally involve the highest company executives. If a manufacturing firm is large, then only lower-level executives, such as district sales managers, may be involved. However, some drawbacks can arise from catering to these customer "prima donnas,"[2] as discussed in the following sections.

The three most common organizational approaches for the handling of key accounts are using (1) company executives, (2) a separate division, (3) a separate sales force.

Use of company executives for major-account selling.   Especially for firms with only a few major customers, company executives tend to be personally involved. Executives may serve as the customer's sole contact or may supplement and reinforce the efforts of a regular sales representative. The company executive(s) involved may range from field sales managers to the top executives of the firm, depending on the customer's importance and the manufacturer's size relative to the customer's.

These executives are authorized to make any necessary decisions relevant to servicing the customer, which results in greater flexibility and responsiveness in customer relations. And the customer is likely to be impressed by dealing with important company executives (although some customers will see it as their right).

We need to recognize, however, several drawbacks to this alternative for handling key accounts. Executives may spend considerable time in contacting these accounts. Less time therefore is available for planning and accomplishing other management activities. Furthermore, catering to large customers can be highly objectionable to smaller but still profitable customers, who see it as detrimental to their best interests.

Use of a separate division to deal with key accounts. A firm may establish an entire separate division to deal with the key accounts. Some manufacturers who produce private-label goods for retailers such as J. C. Penney, Sears, and K-Mart have found this to be the best organizational arrangement. It allows for integrating the manufacturing and selling activities related to these major accounts. However, having a separate division and the concomitant infrastructure for the sole purpose of dealing with a few customers is a costly alternative. But it can be justified if these few customers account for a major part of the manufacturer's total sales volume.

Use of a separate sales force. The most widely used structure for dealing with key accounts is assigning a separate sales force to deal solely with them. This separate sales force may have its own management hierarchy, or it may report to the same sales executives as the rest of the sales force. Sometimes such a national account sales force calls on customers' headquarters and central buying offices, while the regular sales force services individual outlets and stores.

Such national or key account salespeople are the elite of the sales organization. This arrangement provides an outlet for rewarding the outstanding employee who is not interested in a career path in management. Such sales representatives may be paid 20 percent higher and even more than the regular sales staff; some of the more successful firms using this arrangement compensate these sales people at the level of a second-level executive.[3] Provided that competent people are assigned to key account sales to provide such customers a high level of expertise, this approach has little to criticize. It may add somewhat to costs, because some duplication of efforts may result, but the gains in providing better service and tangible evidence of the importance attached to a particular customer should more than offset the costs.

Supplemental arrangements for handling key accounts. Two supplementary adaptations may be used with the above-mentioned organizational approaches: team selling and multilevel selling. If the customer's buying center is composed of people from numerous disciplines, the account manager may need to draw on the services of different functional people in her selling organization. For major equipment purchases, engineers and technical specialists commonly assist in customizing and special design work for the customer's unique requirements. Finance people, production schedulers, and others may also be formed into an ad hoc selling team if the need arises.

Of course, a major disadvantage of such team selling is the high cost involved in bringing together a number of diverse people. Coordinating their efforts and assuring that no one on the team is a negative influence can also be a challenge. Consequently, such team selling is best used only for the most important customers, and usually where major sales are involved.[4]

Multilevel selling is a type of team selling in which various management people in the selling organization call on their counterparts in the buying organization. Thus, a vice president of manufacturing may call on the customer's vice president of manufacturing, while the account manager is calling on the customer's purchasing agent. For major present or potential customers, abiding by the levels of authority can be quite effective, and any concessions or special arrangements can be negotiated quickly.

Company Sales Force Versus Independent Representatives

Should the firm have its own sales force, or should it contract independent sales representatives (often called manufacturers' representatives or, in the food industry, food brokers). Firms usually turn to independent representatives to economize, but they sacrifice control for somewhat reduced selling costs, because the independents represent numerous sellers and cannot be relied on to devote all their selling and servicing to the products of any one manufacturer. They are more likely to concentrate their efforts on the products that are easiest to sell, which may be a major drawback for the new, small manufacturer. However, using independent sales representatives has some important advantages that have induced both small and large manufacturers to turn to them. They can offer advantages in costs, flexibility, and sometimes competence over a company-owned sales force.

In the past use of independent sales representatives was limited to small firms that could not afford their own sales forces; as these firms became larger, they naturally developed their own. But today larger firms are also attracted to independents because of the potential cost advantage. Independents are paid on a straight commission for sales, usually 6 percent. This makes selling costs entirely variable, rising or falling with revenues. In contrast, a company-owned sales force has considerable fixed expenses, such as sales managers' salaries, home and branch office expenses, and base salaries of salespeople, plus travel and entertainment expenses. These costs remain constant whether sales are up or down (commissions and bonuses would, of course, vary). The cost comparisons in a hypothetical example are presented in Table 8.1.

Both examples in Table 8.1 show that a firm is ensured a constant percentage for selling costs with independent representatives—their commission rate remains the same. The higher the fixed costs of a company's own sales force the less predictable the total selling cost during a period of erratic sales. Independent representatives also afford a company considerable flexibility.

TABLE 8.1 Cost of independent sales representatives versus a company-owned sales force ($ hundreds).

	Independent Reps	Company Sales Force
Example 1		
Sales	20,000	20,000
Fixed costs	0	600
Variable costs as percentage of sales (commissions)	6%	3%
Total variable costs	1,200	600
Total selling costs (fixed and variable)	1,200	1,200
Example 2		
Sales	17,000	17,000
Fixed costs	0	600
Variable costs as percentage of sales	6%	3%
Total variable costs	1,020	510
Total selling costs	1,020	1,110

During periods of rising sales, more reps can be used; during periods of falling sales, retrenchment is easier than with a company-owned sales force. Furthermore, when demand for a firm's products has considerable seasonal fluctuation, independent representatives are a logical preference, because a company sales force may not be used effectively during slack periods. Now, in Exercise 8.1 consider two questions regarding the data in Table 8.1:

---

1. If sales climb to $24 million, which method of organizing sales will show a lower cost?
2. Would you expect the fixed costs of the sales department to remain the same if sales climb 20 percent? Why or why not?

EXERCISE 8.1

Some argue that independent sales representatives can actually provide better sales production than company salespeople. Since independents contact the same customers with products of a number of manufacturers, sales calls are more economical—the cost is spread across several products. These representatives may also have more stature in their customers' view because of the breadth of their line and the fact that they may handle several important product lines for the customer. Generally, these representatives are experienced and competent salespeople. Application 8.4 describes one important and widely used type of independent sales representative, the food broker.

APPLICATION 8.4   The Independent Sales Representative: The Food Broker

A food broker performs in a local market the sales function and related services for an average of twenty-five manufacturers (or principals). The food brokerage firm is strictly a selling agent and does not take title or possession of goods. Prices, terms, and other conditions of sale are set by the manufacturer.

In addition to selling principals' products to wholesale merchants, chain stores, supermarket groups, and institutional users, the food broker pushes special deals and promotions developed by the principals. The broker also provides market information on competitors' activities, special promotions, and the like.

The biggest advantage to using brokerage distribution is that manufacturers know their selling costs in advance. The food broker is paid a flat percentage—2 to 5 percent—of sales produced. Often manufacturers cannot operate their own sales forces this economically. And because food brokers are in close touch with local buyers and the market situation—they are local firms themselves—their efforts are often more effective than a company sales force.

VARIATIONS IN ORGANIZATIONAL STRUCTURE

As noted earlier, seldom do two firms evolve into an identical organizational structure. Certain patterns are common, although they may be modified and tailored to the individual firm and its perceived needs, preferences, and resources. Although sales activities can be organized on a functional basis (e.g., developmental, to create new accounts, and maintenance, to service existing accounts), most sales departments are organized by geography, product, or customer. An ancillary organizational arrangement using product managers, usually in staff positions, also is fairly common with large companies having many different products. Each of the four basic organizational structures are described in the following sections and are depicted in Figures 8.2 to 8.5.

Geographical Organization

Organizing by geographical territories is the traditional and most widely used form of sales organization (see Figure 8.2). As a firm grows and adds sales-

FIGURE 8.2   Region-oriented sales organization.

people, the natural tendency is to assign each salesperson to a particular geographical area for selling and servicing. The salesperson then reports either to a regional sales manager, as in Figure 8.2, or, if the company is larger (and has more levels of management), to district sales managers, who then report to regional sales managers; these in turn would report to a general sales manager or a vice president of sales. An obvious benefit of geographical organization is ease of travel time and expense. The major disadvantage for a multiproduct company is that the same salesperson sells all the products to all the customers in a particular territory and may not have sufficient expertise to do so effectively. Further, salespeople tend to concentrate on those products and customers easiest to sell, although sales management supervision and performance evaluation criteria can control this tendency somewhat. If salespeople are evaluated not only on sales produced but also on the gross margin of sales, then they have considerable incentive to sell more profitable products, even if these require more selling effort, as discussed in Chapter 18.

Organization by Products

The problems in geographical organization posed by selling diverse products are, of course, solved by diversifying according to broad product categories, as Figure 8.3 illustrates. Organizing by product lines is sometimes necessary for industrial firms whose products require specialized technical or applications knowledge. In highly diversified companies each division may have a separate sales force because of product heterogeneity. The respective sales forces may report to an autonomous, separate subsidiary or division.

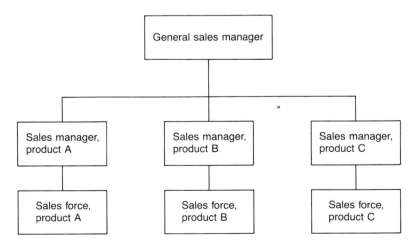

FIGURE 8.3 Product-oriented sales organization.

Because of the costs of separate sales forces for major product categories (which must be weighed against the greater specialization and expertise afforded), another potential drawback is that several different salespeople from one firm may be calling on the same customer. A sportswear manufacturer may have a separate sales force for ski apparel. The rationale is that ski wear is sold in a different department and bought by different buyers in most stores. However, in smaller stores, the same person may buy sportswear and ski apparel. The results are duplicated selling efforts by the manufacturer and, quite likely, customer irritation at being overburdened with sales calls.

The product manager organization.   A subset of an organization by products is the so-called product manager or brand manager, as shown in Figure 8.4. Here the product managers serve in a staff capacity, with a single sales force selling all products. This type of organization is rather widely used by both consumer goods and industrial goods manufacturers. But it is controversial. Usually product managers are staff; they have no line authority over the sales force, and can only advise and persuade. Although they are responsible for advertising and other promotional efforts, for product development, and in general for the profitability of the product or brand, they are essentially thwarted in their ability to control the profitability because they typically do not have the needed authority over prices and costs, the key ingredients of profits. The product manager is the classic example of responsibility without commensurate authority.

Large consumer goods companies have found that the advantages of giving individual products adequate attention outweigh the disadvantages. Indeed, Procter & Gamble and Johnson & Johnson have used the product or brand manager type of organization for well over half a century. (See Application 8.5.)

Other users of the product manager organization include such well-known firms as Lever Brothers, Kimberly-Clark, and Clairol. In recent years industrial product manufacturers have also adopted this type of organization.[5] But some well-known firms, such as Pepsi-Cola, Eastman Kodak, General Foods, Campbell Soup, and Levi Strauss, have moved away from it.[6] And now, even P&G

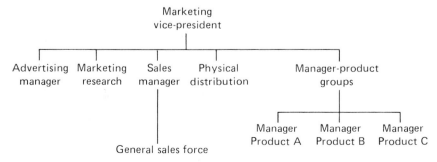

FIGURE 8.4   Product manager (staff) organization.

itself is beginning to modify, by having "business teams" of manufacturing, sales, and research managers work together on problems, such as turning around the languishing Pringle's potato chips. P&G also is establishing category brand managers to oversee an entire group of related products, and is emphasizing cooperation, not competition among brands.[7]

Product management provides major career opportunities. These executives are exposed to a far wider range of marketing problems than are ordinarily found at lower and middle executive levels. Although their responsibility may be limited to a single product or brand, they become intimately familiar with all aspects of the marketing strategy. This is valuable experience for higher-level positions.

Some companies give product managers more authority, treating them as marketing managers for individual product lines. These product managers may have their own sales forces and be responsible for advertising, product planning, and other broad marketing functions. General Electric and Nestlé have used this structure effectively, but decentralization and specialization are costly and best geared to highly diversified companies.

Organization by Customers

If customers are diverse, organizing the sales department by major customer categories, as shown in Figure 8.5, offers a more finely tuned effort to meet customer needs. This structure appears more harmonious with the marketing concept and its implied customer orientation. (See Chapter 1 for a discussion of the marketing concept.) Sales force specialization should improve understanding of the unique problems and needs of the various types of customers. Better customer servicing as well as better communication and cooperation should result.

Some drawbacks are possible. Added selling costs are incurred, because two or more company salespeople may cover the same geographical area. Furthermore, this structure often greatly increases sales territories compared to a geographical structure. Travel time may be increased, which adversely

FIGURE 8.5 Customer-oriented sales organization.

affects sales productivity and may cause poor morale because of the additional time spent away from home. Most firms with a diverse and highly technical product line tend toward organization by products in the belief that no one salesperson can be sufficiently knowledgeable about all the products to be effective. Compelling reasons, however, may lead to a shift to an organization by customer, as NCR did (formerly National Cash Register Company).

NCR products ranged from relatively simple numerical recording and sorting devices (such as cash registers, accounting machines, data entry terminals, and bank check-coding machines) to computers, and it serviced businesses ranging from corner mom-and-pop stores to the largest multinational industrial and financial corporations. As the company grew, sales training and the sales force became increasingly specialized. Reassigning its domestic sales force of 3,000 to specific industries rather than products was a massive reorganization. As a result sales representatives could sell both cash registers and computer systems to department stores. But executives were shifted around, some took early retirement, and 10 percent of the sales force left in "fear and anxiety."

Why would a company make such a sweeping and even disruptive organizational change? Company profits had recently plummeted, but perhaps the most compelling reason for reorganizing was that numerous other industrial and consumer goods companies were already selling by industry, among them IBM, Xerox, Addressograph-Multigraph, and General Foods. A firm organized by customer can have a powerful competitive advantage over competitors who are not, because of the greater servicing and expertise provided.

Combinations of Structures

Many firms have modified the preceding basic structures. The purpose in modifying has been to group activities to best achieve the corporate objectives.

Combinations of structures are particularly common among firms that pre-
serve a fundamental product-oriented structure for most of their business but
also give individual markets more specialized treatment. General Foods has
special sales forces for each consumer product, but it also has one broad-line
division selling all products to restaurants, hotels, and hospitals. Modifications
are also common in international sales, where business volume by individual
product lines may not warrant separate sales organizations, so all products
must be sold by the same salesperson.

ORGANIZATION OF FIELD SALES

First-level sales managers usually are located in the field with their salespeople. Alternatively, they are in the home or regional office, far removed from
many sales territories, which requires communicating mostly by either letter
or phone. When a firm has numerous field or district sales managers, it must
decide whether to have a weak or strong branch organization. In particular
the following questions must be addressed:

- ☐ Should the district sales office be only a central point where salespeople
  get mail and telephone calls and the sales manager (and perhaps one
  clerical person) works?
- ☐ Should the branches have a much more complex structure, with staff
  assistants for sales planning and control, sales promotion and advertising, and personnel and training functions?
- ☐ Should the branch carry stock?
- ☐ If stock is carried, should it be a small back up amount or a full
  warehouse?
- ☐ Should servicing and repair operate out of the branch and under the
  sales manager's control?

Arguments for a Strong Branch Sales Organization

A strong branch will, of course, involve a more complex organization and
will provide more activities and controls. But it will also require much heavier
fixed costs. A strong branch organization permits more flexibility in adjusting
to specific market conditions. It also permits better customer servicing through
fast order filling, prompt handling of repairs and adjustments, and special
tailoring of merchandise and service to customer requirements. Because more
autonomy is possible in this type of organization, sales executives are trained
more thoroughly for higher positions. In addition the deadly parallel evaluation of performance relative to other operational units is enhanced. Finally,
a strong branch is compatible with a decentralized organizational structure
and management philosophy.

Arguments for a Weak Branch Sales Organization

The arguments for the weak branch alternative, as would be expected, are virtually the opposite of those for the strong branch, and can be considered the drawbacks of the strong branch. Costs are considerably less than for a strong branch and all the support that it requires, especially if inventory is involved. A weak branch, which implies more centralized control, ensures more uniform adherence to company policies and dictates. The home office, with its highly specialized staff assistance, can prescribe more effective procedures than are likely to come from harried field executives. And the weak branch requires fewer experienced and capable executives and staff personnel. With efficient transportation and communications facilities (including computer technology and centralized data banks), customer servicing can be almost as quick as (and probably more efficient than) when inventories and repair parts are maintained in the field. Finally, the weak branch permits concentration on selling and avoids diluted sales efforts, as occurs in a strong branch, which requires more administration and more concern with non-selling aspects of the operation.

To a large extent, the decision to develop a strong or weak branch depends on the importance of being closely attuned to the particular market and the amount of flexibility needed in meeting changing environmental conditions and customer demands. Company philosophy toward decentralization also plays a big role in the autonomy and scope of the branch organization. A strong branch is expensive, however, because it duplicates many activities, not only those of the home office but also of the other branches. The decision to have a strong branch sales organization is best made only after careful weighing gains against the costs.

THE INDIVIDUAL IN THE ORGANIZATION

Various elements within the organization and its interpersonal relations can significantly affect an individual's job satisfaction, effectiveness, and personal development. In this section we briefly consider the following elements: management style, pressure for performance, impact of informal groups, and acceptance of authority.

Management Style

A firm's management philosophy (which may be explicit but usually is implicit or unwritten) can take two extremes, autocratic or democratic. Although the preferences and philosophies of various executives result in differences within an organization, the orientation of top management tends to permeate the organization. Management may instill an authoritative, arbitrary, and autocratic dictation of policies and practices, or it may encourage the other extreme—a democratic, participatory, and supportive environment. The organizational structure, whether centralized or decentralized, acts to reinforce the management style. For most individuals, in management or elsewhere, job satisfaction results from involvement in at least some of the planning and decisions.[8] If the organizational structure is relatively decentralized (in which, as described earlier in this chapter, authority exists at lower levels not primarily at central headquarters), the work environment can be particularly satisfying.

Pressure for Performance

Pressure to accomplish also affects job satisfaction and effectiveness. Sales jobs are particularly pressured, and performance is readily measurable in actual sales and perhaps also in profitability. Some firms and managers emphasize performance to the extreme, which might be called a "sales-at-any-cost" philosophy. This not only generates extreme feelings of pressure and anxiety but can also lead to unethical and possibly illegal practices such as commercial bribery, payoffs, and deceptions.

Performance pressure conversely may be expressed in more emphasis on human relations, on helping people develop to their fullest potential. Rewards and punishments are less important than determining the reasons for behavior that detracts from total performance. Most individuals prefer working in this more sympathetic and less coercive environment. However, work may become so pleasant that it results in complacency and poor motivation for performance. The high-pressure situation may be more attractive to those salespeople and sales managers who are highly confident and thrive in competitive and demanding situations. Most people prefer and are most effective in a work environment somewhere between these two extremes.

Impact of Informal Groups

An organization invariably develops certain informal groups or cliques who exchange information, opinions, and sometimes even mutual aid. These informal organizations may help or deter overall sales department goals. A sales manager needs to win the cooperation of informal group leaders to maximize morale and performance. Cliques may impede the full acceptance of new employees; on the other hand, cliques may help during the difficult period of adjustment to a new job in a new location. Cliques tend to be less influential in sales than in other organizations because of geographical separation, but they exist. The sales manager should not disregard the clique's communications (the "grapevine"), which may or may not be accurate, or its influence on the sales force's morale and effectiveness.

Acceptance of Authority

A newly appointed sales manager sometimes faces a trying problem—acceptance of her authority by the organization or by certain of its members.

Sometimes acceptance is hindered by the informal organization, especially if the sales manager is young or inexperienced in management or if the preceding sales manager was well liked and had been in the position for some time. Nonacceptance of the manager's authority may be demonstrated in half-hearted efforts to obey orders, an unwillingness to excell for the new manager, and at the extreme, outright insubordination. The classic example of this problem is represented by the veteran star sales representative who will not accept the young manager's authority. The manager consequently is placed in a dilemma. If she permits rudeness, insubordination, or outright refusal to obey orders to continue, the veteran's informal leadership will completely undermine the new manager's authority. Severely reprimanding, firing, or transferring the offender could severely jeopardize the territory's customer relations and probably would not be supported by top management. The Hewitt Company case at the end of the chapter involves a situation in which a young sales manager confronts a resentful veteran sales representative.

SUMMARY   At the beginning of this chapter I asked you why similar firms are likely to have different organizational structures, and whether these are necessarily a sign of strength or weakness. Firms in the same industry may have considerably different resources and objectives, which may be reflected in different organizational patterns. A large firm with considerable resources may emphasize staff expertise more than a firm with less financial resources is able to and may, therefore, have departments such as planning, marketing research, traffic, and sales analysis. The special abilities or preferences of company executives may dictate one type of organizational pattern—such as emphasis on centralization versus decentralization. The number and buying habits of customers may lead to somewhat different structures, perhaps organized by geographical location or customer type. However, if one organizational structure permits better customer servicing, competitors may need to reevaluate their organizational structure to improve their customer service and satisfaction.

The essentials of organizing are grouping activities, delegating authority and responsibility, and exercising performance control. Grouping of activities is called *departmentalization*. The deadly parallel exists when similar operating units are established that permit performance comparison.

The principal issues involved in organizing sales concern (1) how activities should best be grouped (i.e., by function, customer, territory, product, or some combination); (2) the span of supervision; (3) the extent of centralization or decentralization; (4) the role of staff; (5) handling of national and key accounts; and (6) using a company sales force versus independent representatives.

Sales generally can be organized by geography, product, customer, or some combination of these three. The field sales organization (i.e., the field or district sales managers) may have a strong or a weak branch arrangement, depending on the need to be closely attuned to the market, the flexibility needed, and the company philosophy toward decentralization.

In the organization, management style (autocratic or democratic) affects an individual's job satisfaction, effectiveness, and personal development. The performance pressures and informal groups also impact on the individual. Problems in accepting the manager's authority may sometimes arise, especially with inexperienced managers and veteran salespeople.

QUESTIONS

1. Differentiate between authority and responsibility. Why is their equality preferred?

2. Explain the pros and cons of the deadly parallel, both from the viewpoint of the firm and from the individuals.

3. What are the major arguments for not assigning the sales manager the authority to hire and fire salespeople? Would you be content with such a situation? Why or why not?

4. Would you recommend a company sales force or independent representation for the following firms:
   A small manufacturer with a limited product line
   A small manufacturer with a rapidly increasing product line
   A large manufacturer selling a limited product line to large retailers
   A large manufacturer selling a limited product line to both large and small retailers
   A large manufacturer with a broad product line selling to many customers, both large and small

5. What are the pros and cons of having a product manager organization?

6. What factors should be considered in deciding whether or not to establish sales branches?

7. What are the problems typically encountered with decentralization? What can be done to overcome these difficulties?

PEOPLE PROBLEM: COPING WITH LACK OF AUTHORITY

Please evaluate each of the following alternatives.

As a district sales manager, you dislike the centralization of the sales department. You object in particular to home office dictation regarding planning and most other aspects of the operation, which relegate your role almost entirely to supervision of the sales force. And here you have another gripe, because you do not even have the authority to hire and fire your salespeople—this also is done by the home office. Eventually, you feel that you must do something. But what?

1. You go to your boss and tell him that you will quit unless you are given more authority.

2. You decide to tolerate the situation for now, feeling that nothing desirable is likely to result and that you will simply gain a reputation as a troublemaker.

3. You intensify your efforts to achieve one of the best-performing districts in the company, feeling that this will give your input into this organizational issue considerably more weight.

4. You confer with the other district sales managers at the next national sales meeting and encourage them to join you in demanding a move to more decentralization.

5. You decide to accept the possibility that the home office can better recruit and select high-level salespeople, and in the process relieve you of considerable time and effort. You vow to concentrate on those aspects of the operation—the generation of sales and satisfaction of customers—that you can control directly, and to be content that your authority is not diluted because you still formally evaluate your subordinates' performance.

NOTES

1. See Thomas H. Stevenson, "Payoff from National Account Marketing," *Industrial Marketing Management* (April 1981): 119–124; and Thomas H. Stevenson and Albert L. Page, "The Adoption of National Account Marketing by Industrial Firms," *Industrial Marketing Management* (January 1979): 94–100.

2. Philip Maher, "National Account Marketing: An Essential Strategy, or Prima Donna Selling?" *Business Marketing* (December 1984): 34–45.

3. Gary Tubridy, "How to Pay National Account Managers," *Sales & Marketing Management* (13 Jan. 1986): 50–53.

4. "Specialist Selling Makes New Converts," *Business Week* 28 July 1973, 44–45.

5. For a comparison with consumer goods manufacturers, see J. Patrick Kelly and Richard T. Hise, "Industrial and Consumer Goods Product Managers are Different," *Industrial Marketing Management* (November 1979): 325–332.

6. For example see "The Brand Manager: No Longer King," *Business Week* 9 June 1973, 58; and Richard M. Clewett and Stanley F. Stasch, "Shifting Role of the Product Manager," *Harvard Business Review* (January–February 1975): 65–73.

7. "P & G Makes Changes in the Way It Develops and Sells Its Products," *Wall Street Journal,* 11 August 1987.

8. For a relevant article dealing with job satisfaction, see Robert E. Hite and Joseph A. Bellizzi, "A Preferred Style of Sales Management," *Industrial Marketing Management* (August 1986): 215–224.

cases

8.1 Adjusting to a More Complex Product Line

"Joe, I just goofed up a sale to one of our big customers, the Mead Company."

"How's that, Fred?" you ask tensely.

"The buyer of their lighting products division had asked me about certain performance features of our new 1600 product line, and I gave him the wrong information. When I called on him the other day, he practically showed me the door. I'm sorry, Joe . . . with the product line so big now, I'm having a tough time keeping on top of it. It's not just me.

The other fellows are having the same trouble."

After Fred leaves, you lean back in your chair and ponder his remarks. Were they simply excuses, or were they symptoms of an emerging problem? Your firm is a full-line wholesaler of electrical, plumbing, and heating supplies to a variety of retailers, contractors, and industrial firms. Each of your eleven salespeople sells the complete line. And, undeniably, the product line has grown considerably in the last few years.

QUESTIONS

1. Based on this episode, what course of action should be explored at this time?

2. What further information would you deem helpful in making a decision?

8.2 Reorganizing for a Top Sales Representative

Sandra Chin, the general sales manager for the L. C. Pettiborn Company, a national supplier of small machine tools, was in a quandary. Her top salesman, Stan Mankiewicz, was on the verge of leaving the firm, and Sandra was most reluctant to let him go. She had offered Stan a district sales manager position, but Stan had turned it down: "I'm just not the manager type. I want no part of it. You've been good to me, and I appreciate it. But I think I can make more money and have more challenge selling with some other firm."

Since Stan was adamant about remaining in selling rather than moving up to administration, Sandra pondered how a more challenging and fi-

nancially rewarding sales position might be opened up within the company. She had heard of a few firms that had experimented with separating the sales force into developmental and maintenance groups: A few high-level developmental salespeople created new accounts and then turned them over to maintenance people for the more routine servicing. She thought Stan might be interested in this role, because it would be particularly challenging. Furthermore, he would most likely be a strong asset in the position. She could also assign him to only the key accounts, and she thought he might accept this.

QUESTIONS

1. Evaluate these and other possible alternatives for keeping a top sales representative. What would be the drawbacks to such a change in organizing the sales force?

2. Give an on-balance recommendation for this problem, and support your position as persuasively as possible.

8.3 Mexi-Tacos: Organizing to Handle Geographical Expansion

Bob Pekoc was president of Mexi-Tacos, a franchiser of taco restaurants and, as he liked to say, "a junior competitor of Taco Bell." Although not nearly as large as the very successful Taco Bell, Mexi-Tacos showed a satisfactory growth pattern in the southern and southwestern states. The enthusiasm in these markets for taco and Mexican fast-food restaurants created ample room for several competitors.

Bob wanted to extend Mexi-Taco's market area into the Midwest. Although Taco Bell was already in the Midwest it appeared to be moving very slowly. Bob saw an opportunity for his firm to lead the way into certain eastern and northern metropolitan areas and thus not remain in the distant second place that they occupied in most markets.

In a franchise operation such as Mexi-Tacos, the franchiser extends to independent franchisees the right to conduct the business according to a tested and well-formulated format. Accordingly, although the franchisees owned and financed the individual outlets, they had to abide by Mexi-Tacos Corporation's specifications for decor, signs, menu, service requirements, and so on. If the franchisee failed to comply, the franchiser had the right to withdraw the franchise. Mexi-Tacos, like most other franchised restaurant operations including Taco Bell and McDonald's, maintained close controls and checks on the cleanliness, service, and menus of the outlets, because a few careless operations could result in bad customer perception of all outlets.

From the franchiser's viewpoint the advantage of franchising rather than company ownership is that expansion is possible with only limited finances, because the franchisees put up some or most of the money. Expansion therefore can proceed almost as rapidly as entrepreneurs can be induced to invest. The major selling point to prospective franchisees is that the established format and advertising mean a much lower risk of business failure; they are taking on a unique product or service with established consumer acceptance and wide recognition. Furthermore, the franchiser provides proven managerial and promotional techniques.

Although McDonald's had a waiting list of prospective franchisees eager to invest in what was almost a guaranteed success, Mexi-Tacos—being newer and relatively unknown in many areas—had to exert strong selling efforts to persuade would-be entrepreneurs to invest. The selling job was likely to be especially important and probably difficult in expanding into the Midwest, Bob recognized, because there the concept of Mexican food and tacos was not established and Mexi-Tacos was completely unknown. The firm now had sixty-two outlets. With the growth contemplated in the next several years, plus the efforts to enter a new geographic market, the present marketing and sales organization required change, Bob reasoned, although he was not sure exactly how to accomplish this. The present organization is illustrated by Figure 8.6A.

To facilitate further expansion in their present markets as well as entry into the Midwest and later the East, Bob considered changing to the organization type depicted by Figure 8.6B. He liked the idea of organization by regions but recognized that it would add considerably to the overhead. Research and operations staff would have to be assigned to each region, as well as separate regional general managers and their staffs and secretaries.

Another, less-expensive, alternative would be to keep research and operations centralized, but to break up the sales force (the franchise advisers) into a South and Southwest group under one regional sales manager and a Midwest group reporting to another regional sales manager. Although this arrangement might facilitate selling, separating the research and store location people and the operational executives from the Midwest might hurt the quality of store location studies and of management support and control of the new outlets (see Figure 8.6C).

Of course, Bob recognized that he could continue with the present organization, which had proved effective, simply by adding more sales representatives with new territories in the Midwest, as well as operational store superintendents. This undoubtedly would be the least costly expansion, if the effectiveness of research, control, and selling were not drastically jeopardized. He also knew that other organizational alternatives were possible but had not investigated further.

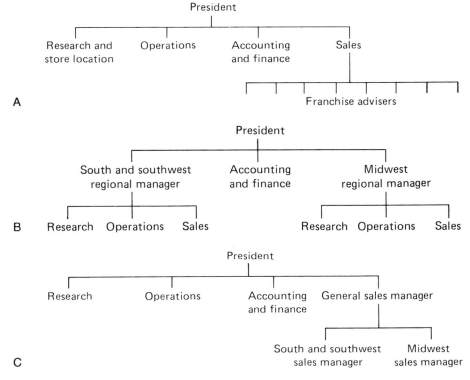

FIGURE 8.6 (A) Present organization; (B) alternative 1, organization by regions; (C), alternative 2, organization by function and region.

QUESTIONS

1. Which of the three organizational alternatives presented do you recommend, and why?

2. Suggest other organizational alternatives that should be considered.
   Optional: You may be invited to take and defend one of the options, while your classmates choose other options. You then would be required to *persuasively* support and defend your position. The possible options follow:
   □ Keep the status quo.
   □ Go with alternative 1.
   □ Go with alternative 2.
   □ Choose some other alternative.

8.4 The Hewitt Company: Problems in Accepting Authority

David Weisman had been with the Hewitt Company, a producer of industrial fasteners, for only 3 years before being promoted and transferred to the Philadelphia district as sales manager. An honor graduate in marketing from Georgia State University, Hewitt Company management quickly recognized his strong potential and marked him for a fast-track career path. They had assigned him to the Atlanta district initially as a sales trainee for 6 months and then gave him a sales territory in central Georgia. His performance fully justified the company's high expectations. Although his sales were not the highest in the district, they approached levels that some of the older sales representatives achieved in well-established territories.

As David grew in experience and value to the company, he was assigned certain nonselling tasks. His district sales manager had made him primarily responsible for planning and organizing the district's participation in the annual sales meeting. Furthermore, for the last year, David had been the primary on-the-job coach of new sales recruits, who had been assigned to him for 2 weeks of field training. He had handled all of these extra duties without complaint, even though they had interfered with maximizing his sales and commissions. The general consensus was that all of these activities had been handled very well and that he welcomed additional duties and responsibilities. When the sales manager of the Philadelphia district retired, 25-year-old David Weisman therefore was named his replacement.

The Philadelphia district was static. It ranked near the middle of the Hewitt Company's eighteen sales districts both in sales and in profit contribution. Its growth was slightly under the median, remaining at about 3 percent annually for the last several years. The sales force consisted of eight people, the oldest of whom was Sam Jamison, a 21-year veteran, while the youngest had been with the company for 2 years.

"David, as the figures show, we are not giving you a problem district," said Annette Coggins, the general sales manager. "However, we think the district can do much better. There has been practically no personnel turnover in the last several years, and we suspect the entire district has become rather complacent. We're counting on you to get things moving again."

Weisman nervously cleared his throat. "I understand. We'll get things moving again." He hesitated, "Ah, do I have the authority to transfer out or terminate anyone who's unable or unwilling to improve?"

Annette looked at David keenly. "We're not bringing you to Philadelphia to be a hatchet man, David. I hardly think the organization is in bad shape. But on the other hand, if you think circumstances warrant drastic action, perhaps as an example to the rest of the sales force, then let's get together and discuss what should be done." She paused. "Incidentally, David, if you can get this district moving again, bigger things may be in store for you in a few years. Let's call Philadelphia a testing ground for your managerial ability, shall we?"

David spent the first few weeks in Philadelphia getting acquainted with his salespeople and going over the records. He also visited each of the major customers in the district. Although he felt some undercurrent of resentment among the older sales personnel (which he judged to be due to his age and limited experience), he hoped to overcome it by being friendly yet businesslike.

He had thought that the sales force had accepted him after a few weeks, but he was quickly disillusioned during what became a confrontation between himself and Sam Jamison. Having been in Philadelphia for a month, David decided that he had spent enough time in getting acquainted with the situation. He was ready to exert some leadership. It seemed best to begin, he thought, through individual discussions with the sales staff. Sufficient performance data had been accumulated to enable him to know each person's weaknesses. He intended to point these out, suggesting improvement techniques and then firmly but diplomatically impressing the need for better performance. Unfortunately, he started with Sam.

Sam Jamison was 56 years old. He was the oldest salesperson in the district. Several times during 21 years with the company, he had been recommended for promotion to sales manager, but he had always declined, noting that he could make more money as a sales representative. And Sam was right, David mused. Last year Sam's total compensation had exceeded $80,000, while David was making less than half that. Sam was consistently the top sales producer in the district. However, his territory, which consisted of a densely populated part of Pennsylvania, also had the most potential. It appeared that Sam was skimming the territory and not developing it to its fullest potential.

David called Sam into his office. After some introductory small talk, during which Sam was polite but coldly distant, David got to the point. "Sam, as you know, the district has not grown as fast as top management thinks it should. I have been told to get things moving again."

Sam nodded, but did not say anything.

David continued, "Now I know you're the best sales rep we've got. At the same time, you have the best territory." He pulled out some papers and pushed them over to Sam. "I'm concerned when I look at these figures, showing that you haven't added any new accounts in over 2 years. We know some new firms opened up in your territory. Don't you think we're missing the boat here?" He looked squarely at Sam. "Have you even attempted to contact these new firms?"

Sam's face darkened. "Are you complaining about my sales?" he demanded harshly.

"Not a bit," David answered, "as far as your present customers are concerned. But I am troubled about not getting our share of the new business."

Sam snorted. "I'll be the judge of the best way to spend my time and sell in my territory. I've been doing it ever since you were a pup and will still be doing it after you leave. So get off my back, mister!"

QUESTIONS

1. How would you, as a newly appointed sales manager, handle this problem with a veteran sales representative?

2. Could the situation have been handled better? If so, how?

3. Can you criticize the way David conducted his first few weeks on the job?

CHAPTER 9
Assembling the Staff: Recruiting and Selecting

CHAPTER PERSPECTIVE

The last chapter discussed organizing the sales efforts. Chapter 9 is concerned with staffing and finding the *best* people for the job, which continually challenges managers. This chapter explores the intriguing difficulties in, and the tools for finding and hiring the best people. Although the chapter is oriented to the sales manager's perspective, much of the material is relevant to entering the job market and making the best impression on a potential employer.

A sales manager knows that sales candidates should be honest, aggressive, persevering, and self-confident. The trick is to identify those candidates who possess these traits in the right degree. Consider how you would determine whether and to what extent an applicant possesses these traits.

CHAPTER OBJECTIVES

☐ Know the major factors that determine a firm's particular requirements for its sales force.

☐ Identify personality characteristics that executives look for in the people they hire. (Trish)

☐ Understand the key relationship between recruiting and selecting.

☐ Become familiar with the recruiting sources and the factors that affect recruiting success.

☐ Know the procedures and tools used in selecting employees. (Joy)

☑ Understand the reliability and validity of these tools, and how they might be improved. (Gabie)

ROLE AND IMPORTANCE OF STAFFING

Staffing entails both recruiting and selecting. Although the importance of selecting good candidates for sales positions is obvious, the costs of selecting unwisely may be overlooked, especially by firms paying a straight commission (no sales, no pay). In addition to the costs of hiring and training, the sales revenue lost should also be considered a consequence of poor selection. For a firm to select wisely it must have a labor pool of qualified candidates to recruit.

Responsibility for Staffing

The field sales manager can recruit and select salespeople, or a regional sales office or centralized home office can administer the process. Each of these alternatives has advantages and disadvantages, although centralizing in the home office seems preferred and is more often the policy of large firms. Small firms tend to saddle field sales managers with staffing their own districts. Generally, the field sales manager has final approval if the regional or the home office performs staffing, thereby preserving the line executive's authority.

Arguments for decentralized staffing. Advocates of decentralizing or staffing in the field see this as improving the district sales force's adjustment to the local environment. Sales representatives coming from the community are likely to be better accepted by local customers. Furthermore, they do not have to make the personal adjustment of relocating when their attention should be concentrated on learning a new job. Selection procedures tend to be less elaborate, and less costly, when conducted in the field than when they are centralized in a home or regional office.

Arguments for centralized staffing. When staffing is centralized more expertise is available and more sources of candidates can be explored. The selection process tends to be more objective and this should produce a higher-caliber employee. Centralizing staffing also leads to more uniform quality, which is hard for individual sales managers to achieve, because some invariably are less capable of making good selections or have less qualified people to choose from, due to local employment conditions. A final argument for centralizing is that field sales managers are thereby relieved of a time-consuming task and freed for their major job of supervising sales generation.

DETERMINING SPECIFIC REQUIREMENTS FOR THE SALES FORCE

Desired Caliber of Salespeople

Before undertaking staffing several general decisions and policies must be established to ensure that people who are likely to be most compatible with the job requirements will be recruited, screened, and selected. Figure 9.1 shows various factors that will affect the desired caliber of sales personnel. Firms can make a mistake in hiring only the best candidates, when the job characteristics do not match the requirements for such high-caliber people. This can result in high turnover, as new salespeople become frustrated and dissatisfied with their jobs' lack of challenge and with rigidities. The best tend to leave for other positions offering better outlets for their talents.

If a sales job requires routine order filling and servicing accounts (which usually entails many sales calls per day), the caliber of person needed to fit this role is not very high. There are exceptions, of course, such as firms requiring this routine work for their management trainees. The management trainee's time spent in low-level selling jobs is finite and moderate, and compensation is at least comparable with that of higher-level sales jobs in other companies.

Turnover expected.   For many firms personnel turnover is a persistent problem, and management exerts considerable efforts to reduce it. The formula for personnel turnover follows:

$$\text{Turnover} = \frac{\text{Number of people hired during the period}}{\text{Average size of sales force during the period}}$$

Thus, a 50-percent turnover, which would be very high, would result if one hundred people were hired in a year, whereas the average size of the sales force was two hundred. A 50-percent turnover rate does not necessarily mean that half of the sales force was replaced during this period; perhaps only 50 to 75 positions had to be filled, but some of these had to be replaced twice.

Many factors affect turnover rate, such as compensation relative to similar firms, challenge of the job, empathetic supervision, and personnel quality.

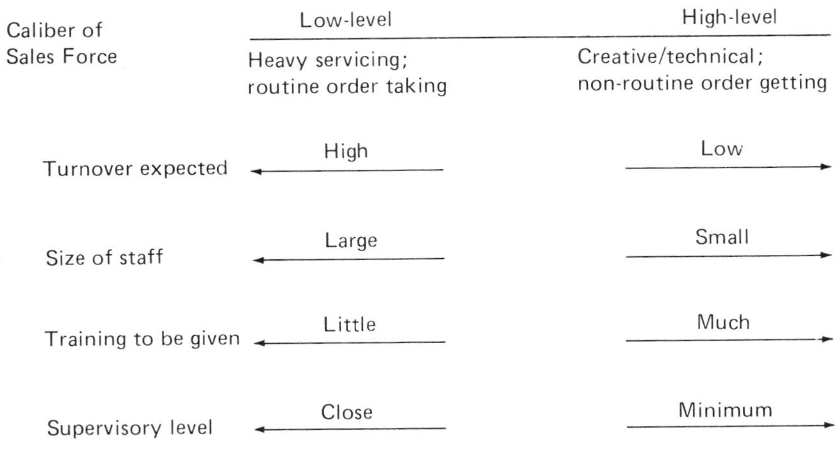

Caliber of Sales Force	Low-level Heavy servicing; routine order taking	High-level Creative/technical; non-routine order getting
Turnover expected	High ←	Low →
Size of staff	Large ←	Small →
Training to be given	Little ←	Much →
Supervisory level	Close ←	Minimum →

FIGURE 9.1   Factors affecting caliber of sales force needed.

For low-level sales jobs, the working conditions often are less attractive and lead to higher turnover than found in high-level sales jobs. A firm can reduce its turnover rate by upgrading the job, screening more carefully, tailoring supervision more closely to the requirements of the job, and hiring more older than younger salespeople, since the young are more likely to quit or to be discharged. The insurance industry in particular has a high turnover rate, with a yearly turnover of 1 million new agents.[1]

Some firms do not find high turnover to be a disadvantage. If minimal training is involved, if finding new candidates is not particularly costly, or if the firm's reputation is not likely to be endangered by less-than-effective selling efforts, then high turnover is not undesirable; it may, indeed, be an important component of the selection process as prospective salespeople are forced to prove themselves on the firing line or otherwise are quickly replaced. This is often the case with straight commission. For example this "cannon fodder" approach is not uncommon in encyclopedia sales. Some insurance and mutual fund firms also view actual sales production as the best way to single out the able; the ineffective do not particularly hurt the company and, in attempting to sell to relatives and friends, may contribute sales that might not have been achieved otherwise.

Training.   The extent of training depends on the job requirements. Selling highly technical products necessitates adequate training. Some life insurance and mutual fund selling, however, does not require extensive training, at least for short-term success; a firm may offer more intensive training only to those who pass the initial hurdle of making sales, whereas it allows the less effective to become discouraged and to quit or be fired.

Another training option is to hire only experienced salespeople. This policy, of course, usually requires paying higher compensation, but the training burden has been shifted to some other firm. The larger company usually prefers to hire novices at lower pay and train them extensively to its particular needs.

Level of supervision.   The closeness of supervision should reflect the capability of the sales force. A high-level sales force would feel restricted and annoyed by close supervision; low-level salespeople would need it to develop.

The desired sales force caliber not surprisingly will affect staffing policies and decisions. A high-caliber sales force requires more rigorous recruiting and selecting as well as more training (either by the firm itself or through prior experience with other firms); compensation, of course, will be higher per person. Turnover, however, should be lower, which should present less demands on staffing; less supervision will probably be needed and, consequently, the span of control could be wider, requiring fewer supervisory levels. Finally, a smaller sales staff might suffice if high-level people are used.

Job Analysis and Job Description

Specific requirements usually must be formulated about the sales force caliber. One should specify job's activities, travel, and technical level. The requirements for education, previous experience, or willingness to travel also should be known. The first step in determining specific requirements involves a job analysis, which leads to a job description.

Job analysis.   In a job analysis the duties, requirements, and conditions of the job are studied. Some businesses perform this analysis informally or almost effortlessly. But many large firms have a more formal and systematic approach to job analysis, not only for sales jobs but for all positions. The rationale is that more detailed specifications should permit a better matching of people to jobs.

The information needed for a job analysis can be gathered by surveys and observation. The researcher may question salespeople, sales managers, other company executives, and customers, seeking their opinions on major objectives and job requirements. The researcher may observe the execution of the job in addition to or in place of conducting a survey. A job analyst might accompany salespeople on their calls, observing and recording tasks as they are performed.

Job description.   The result of a formal job analysis is a job description of the characteristics, duties, and responsibilities of a specific position, as well as the qualifications necessary to fill it. Duties should include selling activities, obligations related to customer service, market research, and trade shows, and other responsibilities to the firm. Working conditions, such as required travel, should be clearly specified. Finally, the minimum qualifications, educational and professional, should be spelled out. Exhibit 9.1 presents a job description for a manufacturer's field sales representative selling electric blankets, bedspreads, and related products primarily to department store buyers.

EXHIBIT 9.1   Job Description: Field Sales Representative, Northern Products Company

General. The position reports to a district sales manager. The job entails selling our complete product line to retail accounts. These customers primarily will be retail buyers, merchandise managers, store managers, and department managers.

Specific Duties

Selling:

Make periodic sales calls on all customers according to Monthly Planning Guide.

Know the key people in each customer organization and maintain friendly relations with them.

EXHIBIT 9.1 *continued*

Be familiar with all the products in the line, as well as their relative profitabilities.

Keep abreast of new products in the line, new uses, as well as new styles soon to be introduced.

Be familiar with and able to explain to customers the company policy on price, delivery, credit, and adjustments.

Call on potential new customers when prospects are not directly competitive with present customers.

Be familiar with company advertising and other promotional programs to be able to inform customers of relevant programs.

Servicing Customers:

If permitted, check stock and displays for customers.

If permitted, write up fill-in orders and submit to customers for their approval.

Handle adjustments, returns, and allowances.

Handle special orders for customers.

Expedite deliveries, when necessary.

If permitted or requested, conduct training sessions for customers' salespeople.

Coordinate cooperative advertising and advertising allowances.

Managing territory:

Plan route for best coverage.

Establish a call schedule so that efforts devoted to particular customers are in relation to their potential volume.

Inform sales manager of special problems, changes in the territory regarding competition, new opportunities, and so forth.

Maintain daily call reports, to be turned in every Friday.

Maintain weekly expense report, to be turned in every Monday.

Submit itinerary for approval of sales manager 1 week in advance.

Maintain an adequate supply of samples, promotional materials, and price lists for distribution to customers.

Send copies of all correspondence to sales manager.

Miscellaneous:

Attend periodic sales meetings and conferences.

Conduct market surveys and assist in market testing if requested.

Report on faulty accounts if requested.

Investigate lost customers and reasons for loss.

Participate in sales volume and expense budget planning.

Participate in coaching and in-field training of new salespeople as requested.

Minimum qualifications:

College degree is preferred, but college work short of degree is acceptable, especially with relevant selling or retail experience.

Persons with selling or retail experience in home furnishings are preferred to those with no experience or with unrelated selling and retail experience.

Candidates must be willing to travel throughout the territory, which may necessitate being away from home during some weeks. Periodic travel to sales meetings and conventions is also required.

The description of the job's duties, responsibilities, working conditions, and required personal and professional qualifications is a valuable tool in the recruitment and selection process. Candidates who do not meet the minimum qualifications can be quickly screened and eliminated.

Should we hire technical or nontechnical salespeople?   When selling complex industrial products, a major controversy concerns determining the ideal background for sales representatives. Should technical experts (e.g., engineers and scientifically educated) be hired and trained to sell? Or should we hire salespeople with marketing and other nontechnical degrees and give them technical training?

In the past a "knee-jerk reaction" sent engineers to sell to engineers. For example in the chemical industry 10 years ago, 80 percent of sales representatives had degrees in technical fields.[2] This is changing because of significant drawbacks, but some sales managers still believe that only the technical undergraduate degrees are suitable. Following are the major pros and cons of technical versus nontechnical sales representatives:

Arguments for using technically trained salespeople:

- ☐ They have technical applications knowledge involving product application, installation, and maintenance.
- ☐ Technical expertise provides better service to customers.
- ☐ If product modifications or customizing must be made for buyers, the sales representative needs a fairly extensive technical knowledge.
- ☐ Technical firms, especially those on the leading edge of technology, use their sales force to provide the expert feedback and ideas pertaining to trends and possible technological innovation.
- ☐ Training nontechnical salespeople can be very expensive in certain industries and may be inordinately time-consuming.

Arguments for using nontechnical sales personnel:

- ☐ Technically educated people often view sales negatively and feel that their education is wasted in a sales position. Consequently, many are difficult to train and to motivate.
- ☐ Technical experts usually lack adequate business knowledge and human relations and communications skills.
- ☐ Salaries of technically trained personnel are up to 15 percent higher than nontechnical personnel, reflecting the higher engineering starting salaries overall.
- ☐ A high degree of technical knowhow is not essential for much industrial selling.

In certain industries requiring a high and frequent level of technical information exchange, the technically trained sales representative may be necessary. In most industries, however, after the initial contact and sale, subsequent orders require less frequent technical information exchange. Even when a complicated component part must be customized, a team approach to selling—in which the sales representative can call in a technical specialist when needed—may provide a better solution than hiring only engineers for sales.[3]

Personality Qualifications

Although the job description should specify qualifications such as education and experience, a firm (or the sales manager in charge of staffing) often will try to identify personality traits presumed to make better salespeople—traits such as self-confidence, stability, aggressiveness, and gregariousness. Many studies have tried to ascertain effective sales personalities but invariably have encountered difficulties.[4] The sales personality is complex, and specific key traits are virtually impossible to identify over a large number of salespeople. Further, the selection tools (most commonly the interview and various tests) cannot reliably determine the sufficient presence of a trait (e.g., self-confidence or aggressiveness). A widely quoted study by two industrial psychologists narrowed the personality traits needed by a successful salesperson to just two, as discussed in the box.

In later research, Greenberg and Greenberg found "job match" to be another key factor influencing success in a selling situation.[5] They defined

---

Personality Traits of a Good Salesperson

Mayer and Greenberg, after 7 years of field research to determine a better method of sales personnel selection, concluded that a good salesperson must have two basic qualities: empathy and ego drive. Empathy was defined as the ability to "feel as the other fellow does," although this does not necessarily mean being sympathetic, according to Mayer and Greenberg. Such empathetic feeling provides "powerful feedback" from the client, which enables the salesperson to adjust the selling message and make "whatever creative modifications might be necessary" to close the sale. Ego drive makes the salesperson want and need to make the sale "in a personal or ego way, not merely for the money to be gained." The sale then becomes a conquest and a powerful means of enhancing the ego. As a result of the two traits, the salesperson "has the drive, the need to make the sale, and his empathy gives him the connecting tool with which to do it."

Mayer and Greenberg discovered that salespeople with empathy but not a strong ego drive may find themselves becoming sympathetic and siding with the customer; they will tend to be less persuasive and poor at closing sales. Salespeople with strong drive but little empathy will tend to bulldoze their way through to close a sale but may repel many customers.

David Mayer and Herbert M. Greenberg, "What Makes a Good Salesman," *Harvard Business Review* (July–August 1964): 119–125.

job match as how well the salesperson's characteristics fit the functional requirements of the job, such as closeness of supervision, handling of detail work, and conceptual ability. Now answer the questions in Exercise 9.1, regarding the initial findings of Mayer and Greenberg:

---

1. Do you see any basic incompatibility in the two traits empathy and ego drive?
2. How would you use Mayer and Greenberg's research information in selecting sales personnel?

EXERCISE 9.1

What are the personality qualifications from the perspective of you, the candidate? What type of personality do sales managers typically look for in the people they hire? What traits should you endeavor to cultivate, or to emphasize, as you seek to enter sales? Table 9.1 lists in the order of importance the most desired qualifications determined from a survey of sales managers. Interestingly enough, enthusiasm received more than twice as many first-place votes as any other characteristic. Experience and recommendations ranked rather far down the list.

Federal Requirements for Nondiscriminatory Personnel Policies

A job description cannot include characteristics that reduce the possibility that minority persons and/or women might qualify unless these characteristics

TABLE 9.1   Sales executives' rankings of hiring qualifications.

Qualifications	Ranking
Enthusiasm	1
Well organized	2
Obvious ambition	3
High persuasiveness	4
General sales experience	5
High verbal skill	6
Specific sales experience	7
Highly recommended	8
Follows instructions	9
Apparent sociability	10

Source: Stan Moss, "What Sales Executives Look for in New Salespeople," *Sales & Marketing Management* (March 1978): 46–48.

are truly essential for the job under consideration. Care must be taken not to discriminate in the staffing procedure.

Federal laws and regulations impact on sales-force selection. *Title VII of the Civil Rights Act of 1964* prohibits discrimination because of race, color, religion, sex, or national origin in all employment practices. *The Equal Employment Opportunity Commission* (EEOC) was created to administer Title VII. In 1972 the EEOC's powers of enforcement were broadened. *The Age Discrimination in Employment Act of 1967* prescribes that an organization cannot discriminate in its hiring or termination practices because of a person's age. The Office of Federal Contract Compliance (OFCC) has jurisdiction over companies that have federal contracts, and any such company with fifty or more workers must submit a written affirmative action program to the OFCC. The *1974 Rehabilitation Act* brought physical handicaps under federal regulation.

These laws and their regulatory guidelines pertain to two employment concepts—nondiscrimination and affirmative action. *Nondiscrimination* requires elimination of all semblances of discrimination, whether based on sex, age, race, or whatever. Any discrimination, whether intentional or inadvertent, is prohibited. *Affirmative action* requires the employer to make *additional efforts* to recruit, employ, and promote qualified people formerly excluded.

These regulations require the firm to demonstrate that its recruiting and selection techniques are not discriminatory. A firm must exercise caution in using ability tests to measure eligibility unless specific evidence proves their validity and that they do not discriminate on the basis of race, color, religion, sex, or national origin. To be acceptable, test results, as well as certain interview answers must be correlated with job performance, which can be difficult to do.[6]

Largely because of federal pressure, the number of women and minority groups entering sales positions has increased markedly for both industrial goods manufacturers and consumer goods firms. With women the trend has also been spurred by increasingly aggressive equal rights groups. As a result, women are moving into sales jobs once held solely by men, such as for machines, factory equipment, and automobiles, as well as representing many consumer goods manufacturers to intermediaries. The change in recruiting and hiring practices is most evident in help wanted advertising, in which sex is seldom specified.

How successful is assimilation? Can women and minorities do the job adequately? Most sales organizations have been pleased with the results. In some instances minority and female salespeople have been more successful than white males.[7] Still, sex discrimination, sometimes inadvertent, can exist in a sales organization.[8] Older people have also proven highly successful in sales situations, and along with the minorities, they represent a large pool of sales talent. Two researchers commented:

Our experience shows that a man of 50 may have more openmindedness and youthful vigor than a man half his age; that women have the same ranges of business talents as men; that race has nothing to do with ability to sell.[9]

Number of Sales Representatives to Hire

Staffing should be planned well in advance to avoid crash hiring and for a systematic and effective procedure. Crash hiring usually results in hiring of "bodies" rather than carefully screening for the most desirable candidates. The future sales force needs should be estimated; the following formula may be used:

$$N = (T + R + P) \pm S \pm C$$

where N = number of additional salespeople needed for the coming period
T = expected turnover of salespeople
R = expected number of retirements
P = expected number of promotions
S = anticipated changes in marketing strategy that should affect the sales force
C = anticipated changes in sales

An example of S is a decision to achieve greater penetration of the Chicago market; such an intensive sales effort probably would necessitate more salespeople in this market. If the decision is to use more mass-media advertising, then perhaps less sales personnel would be needed. Anticipated sales changes would, of course, depend on the approved sales forecast. Expectations regarding salespeople leaving for one reason or another could be made based on past experience; number of promotions planned would encompass both past experience and projections; number of retirements could be specifically determined from employment records.

Using the preceding formula, assume that a company can reasonably expect to lose twelve salespeople through attrition and firings. Four people are ready for retirement. Anticipated promotional openings should involve about eight people. Sales are expected to increase sufficiently that three extra salespeople may be needed. Countering this, however, a change in marketing strategy is planned, with a greater concentration on mass-media advertising, so that some markets are estimated to need less salespeople, for a total of five less. The formula would then give us:

$$N = (12 + 4 + 8) + 3 - 5$$
$$N = 22 \text{ additional salespeople to be hired}$$

In planning for the number of positions to be filled, some constraints may have to be considered. Training facilities can limit the trainee number in any given period (unless the firm decides to eliminate the customary training period until after the new sales recruits have gained some experience in the field). Furthermore, the number of additional people who can be supervised effectively without increasing the number of sales managers and thus incurring additional costs is limited; this is a consideration if the total sales force size is increased well beyond its present levels.

Unless the sales force is paid on a straight commission (no sales, no compensation), increasing its size will increase fixed costs. The firm, therefore, must decide whether increasing fixed costs will generate sufficient additional sales. Unfortunately, most firms do not have a great deal of hard data for making such a decision. Past experience can provide some help, but conditions change, competition may be tougher or react quicker, or environmental factors may restrain greater market penetration.

Mathematical models have been developed to aid in determining the optimum number of salespeople. Unfortunately, despite their sophistication these models have not been very successful, primarily because predicting the sales volume response to changes in the sales force size is difficult.[10]

RECRUITING

Effective selection depends on effective recruiting.

> It is impossible for an organization to be highly selective and to demand the highest caliber hirees *unless* it has a sizable body of candidates to choose from.

Without good recruiting, which produces numerous potential hirees, a firm cannot be selective; it must pick from perhaps only a few marginal people and be happy to fill slots. Recruiting is crucial to the total hiring process.

Factors that affect the effectiveness of recruiting can broadly be categorized as external and internal factors. Figure 9.2 diagrams the major factors that affect recruiting—either by enhancing or complicating the search for potential job candidates. The following paragraphs elaborate on the various inputs of recruiting effectiveness shown in Figure 9.2.

If a firm faces a tight labor market (which is usually the case during economic booms) or wartime (when jobs are plentiful but applicants scarce), then a firm will find fewer good candidates. During a recession or business downturn, ten or fifteen applicants may be available for every opening. Sometimes a community experiences unusually tight or slack employment conditions, depending on local industries or perhaps governmental installations that compete for a limited labor pool. Conversely, a depression of a major local industry, such as steel, may cause an extremely high unemployment. Unfortunately, in this latter situation, many of the unemployed do not have readily transferable skills.

Internal factors affecting recruiting involve the firm's reputation and its growth prospects. As shown in Figure 9.2, a number of factors contribute to

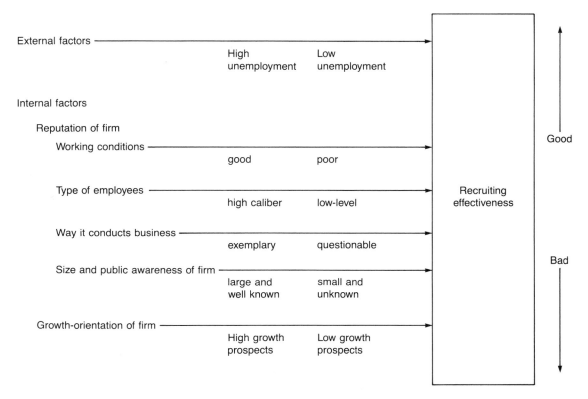

FIGURE 9.2   Major factors affecting recruiting effectiveness.

the firm's reputation. A main contributing factor consists of working conditions, such as fair pay, employee benefits, and supervision caliber (i.e., whether supervision generally is perceived as harsh or empathetic). Reputation also is affected by the type of employees whether they are high caliber or low level. But reputation also is affected by the firm's business conduct. The dependability, quality, and prices of its products and service policies and its adherance to the prevailing business standards of fairness in employment policies, pollution control, and customer and community orientation all affect a firm's reputation. Not only are a firm's sales likely to be adversely affected by a bad or deteriorating reputation but a dearth of good job applicants likely will result.

A large and prestigious company (unless it has permitted its reputation to erode) usually has the advantage over smaller, unknown firms in selecting a work force. An IBM or a Xerox easily attracts numerous highly qualified applicants; but Joe's Electronic Company might be hard pressed to find anyone even marginally qualified. A growth-oriented company that has made spectacular progress in recent years is in an enviable position to attract able people who see great personal advancement opportunities. A firm that is not growth minded, that is more content with the status quo (as characterizes some small- and medium-sized family businesses), has a difficult time attracting good sales and executive candidates.

Sources of Salespeople

Effective staffing depends on having an adequate pool of qualified candidates to select the most able. Effective recruiting is instrumental in providing this pool, although as noted, recruiting is affected by the company's reputation, the state of the economy, and alternative employment opportunities. Recruiting can use a wide variety of sources. A firm may be reluctant to expand the search to other available sources because of the proven effectiveness of those already in use compared with the unknown results with the new source. Using more than one source, however, provides several advantages to the firm that expects to fill a number of positions each year. A wider mix of salespeople—experienced and new, older and younger, from the same industry and from other job experiences—can provide fresh perspectives and can better appeal to heterogeneous customers. Furthermore, during tight labor markets, familiarity with a variety of personnel sources is more likely to produce a pool sufficiently large to select capable employees.

The most widely used sources of salespeople follow:

- ☐ The company's own ranks
- ☐ Competitors
- ☐ Noncompeting companies or organizations
- ☐ Advertisements
- ☐ Schools and colleges
- ☐ Employment agencies
- ☐ "Walk-in" applicants
- ☐ Miscellaneous

The company's own ranks. A firm's present employees provide two sources of salespeople. First, present employees may wish to be candidates for specific sales jobs, or second, they may recommend friends and acquaintances for such positions, and generally, employees are a good source. Employees' job histories are readily available and can help in assessing both their ability and potential. Furthermore, they already are familiar with the firm and probably are loyal to it. Their recommendations of other people can provide an effective screening, because an employee is vouching for these candidates and has probably presold the company to the applicant.

Competitors. A major advantage of obtaining salespeople from competitors is that these people are already trained, are experienced, and should be ready to sell almost immediately. They may even be able to transfer some of their present customers to their new firm. However, many sales managers face nagging questions about loyalty and compatibility with the new organization and management. These doubts boil down to one question: Why does this salesman want to leave his present employer? A satisfactory answer may lead to a valuable new employee. Most firms are careful, however, to avoid the appearance of "pirating" another's employees for fear of retaliation.

Noncompeting companies. Noncompeting firms can provide a good source of trained and experienced salespeople, although these applicants may be unfamiliar with the particular industry and its products. Not uncommonly a salesperson winds up in a dead-end job and desperately wants to leave. Such a candidate's motivation to succeed in a new job may be very high. Of course, those with histories of brief employment with multiple firms must be viewed with caution. Customers' staff can be a source of knowledgeable candidates. Care must be taken, however, to clear overtures with the customer, to avoid jeopardizing good relations.

Advertisements. Classified advertisements in local newspapers and in trade journals constitute a source that sales managers both praise and condemn. Classified ads reach a large audience, which can beseige a firm with applicants, most of whom are second-rate. Furthermore, these ads seldom attract the top candidates, who often can make judicious moves through personal contacts. Local newspaper advertising is a good source in recruiting for low-level sales positions. The national newspapers, such as the *Wall Street Journal,* and the various industry trade journals, such as *Women's Wear Daily,* are used in recruiting for high-level sales and sales management positions. The ad should well describe job qualifications to reduce the likelihood of attracting many unsuitables.

Schools and colleges. Many large firms look to educational institutions for high-level candidates. Although most graduates lack specific sales experience, they have the education and perspective that employers seek, not solely for sales positions, but as potential managers. Smaller firms are less likely to recruit on campus and tend to be less successful when they do, because many graduates prefer large, well-known companies with definitive training programs and benefits. In the past, college students have not always viewed selling favorably;[11] insurance companies in particular have had difficulty in campus recruiting. Attitudes have changed radically, however, as college seniors now realize that selling not only is the entry for higher management positions but is a very lucrative field.

Employment agencies.   Experience with employment agencies varies widely. Some firms consider them only as a last-ditch source of candidates. Yet, agencies can perform a highly useful service by screening candidates so that a firm need spend time only with the most highly qualified. Unfortunately, some agencies lack the ability or the resources to produce eligible candidates. Sometimes the fault lies with the firm in not communicating sufficient information about specific needs and job requirements.

Walk-in applicants.   Some sales managers view walk-ins and write-ins favorably, as aggressive and self-reliant individuals. The best action is to eliminate the obviously unqualified from further consideration, but to evaluate the apparently qualified along with eligible candidates from other sources. The biggest drawback in relying on voluntary applicants as an important recruiting source is that this source tends to dry up in tight labor markets and to be more productive when a surfeit of candidates already exists.

Miscellaneous sources.   The few other occasionally worthwhile recruiting sources include sales executives' clubs, chambers of commerce, and service clubs such as Kiwanis and Rotary. These can help by providing a sales manager with personal contacts who either are interested themselves or know of others who might be.

Conclusions on sources for recruiting.   A sales manager (or a company personnel department, if staffing is centralized) should analyze the success of the company's various recruiting sources. Performance measures (e.g., stability on the job, sales productivity, and promotions) of present and past employees should be correlated with the recruiting sources. Employment agencies generally may not have provided very good employees, but voluntary applicants during times of high unemployment may have been a good source of eligible candidates and effective employees. One firm may find that college recruiting provides the best people; another firm, which has lower-level sales positions, may find that this source produces unstable and short-tenure people. A correlation analysis of sources can be readily performed by computer, even for a large organization with many employees, provided that the recruitment sources were noted in each employee's records. Table 9.2 shows one firm's source analysis results.

The source analysis data will enable a firm to better assign priorities to its sources of salespeople, using the better sources when the labor pool is large and falling back to the second- and third-rate sources when the economy experiences full employment and applicants are fewer.[12] Those involved in the staffing process should recognize, however, that a top-notch candidate can come from any source. One should not be so biased against certain sources as to disregard all prospects from them. For example, even though a firm has not had good experience with people recommended by employment agencies,

TABLE 9.2   Source analysis of salespeople recruited by a castings manufacturer, 1980 to 1987.

Source	Number of Hires	Number of Successful Hires	Percentage of Success
Salespeople from noncompeting firms	17	12	71
Customers' employees	10	8	80
Recommendations by own salespeople	8	6	75
Employment agencies	7	2	29
Unsolicited applications	4	2	50
Competitors' salespeople	3	1	33
Local college recruitment	2	1	50
Total	51	32	63

and may consider such applicants marginal because they could not find a job through other means, this does not preclude the possibility of a highly qualified, strongly motivated person seeking employment in this way.[13]

SELECTION OF THE SALES FORCE

With recruitment hopefully providing a pool of candidates for job consideration, the challenge remains to select the most capable and successful. The selection process should involve initial screening to eliminate the educationally, experientially, and psychologically unsuitable or unqualified from further consideration and further expenditure of company time. Initial screening (even of job candidates already prescreened by employment agencies) can be assigned to staff assistants, with line management involved only in the final hiring decisions among the best qualified.

Procedures and Tools for Selecting

In the intriguing but difficult search for tools to improve the hiring decision, to increase the chances of selecting the most able future employees, a wide range of procedures and techniques are be found. No tool or procedure guarantees the perfect hiring decision. However, the search continues, and the stakes are higher than many executives realize. For example consider the savings from reduced employee turnover.

A conservative estimate of the average firm's losses for each salesperson terminated or departing could well be $25,000 in salary, recruiting costs, training programs, management time, and lost sales. If one hundred persons a year are hired, and twenty of these do not make it and leave in their first year, the total cost is $500,000. Now if through better selection techniques this turnover could be reduced from 20 percent to 15 percent, the firm would save $125,000 (5 × $25,000). Therefore, the payoff from improving the selection procedure can be quite substantial. Many testing services use this argument. If the costs of testing individual candidates are $200 each, and if in testing 300 candidates the costs of $60,000 could be offset by the savings in reduced turnover of $125,000, then testing indeed is a wise expenditure. Of course, in this scenario, the reduced employee turnover caused by testing would need confirmation by the firm's experience.

The steps involved in the selection process vary, usually depending on the company size, the number of prospects, and the importance of the job. The sales manager of a small company looking for a sales representative for a new territory may simply travel to that area and work out of a hotel room, interviewing the available candidates and making the decision at the end of the day or even without talking to all the applicants. Most firms, however, find the most effective selection will result from the following sequence (with perhaps some modification, such as a medical examination and/or a series of interviews, even including one with the applicant's spouse):

1. Preliminary screening interview and/or short application form
2. Formal application form
3. References check
4. Tests
5. Selection interview(s) by line executives

Figure 9.3 shows a model of the typical sequential selection process. Note in particular the elimination variables uncovered in each phase of this selection process.

Preliminary Screening

If a firm has a large number of applicants either for particular advertised positions or as walk-ins and if the caliber of such applicants varies widely, then preliminary screening is particularly important. Obviously, the more steps a candidate completes in the selection process, the more costly it is to the company and the more executive and staff time involved. Consequently, most firms want to eliminate unqualified applicants promptly from further consideration. Preliminary screening is best left to a staff member or subordinate so that more valuable executive time is not involved. Required standards and qualifications should, of course, be well communicated to the people doing the screening. Qualification requirements might include educational levels, type and years of work experience, satisfactory appearance, and so on.

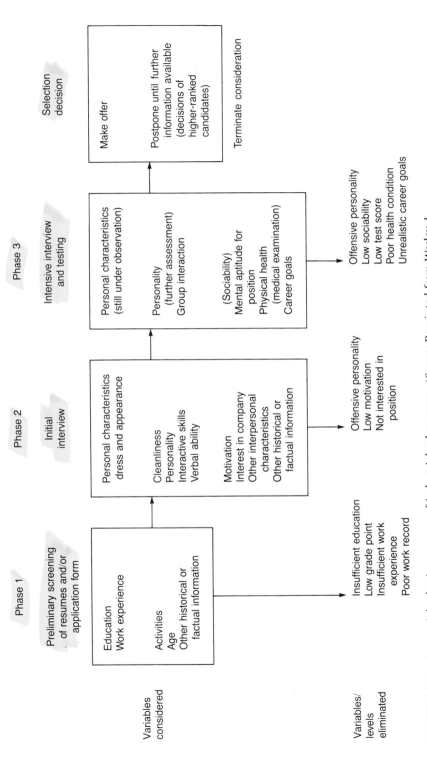

FIGURE 9.3 Sequential selection process of industrial salesperson. (*Source:* Reprinted from Wesley J. Johnston and Martha C. Cooper, "Industrial Sales Forces Selection: Current Knowledge and Needed Research," *Journal of Personal Selling and Sales Management,* Spring–Summer 1981: 50.)

The Equal Employment Opportunity Commission limits the type of questions that can be asked of prospective employees either on application forms or in the interview. Questions related directly to race, color, sex, religion, age, or national origin are taboo. Applicants must not be asked about their religious beliefs or whether the company's workweek would interfere with their religious convictions; applicants may be asked if they are U.S. citizens but not whether they or their parents or spouse are naturalized citizens or native-born Americans; applicants may be asked whether they are minors or age 70 or over but not their age or date of birth. Furthermore, questions such as the following may also be considered inappropriate and discriminatory, whether used in interviews or on application forms:

> *Marital status:* Are you married? Single? Divorced? Engaged?
>
> *Children:* Do you have children at home? How old? Who cares for them? Do you plan to have more children?
>
> *Military status:* What type of discharge do you have? What branch of service?
>
> *Housing:* Do you own your home? Do you rent? Do you live in an apartment or a house?[14]

Formal Application Form

Candidates passing the preliminary screening usually are required to complete a formal application blank. Although the candidate may have submitted a resume, most firms also want their form to be completed for standardization purposes. The application form becomes part of the employee's permanent record, if he is hired. Among the items of information needed for selection decisions are the following:

- ☐ Present employer—type of job, territory, specific sales experience
- ☐ Education
- ☐ Previous positions—time spent with each employer, reason for leaving, record of earnings
- ☐ Personal indebtedness
- ☐ Membership in organizations
- ☐ References

More qualitative questions may also be asked, such as:

- ☐ Have you any geographical preferences?
- ☐ Have you set a goal for yourself to reach in the next 5 years?
- ☐ How did you happen to apply for a position here?

☐ Which of your assets do you feel would be most valuable in any association you might make with us?

Employers increasingly are encountering problems with exaggerated and misrepresented credentials. Common ploys of dishonest job seekers are claiming attendance at a prestigious university when only a noncredit, nongrade workshop was attended and shifting dates to hide periods of unemployment or to expand the length of relevant past experience. For more sensitive and more responsible positions, a firm may be hired to confirm application information.[15]

In addition to providing specific information to weed out the unqualified, the formal application blank provides material that can be followed up later in the interview. (Coordinating the interview with the application form is discussed later in this chapter.) Moreover, some firms have found that certain items on their applications are good predictors of success and failure on the job, based on the firm's experience with its own employees; this is called a scored or weighted application blank. It can be a rather effective selection device that may serve you well as you move up to major hiring responsibilities.

Using a weighted application blank to improve selection. The weighted application blank (WAB) is developed from the regular application form by analyzing the items to determine which answers differ between good and poor salespeople. Usually, some of these items (e.g., educational level, tenure in previous jobs, personal indebtedness, years of selling experience, and previous occupations) are found to be more related to success (as measured by higher sales, longer tenure, less absenteeism, and level of compensation) and are given more weight than less discriminating items. A total score of the weighted items is then determined. Answers of new applicants can then be scored for the discriminating items according to the assigned weights, and those candidates with totals above a predetermined cutoff point would continue in the selection process. Application 9.1 should clarify the procedure in developing a WAB.

APPLICATION 9.1   Developing a Weighted Application Blank

A sample is taken of about 100 to 200 present and recent employees. (This restricts the effective use of the WAB to large sales forces.) Half of these are desirable employees and half are undesirable—in retrospect, the latter should not have been hired. The application blank items are then analyzed to determine those that differentiate between the two groups. Any such differences should be readily apparent, and they are weighted according to their importance in distinguishing the groups.

Figure 9.4 shows a sample work sheet for developing weights for two differentiating personal history items: years of selling experience and educational level. The

APPLICATION 9.1 *continued*

Response category	Number of employees		Assigned weights
	High-performance group	Low-performance group	
Years of previous selling experience			
Less than 1 year	卌	卌 卌 卌 /	−2
1 to 5 years	卌 卌	卌 卌 卌	−1
5 to 10 years	卌 卌	卌 ///	0
Over 10 years	卌 卌 卌 卌 卌 /	卌 卌 /	+1
Educational level			
High school	卌 卌 ///	卌 卌 卌 卌 ////	−1
Some college	卌 卌 卌 卌 卌	卌 卌 卌 卌 /	0
College degree	卌 ///	///	+2
Graduate school	///	//	0

FIGURE 9.4 Work sheet for deriving weights for two items of the application blank.

work sheet shows that tabulating the personal history items (taken from the original application blanks) of the high-performance and the low-performance groups demonstrates a relationship between job success and number of previous years of selling experience. Only five of the successful salespeople had less than 1 year of selling experience, while sixteen of the unsuccessful did. A weight of − 2 accordingly was assigned this category, because it was highly differentiating. One to five years' selling experience was less discriminating between the high and low performers and was assigned a − 1 weight. Over 10 years' experience correlates with the successful group and is weighted + 1. The procedure and rationale is similar for analyzing the educational level (see Figure 9.4) and also for analyzing the other personal history items on the application blank.

  Figure 9.5 shows a work sheet for determining an optimum cutting score. In the example given the greatest percentage difference between the total scores of successful and unsuccessful salespeople occurs at the total score of 6, which is a difference of 44 percent. If applicants are accepted only when the total score of their applications is 6 or higher, then 72 percent of the desirables would be hired and only 28 percent of the undesirables. At any other cutting score, the difference between the two groups would not be as great; in other words there would be more overlap. If the cutting score is raised to 7, then 64 percent of the better people would be hired (with 36 percent eliminated), while 24 percent of the poorer performers would still be accepted.

Total score	Number of employees at given scores				Percentage (cumulative)		
	High-performance		Low-performance				
	Number	Cumulative	Number	Cumulative	High	Low	Difference
10 and above	卌 卌 //	12	0	0	24%	0%	24%
9	卌 /	18	//	2	36	4	32
8	卌 卌	28	卌 /	8	56	16	40
7	////	32	////	12	64	24	40
6	////	36	//	14	72	28	44
Optimum cutting score							
5	卌 /	42	卌 ///	22	84	44	40
4	卌 /	48	卌 /	28	96	56	40
3	//	50	卌 /	34	100	68	32
2	0	50	////	38	100	76	24
1	0	50	////	42	100	84	16
0 or minus	0	50	卌 ///	50	100	100	0

FIGURE 9.5 Work sheet for determining point of greatest differentiation between high- and low-performance groups.

When applicants are plentiful and the employer can afford to be highly selective, the cutting score can be adjusted upward, even if a considerable number of potentially good people must be eliminated because their scores were not acceptable. The score can be adjusted downward in tight labor markets when the employer must accept greater risk of marginal people. To summarize the use of the cutting score: New applicants need to score higher than the established minimum, based on their own personal history characteristics, to be considered further in the selection process. Although a person with a low score on the WAB could prove to be successful, the risks are greater than with those who score high, based on empirical validation with present employees.

Two cautions apply to effectively using the WAB. First, the WAB should be specifically validated for the firm or sales division, and second, it should be reevaluated periodically (preferably every 2 years) to ensure that it is achieving desired results. Now check your understanding of the WAB concept by completing Exercise 9.2.

EXERCISE 9.2

1. What rationale can you offer for personal history items being so predictive of later job performance?
2. What strong arguments can you give for reevaluating the WAB every few years?
3. What arguments would you give for lowering the cutting score in Figure 9.5 to 3? For raising it to 10?

References Check

References often are checked routinely when the application is processed (with the WAB, only if the person has an acceptable score) and before the final interview(s) by line executives; less often, they are checked as the last formality of the selection process. Checking the names supplied by a candidate often is seen as a waste of time, because it is unlikely that serious problems will be uncovered. More is gained by talking with teachers and former employers. The former employers should be asked why the person left and how well he or she got along. The question "Would you hire him again if you had the chance?" tends to elicit more forthright responses.

Although reference checking often does not yield meaningful information about a person's abilities and character, because most persons supplied as references are reluctant to be derogatory, it will confirm factual information about positions, compensation, and dates. Reference checking should not be neglected, because the few falsehoods that may be detected can alert a firm to more serious discrepancies and dishonesties that might result if the person is hired. In the past, credit reference checks were used to provide information about a person's character, scrupulousness, and financial prudence. However, privacy laws have limited the access of third parties to credit information, and credit checks may be used only if credit worthiness is directly related to job requirements, such as if bonding is necessary.

The question of whether reference checking should be done by letter, phone, or personal interview is not easily answered. Personal interviews with references and employers usually is preferred but often is not feasible, especially if out-of-town firms and people are involved. Many employers and teachers refrain from written criticisms. A lukewarm written response may be worthy of a follow-up phone call. Some persons, however, are reluctant to give critical information over the phone to a stranger.

When a candidate is presently employed and wishes these job overtures to be entirely confidential, little will be gained by violating his confidence. Information from previous employers may then have to be relied on more heavily. Sometimes the hiring firm's clients or customers may be a source of information about a candidate.

When checking references, the potential employer should be aware that a person's mediocrity, or even failure, in one job should not permanently label him. Perhaps the fault for the poor showing was the employer's and not the employee's. Or perhaps a powerful learning experience emerged from the situation that improved the person's motivation and effectiveness. An individual's future need not forever duplicate the past.

Tests

Testing is the most controversial selection tool. No one can dispute the need for application blanks, reference checks, and personal interviews (although their predictive abilities are not always as certain as needed); differences of opinion exist about the necessity of tests in hiring, especially for salespeople. Tests are costly to administer and process, ranging from $150 upward per candidate in most instances. But testing services have grown rapidly as firms seek a more objective selection process. Tests obviously are objective, precluding the subjectivity or intuitive hunches that often occur in the personal interview. However, tests are not a panacea.

Reliability and validity.   The selection tool's effectiveness must be considered with regard to reliability and validity. *Reliability* refers to the consistency of the instrument's findings. A test is reliable if a person would achieve about the same score if he were to take the test again under similar conditions. An interview procedure is reliable if different interviewers make the same judgment about the same candidate. *Validity* pertains to how well the instrument actually measures what it is supposed to measure. If success on the job is what is being predicted, then the test is valid if certain scores correlate with job success. Can a selection instrument be reliable but not valid or vice versa? No instrument can be valid if it is not reliable, because without consistent judgments or predictions, no correlation with job success is possible. However, an instrument may be consistent (reliable) but may not accurately predict job success.

Our two main selection tools therefore have the following problems. The personal interview situation usually lacks reliability (i.e., different interviewers often form different judgments about the same individual). Tests usually do not lack reliability (i.e., the same individual will usually score about the same if the test is repeated in a short time). But tests, although reliable, seldom are nearly as valid as one would like, unless they are specifically validated on present and past employees with certain answers and scores differentiating between good and poor performers (much as described with the WAB). Both of our main selection instruments are flawed, which we will explore in the balance of this chapter as we seek to improve the selection process.

Types of tests.   Five basic types of tests are used in selection. Each is described in the following paragraphs. And the efficacy of testing is critically examined.

Measuring mental ability with intelligence tests.   Some of the most popular tests used in selection are those that purportedly measure raw intelligence and trainability. The Otis Self-Administering Test of Mental Ability and the Wonderlic Personnel Test are the most widely used, although a number of other alternatives are available. Three major criticisms can be leveled at these tests, at least in their use for selecting salespeople. First, they discriminate against certain ethnic and racial backgrounds. About 20 percent of the complaints filed under Title VII of the Civil Rights Act have claimed that such tests constituted unfair discrimination against members of minority groups.[16] Because these tests fail to account for different cultural backgrounds, they may underestimate the real ability of disadvantaged minority members, unless the predictability of these tests are validated separately for white applicants and for blacks and other minority groups. Second, although these tests purport to measure usage and comprehension of language and abstract reasoning or problem-solving ability, they do not measure creativity. In many selling situations creativity is essential. Third, these tests may not be needed. If a firm is hiring college graduates, is not a diploma sufficient evidence of satisfactory intelligence? If high school dropouts are the recruiting main source, intelligence tests may be justified to weed out the obviously incompetent; one can still question, however, whether such incompetency would not more easily be detected through the application blank and the personal interview rather than a costly test.

Mechanical aptitude tests.   These tests have little relevance to selling except perhaps in a few cases involving industrial goods. Even then the need for mechanical aptitude to sell effectively can be questioned.

Vocational interest tests.   Interest tests commonly are used in the selection process. These tests assume that a person will be more effective and stable if he evinces a strong interest in that type of work. The two most widely used tests are the Strong Vocational Interest Test and the Kuder Personal Preference Inventory. Although these tests are useful in vocational counseling, they are less so in hiring because of their susceptibility to faking. A man applying for a sales job would be naive indeed if he did not respond that he would prefer spending an evening in a social gathering to remaining quietly at home reading a book. (The first preference, of course, suggests the sociability and extroverted interest that some believe is compatible with selling, whereas the latter hints at an underlying introversion and shyness, which does not match the general notion of the effective salesperson.)

Sales aptitude and social intelligence tests.   A person's innate or acquired social skills and selling savvy can be tested. Some of these tests pose selling situations in which the candidate must select the most effective alternative of the several presented.[17] Other tests attempt to measure tact and diplomacy. But their value is also questionable. Some of the "correct" answers in the sales situation tests are highly debatable; other answers and tests really constitute an examination of basic sales skills. Here a deficiency in an inexperienced candidate should be easily corrected either by a company training program or by study of one of the many books on this topic.

Personality tests.   Certain psychological tests attempt to measure the behavioral traits believed necessary for success in selling, such as aggressiveness, initiative, and extroversion.[18] The most commonly used tests of this kind (e.g., the Minnesota Multiphasic Personality Inventory, the Bernreuter Personality Inventory, and the Edwards Personal Preference Schedule) were originally designed to identify people with personality problems and even psychotic tendencies. One can question whether these same tools can satisfactorily measure normal behavior and inclinations. However, the major criticisms of such personality tests are that they too can be faked easily; their validity is highly questionable, and they eliminate too few candidates.

Conclusions about testing.   Despite testing's popularity and wide acceptance in many organizations, it is an expensive and usually ineffective method to select from a pool of candidates who are reasonably well qualified educationally and experientially. The advantage of testing in the employment procedure is that it is useful in detecting the small number of obvious misfits. But these individuals should have been detected in the initial screening, where tests are seldom used because of their cost. Firms therefore should evaluate their testing program and assess the slight gains in terms of the expense.[19] Such an evaluation is especially desirable today, as charges of job discrimination are commonplace. Only if a firm can prove that its tests are valid and highly predictive of job success is it likely to be safe from charges of unfairness.

As noted earlier in this section, test validation must be conducted separately for minority group members.

Selection Interviews

Decades ago one expert described the interview as the "most used and least scientific" of the various tools for selecting employees.[20] Particularly in the selection of salespeople, one interview—and more often, three or four—almost universally is conducted of the most desirable candidates. It is widely thought that top candidates should be able to sell themselves to be effective. The ability to express oneself, tact, confidence, poise, and even aggressiveness are believed to be readily ascertained through an interview. In the final interview situation with highly qualified candidates, the interviewer must "sell" the company or at least define the job's duties, the benefits, and the salary range and must answer any questions or doubts that the candidates might have.

Types of interviews.   To improve this selection tool several types of interviews have evolved. All have strengths and weaknesses; again, none is the panacea that has been sought for decades.

Patterned interview.   A guided or patterned interview is highly structured. Questions are predetermined, and each person interviewed is asked the same questions in the same sequence. With such a standardized format, the job of the interviewers becomes easier, uniform interviews are ensured, and a better comparison of candidates interviewed by different people should be possible. However, such patterned interviews permit no flexibility for differences in candidates and thwart any probing that might uncover unique abilities or weaknesses.

Nondirective interview.   At the other extreme is the nondirective interview, in which candidates are encouraged to do most of the talking, to speak freely about themselves, their interests, their accomplishments, and so forth. Although nondirective interviews can elicit information about a candidate's fluency, poise, and confidence, much time may be spent dealing with irrelevancies. This type of interview is widely used in psychology and requires more interviewing skill than a patterned interview. Different interviewers may have markedly different opinions about the same candidate in nondirective interviews. A combination of the patterned and nondirective interview is more popular and perhaps more effective than either extreme. In the combined form a set of questions is prescribed for all interviewers, but time is left for open-ended and probing questions at the interviewer's discretion.

Stress interview.   Some firms use a stress interview that puts candidates under severe emotional strain to observe their reactions. In theory this interview simulates the stresses that might be encountered in selling. But its effectiveness in evaluating candidates is contradictory. And one can question whether a severely stressful interviewing situation simulates on-the-job stress. The selling stress is probably far less than that of trying to land the job, and the person brings more experience in coping with selling.

Group interview.   An interview may be conducted before a group or board. Such interviews are more common in governmental hiring than in corporate sales interviewing, but for certain types of selling that involve group presentations, group interviews can be relevant in identifying those candidates with more innate skill in conducting themselves effectively before a group. However, a caution should be noted here: Effective presenting before a group is usually a learned skill. A candidate who may not be particularly strong in this interview may soon be able to develop the skills to be highly effective in presentations before groups.

Common failings of the interview interaction.   Judgments from the interaction between the interviewer and the interviewee are subjective and therefore can be distorted and inaccurate. Sometimes rather minor things can influence this judgment, and following are the more common problems in the interview interaction:

1. Wording of questions. Questions may be ambiguous, suggestive, or stated poorly, so that mutual understanding is difficult.

2. Halo effect. This is the tendency to judge the total worth of a person on the basis of a specific trait.

3. Stereotypes. The interviewer may ascribe certain traits to a person on the basis of his appearance (such as red hair denoting a fiery temper), or nationality, or age, or sex.

4. Personal bias of the interviewer. The interviewer may tend to make a decision about the candidate based on some personal mannerism or characteristic. Personal traits that are objectionable to many interviewers follow:

Interrupting

Talking with cigarette in mouth

Biting fingernails

Using the word "I" continuously

Playing with articles on person

Chewing and snapping gum

Being jittery or fidgety

Talking nonstop

Wearing loud clothing

Avoiding looking interviewer in the eye

Tapping fingers or feet

5. Lack of rapport. This interview problem is not limited to the inexperienced or the young. The interview tends to be a stressful situation, and if the interviewer is not able to establish a friendly relationship with the applicant, the interaction can be strained and communication poor. Differences in rapport can account for interviewers' coming to different conclusions about the same candidate. Some sales managers argue that the sales personality should not suffer from poor rapport during the interview. To some extent the job interview is similar to a sales presentation to customers, but there are differences. Sales presentations can be practiced; confidence increases with product knowledge; and the experience of repeated sales calls should reduce tension far more than is possible in isolated and crucial job interviews.

Now complete Exercise 9.3.

EXERCISE 9.3
1. As an interviewer, how would you attempt to put a nervous candidate at ease?
2. How would you evaluate a person who avoids eye contact? What objectionable personal traits would tend to bias your judgment?

The art of interviewing. Excluding the highly structured, patterned interview, which allows no deviation in wording or sequence of predetermined questions, the interviewing process lends itself to a good deal of art, and some interviewers are highly skilled. Certain questions can reveal a great deal about innate abilities and drives. Yet the inexperienced candidate may have difficulty answering when first encountering these probing questions. How would you answer the following questions so as to put yourself in the best light?

- ☐ How would you describe yourself?
- ☐ What is your greatest weakness? Your greatest strength?
- ☐ What are your career goals?
- ☐ How do you define success?
- ☐ Why do you think you are qualified to work for this company?
- ☐ What have you done that shows initiative?

One consultant advises sales managers to "get behind the candidate's facade," and focus interview questions to elicit proof of candidates' knowledge, skills, and personal attributes. For example, if organizational ability is a prime job requirement, the manager might ask, "Was yesterday a fairly typical day?" Given an affirmative response, the manager might probe for detailed evidence: "Then please describe your day for me. When did you begin? When did you end? Where and how did you spend your time? The consultant further advises: Insist on specific examples of past successes. Without them, critical job dimensions may be impossible to evaluate. When the candidate's response is vague or incomplete, additional probing with evidence-seeking questions elicits specific, measurable proof of performance.[21] Wise interviewers also probe deeper into some of the answers given on the application.

Coordinating the interview and application.   Used alone the interview often fails to predict job success as effectively as sales managers would wish. Used with the other selection tools, the interview's value improves. In particular it should be closely coordinated with the application blank. By carefully reviewing the completed application form before the interview, the sales manager can test and resolve certain hypotheses and possible negative factors. For example:

Response on Application	*Possible Negative Factor to Be Resolved in Interview*
Four jobs in 6-year period	"Butterfly"? Instability regarding job goals?
Reason given for leaving last employment: "Personal"	Evasive? May tend to hold back information?
Several omissions	Evasive? Careless about details?

Furthermore, specific questions such as these might be planned from a careful review of a candidate's application blank:

Response on Application	*Questions for the Interview*
Membership in several college organizations	What was your personal role in the organization? What was your biggest contribution to its success? Why did you join it?
Stated income for present employment higher than starting salary for position under consideration	Why are you willing to cut back on your income? What do you feel you should be earning 1 year from now? Five years hence?[22]

Conclusions on selecting.   The major selection tools and techniques may well be questioned. How widely are these tools used? Do small firms differ from big firms in their use of selection tools? Table 9.3 shows that personal interviews are most widely used, by both big and small firms. Large firms use psychological tests and credit reports almost twice as often as small firms do.[23]

Although selection tools have been tested and improved for decades, no person or firm is likely to perfectly select employees; humans are too complex. Most selection tools, however, are sufficiently precise and valid to eliminate obvious misfits. But despite a sophisticated format (such as used in some of the psychological tests), the tools seldom predict with certainty the more effective employees. Because of the innate deficiencies in selection, few managers are assured of a cadre of superior producers. Management therefore is challenging and crucial in achieving operational objectives.

TABLE 9.3   Use of selection tools by sales organizations.

Selection Tool	Percentage of Small Firms "Extensively" Using	Percentage of Large Firms "Extensively" Using
Personal interviews	91	96
Application blanks	73	70
Personal reference checks	70	62
Psychological tests	22	32
Credit reports	15	36

Source: Alan J. Dubinsky and Thomas E. Barry, "A Survey of Sales Management Practices," *Industrial Marketing Management* (April 1982): 136.

SUMMARY

At the beginning of this chapter I asked you to consider how you, as a sales manager, would identify the honest, aggressive, persevering, and self-confident candidates. What tools would you use to ascertain this information? Did you suggest using some kind of psychological test? A personal interview? What questions would you use in an interview to obtain this information? Although personality tests may provide some insights in aggressiveness and self-confidence, these tests are susceptible to faking, so the answers must be somewhat suspect. The best insights may lie elsewhere. A person's poise and manner and previous handling of leadership positions may suggest self-confidence, but asking a direct question to determine self-confidence is unlikely to elicit valid information. Questions such as "Are you honest?" or "Are you aggressive?" will result in only, "Yes, sure I am." A feeling for the depth of these traits may better be gained from personal history information, such as previous jobs, the individual's contribution to schooling costs, and membership in organizations. References also are a better source of information about honesty than are direct questions.

Staffing involves both recruiting and selecting and can be centralized in the home office or decentralized to the field sales manager. Specific requirements for a particular sales force concern the number and caliber of salespeople needed, personality traits required, and any governmental requirements for nondiscriminatory personnel policies. A job analysis and job description may help to formulate specific job requirements.

Good recruiting is vital to the staffing process because without a sizable body of candidates, a firm cannot be highly selective. Both external and internal factors affect recruiting effectiveness. A tight labor market is an external factor that might necessitate using a variety of recruiting sources.

The selection process often involves a preliminary screening, a formal application form, reference check, testing, and one or more interviews with line executives. The process weeds out candidates at each stage. The major selection tools are interviews and tests, but both are flawed, with reliability and validity problems that are perhaps due to human complexity. A weighted application blank (WAB) may be a useful tool when it has been specifically validated.

QUESTIONS

1. Discuss the pros and cons of hiring only high-caliber candidates when the job calls for generally routine order filling and servicing.
2. In what situations may high personnel turnover be advantageous?
3. Why is a job description generally advocated as a first step in the recruitment and selection process? Is it always necessary?
4. What exogenous factors can affect recruiting efficiency? What internal factors?
5. Would you recommend a policy of recruiting salespeople from competitors? Why or why not?
6. What suggestions do you have for making college recruiting of salespeople more effective?
7. Can personal biases and prejudices of interviewers be eliminated so that the interview situation and the resulting judgment can be completely objective?
8. Which types of tests are most useful in selecting salespeople? Which are the least?
9. Do you think tests should be used in the salesperson selection process? Why or why not?
10. How important are references in the selection process?

PEOPLE PROBLEM: DEALING WITH FALSEHOODS ON THE APPLICATION

Please evaluate each of the following alternatives.

After Charlotte Wilson is hired, you discover that she lied about her age and credit rating. Before long you also discover that she is padding her expenses, although not drastically. She is developing satisfactorily as a beginning salesperson, and you think she can achieve average performance with further experience. What action, if any, should you take in this situation?

1. Discharge her now, because "small" dishonesties tend to become more serious; also, her age and lack of exceptional ability are points against retention.
2. Discuss the situation with Charlotte and place her on probation, with dismissal assured for any further improper conduct.

3. Take no action at this time; these are minor matters, not unique to Charlotte. She is progressing satisfactorily, which is the important thing. However, periodically audit Charlotte's expense reports to check on any further padding.

4. Warn Charlotte about this misconduct, and reprimand the personnel department for not checking on personal history data obtained during the selection procedure.

5. Ascertain the reason for Charlotte's apparent financial insecurity and see if counseling might be needed.

NOTES

1. Bernard S. Rosen, "It's Time They Invested in Field Management," *Managers Magazine* (May 1980): 3; James B. Weitzul, "Building a Sales Force: The Agent, the Managers, and the Marketplace," *Insurance Marketing* (June 1980): 20. For a related article dealing with turnover, see Nicholas C. Williamson, "A Method for Determining the Causes of Salesperson Turnover," *Journal of Personal Selling and Sales Management* (May 1983): 26–35.

2. Joseph A. Bellizzi and Paul A. Cline, "Technical or Nontechnical Salesmen?" *Industrial Marketing Management* (May 1985): 69–74. For another relevant article, see Dan Woog, "Where to Find the Best Salespeople," *High-Tech Marketing* (January 1985): 30–39.

3. This alternative is argued persuasively by Bellizzi and Cline, "Technical or Nontechnical Salesmen?" 72–73.

4. For an overview of early personal selling research regarding predictors of successful sales performance, see James C. Gotham, III, "Selecting Salesmen: Approaches and Problems," *MSU Business Topics* (Winter 1970): 64–72.

5. Herbert M. Greenberg and Jeanne Greenberg, "Job Matching for Better Sales Performance," *Harvard Business Review* (September–October 1980): 128–133.

6. For an approach to validation to satisfy EEOC requirements, see J. Michael Munson and W. Austin Spivey, "Salesforce Selection that Meets Federal Regulation and Management Needs," *Industrial Marketing Management* (February 1980): 11–21.

7. For example, see "Which Sex Does a Better Job of Selling Industrial Products?" *Wall Street Journal,* 5 Feb. 1981; "Tomorrow's Sales Trainees: More Women and Blacks," *Sales & Marketing Management* (17 Nov. 1980): 24; and "Women Often Better Reps, Miller Reports," *Industrial Marketing* (June 1977): 1.

8. For a method of investigating salesforce sex discrimination, see David W. Finn and William C. Moncrief, "Investigating Salesforce Sex Discrimination," in *Proceedings of the AMA Educators' Conference,* ed. R. F. Lush et al. (Chicago: American Marketing Association, 1985), 192–197.

9. Herbert M. Greenberg and Ronald L. Bern, *The Successful Salesman: Man and His Sales Manager* (Philadelphia: Auerbach Publishers, 1972).

10. For a sampling of articles dealing with quantitative models for determining sales force size, see Arthur Meidan, "Optimizing the Number of Industrial Salespersons," *Industrial Marketing Management* (February 1982): 63–72; Leonard M. Lod-

ish, "A User-Oriented Model for Sales-Force Size, Product, and Market Allocation Decisions," *Journal of Marketing* (Summer 1980): 70–78; Charles A. Beswick and David W. Cravens, "A Multistage Decision Model for Salesforce Management," *Journal of Marketing Research* (May 1977): 135–144; and Leonard M. Lodish, "Vaguely Right Approach to Sales Force Allocations," *Harvard Business Review* (January–February 1974): 119–124.

11. To attract the best recruits, some companies offer bonuses as hiring inducements. See Alan J. Dubinsky, Charles H. Fay, Thomas N. Ingram, and Marc J. Wallace, "Market Bonuses: How Attractive Are They?" *Business Horizons* (May–June 1983): 11–14.

12. For recommendations for a more aggressive recruiting effort, see Rick Stoops, "Nursing Poor Recruitment with a Marketing Approach," *Personnel Journal* (March 1985): 92–95.

13. For a broad-ranging discussion of sources for finding high-tech salespeople, see Dan Woog, "Where to Find the Best Salespeople," *High-Tech Marketing* (January 1985): 30–39.

14. For more details about the EEOC's restrictions on the job interview and more "inappropriate" questions, see "How to Keep Bias Out of Job Interviews," *Business Week,* 26 May 1975, 77.

15. For more detail about misinformation and how to detect it, see Robert F. Vecchio, "The Problem of Phony Resumes: How to Spot a Ringer Among the Applicants," *Personnel* (March–April 1984): 22–27.

16. W. C. Byham and M. E. Spitzer, "Personnel Testing: The Law and Its Implications," *Personnel* (September–October 1971): 9.

17. For a recent review of various tests, and in particular, sales aptitude tests, see Stephen Poppleton, "Aptitude for Sales Work," *Personnel Management* (November 1984): 67ff.

18. For an article making a case for the measurement of "personal maturity," see Lester L. Tobias, "Making Tests Pay," *Sales & Marketing Management* (12 Aug. 1985): 87.

19. For a positive view of testing, see Tobias, "Making Tests Pay," 80–87.

20. Roger Bellows, *Psychology of Personnel in Business and Industry,* 3rd ed. (Englewood Cliffs, N.J.: Prentice-Hall, 1961).

21. Phil Faris, "No More Winging It," *Sales & Marketing Management* (August 1986): 90. For other articles offering suggestions for improving the interview interaction, see Nick DiBari, "Closing the Job Interview," *Sales & Marketing Management* (12 Nov. 1984): 63–64; and Robert J. Morris, "Objective Interviewing: Discerning the Best in Sales Candidates," *Business Marketing* (December 1984): 58ff.

22. The examples of the application form questions are adapted from W. J. E. Crissy and Charles L. Lapp, "Sound Selection: First Step in Building an Effective Sales Force," *Advanced Management* (March 1960): 7–8.

23. For an article dealing specifically with selecting people for telemarketing positions, see Leslie Kirby and Joel Linchitz, "Become a Telemarketing Hiring Specialist," *Telemarketing* (February 1985): 44ff.

cases

9.1 Problems in Decentralizing Salesperson Selection

"Jessica, are you aware of the excessive turnover of salespeople in Jim Federico's area?" asked the vice president of sales.

Jessica Seavers, the general sales manager, nodded. "This seems to be a problem peculiar to Federico's district. The other districts are running only about 10 to 15 percent, while Federico's is holding steady at 40 percent. As you know, the salary scale and other amenities are comparable in all districts, so there should be no problem there. I suspect, though I haven't checked this out yet, that Jim just is not a good selector of people. He can't seem to sense from an interview whether a person has the makings to be a top-notch salesperson. I've talked to Jim about this, of course, and he's as baffled as we are with his selection problems."

"What do you think we should do about this situation?"

Jessica replied without hesitation. "It seems to me there are two possibilities. As you know I had proposed using companywide tests to help in selection so that our sales managers wouldn't rely entirely on personal interviews with candidates. Or we could centralize the selection process and bring the most eligible candidates into headquarters for the final hiring decision."

"Tests are expensive, and I'm not sure they're effective," the vice president said. "Still this remains a possibility. Why don't you do this, Jessica? By next Monday draw up a proposal for upgrading the selection process, giving all viable alternatives, and indicate your choice. We can then present this to the executive committee for their approval."

9.2 Randolph Insurance Company: Use of Tests in Salesperson Selection

The Randolph Company, a regional insurance firm in New England, had found a fairly profitable niche in the life insurance market by concentrating its attention on group life insurance plans tailored primarily to small- and medium-sized firms of up to 500 employees. It had twenty-eight salespeople who contacted a variety of firms, some by "cold" calls, others by referrals, and still others in response to expressions of interest from firms that replied to direct mail and trade journal advertising that Randolph did on a small scale.

The "hot" leads from replies to advertising were doled out as equitably as possible to various salespeople, although there were some geographical constraints. A sales representative based in Massachusetts, for example, would not receive a lead for a prospective customer in southern Connecti-

cut. Each salesperson was expected to generate his own referrals, and cold calls were made in the absence of specific hot leads or referrals. The hot leads constituted about 20 percent of the calls, while the ratio of referrals to cold calls varied greatly by salesperson. The better producers tended to develop sufficient referrals, so they rarely needed to make a cold call. The newer salespeople and also those who were less productive tended to have a high number of cold calls.

Although the company had achieved a steady, if modest, growth in its established territory, it experienced high turnover of salespeople and a wide disparity of productivity—problems faced by many firms selling intangibles such as insurance and mutual funds. Ray Travis, vice president of sales, was concerned about these personnel problems. He had requested two reports from the personnel and records departments. The first concerned the longevity of the present selling staff:

Less than 1 year with company	12
1 to 2 years	5
3 to 5 years	6
5 to 10 years	3
More than 10 years	2
Total	28

This lack of experience indicated several problems to Ray. First, the selection procedure apparently did not select enough able and stable people. He concluded that selection was to blame because the compensation plan and amount that successful salespeople could achieve were fully comparable to—if not higher than—that of larger competitors. Randolph salespeople probably were not leaving because pay was inadequate, but simply because they could not make the grade. The second problem resulted from the first. The fact that most of the sales force had been with the firm less than 2 years suggested that additional turnover could be expected and that selling effectiveness was far from optimal. The second report confirmed his assumptions and showed actual sales as a percentage of quota for the various salespeople:

Less than 75% of quota	7
75% to 90% of quota	10
90% to 100% of quota	6
0% to 10% over quota	2
More than 10% over quota	3

The quotas were identical for each salesperson, except two people located in more sparsely settled areas in Maine and New Hampshire. Most of the sales force worked in heavily populated areas, and because there were no specific territorial designations, identical quotas were believed to be equitable and permitted a comparison among sales representatives.

Ray also asked for records of people who had been hired and then quit or were terminated during the last 5 years. A definitive record had not been kept, but the personnel department did think that over 500 had been hired during this time. The evidence definitely suggested that serious problems did exist, and it seemed to point to poor selection as the primary cause of both the high turnover and the mediocre productivity.

Ray knew that most insurance companies used elaborate batteries of tests to help them select the most potentially successful sales candidates. He was not aware that any firms had achieved great success in selecting high-performance people with these tests. But he was sure that Randolph's selection could be greatly improved with a more sophisticated selection process than the series of interviews and evaluation of past history presently used. He therefore contacted Dr. John Phillips of Phillips Psychological Testing Services.

After what seemed to Ray to be a thorough analysis of the personnel situation at the Randolph Company, Phillips returned to Ray's office. "Testing seems indicated for your organization. Most firms use standardized personality tests, interest tests, and sales aptitude tests, and then may use several others that are specialized for their requirements,—such as mechanical aptitude tests for industrial equipment firms."

Ray replied, "I understand that the best way to develop a test is to examine the personality and interest differences between your best salespeople and your worst, or those who have been terminated."

"Yes, that's true and very perceptive," Phillips admitted. "However, my firm has so much material about the characteristics of successful and unsuccessful life insurance salespeople that we don't need to revalidate this for your firm."

"Our sales job is slightly different from the average life insurance sales job. We sell to companies, to groups, and our salespeople often make presentations to committees or to the entire labor force of a small company. Does this require different testing and success patterns?"

Phillips studied Ray briefly. "I don't see that it should. The product is the same, the message and appeals are the same. The same qualities of empathy, aggressiveness, and determination seem to apply to your selling. No, I would not think this should make any difference." He paused. "Should I continue?"

"Please go right ahead."

"All right, then. I recommend giving this battery of tests to all new sales applicants: A Minnesota Multiphasic test, to measure psychological or personality traits; the Kuder test, to determine interest in insurance selling; and finally a sales aptitude test, to detect innate intelligence in social and selling situations. After the tests are completed, you forward them to us, and we'll give you an evaluation of the candidates within 36 hours."

After some further discussion, Ray indicated that the decision about using tests would be made in a few days.

QUESTIONS

1. Evaluate Phillips' recommendations.
2. Do you think tests are the answer to Randolph's problem? If so in what way are they likely to be helpful?
3. To what extent should Ray rely on the tests in the selection process?
4. Is there any other information you would like to have in evaluating the personnel problem and possible solutions?
5. Are there other alternatives that should be considered in improving productivity and longevity?

9.3   State Chemical: Recruiting and Hiring the Best!

State Chemical Company had sales of $1.3 billion. The company manufactured a wide line of heavy inorganic chemicals including alkalies, phosphates, dry bleaches, bariums, phosphoric acid, solvents, and sodium sulfate. Customers were predominantly in the automotive, chemical, food, drug, glass, paper, textile, agriculture, and detergent industries.

Sales were made nationally by 45 salespeople operating out of five district offices located in Los Angeles, Dallas, Chicago, Atlanta, and Philadelphia. The sales representatives called on purchasing agents, production managers, and engineers. Compensation was a base salary plus commission on all sales over a stipulated amount. Each salesperson had unlimited use of a new car every 50,000 miles, as well as an adequate expense account. Compensation for 1987 ranged from $24,500 to $88,000, with the median $51,600.

Because of retirements or for other departures, 6 or 7 trainees typically were hired every year. Recruiting was mostly on college campuses, although occasionally an experienced "walk-in" candidate was hired.

Jeff Maag, the national sales manager, had originally directed the company's recruiter to seek engineering and other technically trained seniors, because these seemed to be more easily trained and had more rapport with customers. However, in some years the number of engineering graduates inter-ested in industrial sales was so low and starting engineering salaries so high that Jeff began recruiting elsewhere. In particular, in the last 5 years, considerable success had been had in hiring MBA graduates, both men and women. Hiring women as industrial sales representatives at first was considered rather risky in this male-oriented industry, but now the sharper women were being readily accepted. All the sales representatives were hired for their management potential, and this was heavily stressed in recruiting and selecting. By paying rather attractive starting salaries, the good earnings potential and management opportunities enabled State often to obtain the top graduates.

The training program was 16 weeks in the home office and various production facilities. Then the new recruit spent from 3 to 6 months in a district sales office as assistant to the manager, while awaiting a sales territory. Occasionally, if an experienced sales representative were hired, the training program's length was substantially reduced. While in training the apprentice sales representatives were paid $25,000 annually. Once they had a sales territory, they could reasonably expect to earn another $10,000 a year.

Jeff first became aware of a possible problem during an exit interview when the employee complained, "The work is just too routine. After a couple years on the same job—even though the pay was OK—well, I need some fresh challenges." And this employee was one of the MBAs hired with high expectations.

"What do some of these young MBAs expect—to be president in a couple of years?" Jeff grumbled to Brenda Kaminsky, the personnel director.

"Maybe we should put the better ones on a faster track," Brenda suggested.

"We can only move them up as management openings develop. The company isn't growing fast enough to generate many new management positions. And some of the good older sales reps are also vying for any openings. So it's survival of the fittest out there. And I've always maintained that competition is healthy for a firm, both internal and external competition."

"Do you know that your personnel turnover has increased from about 10 percent 7 years ago to 15 percent today?"

"No, I didn't. But I think it reflects the changing business environment. With all the mergers and retrenchment in middle-management positions, we see less company loyalty. It's affecting all firms."

QUESTIONS

1. Do you think there is a problem? What further information would you like to have at this point?

2. Evaluate the recruiting and selection process.

3. What recommendations, if any, would you make to Jeff Maag?

CHAPTER 10
Deploying the Staff Through Time and Territorial Assignments

CHAPTER PERSPECTIVE

After recruiting and selecting our sales force, we must deploy personnel most effectively. Usually, this is best accomplished by establishing specific geographical areas, or territories, for accomplishing selling objectives. As Chapter 8 demonstrated, sales efforts also can be organized by customers, products, or functions. In all but the very smallest firms, however, geography enters into the assignment. Time limits that amount of territory that a salesperson can cover. Unless customers are few and widely scattered, a salesperson's time is more efficiently used when limited to a clearly defined geographical area. This chapter describes the procedures for and issues involved in establishing sales territories.

As you read this chapter consider a problem in managing a sales territory. As a sales manager, you find that several of your territories have grown so large that they must be divided into additional territories. The sales representatives in these territories are understandably incensed because they anticipate adverse effects on their income. How would you address this problem, which often accompanies growth?

CHAPTER OBJECTIVES

☐ Become familiar with the reasons for establishing sales territories.
☐ Become aware of general guidelines for establishing territories.
☐ Know the specific procedure for determining territorial divisions.
☐ Understand the response function and its implications.
☐ Consider the need for revising territories and potential problems in doing so.
☐ Become acquainted with territory jumping, overlapping territories, routing, and scheduling.

REASONS FOR ESTABLISHING SALES TERRITORIES

The benefits most commonly attributable to sales territories are better market coverage, reduced selling costs, improved customer service, increased motivation of sales personnel, and more accurate evaluation of sales force performance. These benefits accrue only if the territories are properly designed.

Better Market Coverage

If a sales territory is properly designed, a salesperson can maximize efficiency in calling on customers and prospects. A territory should not be so large that the salesperson has time only to call on a few of the best customers—which is called *"skimming* the cream off the market"—and thereby ignores many other prospects. A territory should be large enough that the salesperson has a reasonable work load without contacting the same customers too often. The proper market coverage should be attainable without incurring disproportionate time and travel expenses, although this ideal situation sometimes must be violated when customers are few and scattered. When a small firm cannot have a sales coverage equal to its sales potential, it should strive to assign its sales coverage to available territories. Thus, it can establish a market core in which it has a strong position and can strengthen its defenses against competitive inroads.

Reduced Selling Costs

Properly designed territories will reduce sales expenses compared to the expenses of no territories or haphazard assignments. Territories should not overlap, thereby avoiding the costs of duplication of efforts. By efficient routing, salespeople incur less road time, thus reducing travel and lodging costs and creating more selling time. Improved market coverage from more productive selling time should decrease the ratio of selling expenses to sales.

Improved Customer Service

Regularly scheduled calls permit both better servicing of customers' needs and better understanding of their problems and preferences. Not the least of the benefits of regular calls is an appearance of perseverance. The more difficult prospects often are won over in the long run by the salesperson who persists in calling and trying to get an order.

Increased Motivation of Sales Personnel

A well-designed territory gives a salesperson a reasonable work load and sufficient potential to encourage best efforts. The fairly compact territory results in fewer nights away from home and increased morale. A definitive territory designates performance responsibility. Being solely responsible for a single territory, being the boss, the manager of that territory, is a powerful motivation for many people.

Territories minimize disputes between salespeople, because they preclude intrusion on someone else's customer. However, territories foster a spirit of competition with other salespeople. If the territories are relatively equitable in potential and ease of coverage, intrafirm competition can stimulate the best efforts of the competitive and ambitious salespeople.

More Accurate Evaluation of Sales Force Performance

An individual's performance can be measured against territorial potential, and the resulting achievement level can be compared with that of other salespeople in other territories. The better producers are thereby identified and problem areas pinpointed for corrective action, which might be additional training, transfer, or termination; or it might rather require additional marketing efforts because of a more intense competitive environment in certain territories. By looking at sales performance in each territory, you can gain better insights into changing conditions and more easily adapt.

Are Sales Territories Always Desirable?

Despite the preponderance of advantages to sales territories, sometimes they are not needed and would even be an encumbrance. For sales made primarily on the basis of personal and social contacts and by leads, territory delineation is unnecessarily limiting. Examples of these sales are insurance, mutual funds and other investments, and real estate. Furthermore, a highly specialized sales force may best serve customers who require technical skill by assigning whichever salesperson is available.

Where the available sales coverage is far below the sales potential (which is often the case with small firms or those introducing a new product), territories may not be assigned because there is more than enough business for all. Failure to assign territories under these circumstances can be a mistake, because territories should enhance sales force effectiveness. Leaving a generous amount of market potential untapped simply invites competition. The better course of action here is to exploit more fully the potential of limited geographical areas and to spread out gradually, as resources permit.

GUIDELINES FOR TERRITORY DECISIONS

Although the benefits of territories are overwhelming for most sales situations, the territories must be designed for equitable distribution and the most efficient overall coverage—an ideal that is not always achieved. If sales managers abide by the following guidelines, a better job of setting up sales territories should result: A territory should have sufficient potential, be of reasonable size, afford adequate coverage, and have a minimum of impediments.

Sufficient Potential

Ideally, all territories should have equal potential, which usually is impossible to achieve because customers tend to be geographically concentrated. Furthermore, customers vary in size, and ease of coverage varies among territories. Competition may be fierce in some regions and practically nonexistent elsewhere. Perhaps the major delimiting factor in achieving equitable sales assignments is geography. Assigning a salesperson in the sparsely populated Northwest the same sales potential as one in the populous East might require a territory of three or four states. The constraints of heavy travel time, increased expenses, and a preponderance of many small accounts would hinder productivity.* Consequently, the goal of designing territories of equal potential usually must be modified by practical considerations, and one must face the reality that not all territories will be equal.

From the sales manager's point of view, there is merit in having territories of differing potential. Smaller territories can be used as training areas for new salespeople or for older ones who are not able to work as hard. Territories of differing potential can then be assigned according to the relative abilities of salespeople; this should yield more total sales and profits, as demonstrated later in the chapter.

In general a satisfactory solution is to structure territories so that each has sufficient potential for a salesperson to meet goals and have a reasonable income. If one territory does not have sufficient potential, the salesperson must work unduly hard to meet even reasonable expectations. More commonly the territory has more potential than one salesperson can fully cultivate, which results in skimming for the easiest customers to sell and giving inadequate attention to other present and potential customers.

Reasonable Size

Relative size rather than total size should be considered. A territory with only a limited number of present and prospective customers requiring only infrequent calls and minimum servicing can be far larger than one requiring

---

*When a firm's customers are widely scattered in certain markets and concentrated in others, some companies use manufacturers' representatives (independent sales agents) in the sparse areas, because covering such territories adequately with company salespeople is too costly. The company sales force might then be reserved for those markets offering more concentration of customers and more sales potential.

continual checking and processing of small orders, such as many route sales-people who work on designated routes encounter.

Territories ideally should be sufficiently large that the salesperson can perform without slighting some customers or disregarding designated sales goals. For example prospecting for new customers often is an important part of the selling job that tends to be neglected if the territory cannot be covered adequately. Some sales managers argue that thin coverage is not necessarily undesirable, because salespeople are thereby forced to operate more efficiently and to seek those customers with the greatest sales potential. The firm with a small sales force may have to tolerate thin coverage if the firm wishes to do business nationally or over a wide geographic area. The alternative is more intensive regional penetration.

Adequate Coverage

Territories should be designed so that customers and prospective customers are properly allocated for selling efforts. Often a compromise must be made between services the customers desire and the firm's market penetration strategy, based on the firm's present resources. Different classes of customers should present different servicing requirements. For example, a firm should give more time and attention to large customers and less to smaller accounts. When selling to different industries, requirements may differ. Some may have complicated technical servicing requirements and may involve many persons in the purchasing decision, while other industries can be serviced less often and more easily with standardized products and procedures. Coverage is a continual problem for the sales manager, because territories with inadequate coverage (either because of a conscious policy dictated, perhaps, by the firm's resources or inadequacies of individual salespeople) are highly vulnerable to competitors who can provide better service.

Minimum of Impediments

In addition to trying to design territories with equal potential, sales managers should try to equalize the work load. Some territories, however, are inevitably more difficult than others, usually because of geography, such as a large and sparsely populated territory or a territory hard to cover in the winter because of heavy snow, cold, or mountainous terrain. Some territories are far from company factories and distribution points, so deliveries are less prompt, and customers consequently are more difficult to sell if competitors offer better service. Competition is an uneven factor. In some territories your firm may be dominant; elsewhere other local, regional, or national firms may create more competition and challenges.

Sales managers should be aware of, and where possible minimize, the obstacles in their territories. With a geographical impediment such as a mountain range (which may preclude reliable servicing during the winter), the sales manager might expand another territory to cover those accounts. The manager's objective should be to minimize traveling during prime selling time.

PROCEDURE FOR DIVIDING TERRITORIES

A firm does not usually begin with carefully designed territories. More often, territories evolve as a few sales representatives in roughly defined parts of the country become unable to cope with growing business. The firm then adds more salespeople until management realizes that a more systematic, equitable, and thorough assignment must be made.

The procedure for dividing territories consists of three major steps: (1) determining the number of territories; (2) determining appropriate focal points (geographical units) and boundaries; (3) assigning salespeople. In the process of working through these three steps, a number of decisions must be made, some requiring rather complex analyses.

Determining the Number of Territories

Deciding on the sales force size (the number of territories) is the important starting point. You should take into account the following factors when making this important decision:

- □ Customer servicing requirements
- □ Sales potential
- □ Attainable work load per salesperson
- □ The firm's resources

These factors, in turn, affect the decision about the degree of market penetration that is possible or established by the firm as a goal. Figure 10.1 illustrates the interrelation of these four factors. For example a firm with limited resources seeking to reach customers with high service requirements and a high sales potential per customer will probably assign fewer customers per salesperson to create a more attainable work load. The mix of these inputs determines the decision to cultivate the market more or less intensively. A decision for greater market penetration and more intensive coverage necessitates more salespeople and smaller territories, whereas a skimming approach requires fewer territories and salespeople.

Customer servicing requirements.   As noted before, the more important a customer is to a supplier, the more attention should be devoted to keeping this buyer satisfied and loyal. You should consider the following in planning adequate coverage of customers' servicing needs:

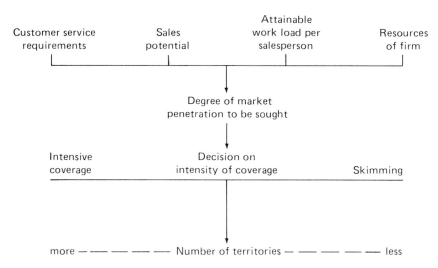

FIGURE 10.1   Decision inputs for number of sales territories.

Call length—how much time should be spent per call

Call frequency—how many calls should be made in a given time period (subject, of course, to geographical constraints in some territories)

Call mix—how much of the total sales effort should be directed to servicing present customers (as individuals and in total) and how much allotted to potential customers

Some firms classify customers into A, B, and C categories, according to size and relative importance. An area with a preponderance of larger A customers has higher servicing requirement than a similar area composed of nearly the same number of smaller accounts. The reason is obvious; larger accounts can be many times more important than smaller ones and deserve more sales efforts to keep their business and sufficiently develop it. The following shows the disproportionate productivity in calling on all customers with the same frequency:

Customer Types	Number of Customers	Number of Calls per Year at 5 per Customer	Sales Volume ($)	Sales per Call ($)
Large	20	100	500,000	5,000
Medium	40	200	200,000	1,000
Small	180	900	90,000	100
Total	240	1,200	790,000	658

The many small customers with their poor sales production per call are taking time that might better be spent with the large customers and might yield more total sales. Reallocating sales efforts according to customer importance could result in the following:

Customer Types	No. of Customers	Call Frequency	No. of Calls	Sales Volume ($)	Sales per Call ($)
Large	20	3 weeks	340	600,000	$1,750
Medium	40	6 weeks	320	240,000	750
Small	180	6 months	360	72,000	200
Total	240		1,020	912,000	894

Total sales to the larger customers have increased because of more frequent calls, and this more than makes up for modest sales losses with the small customers. Overall, sales have increased, sales volume per call has improved, and less calls are needed to service the accounts. The latter result could also permit more time for prospecting or expanding the territory.

A graduated approach to customer servicing.   Rather than placing customers in discrete groups according to size and arbitrarily allocating a specified frequency of calls for each group, you can gain more flexibility by considering customers along a spectrum, as shown in Figure 10.2. The call length and frequency thereby can be tailored more directly to the requirements and importance of each customer. For example if a customer's purchases totaled

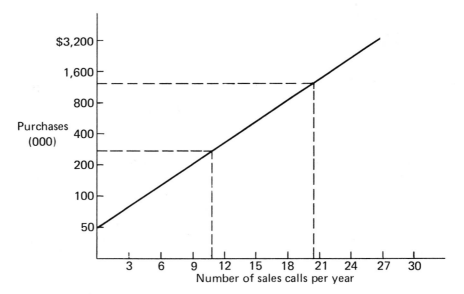

FIGURE 10.2   Allocating number of sales calls to relative size of customers. (*Source*: Adapted from Walter J. Talley, Jr., "How to Design Sales Territories," *Journal of Marketing,* January 1961: 10.)

$1.2 million last year, the number of sales calls can be set at twenty this year; the customer worth $300,000 last year would receive eleven calls. In Figure 10.2 any firms with purchases of $50,000 or less would warrant no sales calls. Of course, for this type of nomogram the slope of the diagonal line should be verified by previous experience as well as customer and sales force opinions regarding the ratio between optimum number of sales calls and customer size.

A portfolio model approach to customer servicing.[1]   Another method for deploying sales force efforts to customers focuses on factors in addition to size that logically have some bearing on the desired amount of customer servicing. A sales manager can consider each customer account as part of an overall portfolio of accounts. Some of these customers are more attractive than others, not only because of their size but also because of their growth potential, their financial resources, as well as other factors that relate to the strength of a vendor's position with them, such as good relationships with important executives, detailed knowledge about the customers' operations, and a history of satisfactory dealings. All these factors will affect a customer's relative attractiveness and importance in our total portfolio or mix of customers. Figure 10.3 shows a matrix for the attractiveness of accounts and the deployment strategy, based on two major considerations: (1) account opportunity, which represents the account's need for and ability to purchase the product, and (2) strength of position, which reflects a firm's competitive advantage in dealing with this customer.

Customers are categorized according to the portfolio model. Those in segment 1 are most attractive and deserve the best efforts, whereas those in segment 4 are least attractive. A two-step analysis can be made (1) by calculating the average number of sales calls and level of sales in each segment for the previous period and (2) by comparing past results with desired deployment strategies, and making any desired adjustments. The results of this analysis for a grocery products marketer are shown in Figure 10.4. Too many sales calls appear to be made to the weaker segments 3 and 4, and more deployment efforts should be given the more attractive segments 1 and 2.

Sales potential.   The sales potentials of a firm's various products affect the decision on how intensively various markets should be penetrated. If sales potentials are limited (perhaps because total potential for the particular industry is limited and static or because competition is severe), then efforts to gain major inroads into the market may be too costly or not worth the effort. Sales potentials that are large and growing, however, provide a strong incentive to penetrate the market intensively before competitors can gain major footholds. More territories and more salespeople also may be invested, subject to the constraints posed by the firm's resources. (Review Chapter 5 for a discussion of market and sales potentials and their calculation.)

Strength of position

	Strong	Weak

	Strong	Weak
High	**Segment 1** **Attractiveness** Accounts are very attractive because they offer high opportunity and sales organization has strong position. **Deployment Strategy** Accounts should receive a heavy investment of sales resources to take advantage of opportunity and maintain/improve strength of position.	**Segment 2** **Attractiveness** Accounts are potentially attractive due to high opportunity, but sales organization currently has weak position. **Deployment Strategy** Additional analysis should be performed to identify accounts where sales organization's position can be strengthened. These accounts should receive heavy investment of sales resources, while other accounts receive minimal investment.
Low	**Segment 3** **Attractiveness** Accounts are moderately attractive due to sales organization's strong position. However, future opportunity is limited. **Deployment Strategy** Accounts should receive a sales resource investment sufficient to maintain current strength of position.	**Segment 4** **Attractiveness** Accounts are very unattractive; they offer low opportunity and sales organization has weak position. **Deployment strategy** Accounts should receive minimal investments of sales resources. Less costly forms of marketing (for example, telephone sales calls, direct mail) should replace personal selling efforts on a selective basis, or the accounts should be eliminated entirely.

Account opportunity (left vertical axis, High to Low)

FIGURE 10.3   The general portfolio model. (*Source*: Reprinted from LaForge and others, *Business Horizons*, "Improving Sales Force Productivity," September–October 1985; pp. 54 and 56. Used with permission.)

If expanding the sales force is no problem, the number of salespeople needed to tap the total sales potential can be determined. This is commonly known as the *breakdown technique* for determining the field sales force size, and it is discussed more specifically later in this chapter (see also Chapter 8).

Attainable work load per salesperson.   Past experience should also indicate the number of accounts that the average salesperson and the better performers can handle. Usually, this information is categorized by customer types; the firm that has not compiled these data must analyze the sales force work and the time needed to sell and service each account effectively. Ana-

Strength of position

		Strong	Weak
Account opportunity	High	Average sales calls: 27 Average sales: 2438 cases Number of accounts: 97	Average sales calls: 21 Average sales: 1248 cases Number of accounts: 15
	Low	Average sales calls: 23 Average sales: 1017 cases Number of accounts: 26	Average sales calls: 17 Average sales: 402 cases Number of accounts: 66

FIGURE 10.4 Portfolio model results for a grocery products marketer. (*Source*: Reprinted from LaForge and others, *Business Horizons*, "Improving Sales Force Productivity," September–October 1985; pp. 54 and 56. Used with permission.)

lyzing sales productivity also may be helpful in uncovering inefficiencies. For example perhaps travel time could be planned more efficiently, a better call schedule could be developed, or waiting time in customers' offices could be reduced by better use of appointments, the telephone, and timing of visits.

Ideally, a firm would determine the total number of customers and their servicing requirements in its selling area and divide the attainable work load per salesperson into this total figure, thereby deriving the number of salespeople and territories required for the desired level of market penetration. This is known as the *buildup method*, which also is discussed in more detail later in this chapter. Although the breakdown and buildup methods likely would produce somewhat different results, these could be settled by compromise. However, another factor affecting the decision on number of territories can be constraining—the firm's resources.

The firm's resources. Although the need for a certain number of territories and salespeople to best allocate sales efforts to customers may be apparent, the present resources and budgets of your firm may necessitate a reduced number of territories and salespeople. For example, consider a corporation with annual sales of about $10 million. It salespeople are paid on a straight salary plus an annual bonus based on sales and profit. The annual costs of salary, travel, and entertainment amount to $40,000 per salesperson. Sales expenses for 1988 are budgeted at 7 percent of sales, or about $700,000. The sales manager must effectively argue that more salespeople and a higher sales expense will produce significantly higher sales than the expected $10 million, or all the other factors influencing the decision on number of territories (e.g., customer service requirements, sales potential, and work load) must bow to the budget constraint. If we assume that of the $700,000 budgeted for sales expenses, $100,000 will be directed to administrative and branch office expenses, then no more than fifteen salespeople and territories can be set up ($600,000 divided by $40,000), even though the perceived need is twenty-four. Regarding this scenario, complete Exercise 10.1.

EXERCISE 10.1

1. As sales manager, what case could you develop to persuade top management to increase the number of salespeople for next year?
2. If top management does not accept your case, what can you do this year to increase the likelihood of getting more salespeople next year?

The four decision inputs previously described (see Figure 10.1) all affect the strategy regarding market penetration, although some factors may be assigned more weight or importance. For example in a small firm with limited resources and a tight budget, budget requirements restrict the number of territories. A larger firm might weight customer service or sales potential as more important. The end result, however, should be a subjective determination of how intensively the market should be cultivated.

Another consideration—the response function.   A sales manager can better make the decision regarding degree of market penetration if she has some idea of the response function—how various customers respond to increased sales efforts, such as number of sales calls. Figure 10.5 depicts some possible response functions. Example (a) shows that additional sales efforts increase the rate of sale up to a point at which total sales potential is perhaps being approached, or competitors are retaliating vigorously, and further increase in sales efforts result in diminishing marginal returns. Example (b) shows sales increases up to a certain point, at which sales level off and even decrease with additional selling effort. This reflects the situation in which too many salespeople and sales calls actually antagonize customers who see their

FIGURE 10.5   Possible effects of increased sales efforts—the response function.

time as being wasted unnecessarily. Example (c) indicates that the sales force is not instrumental in producing sales. Consequently, increasing sales force efforts may not increase business sufficiently to warrant the concomitant increased costs.

Sales responses may, and probably will, differ by territory. For example, in Figure 10.6 the A territory response function indicates that additional efforts will not be very successful, whereas territory B shows an opposite situation. What could explain the dissimilarity between the two territories? This is a very plausible situation, in which the firm is well-known and solidly entrenched in A, but is just getting a foothold in B.

How can you determine which response applies to any given situation, or whether some other response function is more appropriate? The shape of the response function is affected not only by sales force efforts but also by the other parts of the marketing mix. Hence, any determination is complicated. Most sales managers have incomplete data and make judgments intuitively. A few experimental studies have reported that changes in sales were correlated with changes in call frequency and call lengths.[2] A sales manager may want to experiment to determine the response function and to find the best allocation pattern. For example, the sales manager can vary the frequency of sales calls in several selected territories and carefully monitor the sales changes. Sometimes past sales records are helpful if data on call rates also are available. Customers can be asked how often they would like to be serviced. However, customers may express wide variations in alleged preferences: One firm may want to be called on frequently, whereas another does not want to be bothered often, and there may be little correlation to optimum sales productivity.

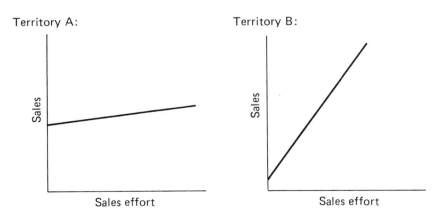

FIGURE 10.6 Territorial dissimilarity in response function.

Objective Procedures for Determining Sales Force Size

Three computational procedures are commonly employed to derive the desired number of territories and sales force size: (1) breakdown technique, (2) buildup method, and (3) incremental method.

The breakdown technique.   The breakdown technique is a rather simple procedure that starts with the overall sales forecast, and then sets an average sales figure per salesperson. This is divided into the overall sales forecast using this formula:

$$N = \frac{S}{P}$$

where:

> N = number of salespeople and territories needed
>
> S = overall sales forecast
>
> P = average productivity per salesperson

Therefore, if the company sales estimate for the coming period is $50 million, and the average salesperson is expected to achieve sales of $1.2 million, then the firm should have between 41 and 42 territories. The sales forecast (sometimes an estimate of sales potential is used rather than the generally more conservative actual sales forecast) should account for potential business in a firm's entire market, as well as the different trading areas and markets. The average productivity per salesperson should be rather easily determined based on past experience and any additional "stretching" that seems reasonable.

With the number of territories determined, the next step is to design the required number of territories by dividing up the entire market so that each salesperson has reasonably equitable potential and work load. (Designing territories is discussed later in this chapter.)

Critics have assailed the breakdown technique as distorting the cause-and-effect relationships of sales effort to sales: Sales efforts should *cause* the sales, and not the other way. Although illogic may be involved, the breakdown technique is a useful approach to determining sales force size and number of territories, especially for industrial firms. The next method, the buildup, overcomes the conceptual weaknesses of the breakdown technique.

The buildup method.   The buildup technique is the most popular approach for determining number of sales territories and involves identifying present and potential customers and classifying them according to desired call frequencies. The number of calls that can be made effectively in one day by an average salesperson then must be determined. Usually, past history can be a fairly good guideline for determining call number. Travel time is a major component of this analysis and will vary according to the concentration and dispersion of customers in the various geographical areas. Consequently, the number of daily calls, which also involves the number of customers assigned to each sales representative, must be determined for each territory because of practical differences in coverage potential (see Application 10.1).

The buildup method has weaknesses. Most important, it does not recognize differences in sales response among customers of the same category. (One customer may respond favorably to increased sales efforts, while another may not.) The buildup method also can be too much wedded to sales force averages and can disregard individual differences in efficient use of time.

The incremental method. The incremental method brings another important factor into the decision on the size of sales force and number of territories, that of profitability. With this method additional territories are created only if their marginal profits exceed their costs. The incremental method recognizes a point of diminishing returns, with a point reached when additional salespeople will result in sales increasing but only at a decreasing rate. A number of studies have confirmed these decreasing returns, as well as the increasing costs that can result when the optimum number of territories has been exceeded.[3] Unfortunately, the incremental method has not been particularly useful. The fault lies in the accounting system. Most firms do not

---

APPLICATION 10.1   Buildup Calculations

A firm is presently doing business with 490 customers of varying sizes: 50 customers are large, 120 are medium sized, 320 are small.

By historical experience and some trial and error, this firm has determined that the large customers should be called on every 3 weeks, medium-sized customers every 6 weeks, and small customers only once every 6 months. The annual call frequencies follow:

large customers	800 calls/year
medium sized	960 calls/year
small	640 calls/year

Because many of the customers are fairly well dispersed, requiring considerable travel time, a sales representative can average only two calls on regular customers per day, to allow time to prospect for new customers. Average calls per day prorate annually as follows:

$$2 \text{ calls/day} \times 5 \text{ days/week} \times 48 \text{ weeks/year} = 480 \text{ calls/sales rep}$$

$$\frac{2{,}400 \text{ total calls per year}}{480} = 5 \text{ sales reps and territories}$$

When designing the territories, however, the differences in concentration of customers and effective travel time must be considered.

have sufficient data to determine sales, costs, and profits that can be contributed at various input levels. With most firms this method is more a theoretical exercise than a practical tool.

Designing Territories

Once you have decided on the number of territories, their actual design can begin. Establishing the territories so that government census data and other market information are readily available is preferred. These statistics are essential for determining market and sales potentials by territory, for readily identifying customers, and for evaluating sales performance.

Find appropriate focal points and boundaries.   *States* are commonly used in establishing territorial boundaries. Statistical data, both governmental and otherwise, certainly are adequate concerning states, their populations, purchasing power, number of various kinds of firms, and so on. One problem with dividing territories by states is that some market areas comprise several contiguous states centering on a single metropolitan area (e.g., Washington, D. C., with adjacent Maryland and Virginia counties in its immediate market area). Furthermore, states are often too large a geographical unit to divide sales territories effectively, except for small firms selling to selective accounts.

Counties afford a better focal point for dividing territories. Because there are almost 3,100 counties in the United States, these can be combined as preferred. Statistical data by county are ample to facilitate the planning and control of territories. The major disadvantage of organizing by counties is similar to that by states—the dissimilarity of some counties in potential and in ease of coverage. A Cuyahoga (Cleveland) county may require several salespeople to cover it adequately, whereas four or five counties may need to be grouped together to offer the same potential in another territory.

Metropolitan areas are becoming widely used as focal points. The federal government has designated over 300 metropolitan statistical areas (MSAs)* with ample statistical data available concerning each. An MSA is an area containing a city of at least 50,000 people, or including an urbanized area of 50,000, with a total metropolitan population of at least 100,000 people (75,000 in New England). The MSAs may embrace contiguous counties and even states that are socially and economically integrated. Because of the heavy urban character and density of population and businesses in the MSAs, some firms gear their sales force primarily to them and disregard rural areas.

Trading areas, which constitute another way of dividing markets, reflect the natural flow of trade rather than political boundaries. Primarily involving

---

*The MSAs have replaced the former standard metropolitan statistical areas (SMSAs) since 1983.

retail and wholesale trade, these geographical areas surround a city and provide it with customers for shopping or transacting business. Usually the larger a city, the more it draws distant customers because of the range of choice, as well as the diversity of entertainment, cultural, medical, and educational facilities. Even a small town in a rather sparsely populated rural area may draw from some distance if no towns of similar or larger size are nearby. For example Mankato, a town of 35,000 in south central Minnesota, regularly draws customers from the South Dakota border, 100 miles to the west, and from the Iowa border, 70 miles to the south. It draws only about 20 miles to the north, however, because Minneapolis is just 75 miles in that direction.

Trading areas are not delineated as precisely as county and metropolitan areas. Trading areas vary according to products, firms, and type of merchandise (e.g., retail shopping and specialty goods or wholesale goods). The trading area for wholesale goods can be several states and even more. A firm's draw can be determined by plotting customer locations on a map. The major drawback of using trading areas as focal points for territorial design is the absence of comprehensive and specific statistical data. Most firms that must use trading areas for sales territories try to adapt their dimensions to the counties that are partially or wholly included. Although the county statistical data may not fit the trading area precisely, they are probably the best available.

Territory shape. The shape of a territory can affect the cost and ease of coverage, and it can increase job satisfaction if it reduces time spent on the road. The two most common shapes are the wedge and the circle.*

The *wedge,* or pie-shaped territory, is commonly used when several sales territories are encompassed by a large city and its suburbs. The tip of the wedge is usually placed in the city proper where customers are concentrated; as the territory is drawn out to the suburbs and rural area, it spreads out to accommodate the smaller number of customers. This blend of urban and rural in each territory permits more equality of sales potentials. The major drawback of the wedge is that the headquarters is usually located downtown, near the tip of the wedge, and thereby is not centrally located within each territory to permit the most efficient use of time.

The *circle* (which actually may be more of a square) represents an efficient design with the branch headquarters located roughly in the center of the territory. The salesperson is never far from customers (unless the circle embraces several states, as it may in sparsely settled parts of the country), and travel time is minimized.

---

*Some books show a third shape, the cloverleaf. However, this is more of a routing pattern, in which the salesperson makes a series of loops for sales calls. It will be discussed later in this chapter.

Assigning Sales Personnel to Territories

Territories are designed with the average salesperson in mind and with the goal of being as equivalent as possible, but two conflicting pulls obstruct these efforts. If a firm attempts to design territories with equal potential, then the work load will not be equivalent, because some territories will require covering much greater distances. A firm may opt instead to design territories with equal work loads, thereby ensuring approximately equal size and ease of servicing within each territory. This decision, however, creates greatly varying potential among territories. The result is that compromises must be made, and some territories will be more attractive than others.

Unequal territories are not necessarily bad. The advantages can be shown mathematically, but a firm must assign its best salespeople to the best territories and its newer and less effective people to second- and third-rate territories. Tables 10.1 and 10.2 show that total sales volume is thereby optimized. As these hypothetical situations in the tables illustrate, if one assigns territories

TABLE 10.1   Assigning salespeople of varying abilities to territories equal in potential.

Territory	Sales Potential ($)	Ability Index of Salespeople Assigned*	Estimated Sales ($)
A	600,000	1.0	600,000
B	600,000	.8	480,000
C	600,000	.6	360,000
Total	1,800,000		1,400,000

*The ability index can be based on relative evaluations of the various salespeople according to such criteria as years of experience, ability to meet quotas, and the like.

TABLE 10.2   Assigning salespeople of varying abilities to unequal territories with regard for ability.

Territory	Sales Potential ($)	Ability Index of Salespeople Assigned*	Estimated Sales ($)
A	700,000	1.0	700,000
B	600,000	.8	480,000
C	500,000	.6	300,000
Total	1,800,000		1,480,000

*The ability index can be based on relative evaluations of the various salespeople according to such criteria as years of experience, ability to meet quotas, and the like.

of unequal potential to salespeople according to their perceived ability—with the best salespeople assigned the best territories (see Table 10.2)—the total sales likely to be realized will exceed those made under the other alternatives (see Tables 10.1 and 10.3).[4]

Now complete Exercise 10.2.

EXERCISE 10.2

1. If the territories are more uneven than in Tables 10.2 and 10.3, with A at $1,000,000, B at $500,000, and C at $300,000, how does the assignment by ability compare with the preceding example?
2. What limitations do you see in permitting territories to be extreme in inequality of work load? Of potential?

Assigning salespeople to admittedly unequal territories can be accomplished in several ways. Newer employees and those who have not measured up to the desired performance level may be assigned the less desirable territories. When their experience and ability increase, they may be transferred to the more desirable areas when these open up. Of course, transfers may be disrupting to individuals and their families and entails considerable moving expenses. In addition it destroys the rapport and confidence that sales personnel may have built up with their customers.

Many firms find sales quotas necessary to achieve more equal compensation and incentive when territories are not as equivalent as preferred. Quotas will be discussed in detail in Chapter 10, but we can note here that quotas should reflect relative sales potentials and work loads in the various territories. Therefore, the territory with less potential and/or a heavier work load would bear the lower quota.

In assigning salespeople the sales manager also should consider personal factors, such as the interests and preferences of individual salespeople. Strong

TABLE 10.3 Assigning salespeople of varying abilities to unequal territories without regard for ability.

Territory	Sales Potential ($)	Ability Index of Salespeople Assigned*	Estimated Sales ($)
A	700,000	.8	560,000
B	600,000	.6	360,000
C	500,000	1.0	500,000
Total	1,800,000		1,420,000

*The ability index can be based on relative evaluations of the various salespeople according to such criteria as years of experience, ability to meet quotas, and the like.

geographical preferences should be given consideration, if possible, because a more contented and motivated work force is likely to result. Age may be a consideration in assigning territories. The older sales representatives may find a large territory necessitating extensive travel too taxing; the salesperson with a large family may see a large territory as disrupting family life. Sometimes abilities and experiences may dictate assigning certain personnel to particular territories because these people are likely to be more effective with certain types of customers. For example a salesperson may have a personality that wears well with rural customers, who are called on infrequently, but is relatively ineffective with urban customers, who have different life-styles and expectations and are called on more frequently.

Stable territorial assignments are preferred to continually shifting and transferring. The person who remains in one territory for some time gains a better understanding of the customers and their problems and needs, and closer rapport likely is established. A salesperson can take pride in her territory and the accomplishments there. Familiarity with the customers and the environment of a particular territory makes a salesperson more knowledgeable in forecasting and in providing market feedback.

Some firms, however, see greater advantages in transferring salespeople frequently. These firms argue that fresh perspectives are useful, and that salespeople tend to thrive in new and challenging environments. Some individuals do become bored and complacent in familiar surroundings and need fresh stimulation and new challenges. But others find their effectiveness optimized when they can see the results of careful building of customers and business. If a firm's product lines change frequently and customers are serviced only sporadically (e.g., with major installations that are purchased infrequently), transfers are justified. To avoid morale problems, however, a salesperson should have a voice in, and should concur with, the transfer decision.

REVISING SALES TERRITORIES

Most firms at some time must revise their sales territories. As a firm grows it usually needs a larger sales force to cover the market adequately. The original territories may have been poorly constructed and established almost by chance, perhaps due more to salespeople's personal preferences and/or work experience than objective decisions about sales potential and coverage. Obviously, market conditions change. Major customers may shift, new markets and industry segments may develop and competition may seriously distort certain territories. Because the environment is dynamic, even territories that originally were carefully designed may need adjustment. Territory adjustment is particularly a problem when a firm is enviably positioned in a rapidly growing market, as illustrated in Application 10.2.

APPLICATION 10.2   Territory Revision: Litton Industries

Demand for microwave ovens skyrocketed beyond all expectations, as industry sales rose from $290 million to $410 million in only 1 year. With one-third of this consumer market, Litton's microwave cooking products division had to maintain a very flexible and constantly expanding sales organization.

Litton salespeople were responsible for all accounts in their territories, and accounts ranged from small mom-and-pop appliance stores to major department stores. The optimum number of accounts that any salesperson could handle had been definitively determined as between thirty and forty, because Litton salespeople had many responsibilities in addition to selling—such as demonstrating the product (knowing how to cook with each of the models, eight of which were introduced in 1 year), helping dealers to plan the merchandising of the products, and spending time on the sales floor, training retail salespeople. Litton found it necessary to review sales territories and personnel planning programs annually, based on growth levels determined at that time. However, the plans were refined whenever the number of accounts for any one salesperson exceeded the thirty-to-forty maximum. Litton continued to add people and territories during the years of rapid growth.

Territorial changes when a firm's growth has slowed down should be made only after carefully studying and eliminating other factors that might impede the most effective coverage. For example the cause of inadequately covered territories may not necessarily be design. Transferring or more closely supervising personnel or perhaps reassessing the quota system might improve coverage.

Handling Morale Problems in Territory Revisions

The most common territorial change is dividing an existing territory into two or more. As business in a territory increases, it may reach the point where one person cannot adequately cover the present and potential customers. Then the territory is being skimmed, and the chances are that the firm will begin losing market share to competitors who can cover the area more intensively. Consequently, although the particular salesperson in that territory may be recording healthy sales increases, the territory potential may be increasing far more rapidly.

The obvious answer in this situation is to split the territory and give part of it to another salesperson, thereby enabling the two to cover the area more intensively than one could. However, the sales manager may encounter serious morale problems. The salesperson who had the original territory faces the very real probability of reduced earnings resulting from a territorial reduction; some of the best customers, perhaps carefully nurtured and developed, will be assigned to someone else to "reap the harvest." Unless the situation is carefully handled, a good salesperson may become so bitter that her performance suffers and she considers resigning. What can be done to ease the morale problems accompanying territorial revisions?

The salesperson can be guaranteed that she will not lose income over the next one or several years and that her quota will be revised downward until the smaller territory can be cultivated more fully. The sales manager may point out the advantages of a smaller territory, such as less travel time, which can mean more time to spend with customers and probably greater sales, more nights at home, and possibly greater opportunities for advancement into sales management because a greater number of territories will create more district sales manager positions. Perhaps the best way to minimize personnel problems arising from territory revisions is to prepare the sales force for these changes so that they are not made suddenly and without warning. Sales personnel participation in the analyses and planning preceding the decision to revise their territories also can minimize problems.

Although most territorial revisions result in splitting or reducing the size, occasionally a territory may have to be expanded. This might happen if, for example, a major customer closed down or left the territory. Usually, increasing the size of territories presents no personnel problems, because salespeople view this as affording more compensation opportunities.

CAUTIONS IN ADMINISTERING TERRITORIES

The sales manager should be alert to the territorial changes that have been discussed—a territory becoming too large for one person to cover adequately or being too small, perhaps because of changes in the market or possibly because of initial poor design. The morale problems in instituting needed revisions have also been mentioned. To be alert to territorial changes, the sales manager must constantly monitor sales results compared with sales potential. Sales performance, of course, is obvious, but changes in sales potential may be more subtle and not quickly recognized. The sales manager must be in close touch with the statistics that are relevant to her products' market potential in the the district or region. Sales and market potential evaluations should be conducted at least annually, when sales quotas are developed (this is discussed further in the next chapter).

Territory jumping, one salesperson entering another's territory in quest of business, may be tolerated or sometimes even encouraged, but the practice is basically bad. It distorts the efficiencies that should ensue from having territories, and it obviously can cause serious friction. Territory jumping is sometimes permitted when one territory has a strong sales representative and the adjacent area is assigned a new and inexperienced person. But when territory jumping is practiced, it often is a symptom that territorial adjustments are necessary because sales potentials are too high in some and insufficient in others. It also may be evidence of poor supervision. Some salespeople are interested only in selling the easy customers and not in developing their own territories. So they sell outside their territories unless the supervisor steps in and stops the practice.

Overlapping territories may result from a territory's being split. To maintain the morale or appease the complaints of the salesperson involved, a sales manager may permit keeping some of the key accounts in the former territory. Overlapping is a sign of territorial weakness that generally should not be tolerated on any but the most temporary basis. But certain arrangements sometimes must be continued. For example if an important customer insists on dealing with the old salesperson and the account is in danger of being lost otherwise, the situation may have to be tolerated.

TIME MANAGEMENT—ROUTING AND SCHEDULING

The Manager's Role in Maximizing Productive Selling Time

We discussed in Chapter 3 the importance of managing time for more effective selling, but we did so from the perspective of the salesperson. Now let us consider how the manager can help. Time management is really an allocation problem. *The objective is to allocate a limited resource, time, in the most efficient manner to maximize productivity.* Some allocation problems follow:

☐ How best to apportion time between new calls and service
☐ How to balance office work with field work
☐ How much time to give the overly demanding prospect or customer
☐ How to minimize travel and waiting time

Sometimes the firm creates undue impediments to the best allocation of its sales force's time by being unreasonable in requirements for field reports, especially when these reports are not used effectively by management. The value of field reports should be assessed and, if possible, they should be simplified. The effective sales manager does not simply leave sales representatives to fend for themselves within their designated territories. Rather, she guides them in best using their time, because this is critical to their ultimate productivity.

Unfortunately, the nature of the sales job is such that time spent in nonproductive activities tends to increase, unless continual attention is given to this problem. For most salespeople the greatest proportion of unproductive time is spent in traveling to customers and waiting to see them. Consequently, salespeople need the most efficient routing and scheduling. The question arises as to how formally management should direct salespeople to present and potential customers. A sales manager may even need to assign the time of day and day of week for sales calls to particular customers. For example salespeople calling on retail store buyers may find that the latter part of the week is not good for sales calls because of heavy demands on buyers' time in preparing for the peak weekend business. Similarly, the Christmas and Easter seasons may impede effective selling efforts.

Should Salespeople Be Routed?

Routing refers to the formal patterning of sales calls in a territory. In some firms staff people prepare routes using complex operations research techniques; in others the sales manager designs the routes; or the salespeople devise their own routing, either solely by themselves, probably informing their sales manager, or in consultation with the sales manager. Some firms allow salespeople to plan their sales calls and routes independently, with little or no interference, unless serious performance deficiencies occur.

In general the extent to which routing is formalized depends on (1) the nature of the product and (2) the caliber of the sales representatives. If the product requires regular and frequent servicing (e.g., soft drinks, hardware, tobacco, and many grocery items), then routing is necessary to ensure adequate and efficient coverage. If the sales force is relatively low level and inexperienced, routing is often instituted. But most high-caliber salespeople resent the intrusions imposed by routing and think it is suited only to low-level servicing, not creative selling.

Careful routing includes advantages such as reduced travel time and costs and thus more time for productive selling. Routing facilitates communications between the field sales office and the sales force, because each person's whereabouts should be known at all times, but this advantage is not unique to formal routing; it can be attained simply by having each salesperson file a travel plan for the following week.

The major disadvantage to routing is reduced initiative and flexibility. Sometimes a particular customer requires emergency servicing, or perhaps a major sales commitment could be made with just a little more time and effort, which a formalized routing plan may impede. Routing is impractical for new firms or for firms that have just expanded into a new geographical area, because the number and location of prospective customers is usually not readily known.

Procedure for Routing and Scheduling

A first step in routing is to pinpoint present and potential customers on a map of the territory. The number of calls that can be made and the desired call frequency for each account should be ascertained. Some sales managers use a map and colored pins to represent customers. Each color may represent a different desired frequency of sales calls. By using various highways and transportation modes and by recognizing any geographical impediments, you can plot the route's path without great difficulty to minimize any backtracking and crisscrossing, permitting the most efficient territorial coverage.

Route patterns may be simply a straight line or may be more or less circular. More sophisticated patterns are the cloverleaf and the hopscotch, depicted in Figure 10.7. The advantage of both the cloverleaf and the hopscotch is that the salesperson arrives back at the home base at the end of the sales trip with a minimum of unproductive travel time. In the cloverleaf the salesperson makes a loop of sales calls, starting and ending with the headquarters. With the hopscotch pattern the salesperson starts from the farthest point and works her way back.

Use of Mathematical Models

The routing and scheduling problem permits computer applications and mathematical modeling to minimize either total travel time or travel cost. Linear programming can be used in any case in which the number and location of accounts, the call frequency, and the number of calls that the salesperson is capable of making are all known.[5] However, these mathematical models seldom are sufficiently representative of the real world, in which some backtracking may be necessary to meet customer needs and not every sales call and its duration can be precisely programmed.

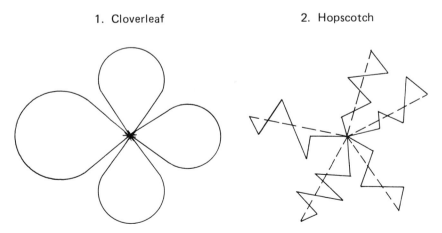

FIGURE 10.7   Route patterns. (A) Cloverleaf (B) hopscotch.

SUMMARY   At the beginning of this chapter I asked you to consider how you as sales manager would handle the personnel problems that arise when sales territories must be revised and divided into smaller territories. What rationale would you give the disgruntled sales representative who sees her future earnings being drastically reduced? Congratulations if you gave the sales potential argument. You may likely need to give temporary guarantees of compensation to salespersons facing greatly reduced territories. The guarantee might be no salary loss for 1 year, which permits time to build up the revised territory without being penalized. If business is growing as expected, sales should soon reach former levels, and the ease of covering a smaller territory will be significantly improved.

Firms establish sales territories to obtain better market coverage, reduce selling costs by eliminating duplication of efforts, improve customer service, increase motivation, and provide a more accurate performance measure. But territories are not always preferred, such as when sales are made on the basis of personal contacts and leads, and when sales potential greatly exceeds the available sales coverage.

A territory should have sufficient potential, be of reasonable size, afford adequate coverage, and have minimum impediments. An important first step in dividing territories is to determine the number of territories needed. In general the factors that should influence this decision are customer servicing requirements, sales potential, attainable work load per salesperson, and the resources of the firm. The sales manager's knowledge of the response function (i.e., how customers respond to increased sales efforts) is helpful. Objective procedures for determining number of territories are the breakdown technique, the buildup method, and the incremental method.

The second step is to design the territories and find appropriate focal points and boundaries. The final step is to assign salespeople to the territories.

Revising territories is usually necessary with growth and can present some management and morale problems. Other management concerns may include territory jumping, overlapping territories, and the issues of routing and scheduling.

QUESTIONS   1. Should sales territories be established for all firms? Why or why not?

2. How can the use of territories reduce selling costs?

3. How often should sales territories be revised?

4. Under what conditions is routing most desired? When is it least desired?

5. What is a response function? How does this concept relate to the establishment of sales territories?

6. Is it good practice purposely to design gradations in the desirability of territories, with the intention of using the best territories as promotions for the better salespeople?

7. Discuss the rationale and any limitations of overlapping territories.

8. Is it a good practice to reduce a territory to prevent a salesperson's earnings from becoming disproportionately high, relative to other salespeople and executives? Why or why not?

9. Do you think territories should be reserved as training grounds for new salespeople? Why or why not?

PEOPLE PROBLEM: WHETHER TO DIVIDE A GOOD TERRITORY

Please evaluate each of the following alternatives.

You are faced with the decision of whether or not to divide a territory. Sarah Shorrock, a veteran salesperson, has had the Houston territory for 8 years and has developed it into one of the top five in the nation. However, you are sure that she is only skimming the cream of the territory. Because of the rapid growth of the Houston area, sales could be two or three times greater, even with the healthy growth rate that Sarah has realized. Sarah has hinted rather strongly that she has a strong proprietary interest in her territory and will tolerate no intrusions. Furthermore, if she should leave the company in a huff, she might take some of her customers with her to another firm. As sales manager, what would you do in this situation?

1. You are the boss and must look at the overall picture. No single subordinate should be allowed to dictate procedures that are against the best overall interest of the organization, even at the risk of losing the employee.

2. Personal elements must be considered in management decisions. Although theoretically the territory should be broken up, the time is not ripe. The decision should be delayed and reexamined in another year.

3. Would splitting up this highly successful territory destroy the morale of other salespeople with growing territorial business? Even though change might be desired, morale must come first. The decision should be to leave the present size indefinitely.

4. Can Sarah be mollified if she is permitted to keep her major customers, with a junior salesperson taking over certain parts of her territory? This is a compromise decision, and compromise often is the better course of action.

5. Can Sarah be reasoned with? Is it possible to break up this thriving territory without losing a star salesperson? Try giving her a guarantee of a certain level of compensation for a 3-year period, by which time she will probably have built up a smaller territory into one even more lucrative than the larger one that could be only partially covered.

NOTES

1. The material dealing with a portfolio model is adapted from Raymond W. LaForge, David W. Cravens, and Clifford E. Young, "Improving Salesforce Productivity," *Business Horizons* (September–October 1985): 50–59.

2. Most of these studies are dated, for example, Clark Wald, Donald F. Clark, and Russell L. Ackoff, "Allocation of Sales Effort in the Lamp Division of the General Electric Company," *Operations Research* (December 1956): 629–647; and Arthur A. Brown, Frank T. Hulswit, and John D. Kettelle, "A Study of Sales Operations," *Operations Research* (June 1956): 296–308.

3. See, for example, Zarrell Lambert and Fred W. Kniffen, "Response Functions and Their Applications in Sales Force Management," *Southern Journal of Business* (January 1970): 1–9; Henry C. Lucas, Jr., Charles D. Weinberg, and Kenneth W. Clowes, "Sales Response as a Function of Territorial Potential and Sales Representative Workload," *Journal of Marketing Research* (August 1975): 298–305; and C. Davis Fogg and Josef W. Rokus, "A Quantitative Method for Structuring a Profitable Sales Force," *Journal of Marketing* (July 1973): 8–17.

4. Adapted from James G. Hauk, "Research in Personal Selling," in *Science in Marketing,* ed. George Schwartz (New York: Wiley, 1965), 236–242.

5. For example, M. Bellmore and G. L. Nemhauser, "The Traveling Salesman Problem: A Survey," *Operations Research* (May–June 1969): 538–558; Robert L. Karg and Gerald L. Thompson, "A Heuristic Approach to Solving Traveling Salesman Problems," *Management Science* (January 1964): 225–248; and William Lazer, Richard T. Hise, and Jay A. Smith, "Computer Routing: Putting Salesmen in Their Place," *Sales Management,* 15 March 1970: 29.

cases

10.1 Customer Intransigence to a Territorial Realignment

You have found you must reduce and redefine some territories because of expanding business. To avoid overlapping territories, you decided to make a clean break with no salesperson keeping any former accounts if they are outside her new territory. Now, however, you find a major challenge to your decision. A large customer has refused to do business with the new salesperson. The customer insists on dealing only with the former sales representative, who has been reassigned.

QUESTIONS

1. Should you make an exception to your policy of no overlapping in view of this obdurate customer?
2. What is another solution in this situation?

10.2 Dividing an Area into Sales Territories

Jim Barnet had earned a reputation as a troubleshooter with the General Dental Supply Company. The Minneapolis–St. Paul sales district had been losing market share for the last 2 years, so Jim was brought in as sales manager to reverse this trend. The district had six salespeople in the metropolitan area selling to dentists, hospitals, dental labs, and pharmacies. A variety of products were sold, ranging from large dental equipment, such as chairs and drills, to dental floss.

Jim was surprised to learn that instead of each salesperson's having a defined geographical territory, customer accounts were assigned without any particular regard for geography. The result was an indeterminate amount of crisscrossing and inefficient travel time. He determined, as a first step in rejuvenating this district, to reassign the salespeople geographically.

Jim determined that each salesperson could average eight calls a day. Large customers—hospitals and labs—should be called on once a week; smaller customers, such as smaller pharmacies, once every 2 weeks; and dentists, once a month.

QUESTION

Using a telephone directory and a map of the metropolitan area, divide this district into six sales territories. (Another similar metropolitan area can be selected for this exercise.)

10.3 Petite Dress Company: Are Sales Territories Necessary?

Sid Arnow was one of four salespersons for Petite Dress Company, a small garment maker that sold medium-priced casual dresses primarily to department stores and specialty chains. His home was in Cleveland, Ohio; another salesperson operated out of Chicago; the third had the entire Far West; and the last was based in Atlanta. Although each of the four had a focal point, or home base, no formal territories existed. The absence of territorial delineations caused no particular problems with the people in the Far West and the South, because they were hundreds and even thousands of miles from any other Petite salespeople. But Sid, and Jane Gabriel, his counterpart in the Chicago area, occasionally had some problems. Sid had a very lucrative account headquartered in Chicago, a chain of eight department stores that he called on at least four times a year. And Sid thought that Jane had done some business in the Columbus and Toledo areas in the past year. Although this did not bother Sid particularly—and he was not about to give up his lucrative account in Chicago—he recognized that this arrangement was not very effective.

Sid knew that he was spread too thin to adequately cover an area that roughly included the northeastern United States. The major buyers in New York City and the greater metropolitan area usually went directly to Petite's sales office in the garment district. Although Sid could have called on some of the more important accounts, he was so busy with distant customers that he had never called on a retail account in New York City. He could not possibly contact all the stores that might be potential customers. He usually made his rounds of present and preferred customers to show the new dress lines. Only if time permitted did he attempt any prospecting for new accounts. In the last year he had made six prospecting calls, two of which had sampled some of the line. One of these new accounts reordered in quantity, so Sid considered it a regular customer.

Several times Sid had told Rosalind Wellman, director of sales, about the need to add additional salespeople.

"I know we should, Sid, but we're a small firm," she had replied. "We just can't afford now to enlarge the sales staff. I'm not even sure we have sufficient production capability to handle increased sales."

One day Rosalind called Sid into New York. "Sid, we've been thinking about your strong recommendations last year that we add more salespeople, and I think we can add two right now. You also mentioned the need to draw up more definite territories if we increased the sales force. Sid, I've talked to the president, and he agrees with me that we should let you run with this, be some kind of informal sales manager."

Sid frowned. "I like selling. I don't think I want to give it up."

"Of course," Rosalind said. "We don't want you to give it up—you're too good a salesman. But if your territory is cut down a bit, don't you think you could also find some time to do some managing, especially of the two new people? We need you, Sid. You're the best person we have for this. And I think we already have your two new recruits. They both work here at the plant, so they're familiar with the products and the industry, and they want to get out in the field and do some selling."

Sid reluctantly agreed.

Rosalind continued, "The first thing we'd like you to do is to draw up six definite sales territories and to decide where you want to base these new people." She paused. "Try to do this as quickly as you can, Sid, because we cannot send the new people out until we know where they should go. If you want, Jane over in Chicago can back up for a few weeks."

QUESTIONS

1. Based on retail sales potential, draw up six new territories, specifying the territorial base city for each. (Hint: Use the *Survey of Buying Power* data.)

2. Do you think this firm really needs definite and well-defined sales territories? Why or why not?

3. Sid's newly defined territory will not include the Chicago area, because Jane is firmly established there. What should be done about the lucrative account that Sid has been servicing in Chicago?

4. Do you think in this particular case that Sid can handle both his own territory, albeit somewhat reduced in size, and the details of sales management?

5. Do you have any other recommendations to make for this case?

10.4 Midwest Paint Company: Are Territories a Mistake?

Tina McCoy was a sales manager for a growing firm. She felt that having designated territories should give more structure to the operation, enable potential to be more fully tapped, and reduce sales force expenses. "I thought we had a happy ship," Tina ruefully told Amos Patterson, general manager of the division. "But now that we're organized into territories all hell is breaking loose."

Midwest Paint was a subsidiary of a larger national firm, who had acquired it 5 years ago. Previously, Midwest had operated independently and primarily in the three-state area of Missouri, Illinois, and Iowa. Most of its business was still in these three states although some uncontrolled growth had occurred elsewhere.

The industrial line was Midwest's most important paint classification. Here, products were developed specifically geared to the needs of individual industrial customers, and hundreds of unique and customized items resulted. Research and development was conducted as a result of customer contacts by the sales force. Any firm that used paint somewhere in its operation was a potential prospect. Over the last 5 years, sales had been growing at a 10 percent annual rate.

Competition was keen, with the biggest competitive threats from such national firms as Du Pont, Sherwin-Williams, and Glidden. Another competitive threat came from certain small local paint manufacturers in the St. Louis, Chicago, and Kansas City markets. These firms had lower overhead and sometimes obtained business by cut-throat pricing. Midwest Paint fell in somewhat of a middle position, unable to match some of the local prices but offering good alternatives to the national brands. And it excelled in developing paint and service to meet its customers' needs more effectively than most of its competitors. To a large extent this competitive advantage was due to the expertise and dedication of the sales representatives, all of whom had an intimate knowledge of both products and customer operations, mostly gained by years of experience.

Tina McCoy's sales staff consisted of 9 salespeople, most of whom had been with the company for over 10 years. They were compensated by a substantial base salary, whereas commissions were paid beyond a certain quota based on profitability. For example after a sales quota was reached, commissions were 2 percent on 15- to 17-percent profit items, 3 percent on 17- to 25-percent profit items, and a 4-percent commission on products carrying a 25 percent and better profit. Total compensation of the sales force ranged from $45,000 to slightly over $100,000 for Bill Richardson, the ace. Sales force travel and entertainment expenses were budgeted quarterly up to a fairly generous fixed amount. But if the allotted expense budget was exceeded, the difference was subtracted from the commission.

Until 6 months ago, there had been no sales territories. Consequently, each salesperson could go anywhere that allotted expenses allowed. This had resulted in considerable expansion of sales efforts beyond the three-state area. For example, there were several accounts in the Carolinas, and one even in Georgia (some of the sales force liked to venture south in the colder weather). Because such uncontrolled sales coverage was resulting in spotty coverage in the primary selling area as well as constant sales force pressures to increase the expense budget, Tina had convinced Amos, the general manager, of the need to draw up territories.

In the switch to sales territories, however, some rather serious problems developed. Bill Richardson had lost almost $5,000 in commissions in the last 6 months due to the realignment and the necessity of turning over some of his accounts to other territories. His complaints were loud and vigorous, and they primarily focused on the fact that he had built up certain accounts and serviced them for several years, only to have to give them up now. "Things were great before you constrained us with these blasted territories," Bill had complained. "Now I'm not sure I even want to continue in this rat race."

Although Tina did not take Bill Richardson's threat too seriously, nevertheless she saw a potential danger that one or more of the other representatives might quit, which could have serious consequences for Midwest. Most of the products sold were not covered by patents, and competitors would easily duplicate the product and take the business if a disgruntled salesman gave them the information.

"I hate to go back to unstructured sales and no territories," Tina admitted to Amos. "But maybe this territory idea was a mistake."

QUESTIONS

1. Do you think territories are inadvisable in this situation?

2. Evaluate the present policies of this company.

3. Recommend a course of action for Tina McCoy at this point, and support your recommendations as fully as possible.

CHAPTER 11
Deploying the Staff Through Quotas

CHAPTER PERSPECTIVE

As discussed in Chapter 10, even the most carefully designed territories entail disadvantages. Invariably, territories will not be equivalent in potential and in work load. Using quotas, however, can balance some of the inequities among territories. For example the salesperson in a territory requiring a heavier work load because of geographical conditions, customer mix, or more intense competition may receive a lower quota than a salesperson in a more desirable territory. The sales manager then can better ascertain the effects of deployment on sales production. This chapter examines the benefits and drawbacks with quotas, as well as effective techniques to develop quotas.

Consider this issue as you read the chapter: If your quota is higher than that of your colleague in the adjacent sales territory, do you have cause to complain bitterly that this is unfair? Why or why not?

CHAPTER OBJECTIVES

☐ Understand why quotas are used.
☐ Know the various types of quotas.
☐ Become familiar with the characteristics of a good quota.
☐ Grasp the steps involved in developing a quota.
☐ Understand when the quota base should be adjusted for the human factor.
☐ Become aware of the various problems involved in administering a quota.

DEFINITION OF A QUOTA

A *quota* is the expected performance of the overall sales task assigned to an individual salesperson or other marketing entity. Although this chapter focuses on the design and use of quotas for individual salespeople, quotas can also cover large entities, such as geographical areas, types of customers or distributors, and branch offices. The quota is set for a specified time period, perhaps a year, a quarter, or a month; sometimes, for a season or the duration of a sales contest.

A sales quota sometimes is confused with the sales forecast, sales potential, or market potential. Although the quota may incorporate the sales forecast or estimates of sales potential, it is seldom the same. A review of their definitions clarify the differences. A *sales forecast* is the estimate of sales for a specified period of time under a particular marketing plan. *Sales potential* is the share of the market potential, or the total realizable sales, that a firm can expect to achieve. *Market potential* is the total realizable sales of the industry (e.g., the firm and its competitors) during a specified period of time. The sales quota may use the sales forecast or the estimate of sales potential as a base figure. But other factors usually will lead to adjusting the quota from the base figure.

USES OF QUOTAS

Quotas are primarily used in making sales territories more equitable, measuring performance, providing an incentive, serving as a basis for compensation, and directing sales force activities.

Making Sales Territories More Equitable

As discussed in Chapter 10, the impossibility of making all sales territories equivalent in potential and work load can be ameliorated by quotas, which can be set higher for the better territories and lower for the less desirable ones. This equalizing factor of quotas increases the relevance and validity of the other uses of quotas.

Measuring Performance

Quotas are widely used to evaluate performance, including but not limited to performance in sales production. When other activities, such as servicing customers or producing new accounts, or profitability of the business generated are thought to be important, then quotas can be established to measure their effectiveness in achievement. If a quota is to be used effectively and equitably to evaluate performance, it should be realistic and achievable. This would seem to require gearing quotas closely to the sales potential of the particular territory and, furthermore, systematically and thoroughly calculating this potential. You may want to review Chapter 5 for procedures for measuring market and sales potentials.

Providing an Incentive

Quotas sometimes are set above a point that is reasonably achievable, to inspire the selling staff. These quotas may not be closely related to the estimated sales or sales potential. "Incentive" quotas, however, may be placed so high that they will not inspire but will discourage. Sometimes special quotas are used in conjunction with sales contests and only for the period of time of the contest. Unless regular quotas are in effect before and after the contest period, sales may suffer in those periods because of overselling during the contest. In general, incentive quotas must be attainable to be effective, and the reward for success in reaching the quota should be worth the effort.

Serving as a Basis for Compensation

Quotas usually are tied to the compensation plan. Every salesperson then should be expected to exceed the assigned quota and should receive incentive pay when they do. When used as compensation, quotas can be set quite low, as low as at the break-even point of the base salary and expenses, or they can be set at a higher, more realistic measure of the job. These quotas generally would be set below the estimated sales and sales potential. Only a few firms purposely set quotas high in order to "inspire" their salespeople. Most firms think there is sufficient incentive with quotas that are realistic and attainable and use them as a benchmark for their compensation plans.

Directing Sales Force Activities

Quotas can be used to direct sales force efforts to the highest-priority areas and activities. The appropriate type of quota can encourage giving more attention to high-margin products, attaining new accounts, and conducting an appropriate level of service to customers.

TYPES OF QUOTAS

Although we commonly think of quotas as dealing with sales, four categories of quotas are in fairly wide use today: (1) sales volume, (2) budget, (3) activity, and (4) combination quotas. These reflect the different objectives and activities considered most important by management. They should reflect market conditions and how best to serve the market.

Sales-Volume Quotas

Sales-volume quotas are most popular because sales managers, as well as sales representatives, have been nurtured on the idea of maximizing sales volume. Quotas based on sales volume are relatively simple to compute and to understand. They present the disadvantage, however, of overemphasizing sales production, at the expense of a more balanced performance. A sales quota does not account for the profitability of the items sold. Disregarding substantial profit diversity in a firm's product line may result in overemphasis on low-margin, fast-moving items at the expense of higher-margin, more profitable items. A sales quota may be based on units sold or on dollar sales. For relatively expensive and infrequently sold products, a quota based on units is common.

Budget Quotas

Budget quotas change the emphasis from maximizing sales to either reducing the cost of selling or increasing the gross margin. The former may be called an *expense quota,* and the aim is to foster a cost-consciousness with respect to travel, entertainment, and other expenses. An expense quota may be expressed in dollars or as a certain percentage of sales. A limit, perhaps 6 percent of sales, may be stipulated; and if the salesperson remains within the limit, a bonus may be given. The objective of cost-consciousness can hardly be criticized. Yet, when carried too far, such a quota may focus undue attention on expenses, to the detriment of sales. In extreme cases the firm's image may be jeopardized as the sales force shifts to cheaper hotels and reduces entertainment.

Another type of budget quota uses *gross margin* or *net profit.* Here attention is focused on the relative profitabilities of the various items in the line, thereby curbing the salesperson who unduly emphasized the lower-profit, higher-volume items. The major drawback of this type of quota is the analysis and recordkeeping involved in measuring profitability on an item-by-item basis.

Activity Quotas

An activity quota de-emphasizes sales volume, and its base of desired performance is one or more nonselling activities, such as calling on new prospects; opening new accounts; reactivating accounts; demonstrating; setting up displays; conducting sales training meetings for customers; service calls; making bids; and conducting surveys. Activity quotas are used to encourage a more balanced sales job and thereby provide recognition that some aspects of the sales job do not provide an immediate payoff in sales but have longer-term effects. Unless these activities are given formal standing through some sort of activity quota, they tend to be downgraded in the quest for immediate sales accomplishments.

Although a balanced sales job is preferred, activity quotas can present difficulties if used alone. First, there is the possibility that not all the reported activities claimed actually were completed. Calls on customers are not as easily monitored or verified as are sales. Second, the quantity of work tends to be rewarded, but these quotas do not measure the quality of the work. Consequently, the sales manager must increase contact and supervision to ensure that the activity quota is a valid measure of performance.

Combination Quotas

Combination quotas can be used to obtain the best balance between sales, profitability, and desired nonselling activities. This method combines two or more of the quotas described previously. And management may weight the various factors according to their perceived importance. Table 11.1 shows such a combination quota, weighted so that more importance is given to new accounts gained and to the gross margin of sales.

Combination quotas are, of course, more complex, and problems may be encountered in defending the choice of weighting. Their use does not guarantee that proper attention is given to all factors that management wants emphasized, because a satisfactory overall showing can still be achieved by overemphasizing one or a few components of the quota to the detriment of others. Furthermore, they may become so complex that even though they are a fair and accurate measure of performance, they are not trusted and accepted because salespeople cannot assess their own performance.

TABLE 11.1   Combination quota and attainment by salesman X.

Factors	Weight	Quota	Actual Results	Percentage of Quota	Percentage × Weight
Sales volume	2	$30,000	$33,000	110%	220
Gross margin	3	$12,000	$10,000	83	249
New accounts	3	10	6	60	180
Displays erected	1	30	40	133	133
Customer training sessions	1	30	36	120	120
	10				902

$$\frac{902}{10} = 90.2\% \text{ attainment of quota}$$

Now perform Exercise 11.1 to compute a combination quota and to consider specifically some implications arising from its use.

EXERCISE 11.1

1. If, in the example in Table 11.1, salesman X had attained the following results, what would his overall quota attainment be?

Sales	$24,000
Gross margin	$ 8,000
New accounts	8
Displays	90
Training sessions	100

From this hypothetical example, what implications regarding the desirability of combination quotas do you see? How would you as sales manager now evaluate salesman X?

2. What percentage of quota would salesman X have achieved if the factors had been weighted as follows: sales volume at 2 and the other factors at 1 each?

CHARACTERISTICS OF A GOOD QUOTA

The use of sales force quotas does not guarantee that quotas are effective in accomplishing the desired objectives. Quotas imperfectly constructed and communicated to the sales force can cause morale problems; they may confound the best use of sales efforts; and they may be so rigid that they ignore important changes in the environment. Certain qualities seem inherent in most effective quota systems:

Fair

Challenging

Easily understood by salespeople

Flexible

Measure the most important managerial priorities

The quota should be fair to the employees. It should accurately reflect a territory's potential and constraints, and it should do so on a par with the quotas of other territories. It should be attainable with reasonable efforts. A quota that is inaccurate and not equitable with other territories becomes counterproductive.

A quota should be challenging. In general it should be sufficiently high that the salesperson must "reach," but not so high that it is practically unattainable. As noted previously, quotas that are an important part of the compensation plan may be set relatively low with the expectation that they will be easily exceeded. Such easy quotas are challenging because commissions or bonuses are paid only after the quota has been achieved. Thereby, sales beyond the quota are richly rewarded. The challenge then becomes similar to that of a straight commission—to reap the greatest-possible harvest.

A quota can be complex and difficult to understand, and this may lead to the suspicion that it is slanted in favor of the firm and contrary to the employee's best interests. One of the disadvantages of combination quotas is that they are more difficult to understand than most other types, and their measuring factors and weightings are sometimes difficult to defend. A quota should be easily understood by the participants. When a more complicated quota is deemed necessary, a heavier burden is placed on the sales manager to explain the procedure satisfactorily to the sales staff.

A quota should be flexible so that if conditions change in a certain territory it can be adjusted accordingly. A major customer may undergo a lengthy strike or experience a fire or flood, or competition may make a major effort in a particular territory. Unless a quota is modified according to such changed conditions, it becomes meaningless and frustrating until conditions have normalized. Similarly, if the economy experiences a downturn after quotas have been prepared, then their value is reduced unless adjustments are made that more correctly mirror the external situation.

Finally, a quota should implement the most important management concerns and goals. For many firms sales are the most important goal. But for other firms, increasing the profitability of sales, gaining new accounts, or servicing customers better may be most important. When designed with key management goals in mind, the quota system can help management better direct sales efforts.

DEVELOPING THE QUOTA

Quota setting involves basically a three-step process, as shown in Figure 11.1. First, a decision must be made as to the type of quota to use. Is a sales-volume

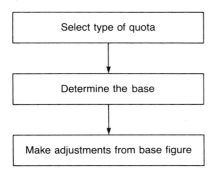

FIGURE 11.1   The quota-setting process.

quota sufficient, or should various other activities be encouraged, and even measured? If more than sales volume should be made part of the quota, what should be the relative importance of the various activities, that is, how are they to be weighted? For a sales quota the base figure will be the sales that can be achieved reasonably under normal conditions by the average salesperson in the particular territory. This base figure is seldom sufficient, however, because circumstances vary among territories and salespeople differ in experience and general ability. Therefore, most sales managers find that adjusting the base figure will improve quota effectiveness. Most of the these adjustments are for the human factor.

Determining the Base

For the most common type of quota, the sales-volume quota, the base can be determined in several ways that range from sophisticated and objective to arbitrary and suspect. (1) The base can be determined by calculated sales potential. (2) Or the base can be set without any objective consideration of potential.

Base directly related to territorial potentials. If competently ascertained, territorial potentials provide the best estimates of relative sales opportunities in the various geographical areas. (At this point you may want to review Chapter 5, on assessing market potential.) If the territorial sales potentials have already been calculated, the bases for the quotas in the various territories are also determined. For example if one territory has a sales potential that is 2.5% of the total company potential, and if total company sales are forecast at $40 million, then the base for quota purposes would be $40,000,000 \times .025 = \$1,000,000$. The total of all territorial quota bases would then equal the company forecast.

If there are no territorial breakdowns of sales potential, the sales forecast for the entire firm may be allocated according to some of the methods explained in Chapter 5. As an alternative, when a firm has not analyzed in detail the relative sales potential for its various geographical units, each territory's proportion of total industry sales may be used to derive a base figure for the sales quota.

When potentials are not directly considered. Not all firms use objectively derived sales potential calculations in developing the quota base. Other alternatives are (1) setting quotas strictly on the basis of past sales; (2) setting quotas according to executive judgment; (3) relating quotas to the compensation plan; (4) having salespeople set their own quotas. Although these alternatives represent an easy approach to quota determination, they are all significantly flawed, as we will examine next.

Past sales. When past sales are used as a base, usually some arbitrary percentage increase is assigned for the next year. For example a 7 percent sales increase may be established for the next year, and sales planning and quotas will be geared to this projected figure. The base quota in each territory therefore would be raised by 7 percent. This approach is simple, inexpensive to compute, and easy to understand, and it implies progress. But there are some serious flaws in the charge to "beat last year." An assumption is made that past sales achievements represent the maximum use of potential, when in reality performance may have been poor in some territories, resulting in sales far below those attainable with better efforts. Such poor performance is in effect condoned when a uniform increase is set for quotas in all territories. Furthermore, arbitrarily determined sales objectives do not acknowledge changes in the economy, competition, or new customers that may affect sales potential in some territories. For example if a salesperson in territory D sold $250,000 during 1 year, an arbitrary 7 percent increase would put his new quota at $267,500. But if the sales potential in the same territory is realistically valued at $400,000, then the quota is set far too low relative to other territories where achieved sales are closer to the sales potential.

Executive judgment. Instead of simply projecting past sales, one may make an educated guess that supposedly reflects local conditions, economic projections, and any anticipated company strategy changes in the coming period. The quality of such estimates depends on the competency and objectivity of the people making such judgments. Although executives may be very experienced, and perhaps have some definitive plans that should impact on sales for the coming period, still these judgments usually ignore quantitative marketing measures and are often overly optimistic. When used alone in the quota determination, they often have an added drawback: The sales force may chafe under unilateral dictates affecting their performance evaluation and their compensation. They may only grudgingly accept these budgets, and morale may be affected. If these executive judgments are but one component of the quota deviation, with one or more other factors also considered, then the process and its acceptability often will be improved.

Quotas related to compensation. Sales volume quotas sometimes are related to the fixed salary component of the sales force compensation plan. The higher the base salary, the higher the quota before any commission is paid. Consider two sales representatives having different base salaries based on their years of seniority (see Table 11.2). Often the increase in quota will lag behind the difference in base salary, thus enabling the senior salesperson to have a total compensation advantage. But the lack of quantitative market measures, which would identify differences in territorial potentials, give this method the same limitations as basing the quota on direct sales alone.

Sales force responsibility for setting quotas. Allowing salespeople to set their own quotas may result in lack of objectivity and biased judgments. If the quota is tied in with compensation, as it usually is, then salespeople may seek the more easily attainable quotas, although some evidence suggests that

TABLE 11.2 Determining compensation-related quotas.

Comparative Factors	Sales Rep A	Sales Rep B
Years with company	2	10
Base salary per month	$800	$1,000
Quota per month	$10,000	$12,000
Sales made this month	$16,000	$16,000
Commission is at 6% of all sales over quota	$360	$240
Total compensation	$1,160	$1,240

this is not necessarily the case.[1] The major rationale for letting salespeople set their own quotas is that they are closer to their customers and therefore should be able to better assess market conditions. Also, it is argued that if allowed to set their own quotas, salespeople will have higher morale and strive more to attain their personally committed objectives. But salespeople do not usually have the exposure to gain a wide perspective and tend to be either overly optimistic or pessimistic. More objectivity is desired.

In determining the base figure to use in setting the quota, a firm can use all of the preceding approaches. Past sales can be included for realism, and the sales guesstimate can allow for probable strategy changes in marketing efforts, while sales potential can reflect relative share of market and sales opportunity. These various inputs can be weighted according to their perceived relative importance.

Adjusting the Base for the Human Factor

After the base has been designated for a territorial quota, it can be adjusted for the person who has the territory according to such factors as the following:

Age

Experience with the company

Other relevant selling experience

Past performance

Special circumstances

Age or other physical limitations may necessitate a downward modification of the base quota figure to keep the quota realistic and attainable. This situation is more likely to occur with older employees who have faithfully served the firm, but who now are forced to slow down either temporarily or permanently, such as employees nearing retirement or recovering from a heart attack or other physical infirmity. Even though a modified quota may not fairly reflect the sales potential of a territory, the result may be in the best interest of all concerned. Of course, an alternative to arbitrarily reducing the quota would be assigning smaller territories with smaller potentials. But transfers might be disruptive to the individuals, their families, and long-standing customer relationships.

Newer salespeople understandably may have more trouble converting a territory to its fullest potential than more experienced personnel. Therefore, establishing a quota that is reasonably attainable by a relatively new employee, may again require adjusting the base downward. Sometimes selling experiences with other companies and industries may enable a newcomer quickly to achieve standards comparable with colleagues, and the quota should not be modified. But not all kinds of selling experiences are easily transferable. New employees who have worked in some other industry or in some other type of selling (e.g., products versus intangibles) may still require a period of adjusting and learning, which may warrant at least briefly moderating the quota. Although the sales manager can place newer people in smaller territories to compensate for differences in experience, this is not always possible. Quota modifications therefore may be the better alternative.

Similar reasoning applies to salespeople with differing abilities. For challenging but reasonably attainable quotas, those persons of lesser ability (indicated by past performance levels) might justifiably receive a somewhat lower quota than that warranted by sales potential. This point is controversial. It can be argued that better training and supervision or, if necessary, replacement should upgrade the selling in a particular territory. However, given that the person is trainable, several quarters or more may still be necessary to bring performance up to a satisfactory level. To prevent discouragement a sales manager may want to modify the quota for a limited time.

A base figure for the effective producer may be adjusted upward to make the quota sufficiently challenging. There is the expectation, and the pressure, for increased sales—the obvious consequence is to increase the quotas. As salespeople develop their territories (given that general economic conditions, level of competitive activity, and the firm's competitive strength in products and marketing efforts remain about the same), an increase in quotas can be supported. However, the practice of always raising quotas can create serious personnel problems, as the next section describes.

Fallacy of continually increasing quotas. Continually raised quotas, although sales potentials have not increased significantly, is one of the actions most destructive to morale. This is especially detrimental when the quota is tied into the compensation plan and a bonus is paid on all sales over the quota (see Exercise 11.2 and Application 11.1).

---

1. How would you as sales manager respond to this protest by Bill Van Zandt?	**EXERCISE**
2. What do you think Bill's sales performance will be next year?	**11.2**

APPLICATION 11.1   Continually Increasing Quotas

In his first year of selling, Bill Van Zandt fell slightly below his quota of $180,000. The next year, with more experience and the new accounts that he was able to develop, his sales were $184,000. Immediately, the quota was raised to $200,000. Bill struggled hard that year and had the real satisfaction of achieving sales of $212,000. With the bonus of 20 percent for sales over the quota, his family had an extra $2,400 just in time for Christmas. But for the next year his quota was again raised, this time to $220,000. By now he was working his territory to its fullest potential; still, he did reach $223,000 in sales, and the bonus, although considerably less than the previous year, was welcome. Then Bill was shocked to find his new quota set at $232,000.

"But there are no other customers I can possibly contact," he told his sales manager. "And I can't load up our present customers any more or they won't even let me in the door."

A sales manager should be careful not to make quotas so high that morale and performance suffer. If the superior salesperson feels his quota is inequitable relative to those of other salespeople, morale can suffer greatly unless base pay or other perquisites are relatively higher also.

Other adjustments to the base.   As discussed in Chapter 9, when a veteran salesperson's territory is split to service a growing sales potential more efficiently, the quota in the reduced territory may be adjusted so that no compensation loss will result before the salesperson has had ample time to build up the revised territory. Other special circumstances that may make adjustments from the base desirable can arise from special sales assignments, such as greater involvement in training, a special servicing or research assignment, or perhaps assuming an understudy role for the sales manager.

Most modifications from a base developed through careful analysis of relative sales potentials should be temporary and not be permitted to become institutionalized. But a sales manager who does not recognize extenuating circumstances that warrant quota adjustment may be just as misguided as one who either disregards performance relative to quotas or is quick to modify the quota with little justification (see Application 11.2).

Now, in Exercise 11.3, give your recommendations for scenarios regarding Mark's performance.

EXERCISE 11.3

1. If Mark sold $180,000 in his first year, what quota would you set for the following year, assuming that sales potential and executive estimates were 10 percent higher?
2. If Mark sold $280,000 in his first year, what quota would you set the following year? Defend your rationale.

APPLICATION 11.2   An Example of Setting a Sales Quota

Mark Hubbard was assigned the Oklahoma City territory for the Apex Company, a manufacturer of dental equipment and supplies marketed to dentists and dental labs. Mark was 26 years old, had a college degree in marketing, and had been a salesman for Procter & Gamble for 2 years before joining Apex. After a 6-month training program during which he worked under a more experienced salesman, he was assigned his own territory with the following characteristics: (1) Sales potential was estimated at $300,000 annually. (2) Last year's sales—by a more experienced, but not particularly competent salesman—were $210,000. (3) The judgment of company executives was that a new warehouse just opened in Dallas would permit much better servicing of the Oklahoma City area; thus, reasonable sales should be $330,000.

The company had a policy of placing sales quotas at 90 percent of sales expectations. A 5-percent commission was paid on all sales over the quota. Tom Hay, the sales manager, computed Mark's quota as follows:

$$\text{average of sales potential } + \text{ last year's sales } + \text{ executive estimate } =$$
$$\frac{\$300,000 + \$210,000 + \$330,000}{3} = \$260,000, \text{ the base for sales expectations}$$

Tom felt that Mark's 2 years of route selling for Procter & Gamble did not provide transferable experience and that Mark was therefore inexperienced. Tom therefore reduced the sales expectation 20 percent from the base:

$$\$260,000 - (\$260,000 \times 20\%) = \$208,000, \text{ the base adjusted for the human factor}$$

The quota was then computed as 90 percent of the adjusted base:

$$\$208,000 \times 90\% = \$187,000$$

Tom hoped Mark would prove himself sufficiently capable that any adjustment from the base would not be necessary during the next year.

ADMINISTERING THE QUOTA

Good quota administration requires that the sale representatives accept the quota-deriving process and the individual quotas. Furthermore, to use the quota to its full potential, the quota should be a tool for managing people by exercising controls to improve performance.

Acceptance Problems

A sales manager reports:

> We find that quotas are a psychological sore point. Nobody is content with their quota—they all think their quota is unfair. And when a quota is raised, all Cain

breaks out. I'm tired of this whole thing. I am recommending to top management that quotas be eliminated.

Salespeople mistrust quotas and see them as performance requirements that were developed through arcane analyses and are intended to expose weak points and goad them to unreasonable efforts. When these attitudes exist, the manager's job of directing and motivating the sales force becomes difficult, and the benefits of quotas may be jeopardized.

Minimizing acceptance problems.   Acceptance problems can be minimized in three ways. First, the quota must be as equitable as possible, based on objective data modified by human factors. Unfortunately, the more obvious it is that quotas deviate from purely objective factors, the more likely it becomes that one will encounter criticism and complaints of unfairness. Second, the quota should be easily understood. If this is not possible (perhaps because a sophisticated combination quota is used), special efforts should be made to explain it thoroughly to those involved. The sales force should be informed of both the derivation of the quotas and the rationale for the method and inputs used. Finally, an almost essential ingredient for attaining acceptance is to allow the sales force to participate in the quota setting. When each salesperson has an active part in helping to derive his or her particular quota, acceptance is far more likely. Management must be careful, however, in espousing such participation. If management invites the sales force to participate, but then firmly controls the final results, the process is wasted. Quota setting by decree probably would be just as effective and would save time. Active participation may require compromises between management and the sales force.

Managing and Controlling People Through Quotas

Certain types of quotas, notably the activity and combination quotas, enable management to direct the sales force toward priority activities. If management provides sufficient motivation for salespeople to strive earnestly to meet and exceed their quotas, management can exercise this direction without close personal contact. Actual results against expected goals can easily be ascertained.

For quotas to be an effective control tool, they must be constantly monitored, salespeople must be kept informed of their own progress toward quotas, and the sales manager must follow up on performance inadequacies. When the quota or certain aspects of it seem out of reach, follow-up may involve special coaching, additional training, or if uncontrollable extraneous factors seem to be operative, modifying the quota to reflect the factors.

A common question confronting the sales manager is how to respond to quota deviations. Should these be ignored, should the unmet part of the quota be carried over to the next period, should a penalty be attached to serious deviations, or should the sales results of the preceding period be reduced accordingly? Most firms affix no penalty for failure to achieve the quota, although a minority add any deficiency to the next quota period.

Drawbacks to Using Quotas

Although the advantages of using quotas are undeniable—assuming that the quotas are fair, reasonably attainable, challenging, and well accepted—sometimes their use is not advantageous and may even be detrimental. In assessing the desirability of quotas, however, one must carefully identify those alleged drawbacks that are due to poorly designed quotas and those inherent in the quota concept itself. Some salespeople and sales managers argue that quotas may result in using high-pressure techniques and overstocking customers. The quotas can overemphasize the wrong aspects of the selling job or can reward short-term sales generation at the expense of longer-term customer satisfaction. But misguided selling emphasis can be corrected by redesigned quotas, such as quotas based on gross margin, perhaps, or combination quotas. The quota concept itself should not be blamed for this situation.

A firm's sales may be fully dependent on the business of its customers, such as is experienced by a firm selling component parts to other manufacturers. The efforts of salespeople in generating sales consequently are dependent on factors beyond their control, and the use of quotas is then questionable. Similarly, in sales involving infrequently made major expenditures such as heavy equipment, the quota becomes a meaningless exercise; the salesperson may record no sales at all in one period and may far exceed any imaginable quota in another period.

Quotas should stimulate selling efforts and provide a basis for measuring performance and controlling sales efforts. The potential benefits sometimes are not worth the time and effort required to develop quotas. For example a quota is not necessary if the sales force is on straight commission—which should induce maximum efforts and challenges in itself—or if the sales force experiences rapid turnover—such as in some kinds of door-to-door selling, such as encyclopedias.

Like most sales management tools, quotas can be highly useful. But only a firm's unique situation and requirements can determine whether quotas are likely to produce sufficient benefits to be worth the effort.

At the beginning of this chapter I asked you to consider the issue of a salesperson whose quota is higher than that of another, adjacent territory. Is this a blatantly unfair situation? Your answer should involve considerations such as differences in potential, ease of coverage, and the human factor. If the neighboring salesperson is more inexperienced, perhaps his quota should be lower for a short period of time. Quotas should reflect differences in expected territorial attainment, based on past results and present expectations.

SUMMARY

A quota is the salesperson's expected performance; it can also be expanded to cover other marketing entities, such as a distributor or a branch office. The value of quotas lies in their use to measure performance, to provide an incentive, to serve as a basis for compensation, to channel sales force efforts in the most desired directions, and most important, to make disparate territories more equivalent.

Most quotas are sales volume, budget, activity, and combination quotas. A quota should be fair, challenging, easy to understand, flexible, and capable of monitoring managerial priorities. The steps usually involved in developing a quota are (1) selecting the type of quota, (2) determining the base, (3) making any desired adjustments. Adjustments are most commonly made for the human factor, such as lack of experience.

Quotas are not without drawbacks, chief among them are lack of acceptance and mistrust by sales representatives. The drawbacks can be minimized by making quotas as equitable as possible, easily understandable, and by including the sales force in setting the quota.

QUESTIONS

1. Distinguish between a sales forecast and a sales quota. Are they usually the same?

2. How can quotas be used to direct efforts into the highest-priority activities?

3. Would you recommend using an activity quota for an insurance salesperson? Why or why not?

4. "We have always used past sales as the base for figuring next year's quotas. Nothing is to be gained by making the quota more complicated." Would you agree with this statement?

5. What arguments can you give for not adjusting the quota base for the human factor?

6. Under what circumstances may quotas be useless or even detrimental?

7. Why should each salesperson be involved in determining his own quota?

8. How can a quota be set in order to emphasize profitability?

9. Should a quota be tied in with a compensation plan? Why or why not?

PEOPLE PROBLEM: FAIRNESS IN ADJUSTING A QUOTA

Please evaluate each of the following alternatives.

A problem has arisen in adjusting one of your territorial quotas. The procedure is to determine quantitatively the base for the quota considering past sales and estimates for future potential. You then adjust this quantitative base for the human factor. But this is causing serious morale problems with your sales force. You have lowered the quota for Anthony Scarpino, one of the older salesmen, because of his age and also because of an arthritic condition that is slowing him down. As a result, last year Anthony earned as much commission as several other salespeople whose sales were 10 to 25 percent higher. They are calling this discrimination. What should you do?

1. Stand on your principles. You are the boss, and your judgment should not be disputed. Get tough if you have to: the cause is right.

2. You have to face up to the realities of the situation. Anthony is no longer as valuable to the firm as he was in his younger days. His compensation should reflect this diminished contribution. The full quota should be reinstated.

3. Perhaps short-term morale might be affected adversely. But the other employees eventually will positively view the consequences of sympathetic treatment of faithful employees. Do not let petty bickering and jealousy sway your decision to let Anthony have the special treatment he deserves. You may explain your reasoning, but do not be apologetic.

4. The morale of the rest of the sales force must be acknowledged. Their perception of rampant favoritism is bound to have an adverse effect. Make the quotas more equal.

5. Try to convince the rest of the organization that this person has given years of loyal service to the company. He deserves special consideration.

---

1. Thomas R. Wotruba and Michael L. Thurlow, ''Sales Force Participation in Quota Setting and Sales Forecasting,'' *Journal of Marketing* (April 1976): 11–16.

NOTES

cases

11.1 Carrying Over Quota Deficiencies

"I'm sick of the whole thing," Jessica Simcox, one of your newer salespeople is telling you. "I'm trying my darnedest, and I know I'm improving, but I'm never going to make up my quota deficiencies and be able to make any money."

Jessica has a point, you must admit. She has been with the firm almost a year and a half now. You hired her fresh out of college, and she had a lot of trouble at first. Maybe the company should have had a better training program, or maybe hiring inexperienced people for a rather complex product line was a mistake. However, Jessica has worked very hard, and she finally appears to be improving. This last quarter she moved out of last place in sales. The company policy, however, was to add any deficiency in meeting the quarterly quota to the next quarter's quota.

"What is your quota for this quarter?" you ask her.

"It's $450,000, of which $225,000 are deficiencies carried over from previous periods. I think I did well last quarter, with sales of $305,000, but I was still almost $70,000 deficient, which makes this quarter that much more impossible to reach. I don't know what to do. Maybe I should quit."

QUESTION

As sales manager, what would you do in this situation?

11.2 Revising Quotas for Better Control

John Severson, sales manager for Miss Traci, Inc., a wearing apparel manufacturer, is dissatisfied with the sales volume quota presently used. His salespeople are paid a base salary and a commission of 5 percent on all sales over the quota, which is based on 60 percent of expected sales in each territory. Most of his men and women have exceeded their quotas and achieved a major part of their total compensation in the form of commissions. Sales overall have been satisfactory.

The trouble is that other activities—prospecting for new customers and servicing present accounts, particularly regarding handling complaints, making adjustments, and helping with displays—are being neglected. Several large retail customers have complained to John about this lack of servicing. The problem has recently come to a head. The home office wants specific feedback on customer intentions for the coming season, and the sales force has been charged with formally querying all customers about their future product needs. But the material that John has received from the field has been left incomplete, done carelessly, or not done at all.

QUESTIONS

1. What revision of the quota would you recommend to give management better control over the sales force?
2. Or do you have some other suggestions for encouraging nonselling activities?

11.3   Williamson Company: Setting Sales Quotas

Williamson Company marketed commercial security systems primarily to small businesses. It planned and installed appropriate theft and fire detection systems for its clients, and it also had a monitoring office for early warning, at which point the appropriate fire or police departments were quickly notified. The degree of protection varied according to the needs and budgets of the clients and could range from a little over $1,000, for minimum protection, to over $10,000.

Williamson employed nine sales representatives in the metropolitan St. Louis area. They contacted prospective businesses either through cold calls or referrals from the direct mail brochures that were periodically sent out or from other sources. The salespeople, after convincing a contact of the need for a security system, then designed or customized a system according to the customer's needs. A service department performed the installation according to the plans drawn up by the sales representative in consultation with the customer.

Salespeople were assigned specific territories or parts of the metro area, and these territories were fairly equitable regarding the perceived potential. Yet, wide sales disparities were realized among the nine. Invariably, salespeople who had difficulty in achieving their quotas complained that the calculation was patently unfair.

The quota was an important factor in the total compensation that each salesperson could receive. They were paid on a straight salary plus commission. Only after the quota had been achieved was a commission earned, but this was quite lucrative: 7 percent of sales over the quota.

The quotas were simply calculated and were based entirely on the estimated sales potential in each territory. From telephone directories and other data sources, Williamson had obtained a listing of the number of small firms in each territory. An effort was made to weed out the very smallest firms because they probably had less need for the security system Williamson marketed. Because the industry was rapidly growing, the company felt a 10-percent annual growth factor in the quota determination was reasonable, despite the inroads of competition. In territory A the quota for 1988 was calculated as follows:

$$1987 \text{ company sales} = \$1,520,000$$
$$10\% \text{ increase projected for 1988} = \$ 152,000$$
$$\text{Sales forecast for 1988} = \$1,672,000$$
$$\text{Quota for territory } A =$$
$$\$1,672,000 \times \frac{\text{no. of small firms in } A}{\text{total no. of small firms in metro St. Louis}}$$
$$= \$1,672,000 \times \frac{1,680}{20,200}$$
$$= \$138,776$$

The salespeople particularly complained about the arbitrary 10-percent increase in sales for each year. They claimed that this was unwarranted and not based on sound reasoning. Indeed, some of the salespeople habitually argued, the entrance of new security system firms into the St. Louis area should have led Williamson to change its unsubstantiated and arbitrary sales increase into a decrease. However, management refused to accept this argument, pointing out that Williamson had been achieving better than a 10-percent gain in sales for each of the last 3 years.

Other complaints were directed at the use of total number of small firms in a territory as a percentage of total number of small firms in metro St. Louis. The sales force pointed out that certain types of businesses, notably retailers and wholesalers, had been the major customers for security systems. Management countered this argument by stating that all small businesses, except the very smallest mom-and-pop establishments, could benefit from this system and that the potential of becoming a client was the same for all types of firms.

The final major complaint against the quota was that it did not reflect personal factors among the salespeople, such as differences in experience, age, and so on. Company management also refused to concede this point, maintaining that whereas such personal differences existed, they saw no reason to favor or penalize anyone because of these factors.

So the quota system and calculation remained rigid, despite continual complaints and considerable agitation.

QUESTIONS

1. Evaluate the Williamson method for quota calculations—both pros and cons.
2. Do you think sales force criticism of these quotas was justified? Why or why not?
3. Can you recommend alternative calculations to develop the quota? Would this have been more equitable?
4. What recommendations, if any, would you as a consultant make to the Williamson Company?

PART IV
IMPLEMENTING SALES EFFORTS

CHAPTER 12
Training for Selling Effectiveness

CHAPTER 13
Directing and Motivating Through Compensation

CHAPTER 14
Directing and Motivating Through Supervision

CHAPTER 15
Implementing Effective Distributor–Customer Relations

CHAPTER 12
Training for Selling Effectiveness

CHAPTER PERSPECTIVE

In Chapter 2 we debunked the myth that "salesmen are born, not made," that no amount of training will produce the able salesperson and some innate aptitude is needed. This is nonsense! Firms now recognize the benefits of sales training and the need for it in today's competitive environment. The well-trained, confident, and knowledgeable salesperson invariably wins out over the poorly trained. This chapter examines the benefits of training and how to do it.

As you read this chapter, consider how you would determine the training needs of your firm. What information would you want in planning the training program?

CHAPTER OBJECTIVES

□ Know the four types of sales training.
□ Become familiar with the particular benefits of training.
□ Become aware of formality and duration issues in training.
□ Know the various topics that can be covered in sales training.
□ Become familiar with the methods and procedures that can be used for conducting sales training.
□ Become aware of administrative issues such as who should do the training, when it should be done, where it should be done, the amount that should be spent, and how training can be evaluated.
□ Become aware of cautions regarding training programs.

TYPES OF SALES TRAINING

Training normally is thought to occur in the first days or weeks on the job. But sales training can and often should involve considerably more than that. We can identify four categories of sales training:

1. Salespeople new to the organization receive *initial training*.
2. Present and experienced salespeople receive *continuous* or *refresher* training.
3. Sales personnel of distributors and dealers are trained by the manufacturer, who is most knowledgeable about the product(s). These salespeople, in turn, will pass it on to their customers.
4. Customers are trained by the manufacturer. Customers are given adequate information so that they may correctly use and maintain the product and achieve better satisfaction with it.

Most firms limit sales training to initial and refresher. Because there are many similarities in all training, we will discuss training in general, but where appropriate, we will differentiate between initial and refresher training. And we will discuss an aspect of training that usually receives scant attention—training sales managers to train.

BENEFITS OF TRAINING

Deficiencies of Trial-and-Error Learning

Some sales managers still argue that training is not really necessary. They maintain that salespeople can learn on their own by trial and error, on the "firing line," where "it really counts," and not merely in some artificial training program. Trial-and-error learning, however, has several notable disadvantages. Sales are lost before the desired level of competence is reached, and trial and error is not an effective learning method.

Undoubtedly, sales will be lost and potential business missed during the learning period. For many firms the desire to avoid business losses is a crucial argument for developing more formal training programs. But for those firms with a large body of potential customers who can never be entirely covered (e.g., insurance, financial services, door-to-door selling, and recreational land), the loss of some business during the process of weeding out the less competent salespeople is of little concern.

Perhaps the best argument against the position that formal training is not really necessary is that trial and error is not a very effective training technique. Often people cannot recognize specific problems that make them less effective. Continued trial-and-error efforts may only reinforce bad habits. Unless a firm has such a high turnover of salespeople that formal training would be largely wasted, the trial-and-error approach is not recommended. Even for firms with high turnover, a better training program might create stability. The obvious objective of training programs is to increase sales. However, one should recognize more specific benefits that can translate into increased sales (see Figure 12.1).

Figure 12.1 shows that training can help salespeople to develop faster and become more competent. The knowledge, and competence, and enthusiasm that a good training program can engender can improve morale. Better knowledge and improved morale result in less discouragement and less personnel turnover. A more competent and stable sales force, as the figure indicates, also promotes better customer relations. All of these factors should have a healthy effect on sales. Simultaneously, increased sales boost self-confidence and increase earnings, producing an enthusiastic and dedicated sales force.

Faster Development

The new salesperson requires initial training to learn the right way to present the product, its specific features, its capabilities and limitations, price information, and included servicing or warranties. Furthermore, certain procedures for handling orders and promising deliveries must be communicated to the fledgling salesperson. The more complex product lines and order-processing systems generally require more time for initial training before the new representative can function without close guidance.

Instruction on planning—its importance and the best approach—also can expedite the new person's effectiveness. To best use time, sales calls must be scheduled to minimize waiting and backtracking. In addition most businesses treat their various customers somewhat differently, giving more time to the larger, more important accounts, and calling on smaller accounts less fre-

FIGURE 12.1   Benefits of sales force training programs.

quently. Classifying customers and other developmental planning rarely is done well without some training. The importance of other selling activities (handling complaints, prospecting for new customers, perhaps setting up dealers' displays) must also receive due emphasis.

Finally, both new and old sales representatives can use training to help them develop their selling techniques as quickly and thoroughly as possible. Although selling is more of an art than a science, many aspects of selling can be comprehended more quickly and proficiency acquired through instruction that may involve role playing and demonstrations, as well as more common teaching techniques. Even experienced salespeople sometimes find aspects of their performance falling below par and can address these with refresher training.

Improved Morale

Confidence translates into better morale, which contributes directly to increased sales, and confidence accompanies knowledge. Successful experience and minimal training breed confidence, but adequate training speeds up knowledge acquisition.

A by-product of good morale is lower personnel turnover and more enthusiasm about the job and the employer. The firm that argues against comprehensive training on the grounds that its salespeople do not stay with the company long enough for it to pay off is missing the point. Better training would probably result in more stability. Enthusiasm and optimism are contagious. The sales manager who can keep a sales force enthusiastic is successful. Adequate training (both for new employees and the more experienced) can instill the good morale and motivation desired. The problems and opportunities of motivating a sales force are examined in greater detail in Chapters 13 and 14.

Better Customer Relations

Some firms fail to consider the consequences of a training program on customer relations. A well-trained sales representative should be oriented to ascertaining customers' needs and presenting products and services that effectively satisfy those needs. Few firms now use training programs that indoctrinate a salesperson with high-pressure techniques, because high-pressure selling is incompatible with customer goodwill and loyalty. A sound training program rather should instill a commitment to customer satisfaction and customer service.

Knowledge of the firm's products and policies is important in achieving customer satisfaction. The salesperson who has more than a passing knowledge about the customer's operation and problems, can better match products and services to the customer's needs. Customer information can come with experience, but a well-trained sales representative is in the best position to cultivate the mutuality of interests that characterizes good buyer–seller relationships. When a sales force is relatively stable, when the same salesperson calls on the same customer over a considerable period of time, the rapport and confidence gained from past satisfactory service instill loyalty and give a competitive advantage over the firm with a high personnel turnover and a constantly changing sales force.

DETERMINING THE SCOPE OF THE TRAINING

Scope refers to the formality and duration of the training program. Companies vary widely in their scope. A firm's own particular requirements should govern, which essentially means that the difficulty of the selling job should be the major determinant of the scope of training.

How Formal Should Our Training Be?

Figure 12.2 depicts a continuum of the formality possible in sales training. At one extreme no formal training occurs; rather, the sales manager and/or other experienced salespeople provide field coaching, or the selling techniques of fellow salespeople are observed. In the latter situation the novice may accompany an experienced salesperson on her rounds for a period of time considered sufficient to learn the art of selling the company's products. At the other extreme are formal training sessions that may occur at headquarters or a manufacturing plant. In formal training sessions the new employees receive information and practice selling techniques before being permitted to go out into the field. Of course, as the continuum suggests, various combinations of formality are possible and are more common than either extreme. But the amount of formality is controversial.

An alternative to a formal and lengthy training program is interspersing formal training sessions with field experience. The new salesperson therefore can practice some of the techniques learned in formal training sessions, while periodically returning to compare experiences with other trainees and to receive additional instruction in areas that are still weak.

no formal training; reliance on field coaching and/or observation of other salespeople	combination of formal and informal	formal training, of the classroom type, away from the field

Substitute model is the hand-out given

FIGURE 12.2   Range of formality of training programs.

A Controversy: Formality of Training

A sales manager of a small apparel manufacturer speaks out against any formality:

> How can effective selling be learned from a lecture, a book, or movies? Or even from some artificial role-playing exercise? I don't think it can ever really be learned except on the firing line. Now, I'm not talking about trial-and-error, sink-or-swim situations with no training. No, what I favor is personal coaching—by the manager and/or experienced associates—in the real job environment, making contact with real customers, and experiencing the true flavor of the selling challenge.

The personnel director of a medium-sized industrial chemical firm defends formal training:

> Sure, on-the-job experience is good. But it should only come after careful preparation. Otherwise, there may well be a long transition period before the salesperson can learn to sell effectively, and during this time sales will be lost. But even more important, we're conveying a poor image of the company to our customers—not the image of an experienced and professional sales staff. And what sales manager has time to do much personal coaching?

How Long Should the Training Be?

Initial training programs vary in duration from a few hours of indoctrination or tips to several years. Table 12.1 shows the length of sales training programs for new recruits for manufacturers of industrial products, consumer products, and for service firms such as insurance, banking, public utilities, and transportation companies. Although most manufacturers limit their formal training to 3 months or less, service firms generally have longer sales training programs. The best length depends on the difficulty of the selling job, and the combination of formal and informal training should be a function of this characteristic. A lengthy training program is necessary when products are technologically complex and customers' requirements are diverse, thereby necessitating special tailoring of the product or service to customers' needs (which is often the case with expensive machinery and even with insurance and financial planning). Some firms, however, tend to drag out the formal

TABLE 12.1   Length of training programs for new salespeople.

Time Period	Percentage Industrial Manufacturers	Percentage Consumer Manufacturers	Percentage Service Firms
Three months or less	50	55	17
Over 3 months, up to 12 months	41	45	83
Over 12 months	0	0	9

Source: Adapted from *Sales & Marketing Management* (20 Feb. 1984): 73.

training program longer then necessary. Although there are advantages to gaining familiarity with all aspects of an employer's operation, including production, this can be overdone. The longer formal training programs increase cost and postpone demonstrating capability and increasing earnings.

A policy of flexibility rather than a fixed duration for the training programs is recommended. Trainees' prior experiences then can be recognized, as well as the characteristics of the jobs to be filled. An experienced salesperson, for example, will probably require less training time than a recent college graduate who has never sold before. If a firm's customers are primarily technical experts and high-level executives, more training time seems required than for another selling job that involves mostly smaller customers with less sophisticated needs. A further, major argument for flexibility in duration or training is the urgency of filling the job. A sudden vacancy, because of resignation, illness, or unexpected promotion, may need to be filled promptly. If no experienced person is available, the sales manager cannot wait for a hiree to complete a lengthy formal training program before being placed in that slot. The training may have to be limited to informal on-the-job guidance, perhaps interspersed with some formal training sessions at a later date.

Refresher or *follow-up training* may be given periodically or sporadically. If technology changes or major new products are developed, the sales force must be adequately informed. But problems can arise with refresher training. Usually time must be taken from selling activities. If the salesperson is on commission—as most are—some reduction in income may result. But the company also loses in decreased productivity because of the training period. Some firms attempt to overcome this drawback by encouraging or requiring their salespeople to attend "self-development" sessions during their own time. These efforts tend to be checkered at best. New sales representatives may be more interested than older ones, and serious morale problems can develop unless such free-time training readily is identified as self-development, such as a public speaking course or one on leadership development.

SELECTING TOPICS

Training programs cover some or all of the following topics:

1. Product and company knowledge
2. Customer and industry orientation.
3. Sales techniques
4. Territory management - Skills
5. Inspiration (Ignore)

Table 12.2 shows how companies, on average, distribute the training time. Product information receives the most attention in training programs—as

TABLE 12.2   Training time spent on various subject areas.

Subject Area	Percentage Training Time, Median all Companies
Product knowledge	42
Selling techniques	24
Market–industry orientation	17
Company orientation	13
Other topics	4
	100

Source: Based on 152 firms, reported by David S. Hopkins, *Training the Sales Force: A Progress Report* (New York: The Conference Board, 1978), 6.

much as 90 percent of the total training in some firms. A salesperson therefore must know the products well to capably present them to customers. (An often-heard criticism of retail salesclerks is that they know little or nothing about the products they sell and "sometimes could care less.")[1]

Product and Company Knowledge

To give sales trainees sufficient product information, some companies assign them to the factory to observe production. The trainee may be transferred to various departments to gain sufficient breadth. The amount of time spent on technical matters, however, does not always translate into the kind of product knowledge necessary to sell effectively. One might question whether a lengthy stay in the factory or warehouse is worth the investment in time and money.

What kind of product knowledge is important?   *1. The product line.*   The sales representative should know the products available to sell, which may involve considerable study, because there may be hundreds of different products and variations. Of course, brochures, catalogs and other listings, and samples help, but a more detailed knowledge is desired, including the characteristics of at least the more important products, their end uses, and their differences.

2. Special provisions.   The salesperson should know the available product options, delivery conditions, servicing and maintenance standards, and any special set-up problems or requirements.

3. Relative profitability.   An additional category of information often is neglected in sales training and sometimes is not even definitively known by the firm. This is the relative profitability of the various products in the line—which should be stressed in the sales presentation to produce the most profitable business.

Information about the firm is necessary, but sometimes training programs are too zealous in devoting time to this topic. Just as one may question the productivity of giving sales trainees lengthy exposure to manufacturing, so a policy of transferring to various jobs in the company can be overdone and can delay the contribution of the new sales recruit. However, certain company information is vital and must be conveyed to customers. This information includes company policies regarding credit, product warranties, handling of defective goods, exclusivity of merchandise, price guarantees, discounts, and terms of sales. Delivery and servicing information also is important. The sales trainees should be informed about the amount of latitude they have in pricing. They must know how to expedite an order for customer emergencies.

Some information should not be limited to the initial training period. Sales representatives must be constantly informed of advertising and the products and product features that are emphasized. Furthermore, information on planned promotions should be promptly communicated to the sales force to achieve good coordination of sales and promotional efforts.

Customer and Industry Orientation

A customer orientation is essential to effective marketing today. The firm—or the sales representative—that does not take this position is at a competitive disadvantage with other firms and salespeople who do. *A customer orientation* implies knowing about the customers' needs, wants, and problems, and the practices of their industry.

The salesperson's job sometimes involves problem solving, showing how particular products and service can help solve some of the customer's problems. Although the more intimate knowledge about particular customers cannot be gained in an initial training program, characteristics of the industry and present and potential customers offer a starting point.

The types of customer assistance needed (e.g., setting up displays, training dealer salespeople, or handling defective goods) deserve attention in the training program when these services are important to customers, as is the case with many small retailers and with larger self-service firms. Knowing who makes buying decisions in various firms can simplify the new salesperson's efforts and can permit more productive use of time. Sometimes this must be learned on the job, but general organizational patterns, discussed in training, can provide clues.

Salespeople must have information about competitors and competitive products to answer customer objections and present products effectively. Salespeople particularly must know how their own products compare with competitors in specific features, quality, and capabilities and limitations. Only in this way can salespeople counter price objections by showing specific product advantages over competitor's lower-priced goods.

Sales Techniques

As Table 12.2 shows, most firms emphasize teaching sales techniques. A firm may show trainees how to prospect for customers, how to gain attention and interest, and the best responses to the more common objections. Training will also include discussion and demonstration of effectively initiating the close of the sale. In addition to lectures and demonstrations of proper sales techniques, trainees may also role play in simulated sales situations. Increasingly, firms are using role-playing videotapes to more vividly show weak and strong points.

When a salesperson with minimal training must be moved quickly into the actual selling situation, a prepared sales pitch is often rehearsed. This may be memorized or *canned* (as discussed in Chapter 3). Although "formula" selling uses the most persuasive language that line and staff specialists can devise, it has its drawbacks. Giving the same memorized presentation to all customers destroys flexibility. Situations differ, and the same sales talk is not appropriate or effective in all instances and with all customers; and it sounds like a poor actor saying a script. Furthermore, this type of selling is incompatible with the problem-solving approach, which is generally more effective.

One may question whether selling really can be taught. Selling is difficult to teach, because salesmanship requires skill and practice, and not just reading about it out of a book. As discussed throughout this book, however, certain selling techniques have proven to be quite effective. Hearing or reading about these techniques does not guarantee their best use, but knowledge, combined with practice, can encourage more rapid improvement in selling.

Refresher training in sales techniques can be useful when particular problems are encountered, such as customer objections, difficulty in closing, and unsuccessful prospecting. Individual coaching sometimes is satisfactory in these situations; or a sales staff round-table discussion can disclose successful techniques used by other sales representatives.

Territory Management

Training programs should devote some attention to helping individual salespeople better manage their own selling. Advice can be given for making the best use of time, minimizing waiting to see customers, and routing efficiently to avoid backtracking. Trainees should be taught how to plan sales calls, materials and handouts to use in presentations, and how to record important information about each customer. In particular attention should be given to the proper allocation of sales calls and sales efforts according to the importance of customers. The need for field reports can be demonstrated, as well as the best time for making such reports to minimize the loss of productive selling time.

Of course, when salespeople are routed and call schedules specified, much of the management function has been removed from the salesperson and assumed by the company. But for most high-level sales jobs, individual sales representatives still do their own scheduling and routing, sometimes subject to approval by management. Better territorial management can separate the good from the mediocre, as well as improve district selling production.

Inspiration

As you might expect, heavy and obvious doses of inspiration are better for low-level salespeople—for example, the untrained college student earning money during the summer by working a grueling schedule. High-level salespeople often resent exhortative efforts. As selling becomes more professional, and as greater recognition is given to the value of better meeting customer needs and using a problem-solving approach, the popularity of inspirational content in training sessions is decreasing. Confidence, morale, and a better job of selling are more likely to result from a well-designed training program than from one heavy on inspiration.

METHODS AND PROCEDURES

Figure 12.3 shows a continuum of the various conventional media and techniques used for sales training, from the most indirect to the most direct. They culminate in actual work experience.

Training methods can be classified as group or individual. Group methods include those commonly encountered in education of any kind such as lecture, case and panel discussion, and audio-visual demonstration, as well as role

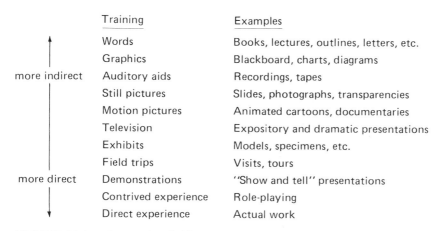

	Training	Examples
	Words	Books, lectures, outlines, letters, etc.
	Graphics	Blackboard, charts, diagrams
more indirect	Auditory aids	Recordings, tapes
	Still pictures	Slides, photographs, transparencies
	Motion pictures	Animated cartoons, documentaries
	Television	Expository and dramatic presentations
	Exhibits	Models, specimens, etc.
	Field trips	Visits, tours
more direct	Demonstrations	"Show and tell" presentations
	Contrived experience	Role-playing
	Direct experience	Actual work

FIGURE 12.3 The training ladder. (*Source*: Adapted from James F. Bender, "Training and Developing Sales Personnel," in *Handbook of Modern Marketing.* New York: McGraw-Hill, 1970, 12–46.)

playing, which is particularly suited to sales training (though not limited to it). Individual training methods include on-the-job training, company-sponsored home study, and self-development programs, which the company may subsidize.

Group Methods — Know Prob't Cas

Lectures. The most common method of teaching is the lecture. It is the most efficient method in terms of time, because one trainer or lecturer can handle almost any size group. For information such as company and industry characteristics, planned advertising and promotional strategies, or sales expectations, the lecture method is ideal, if conducted properly. The lecturer or speaker must be competent, have a good voice, and be well prepared. Nothing is more deadly to the sustained interest of the audience and their ability to absorb the material than a lecturer who reads from notes in a dry monotone.

For sales training the lecture method has some important limitations. It is ill suited for training in sales techniques. Words cannot convey the finer points, or the art, of selling. Furthermore, for a mature audience, eager to begin producing, a lengthy training period of lecturing or sermonizing will not improve interest, learning, or morale. Some modifications of the lecture format can increase interest and learning, however. It may be used to introduce certain points that the trainees may then discuss in small groups. Or a movie or slide demonstration might supplement the lecture material.

Discussions. Discussions can be effective for training in sales techniques and problems by dramatizing and providing an in-depth development of certain topics. Cases are commonly used to give practice both in finding creative alternatives and in solving problems. Round-table discussions of certain topics, issues, and problems can reveal diverse viewpoints and solutions. Panels sometimes are used for similar purposes, but the discussion is before an audience. Obviously, discussion techniques have more value if the participants are relatively experienced. For the completely inexperienced, discussing actual selling situations and offering solutions may be premature. The discussion technique therefore can be particularly fruitful for refresher training, but is less so for initial training except in moderation and for a change of pace.

Demonstrations. Demonstrations include visual aids such as movies and slide presentations. Correct and incorrect sales techniques can be shown and analyzed. Demonstrations are particularly effective in sales training, and retention is enhanced because both the eyes and the ears are involved. For most persons dual perception has more impact and causes longer retention than either sight or hearing alone. So demonstrations can be important in both sales training and customer presentations.

Role playing.   Role playing can be one of the most effective training techniques for the art of selling. In role playing one trainee assumes the role of salesperson and one or more persons take on the role of customer(s). The result is a simulated selling situation that conveys the buyer-seller interaction, although it can be criticized justifiably as artificial. But role playing is particularly effective if done before an audience of other salespeople. Their comments can provide valuable feedback on effective and ineffective techniques. Furthermore, certain nervous tendencies or idiosyncrasies are readily evident to the audience and can be constructively pointed out.

Videotape in role-playing episodes can be a powerful learning tool. The participants can see and hear their actual performance repeatedly to identify weak points for corrective action. Seeing oneself unfavorably on tape, however, can be traumatic unless coupled with tactful and constructive suggestions for improvement.

Individual Methods

On-the-job training.   Nothing in a training program can duplicate the actual job experience. Although role playing comes closest, its artificiality tends to mask the apprehension, the interaction, and the possible triumph of the real selling situation. In some on-the-job training sessions, the beginning salesperson may accompany an experienced one and observe. Only after some time may the fledgling actually be turned loose. In some on-the-job training, the sales manager accompanies the trainees on sales calls. The sales manager then should remain a background observer, simply observing the apprentice's skill or lack of skill (unless a major sale is in jeopardy), to offer constructive advice later. The major disadvantage of supervised on-the-job training is the managerial time involved. When a sales manager has many responsibilities and a sizable sales staff to supervise, personal training, although possibly desired, likely is impossible without neglecting other important functions.

Home study.   Home study, usually involving correspondence training, occasionally is used. Individual motivation and willingness to study can be relied on when the selling task and the product are standardized and when the selling situation is routine. Home study therefore is generally limited to circumstances requiring little training other than indoctrination. For some firms that recruit by mail, especially if recruits work on a straight commission, home training is practical, because it provides basic information and orientation at a minimal cost.

Sales training by correspondence can also be used for introducing product changes to a regular sales staff. By conducting indoctrination training without assembling the sales staff in central or regional groups, management can minimize costs. With programmed learning, in which the learner receives prompt feedback, individual home study is more practical. The major drawback is diminished motivation resulting from the absence of competitive contact in group training.

Self-development.   Some firms encourage their sales representatives and other employees to take self-development courses, which may be formalized undergraduate- or graduate-level instruction or may consist of more specialized, shorter sessions on topics such as public speaking and conference leadership. The firm often pays part or all of the program fees, but the employee contributes her time in nonworking hours. The company expects training to result in a more effective employee, more strongly motivated to performance excellence. A willingness to engage in free-time self-development activities may be considered tangible evidence of a person's drive and future promise.

Encouragement and subsidies of employee self-development raises some interesting issues. Should a firm make a commitment to "total personal development," rather than sales and management training per se? Does a firm have a moral responsibility to help its employees and salespeople become better adjusted, happier individuals? Some argue that the company's responsibility ends when the daily job duties are finished, that any concern beyond strictly job-related aspects of life is an infringement on personal freedom. A more enlightened approach recognizes that both firm and employee can benefit from encouragement and support of total personal development.

ADMINISTERING THE TRAINING PROGRAM

Who Should Conduct the Training?

Training can be done by line executives, by staff personnel, or by outside specialists. Often a combination of these sources can be used to advantage.

Line executives.   Sales executives can achieve better rapport with their people and gain a better insight into their abilities and potential when they are actively involved in the training process. Because most sales executives came up through the ranks, they should have a better understanding of the problems and challenges in the sales situation than can staff personnel, who are isolated from the field.[2] A major disadvantage of using line executives in formal training sessions is their lack of adequate time. Furthermore, although a particular sales manager may once have been an excellent salesperson, this is no assurance that she can communicate her knowledge and skills to others,[3] unless she is trained to train (see Application 12.1).

Staff personnel.   Staff training personnel can give more expertise to the training function than can line executives who may give it only cursory

---

APPLICATION 12.1 Training Sales Managers to Train

Even if sales managers are not directly involved in formal training sessions, they almost certainly will still be involved in training because they are coaches and role models for their salespeople. Unfortunately, skilled salespeople and sales managers often are not the best trainers; they are "amateurish" without some formal training. To demonstrate the shaky correlation between success in selling and effectiveness in teaching, some professional sales trainers were rather poor sales representatives. Teaching skills seem more important than knowledge of the subject matter.* But teaching skills can be learned. Sales managers particularly need training in subjects such as the following:

The most effective training techniques
How to coach
How to praise and how best to criticize
How to prepare and conduct a performance evaluation
How best to conduct pre- and post-call reviews with salespeople†
How to adapt training to the needs of individual trainees
How to interact with trainees so that each is motivated to learn‡

These recommendations suggest that the sales manager's involvement with training exceeds initial formal training. It is an ongoing process, as the sales manager guides and directs.

*Dennis A. Miller, ''Ten Ways to Improve Sales Training Programs,'' *Marketing News* (22 Aug. 1980): 4.
†Bernard L. Rosenbaum and Nick Ward, ''Why Sales Managers Need More and Better Management Training,'' *Training/HRD* (August 1982): 45.
‡Robert E. Lefton and V. R. Buzzotta, ''Trainers, Learners, and Training Results,'' *Training and Development Journal* (November 1980): 12–18.

---

attention. Staff experts should have more know-how on teaching methods, on the use of audiotape supplementary aids, and the like. They should be more familiar with other firms' successful training methods. In general staff people bring more sophistication and objectivity into the training program, although they may lack the practical experience of line executives. A temptation of staff specialists is to overdo sales training, to present more than is really necessary, and thereby prolong the training process. Staff participation usually stops at the end of the formal initial or refresher training program. Ongoing involvement with indirect training aspects such as establishing goals with the sales representatives, holding progress reviews, coaching and motivating to correct deficiencies—all are the responsibility of the sales manager, although these activities are not always recognized as training.

Outside specialists. Outside consultants and sales training firms supply a needed service for many smaller businesses that cannot afford their own sales training departments. Specialists can handle an entire training program or the part for which a firm most needs outside help. Specialists therefore provide great flexibility. And because outside training specialists depend on their clients' satisfaction for repeat business, they usually are knowledgeable and interesting.

When to Conduct Training?

As noted before, in many firms sales training consists of both initial and refresher training. Although the inexperienced new employee obviously needs sales training most, many firms find a need for some continuous, periodic training, called refresher training.

Refresher training may be remedial, aimed at improving poor performance.[4] Or it may be directed at better-than-average salespeople under the assumption that the payoffs of further training will be highest with superior performers. The general objective is to help the experienced person grow and develop rather than continuing to operate on a plateau. Updating skills, providing current information, tackling recurring problems in selling, and re-motivating are arguments for refresher training. Admittedly, trainers face greater challenges in refresher sessions than in initial training, because experienced salespeople resent time taken from productive selling unless its usefulness is readily apparent. Resentment is particularly likely if training requires the salespeople to do some work on their own, during their own time, reducing the perhaps already limited time that could be spent with their families.

Firms differ in their timing of *initial training.* Some firms like salespeople to prove their worth by achieving a certain sales level before the firm invests in sales training. This sink-or-swim philosophy is best used when the loss of a few customers will not affect the firm. Some insurance companies have this policy, but few industrial firms can afford the loss or alienation of customers that might result.

Where to Train?

Training can be centralized or decentralized. The distinction relates to who should do the training—central staff and/or consultants versus field management. A combination of centralized and decentralized training is probably best for most firms, except the very small, which must rely on centralized training.

Should training be centralized?   Several options are possible for centralized training. A firm can maintain permanent facilities and training schools or use temporary locations through periodic conventions and either national or regional sales meetings (depending on the size of the sales force). Permanent facilities may be at the home office or major plant; special rooms or even a separate building may be set aside for training purposes. When facilities are not needed, customers' employees may be invited to upgrade their knowledge and skills.

Advantages.   Proponents of centralized training offer the following persuasive arguments. It permits use of more capable training specialists than when training is assigned to the field. Centralized training can offer a standard training package, exposing all sales representatives to the best information and techniques. It results in better facilities, more and better equipment (such as videotape, which can be highly effective in role playing), training manuals, and the like. Contact with salespeople from all parts of the country creates a feeling of camaraderie that encourages improved morale and company loyalty. Whether or not training is conducted at the home office, top executives usually are present, and their presence can build morale. Training may occur at conventions, which are often held in resort hotels and can be a pleasant experience. In this situation, however, proper balance between recreation and business must be maintained; sometimes recreation becomes so important that the training impact is practically nil.

Disadvantages.   Centralized training has only two general disadvantages, but they are major: cost and time. A firm's training costs are greatly increased when it centrally groups its executives and sales representatives, whether in a permanent facility, a hotel, or resort. Transportation, food, and lodging costs must be considered, as well as the loss of sales production. In addition the logistics in planning and accommodating a large group of people may involve the full-time attention of several staff people.

Time constrains the training program's length. Obviously, experienced salespeople cannot be taken from their productive selling jobs for very long. Not only would sales suffer, but the amount of time that individuals can be absent from their families is limited. The sales productivity loss sometimes can be minimized by holding training sessions and meetings during slack periods. Many textbook publishers hold sales meetings during the Christmas holidays, because sales calls cannot be made during this time. For new trainees a lengthy training program that involves working first at the factory and in various departments of the firm before assignment to a territory may require several relocations, with the consequent expenses and personal disruption. Management must determine whether advantages gained from centralized training are worth the drawbacks.

Should training be decentralized?   Several varieties of decentralized training are common. These may range from on-the-job coaching by the branch sales manager to more formal training sessions at the branch, perhaps with a headquarters personnel assistant, to sales clinics traveling between the districts.

Advantages.   A major advantage of decentralized training, in any form, is that it is much cheaper. Salespeople can intersperse productive work with the training. Therefore, they can put the training ideas and techniques into immediate practice, test them out, refine them, and, if necessary, receive prompt remedial follow-up. Because decentralized training is usually less intensive, the material is likely retained longer than that gained in a more centralized, more intense atmosphere. With the branch manager involved, conditions are favorable for creating better rapport with the sales force.

Disadvantages.   A major disadvantage concerns the training ability of the branch manager. One would expect a field sales manager to be less skilled at training than specialized staff members. The sales manager may even resent the time spent on this training and give it short shrift.

Combination.   A combination of centralized and decentralized training is best for most firms. Some centralized orientation for new employees is followed by longer on-the-job coaching and training sessions. Sales meetings, conducted either regionally or nationally (depending on the size of firm), can be used to upgrade skills, to inform the sales personnel of newest developments and products, and also to increase morale. Table 12.3 shows the frequency of sales meetings among reporting firms. One to four meetings per year are most common.

Costs of Training

Sizable costs are involved in any but a completely decentralized training program. If a lengthy centralized program is necessary, as it often is for technical selling of complex products, the costs are formidable. A firm must weigh the costs of not training (or of reduced training) against those attributable to a more intensive training program. Figure 12.4 shows the more common costs associated with a training program, as well as those intangible costs of sending improperly trained salespeople into the field.

The direct costs of training can be estimated fairly accurately. These include salaries, instructional materials, transportation and living expenses in-

TABLE 12.3   Frequency of sales meetings.

Number of Meetings per Year	Percentage of Firms
Less than 1 meeting per year	3
1 meeting	16
2–4 meetings	47
5–12 meetings	26
More than 12 meetings	8

Source: Based on 152 firms, reported by Hopkins, *Training the Sales Force*, 16.

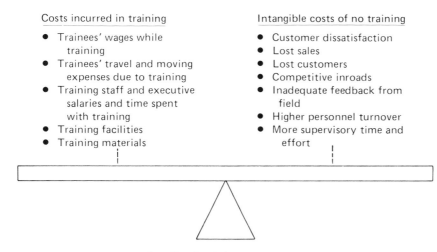

Costs incurred in training

- Trainees' wages while training
- Trainees' travel and moving expenses due to training
- Training staff and executive salaries and time spent with training
- Training facilities
- Training materials

Intangible costs of no training

- Customer dissatisfaction
- Lost sales
- Lost customers
- Competitive inroads
- Inadequate feedback from field
- Higher personnel turnover
- More supervisory time and effort

FIGURE 12.4 Cost trade-offs of training.

curred during training course, instructional staff, management time spent as part of the training program, and outside seminars. Table 12.4 shows the increase in average annual cost of sales training per salesperson by industrial products, consumer products, and service firms, such as insurance, financial, utilities. With training costs running near $20,000 and over per person, full-scale training is costly indeed, and may exceed the reach of small- and medium-sized firms. And if the firm has a fairly high personnel turnover rate, it can ill afford heavy costs of training an unstable work force. (Some would argue here that if training were better, the high instability would be corrected. Factors other than training, however, can also contribute to employee dissatisfaction and instability.)

The intangible costs of no training, as shown in Figure 12.4, are more difficult to estimate. How can you determine specifically the costs of lost sales and customer dissatisfaction, for example? Since customer dissatisfaction and

TABLE 12.4 Average annual cost of sales training per salesperson.

Type of Company	1985 ($)	1983 ($)	1980 ($)	Percentage of Change 1980–1985
Industrial products	26,670	24,600	20,093	32.7
Consumer products	18,560	16,600	13,625	36.2
Services*	19,320	16,000	12,772	51.3

*Includes insurance, financial, utilities, transportation, retail stores, etc.
Source: Adapted from "Survey of Selling Costs," *Sales & Marketing Management* (February 1981, 1984, 1986).

Montrose's training manager, Debra Schlitz, faced an arbitrary 35 percent budget cut. Yet she had an important new product to introduce to the sales force. Traditionally, the entire sales force was brought to the factory when new product lines were introduced. As a first cost-cutting move, this practice was eliminated. Instead, Debra had staff people travel to each regional office, train branch managers on the new line, and then give them the materials such as slides, tapes, and samples to train their salespeople.

Montrose had also sponsored intensive training programs for distributors' personnel, during which they were brought to the plant several times a year for week-long courses. Debra reduced this program to 1- and 2-day field training sessions. The change proved serendipitous; not only were costs reduced, but feedback from the more informal field sessions revealed the need to talk more about local market applications and opportunities and less about the nuts and bolts of products. Sessions began to stress advantages over competitive products, local market applications, and selling techniques such as closing the sale. Distributor reactions became highly positive.

---

alienation is often not even expressed except under the most serious situations, this lulls some firms into complacency. Its lack of measurement unduly worries other firms, who then incur more training and more costs than are really necessary. Sometimes a firm must take a fresh look at the training procedure to reduce some of the costs judiciously (see Application 12.2).

Justifying the Cost of Training to Top Management

As Application 12.2 implies, many firms should evaluate their training to determine if they indeed are getting their money's worth from it or if it can safely be reduced. Unfortunately, the benefits of training and the trade-offs from certain cost reductions cannot be definitely determined, as Figure 12.4 suggests. For example it would be useful to know more about the cost results and return on investment of the following:

- ☐ Audiotape home study versus printed, programmed instruction
- ☐ Premeeting reading assignments versus coverage of the same materials as part of the meeting.
- ☐ Canned training programs versus those specifically designed for one company's products, sales strategies, and personnel
- ☐ The optimum combination—in skill development—of self-study materials, group training, and field coaching
- ☐ The use of videotape in role playing (does it enhance or inhibit the desired learning?)
- ☐ Value versus cost of field follow-up after a sales training meeting[5]

Management is fully justified in demanding that training justify its costs for continued funding. If management is asked for an increased appropriation for training, they have a right to know what improvements they should get for their money. So, training programs must be evaluated, despite the difficulty in evaluating as specifically as preferred.

General methods for evaluating training. Three evaluation methods are commonly employed, although all are flawed. They are (1) interview the trainees, (2) interview sales managers, (3) interview customers.

The trainee participants of a training program can be surveyed to determine "what they got out of it," which will fairly well evaluate training programs for experienced salespeople. But new trainees are not experienced enough to judge the benefits. New trainees can be tested to determine what they learned and can be questioned about whether they were interested in and understood the presentations and methods. Unfortunately, an entertaining speaker does not always provide the best learning experience, but one who is totally boring can never do so.

Selling skills after a training program can be subjectively assessed by the field sales supervisor. Sometimes before-and-after role playing may detect improvement in selling techniques as well as improved attitudes and motivations.[6] Any judged lack of improvement, however, may not necessarily be the fault of the program; rather, the trainee or other factors may be responsible.

Contacting customers for their opinions of any changes in the salesperson's performance before and after the training may indicate some strengths and weaknesses in the program, especially because customers observe actual behavior. These contacts can be in person or by mail, and customers are usually quite pleased to have their opinions solicited, "so that we can serve you better."[7]

These three general methods all involve subjective opinions of various parties. Evaluation would be greatly improved by objectivity. Different degrees of training could be used in different sales districts and the results compared, as is done in test markets (where different inputs of advertising, prices, and product characteristics are used to ascertain which result in the most profits). However, this type of assessment is seldom done in evaluating training and would be unwieldy at best, because the training output is far less definable than the sales results in market tests.[8]

Evaluating specific benefits. The merits of a training program can be evaluated more concretely if the purpose of the training has been specifically established and communicated. A problem can arise if the objectives are stated too broadly. For example, maintaining that training should produce better sales productivity, or improved morale, is too general. If sales are examined before and after the training period and an increase is shown, how should it be interpreted? Was the training program very effective? So many factors affect sales (e.g., competition, seasonal factors such as the weather, the economy, pricing or advertising changes) that no single one, such as training, can be identified as the major contributor. But with more humble objectives, one can assess achievement. These objectives might include the following:

Improving prospecting for new accounts

Closing sales more efficiently

Improving time management

Better report writing

Better customer knowledge

If a week-long training session concerns primarily improving prospecting and closing sales, then improvement in the number of new accounts gained in the period after the training and the ratio of sales made to number of calls give quantitative measures of short-term training results. Improvement in time management could similarly be measured objectively by any increase in number of sales calls made. Better report writing could be evaluated by simple observation as well as more on-time reports. Improved customer knowledge might best be measured by giving salespeople a quiz concerning their customers' characteristics.

Although analyses and surveys can provide a rough idea of the training program's effectiveness, they do not determine the amount that can be spent for training and whether present expenditures can be reduced without jeopardizing customer relations and losing sales. The problem is very much like that faced by the marketing manager in budgeting advertising. Our tools for evaluating advertising effectiveness also have not progressed to the point at which the optimum allocation of efforts can be ascertained.

CAUTIONS IN PLANNING AND EXECUTING TRAINING PROGRAMS

A point of diminishing returns can be reached in the design and commitment to a sales training program. Application 12.2 shows that a firm can drastically cut the training budget without ostensibly hurting the training effort and perhaps even improving it. Centralized training must be carefully evaluated based on its scope (that is, should all salespeople periodically be brought in for such training?) and duration.

Many training programs lack clearly defined objectives. As a result they are not tightly organized, and any definitive evaluation of their effectiveness is practically impossible. Boring speakers, unrealistic sales demonstrations, and too much information on the company and not enough on other aspects of the selling job, such as customer and market orientation, plague many training programs. Topics for sales meetings often could be improved. As

Application 12.2 indicates, centralized meetings do not always address topics of most concern to the field representatives.

Training is one of the many challenges facing sales managers. Effective sales training will make other parts of their job easier. But the need remains for continual follow-up, remedial advice, and motivation of the sales force.

SUMMARY

At the beginning of this chapter I asked you to consider how you would determine the training needs of your firm and what information you would want in planning the training program. Obviously, training needs could be determined by research into problems and weak areas of performance. A survey could be conducted, perhaps of sales managers as well as sales representatives, to identify what they see as the most urgent training needs. A customer sample also might be surveyed to determine deficiencies they would like to see improved. Perhaps sales meetings would be more beneficial if, several weeks previously, district sales managers, sales representatives, and others such as product and brand managers, were queried about appropriate subject matter. Topics with the widest appeal or the most urgent need then would be developed for the forthcoming meeting.

Sales training is not limited to initial training at the hiring point and includes refresher, or ongoing, training. Benefits of training are better personal development, enhanced customer relations, and improved morale. Issues concern the degree of formality and duration. Topics that can be covered in training programs include company, product, and customer knowledge, sales techniques, and territory management. Inspiration is a dubious but sometimes effective topic.

Training methods include lecture, case and panel discussions, demonstrations, role playing, as well as individual training methods such as on-the-job training and home study. Issues regarding training include who should do the training, when it should be done, where it should be done (centralized or decentralized), and cost.

Although there are various methods for evaluating training it is easier to evaluate specific benefits—such as improving prospecting—than overall accomplishment.

Finally, one must recognize that a point of diminishing returns can be reached in training. More is not necessarily better, and the benefits of intensive training may not always outweigh its costs.

QUESTIONS

1. Discuss the drawbacks of trial-and-error learning. Should it ever be recommended?

2. "Good morale and enthusiasm are not necessarily by-products of training. On the contrary, training programs impede or delay progress toward individual goals and may be detrimental to morale."

"The salesperson with good potential does not welcome a formal training program; the dud, on the other hand, thinks formal training programs are great—the longer the better."
Evaluate these two statements.

3. What criteria would you establish to indicate the need for refresher training?

4. Evaluate the effectiveness of pep talks and inspirational sessions in training programs.

5. Compare the relative effectiveness of the various group training methods.

6. Under what circumstances might a firm postpone initial formal training until sales representatives have proven themselves? Do you think this policy is wise?

7. How can the effectiveness of an individual instructor be determined?

8. Discuss the pros and cons of using on-the-job training exclusively.

9. How can a trainee best learn how to approach a customer? How to handle objections? How to close effectively?

PEOPLE PROBLEM: JUSTIFYING A REFRESHER TRAINING PROGRAM

Please evaluate each of the alternatives.

You are faced with somewhat of a dilemma. In the latest industry downturn, headquarters is asking for greater economies in operation. One of the suggested areas for cutting back is the refresher sales training. The company currently spends $125,000 annually for this training program in equipment, teaching, facilities, and time lost from the job. To justify the need for refresher training, you are asked to evaluate the training. How would you respond to this directive to justify the refresher training program?

1. You admit that it is impossible now to evaluate your training effects. However, you propose to aim future training at specific objectives, such as prospecting for new customers and increasing the average order size, so that before-and-after performance can be checked. In the meantime you continue the present program because there is no proof that the money and time are not well spent.

2. You are forced to admit that there is only subjective proof of the refresher training's effectiveness. You believe your people return to the field with more enthusiasm and improvements in some of their deficiencies.

3. You survey the participants at the most recent refresher session and find that 69 percent considered the session worthwhile.

4. Lacking any specific and objective evaluation criteria for past training, you suggest maintaining the present level of training but checking the before-and-after performance of selected salespeople.

5. Your doubts about the effectiveness of this refresher training are finally surfacing. You wonder whether problems of boredom or careless techniques can be handled in the field. Accordingly, you have no major objections to cutting the refresher training drastically.

NOTES

1. For an article on training for telemarketing, see Andrea A. Crane and Thomas Carmichael, "Tactics for Selecting an Effective Telemarketing Training Approach," *Telemarketing* (June 1983): 42–46.

2. A strong case for using first-line sales managers for training is presented by Jack R. Snader, "Why Most Sales Training Doesn't Work . . . and What You Can Do About It," *Business Marketing* (May 1984): 86–90.

3. Robert Evans, "Training, Employee Orientation Hike Sales Rep Performance," *Marketing News* (13 Nov. 1981): 1.

4. For an interesting article involving the sales training of a blue collar route sales force, see Linda Segall, "Turning Order-Takers into Salesmen," *Training and Development Journal* (Jan. 1986): 72–73.

5. Adapted from Eleanor Brantley Schwartz, "Increasing Sales Productivity through Innovative Training" (Monograph, Cleveland State University, n.d.), 25.

6. Related to evaluating training, see Alan J. Dubinsky and William A. Staples, "Sales Training: Salespeople's Preparedness and Managerial Implications," *Journal of Personal Selling & Sales Management* (Fall/Winter 1981–1982): 28–32.

7. See Gerry Marx, "Let Customers Write Your Training Programs," *Training and Development Journal* (November 1982): 40–43.

8. For a discussion of problems in evaluating training methods, see Dale C. Brandenburg, "Training Evaluation: What's the Current Status?" *Training and Development Journal* (August 1982): 14–19.

cases

12.1 Evaluating Training

"Marc, we are spending $725,000 a year on training. I wonder if it's worth it," the company president queried Marc Fernandez, vice president of sales.

"It's hard to measure with any precision the value received from training programs, as you know. However, sales in general have been satisfactory and according to expectations. Turnover of the sales staff has been a modest 8 percent; customer complaints—at least those that have come to my attention—have been minimal. All evidence indicates that the training is good—maybe excellent—and well worth the costs involved."

"Could we accomplish the same thing with less cost?" the president persisted.

"I can't answer that. I don't know."

"Marc, I would like a formal evaluation of the effectiveness of the sales training program. Can you have such an appraisal on my desk by the first of the month?"

12.2 Washington Mutual Fund: Need for Formal Training

Karen Waite was a district sales manager for the Atlanta area of the Washington Mutual Fund Company. The sales increase in her district lately had been comparing unfavorably with certain other districts. She was particularly concerned with the individual productivity as well as the turnover of her part-time salespeople. More formal training might be the answer, she thought, but she was uncertain about what kind and how much would be effective. In addition the home office eschewed centralized formal training, outside of an annual sales meeting, so she could expect little or no support. The burden of training would fall on her shoulders.

Karen had about sixty part-time salespeople in her district. Unlike other mutual fund companies (notably the large Investors Diversified Services), who relied on full-time salespeople, Washington used "moonlighters." Many of these were teachers who found that selling mutual funds part-time, mostly in the evening, provided a welcome supplement to their salaries. So about 60 percent of the Atlanta district's salespeople were teachers, 20 percent were housewives or retired people. The other 20 percent were employed full-time in various types of work; they ranged from policemen to college students to artists.

Rather than being sold through brokerage houses, shares in mutual funds were sold directly to prospective investors, usually to couples in their homes. The better producers developed a sizable list of prospects through referrals and other leads; the less successful salespeople found that after they had exhausted their list of friends and neighbors, leads were so sparse that frequently they left the company.

The mutual fund program sold most often was a periodic payment plan, in which the customer agreed to pay from $10 up to several hundred dollars a month (in unusual cases) for the life of the plan, essentially resulting in a forced savings. There was also a single-payment plan for those persons (few in number) who had $1,000 or more to invest at one time. The typical customer was a lower-middle-class, blue-collar employee who had limited income and no investment experience. The major incentive for purchasing mutual funds was to provide for retirement or to save for their children's college educations. The 8.5-percent front-end load required purchasers to stay in the plan for a number of years before they were likely to profit, depending on the stock market, of course.

The salespeople were paid a straight commission, so the company incurred no fixed selling costs except for a base salary for Karen and a part-time secretary. Karen used her home for her business office, thereby again ensuring minimal fixed selling costs. The fact that the salespeople were paid on straight commission, Karen believed, accounted for home-office indifference both to training and turnover. But the home office did expect sales performance and gains over previous years. The company philosophy was to hire as many salespeople as possible. Even if attrition was high, most would make some sales to friends and relatives before they quit.

Although Karen was the sales manager, she was expected to do some selling, too. Indeed, she spent more time selling than she did in sales management. In addition to handling reports and correspondence with the home office, Karen conducted a sales meeting for her salespeople one night a month. In these meetings she conveyed communications and directives from the home office; the salespeople's problems were discussed. Karen also liked to have several of her successful producers give brief inspirational talks and tips to the rest of the sales force. Karen constantly encouraged her sales force to persuade their friends and acquaintances to join Washington. She even gave small bonuses to those who recruited the most people in a 6-month period. Karen also did some on-the-job coaching. If a salesperson was having particular difficulty and requested help, Karen scheduled the salesperson to accompany her on some sales calls, thereby profiting from her example. Occasionally, Karen accompanied a salesperson on calls to observe and lend support. The problem was a lack of time to do as much individual coaching as desired. Most of the sales calls were limited to weekday evenings from 7:00 to 9:30. Sometimes appointments could be made for the weekends (especially during the winter), but the productive selling time was necessarily limited.

Karen was never sure whether the evening per month devoted to the sales meeting was worth the time taken from productive selling efforts. But the home office encouraged these monthly meetings. The only other formal training was a series of annual sales meetings. High-level company executives visited about twenty different cities, holding one-day sessions in plush hotels. Salespeople, their spouses, and even prospective recruits were invited to the banquet and closing speeches. These meetings were primarily exhortative and motivational, rather than focusing specifically on training. The executive vice president who usually conducted the meetings was a particularly inspirational speaker.

QUESTIONS

1. Evaluate the sales and training efforts for this company and product.
2. Discuss ways to increase productivity and decrease turnover.
3. What recommendations, if any, do you have for improving the situation? Support these as fully as possible.

12.3 Allen Drug Company: Need to Rejuvenate a Sales Force

Allen Drug marketed a number of consumer products such as dental cleaners, medicated shampoo, and sleeping tablets. It traditionally depended on a heavy advertising budget to pull its products through distribution. In 1984 it budgeted $47 million for advertising, and this amounted to 40 percent of its total selling, general, and administrative costs. Over 60 percent of this ad budget went for network television.

Allen was a small company compared with other national advertisers. Its sales were only $144 million in 1985. Its marketing organization in 1985 is shown in Figure 12.5. Until the late 1970s it had faced no strong competition, but then the serious challenges began. Behemoths such as Procter & Gamble (the world's largest advertiser, with national advertising expenditures approaching $800 million) entered the scene with competing products and began to clobber Allen.

Although it could not possibly match the amounts budgeted by its major competitors, Allen relied solely on mass-media advertising. It was slow

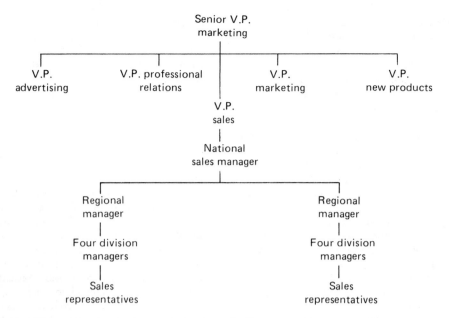

FIGURE 12.5 Marketing organization of Allen Drug Company, 1985.

to offer drugstores, chains, and wholesalers the co-operative advertising funds and other trade promotions that other firms had found to be effective alternatives to heavy-pull, mass-media advertising. But in 1983 and 1984, Allen began trade promotions on a trial basis, and initial results were encouraging. As a result in 1985 it cut back on its mass-media advertising and put the money into trade promotions instead.

The results were disastrous. Sales of the domestic drug division, which accounted for about 65 percent of Allen's sales, were down 8.5 percent for the first half of 1985, resulting in the first sales decline in the firm's long history. On top of this a major merchandising program that Allen had initiated for its 10,000 retail and wholesale accounts was a complete failure.

Something obviously had to be done, and it would probably have to be drastic, but first the cause or causes of the decline had to be identified. The vice president of sales, Clint Robinson, and the senior vice president of marketing, Louise Blake,

reevaluated sales and marketing activities. They came to the dismal conclusion that most of the salespeople just could not sell. As Clint described it, ''Our sales reps are lethargic. Training efforts have been poorly received, and our compensation plan, which bases bonuses on sales increases, just is not working as an incentive for improvement.''

The blame for this situation, however, could not necessarily be attributed directly to the sales force. In the past they had been primarily routine order takers, due to Allen's heavy pull-type consumer advertising. Furthermore, the company's territory administration policy was identified as part of the problem for the failure to penetrate mass-merchandising outlets, which had become the fastest growing retail market for proprietary drugs. The sales force called on each of the 10,000 accounts once every 6 weeks. The average sales representative made 5.8 calls per day. But the big-volume customers were not effectively contacted.

Immediate steps were needed to upgrade the sales force.

QUESTIONS

1. How would you recommend that the sales force be upgraded? What facets would you change or work on? Be as specific as possible and be prepared to defend your recommendations to a skeptical audience.

2. Would you make any organizational changes and, if so, what?

3. Do you really think Allen can be turned around at this point?

CHAPTER 13
Directing and Motivating Through Compensation

CHAPTER PERSPECTIVE

Success in sports, most observers claim, depends on talent or ability. But sports history is replete with examples of underdogs who rose to inspired performance and trounced teams greatly superior in talent and experience. Selling is not all that dissimilar to sports. Although ability (which might be equated with good training and experience) is important in selling, the intangible quality of motivation or desire may be even more important. The sales manager who can encourage this in employees is as valuable to the firm as the coach who can fire up an athletic team. This chapter examines how the various aspects of the compensation plan

can help motivate and direct sales efforts. The next chapter explores the role of supervision in motivating and directing.

As you read this chapter, consider two problems that sales managers often face. (1) Salespeople tend to push the easier-to-sell items and give less attention to the harder-to-sell. But often the harder-to-sell products carry the most profit. (2) Developing new customer accounts often is neglected, because this usually requires more effort than servicing existing accounts. How would you design a compensation plan to overcome these problems?

CHAPTER OBJECTIVES

☐ Be able to differentiate between morale and motivation, and their influence in organizational well-being.

☐ Know the characteristics of a good compensation plan.

☐ Know when a compensation plan ought to be revised.

☐ Understand the steps in developing a compensation plan.

☐ Become familiar with the three types of compensation plans and their strengths and weaknesses.

☐ Be able to identify the more common fringe benefits offered sales employees.

☐ Understand the various problems having to do with compensation.

☐ Know how selling expenses can best be handled.

MORALE AND MOTIVATION

The term *morale* often is confused with *motivation*. *Morale* refers to the attitude an employee has toward the employer and job environment. *Motivation* refers to how strongly an individual wants to do his job well; it refers to the desire to succeed.

Morale

Generally, the most productive workers are those with good morale, but good morale in an organization does not ensure that everyone will be highly motivated to produce. Instead, some employees may be complacent, comfortably secure, and unwilling to exert greater efforts. An environment that is less pleasant but more challenging may elicit the best efforts of more individuals.

The consequences of poor morale are more easily seen. These range from high personnel turnover to disparaging remarks about the company to friends and customers, and even to unionization. Sales are often adversely affected by poor morale. We can identify a number of causes of poor morale. Some are external and often are beyond the firm's control. But the sales manager who is alert and attuned to friction points and negative employee attitudes toward management can eliminate other sources of poor morale, such as the following major work-environment causes of poor morale:

Poor communication tends to foster suspicion, uncertainty, and a feeling of lack of concern by management

Unfair and inequitable treatment, perceived or actual

Poor working conditions, such as difficult-to-cover sales territories, time-consuming reports, and stingy expense accounts

Lack of recognition, especially for efforts beyond the ordinary and expected

Unsatisfactory status

Coercive and dictatorial supervision

Poor compensation plan

Management can control and correct all of these factors of a negative work environment, but management must recognize and act on them. The following causes of poor morale are personal and are usually beyond management's control (except the last):

Domestic difficulties

Financial problems

Health conditions

Overqualified for the job

These factors also should be recognized and if serious, outside counseling should be encouraged. After all, these personal factors probably affect performance. Furthermore, the empathetic sales manager is concerned with the welfare of subordinates.

Some firms make a practice of hiring top college graduates, both at the undergraduate and MBA levels. Yet the training program may be rather lengthy, and may require considerable time in rather routine jobs, such as missionary sales, before the person is finally moved into more responsible and challenging positions. Sometimes too many people are hired for the available openings and the waiting period for advancement may drag on. A person overqualified for the particular job who does not see advancement as coming soon tends to rapidly lose morale. Typically, the better people are more mobile and will leave; the less able people will stay, but discouraged and complaining.

Despite careful efforts to minimize possible morale problems, they may still arise and may not be immediately evident to management. What can the sales manager do to detect deteriorating morale in the work force? If he is receptive to employee complaints and if subordinates feel free to communicate with the manager, a great deal is gained.[1] Of course, some employees are perpetual complainers. The justifiable complaints then must be differentiated from the imaginary. But if the same concerns are expressed by other employees, these problems are probably real and may not be trivial. They should be corrected if at all possible. *Exit interviews* can also be important information sources. Because the employee is leaving, it is usually too late to correct the situation to his satisfaction, but other employees may benefit from the detection and correction of problem areas.

Motivation

Considerations of morale usually focus on the negatives of an operation, because poor morale can have such a negative impact. Motivation is more concerned with accentuating the positive, but this is a murky area of human relations, because motivation varies greatly among individuals. Some persons are motivated with little or no outside stimulus. These are the "self-starters." Others are motivated by certain job-related factors, such as money, working conditions, an understanding supervisor, status, and even harsh criticism.[2] Salespeople are particularly vulnerable to depression and loss of confidence. The loneliness of the typical selling situation, the destruction of self-confidence engendered by losing an important sale, the difficulty of remaining in high gear at all times and under all circumstances—all create a need to stimulate motivation and to rekindle interest and desire.[3]

Chapter 14 examines motivation in greater detail. It can play such an important role in sales productivity that any sales manager should be aware both of the concepts underlying motivation as well as the more practical techniques to foster it, of which compensation is only one.

Importance of Financial Incentives

A major reason that people change jobs is to get more money. Money, however, should not be presumed to be the only factor motivating employees and creating job satisfaction, nor even the most important. Numerous studies, dating back decades, have found that several factors are often cited by workers as even more important than pay:

- ☐ Social status and respect
- ☐ Security
- ☐ Attractive work
- ☐ Opportunity for personal development
- ☐ Worthwhile activity
- ☐ Personal power and influence
- ☐ Voice in one's own affairs
- ☐ Just and diligent supervision
- ☐ Treatment as an individual
- ☐ Sense of accomplishment[4]

Some evidence suggests that salespeople are more motivated by money than are other workers.[5] But one recent study showed that financial motivation varied among firms. In one firm the salespeople ranked "more pay" as most important to them, whereas another firm rated it third, behind "opportunities for personal growth," and "sense of accomplishment."[6] If employees feel that the pay scale is unfair, serious morale problems can result. And when pay scale is considered unfair, compensation appears to be the most important factor, which, the preceding study suggested, may reasonably explain the differences in employee attitudes in the two firms.

Problems with the compensation plan are particularly likely if the pay scale is lower than that of similar jobs with similar firms (unless there are good offsetting features, such as higher status of company, more fringe benefits, or greater advancement opportunity) or if favoritism is perceived to affect pay or frequency of raises. Consequently, a firm should seriously attend to its compensation plan to ensure that it is not a source of employee dissatisfaction and positively contributes to morale, motivation, and direction of selling efforts toward company objectives.

CHARACTERISTICS OF A GOOD COMPENSATION PLAN

A good compensation plan has certain characteristics or requirements that should be met: It should be fair, direct efforts toward company objectives, afford flexibility, provide incentive and motivation, give security, and be easily administered and understood. Unfortunately, some of these requirements are not wholly compatible with each other, necessitating compromise between the preferred and the practical.

Fairness

Above all else, the compensation plan should be perceived by employees as fair. Even fairness, however, may require compromises. For example should compensation be based on longevity or on job performance? Often performance is not related to years of service, yet, what should be the reward for a person's loyalty and service to a firm?

If compensation can reasonably be related to the salesperson's contribution, especially if the contribution can be expressed in relation to the contribution of others, a stronger feeling of fairness will result. However, the contribution must be adequately spelled out and measurable. It must be as tangible and objective as possible. Although contribution in sales generated is the most common measure of selling performance, other contributions also may deserve recognition, such as servicing customers, helping novice salespeople, and the like.

Finally, the compensation package should be equitable with that offered by other firms for similar work. Individuals should feel that they are being paid "enough." Relative pay, rather than absolute, seems the more important factor. An example taken from another field best illustrates this fact. Harry Reasoner, long-time news commentator for ABC, earned a comfortable $300,000 a year when the network persuaded Barbara Walters to join him as co-anchor for network news at the widely publicized salary of $1 million. The result was predictable: Reasoner felt grossly underpaid and ill-treated.

Direction of Efforts Toward Company Objectives

The compensation plan should be designed to direct efforts to the firm's highest-priority selling and servicing activities. If performing missionary work and customer service, training junior salespeople, and prospecting for new accounts are factors on which raises and promotions are based, then these objectives should be well communicated to the employees so that they can give these activities adequate attention. The compensation plan that is compatible with an emphasis on such activities would not be straight commission, which provides remuneration only on sales production, not on servicing and other nonselling activities.

Flexibility

The compensation plan should be flexible enough to acknowledge territorial differences that make one person's job much more difficult than another's.

The plan should be flexible enough to reward outstanding performance that is not tied directly into the compensation plan. For example the salesperson who is outstanding in gaining new accounts should be rewarded although his sales do not realistically reflect his contribution because of the time spent in developing accounts. Furthermore, sufficient flexibility should be built in that a period of recession will not devastate the sales force and that a booming economy will not result in a windfall for exceeding the salesperson's contribution.

Some flexibility therefore is desired, as compared to a rigid and unwavering plan that is oblivious to inequities. But the other extreme—too much flexibility, or a tailor-made plan for every individual and situation, or one that is constantly being changed—is not good either. Moderation is the better course of action.

Incentive and Motivation

The compensation plan can be the major stimulating or motivating factor in maximizing sales force production. Rewards in the form of increased compensation for higher sales production (or other desired objectives) can be a powerful spur. Unless a sales force is engaged solely in missionary work, in which no sales are made directly, or in highly technical selling, in which a number of company representatives will necessarily be involved, then some form of commission or bonus arrangement should be provided for greater incentive.

Security of Steady Income

In contrast to the opportunity to maximize reward, most salespeople prefer some assurance of steady income. In those types of selling in which sales are infrequent but sizable or are highly seasonal, sales can fluctuate to the extreme, with no sales in one period and high productivity in the next. A salesperson could be ill for part of a period and thus unable to bear his normal work load. In this situation it seems best to design a compensation plan that guarantees a minimum level of pay, thereby giving some security for the sales force and their families.

Ease of Administration and Comprehension

A plan should be simple enough that individual salespeople can understand it and keep track of their commissions and/or bonuses. Furthermore, bonuses and commissions should be paid promptly, both to provide immediate reward for the work performed and also to allow easier calculation.

A relatively simple compensation plan, which avoids complicated and varied computations of commissions earned, is also easier to administer and less costly to operate. Sometimes through efforts to be as equitable and flexible as possible, a compensation plan may become rather complicated, and simplicity might have to be sacrificed. Complexity burdens the sales manager with ensuring that salespeople understand their pay package and have no major complaints about it.

Conclusions About the Characteristics of a Good Compensation Plan

No compensation plan can be strong in all the preceding attributes. Trade-offs and compromises are necessary, and certain qualities, such as simplicity, may have to be sacrificed for other objectives considered more important. Seldom is a plan optimal for all salespeople under all conditions, but if a plan does not attract, motivate, and retain good people (as well as stay within the company's budget[7]), then it is seriously flawed. However, we cannot expect the compensation plan to overcome basic flaws in supervision or in operational factors such as territorial assignments.[8]

SHOULD THE PRESENT PLAN BE REVISED?

Seldom will a firm need to develop a completely new compensation plan. Usually some revision of the present plan should suffice and is less disruptive than a complete overhaul. Before any changes are made, however, it should rather firmly be established that there is a problem and that the compensation plan is at least partially to blame.

If sales productivity is decreasing, if selling costs are consistently above a reasonable budget, if salespeople appear insufficiently motivated, the blame may lie with the compensation, but other factors, such as inadequate training, weak supervision, or sheer incompetence, should not be ruled out and should be investigated. Certain problems suggest that the present plan may not be satisfactory. The most obvious indicators are increasing complaints by salespeople about the compensation plan, regarding lack of security, lack of fairness, insufficient incentive, difficulty in understanding, and so on. Another indicator is consistent failure to meet sales objectives, such as new accounts, customer servicing, and sales of more profitable products. Finally complaints by customers about poor servicing, high pressure, overselling may indicate a compensation problem.

If it is determined that the compensation plan is not producing the intended results, further investigation is needed to determine why. Perhaps the plan creates too much incentive for sales production or perhaps not enough. Perhaps it does not reward effective nonselling activities. Perhaps it is too encouraging of short-term productivity at the expense of long-term customer satisfaction. With an investigation of deficiencies and a reappraisal of the desired objectives for a compensation plan, the task of revising is at hand.

DEVELOPING A COMPENSATION PLAN

In either revising a compensation plan or developing a completely new one, certain decisions need to be made. They are (1) determine specific objectives for the plan, (2) establish the desired level of earnings, (3) choose the method of payment, (4) decide on the role and nature of quota, and (5) implement the plan. A further policy may be stipulated regarding the role, if any, that contests and short-term incentives should play in the total compensation package.

Determine Specific Objectives

For a compensation plan to be most effective, specific objectives must be determined. Stating a desire "to increase sales," or to "beat last year" is insufficient. More specific goals should be established, such as increasing the number of new customers; increasing sales volume of certain categories of goods; stimulating customer servicing, such as building displays, training dealer salespeople, or handling customer complaints. With such specific objectives clearly in mind, a compensation plan can then be devised to encourage such actions.[9] For example a bonus might be paid for new customers. A commission or bonus paid on profitability of sales would encourage sales efforts of the more profitable goods. Missionary sales work involved in better customer servicing would suggest a compensation plan in which a fixed salary was the major component, and any commission or bonus a minor part of the total compensation.

Establish Desired Level of Earnings

Level of earnings refers to the target income or average earnings of the sales representatives, or in other words, the income that should be achieved with average performance from the total compensation package of base salary, commission, and any group incentives or bonuses. The earnings level for individual salespeople should reflect their experience and ability and should place the firm in a competitive position with respect to pay scales to assure reasonable job satisfaction and the desired caliber of employees. Figure 13.1 shows how the level of income for each salesperson should fall within a designated range—depending on education, experience, and ability—that ensures consistency among sales districts.[10]

Factors influencing level. A number of factors can affect the level of compensation. The most common follow:

- □ Competition, "the going rate"
- □ Reputation of the firm

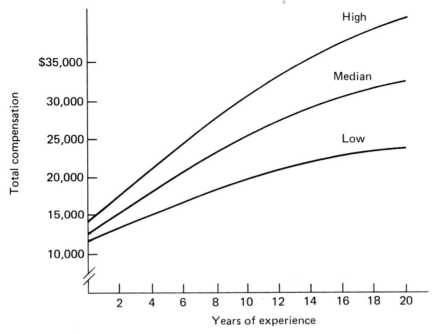

FIGURE 13.1   Range of income for salespeople. (*Source*: Adapted from Frederick E. Webster, Jr., "Rationalizing Salesmen's Compensation Plans, January 1966, p. 56. Reprinted from *Journal of Marketing* published by the American Marketing Association.)

☐ Effectiveness of the sales training program

☐ Resources of the firm

We would certainly expect competitive compensation levels to be a major factor. The problem is that earnings figures vary both among industries and among firms in the same industry. Partly this is due to the proportion of base salary to commission in the total compensation plan. Sales representatives paid on straight commission characteristically earn far more than those mostly on straight salary.

The well-known firm will often pay its sales representatives less than the smaller firm, because it has less difficulty attracting a large body of sales candidates, and with a heavy advertising budget the selling job should be less difficult. Similarly, a firm with an intensive training program usually pays its sales force less relative to the firm having less training. The latter firm will often have to hire more experienced people and, of course, pay them more.

Typically, smaller firms pay their sales forces more than larger firms do. With limited advertising budgets, smaller firms usually are forced to rely heavily on a competent sales force. The amount a firm can afford to pay is a limiting factor and may force the firm to pay under the prevailing competitive level and/or resort to straight commission to tie earnings directly into sales productivity.

Should there be a cap on earnings?   A problem that occasionally must be confronted is whether to place an upper limit on a salesperson's earnings. Proponents for establishing a limit point out that this avoids windfall profits from situations in which the salesperson had little influence, such as a major new customer's moving into the territory or an important competitor's leaving. Furthermore, without such an upper limit, some salespeople can earn more than their executives. This can be demoralizing for the executives and lessen their prestige and influence. Able salespeople may be less eager to advance into executive ranks when a promotion would necessitate a pay cut. (A possible solution to a salesperson's earning an ''unreasonable'' amount is a regressive sliding scale commission plan, discussed later in this chapter.)

It also can be argued that placing limits on a salesperson's earnings effectively discourages maximum sales production. In this case both the company and the salesperson are hurt. However, sales productivity far in excess of that achieved by reasonable efforts of the rest of the sales force suggests that some territorial realignment may be desired. A few territories, perhaps because of changed conditions, may now have sales potentials much greater than assumed when the territories were first designated.

Dangers of overpaying and underpaying.   Some firms overpay their salespeople, assuming that this will result in attracting the very best people, increasing motivation, and maximizing sales productivity. But there are some serious flaws with this practice.[11] Higher selling costs than the competition can place the firm at a competitive disadvantage and hurt profits. Furthermore, the disparity between sales force earnings and those of management may become great enough to pose a morale problem with many managers who find their jobs relatively less attractive and their authority diluted by higher-paid salespeople.

Underpaying presents considerable problems. Less able people generally will have to be hired, which will adversely affect sales productivity. Typically, in a situation like this, the more able salespeople will not stay long—perhaps just long enough to gain a little experience. Then they will seek more productive employment, either on their own or due to pirating by other firms. And the firm that consistently underpays will be left with a group of second- and third-rate salespeople.

Method of Payment

Method of payment for most sales compensation plans is a combination of fixed and incentive income. The incentive income is further differentiated between individual and group incentive income. Usually, individual incentives consist of commissions on total sales or, more commonly, commissions on sales above quota. The higher the percentage that commission contributes to the total compensation package, the more incentive theoretically exists. The lower the percentage of commission, the more security results and also the greater is management's control over the selling activities. Some firms give individual salespeople their choice of how much of the total compensation will be base pay or secure guaranteed income and how much will be commission, providing the chance of higher earnings but less security.

A *bonus* is often paid to all salespeople in a particular district when the quota for the entire district is exceeded, the amount of bonus depending on total group performance. Although bonuses are uncertain, they can furnish the extra fillip that adds to teamwork and esprit de corps, especially when the district sales manager can instill a sense of friendly competition and group cooperation and support. The various types of compensation plans are discussed in greater detail shortly.

Quotas, as discussed in Chapter 11, can be the equalizer between disparate territories and selling jobs. When commissions and bonuses are paid for achievements beyond the quota, they are intended to achieve equity in both the compensation plan and the performance evaluation. Unfortunately, despite best efforts, quotas do not always have this equalizing effect.

Implementing the Plan

Three steps generally are preferred in the introduction and implementation of a new or revised compensation plan. (1) It should be pretested, (2) it should be sold to the sales force, and (3) it should be monitored periodically.

Pretesting. Pretesting is desired before introducing the new plan companywide. Pretesting likely will indicate that some modifications are needed, and these are much more easily made at this stage than after a full-scale introduction. In particular attention should be focused on how well the plan achieves the desired objectives, and how well it fits into budget guidelines. Furthermore, this is the chance to empirically test the plan's fairness and ease of administration and understanding.

Pretesting is most easily accomplished by introducing the plan in one or several districts or regions. If there are any doubts about the plan, it is best not to introduce it companywide too quickly. Rather some time should be taken to compare the performance in the territories with the new plan versus those under the old plan. Definite improvements may be clearly indicated, or the desired improvement may not result, and management might question further expanding the new compensation plan.

Selling. A new compensation plan must be introduced to the sales force rather carefully. Some salespeople will see any change as a threat to their present level of earnings. There is always resistance to change. The common notion is that management is only interested in cutting selling costs so that any change is most likely to lower individual earnings. The change in the plan therefore must be carefully sold to the organization, stressing the benefits to the sales force. The salespeople should have been involved in the early development of the plan and their suggestions and criticisms solicited and recognized. Given such participation by the sales force, the task of selling the finished product becomes much easier, but still the plan should be introduced with full explanation and opportunity for answering questions.[12] An introduction probably is best done in small conference groups and not in a large gathering that does not foster easier questioning and discussion. Worse yet is to announce the change by letter or by the house organ. Lack of acceptance can scuttle even the best compensation plan.

Periodic monitoring. Compensation systems become outdated or out of touch with new company objectives. Competition and the environment change, new employees may have different backgrounds and abilities, customers may develop different sales and servicing requirements. Or over several years insidious flaws in the existing compensation plan may have become painfully evident. Hence, periodic appraisals should be made of individual performance under the plan and whether these are meeting expectations with minimum friction.

TYPES OF COMPENSATION PLANS

A firm has three basic methods of paying salespeople: (1) straight salary, (2) straight commission, and (3) a combination of salary and commission and/or bonus. The advantages of the latter, which offers some of the strengths of the other two methods without suffering from their full limitations, have made the combination plan the most widely used method of compensating a sales force today. Table 13.1 shows the percentage of use of various compensation plans.

Four factors are involved in selecting a compensation plan: security, incentive, control, and cost. Security gives the salesperson assurance of a steady income through good times and bad. Maximizing incentive, as in a straight commission, contrasts with the maximum security of a straight salary. Management's control over the sales force, especially regarding nonselling activities, is maximized under a straight salary plan and minimized under straight commission, where the sales force will bitterly resent any efforts to remove them from productive selling time. Costs differ greatly by type of compensation plan, as we will discuss shortly.

A straight salary plan normally offers the greatest security and least incentive for the salesperson, whereas straight commission is at the other ex-

TABLE 13.1 Percentage of firms using different compensation plans.

Type of Plan	Percentage of Firms Using Each Plan
Straight salary	17.4
Draw against commission	6.5
Salary plus commission	30.7
Salary plus individual bonus	33.7
Salary plus group bonus	2.7
Salary plus commission plus bonus	9.0
Total	100.0

Source: Adapted from *Sales & Marketing Management* (17 Feb. 1986): 57.

treme, providing maximum incentive and minimum security. This is shown as a continuum in Figure 13.2, which also depicts the combination plans as a middle ground, a compromise between maximum and minimum in security and incentive.

Two other diagrams are useful in showing the relationships between these three types of compensation plans. Figure 13.3 shows the relationship from the salesperson's standpoint—how total compensation will be affected. With straight commission, compensation can rise to astronomical heights as more sales are achieved; with straight salary, compensation remains constant regardless of sales. Figure 13.4 shows the relationship from the perspective of the sales manager, whose concern is selling costs as a percentage of sales. With straight commission, selling costs as a percentage of sales will remain

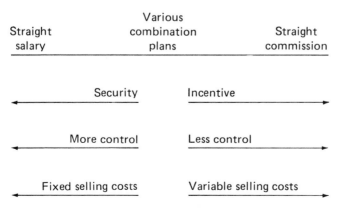

FIGURE 13.2 Range of salary plans and their major attributes.

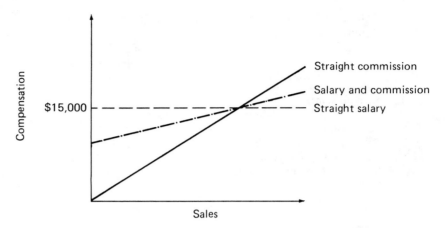

FIGURE 13.3   Relationship between basic compensation plans and sales volume on total compensation.

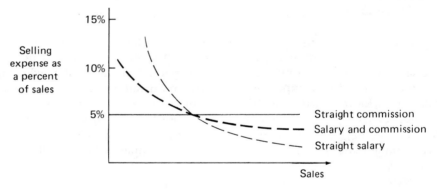

FIGURE 13.4   Relationship between basic compensation plans and sales volume on selling expenses.

the same at all volume levels; but with straight salary, selling cost percentages rise drastically with decreases in sales and fall just as drastically as greater sales are achieved. The plans combining salary and commission fall in a middle ground, depending on the proportion of salary to commission actually included in the total compensation package.

Straight Salary Plan

In addition to offering maximum security, which tends to minimize employee turnover, a straight salary enables management to exercise better direction and control, because the salespeople do not depend on sales for their pay.

Therefore, if some missionary work is needed, or a credit check is advised, or if a new employee should be coached by an experienced one, these duties can be assigned without generating dissatisfaction. Customer goodwill is often best cultivated when incentives for sales are lower pitched than they would be under a substantial commission plan. Drug salespeople (or detail persons), who contact doctors and other professionals, are usually paid on a straight salary (with perhaps a bonus arrangement based on territorial sales) because part of their job is missionary and because customer goodwill must not be jeopardized. New salespeople are often paid a straight salary, as are those opening up new territories and those selling technical products involving lengthy negotiations.

Aside from minimizing incentive, a straight salary plan may drastically affect the profits of a firm during periods of declining sales. With salaries fixed and not tied in with sales, these selling costs will represent a larger percentage of the cost of doing business and may even lead to a net loss. Of course, during periods of rising sales the reverse is true: Selling costs as a percentage of sales will decrease, to the benefit of profits. A fixed salary can lead to complacency among some employees, whereas it may frustrate the eager and capable new employee who feels that the firm bases maximizing compensation more on longevity and perhaps friendship than ability and effort.

Straight Commission

The principal limitations of the straight salary—the lack of incentive and a fixed cost not related to sales production—are certainly overcome by a straight commission. This method is particularly useful when the selling is on a part-time or irregular schedule, such as a moonlighter who sells mutual funds.

Sales managers whose personnel receive straight commission frequently complain that it leads to overselling, which often increases customer complaints, returns, and general ill will. Furthermore, sales managers see their salespeople acting too independently, being very difficult to control. Of course, the absence of security with the straight commission arrangement attracts only a certain kind of person and turns away many others who might be more competent overall. The result is that a firm's pool of sales applicants tends to be smaller than it would be under other compensation plans. This disadvantage can be overcome by having a *drawing account,* by which the salesperson receives a fixed amount regularly, even if sales for that period are not sufficient to cover the draw. The guaranteed draw essentially has the features of salary and commission, which is a combination plan, although the salesperson might perceive it somewhat differently. When the product is expensive and technologically complex and requires a lengthy period of negotiation and research into specific requirements, perhaps with one or more technical specialists aiding the sales representative, the straight commission is impractical.

Sliding-scale commissions.   Commissions sometimes are computed on a sliding scale, with the percentage moved up or down as sales change. The primary rationale for such progressive or regressive commissions is to motivate sales force efforts beyond what they might be under a constant commission rate. As an example of a progressive commission, the following rates might apply to monthly sales:

Sales to $10,000	4.0%
Sales from $10,001 to $25,000	6.0%
Sales over $25,000	7.5%

Commission rates may also be on a downward-sliding or regressive scale:

Sales to $20,000	7%
Sales over $20,000	5%

Figure 13.5 illustrates the relationship between progressive and regressive pay scales.

The following example shows the computation of pay using the progressive scale previously given for a straight commission plan (it can also be used for the commission part of a combination plan):

Bob Kirkpatrick had a good month in April, recording sales of $58,000. His total compensation for April may be calculated as follows:

$10,000 × 4.0%	=	$ 400
$15,000 × 6.0%	=	$ 900
$33,000 × 7.5%	=	$2,475
Total compensation		$3,775

Now complete Exercise 13.1.

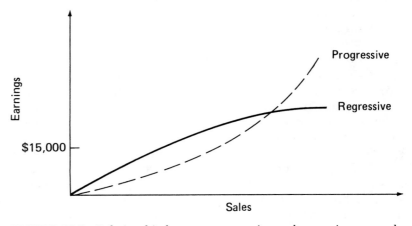

FIGURE 13.5   Relationship between progressive and regressive pay scales.

EXERCISE 13.1

1. What would Bob Kirkpatrick's compensation be with the regression scale given previously?
2. Compare the compensation under both methods if his sales are only $24,000 for the month.

As you can imagine, the progressive and regression approaches are controversial. Application 13.1 exemplifies two typical positions of sales executives.

Combination Plans

To attain some balance between incentive and security, a multiplicity of combination plans are used involving a base salary and a commission or bonus arrangement in various proportions. The popularity of combination plans is clearly seen in Table 13.1, in which 75 percent of the firms reported using this type of plan.[13] The proportion of fixed versus incentive pay can be tailored to specific job requirements as well as management's and salespeople's preferences.[14] New employees sometimes are paid mostly on a straight salary, but with the option of switching later to a lower fixed salary and a higher commission rate.

Bonuses. A bonus is sometimes used in combination with a salary or commission. It is a lump-sum payment as a reward for individual or group (such

---

APPLICATION 13.1 *Controversy:* Progressive Versus Regressive Commission

A sales manager of a paper company strongly supports the progressive rate:

> We use a progressive rate because it is a real motivator for our sales force to get out and push. And let's face it. Sales are more difficult to achieve beyond a certain point, so we should reward accordingly. Even the controller likes this arrangement. We have certain economies of scale with greater production. This means that our costs per unit are lower with more sales, so that this business is more profitable.

The general account manager for a Midwestern railroad favors the regressive commission plan:

> We have found that a progressive scale leads to bad overselling. We had this arrangement, and it was a real source of customer complaints. That, and the inattention given to nonselling activities—all our people wanted to do was push, push for more sales. Then, occasionally someone would stumble into a windfall situation—you know, a really big sale—all out of proportion to his efforts, and reap a big harvest. No, we didn't like it, and have even moved to the opposite, a regressive rate. We find that getting the first sales is by far the most difficult. Once the ice is broken, additional sales are easier. And we don't believe these should be rewarded as generously.

as the entire district) performance, which may be the attainment of a sales quota or goal. But a bonus also may be based on other factors. Following are the most common bases for bonus payments:

- ☐ Performance compared to quota or budget
- ☐ Dollar sales volume
- ☐ Gross margin or profit[15]
- ☐ New business gained
- ☐ Performance of group
- ☐ Management judgment

Important differences exist between bonuses and commissions, despite some confusing similarities. Bonuses are not tied directly to a unit of accomplishment such as sales, but commissions are, so each additional unit sold will affect the commission. Bonuses are often given for achievement other than sales performance, as noted previously. A Christmas bonus is traditional with many firms, whereas other bonuses may be based on length of service. Sometimes a firm that has a particularly profitable year will pay an extra bonus to those employees it sees as having been instrumental in the success. This identifies another important difference between bonuses and commissions: *A bonus is discretionary,* because the firm has no obligation to pay either a particular amount or any bonus whatsoever. The employee therefore, cannot depend on a bonus, at least during bad times. The commission, however, is a definite part of the compensation package and will be paid in proportion to sales production (provided that sales exceed the quota or the amount designated for the draw in certain compensation plans). Most commission plans pay monthly, whereas most bonuses are distributed annually or sometimes quarterly.

Bonuses are considered part of the incentive features of the compensation package, but unless this is fully explained in advance, the incentive feature is suspect. Furthermore, when paid only once a year, the incentive features tend to be diluted, because the rewards for an individual's effort may be long delayed. A disadvantage of bonuses based on group performance is the lack of direct relationship to individual performance. Yet, as noted previously, for certain types of selling involving several people before the sale and in after-sales servicing, bonuses may be the only practical way of rewarding performance and offering incentive.[16]

Using Point Systems in Compensation Plans

A point system sometimes is used as part of the compensation plan to give management more control over various aspects of the sales job. A point system is not a separate basic compensation plan but rather an adaptation of the

---

APPLICATION 13.2 Using a Point System in Compensation Plans

An industrial fastener manufacturer saw a need for its salespeople to improve their sales profitability and also to do a much better job of gaining new customers. Yet, sales productivity was still important. The sales force was paid a substantial base salary and a 3% commission on all sales over the quota. The base salary was not changed, but the commission was restructured around the following points:

5 points for meeting sales quota
3 points for every 3% of sales over quota
5 points for each order from a new customer
5 points for attaining an average gross margin of 22%
3 points for every 2% attained over the average gross margin of 22%

For each point earned during the month, the sales representative would receive 1% of his base salary for the month. Thus, if one sales representative had a base salary of $1,800 for the month, and had exceeded both his sales quota and the gross margin goal, as well as gaining several new customers, conceivably he could earn 40 points, and receive an additional $720 for the month.

---

other three. Although it can be used with the straight salary, it is more commonly attached to the incentive portion of the compensation. Essentially, under the point system management assigns "points" to various activity achievements. The payoff then depends on the number of points accumulated during the period. To better clarify this, Application 13.2 shows one firm's solutions.

A point system, in addition to giving management greater control, also affords considerable flexibility. Points can easily be changed and new activities added if desired to greater emphasize certain parts of the selling job. However, as with the combination quota plan described in Chapter 11, a salesperson can overemphasize certain aspects of the job and still neglect other important parts. This is more a problem if nonselling activities, such as displays erected and customer training sessions, are also brought into the point package.

FRINGE BENEFITS

Salespeople were one of the last groups of employees to receive many fringe benefits. Partly this delay was due to the general belief that sales representatives would rather have the money than the benefits. A widely circulated survey in 1959 found this to be clearly indicated.[17] A further inhibiting factor was that fringe benefits were difficult to compute and administer when salary levels fluctuated widely, which is possible in sales, especially under the straight commission plans that were more popular in the past. Now salespeople have most of the fringe benefits offered to other nonmanagerial employees. Benefits include paid vacations, hospital insurance, life insurance, accident insurance, moving expenses, salary continuation program, educational assistance, pension plan, profit sharing, dental insurance, and stock purchase. Some major companies offer the sales force a so-called cafeteria-style approach to benefits. Under these plans employees select those benefits that they deem most important from a complete package of benefits.[18] Salespeople on straight commission tend to have fewer fringe benefits than those who are primarily salaried, particularly regarding paid holidays and vacations. Most firms, however, now offer pensions, life insurance, hospitalization, and major medical insurance.

A company's sales force usually has several additional benefits denied most other employees including most executives except the highest. Expense accounts are discussed more thoroughly later in this chapter. But several other benefits should be briefly noted:

☐ Personal use of a company car

☐ Club or association memberships

☐ Meetings and conventions in exotic places

Because of the amount of travel required of most sales representatives, they commonly are provided either a company-owned or -leased car. Usually they can also use these cars for personal activities, although tax laws require them then to pay part of the car's operating costs. Company-paid memberships in country clubs and other associations are not uncommon, because firms recognize that these provide excellent ways to meet prospects and to entertain clients. Finally, many companies hold periodic sales meetings and conventions in resort hotels with a wide range of amenities, and often the spouse may be invited.

COMPENSATION PROBLEMS

Problems concerning compensation can be particularly disruptive to an organization. When specific policies have been formulated and well communicated to all concerned, less difficulties arise. Consistency in treating similar problems is essential to avoid morale problems and charges of unfairness or inequity. Following are the more typical problems related to compensation (assuming that quotas and territory assignments are not focal points of disagreement; when they are, the problems are multiplied):

☐ Telephone and mail order sales

☐ House accounts

☐ Dual contribution to a sale

☐ Sales returns and allowances

□ Bad debts

□ Windfalls

□ Nonselling assignments

Telephone and mail order sales. Although placed by customers in a particular territory, telephone and mail order sales are not directly attributable to a salesperson's efforts. The issue is whether or not the salesperson in that territory should receive credit (and compensation) for these orders. More firms lean toward giving the salesperson credit, assuming that these orders reflect customer developmental efforts, servicing, and goodwill attributable to the salesperson in that territory. Sometimes management may designate a smaller commission arrangement for these than for other sales. But in all cases an understanding should be communicated and accepted by all parties concerned about how such transactions should be handled.

House accounts. Usually house accounts are large, lucrative accounts that are handled directly by the sales manager (or home office personnel). They can present serious morale problems if improperly handled. Several assumptions are made in removing these customers from the salesperson's responsibility and recompense. Being large and important customers, they may require different handling than the field sales representative is in position to provide. For example special price concessions or inducements may be needed; or perhaps top executives of both companies are friends and conduct business at the highest levels. Or perhaps these accounts provide so much volume that one salesperson's earnings would be excessive and out of proportion with all the others' if credit were given for such sales.

Abuses can occur, however. The sales manager may arbitrarily take over the most profitable accounts, disregarding the efforts of the salespeople involved. For morale purposes the parameters of house accounts should be clearly specified and accepted by the sales force.

Dual contributions to a sale. Sales with important customers and large sales transactions involving more than one salesperson are the usual causes of dual contributions to a sale. Sometimes these dual contributions involve selling efforts spread through several territories, such as when the sales representative in one territory makes the initial contact and arouses interest, but the sale is closed at the customer's headquarters, which is located in another territory. Presumably, the salesperson who made the major contribution should receive more of the commission, but this should be clearly spelled out and guidelines established for such situations, which in many firms are fairly common.

Merchandise returns. Returned goods are a common source of friction. Should customer returns be deducted from the salesperson's sales, or should the company absorb the loss? Sometimes quality control is faulty; perhaps the delivery was late; or the order may have been filled incorrectly. At other times the salesperson may be at fault. Perhaps the customer was persuaded to buy more than could be sold in a reasonable time period; perhaps the salesperson misrepresented the goods—puffed too much—to get the sale; or the order could even have been written up incorrectly. So customer returns can reflect both company and salesperson errors. Some companies make a practice of absorbing the losses when returns are within modest limits. Other firms routinely base commissions only on net sales, not on gross. Regardless of the policy, it should be well understood to eliminate surprise and dismay.

Bad debts.   Bad debts, such as a firm's defaulting because of bankruptcy, can be devastating to the salesperson who has worked hard on a particular account. Some firms deny commissions for aborted sales, and the salesperson must accept this situation as the luck of the draw. Other firms, recognizing that moderate credit losses will occur, cover the bad debt losses themselves.

Windfalls.   A windfall is an unexpectedly large order. The salesperson may be eligible for exceptional commissions, and the windfall should be a welcome, albeit rare, situation. Unfortunately, windfalls can cause a serious management dilemma and can jeopardize morale of the sales and management organization. For example see Application 13.3.

With Application 13.3 in mind, complete Exercise 13.2.

APPLICATION 13.3   Windfalls

Joe LaMarche entered the office of Madeleine Stillson, purchasing agent for the Vista Machine Company, for what he hoped was the last time in this sales transaction. For 3 months he had shown his company's machines to Madeleine, to her production engineers, and even to the plant manager. Now he expected to close the sales for two $20,000 machines. Joe was paid 5 percent on all sales over his quota, and he had already achieved quota this quarter. Consequently, he was anticipating a $2,000 commission on this sale.

Madeleine greeted him warmly. After the preliminary small talk, she calmly announced:

"By the way, we're impressed with your machines and also with your company's service. I didn't tell you before, Joe, but we are in the final stages of site selection for a new plant. I am prepared to sign an order for ninety-four of your machines."

Joe gulped, then rapidly calculated this exhilarating news: 94 × $20,000 × 5% = $94,000 commission. But he sobered. His sales manager, he knew, earned only about $50,000 a year, and the president of the company made $90,000.

1. Do you think Joe should receive the full commission on this windfall? Why or why not?
2. How do you think his sales manager would react if Joe receives the full commission? What would you expect Joe's reaction to be if this windfall is denied him?
3. As general sales manager, draw up a policy statement regarding such windfalls. Be as specific as you can, and defend your recommendations.

Nonselling assignments. Occasionally, nonselling assignments occur. When the sales force is on straight salary, these present no problems, but when the compensation is mostly incentive commissions, difficulties can arise. A salesperson may be asked to perform missionary work, to indoctrinate a new employee, or perhaps to prepare a presentation for the annual sales meeting. All of these activities take time from productive selling and affect compensation accordingly. Although I can make no specific recommendations here, it seems only fair to adjust income to cover these nonselling activities. The adjustment could be in the form of a reduced sales quota for the period involved or an increased bonus. But if a sales manager intends to use the talents of the sales force regularly for nonselling activities, he should make some provision to protect these people from pay disadvantages and to reflect their real worth to the company.

SELLING EXPENSES

The expenses incurred in making a sale are a substantial part of a firm's total direct sales cost. Expenses such as automobile, entertainment, food, and lodging can easily run from $10,000 to over $30,000 a year. The expenses of making a sale range from one-fourth to over one-third of the total compensation of field sales representatives. And these costs inexorably rise annually. Obviously, any measures that can help to reduce these expenses—or, rather, to slow down the rate of increase—without antagonizing salespeople or giving customers a bad impression is desired and worth investigating.

Types of Expenses

Travel expenses and living expenses while away from home are usually reimbursed. These include a variety of expenses, from meals and taxis to valet and laundry costs. Postage and telephone costs are usually covered, and in this area some cost savings can be made. The use of letters or mailgrams can result in substantial savings over long-distance telephone charges, although care must be taken that sales are not jeopardized.

Many alternatives are possible with transportation. Should a sales representative travel by coach or first-class air? Should the firm provide company cars or lease automobiles, or should salespeople use their own cars, being reimbursed for business use? It is impossible to generalize on these issues, because conditions vary greatly by company and sales territory. However, a strong trend seems to be developing toward auto leasing.

Entertainment and gifts are the most controversial expense categories. In some industries it is accepted practice to buy lunches as well as provide tickets for the theater and sports events. Gift giving at Christmas time is still commonplace, although some firms attempt to monetarily limit gifts, such as a maximum of $50. The problem is that no supplier wants to suffer competitively, and so the practice is perpetuated and, at extremes, is akin to bribery and payoffs.

Objectives of a Sound Expense Plan

Expenses incurred by sales representatives should be reimbursed. However, the following issues arise:

1. Should the expense plan result in additional income for the frugal salesperson?
2. What limits, if any, should be imposed on entertainment, food, and lodging expenses?
3. How can salespeople be motivated to curb these expenses?

Ideally, the expense plan should result in the salesperson's breaking even on expenses, not making money on the expense account, but not being out-of-pocket either. In practice this is difficult to achieve. The person determined to come out ahead may cut expenses to the bone, or may pad the expense statement, or both. Neither is satisfactory from the firm's viewpoint. The former may cheapen the company's image and the sales representative's prestige whereas the latter is dishonest and can lead to bigger problems and deceptions.

Some firms consider that liberal expense budgets, permitting first-class air travel and lodging accommodations along with deluxe model cars are part of the motivational package, as well as a means of enhancing their image. The question can always be raised, however, whether such frills have sufficient payoff or whether motivational efforts could not be better directed elsewhere, such as an improved compensation package, or better fringe benefits.

A frequently encountered problem with expense plans is that they do not allow variations in costs in different territories. Some parts of the country are more expensive, particularly in lodging and meals, than elsewhere. The South and the Midwest generally are less expensive than the major cities of the

Northeast or those of the West Coast. Some provision should be made to treat these differences equitably.

Expense accounts should be easily understood and inexpensive to process. Complex reports requiring considerable attention by salespersons, management, and clerical staff create diseconomies affecting overall sales performance. Policies should be specific to avoid disagreements that result from hazy instructions. Finally, payment should be prompt; the sales representative should not be out-of-pocket very long for expenses incurred in pursuing sales.

Types of Expense Plans

Expense plans can be categorized as (1) unlimited plans, (2) limited payment plans, (3) fixed allowance plans, (4) expense quota plans, and (5) no reimbursement, with salespeople paying their own expenses.

Unlimited plans. With unlimited plans the company pays all "reasonable" expenses. The definition of what is reasonable may vary with the stature of the salesperson or executive, years of service, and the level of sales performance. Unlimited plans provide the utmost flexibility, but they can also lead to abuses. In practice, however, if a salesperson is achieving a satisfactory level of sales, his expense statements are less likely to be questioned; the salesperson who is not doing so well may feel hounded.

Although company practices differ regarding the amount of detail required in reporting expenses, the Internal Revenue Service requires substantiating expenses with detailed records on the amount, time, and place of the expense, the business purpose, and the business relationship to the recipient of any entertainment or gifts, with receipts required for all expenditures over $25.

Limited payment plans. Limited payment plans stipulate the maximum amount to be paid for each expense category. Accordingly, the salesperson is allowed specific amounts for automobile transportation, meals and lodging, and entertainment. Auto transportation most likely is on a fixed mileage rate. Meal allowances may further designate specific sums for breakfast, lunch, and dinner. These plans permit strict control, but may not always be sufficiently flexible for different clients and different territories and may be unduly restrictive. Furthermore, as costs continue to rise, the plan must be frequently updated to represent actual field conditions.

Fixed allowance plans. With the fixed allowance plan, the salesperson receives a flat sum, perhaps per diem, or per month or quarter. This plan provides flexibility because the salesperson can vary the various expense categories according to his judgment and still remain within the overall allowance. Management is tempted to be unduly penurious with this plan, because the salesperson keeps the fixed allowance whether or not it is spent.

Expense quota plans.   Essentially, the expense quota plan is a percentage-of-sales method, which presumably represents the optimum relationship of selling expenses to sales volume. A salesperson in lean times may incur some out-of-pocket expenditures under this method, whereas undue extravagance may result when sales are good. Like some of the other plans, this does not recognize territorial difference or special needs.

No reimbursement.   Occasionally, a firm may have its salespeople pay their own expenses, thereby having no expense account. Certainly, this provides the utmost flexibility. Presumably a higher commission rate is given to cover such expenses, although the temptation is for the salesperson to be too frugal.[19] These plans usually are limited to salespeople selling for more than one manufacturer (e.g., manufacturers' representatives) and for part-timers.

Control of Selling Expenses

Some checking or auditing of expense reports is reasonable to detect mathematical errors and any questionable entries. Padding or faking is not uncommon with expense reports, but auditing should curb extreme abuses. If receipts are easily obtained, such as those for air transportation and lodging, they should be turned in with the expense report. Even if an employer is negligent on this requirement, the IRS necessitates rigorous recordkeeping.

Calculating the cost per call.   Sales managers can calculate the cost per call of their salespeople. This can serve as a basis for comparing selling costs with previous years as well as identifying the more efficient producers. As a result, areas in which corrective action is needed can be spotted, and the importance of such expenses can be more readily appreciated.

Four steps should be involved in calculating the cost per call. (1) Calculate the actual number of sales calls made per year, both by the individual salespeople and by the total sales force. (2) Compute the direct sales costs of the individual salespeople as well as those of the total sales force. These direct sales costs include total compensation plan, transportation, and expense account costs. (3) Divide total costs by total calls, both for individual salespeople and for the total sales force. (4) Finally, and this is optional but very important with a widespread salesforce, divide this average cost per call by the "index" for that metropolitan area to obtain the adjusted cost per call. (See Application 13.4.)

How to encourage lower selling expenses.   A firm can encourage lower selling expenses by giving a bonus to those whose expenses come in under plan. This may, however, strongly motivate niggardly spending, which is especially risky when important customers are involved. Motivating personnel

APPLICATION 13.4 Calculating the Adjusted Cost per Call

In 1988 Ellen Tamasi made 950 calls. Her compensation, including salary and commission, amounted to $30,500, and she incurred selling expenses of $11,000. The ten salespeople in the district made a total of 11,250 sales calls, and total direct selling costs were $430,000. Ellen's cost per call compared with the total for the district may be computed as follows:

$$\frac{\$30,500 + \$11,000}{950} = \$43.68 \text{ Ellen's average cost per call (unadjusted)}$$

$$\frac{\$430,000}{11,250} = \$38.25 \text{ the district's average cost per call (unadjusted)}$$

At this point, Ellen's higher-than-average selling cost can be identified for possible criticism and corrective action. But her territory may be a high-cost area. *Sales & Marketing Management's* annual *Survey of Selling Costs* indexes average selling costs for the various metropolitan areas. One index provides the city's per diem average of meals and lodging expressed as a ratio of the U.S. average. A value of 102, for example, means that the area's total costs are 2% above the national average. Suppose Ellen sells in San Francisco, 145 on the per diem index, whereas another salesperson works in Sacramento, where the per diem index is only 87. An adjusted cost-per-call figure would then be necessary to reflect the true performance:

$$\frac{\$43.68}{145} = \$30.12 \text{ San Francisco's adjusted cost per call}$$

to reduce costs is not easy; but sales meetings should address cost reduction and explore more economical ways to service customers. Sometimes better routing and scheduling can reduce costs. Management also can encourage less expensive modes of transportation (e.g., shuttle van service from airports instead of taxis), more modest lodging, and letters instead of long-distance calls. Renting or leasing cars rather than using company-owned vehicles should be analyzed. Numerous other expense-reducing measures are possible without jeopardizing the company's image, reducing customer service, or causing the salesperson distress or embarrassment. But unless conscious attention is given to this important cost category, a lot of fat and extravagance likely will develop.

Now, what should be done about the sales representative whose expenses exceed the designated fixed allowance? In the interests of flexibility, exceptions may have to be permitted, although in most firms the sales manager must approve. The salesperson therefore must make a suitable explanation regarding these exceptions. Neither extreme—rigidity or laxness—is best. But the expense budget generally should not be taken lightly; when carelessly handled it can be a significant profit drain.

SUMMARY   At the beginning of this chapter, I asked you to think about designing a compensation plan to overcome two problems: (1) salespeople over-emphasizing the easier-to-sell parts of the product line, and (2) salespeople neglecting new customer accounts. Did you suggest a commission plan based on gross margin for the first situation? Good. Usually, the easy-to-sell items are also the low-margin items. So, paying commission on gross margin will discourage emphasis on these items. I hope you didn't suggest a straight commission plan for the second problem. Having a base salary as a major component of the total compensation plan enables management to require salespeople to perform nonselling activities. When commission is the major component, this is more difficult, because developing new accounts can be time-consuming and not yield any immediate sales results. A point system based on the number of new accounts called on or sold also could solve this problem.

Compensation is an important factor in morale and motivation, although it is by no means the only influence. Problems with compensation plans are particularly likely if the pay scale is lower than that for similar jobs. A good compensation plan should be fair, direct efforts toward company objectives, afford flexibility, provide incentive, give security, and also be easy to administer and understand. A plan should enable the average level of earnings to be reasonable from the company's viewpoint.

The three basic compensation plans are straight salary, straight commission, and some combination of the two. Factors favoring a greater emphasis on base salary are security and better management control; the higher the commission factor, the less the security and control, but the greater the incentive. A progressive or regressive commission structure is sometimes used. Indirect compensation often includes fringe benefits such as liberal expense accounts, company cars, and sometimes club memberships, as well as the more common benefits.

Selling expenses can be a substantial part of total direct sales costs of a firm. A number of different methods are used to handle travel and entertainment expenses in particular, but whichever is used, management should exercise some control to keep these necessary costs sufficient but not exorbitant.

The most common compensation problems concern telephone and mail order sales, house accounts, dual contribution, returns, bad debts, windfalls, and nonselling assignments.

QUESTIONS   1. Differentiate between motivation and morale. Which is more important to an organization?

2. "I would do anything for a buck!"
   "Compensation is important only in relation to what other people are

making; therefore, its value lies in the status implications.''
Which of these two statements do you think is more nearly correct?

3. Some top salespeople earn more than their sales managers. Does this mean that they would never consider a step-down in earnings in order to get into management? What would be your attitude toward this if you were a star salesperson?

4. Why were fringe benefits so slow in coming to salespeople relative to other types of employees? Did this make sales jobs less attractive in the past?

5. Should telephone and mail order sales be credited to the person in the particular territory? Why or why not?

6. What are the advantages and disadvantages of unlimited expense plans?

7. What would be the most appropriate compensation plan for salespeople in the following jobs:
   (a) computer sales to large firms,
   (b) retail sales in a men's clothing department,
   (c) missionary sales,
   (d) mutual funds sales,
   (e) real estate sales,
   (f) new car sales?

8. Is compensation the most important motivation factor? Discuss it in relation to other factors.

9. Describe the type of salespeople who would most likely have a strong preference for straight salary compensation.

Please evaluate each of the alternatives.

You are confronted with rebellion in the ranks. Several of your top salespeople are agitating in your office. They are upset because you have asked them to take some time out from their direct selling duties to handle a rash of recent customer complaints including improperly filled orders, defective or damaged products, and lack of sufficient instructions for proper use. The sales representatives are on straight commission and resent having to take time out from selling to handle these problems, for which they feel blameless. How would you handle this confrontation?

PEOPLE PROBLEM: DIFFICULTY WITH STRAIGHT-COMMISSION SALES-PEOPLE

1. You remind these salespeople, tactfully at first, then more forcefully, that they are employees of the company, are being well compensated, and are expected to perform those necessary duties prescribed by the firm.

2. You agree with these salespeople that their earnings should not suffer from nonproductive activities. Accordingly, you promise to adjust their income to cover these nonselling activities.

3. You ask the salespeople if they would rather have the compensation plan changed from a straight commission to a salary and commission or bonus so that nonselling assignments can be better accommodated in the pay structure.

4. You promise to complain about the defective servicing of customers to those other departments of the company that are most at fault, such as quality control, order filling, and engineering. Meanwhile you tell your salespeople that customers must be serviced to their full satisfaction; otherwise, neither you nor the sales force will have a job.

5. You promise to develop a supplementary compensation package that will give bonus points to nonselling activities according to both the time taken away from selling and the effectiveness of the nonselling activities.

NOTES

1. For further discussion of the sales manager's role in maintaining morale, see R. Kenneth Teas and James F. Horrell, "Salespeople Satisfaction and Performance Feedback," *Industrial Marketing Management* (February 1981): 49–57.

2. Gilbert A. Churchill, Jr., Neil M. Ford, and Orville C. Walker, Jr., "Personal Characteristics of Salespeople and the Attractiveness of Alternative Rewards," *Journal of Business Research* (January 1979): 25–50.

3. Related to this, see Alan J. Dubinsky and Mary E. Lippitt, "Managing Frustration in the Sales Force," *Industrial Marketing Management* (June 1979): 200–206.

4. For example C. E. Jurgensen, "What Job Applicants Look for in a Company," *Personnel Psychology* (Winter 1948): 433–435; Charles D. McDermit, "How Money Motivates Men," *Business Horizons* (Winter 1960): 94–100; Edward E. Lawler, III, *Pay and Organizational Effectiveness: A Psychological View* (New York: McGraw-Hill, 1971).

5. For example Richard C. Smyth, "Financial Incentives for Salesmen," *Harvard Business Review* (January/February 1968): 109–117; Neil M. Ford, Orville C. Walker, Jr., and Gilbert A. Churchill, Jr., "Differences in the Attractiveness of Alternative Rewards Among Industrial Salespeople: Additional Evidence," *Journal of Business Research* 1984.

6. Gilbert A. Churchill, Jr., Neil M. Ford, and Orville C. Walker, Jr., *Motivating the Industrial Salesforce: The Attractiveness of Alternative Rewards.* Report #76–115 (Cambridge, Mass.: The Marketing Science Institute, 1976).

7. Leon Winer, "A Sales Compensation System that Maximizes Motivation and Economy," *Advanced Management Journal* (Spring 1982): 46.

8. John K. Moynahan, "Nothing Can Compensate for a Poor Organizational Climate," *Sales & Marketing Management* (16 March 1981): 112–114.

9. See Rene Y. Darmon, "Compensation Plans That Link Management and Salesman's Objectives," *Industrial Marketing Management* (April 1982): 151–163.

10. See Douglas J. Dalrymple, P. Ronald Stephenson, and William Cron, "Wage Levels and Sales Productivity," *Business Horizons* (December 1980): 57–60. For an interesting article describing the role of negotiation in setting individual compen-

sation levels, see Ken Swift, Tom Perseput, and Brian Kleiner, "Salary Negotiation: A Strategy for Success," *Office Administration and Automation* (February 1985): 30–32.

11. For ideas on adjusting a compensation plan that is overpaying sales people, see John K. Moynahan, "How to Correct an Incentive Plan That Pays Sales People Too Much," *Sales & Marketing Management* (29 Aug. 1977): 112–115.

12. See Matt S. Walton, III, "How to Draft a Sales Compensation Plan," *Personnel* (June 1985): 71–74.

13. Combination plans are more commonly found in larger than in smaller firms. See Alan J. Dubinsky and Thomas E. Barry, "A Survey of Sales Management Practices," *Industrial Marketing Management* 11 (1982): 137.

14. David M. Gardner and Kenneth M. Rowland, "A Self-Tailored Approach to Incentives," *Personnel Journal* (Nov. 1979): 907–912. Also see Mary Lynn Miller, "Motivating the Sales Force," *The Conference Board Information Bulletin* 64 (1979): 2.

15. For a cautionary view of sales compensation tied to gross margin, see Douglas J. Dalrymple, P. Ronald Stephenson, and William Cron, "Gross Margin Sales Compensation Plans," *Industrial Marketing Management* (July 1981): 219–224.

16. For a strong case on the use of bonuses, see Fred K. Foulkes, "Why Bonus Plans are Good for Business," *Personnel* (August 1985): 72–73.

17. Marvin Hoffman and David J. Luck, *Salesmen's Fringe Benefits*, Marketing and Transportation Paper, no. 6 (East Lansing, Mich.: Division of Research, Graduate School of Business Administration, Michigan State University, 1959).

18. Deborah Randolph, "More Workers Are Getting a Change to Choose Benefits Cafeteria-Style," *Wall Street Journal*, 14 July 1981. Also see David M. Gardner and Kenneth M. Rowland, "A Self-Tailored Approach," 907–912.

19. For a comparison of expense practices by type of compensation plan, see John P. Steinbrink, "How to Pay Your Salesforce," *Harvard Business Review* (July–August 1978): 114–121.

cases

13.1 The Problem of Inequitable Relative Compensation

"This is intolerable. How can you do this to us old-timers?"

"I know how you feel," you reply. "But I can't do anything about it. These are simply the facts of life in today's job market."

The problem is that you must hire six to eight new salespeople to meet expansion and retirement needs. The job market is such that to get reasonably qualified people you must offer them as much as some of your 10- and 15-year veterans receive. Understandably, your people are resentful.

QUESTION

What, if anything, can you do about the potential major morale problem arising from inequitable compensation?

13.2 A Problem with Dissimilar Compensation Plans

The John O'Day Company, distributor of plumbing fixtures and equipment, always gave its salespeople their choice of compensation plan. Consequently, some are on straight salary, a few are on straight commission, and the majority receive some combination of salary and commission. In the past this hodgepodge presented no real problems. However, with construction and housing booming, the few people on straight commission now reap the har-

vest. One salesman, in particular, has earnings that total twice as much as anyone else on the sales force and are approaching those of the executive vice president. As a result there is severe agitation among the sales representatives. Few want straight commission, but all think their level of earnings should be drastically raised. There is even talk of contacting a union. Management most fears this last possibility.

QUESTION

What course of action seems advised?

13.3 Door-to-Door Encyclopedia Selling: A Radical Idea in Compensation

Dan Hasbro was sales manager of the Great Lakes region of the Moore Encyclopedia Company. Door-to-door sales, most often cold calls, are traditional in this business. Dan recognized that this was the most difficult selling imaginable—attempting to sell an item retailing more than $400 to people selected

at random, the vast majority of whom were disinterested and even hostile. Like most of the other sales executives of the company, he had advanced through the ranks, had been a successful salesman who had persisted when the vast majority of salespeople quit, sometimes in only a few weeks. Training was minimal. All salespeople were supplied a canned sales presentation, which they were expected to memorize along with responses to the most common objections raised by prospective customers, but this was all they received. Compensation was straight commission.

In such an environment, only the most capable stayed with the company. Dan sometimes chuckled to himself as he referred to it as the "law of the sidewalk jungle—survival of the fittest." But the high attrition rate (as high as 300 percent) meant that he and all the other sales managers were constantly combing their areas for new recruits. Requirements for such recruits were not high; a high school diploma was not required. The ads that Dan frequently placed in newspapers in his region were somewhat deceptive. He had found that advertising for an encyclopedia salesperson seldom elicited much of a response. But advertising for someone to conduct "research" or to do "creative selling," drew a much better response. He often persuaded candidates to try encyclopedia selling by showing them truthfully the rather high rewards that a few of the top-notch people were achieving. One woman, for example, was earning over $45,000 a year, and several other top producers were in the high thirties. During the perpetual, frustrating, and time-consuming job of recruiting, he increasingly thought that something could be done to develop a more professional and stable sales force.

Better training would help, Dan thought. Perhaps the new recruits could be given a 2- or 3-week indoctrination period and accompany a successful salesperson for a few days or longer. However, Dan concluded that the compensation plan of straight commission was the biggest single deterrent to pro-

ducing stability and effectiveness among more than just a handful of salespeople. If some part of the compensation could be a salary, not dependent on sales, more time could be spent in training and developing people. Then more individuals should become effective producers, and there should be far less turnover, and also perhaps fewer "high pressure" tactics (for which the company and other door-to-door marketers were being criticized by consumer groups and the government).

Deeply concerned about the existing situation, Dan compiled some material to present to top management to support his contention that the straight commission plan should be modified. Excerpts follow:

Gross sales in our region for fiscal 1987 were $1,206,800 and resulted from the sales of 3,446 sets. Table 1 summarizes those sales (volume is grouped by specific volume levels per salesperson).

Table 1 clearly shows that our top 19 salespeople (15% of the total who sold anything at all, and only 5% of everyone on board in 1987) accounted for 85% of gross volume. Certainly, this severe imbalance suggests that we should be concerned about the stability of our sales dollars.

Perhaps even more worrisome is that of the 361 salespeople on board at one time or another during 1987, only 129 sold even one set, and 232 people sold nothing. Moreover, our turnover in 1987 resulted in 265 new hires, for a turnover rate of 288% based on an average sales force of 92. Because of this alarming statistic, I requested an analysis from accounting on those costs associated with recruiting 265 new hires. These costs are shown in Table 2.

Table 2 clearly shows that our "minimum investment" policy does have associated costs. In fact recruiting costs in 1987 were ($78,900/$1,206,000) × 100 = 6.5% of gross sales.

Beyond these recruiting costs we no doubt also experience lost opportunity costs due to the lack of

TABLE 1 Sales breakdown.

Gross Annual Sales Per Sales Rep ($ Hundreds)	No. of Sales Reps in the Range	Summation of Gross Sales ($ Hundreds)	Sets Sold
120–160	1	125	357
80–119	4	400	1,143
10–79	14	500	1,429
less than 10	110	181	517
Yearly Totals	129*	1,206	3,446

*129 people sold at least one set; 361 were considered salespeople in 1987.

TABLE 2 Recruiting costs in 1987.

Item	Cost ($)
Newspaper ads (average cost at $1.85/line/day, run 30 days on, 30 days off, 15 lines per ad for 1 year)	
Chicago, *Calumet*	7,300
Detroit, *Free Press*	3,600
Cleveland, *Plain Dealer*	6,200
Toledo, *Blade*	2,800
Erie, *Penn*	5,500
Pittsburgh, *Post Gazette*	5,600
Total	31,000
Secretarial/administrative (1.5 full time)	28,000
Executive administration (3 hours/hire, $25/hour)	19,900
Total recruiting costs, 1987	78,900

sales training, as well as the lost management time associated with a 300% turnover. From these data I respectfully submit that a reevaluation of our compensation and training policies may be worth considering.

The reaction to Dan's memorandum was completely negative. The executive vice president sharply defended the company's policies, "Paying these people a salary when they're not producing would destroy the already slim profits we have. The losers would stay on, and the good people, the ones we keep now because of the high commissions they are able to achieve, would quickly leave us." The vice president said in a lower voice, "Just between you and me, if we paid anything less than a straight commission, I doubt that we'd get the kind of high-pressure selling that we need in this business. So, no way, Dan. Our present compensation method is tried and proven. All the other major door-to-door firms have exactly the same compensation method. Doesn't that tell you something?"

Dan shrugged. "What's the use of batting your head against a brick wall?" he told himself. Still, it would have been interesting if he had been permitted to test out his theory on a small scale.

QUESTIONS

1. Evaluate the position of the executive vice president.

2. Evaluate Dan Hasbro's recommendations. Do you think he could have been more persuasive or presented a more convincing argument?

3. If the vice president had expressed some interest in changing compensation to salary and commission, what percentage would you recommend for this situation? How would you handle the problem of "deadwood" if the salary was sufficient to provide a living wage?

13.4 Monarch Machine Company: Devising the Best Compensation Plan

The Monarch Machine Company manufactured, usually to customers' requirements, specialized machinery for firms primarily in the garment- and shoe-manufacturing industries. Although some of the machines were small and multipurpose, requiring no great expertise, others were expensive and complex. Sales of the latter might take months to close, and a number of Monarch people might be involved as well as the sales representative. In addition to its sales force of eight, most of whom had nontechnical backgrounds, three technical specialists with mechanical engineering degrees customarily assisted the sales force in assessing customers' special requirements and designing equipment accordingly. For some of the larger potential sales (a large machinery order could comprise as much as 10 percent of Monarch's annual sales volume), some of Monarch's top engineers might be involved, and even the vice presidents and company president might contact the customer firm's top executives.

Brenda Rizzo, Monarch sales manager, was not pleased with the present compensation plan. The sales representatives were paid straight salaries, ranging last year from $27,500 to $48,000 and depending mostly on years of experience with the company. The three technical specialists were also paid on a straight salary, ranging from $34,000 to $45,000. Brenda considered their expense budgets to be realistic but not excessive. What bothered her most about the present plan was the lack of sufficient incentive. Because no bonus or commission was paid on sales, she suspected but could not prove that several sales representatives were not producing to their maximum potential. And she received some complaints from the sales force that the technical specialists, although they might know their machinery, were particularly weak in customer relations and sometimes even jeopardized a sale.

Finally Brenda spoke to Robert Pembrook, vice president of sales. "I think we must reevaluate our compensation plan. We must develop more incentives for our people."

"Brenda, I know more incentives would be preferred. But we can't pay these people a commission. How can we ever single out the contribution that each person has made to the sale?"

"I know, Bob. That's the rub. But I'm not advocating that we go whole commission or that the commission be a major part of the total compensation package. Maybe the incentive shouldn't even be a commission, but rather a year-end bonus."

"I'm not particularly sold on the idea of a year-end bonus—although traditionally executives are given extra compensation through a bonus. It seems to me that as far as the sales force is concerned, a remote year-end bonus possibility probably has no more incentive value than the straight salary we have now." The vice president scratched his chin reflectively. "And if we go with either commission or bonus, how do you determine the contribution of the sales representative to the sale, when we have two, three, or more other people also involved?" As Brenda began to respond, Pembrook said, "Let me raise another problem, and as I see it, this may be the most serious problem. Some of these sales may take more than a year to finalize. Then, as you know, as much as half a million dollars may be involved. This situation creates a feast-and-famine scenario for the person depending on either a commission or a bonus. Brenda, although I agree that more incentives should foster our compensation plan, I'm not sure that in our case it is workable. Maybe you'd be best off developing some other kinds of incentives, rather than anything tied in with the compensation plan."

"I don't think so, Bob. In the first place, sales contests or special recognitions still face the same impediments we discussed with the compensation idea—that of recognizing the contribution that each person makes to the final sale."

"Would you bring the technical specialists and any other engineering people into the incentive payment?"

"I think so. The incentive should not be limited just to the sales reps. The other people are fully as instrumental, if not more so, in making the sale."

Pembrook frowned and drummed his fingers on the desk. "Brenda, I recognize the need to develop some incentives. Yet, the obstacles to a workable system seem almost overwhelming. Tell you what . . . let's bring in a management consultant to advise us. He probably has had experience with similar situations in other companies."

QUESTION

Assume the role of the management consultant in this case. How would you advise Monarch to develop more incentive? Develop in detail a change either in the compensation method or in the use of other nonmonetary incentives or in both. Be as specific as you can and be prepared to support your recommendations as fully as possible.

CHAPTER 14
Directing and Motivating Through Supervision

CHAPTER PERSPECTIVE

Advancement through the ranks of management in any organization mostly is related to how much one can accomplish through people. Supervision is a vital part of people management. Beginning supervisors can be exhilarated by their new job, but effective supervision is complex. Certain principles of human relations and motivation are involved. Furthermore, good supervisors are continually challenged by the variety of problems they encounter.

The field sales manager's job of supervising differs from and often is more difficult than that of managers in offices, factories, and stores. Because the sales force may be widely scattered, face-to-face observation and direction is necessarily lim-

ited. More emphasis must be given to indirect supervision through correspondence, reports, periodic sales meetings, and the like. The need for motivating and directing the sales force is not mitigated, despite the constraints of distance. Chapter 14 examines the heady opportunities, and the inevitable problems that will be confronted, and how these can best be handled by the effective supervisor. By you!

As you study this chapter, consider what the sales manager can do both to encourage better acceptance of report requirements and to ensure that reports are used only to extract meaningful and important information.

CHAPTER OBJECTIVES

☐ Attain a perspective of what is involved in supervision, and especially in effective supervision.
☐ Understand the factors needed for good directions.
☐ Become aware of the contributions of motivational theory to effective supervision.
☐ Consider the factors that should influence how closely you need to supervise.
☐ Know the various methods of supervision, including indirect methods.
☐ Become familiar with an important application of supervision, delegation.
☐ Become aware of the more common problems in supervision, including the inevitable need to discipline.
☐ Know the use and effectiveness of incentives of various kinds, including the role of contests.
☐ Become aware of career paths, their role in motivation, as well as the implications for the ambitious.

INGREDIENTS OF SUPERVISION

Supervision refers to the directive relations between executives and their immediate subordinates. *Effective supervision* may be defined as the act of providing a job environment that encourages high-level, goal-directed accomplishment. The following elements are involved in supervision: planning, making work assignments; directing, issuing instructions; motivating, stimulating good performance; following up, checking to see that instructions are followed and that performance is satisfactory. All these supervision duties are closely related. Planning and direction are almost inseparable, and the manner of directing is closely associated with problems of motivation. Permeating all is leadership, a skill that is complex and not easily defined, but supervisory and leadership skills can be learned.

Planning Work

Before a sales force can accomplish a high level of productivity, some plans must be made. For example what customers will be called on today? This week? What nonselling activities will be conducted? What products and/or promotional ideas will be emphasized in sales calls? *Planning* is deciding in advance what is to be done in the future. The individual salesperson must plan each customer visitation to do an effective job. And the sales manager, in the role of supervisor, is involved in planning when assigning salespeople to various territories, perhaps based on their experience and ability. Although some salespeople may operate quite independently, others may require that the supervisor plan the routing and call schedules to ensure proper coverage. Where selling efforts are coordinated with advertising and other promotional devices or with new product introductions and customer orientations, careful planning is necessary to ensure unified, goal-directed activities.

Directing

Directing is issuing instructions to subordinates or otherwise indicating what should be done. Although the compensation plan, the components structure of the quota, and the expense budget should all contribute to the desired goal-directed behavior, invariably some verbal or written directives also will be needed. Certain characteristics that typify a good instruction or directive are discussed in the following paragraphs.

An instruction should be clear.   Common sense dictates that instructions should be clear, but this often is violated. Although a directive may be clear to the issuing supervisor, it is not always clear to the recipient. Especially with new employees and those who are relatively untrained, clear instructions are most important.

An instruction should be complete. To tell a salesperson, "We need to do a better job of servicing our accounts" is vague. It does not indicate why the change is necessary, what was being done wrong before, and what particular extra services are now desired. A complete order should leave no question in the mind of the person receiving it about what should be done. Usually a time factor should also be indicated. If other tasks also must be done, the supervisor should indicate the *priority*—which should be done first, and what is the relative importance among all activities.

An instruction should be reasonable. A supervisor must consider whether the person receiving the instruction has the necessary experience and ability to perform it satisfactorily. Asking a new sales representative to handle customer complaints might be unreasonable and might result in a bungled or unfinished job. Furthermore, company policies, resources, and other aspects of the operating situation must be considered when issuing an instruction, so that the employee can comply with reasonable effort and ability.

Explain why a particular order is being given. Most effective supervisors explain the reasons for an order. Explanations are good for morale because they give subordinates an increased sense of personal importance. Subordinates also may be better able to carry out the instruction because they can see the relation between their actions and the larger goal. Especially when some initiative can be exercised in carrying out the order (when some of the detailed planning can be left to the subordinate), an understanding of why it was given may be important to the interpretation and sense of priority. For example the instruction to "spend time on each visit instructing the customer's salesclerks" may become more effective when the reason for doing so is given, "We are receiving a large number of returns of damaged goods because the buyers were not given adequate instruction by the retailers on correct use."

Evaluating Participatory Direction Versus Autocratic Direction

Direction can take two extremes. In *participatory direction* the supervisor consults with the people responsible for doing the task about its workability and better ways to accomplish the same results; the subordinates participate in the decision. The sales manager may consult senior salespeople about a slow-selling product category. The sales manager may ask for suggestions to increase sales or modify some product features. This discussion may result in a program to promote these items through more aggressive selling efforts, an improved package, or a price reduction; or the consensus may be to eliminate these products from the line. The sales manager may not have thought of some of the solutions.

Autocratic direction is simply issuing orders unilaterally, without any consultation with or participation by subordinates. For example in the preceding situation, the sales manager might have a sales meeting and tell the salespeople: "These items are not selling, and we are receiving pressure from the home office about it. I want everyone here to make a real effort to sell one dozen a day until they're all gone."

Benefits of participatory direction.   One benefit of employee participation obvious is greater cooperation and enthusiasm for one's work. A person will work much harder for a plan to which she has made a contribution. Subordinates sometimes can point out practical difficulties in a plan and suggest modifications, and an innovative idea may emerge. The work environment can become more harmonious if the executive is more a coordinator of ideas than a "boss." Such an environment promotes the personal development of subordinates. They can begin to generate ideas and develop judgments, and they are motivated to seek more responsibilities. This is especially preferred for management development, because trainees exposed to a democratic superior learn more quickly than they do from one who issues orders autocratically.

Dangers of participatory direction.   Participation should not always be used, even by the executive who prefers this management style. The time and expense of consulting with subordinates are often impractical, especially if minor decisions must be made, or if action must be taken quickly, or if the sales force is widely scattered and communications not always prompt. The caliber of the sales force may weigh against inviting participation. If most of the salespeople are new and untrained, if they lack interest (perhaps because of a straight commission plan, in which all activity is subordinate to sales production), or if they are not very competent, no benefit would be likely. By participating in the development of a plan, a salesperson may feel free to change it later without consulting the supervisor. Furthermore, there is some possibility that the instructions finally developing in extended group participation will be fuzzy rather than complete and clear.

The supervisor can avoid or minimize most of the preceding dangers by taking care with employee participation. The sales manager can look for opportunities to use and to experiment with employee participation. It can be used with just one or two subordinates or with a whole group at a sales meeting, depending on the situation.

Motivation

In Chapter 13 we took an initial look at motivation and considered specifically the role of the compensation plan in sales force motivation. In this section the major psychological theories of motivation are briefly described, followed by supervisory inputs into the challenge of motivation.

Theories of motivation. Chapter 13 defined motivation as a person's desire to do her job. To lead most effectively, the manager must understand factors that affect and stimulate this desire. Motives are tied in with an individual's needs and life goals, and as shown in Chapter 13, these vary among individuals. But psychologists generally agree that needs can be classified and ranked, which presents some useful concepts concerning motivation.

Primary needs are the basic needs for food, clothing, and shelter, whereas *secondary needs* are those that can be postponed and are often psychological, such as love and esteem. The primary needs must take precedence over secondary needs because health and life obviously depend on primary needs.

Maslow developed a pioneering theory in arranging needs according to their order or importance. *Maslow's hierarchy of needs* is well-known and widely accepted.[1] Figure 14.1 shows the basic theory. According to Maslow, the lower-level needs must be satisfied before higher-level needs become important motivating forces. One should recognize that a person more likely will work simultaneously toward several levels of need satisfaction, although needs at any single level will probably never be fully satisfied.

Now, what is the sales management significance of Maslow's concept?[2] Presumably, money is a more important motivator at the lower level of needs. Nonfinancial honors and recognition may be more effective for those who are reaching for esteem and self-actualization and not merely for money to keep a family at a reasonable standard of living.[3] Maslow's theory strongly

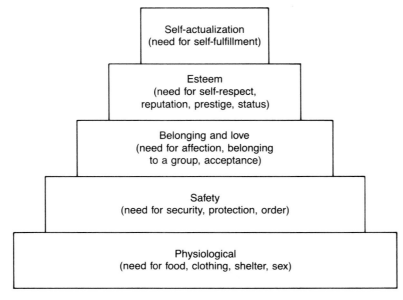

FIGURE 14.1   Maslow's hierarchy of needs. (*Source*: Based on Abraham H. Maslow, ''A Theory of Human Motivations,'' in *Motivation and Personality*, 2nd ed. New York: Harper & Row, 1970.)

supports the idea that motivation differs among individuals, that individuals are at different stages of a hierarchy of needs.

Herzberg's motivation-hygiene theory is similar to Maslow's hierarchy.[4] Herzberg, however, recognizes only two levels of needs, which he calls motivator needs (the higher level), and hygiene needs (lower level). Examples follow:

Motivator Needs	*Hygiene Needs*
Recognition	Salary and fringe benefits
Achievement	Work conditions
Responsibility	Job security

These needs are comparable to those identified by Maslow, but Herzberg develops a relationship between the two levels of needs and the ideas of job satisfaction and dissatisfaction. According to Herzberg the worker does not necessarily have an either–or attitude toward the job, but also sometimes has a neutral attitude, being neither satisfied nor dissatisfied but rather indifferent or neutral. For example if the hygiene needs—those of salary, working conditions, and the like—are not fulfilled, then the worker will experience job dissatisfaction. But even if these needs are met, there may still be no job satisfaction unless the motivator needs are met, such as recognition and achievement. The significance of Herzberg's theory for sales management is clear. Meeting an employee's hygiene needs for a decent salary and working conditions is insufficient. Although meeting these needs may prevent the morale problems of job dissatisfaction, this will not be enough to spur motivation beyond the neutral area. The sales force therefore must be provided opportunities for recognition and personal growth; only then will job satisfaction truly exist, and with it, a positive motivation.[5]

The *expectancy theory* of sales-force motivation surpasses the two need-oriented theories and is probably more realistic.[6] The term *expectancy* is based on the idea that salespeople have expectations of rewards for the effort expended and the results achieved. The concept unites three factors: (1) effort (of the individual), (2) performance, and (3) rewards provided by management. If the rewards for the successful effort are not considered worth the effort, motivation will be severely jeopardized. A number of research studies have supported the motivational stimuli of rewards such as membership in the $1 Million Club, and attendance at annual conventions, as well as some other nonfinancial sales incentives.[7]

Job clarity and *role ambiguity* have received considerable research attention regarding motivation. Job clarity is present if the salesperson fully understands her role in the company, what is expected, and how she will be evaluated. Role ambiguity exists when clarity is absent.[8] Good communication is needed between management and the sales force, with good channels of communication both down from management as well as up from the sales force. The job clarity and role ambiguity concepts also suggest the importance of fully informing candidates during the hiring process exactly what is expected of them, even taking them out into the field and showing them the job conditions. The concepts also suggest the need for training that as realistically as possible represents actual field conditions and management expectations.

Practical supervisory inputs.   Supervisors should be keenly interested in motivation. It is understandably one of the most common topics in sales management publications and in seminars. Well-motivated subordinates perform better on the job, and as the theories of motivation suggest, motivation is affected by their feelings of job satisfaction. But supervisors also should recognize that different supervisory techniques may be called for with different salespeople. One salesperson may perform best under the critical eye of an authoritarian boss, whereas another would resent this or be so upset that efficiency would suffer.

Perhaps the greatest influence a manager can have on individual motivations is in relieving sources of employee dissatisfaction. For example a supervisor may recognize that the present compensation plan is lacking, and that one offering more potential income through greater emphasis on commissions would be a good motivator. But company policies may prevent changes in method of compensation. Perhaps the supervisor could improve working conditions by offering clerical assistance or by a different routing that would allow salespeople to be home more nights. Table 14.1 shows other frustrating situations that salespeople face and how management can relieve or improve the situation.

Motivation can depend on how well a salesperson identifies with the company. Such identification may be determined by the public image of the company—whether the employee can be proud to work for it—and by the quality of its products. Over these aspects the sales manager may have little control. But perhaps she can influence some elements that contribute to a positive identification.

One key to motivation: Identification with company.   Identification is a deep-seated primal tendency. As children we identify with our parents; later we identify with our school and our country. Identification implies that company or institution goals become individual goals. How can the sales manager influence people to form a positive identification? If employees perceive that management and the company care about them, they will, in turn, tend to care about the company. Above all, the sales manager should have a positive identification toward the company, because supervisors' attitudes are quickly sensed by subordinates.

Although some salespeople can sell products about which they themselves feel doubtful or cynical, to be effective, most people must believe in what they sell. The sales manager, and higher management and the training staff as well, should have a major commitment to convincing salespeople of the merits of the products they must sell; and this is difficult if shoddy work-

TABLE 14.1 Common frustrating sales situations and recommended managerial action.

Situation of Interest	Probable Type of Behavior Exhibited by Salesperson	Probable Source of Frustration	Management's Remedial Action
1. Salesperson's failure to consummate a sale	Aggression Regression Fixation	Salesperson's management Salesperson's customers Environment*	Provide better sales training Give salesperson more discretion on key bargaining points Employ team selling approaches
2. Salesperson being below sales quota—low sales volume	Regression Psychological resignation	Salesperson's management Salesperson's customers Environment*	Set realistic and fair quotas Permit sales personnel some input in quota setting Provide "refresher" sales training courses Have manager accompany salesperson on sales calls
3. Salesperson's failure to obtain prospects	Psychological resignation Aggression	Salesperson's management Salesperson's customers	Allocate sales territories fairly Provide "foot-in-the-door" sales training Express management's confidence in the salesperson Provide problem-solving aids
4. Salesperson's inability to grant a prospect's request	Regression Aggression	Salesperson's management Salesperson's customers Organizational ability Environment*	Permit salespeople more discretion, within a prescribed range Have manager accompany salesperson on sales calls Provide more sales training to help salesperson problem solve more adequately and overcome customer's resistance to buying
5. Salesperson's failure to achieve a promotion	Aggression Fixation Psychological resignation	Salesperson's management	Clearly define guidelines for promotion to sales personnel Periodically review performance with salesperson Employ nonpromotion forms of recognition Use company's goals and promotion policies during recruitment to ensure a proper "match" between company and recruit
6. Salesperson's failure to circumvent "closed door" tactics	Regression Aggression	Salesperson's management Salesperson's customers	Teach "getting-in-the-door" approaches in sales training Have manager accompany salesperson on sales calls

*The environment consists of elements not under the control of the salesperson's management (e.g., competition, business conditions, suppliers).

Source: Reprinted from Alan J. Dubinsky and Mary E. Lipitt, "Managing Frustration in the Sales Force," *Industrial Marketing Management* (June 1979): 203.

manship, poor quality control, and carelessness in delivery and servicing are commonplace. Employees identify better with a company if there is occasional contact with top management, perhaps at training sessions or through periodic visits to the home office. The house organ can help with communication and identification if used judiciously, and not for obvious propaganda purposes. Above all, the work environment must foster positive employee attitudes, and positive attitudes are more likely to occur if policies are consistent and clearly communicated, if the company appears to be a good place to work, if it is responsive to the environment in which it does business, and if it is obviously concerned about the attitudes of employees, customers, neighbors, and suppliers.

Now complete Exercise 14.1.

---

1. Do you think that a company that is primarily interested in short-term profits, as opposed to long-term profits, can succeed in generating a positive identification by its employees? Why or why not?
2. A salesman who has been with the company for 10 years and has been passed over for promotion twice has a poor attitude toward the company and has even disparaged it publicly. What, if anything, can the sales manager do to encourage a more positive identification with the company? What would you recommend?

EXERCISE 14.1

Employee self-esteem.   As noted before, permitting subordinates to participate in some planning and decision making can be an effective motivator. Many other little things can be done to enhance a salesperson's self-esteem and thus to make the work environment more attractive. An executive can contribute to an individual's stature in the eyes of her associates by publicly recognizing accomplishments and explaining to others the importance of a person's work. A sales manager can motivate at least some salespeople by encouraging them in self-development, giving them the opportunity for it, and counseling and challenging them. Some people are eager to take on more responsibilities, to prove themselves. The supervisor who is quick to delegate new tasks and responsibilities to eager people not only aids their training but also enhances their self-esteem and simultaneously makes her own job easier. Delegation is so important that it is further explored later in this chapter.

Security.   This discussion of security does not involve supplying old age benefits but, rather, building a work environment that reduces uncertainty. Uncertainty breeds feelings of insecurity. Change is inevitable, including change in executives, methods of operation, and many other features of the work situation. Rumors and uneasiness abound and are spread in many organizations by the grapevine (informal communication channels). The sales manager can remove most of this source of insecurity by sharing information with the sales force, by telling them as far in advance as possible about any changes that will affect them. Sharing with subordinates information about current problems and future plans (even if subordinates will not be directly affected) puts them in the comfortable position of being informed. Keeping communication channels open by two-way personal communication not only builds morale but may also give the manager a better grasp of a situation through feedback from the field.

Just and empathetic supervision. *Empathy* is the quality of being able to put oneself in another's position, to see and feel from another's viewpoint their feelings about the job, hopes and aspirations, and worries and problems. *Just* supervision suggests consistency and fairness. These ingredients of effective supervision can have a powerful effect on the loyalty and motivation of salespeople.

Favoritism can badly affect motivation and harmony. A common complaint is that some other employee gets all the soft assignments. Furthermore, determining fairness is not always easy. Equal treatment is not really the answer, because employees differ in length of service, abilities, and strength. Fairness may actually require giving special treatment to those salespeople with long service or poor health.

Supporting subordinates. Sales managers should support their people, represent their needs to higher management, and back them up. This might mean vigorously seeking every salary increase an employee deserves, pushing for better working conditions, or negotiating frictions with other departments. Able salespeople should be identified to superiors and their promotions urged (even if this means losing a good person to the ranks of management). Managers should be willing to take the blame for subordinates' mistakes (rather than passing the buck); supervisors are responsible for what happens in their areas, and sufficient training or follow-up might have prevented any errors.

Some managers have the mistaken notion that able subordinates are threatening, attempt to downgrade their accomplishments, and in extreme cases, even create obstacles for effective performance; this is anathema to a smoothly functioning organization. Some firms try to overcome such potential problems by insisting that executives train adequate replacements for their own positions before they themselves can be promoted.

Now perform Exercise 14.2.

EXERCISE 14.2

1. What would you assume about the personality and ability of managers who refuse to back their subordinates?
2. Can a manager be too supportive of salespeople? If so, what guidelines would you recommend for a desirable level of support?
3. What additional incentives can you suggest for encouraging managers to do a better job of developing their subordinates?

Following Up

Unless a supervisor checks up on instructions and the way they are being followed, the end result may differ from expectations; both the manager and the employee may be embarrassed or worse. *Following up* simply means checking to ensure that everything is proceeding well, that work is on schedule, and that no problems are unresolved. It is a naive supervisor who issues instructions to an untried employee and assumes that, without some checking, everything will be done as ordered.

Follow-up need not reflect negatively on the employee. Sometimes instructions are misunderstood or misinterpreted. Often an order's priorities are not made clear, so that a particular assignment is put aside until later. For the new or relatively untrained salesperson, some follow-up and consequent support or assistance may be indispensable to the successful accomplishment of the assignment. Furthermore, the wise sales manager can prevent considerable wasted effort by training employees to ask questions if they do not understand the instruction.

Admittedly, following up on a sales staff spread over a fairly wide area is decidedly more difficult than the task the supervisor faces in a store, factory, or office. However, salespersons' reports and other feedback from the field, as well as periodic visits by the sales managers and other communications from the sales office, can be adequate. Part V of this book is devoted to the important topic of controlling sales efforts.

HOW CLOSELY SHOULD YOU SUPERVISE?

Close supervision implies constant follow-up and detailed directives with little room for individual initiative. The manager is continually observing and making suggestions to the subordinate. Although most would condemn such an extreme of supervision, with some employees and in some situations this is necessary. At other times such close supervision is not in the best interests of a smooth-running organization.

Figure 14.2 depicts the two major factors that should dictate the amount of supervision: (1) the caliber of the salesperson and (2) the relative importance of each customer contact or transaction to the firm's overall success. The higher the caliber of salesperson, generally the less supervision needed. But with inexperienced, low-level, or poorly motivated workers, usually much more supervision is required for effective selling performance. The exception here is when a lost sale or customer is unimportant to the firm, as is the case with door-to-door selling. The more important each salesperson's performance is to the overall success of a firm (at the extreme, where customers and sales are few, but large) then enough supervision is needed to ensure that each person is performing effectively.

Most supervision falls somewhere between the extremes of too little and too much; otherwise, worker frustration or anarchy would reign in many

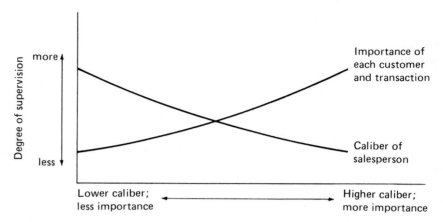

FIGURE 14.2   Factors affecting closeness of supervision.

organizations. Poor supervision results when the caliber of the salespeople and the nature of the selling situation are ignored, so there is either too much or not enough supervision. The consequences of poor supervision are numerous.

Too much supervision can result in wasted time for both the manager and the salesperson, with time taken from productive selling activities and spent on reports, conferences, and other communications and meetings. It also can destroy the morale of competent employees. Too little supervision may stifle the full and productive development of individual sales representatives and may be as destructive to morale as oversupervising, because some will feel unsupported and ignored by management. Furthermore, too little supervision usually implies a dearth of communications and feedback, which can result in undetected and unaddressed problems in the field.

Several other factors also affect the closeness of supervision and can act as constraints. The geographical distribution of a sales force may prohibit direct supervision because of distance and associated expenses. A compensation plan based heavily on incentive income can impede the sales force's acceptance of most types of supervision unless the plan clearly demonstrates direct benefits for sales productivity and income. However, it can also be argued that a strong incentive-pay policy accomplishes most of the objectives of close supervision by stimulating conscientious performance.

METHODS OF SUPERVISION

Supervision can be done by direct, or face-to-face, contact with subordinates. As noted before, the sales manager's sales force often is dispersed over a large geographical area, making direct supervision difficult and spasmodic at best. Consequently, the sales manager may rely more on indirect supervisory methods than do other types of managers. Indirect methods include telephone calls and correspondence, sales meetings and conferences, as well as programmed supervisory adjuncts such as the compensation plan, quotas, territorial assignments, routing, expense accounts, and reports.

Personal Supervision

Face-to-face contact with subordinates is the best kind of supervision, even if personality conflicts occasionally jeopardize its effectiveness. In sales personal supervision often involves the sales manager's accompanying the salesperson on visits to customers, observing the effectiveness of the visit, suggesting ways to improve performance, and also perhaps helping the salesperson with a difficult or important customer. Such a day-long or longer contact can promote a high level of rapport and rejuvenate a slipping motivation. Any personal problems bothering the salesperson may be brought to light and perhaps solved. The manager can better recognize the salesperson's concerns, and the salesperson likely will better understand the sales manager's specific expectations. Communication can be optimized through personal supervision.

Obstacles to personal supervision.   Time demands on the sales manager often preclude more than token visitations with individual salespeople. When visits are limited—perhaps to occasions when particular problems in the territory have surfaced—they tend to be critical in nature and, thus, destructive to morale. The sales manager may face the problem of whether this limited time should be spent with the weaker members of the sales force, trying to bring them up to par, or whether the time would be better spent working with the top producers to help them become even more effective. More often than not, the decision is to spend more time with the weaker, while permitting better producers to fend for themselves. This issue is examined more specifically in Chapter 18 on evaluating individual sales performance.

Indirect Supervision

Telephone calls and correspondence.   Letters and phone calls may be the best alternative to face-to-face supervision. They allow sales personnel to feel that they are not neglected, that their problems and accomplishments are being recognized. But a constant barrage of phone calls and letters requiring return correspondence can negatively affect salespeople who thrive on independence and assumption of initiative. Effective supervision can be a delicate balance between frequent communications and "nit-picking."

Sales meetings and conferences.   Many firms insist on periodic meetings for their salespeople. These gatherings can inform personnel about new policies and new goods; they can be used to correct certain deficiencies, such as carelessness in handling credit authorizations; and they can generate fresh enthusiasm. At the very least, all meetings should provide better communication and thereby increase job involvement.

Too often meetings are routine, uninteresting, uninspiring. Some sales managers conduct more stimulating meetings than others (just as some professors conduct more stimulating classes). But sales managers do not always realize possibilities for using meetings for training, motivating, and even inspiring. The following are guidelines for conducting better meetings:

- ☐ Have a definite purpose for the meeting.
- ☐ Plan the general course of the meeting and the timing of the various topics.
- ☐ Brief participants in advance about the meeting, its purpose, and the items to be covered.
- ☐ Lead the meeting but do not dominate it. Ask for creative solutions. Involve the audience.
- ☐ Keep the meeting moving and on track, without getting bogged down with irrelevant matters and discussions.
- ☐ Assign actions and responsibilities as needed.
- ☐ Try to end the meeting on an up-beat note.

The opportunity that sales meetings afford for face-to-face contact between managers and individual salespeople should be fully cultivated.

Programmed supervisory adjuncts.   The role of the compensation plan, the assignment of territories and determination of any routings, the components of the quota system, and the various elements of the expense budget in directing sales efforts have already been described. If these are compatible with supervisory objectives, they can be important adjuncts. Sometimes, however, they are developed without any particular coordination and compatibility. For example the sales manager may need more control over salespeople but may be constrained by a straight commission plan that encourages independence and by a nondeviating commitment to maximizing sales to the exclusion of all other activities.

The role of reports.   Sales force reports are a major supervisory tool. Field reports have at least three objectives or benefits. (1) They provide some assurance that salespeople are following company policies. (2) They provide a basis for performance evaluation in reporting the number of calls made, orders received, new customers contacted, and the like. (3) They provide information from the field that can be invaluable in keeping abreast of competitive activities, changing habits and preferences of customers, local economic factors affecting business now and in the future, and potential problems concerning products, servicing, prices, and so on.

Salespeople tend to view their reports as anathema. Often reports must be completed during time off, to avoid taking productive hours from selling. Report forms may be unnecessarily detailed and complicated. Because they do provide some measurement of performance, the salesperson is tempted to disguise any negative items, which is especially likely to result when reports are used as a basis for criticism and corrective action against the employee.

The sales manager should use care in report requirements, or they may become useless fictions. Report forms may need to be reviewed to eliminate any useless data requirements, to simplify their complexity, or perhaps to reduce the frequency of reporting. Requiring daily reports may be akin to supervising too closely. Weekly reports are more practical for many firms and will be less onerous. A sales manager may create more incentive for accurate, timely, and complete reports by reminding salespeople that prospective managerial material may thereby be identified. As a deterrent to falsifying, a sales manager occasionally may want to spot-check some data entries, such as number of calls claimed. When deliberate inaccuracies are encountered, severe reprimands are appropriate. Repetitive offenses may justify termination, as an example to the rest of the sales force.

A Special Application of Supervision: Delegation

Delegation is one of the mainstays of effective supervision. *Delegation* simply is giving and entrusting work to other persons, and three steps are involved in this process:

1. The manager assigns duties.
2. The manager grants the subordinate the authority to act (e.g., to spend money, to direct the actions of others, or to take any other steps necessary to fulfill the duties).
3. The manager creates an obligation to act, with the subordinate taking on the obligation or responsibility to complete the job.[9]

The degrees of delegation can range from simply giving an order to a subordinate to do the most routine task (which one cannot consider true delegation) or assigning a critical project, giving the subordinate wide-ranging authority and freedom to accomplish the task. Some bosses go to such an extreme of delegation that they engage in "dumping." The classic example of dumping is the executive who believes in a clean desk (for herself), and dumps all the mail and reports on the secretary's desk, "to take care of." Dumping is not true delegation.

Reasons for delegating.   The need for delegation is obvious. Managers cannot do everything themselves (although some are reluctant to relinquish all but the most routine tasks) and so must decide what to do themselves and what to assign to others. Only then does the manager free up time to devote to planning and more important pursuits. A manager who delegates rather freely to competent subordinates can take on more and larger overall tasks and responsibilities and can advance much farther on the career path than someone else who is reluctant to delegate much.

Subordinates also benefit from liberal delegation. To be assigned increasingly more important tasks with reasonable freedom to exert initiative is superb management development training. Delegation heightens morale and motivation and can imbue the entire organization with an attitude conducive to creativity and enthusiastic job satisfaction.

Reasons for not delegating.   But many managers hesitate to delegate. They find all kinds of excuses for not doing so, such as the following:

"If you want a job done right, you have to do it yourself."

"I have no confidence in my subordinates."

"I can't make them understand what really is to be done and what is expected."

"I don't have adequate controls to detect mistakes before they become serious."

"I'm really reluctant to take a chance."

Another reason for not delegating, which no manager would express, is fear of the understudy. How valid are all these reasons? Excluding the unstated fear of the understudy (which reflects an insecure manager who recognizes the training and developmental consequences of delegation), all these reasons can be attributed to the key principle of delegation: The manager remains responsible for the actions and outcomes of subordinates' efforts.

Ultimate Responsibility Principle of Delegation

Although the manager can delegate responsibility for an action to a subordinate, the ultimate responsibility remains with the manager.

If mistakes are made and the work is not satisfactorily accomplished, the manager remains accountable to her superiors or perhaps to the stockholders. So the central issue in delegating is *trust*. If the manager does not trust subordinates to do an important task, then a real reluctance to delegate results. Lack of trust, which may or may not be valid, hardly excuses a manager from disavowing delegation. Rather, it suggests that better employees may need to be hired, that better training and coaching must be done, or perhaps that motivation should be improved. Where lack of communication is an obstacle, greater stress must be placed on complete understanding of all directives, perhaps with any complex instructions being clearly written down and re-viewed for understanding. When subordinates are unproven, control points may need to be established so that the supervisor can more closely monitor the progress of the task assigned.

For better delegating.   Some managers, after they have delegated, still have the urge to hold on. They monitor closely and even may involve them-selves in the activity that they "delegated." Postdelegation hovering gives the subordinate no freedom to act and conveys the feeling to all participants that the manager is trying to take the delegation back, that there is no trust. And the subordinate's authority is undermined.

True delegation gives a subordinate enough authority and enough free-dom to do the task, but the manager should be aware of what is going on and can act to correct a worsening situation. Effective delegation requires (1) setting clearly understood objectives; (2) establishing a time frame (when is the task to be completed, and what are its priorities relative to other job commitments); (3) making periodic reviews and progress reports to clearly inform the manager of progress and to catch any errors or problems before they become serious. The better managers are quick to delegate because it can advance their career. Although delegation involves risks, these can be minimized.

PROBLEMS IN SUPERVISION

Problems encountered in supervising can be broadly placed into three major categories: (1) handling grievances, (2) disciplining, and (3) motivating. Grievances and disciplining can be resolved positively so that harmony and morale may even be strengthened. But ignoring or clumsily handling these problems can easily create more serious problems. Motivational problems arise when an individual salesperson or the entire sales force begins to slow down. Although a good compensation plan and effective supervision heighten motivation most sales managers need other supplementary incentives.

Grievances

Grievances usually are minor, yet if not handled carefully and promptly, they can fester and become serious. Minor grievances that can easily be rectified or settled include a small error in computing the expense budget or in the amount of commission due, a belief that other salespeople receive more prompt processing of their orders and commissions, a lost telephone message, a feeling that other salespeople are burdened with fewer nonselling chores. But these grievances require some supervisory attention to be handled satisfactorily.

The manager should be careful not to appear to play favorites. Some employees perceive favoritism, even when the situation does not exist. Salespeople at the same level and with approximately the same length of service should be treated similarly, as much as possible. Admittedly, having entirely equitable territories is practically impossible, so this source of friction frequently exists. Most managers lean toward giving some preferential treatment to older employees who have provided long and faithful service.

Some grievances are major, and these often involve a subordinate feeling mistreated, especially by the boss. When there is a simple misunderstanding, a quiet talk may resolve the situation. But sometimes things cannot be so easily settled; perhaps the subordinate feels that disciplinary action was unfair or unwarranted. Other major grievances may concern other departments of the firm, and these complaints may require the sales manager to intervene. Higher-level executives may even have to be involved in recurring problems that cross departmental lines, such as late deliveries, frequent out-of-stocks and partially filled orders, too many defective items, and overly rigid credit approvals.

Disciplining

Disciplining is one of the more unpleasant aspects of a manager's job. The supervisor must act on carelessness, insubordination, lack of cooperation, disregard for instructions or policies, laziness, and alcoholism. Failure to discipline an employee when the standard of performance or behavior falls below an acceptable level encourages more poor attitudes, not only for the offender, but also for employees observing their colleague's "getting away with something." A general deterioration of productivity can result.

The other extreme is also bad. Discipline can be too severe and can be administered harshly without considering circumstances. Today, many salespeople will not tolerate a situation of harsh and unjust discipline and supervision; they feel they are mobile, and can easily get another sales job. Sometimes, however, a sales representative or an executive dependent on a superior for a promotion may be forced to accept less-than-desired treatment.

Reprimands, demotions, temporary layoffs, withheld promotions and/or raises, poor evaluation reports, and outright discharges are penalties that can be imposed. Disciplining can vary from the minor, such as a quiet reprimand perhaps by letter or phone, to the most drastic, such as disrupted career advancement through a poor evaluation report, vetoed promotion, or even firing.

Principles of good disciplining. Several general principles for effective disciplining are rather obvious, though not always practiced. They simply bring to the situation good human relations practices.

Disciplining should not be used as punishment. Less than optimum behavior on the job is not reason for punishment. Rather, the purpose of disciplinary action should be solely to improve future behavior, of both the employee being disciplined and other personnel. The rest of the work force will be influenced by the promptness and type of disciplinary action imposed on one of its members.

Disciplining should be in private.   Simple reprimands or more drastic action should be performed in private. Privacy not only saves the subordinate from acute embarrassment but also offers the opportunity to defend or explain the conduct. Reasons may excuse the employee's actions. Violations of this principle of good supervision, of course, occur more seldom in the field selling situation with its far-flung sales force than in the confined environment of an office, store, or plant. Violations may occur, however, in conferences and sales meetings. And possibly even worse is to reprimand a salesperson in the presence of a customer.

Misconduct should receive prompt, objective attention.   The manager should take action when facts are fresh in mind. To wait until details are half-forgotten destroys the effectiveness of discipline and may result in undue resentment. For example if a salesperson was rude to a customer or performed so poorly that the customer complained about service, the manager should issue the reprimand shortly after the event and not later, in conjunction with another type of misconduct. A caution should be noted here, however. Discipline should be objective. A manager should not act when angry or emotionally upset, so it may be necessary to delay action until everyone has had time to cool down. Perhaps additional facts must be gathered to make a wise discipline decision.

Warn before acting.   Except in cases of serious misconduct, such as dishonesty or unethical behavior, employees should not be reprimanded for something they did not realize was wrong or did not understand the importance of. This suggests that a person should be formally warned for the first offense and disciplined only if the action is repeated. It also suggests that the manager is responsible for informing sales personnel of rules and policy violations for which disciplinary action may be taken. For example falsifying a report may be viewed as a serious misdeed. Disciplining a new salesperson, however, who was unaware of how seriously management viewed padding a call report or an expense account would be unjust.

Disciplining should be consistent and fair.   Nothing is more destructive of morale than allowing one member of a group to get away with something for which others are punished. For example one salesman may be the "big spender," always exceeding her expense budget, while other salespeople are reprimanded if they do. If this big spender is also the star salesperson, the sales manager may be tempted to overlook her handling of expenses, but consistency of enforcement would be sacrificed unwisely. In the interest of consistency, discipline should not be harsh and unbending. Exceptions sometimes must be made and rules bent a little. The inexperienced salesperson may deserve a different action than the experienced. Special problems at home may force one person to have a modified territory or routing or to work on a somewhat different schedule. As noted before, older employees may deserve special consideration, especially if they suffer physical impairments.

Practical guidelines for effective disciplining.   Certain practices seem to produce better results in modifying employee behavior for the better. Admittedly, with a recalcitrant employee nothing may work, and termination may be the only remedy, but this is the exception. The best way to change a person's behavior is to sit down with the person in private, focus on the problem, explain why it is important that the person conform to the rules or what is expected, and then ask what she plans to do about correcting the situation. Both parties must recognize that the employee, not the supervisor, is responsible for changing behavior. The employee thus is treated as an adult, with a problem to solve.

The supervisor should strive to convince the employee to agree to change and then set goals for doing so, which again reinforces the idea that the worker is responsible. The supervisor must follow up on the commitment. If the goal is not reached, the supervisor can offer the alternative of correcting the problem or taking the punishment, "Do you still want the job?" Improvement should be recognized and encouraged. Essentially, a three-step procedure is involved in the most effective disciplining: (1) focus on specific performance, (2) obtain the employee's agreement to change, and (3) follow up.

Alcoholism

Bill Bledsoe has been with the firm for over 15 years, and for much of this time he has been one of the top producers. In the last few years his performance has eroded somewhat. You, Bill's sales manager, became concerned after you received an unexpected complaint from one of Bill's smaller customers that he had been drinking when he called on the customer. Then you recalled that Bill had appeared tired and out of sorts at several recent sales meetings.

You decide to examine Bill's sales records over the last year, and discover several things that concern you. Although total sales of most of Bill's accounts have held fairly steady with preceding years' levels, four accounts show drastic declines in orders. Furthermore, you find no indication that any new accounts were opened in the last year. Because Bill has been a successful and conscientious sales representative for many years, you decide to gather more information, if possible, before confronting. Accordingly, you personally contact two of the accounts showing diminishing orders over the past year. Neither customer is very informative, but one expressed disappointment with service. Bill's drinking was not brought up either by you or by the former customers during these visits.

Supervisory disciplining problems. Two rather typical problems that can face sales managers follow. At the end of each example, consider how you would handle the particular situation.

Now perform Exercise 14.3.

What would you do about Bill Bledsoe's performance at this point?	**EXERCISE 14.3**

Making False Promises to Customers

Jim Edwards has been with the company for only 2 years, but already he is a star. He is good-looking, a good talker, a fancy dresser, and is reputed to have "a way with the ladies." You do not particularly like Edwards; in fact when you have reprimanded him (he usually overspends his expense budget), his ego and abrasive personality have irked you on more than one occasion. Some of the other members of the sales force apparently feel the same way, because you have received complaints that he is using high pressure and creating customer ill will. You note that several smaller accounts have been lost, but the larger, more profitable customers are doing more business with the company than ever before. Furthermore, his record of new accounts opened is the best in the district. You attribute some of the undercurrents simply to criticism of an aggressive and successful newcomer by jealous colleagues. You have managed to hide your own irritation because of Jim's successful performance.

At the regional sales meeting, Donna Schultz, who had had part of Jim Edward's territory before it became too big and was split up, asks to speak to you privately.

"I don't like to carry tales, chief," she begins, "but several of my old customers in Edwards's territory have told me that he's been making false promises to them about the product life of the X-100 line. They say these items have been falling way short of what they were led to expect."

"Jim's sales have stayed good," you say. "Could there have been some misunderstanding?"

"No way," Donna retorts. "I think you're going to see a drastic erosion of business in that territory as more and more customers find out they've been lied to. You'd better do something about this now!"

Now perform Exercise 14.4.

What would you do about Jim Edwards?	**EXERCISE 14.4**

USE OF INCENTIVES

Many types of incentives are commonly used in motivating salespeople. Management assumes that the incentive will produce a well-motivated salesperson who likely will be more effective and aggressive. Further, management assumes that the compensation plan, empathetic and conscientious supervision, and the inherent challenges of the job are not enough to produce the best efforts day in and day out. Accordingly, supplemental incentives must be provided, and the major supplemental incentive devices are sales meetings and conventions, contests, recognition awards, and career promotional possibilities.

Conferences, Conventions, Clinics, and Meetings

Meetings, conferences, conventions, clinics, and the like are often thought of primarily as part of the training program, with the major objective being to update selling skills and furnishing information on new products and promotions. But in most sales organizations these events have a broader function and consume considerable amount of sales manager time as well as that of higher-level executives. And the costs are by no means inconsequential. Yet, most firms find sales meetings and conventions to be worth the effort and expense.

Objectives.   In general conventions and the like have three purposes: training, communication, and inspiration. When handled effectively, these events should motivate a sales force to work harder. The enthusiasm is often rather transitory, but the sales force's anticipation of meetings held in elegant places may last for months. More permanent results can be achieved if specific objectives such as the following guide the meeting:

- ☐ Introduce new products, as well as planned additions.
- ☐ Explain planned changes in advertising and marketing strategy.
- ☐ Provide training for salespeople on advanced selling techniques, or perhaps areas of general weaknesses.
- ☐ Give predictions of coming business and economic patterns, how these will affect the sales force.
- ☐ Honor outstanding sales representatives.
- ☐ Gain better rapport with management.
- ☐ Provide inspiration.

Group gatherings provide an ideal platform for inspirational, motivational messages—pep talks. Sometimes celebrities—such as noted football coaches, authors of best-selling management books, or others who have gained reputations as charismatic speakers—are hired to give the pep talk, and their fees are not low.[10] The major danger is that inspirational messages may over-shadow the training and information-providing aspects. A 2- or 3-day meeting devoted primarily to goading and inspiring may fade from memory unless more substantial input is also provided. Informal counseling and the rapport and communication that can be achieved among the salespeople themselves and also with management are not the least of the benefits of group events, despite the cost in time taken away from selling and the considerable direct expenses involved. Expenses (excluding travel) can run $50,000 and up.[11]

Meetings can be routine, uninteresting, and uninspiring. Some executives conduct more stimulating meetings than others. Recognizing this, a firm should assign its most capable people to meetings, even if other tasks must be temporarily tabled. The costs involved mandate the most effective use of this time by the most capable speakers and leaders. Planning is important, because a meeting should be designed to accomplish one or more specific purposes.

Planning meetings and conventions.   Large meetings or conventions held off company premises require considerable preparation. The time and place must be established, often from among many alternatives. The objective(s) and theme must be clearly determined. The program must be developed in detail, with speakers and meeting aids and perhaps new products arranged well in advance. Arrangements must be made for space, meals, transportation, and even recreation. When spouses are invited, activities, such as sight-seeing tours and similar activities, should be planned to fill the time when the salespeople are in meetings. Application 14.1 presents some specific planning suggestions for controlling meeting costs.

Picking a site.   The choice of a meeting site will affect the cost. Table 14.2 shows sales meeting site preferences. A company site would be much less costly, but Table 14.2 shows more preferences for noncompany sites including hotels, conference centers, and resorts. Why? The home office or plant often does not have an adequate number of banquet or meeting rooms, and a more isolated site is thought to eliminate distractions and lead to better participant interaction. And company executives probably want to get away to a possibly exotic location at company expense.

What should be the scope of the meeting?   Another decision to be made is whether meetings should be national or regional. The relative pros and cons of centralized versus decentralized training are discussed in Chapter 12. For a small sales force, the decision almost always must be for a national or centralized meeting, because the participants otherwise would be too few. For sales forces of fifty or more, regional meetings may substitute or supplement. Obviously, closer individual attention can be given in smaller meetings. However, this advantage may well be offset by the greater demands on management time in attending a number of regional meetings. If individual counseling is deemed important (and it often is far more important than management

APPLICATION 14.1   Specific Suggestions for Controlling Meeting Costs

Considerable money can be frittered away by an unconcern with minimizing meeting costs. The quality and the comfort of the meeting should not be reduced, but planners should be sophisticated regarding meeting arrangements and should achieve full values. Following are a sample of possibilities for maximizing value received:

1. Negotiate for complimentary rooms commensurate with your use of site facilities.

2. If you pair two salespeople to a room, make sure they will both arrive on the same day. This avoids single-room charges for the one night the partner is not there.

3. Make sure there is no charge for meeting-room setups such as water pitchers, pads, and pencils unless you agree to it.

4. Evaluate your use of each piece of audiovisual equipment according to cost, quality, and convenience in renting at the site versus bringing you own.

5. If you want to slow down appetizer consumption, use napkins instead of plates for the appetizers.

6. For refreshment breaks, consider coffee by the gallon instead of by number of people; arrange credit for unopened soft drinks; eliminate the afternoon refreshments and use a stretch break instead.

7. Set the rules and monitor the bar operation relative to measured drinks, accounting for empties, and closing time.

8. Negotiate for lower weekend rates that most sites offer, if you can hold your meeting then.

For many more specific suggestions for reducing costs and getting full value, see Homer Smith, "Balance the Budget for Better Meetings," *Sales & Marketing Management* (March 1986): 73–76.

TABLE 14.2   Sales meeting site preferences.

	Percentage of Preferences	
*Site**	*1982*	*1986*
Company site	61	44
Hotel	62	40
Resort hotel	51	38
Conference center	23	14
Airport hotel	26	9
Budget motel	1	1

*Replies total more than 100 percent because of multiple answers.
Source: Sales & Marketing Management (14 Nov. 1983): 67; (11 Nov. 1986): 100.

realizes), it can be accomplished at a national meeting by setting aside sufficient time for this activity.

Timing.   How often should meetings be held? In Chapter 12, Table 12.3 shows the frequency of sales meetings reported by sampled firms. Although 19 percent held only one sales meeting or less a year, 81 percent held two or more a year. The decision about frequency often rests on the perceived effectiveness of meetings, although extent of major new product introductions, size and concentration of the sales force, and the firm's financial resources will have major bearing on both frequency and site. If the meetings are deemed effective, a firm will probably plan more and better meetings. Unfortunately, the evaluation of effectiveness usually rests on the shaky ground of subjective opinion and sporadic comments.

Evaluating.   A preferred way to evaluate the effectiveness of a convention or sales meeting is to measure improvement in certain areas of sales activity, for example, in new accounts opened, or improved time management as evidenced by increased frequency of sales calls. However, concrete measures of improvement would depend on the theme of the meeting and the items stressed. The biggest drawback of using objective measures is the time required to measure results. Weeks and even months may be needed to tabulate this information. Sales meeting planners usually evaluate during the meeting or as soon as it concludes.[12]

For these reasons most evaluations involve a survey of participants regarding satisfaction with the meeting and suggestions for improvement. These surveys can be a formal questionnaire, which can cover all aspects of the meeting or convention, from facilities to program to speakers, or they can be informal discussions during breaks.[13] The major limitation of subjective feedback from participants is that the entertainment element of the meetings is often valued higher than more important aspects.

Contests

Contests are essentially competitions that reward the winners. A contest is most appropriately used for a limited time to accomplish one or a few specific short-run objectives. They are an important incentive tool and widely used. A recent survey by *Sales & Marketing Management* found that 61.4 percent of responding firms were planning to use special incentive programs (contests) that were not part of the regular compensation plan.[14] *Sales & Marketing Management* annually devotes two large special sections to sales contests, which indicates their importance as a sales management tool, despite some drawbacks that will be examined shortly.

A company's sales force is not the only group to whom firms offer contests. Table 14.3 shows that distributors also frequently participate, and even field sales managers themselves can participate.

TABLE 14.3   Participants in incentive programs (contests).

Participants	Percentage of Firms
Own field salespeople	83.6
Field sales managers	49.1
Distributor salespeople	30.1
Reps, brokers, or other outside agents	26.7
Own inside salespeople	21.5
Other	5.1

Note: Percentages total more than 100% because of multiple answers.
Source: Sales & Marketing Management (April 1986): 99.

TABLE 14.4   Reasons for running an incentive program (contests).

Reasons	Percentage of Firms
Achieve immediate sales gains	72.4
Achieve long-range sales gains	62.0
Focus attention on specific products	59.4
Improve sales force morale	54.3
Sales force expects it	9.4
Forced to by competition	4.3
Other	6.0

Note: Percentages total more than 100% because of multiple answers.
Source: Sales & Marketing Management (April 1986): 99.

Table 14.4 shows the reasons firms give for using an incentive program. The major reason is to achieve an immediate spurt in sales. But for more than half the firms, an improvement in sales force morale is a good justification.

Awards for winners can include cash, merchandise, trophies, pins, or travel. Many companies involve the salesperson's spouse in the contest, with awarding merchandise for the home or travel for two. Trading stamps exchangeable for merchandise are commonly used because of their divisibility and versatility. Because different values of stamps can be given for the various award categories, an equitable distribution of awards is more easily achieved. And the winners of stamps can use them to obtain the most desired merchandise from among many alternatives. Thus, increased satisfaction with the awards is more likely, which should enhance motivation.

Planning and conducting the contest.   For a contest to be effective it should be carefully planned to be as stimulating and equitable as possible, as well as accomplish the desired objectives.

Determine objectives.   As shown in Table 14.3 a sales contest can be aimed at the company sales force, or dealers, or others. Table 14.5 shows a sampling of specific objectives that can be established for sales incentive programs for the sales force and for a firm's dealers and distributors. As Table 14.5 shows, numerous specific goals can be established, which helps account for a proliferation of contests as a firm shifts its areas of greatest concern.

The time spent in achieving the objectives should be relatively short to maintain interest and enthusiasm. But sufficient time should be allowed so that the sales force can cover the territory adequately. The average sales contest lasts about 3 months.

Contest theme.   A central theme should be established to promote the event and build enthusiasm, while retaining the specific objectives. The more innovative and exciting the theme, the greater the interest generated. Sports themes are common, such as a sales "world series," because of the stress on competition. But many other themes are possible, and creativity is desired so the sales force will not view the contest as just another "ho-hum" game.

TABLE 14.5   Examples of specific contest objectives directed to the company sales force and to dealers.

Company salespeople
    Improve working habits
    Improve creativity in selling
    Increase dealer calls
    Open new outlets
    Sell high-profit items
    Accomplish broad-line selling
    Help move off-season products
    Introduce new products
    Move discontinued merchandise
    Spur recruitment
    Recognize outstanding performance

Dealers (the trade)
    Lessen out-of-stocks
    Serve as thank-you gifts to customers
    Induce large-quantity buying
    Introduce dealers to a wide selection of the company's
        products
    Promote displays
    Offset competitive programs
    Boost sales during slow-selling seasons
    Change old buying habits
    Communicate important sales points

Contests should be fun.   Appropriate gimmicks, give-aways, posters, sweat-shirts, and other hoopla can add to the excitement—unless this paraphernalia is used too frequently. Salespeople should promptly receive feedback during the contest regarding how much more they must do to win an award. Awards should be distributed promptly at the end of the contest.

Criticisms of contests.   Although the desirability of providing special incentives to spur flagging motivations rarely is questioned, still not all firms use them. And those that do sometimes overuse them. Table 14.6 shows the reasons firms give for not using contests. The majority felt that contests were not really necessary, that the compensation plan provided enough incentive. Admittedly, professional salespeople should be self-motivated and should not require artificial stimulus to do an effective job. But sometimes a game can promote greater efforts, primarily because of the aura of intense competition it may engender for the contest's duration.

Overselling and high-pressure tactics, however, may antagonize customers. Aggressive selling efforts during a contest may result in less-than-normal business after the contest ends, perhaps because a psychological letdown occurs or because customers were overstocked for contest credit. The latter is known as "borrowed business"; that is, it is borrowed from future sales, rather than adding to overall sales as is desired. Another objection inherent in any contest is that not everyone can win. Although the winners' morale may be boosted, losers may feel less motivated than before the contest. In planning a contest efforts should be made to ensure that all participants have a reasonably good chance of winning a prize. If the same persons win repeatedly, the requirements must be changed or the contest idea discarded.

TABLE 14.6   Reasons for not using contests.

Reason	Percentage of Firms
We don't feel they are necessary	35.6
Against company policy	13.6
Too costly	13.6
Too time-consuming and difficult to administer	10.9
Tried them and they didn't accomplish our objectives	5.4
Our salespeople don't like them	4.1
We feel they are unfair	1.3
Other	30.1

Percentages total more than 100% because of multiple answers.
Source: Sales & Marketing Management (April 1986): 100.

Contests should not be used as substitutes for good compensation plans. They should not be used so frequently that their excitement is lost. But when properly done, sales contests can be an effective motivational device.

Recognition Awards

Public recognition is an easy way to motivate employees. Recognizing a job well done builds an employee's self-esteem and is a good supervisory approach. Some firms have sales achievement clubs and award certificates to outstanding salespeople as well as publishing their names in a special roster. Newspapers often publish names and photos of insurance agents who have been designated members of their companies' "million-dollar clubs" for selling policies totaling that dollar value.

Recognition can take many forms, some tangible (such as medals and certificates) and others more intangible (such as a personal greeting from top executives). The more common types of recognition awards are titles, such as "sales rep of the month"; trophies; congratulations from high-ranking executives; recognition for successful salespeople's spouses such as flowers, medals, and so on; membership in honorary clubs or organizations; recognition in house publications; pins and rings; and certificates, diplomas, and the like. The costs of such recognition are slight, whereas the benefits in stimulating employees can be significant.

Related to recognition is the posting and disseminating of sales standing of the sales representatives in the district and throughout the organization. These public comparisons of performance can provide positive recognition for the top producers as well as a spur for the less productive. The discouragement and pessimism that those consistently at the bottom of the list may feel generally is outweighed by the spirit of intrafirm competition fostered throughout the sales organization.

Promotion Opportunities

The subordinate's desire for advancement and promotion can be strong motivation for dedicated job performance. The sales manager should not overlook the importance of this type of incentive. Of course, not all salespeople aspire to managerial positions. Some welcome the independence, earnings potential, and freedom from responsibility for the work of others that career sales affords. Most, however, desire better positions in sales, such as larger and more important territories, more expensive product categories, and bigger customers, such as national accounts—all of which translate into the opportunity to make more money. Many college-trained people, on the other hand, think of their sales jobs as only a stepping-stone to management careers. These ambitious people constitute a resource that can stimulate the entire sales force to greater efforts. However, management usually must foster this happy situation and must encourage the able and ambitious in their expectations. Furthermore, the advancement route must be clearly evident and not based primarily on seniority and years of experience. A well-designated program for advancement is termed a *career path*.

Not all career paths are attractive. Figure 14.3 shows an unattractive career path, in which advancement comes slowly and is related to age and years of service rather than ability and ambition. The result is that the able soon leave for a "faster track." Good people may be held back, not because their abilities are unrecognized, but because there are no higher-level positions available. Of course, a rapidly growing company requires an increasing number of management and key positions and is particularly attractive to the ambitious. But a slower-growing firm can partly overcome the obstacles in the path of able and ambitious young salespeople by not allowing mediocre performers to remain in key jobs. In providing an accelerated career path, a firm may stipulate that new employees must be promoted within a certain length of time, perhaps 4 years (provided, of course, that their performance warrants this), or they will be terminated so that room can be made for more capable people.

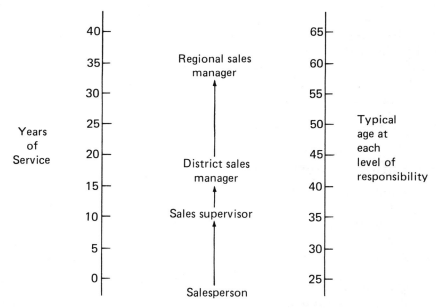

FIGURE 14.3   Unattractive career path. (*Source*: Reprinted from Andrall E. Pearson, "Sales Power Through Planned Careers," *Harvard Business Review*, January–February 1966, p. 109. Copyright © 1965 by the President and Fellows of Harvard College; all rights reserved.)

SUMMARY

At the beginning of this chapter I asked you to think about what the sales manager can do both to encourage better acceptance of report requirements and to ensure that reports are used only to gain meaningful and important data. Few salespeople welcome having to do reports; however, they are more likely to accept report requirements and conscientious and honest reporting when (1) reports are not used as a basis for criticizing, (2) the reports are obviously used by management, and (3) the report requirements are streamlined as much as possible and useless and extraneous data requirements are eliminated. The first condition, of course, is most difficult, because reports necessarily measure performance and provide a comparison with other salespeople. The spirit with which management acts on report data is the key here. When obvious deficiencies are seen, suggestions for improved performance can be constructive, rather than critical, and can be offered from the viewpoint that both the company and the salesperson will gain when better sales and profits are achieved. Indicating to the more ambitious salespeople that prospective managerial material may thereby be uncovered also creates more incentive for accurate, timely, and complete reports.

The essential ingredients of supervision are planning, directing, motivating, and following up. Directing is involved with issuing directions. An instruction should be clear, complete, reasonable, and with adequate explanation. Two extremes of direction are participatory and autocratic, and each is advantageous and appropriate in certain circumstances.

A number of theories have been developed concerning motivation, such as Maslow's, Herzberg's, the expectancy theory, and role ambiguity. Each have practical supervisory applications.

The level of supervision or follow-up should depend primarily on the caliber of the sales force and the relative importance of each customer or transaction. For example inexperienced salespeople dealing with important customers should be closely supervised.

Supervisory methods usually involve face-to-face contact with subordinates. With sales organizations this is often not possible, and indirect methods must be used, such as telephone calls and letters, sales meetings and conferences, and of course, reports.

Delegation is important in effective supervision. This involves entrusting work to the subordinate, which some managers are most reluctant to do for various reasons. The most important reason for reluctance to delegate is that the ultimate responsibility for the task remains with the manager.

Common problems in supervising are handling grievances, disciplining, and motivating. Motivation can be promoted with incentives such as conferences, conventions, meetings, contests, and recognition awards. Opportunity for promotion also can be a powerful incentive. A firm's career paths therefore should be reasonably attractive, or the more able employees may become disillusioned and leave, thus relegating an organization to mediocrity.

QUESTIONS
1. What are the ingredients of indirect supervision? How effective are these likely to be?
2. Discuss the role of empathy in good supervision.
3. When would you follow up on your orders and instructions?
4. What is the role of accountability in delegation?
5. How would you determine why one of your salespeople was performing unsatisfactorily?
6. Should a sales manager periodically accompany each salesperson on customer calls?
7. For what types of situations is close supervision most important? Least important?
8. Discuss the desirability of participatory direction in the selling situation.
9. "Disciplining should be viewed by the supervisor as providing an example for the rest of the organization on the consequences of misconduct." Evaluate this statement.

PEOPLE PROBLEM: IMPROVING THE EFFECTIVENESS OF SALES CONTESTS

Please evaluate each alternative.

You are displeased with the effectiveness of your last four or five sales contests. Theoretically, these contests should renew the sales force's enthusiasm, but almost the opposite seems to occur. The fault, you believe, lies in Amanda Malock being too good. She has walked off with the top award in all recent contests, to the point that some of the other salespeople are throwing up their hands and muttering, "What's the use?" What recourse do you have for this dilemma?

1. Maybe it would be best to give up contests temporarily.
2. You seriously consider disqualifying Amanda for any new contest by making past winners ineligible.
3. You toy with the idea of basing a new contest on the greatest percentage sales increase over an individual's previous year's sales. For those who have joined the firm within the past year, an adjusted figure should present no problem for comparison purposes.
4. Because Amanda is so good, you seriously consider promoting her to the position of your assistant, although you are reluctant to throttle her sales contribution. If you promote her, contests of course would present no further problems.
5. You consider basing a new sales contest on a team approach, rather than on individual achievement. Many prizes could be offered, not just the few for the top individual winners.

1. Abraham H. Maslow, *Motivation and Personality,* 2nd ed. (New York: Harper & Row, 1970).
2. For an article questioning the usefulness of Maslow's work for sales management, see Robert L. Berl, Nicholas C. Williamson, and Terry Powell, "Industrial Sales Force Motivation: A Critique and Test of Maslow's Hierarchy of Needs," *Journal of Personal Selling and Sales Management* (May 1984): 32–39.
3. Bernard L. Rosenbarm and Nick Ward, "Why Sales Managers Need More and Better Management Training—and How You Can Give It," *Training,* (April 1982): 45.
4. Frederick Herzberg, Bernard Mausner, and Barbara B. Snyderman, *The Motivation to Work,* 2nd ed. (New York: John Wiley & Sons, 1959).
5. Victor H. Vroom, *Work and Motivation* (New York: John Wiley & Sons, 1964); Edward C. Tolman, *Purposive Behavior in Animals and Men* (New York: Appleton-Century-Crofts, 1932); and Kurt Lewin, *The Conceptual Representation and the Measurement of Psychological Forces* (Durham, N.C.: Duke University Press, 1938).
6. For a study questioning the validity of Herzberg's Motivation Hygiene Theory, see Robert Berl, Terry Powell, and Nicholas C. Williamson, "Industrial Salesforce Satisfaction and Performance with Herzberg's Theory," *Industrial Management* (February 1984): 11–19.
7. For example Richard L. Oliver, "Expectancy Theory Predictions of Salesmen's Performance," *Journal of Marketing Research* (August 1974): 249; A. J. Dubinsky and T. N. Ingram, "Examining Industrial Salespeople's Reward Valences: A Multi-Level Analysis," *Journal of Sales Management* 1, no. 3: 25–29.
8. Douglas N. Behrman, William J. Bigoness, and William D. Perreault, Jr., "Sources of Job Related Ambiguity and Their Consequences Upon Salespersons' Job Satisfaction and Performance," *Management Science* (November 1981): 1246–1260.
9. William H. Newman, Kirby E. Warren, and Jerome E. Schne, *The Process of Management, Strategy, Action, Results,* 5th ed. (Englewood Cliffs, N.J.: Prentice-Hall, 1982), 221.
10. For an article questioning the desirability of celebrity exhortatory speakers see Kevin T. Higgins, "Motivating the Sales Force: Does 'rah-rah' Talk Still Translate into Action?" *Marketing News* (4 July 1986): 10.
11. "New Meaning for Meetings," *Sales & Marketing Management* (11 Nov. 1985): 95.
12. Rayna Skolnik, "Helping Sales Meetings Make the Grade," *Sales & Marketing Management* (12 Nov. 1979): 49.
13. For other relevant articles dealing with planning and evaluating sales meetings, see "A Guide Through the Minefields," *Sales & Marketing Management* (July 1986): 96–101; and "Sales Meetings with a Plan," *Sales & Marketing Management* (12 Nov. 1984): 79ff.
14. "Incentives Get Specific," *Sales & Marketing Management* (April 1986): 98.

cases

14.1 Handling a Complaining Subordinate

Mike Rothenberg is a complainer, but he is also one of your better salesmen. Outspoken, aggressive, and short-tempered, he is not your favorite employee, although you grudgingly respect him and do not want to jeopardize his effectiveness. He continually gripes about his quota. It is always "far too high"; he complains about slow deliveries on his orders and warehouse out-of-stocks; he thinks other salespeople are given preferential treatment; he complains about you as either always "nit-

picking" or else totally neglecting his territory. You now ignore the gripes, categorizing them as unwarranted and worthy of no further action.

Lately, Mike has focused on another area for complaining—credit approvals. He vehemently proclaims that too many of his customers are refused by the credit department as poor risks. He further claims that his territory is being discriminated against, because he has more small customers than most other territories.

QUESTION

What, if anything, would you do?

14.2 Supervisory Problems for a New Sales Manager

Sarah Lindstrom has been sales manager for the Dallas district of the Harriet Beame Cosmetic Company for 9 months. A small firm compared to the likes of Revlon and Avon, Harriet Beame has been able to compete fairly successfully by selling specialized products for teenagers primarily to department stores and drug chains. Entry into these large retailers is not always easy and usually requires aggressive selling, demonstrations, and display assistance.

Sarah had been the most successful salesperson in the Richmond area before her promotion to management. She still has major accounts to service personally. Under her are eight salespeople, three of whom are experienced, while Sarah had

recently hired the others in anticipation of expanding sales in the Dallas district.

The sales buildup, however, continues to be disappointing. Sarah had thought that as the inexperienced salespeople gained experience on the job, their production would rise, but it is doing so quite slowly. Of even more concern is the inability of the older salespeople to make their quotas. When Sarah queried them about their poor performance, they invariably responded that competition was keen and the quotas were too high. Sarah is in a quandary. Servicing her own accounts is taking much of her time, and yet much more personal supervision of her sales staff seems necessary.

QUESTION

What should Sarah do to overcome the weak start and to build satisfactory sales volume in her district? Be as specific as you can.

14.3 Bailey Company, Air Conditioning Division: Use of Incentives

Jeff Bell, vice president of sales for the air conditioning division of the Bailey Company, reached

his phone to call Lisbeth Roberts into his office for a conference. Lisbeth, the newly appointed sales and promotion manager, was on a fast track, he mused. After obtaining an undergraduate degree in marketing, she had entered a male-dominated field, technical selling. She had quickly become a top producer and constantly sought out more responsibilities. Somehow she had also completed an MBA at night school, and shortly thereafter she was promoted to sales manager in another division of the company, where she had compiled an outstanding record. Jeff had thought she was just the person he needed for his air conditioning division, which had experienced static sales over the last several years. He had persuaded corporate management to set up a new position, sales and promotion manager, and to transfer Lisbeth to it about 6 months ago. The position was roughly equivalent to general sales manager, however. Lisbeth also had responsibility for sales promotion and trade advertising.

The air conditioning division sold window air conditioners through forty-two distributors to some 4,500 dealers. The sales force comprised 280 people, who contacted the distributors as well as most of the dealers (except a few hundred of the very smallest). The sales force was paid primarily by salary, with a limited bonus if the district achieved its sales goals. About one-third of the salespeople had been eligible for a bonus the previous year.

As Lisbeth Roberts entered his office, he greeted her pleasantly. "I've called you in because production has been complaining again. They're most unhappy about the peaks and valleys of the business."

"The peak retail selling months are May, June, and July," Lisbeth noted. "By the end of July, sales trail off almost to nothing."

"That's the trouble, from production's viewpoint. Their employment swings seasonally from 1,500 to 7,500 people, with a lot of overtime as well in the busy season. They're practically begging us to do something to flatten the peaks and valleys of demand."

"We are offering special discounts from the regular price as well as extended dating and financing to induce the dealers to buy in advance of the sea-son," she reminded Jeff. "Not that this has had any appreciable effect, although some customers buy a month or 6 weeks earlier than they otherwise could. Can we give any better price concessions?"

"I'm afraid not, not if we are to make any money on these off-season sales." Jeff looked keenly at Lisbeth. "Do you have any other suggestions?"

"Not right now," she admitted. "I'd like to discuss this with my sales managers and maybe with some of the sales staff, too. Can you give us a few weeks to come up with some definite ideas?"

"We've had this problem ever since air conditioners first came on the market. A few more weeks certainly won't make any difference."

"Good," she responded. "I'd also like to talk with a few of our more important dealers, to get the opinion of those on the firing line."

Exactly 2 weeks later, Lisbeth Roberts submitted a report and recommendations for flattening the peaks and valleys of air conditioning demand. The following are excerpts:

> The consensus in the field is that the peaks and valleys of air conditioning sales can be moderated if aggressive dealer promotions and push are instituted to persuade consumers to buy either ahead of the season or at close-out prices at the season's end.
>
> It appears that our 20-percent price discounts to dealers for off-season commitments, as well as the extended dating (so that purchases made early in the season do not have to be paid for until the peak) should present adequate incentive for dealers. However, more effective persuasion must be employed.
>
> Accordingly, we recommend instituting a concerted incentive program for our salespeople to push dealers during the off-season. (Our salespeople are paid primarily on a straight salary, which offers little incentive to maximize sales.) Both short-term and long-term (lasting the entire off-season) contests are recommended for our field sales force. Awards should include individual pieces of merchandise, cash, or catalog prizes, as well as recognition, via plaques, mugs, and diamond rings. We might consider giving the top quota breakers and their spouses a trip.
>
> Although these recommendations are couched in general language, if the Executive Committee approves, we will propose specifics for such a comprehensive incentive program.

QUESTIONS

1. Evaluate the recommendations offered by Lisbeth Roberts. Do you see any problems or deficiencies?

2. Given that top management accepts these recommendations, draw up a specific implementation program.

3. Do you have any other suggestions for flattening out the peaks and valleys of home air conditioner sales?

CHAPTER 15
Implementing Effective Distributor–Customer Relations

CHAPTER PERSPECTIVE

A sales department's success in cementing long-lasting relations with its customers greatly determines its effectiveness. A sales department also should develop greater dealer push (i.e., to increase the sales volume of each account) and win new customers. Few manufacturers sell directly to final users; most sell to distributors, who in turn sell to final buyers. The manufacturer must influence and motivate its dealers to extend their best efforts, much as it must motivate its own sales force. But the manufacturer can exercise much less control over these independent dealers.

The term *symbiotic relationship* is used to describe the relationship between the manufacturer and the dealers and distributors who comprise the distribution channel. A *symbiotic relationship* exists between a producer and a dealer simply because they depend on each other. Although dissimilar, the parties involved have a mutual advantage in working together, they both will benefit from the success of the product(s). This chapter examines the pitfalls in and opportunities for developing the best distributor–customer relations.

CHAPTER OBJECTIVES

□ Acquaint yourself with the major sources of channel of distribution conflicts.
□ Become familiar with the importance of the distributor and what is needed to build customer loyalty.
□ Consider how a manufacturer can induce dealers to give its products more push or emphasis, and investigate the possibilities of being a channel captain.
□ Know the different degrees of intensity of distribution and the implications for the sales organization.
□ Understand the various facets of customer services.
□ Become familiar with the various methods of measuring customer satisfaction and their benefits.
□ Become aware of unreasonable customer demands and actions that are appropriate in such circumstances.

CHANNEL CONFLICT

One would expect harmony and cooperation to develop naturally among the various members of a distribution channel. The manufacturer will benefit from aiding wholesalers and retailers by providing the following:

☐ Training aids and promotional material, such as advertising mats and displays

☐ Help with servicing problems and the handling of customer complaints

☐ Financial help and flexible credit arrangements to enable distributors to stock up in advance of a big selling season

☐ Ample warnings of model and price changes, and even protection against price changes

☐ Helping channel members avoid heavy markdowns on merchandise in stock

The dealer and distributor reasonably can be expected to be motivated to merchandise the product favorably and also to furnish feedback through the channel so that any difficulties can be corrected. Despite strong incentives for cooperation, conflicts may arise from actions by either the producer or the middlemen. Table 15.1 lists the major sources of channel conflicts, some emanating from the producer, others from middlemen.

The Importance of the Distributor

The distributor can play a key role in the effectiveness of the manufacturer's selling efforts, because the distributor may well be the only contact with the ultimate buyer. How well this middleman then presents the goods (and if he has adequate goods on hand, with no out-of-stocks) becomes a major factor in the manufacturer's success in that market area.

The distributor may play an even more important role, that of permitting or denying entry to the market itself. For example when the number of possible distributors is limited in a geographic area and most of these are committed to handling competitors' products, a distributor may represent the manufacturer's only entry to this market. If this distributor proves to be recalcitrant, the manufacturer may be forced to either leave that market to competitors or try somehow to placate and appease, and be satisfied with less-than-optimum distributor efforts. Hence, the manufacturer has a vital interest in maintaining the most harmonious and effective dealer relations.

BUILDING LOYALTY

Good customer relations translate into satisfied customers and customer loyalty, without which, customer turnover will be high and the costs of contin-

TABLE 15.1   Sources of producer–distributor conflict.

Producer-created conflicts

Making heavy demands on middlemen, such as requiring large and varied inventories, special promotional support, extensive service facilities, and burdensome payment terms

Refusing to protect middlemen against model changes and price changes, so that heavy markdowns are incurred.

Making similar goods available to a middleman's competitors, either similar firms or firms of a different type, such as discount stores and catalog showrooms, who may undercut prices

Selling to the middlemen's customers and thus competing directly with the distributors

Promising ''expert'' promotional and merchandising assistance that never materializes

Refusing to handle adjustments due to faulty products or not reimbursing dealers fully for their costs in servicing products still under warranty

Middlemen-created conflicts

Demanding large discounts, special promotional allowances, and more favorable pricing terms

Demanding special shipping arrangements and quicker deliveries

Handling competing products, especially their own private brands, and not giving adequate effort to selling the manufacturer's brand

Giving careless servicing and disregarding product information

---

ually replacing dealers and customers become burdensome. In general customer loyalty depends on the following:

☐ Sales and distribution policies must be congruent with distributor requirements and must be at least as favorable to customers as those of competitors'.

☐ Communication should flow freely, both up and down the distribution channel.

☐ Customer service must not be meager. The customer should be able to depend on the backing of the manufacturer.

Congruent Policies

The manufacturer's distribution policies should be compatible with those needed by customers to make the relationship satisfactory. The manufacturer and the distributor should represent a valued partnership—the symbiotic relationship: This is especially important if competitive and alternative suppliers are readily available. The following policies in particular should be congruent.

Prices and discounts.   The pricing structure should allow all dealers, large and small, a reasonable profit. Granting excessive discounts for large orders puts smaller dealers at such a price disadvantage that they may seek alternative brands. Failure to warn dealers adequately about price changes may force them into costly markdowns when the manufacturer unexpectedly lowers his price. Or dealers may incur unexpected replenishment costs if prices are raised. Many manufacturers protect their dealers against unexpected price changes, even if the manufacturer must absorb some markdowns or other costs connected with the price change.

Advertising and promotional efforts.   The manufacturer should coordinate its advertising and promotional efforts with the dealer's to provide the greatest impact for mutual benefit. The company sales force can play a key role here in providing information about forthcoming promotional efforts and in furnishing matching displays and other materials.

Products and service.   Policies regarding products and service should be compatible with dealers' expectations and needs. A proliferation of models, colors, and styles may unduly burden dealer investment and available space. Large minimum order quantities force the smaller dealer either to overstock, thus tying up resources in unneeded inventory investment, or else miss out on attractive products that larger customers can more easily handle. Quality control, manufacturer-provided service, and delivery dependability are other areas where the manufacturer's and distributor's policies and practices should be in harmony. The manufacturer of packaged consumer goods should ensure that the container size is uniform with those of similar products; otherwise, shelf space may be inadequate or require redesigning. Some years ago an expensive foul-up occurred when Royal Crown Cola introduced an attractive new aluminum can that had been carefully designed to fit supermarket shelves. Unfortunately, it was too tall for vending machines. Size selection, shipping cartons tailored to the needs of retailers, and ease of opening and marking are other important packaging considerations in better meeting the needs of middleman customers.

Distribution.   When a manufacturer has a limited distribution policy, problems can arise unless the manufacturer carefully avoids making the same goods available to a middleman's competitors, especially if competitors are likely to undercut prices. This problem is more prevalent with consumer goods manufacturers, who deal with a variety of retailers, such as department stores and discount stores, who practice different pricing policies. For example no department store can tolerate having its same brands and products offered by a discount store at 20 percent less. It could match the discounter's price and lose money because its operating expenses are higher, or it could maintain its higher prices and risk lost sales and, more important, the ill will of its customers, who can see tangible benefits in buying at the discount store's prices. The department or specialty store thus is virtually forced to look for another brand that is not sold to discount stores.

Frequently, the best interests of the dealer and the manufacturer would be better served by different sales and distribution policies regarding matters such as prices, discounts, and advertising and promotion. For example the manufacturer needs the flexibility to institute price changes whenever warranted; the dealer on the other hand needs ample advance warning (so inventories can be adjusted) and needs full protection against any unexpected markdown or replenishment costs. A compromise may be needed, with both parties giving up some benefit through negotiation.

Negotiation. Negotiating, or bargaining, involves a resolution of one or more issues between at least two parties. It usually is achieved by presentations of demands or proposals with a compromise eventually reached. Books on negotiation abound; the subject has variously been treated by economists, game theorists, social psychologists, labor relations experts, and others.[1] And numerous ''how-to'' books offer tactics for better negotiating,[2] as do some successful seminar speakers. A few examples of common negotiating tactics follow:

Acting crazy

Trial balloon

Surprises

Wet noodle

Acting crazy involves putting on a good show by visibly demonstrating your emotional commitment to your position. This increases your credibility and may give the opponent a justification to settle on your terms. With a *trial balloon* you release your decision through a so-called reliable source before the decision is actually made. This enables you to test reaction to your decision. *Surprises* are used to keep the opponent off balance by a drastic, dramatic, sudden shift in your tactics. Never be predictable; keep the opponent from anticipating your moves. The *wet noodle* gives no emotional or verbal response to the opponent. Don't respond to his force or pressure. Sit there like a wet noodle and keep a ''poker face.''[3] Note that even in this small sampling of tactics, the term *opponent* is used frequently.

Negotiating skills undoubtedly can be improved, so that one side will achieve a more favorable compromise than the other party. The sales manager, or sales representative, must realize, however, that in negotiations, customers and other channel members should not be considered as opponents. Rather, they should be viewed as valued associates, whose reasonable best interests should be observed, no matter how strong the manufacturer's bargaining position. Some of the tactics aimed at achieving an advantage may not be compatible with the symbiotic relationship.

Equitable treatment. In dealing with its various middlemen, a manufacturer carefully avoids giving the impression of playing favorites and giving preferential treatment to certain customers. The Robinson-Patman Act can make certain kinds of preferential treatment, such as price advantages and advertising allowance, illegal under conditions that are discussed in Chapter 19. However, more common preferential treatment occurs during times of short supply when certain distributors are given priority over others.

Good Communications

To enhance distributor loyalty, communication should flow freely up and down the channel. A distant manufacturer who maintains little close contact with dealers can often be vulnerable to competitors who work at developing close personal contacts, even if products and prices are not as good. The manufacturer can foster better communication through such actions as the following:

□ Using missionary salespeople to back up wholesalers' efforts with retailers

□ Periodic visits by company executives to major distributors

□ Sponsoring conventions and/or training sessions for distributors and dealers

□ Personal letters and telephone calls from the home and regional offices

□ Development of close personal relationships through company salespeople

□ Prompt handling of correspondence, often involving queries and complaints, from dealers

Regarding dealer complaints, building loyalty entails responsiveness. Usually, communications procedures should be developed so that areas of customer dissatisfaction can be quickly identified and prompt corrective action can be taken if the manufacturer is at fault, or at least some compromise can be made if the blame is more questionable. Salespeople normally represent the best channel of communication, so they should be encouraged to relay this information. To promote goodwill and to encourage better communications with customers, however, sales managers and higher-level executives may visit at least the more important customers periodically.

Small-account problems.   Small accounts may not be economical to service. The 80/20 rule is often cited as a factor. (The 80/20 rule and its implications are discussed in detail in Chapter 17.) The rule suggests that only 20 percent of customers yield 80 percent of the profits, and most of the rest are marginal and even unprofitable accounts. In building customer loyalty when data consistently show that a small minority of the customers produce most of the sales volume and profits, sales managers face a major decision on how to handle these marginal accounts. Whatever the decision regarding smaller customers—whether to drop them, call on them less frequently, or not call on them at all—the larger, more important accounts must be called on with regularity, even if an order is not sought or expected each time. The sales manager must guide salespeople in this respect to ensure that present customers are not neglected during efforts to obtain new business. Little is more damaging to good buyer–seller relations than taking the buyer for granted.

Customer Service

One of the sometimes neglected, yet most important, aspects of selling is customer service, which will affect customer satisfaction with the product as well as its accompanying service. Every sales manager has a golden opportunity to cement customer loyalty and gain differentiation from competitors by effectively attending to customer service. This topic is so important that it is covered in greater detail later in this chapter.

DEVELOPING DEALER PUSH

Most manufacturers do not sell directly to the final consumers or users; as noted before, they sell instead to a go-between—a dealer or a wholesaler. Consequently, manufacturers depend on third-party efforts for their products' success. But the middlemen usually carry the products of numerous manufacturers, with a large retailer or wholesaler carrying hundreds, even thousands of products. Each manufacturer's sales department then must vie with competitors in inducing dealers to exert more push on its particular products, to give them more prominent displays, better inventory assortment, more suggestions by dealer salespeople, more prompt servicing, and the like. How can a manufacturer (who usually can only persuade, rather than coerce) induce its dealers to use more push and give its products more emphasis, while competitors simultaneously attempt the same thing? Before examining this challenge more specifically, let us discuss channel captaincy.

The Channel Captain

A strong member of a channel can supply needed leadership in planning coordinated efforts by the various members of the channel and in stimulating

---

APPLICATION 15.1   Assumption of Channel Captaincy

Oshkosh B'Gosh, Inc., was family-owned and tiny (sales were only $48 million) compared to competitors such as Levi Strauss (with sales of $2 billion). Oshkosh had made traditional overalls for 86 years without much fanfare and had distributed primarily through men's and boy's clothing stores.

Then an Oshkosh-based mail order firm, Miles Kimball Co., included a pair of Oshkosh B'Gosh children's overalls as a novelty item in its Christmas catalog. Oshkosh had been seriously considering discontinuing its children's line of overalls because of few sales, but these thoughts were quickly dispelled when 15,000 orders poured in. Charles Hyde, Oshkosh's president, began to wonder why the regular retail outlets were finding no such popularity. "Maybe our traditional outlets are the wrong outlets," he pondered.

Hyde decided to issue direct mail solicitations to hundreds of children's clothing stores across the United States, and orders mushroomed. Demand for children's overalls became so great that even with production increased by 65 percent, the company could not make enough to satisfy demand, and all stores were on allocation. Oshkosh had become the profitability leader of the industry, and kiddie overalls accounted for 44 percent of Oshkosh sales and 50 percent of profits.

For more detail about Oshkosh, see "Fashion is Fickle," *Forbes*, 22 June 1981, 102–103.

their cooperation and support. Who is to be the captain depends on the size and general market power of the firms involved. Small retailers and wholesalers usually are not in a position to lead. Although they provide access to the market, their influence is limited because of their size and consequently their bargaining position is less than that of large firms at any level in the channel. Small manufacturers, however, may be channel leaders if they have a desired product and can therefore exercise control by offering or withholding it. Sometimes a small manufacturer must assert authority when it realizes that regular channel members are overlooking sales opportunities, and thereby it advances from following to leading. Application 15.1 shows an example of assumption of channel captaincy.

The more common channel captains are large manufacturers, large retailers, and sometimes large wholesalers who have established strong private brands and wholesaler-sponsored voluntary chains. The power of a General Motors or a Ford can be almost dictatorial regarding prices, discounts, bonuses, warranty reimbursements, and even inventories. At the other extreme the market power of a Sears, a J. C. Penney, or a Safeway is indisputable, even with large manufacturers. Smaller manufacturers whose entire output is marketed under the private brand of a big retail chain may depend on the retailer even to the design of the product.

Sometimes the market power of a big retailer and a big manufacturer may be almost evenly balanced. Especially with supermarkets, a few chains may dominate a metropolitan area and can substantially influence the success of the manufacturer in that area through granting or denying market access. The strong product acceptance of Gillette or Procter & Gamble, for example, based on well-known products and heavy mass media advertising, unlikely would be denied market access.

How Can the Manufacturer Motivate the Channel?

If a particular brand has strong consumer recognition and demand—usually gained by a reputable product through heavy consumer advertising—then dealers will be forced to push it, even if profit margins are not as attractive as those of competing products. Lacking such final user acceptance, the answer to manufacturer channel motivation and leadership lies in making the particular brand or product more attractive for the dealer to handle and to push than are competing products. This may be achieved by giving the dealer a better margin and profit or by better-designed point-of-purchase displays furnished to the dealers. The manufacturer might also supply better advertising allowances or cooperative advertising arrangements. Manufacturers sometimes reimburse retailers for part of the costs of ads featuring their goods. This is known as *cooperative advertising,* and a manufacturer may pay as much as 50 percent of the cost, up to a certain percentage (often 5 percent) of the retailer's total purchases from the manufacturer.

Figure 15.1 lists the most important "push" techniques and also shows the relationship with "pull" techniques, in which the consumer is influenced via heavy advertising, sampling, and discount coupons or premiums to demand the product from the dealers, thereby "pulling" it through the distribution channel.

The sales force can be a major factor in generating dealer push. If the sales force can develop a good rapport with the dealers, if salespeople make calls regularly and stress the benefits of their products, then dealer cooperation is likely. If a customer has a particular problem, perhaps the salesperson should try to help him out. For example a retailer might find himself with a heavy inventory of a manufacturer's goods, perhaps because of unseasonal weather or a major strike in the community. An alert salesperson might arrange to transfer the goods to another customer or might gain permission to return the overstock to the manufacturer. Perhaps the dealer could receive a special allowance to reduce prices, without losing money. A salesperson's extra efforts often result in gaining preference over competing firms.

Sales meetings and training aids for dealers' salespeople can also be fruitful in increasing dealer push. Because many products today are becoming more technical and more complex, the knowledge and persuasiveness of a retailer's salespeople are often the deciding factor in clinching a sale. To stimulate greater efforts by dealer salespeople, a manufacturer's sales department may

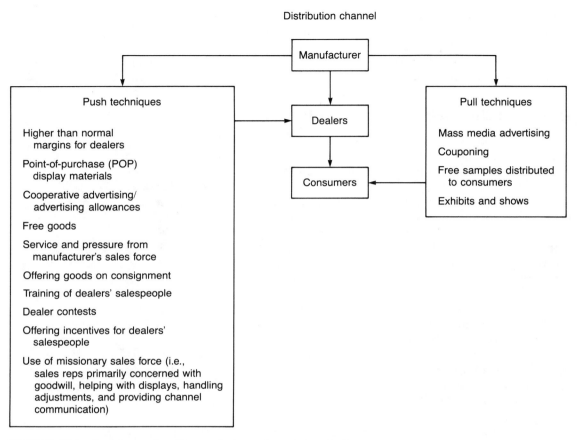

FIGURE 15.1   Pushing and pulling techniques for gaining dealer acceptance.

give dealers special premiums, such as prizes or trading stamps. In cosmetics the manufacturer commonly pays a small commission for each item sold by a retail sales clerk. And as shown in Chapter 14, contests and other incentives may be offered dealers to increase their motivation.

Many sales departments use missionary salespeople to aid dealer push. This is true particularly in selling to self-service outlets (e.g., supermarkets, discount stores, and drug stores). Because these outlets normally do not involve retail clerks in selling to customers, sales success depends on the amount of shelf space and its location. Table 15.2 shows the importance of spacing and display in the supermarket. If the retailer can be induced to give a brand an eye-level space, sales can improve as much as 78 percent compared with sales from floor-level shelf space.

TABLE 15.2   Importance of spacing and display in the supermarket.

Procedure	Percentage Change in Unit Sales
Maintaining a fully stocked shelf rather than a normally stocked shelf, which would result in some low-stock and even out-of-stock conditions	+20
Using special shelf signs to highlight certain items	+152
Displaying individual items in combination with related goods rather than presenting by themselves elsewhere in the store	+418
Using "as advertised" and "cents-off" signs	+124 and +23
Moving an item	
From waist level to eye level	+63
From waist level to floor level	−40
From floor level to waist level	+34
From floor level to eye level	+78

Other studies reported that a display can boost sales as much as 536 percent over original shelf position.

Sources: "Colonial Study," *Progressive Grocer* (January 1964): 123–127; "How In-Store Merchandising Can Boost Sales," *Progressive Grocer* (October 1971): 94–97; "How the Basics of Special Display Affect Sales and Profits," *Progressive Grocer* (January 1971): 34–35; "How to Make Displays More Sales Productive," *Progressive Grocer* (February 1971): 34–45; and William W. Mee, "How Point-of-Purchase is More Efficient as an Advertising and Sales Medium," *Media/Scope* (September 1963): 55–56.

In helping to generate more dealer push, missionary salespeople also aid the dealer in operating more efficiently. They may check the dealer's inventory, arrange displays, clean and straighten stock, and generally attempt to maintain friendly and helpful relations. Some manufacturers exert additional efforts to help their smaller dealers and distributors. They may provide advice and assistance on general management problems such as store layout, accounting methods and controls, advertising, credit and collection policies, in addition to the more common help in training dealer salespeople when products are fairly complex (e.g., appliances and sound systems).

Screening Customers

For some types of selling, the sales force is free to sell to every possible customer. In insurance, mutual funds, and door-to-door sales, screening customers systematically usually is unnecessary, unless a lack of ability to pay is obvious. For selling to resellers such as retailers and wholesalers, the sales force may need to screen and to limit customers in some way to enhance the quality of those who are finally accepted. The terms *intensive, selective,* and *exclusive* distribution are used to refer to the degree of market exposure that a consumer goods manufacturer can achieve with a product (see Figure 15.2).

Intensive distribution.   In intensive distribution the product or service is available to as many dealers as possible. The manufacturer's sales force is involved less in selling than in servicing many accounts. Routing and definitive scheduling of the sales force are often needed with this type of distribution.

Selective distribution.   In selective distribution the manufacturer limits his dealers to those considered the best available. They may be the largest or those with the best service standards, the most effective sales organization, and the best reputation. This more limited distribution should produce a much closer working relationship and rapport between manufacturer and dealer than under the more intensive distribution, because both are important to each other and will gain from the product's success.

Exclusive distribution.   The extreme of selectivity is exclusive distribution; product or brand distribution is severely limited. The manufacturer provides the distributor the fullest support and protection from competition and

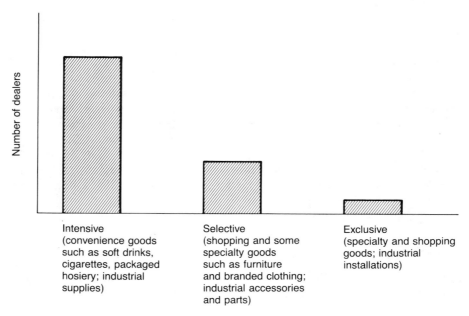

FIGURE 15.2   Degree of market exposure: Intensity of distribution.

exclusive rights to handle the product within a territory. The manufacturer expects maximum service and control, and the closest relationship is fostered.

In selective and exclusive distribution the sales representative may be involved in screening dealers, seeking those with the most ability and the best reputations. If the seller represents a large and well-known manufacturer, he can be very selective. But if the salesperson represents a smaller firm that cannot spend millions of advertising dollars to become a sought-after brand, the job of inducing sufficient and able dealers to handle the product may be very difficult.

CEMENTING CUSTOMER RELATIONS WITH GOOD CUSTOMER SERVICE

Definition

In the broadest sense *customer service* includes all offers of value to a firm's customers beyond the product itself. Although repair and warranty service generally receive the most attention (and complaints), customer services include such diverse aspects as guaranteed sales, protection against price changes, faster and more dependable delivery, dealer displays, and training aids and training for customer personnel.

Some services involve promotional activities. For example *guaranteed sales* and *protection against price changes* are inducements to buy. Guaranteed sales may enable a relatively unknown firm to gain market entry by guaranteeing to take back for refund any goods unsold by dealers. Price change protections may encourage customers to buy in larger quantities and further in advance, with the assurance that the manufacturer will reimburse for any detrimental price changes made before the goods are sold. Dealer aids, such as point-of-purchase displays, are a service that manufacturers render to dealers, but these aids also may be considered as promotion. Manufacturers' efforts to train dealers in maintenance and repair techniques or to train users when products are technically complex are genuine customer services. Although the distinction from promotional efforts is somewhat hazy, in this text, activities are considered customer services when they are only indirectly geared to sales generation and are not part of the promotional strategy.

Benefits of Good Customer Service

Good customer service produces customer satisfaction, loyal customers and repeat business, and word-of-mouth influence, which is potent if not easily measured. Profits can be increased by the following:

□ Attracting new customers

□ Increasing sales to present customers

□ Permitting higher product prices

□ Reducing vulnerability to price competition

□ Providing miscellaneous indirect benefits[4]

The effect of a firm's reputation on attracting potential customers and preventing the loss of existing customers is obvious. Less obvious is the protection from price competition that a good reputation for service can provide. Although some customers are swayed by a better price, many place a higher value on a firm's reputation for dependable service. Some services, such as extended warranties, are easily imitated. Others, such as prompt and dependable delivery and high-caliber maintenance and repair facilities, are less easily imitated, and their effective performance slowly builds reputations.

A customer service program can also provide indirect benefits. A firm's good reputation can make customers more receptive to the company's sales representatives (can make customers easier to sell to) and more tolerant of the inevitable foul-ups. Recruiting salespeople tends to be easier if a company has a good public image, and higher morale and lower personnel turnover should result. Even dealings with governmental agencies and regulatory bodies may be smoother.

Costs of Service

Services sometimes are furnished for an extra charge, such as an extra fee for expedited delivery. Service contracts having the characteristics of insurance policies may be offered for complex products. Other customer services may be provided without extra charge, although their expenses must be considered in pricing decisions.

Unless they can be passed on directly to the customer, as in a service contract, service costs constrain the extent to which services can be offered without forcing selling prices to exceed market demand and competitive offerings. There is danger of a firm's going to either extreme—either not enough service or too much. For many firms a careful study of market needs is desired and may result in developing a strategy different from competing firms or in using different service mixes in different market segments.

Types of Customer Service

Services can be classified by the type of value they provide for customers, as shown in Figure 15.3.

Risk reduction.   Services that reduce a customer's risk of receiving the wrong product or a defective product are *adjustment and return-goods privileges*

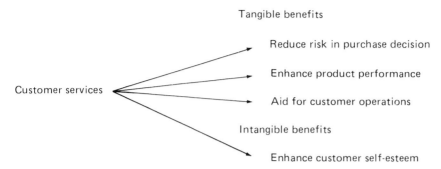

FIGURE 15.3 Customer services categorized by value to customers.

and *warranties and guarantees*. Retailers have led the way in offering adjustments and refunds to their customers, even though the product may not be at fault. The customer thus may examine the goods at home without risk or a rigid commitment. Warranties and guarantees have caused the greatest problems. These are seller-assumed obligations, designed to give the buyer greater assurance. Warranties may be explicit or implied. Implied (nonwritten) warranties have been delineated by the Uniform Sales Act, which is in force in over thirty states, and have been interpreted in numerous court cases. Usually, buyers have some protection without a written warranty, even though they examined the goods before purchase, if latent defects are later discovered. Written warranties often are stated in ambiguous language. They may be unnecessarily complex, and terms such as "unconditionally guaranteed" and "lifetime guarantee" often conceal disclaimers and qualifications that make the warranty effectively worthless.

Recognizing that good warranties provide the purchasing assurance that creates more satisfied customers, Maytag eliminated "all exceptions" and stipulated that its warranty would be carried out even if the customer moved out of the selling dealer's area. Automobile makers, to be competitive, have been extending their normal 12-month, 12,000-mile warranties to 6 years and 60,000 miles.

A federal warranty law was enacted in 1975. Although it does not require manufacturers to issue warranties, it does specify that if a manufacturer promises a "full" warranty, then repair must be made "within a reasonable time and without charge" for any defects and replacement of merchandise or a full refund must be given if the product still does not work. If the manufacturer does not want to meet this tough standard, then the warranty must be "conspicuously" promoted as a "limited" warranty.

Performance enhancement. Services that improve product performance include the tailoring, alteration, or adjustment needed to fit the product to the particular customer's requirements. Also included are special training or instructions that help the customer to use the product properly. Instruction may prevent costly warranty repair work.

Effective and fairly priced repair and maintenance service is a major factor in performance satisfaction, and it often involves expediting delivery of parts orders. Beech Aircraft, for example, has a policy that 90 percent of its parts orders needed to restore planes to working condition must be shipped within 24 hours after an order is received. Training dealers, their service representatives, and customers in the latest maintenance and repair techniques can greatly help product service. Some manufacturers are seeking to simplify their products and make them more easily repaired. (Designing products that consist of plug-in modules is another possible solution, because relatively inexpensive replacement units would make repair unnecessary.)

Statistical quality control, which accepts a predictable number of defective units, could be replaced by a complete quality control, which accepts "zero defects" for items whose serious servicing problems cannot otherwise be eased. Most firms reject multiple inspections of critical parts as too costly. But compared to the costs of customer brand switching and costly call-back programs, improved quality control might sometimes offset the increased costs.

Aid for customers' operations.   Services such as the following can broadly be categorized as helping customers to operate more efficiently:

- □ On-time delivery according to customer expectations and needs
- □ Reasonable distribution costs in relation to the competition's customer expectations
- □ Responsibility for a minimum of damage in transit and handling
- □ Prompt and courteous handling of any service problems that inevitably will arise
- □ Information and/or business consultation to help customers do a better job and avoid possible problems

Reliable and on-time delivery primarily depends on goods being available for quick order processing and filling. (Sometimes poor delivery also can be due to unreliable and slow transportation, which must be detected and resolved.) The number of field warehouses, their proximity to the market, and the inventory control system all affect delivery time.

Importance of inventory control for reliable delivery.   In addition to good warehousing and physical handling facilities, an effective inventory-control system is needed to provide a balanced inventory. With too high an inventory, unnecessary goods take up storage space, increase the required investment, and face greater risks of obsolescence, price declines, destruction, and the like.

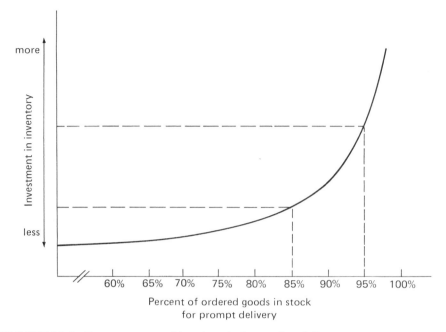

FIGURE 15.4 Investment considerations in improving delivery promptness to customers.

Too little inventory, which is manifested in out-of-stocks, so that customer orders cannot be shipped, results in loss of sales and customer good will; if it occurs too frequently, customers may be lost permanently.

Unfortunately, the total amount of goods found in inventory is seldom a sufficient criterion of an in-stock condition or an ability to promptly fill customer orders. A heavy inventory often may reflect a preponderance of slow-moving items, while fast-moving goods are out-of-stock. Careful attention and control are needed to ensure that fast-selling items are replenished in time to meet customer demand.

The ability to fill 100 percent of orders promptly, however, may require an excessively large inventory with its accompanying costs. It has been estimated that 80 percent more inventory is required to fill 95 percent of the orders than to fill only 80 percent.[5] Figure 15.4 shows the much greater investment typically required to maintain an inventory that will minimize out-of-stocks. The computer and operations research models can help to establish the optimum quantity to reorder (known as the economic order quantity) when inventory stocks must be replenished.

Now do Exercise 15.1.

EXERCISE 15.1	A company's executives have estimated that the cost of lost sales and customer switches is $100,000 if an 80-percent inventory level is maintained. If a 90-percent inventory level is achieved, the increased cost would be $50,000, but the cost of lost sales and customers would be reduced to $75,000. If a 95-percent inventory level is attained, the increased cost would be $100,000, but the cost of lost sales and customers would be only $25,000.

1. Based on these estimates, which level of inventory should be planned?
2. If it is deemed impossible to estimate the cost of lost sales and customer switches, what would your answer be? Why?

Minimizing problems with customer service.   The shipper cannot disavow distribution costs and responsibility for ensuring minimal damage in transit and handling, even though the carrier may be to blame for problems. The shipper should take reasonable care to determine and specify the most competitive transport method, subject to customer designation, of course. Furthermore, adequate packing on the manufacturer's premises should minimize damage claims.

Promptly and courteously handling service problems and customer complaints can greatly lessen any detrimental effect of shipping problems. Most executive time, however, is spent in supervising aspects of the operation other than customer relations, and with good reason. Managers must resolve operational crises and problems such as determining promotional scheduling that cannot be delayed; breaking in a salesperson in a new territory; devoting immediate attention to several territories whose planned sales were not reached. The customers who are antagonized, who are ill treated, whose special requirements are disregarded, whose sales quietly are lost—all these may be overlooked in the pressure of "more important" matters.

The reason that many firms neglect the customer relations aspect of their business largely is a lack of awareness of the depth of these problems. Sales and profit figures usually cannot detect the extent of customer dissatisfaction until these problems may have assumed major proportions. Figure 15.5 shows a model of how customers lost can be offset by new customers gained so that, over succeeding time periods, the level of sales and profits remains steady. One can only speculate on the probable long-range consequences of unrelieved customer erosion. And one can wonder how profit performance would change if the ratio of customers lost to customers gained were greatly reduced. Moreover, because responsible executives hear about only a small proportion of total complaints, they frequently are induced to believe that dissatisfaction involves only a few customers who have mostly unjustified complaints. In a report to the Federal Trade Commission, General Motors lightly dismissed 129 warranty complaints that the FTC had received by saying they amounted to "only .0015 percent of the new cars sold in that year."[6]

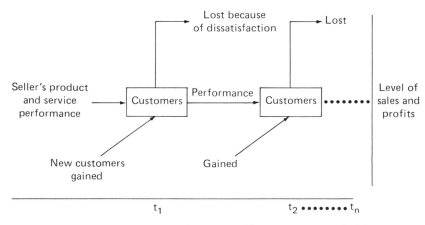

FIGURE 15.5   How customer relations problems can remain hidden.

A firm should establish procedures for prompt feedback on service problems and customer complaints to responsible executives. Usually, some centralized and standardized procedures should be established both to obtain service feedback and to handle complaints. Some firms have found that "hotlines," toll-free direct lines to company headquarters for customers whose problems are not being handled to their satisfaction, are effective both as a service and a sales tool.

A number of firms now offer information services to their customers. For example Cessna helps customers using Cessna planes for crop dusting by furnishing information on professional aerial application and publishing a directory of Cessna-equipped crop dusters. Mattel toy company provides sophisticated information to its retail customers on controlling inventory levels. Other firms keep their customers informed of order status, especially when shipments will be delayed or reduced due to shortages, strikes, or other unforeseen circumstances. Sales force use of portable computers is vastly improving customer service in speeding up order delivery (see Application 15.2).

Intangible Customer Service

In addition to the tangible services, another type of service can provide a powerful edge in customer relations, and this has been termed *overtones,* that is, efforts that enhance a customer's needs for self-esteem and self-respect.[7] Overtones are simply courtesy and respect, prompt attention, and consideration. They occur (or do not) at the point of contact between a firm and its customers and are vital ingredients for establishing a positive or negative public image.

Wrangler salespeople began using portable computers in 1984 on a trial basis. By 1986 all 70 of its salespeople had computers. Sales productivity and customer service substantially improved as a consequence, although not without cost. The Wrangler experience typifies the gains and costs of computers for a sales force.

The apparel industry is characterized by seasonality and the transient life of fashions. Retailers' biggest need, therefore, is quick order delivery. The portable computers of Wrangler strikingly meet this crucial customer need. Wrangler salespeople can use their portable computers to interact with the company's mainframe and can send and retrieve messages. The sales representative can immediately give a retailer information on garment availability and delivery. The speedup in entering orders has been reduced from 21 days to 24 hours.

The following costs, however, must be recognized by any firm contemplating equipping its sales force with computers:

☐ The total company investment per salesperson for computer hardware and software can run over $5,000.

☐ Many salespeople do not like to type, and some have a phobia against computers.

☐ Significant benefits may not appear until the system has operated for a year or more.

☐ All relevant data must be converted from print into the computer, which can be a massive process.

For more information on the Wrangler experience, see Peter Finch, "How Computers Are Reshaping the Sales Process," *Business Marketing,* (August 1985): 108–118.

Even the promptness and the quality of responses to customer mail can result in positive or negative overtones. A firm is well advised to devote some attention to this aspect of the firm–customer interaction. Special training may be needed, special policies established, and some type of periodic follow-up used to ensure that the company's image does not deteriorate. The telephone is another point of contact that has overtones yet is seldom checked for its positive or negative contribution.

A successful overtones program requires a commitment by top management. It must be a frequent topic of meeting and training sessions; it must be given high priority, or other matters will intrude and monopolize attention. Without constant pressure and without suitable controls to provide feedback, an organization tends to become indifferent to customer relations. This is true for all manner of organizations, from government agencies to hospitals, schools, police departments, and business firms large and small.

MEASURING CUSTOMER SATISFACTION

To determine whether customer service is adequate, and to pinpoint areas where improvement is desired and perhaps even vitally needed, a firm should have a method to measure customer satisfaction. In most firms, however, methods for evaluating customer satisfaction are not as well established as those for evaluating profit; indeed, many firms do not measure customer satisfaction.

Table 15.3 shows the results of two surveys of major firms in which they were asked, "How do you determine the degree to which you are satisfying your customers?" The most common formal and informal measurement factors were the following:

Sales volume and trends

Market share

Opinions of distributors, dealers, and salespeople

Unsolicited customer responses

Customer research studies

Most of the preceding measures are flawed. Sales and market share results, for example, are very indirect and lack sensitivity, because many other de-

TABLE 15.3   Reported measurement factors of customer satisfaction, 1968 and 1977.

Measurement Factor*	1968		1977	
	Number of Companies Using Factor	Percentage of Companies Using Factor	Number of Companies Using Factor	Percentage of Companies Using Factor
Consumer research studies	34	65.2	31	68.9
Unsolicited consumer responses	34	65.2	17	37.8
Sales volume/trends	29	56.0	9	20.0
Share of market	22	42.0	11	24.4
Opinions of middlemen and salespeople	20	40.0	21	46.7
Market test results	7	13.0	11	24.4
Profit	1	2.0	3	6.7
Repeat business			15	33.3

*Some companies reported using more than one measurement factor. In 1968 the number of companies surveyed was 52; in 1977, 45.

Sources: James U. McNeal, "Consumer Satisfaction: The Measure of Marketing Effectiveness," MSU Business Topics (Summer 1969): 33; James U. McNeal and Charles W. Lamb, Jr., "Consumer Satisfaction as a Measure of Marketing Effectiveness," Akron Business and Economic Review (Summer 1979): 41–45.

terminants (e.g., environmental elements and quality of competition) affect sales and market share. Furthermore, these data do not indicate the degree of satisfaction. Are customers well pleased? Are they mostly dissatisfied but have no other reasonable alternative choices to do business with? Sales results generally lag behind changes in customer satisfaction.

Feedback from distributors, dealers, and salespeople often gives biased results. Dealers tend to be overly pessimistic, to the point that legitimate communications about problem areas may be discounted. The sales force, on the other hand, also cannot be relied on for objective reporting. Salespeople sometimes tend to withhold information about problem areas from higher management under the assumption that the salesperson will somehow be held accountable for customer dissatisfaction. The opposite may occur when the salesperson exaggerates customer complaints and problem areas to find an excuse for poor sales production.

Most direct feedback from customers that reaches responsible executives comes from occasional letters of complaint directed to the president. This feedback is fragmented at best and seldom represents most customer attitudes because it comes from a vocal minority of customers most difficult to satisfy (or most desperate to have product or service deficiencies corrected). Other dissatisfied customers simply take future business elsewhere. For most firms the gain of new customers offsets the loss of old customers, and this can disguise the full seriousness of business erosion.

In Table 15.3 the 1977 study, almost an exact replica of the 1968 study, gives some trend information. Less reliance justifiably is being given to unsolicited customer responses, sales volume, and market share. One-third of the firms surveyed in 1977 regard repeat business, not mentioned in the earlier study, as an important measure. Although customer loyalty can be readily ascertained by manufacturers selling to industrial and commercial customers who are usually relatively few in number, this becomes much more difficult or even impossible for firms dealing with final consumers, who may number in the thousands and even millions.

A more positive approach can be taken to ascertain the existence and sources of customer dissatisfaction and to provide feedback on their views about the firm's policies and actions. The opportunity exists both to win new customers and to cement the loyalty of present customers. Customer attitude surveys can be effective, and about two-thirds of the companies surveyed did mention customer research as a major source of satisfaction information.

Use of customer surveys to measure satisfaction. Attitude surveys commonly are conducted in either of two ways. Brief questionnaires inviting customer opinions may be inserted in shipments or in monthly statements. Or salespeople during their calls can formally invite customer opinions and expressions of satisfaction level. Both methods assume that the more serious complaints or the strongest customer feelings will be revealed.

Unfortunately, each of these survey methods can be criticized. The use of questionnaire inserts raises serious questions about the reliability and validity of the results because of the unknown response rate. Using salespeople to make inquiries during sales calls can also yield poor data unless research controls are established. Three considerations affect the usefulness of salespeople in research. (1) A survey may result in either unusual praise or the airing of gripes—responses that may not accurately reflect attitudes because of the presence of the salesperson, who has much to do with the existing degree of customer satisfaction. (2) The salesperson's report may not be completely objective, especially when some emotional involvement in the relationship is surveyed. (3) The use of salespeople to collect this kind of information conflicts with the fundamental purpose of the sales call. If, in spite of these drawbacks, salespeople are used to collect information, they need training in what is expected and how they are to do it.

Periodic surveys conducted by objective researchers are better recommended. Outside consultants or the firm's marketing research department could be used. If respondents are carefully selected, the sample need not be large. These surveys, however, should be systematic and continuous; otherwise, trends in attitudes go unnoticed and danger areas are not spotted until serious erosion of customers has occurred.

Direct measures of customer satisfaction have three main advantages. (1) Trends in customer attitudes can be established and problem areas detected early, before they become serious. (2) Good will can be fostered and a reputation as a "caring" firm gained. (3) Unfilled customer needs and wants may be revealed, suggesting opportunities.

ABUSES OF SERVICE

Buyers occasionally will abuse the service, will try to take advantage of the supplier, will be overly demanding and impossible to satisfy. Sometimes when large buyers deal with smaller suppliers, coercion results, as the constant threat of losing an important customer looms over the heads of the sales representatives and the sales manager. These customers may demand special low prices or sale terms; they may insist on priority over other customers for their order processing and deliveries; they may demand that certain goods be returned for full credit even though the merchandise has become shopworn or damaged through their own negligence. Sometimes the situation becomes such that the supplier is faced with the legal consequences of giving preferential treatment to one or a few customers. (This is generally a violation of the Robinson-Patman Act, as mentioned earlier in this chapter.) How should a sales manager react to customers' attempts to abuse their service privileges or to demand special treatment? A range of alternatives is possible.

☐ The buyer's demands may be fully met.

☐ Some compromises may be made, with both parties giving a little to reconcile their differences.

☐ The sales manager may adamantly refuse to bend, even at the risk of losing the customer.

The sales manager should consider the seriousness of the problem or dispute, the importance of the customer, and past customer relations. A minor problem (e.g., replacing a part damaged due to customer negligence or misunderstanding of correct use) probably should be resolved without quibbling, at least if it is the first time and if the cost is modest; the good will gained should more than compensate the manufacturer for any monetary loss. If more serious problems and more costly issues are involved, resolution is less easy. The sales manager should consider, however, whether the customer genuinely feels that the seller has an obligation and is at fault, or whether the buyer is attempting to take advantage of a smaller seller or of a seller who is unlikely to risk offending and possibly losing an important customer. If disputes with one customer recur regularly, the sales manager may have to resolutely question whether the costs of handling the account and the continual travail are worth the business. An alternative to consider in extreme cases may be threatening to terminate business with the buyer.

When the buyer persists in demanding lower prices and better terms, more advertising and promotional allowances, and more costly display aids (proportionately better offerings than those given to other customers), the probable violation of the Robinson-Patman Act should deter the seller from accepting. A big customer's coercive power should not lead a supplier to violate federal laws.

SUMMARY   Channel conflict exists, despite apparently strong incentives for cooperation between manufacturer and dealers or distributors. The distributor obviously is important to the manufacturer, as are congruent policies and good communications between manufacturers and distributors, and dependable customer service in building loyalty.

A channel captain supplies leadership in securing coordinated efforts by the various members of the channel in pushing the product. Motivating the channel depends on strong final user acceptance or in making the product more attractive for the dealer to handle than are competing products.

A strong manufacturer sometimes wants more limited distribution, and some screening of dealers may be desired to gain the best dealers. Maximum control over dealers can be achieved with the more limited or exclusive type of distribution.

Good customer service is needed to gain loyal channel members, although the costs of some services must be weighed against the benefits. Customer services can be categorized as reducing risk, enhancing product performance, aiding customer operations, and building customers' self-esteem.

A manufacturer should periodically measure customer satisfaction to be sure that this is not deteriorating because of unrecognized deficiencies and problems. Although many firms consider sales and market share as good indicators of customer satisfaction, these are not precise enough, because so many other factors can affect satisfaction levels. Systematic customer surveys generally provide the best measure.

Occasionally, a customer will abuse a firm's liberal service policies or demand inequitable special treatment. In handling these situations the sales manager should consider the problem's seriousness, the customer's importance, past customer relations, and legal ramifications.

QUESTIONS

1. Discuss how a manufacturer can build customer loyalty among his dealers and distributors.

2. Discuss the sometimes incompatibility between the idea of a symbiotic relationship and negotiating skills.

3. What should be the sales force's role in developing push?

4. Discuss the pros and cons of screening customers.

5. Why would any manufacturer want exclusive distribution, thereby severely limiting the number of outlets carrying his products?

6. "Good customer service doesn't do you much good, but poor customer service can kill you." Evaluate this statement.

7. "We can readily determine the extent of customer satisfaction by looking at our sales and profits. If they are up and healthy, how can our customers be anything but satisfied?" Evaluate this statement.

8. Design as specifically as you can a customer relations program for a firm that previously has ignored this. (Make assumptions, if needed, but state them fully.)

9. How would you determine the payoff for the effectiveness of your customer relations program?

10. Why do firms have statistical quality control rather than complete quality control? What arguments can you raise for having complete quality control?

11. How would you design a survey to determine customer attitudes toward your company? (You may want to differentiate between industrial and consumer goods manufacturers.)

PEOPLE PROBLEM: COPING WITH DEFECTIVE QUALITY CONTROL

Please evaluate each alternative.

As sales manager you are continually in conflict with the production manager over quality control. You are concerned with the number of customer complaints of defective products. This is not the first time that you have expressed concern to the production manager about the need for tighter quality control. His argument has always involved cost; improved quality control would knock costs out of line. What action, if any, do you think you should take?

1. Complain to the vice president of manufacturing.

2. Instruct your salespeople to give priority to customer complaints.

3. Before taking any further action, document the extent and seriousness of customer complaints and the success rate in reconciling them to the customers' satisfaction.

4. Complain to your boss, the vice president of sales, that your job is being undermined.

5. Talk in a conciliatory manner with the production manager and see if some compromise can be made.

PEOPLE PROBLEM: DEALING WITH AN UNJUSTI-FIED CUSTOMER COMPLAINT

Please evaluate each alternative.

A medium-sized customer is demanding that you replace a damaged part on a machine purchased from you 4 months before. On investigation your technical people report that the damage was due solely to customer negligence. Correcting the difficulty would cost at least $70,000. What should you do?

1. Point out that the damage was due to the customer's negligence and that your firm has no obligation to honor the claim.

2. Replace the damaged part, but point out that you are doing this reluctantly and should not be doing it.

3. Replace the damaged part without quibbling, and then send in your technical people to thoroughly instruct the customer's staff in correct maintenance.

4. Replace the damaged part after obtaining agreement from the customer that each of you will pay half the cost, a big concession on your part because the fault was not yours.

5. Do not honor the claim unless your investigation shows that other customers have experienced similar difficulty in correct maintenance of this type of machine.

NOTES

1. For example, Ian Morley and Geoffrey Stephenson, *The Social Psychology of Bargaining* (London: George Allen & Unwin Ltd., 1977); John Dennis McDonald, *The Game of Business* (New York: Doubleday & Co., 1975); Howard Raiffa, *The Art and Science of Negotiation* (Cambridge, Mass.: Harvard University Press, 1982); Chester L. Karrass, *The Negotiating Game* (Cleveland: World Publishing Co., 1970).

2. For example, Roger Fisher and William Ury, *Getting to Yes: Negotiation Agreement Without Giving In* (Boston: Houghton Mifflin Co., 1981); Herb Cohen, *You Can Negotiate Anything* (New York: Bantam Books, 1980); Samuel H. Bacharach and Edward J. Lawler, *Bargaining: Power, Tactics, and Outcome* (San Francisco: Jossey-Bass, 1981).

3. From a list of many tactics prepared by Professor Donald W. Hendon, University of Hawaii, in seminars, "How to Negotiate and Win."

4. Alfred R. Oxenfeldt, *Executive Action in Marketing* (Belmont, Calif.: Wadsworth, 1966), 604.

5. John F. Magee, "The Logistics of Distribution," *Harvard Business Review* (July–August 1960): 92.

6. Ronald G. Shafer, "Buckpassing Blues," *Wall Street Journal,* 3 Nov. 1969.

7. Oxenfeldt, *Executive Action,* 628–641.

cases

15.1 Dealing with Carelessness in Handling a Customer's Order

Lately you have noticed a marked decline in your firm's quality control standards. Defective goods increasingly are called to your attention by irate customers. Although you and your salespeople have tried to be very responsive in promptly handling adjustments, customer dissatisfactions are rising, and sales to some accounts have dropped drastically.

The situation came to a head last Friday, and it concerned not a defective product but simple carelessness in filling an order. The Smithview Company, one of the oldest regular customers in your district, had called in a rush order for spare parts the day before. One of their key machines was down until the parts could be installed. Recognizing the urgency of the situation and the needs of an esteemed customer, you and your salesperson in that territory managed to expedite the order so that with special handling the parts reached the customer the next day, Friday. You breathed a sigh of relief, until the phone call from Smithview came just as you were leaving the office for the weekend.

"The parts you sent us are all wrong! You people goofed again! Now even if you get the correct parts to us by Monday, we'll be out $10,000 of business. I think we've had about enough of this inefficiency from you people."

QUESTION

What would you do in this situation?

15.2 Developing a Customer-Relations Strategy

John Torrentino was filled with doubt. He was pressured by top management to improve customer service, and John and the other sales managers had received numerous memos dictating how, specifically, to accomplish this. The latest directive's preamble follows:

> We are determined that our company will stand at the very top in the minds of our customers in the way of service and customer satisfaction. This is how we intend to differentiate our company from competitors who, we must admit, offer products similar to ours in quality and price. Our forte from now on is to provide superlative service, second to none. Each and every sales manager is responsible for ensuring that this philosophy permeates your sales organization. No exceptions will be tolerated.

The problem was that the salespeople were paid on straight commission, and the only individuals whom the personnel department would hire were uniformly aggressive and hard sellers. Although they paid lip service to the idea of customer service, John knew that their primary motivation was financial, making a buck as quickly as possible.

QUESTION

Design a program or a strategy for John Torrentino to implement a positive customer relations philosophy in his sales organization. Consider both short-term and long-term approaches.

15.3 Jessup Supply Company: Minimizing Unreliable Deliveries

Marge Jankowski, sales manager of Jessup Supply Company, had a serious headache. One of her oldest customers had just called in an irate mood, threatening to terminate all relations with Jessup. The problem was not the sales department's doing; the customer had admitted that. But the blame for a loss of business would still be her's, Marge reflected. "How in the world am I to get such problems and messes straightened out?" she sighed.

Jessup Supply Company was a distributor of engine parts, primarily for trucks. It covered a six-state area in the southeastern United States. Headquarters were in Atlanta, and there were two other distribution points or field warehouses, one in Jacksonville, Florida, and the other in Mobile, Alabama. Jessup distributed to parts dealers and large trucking companies. Fast and dependable delivery was essential; otherwise, a customer's trucks could be inoperative until parts were finally obtained. Marge had tried to convey the importance of prompt and reliable deliveries to her superiors, but they only seemed interested in minimizing costs and maximizing profits. Marge tried to point out that profits would not be maximized for long if customers were dissatisfied because of slow deliveries or because of out-of-stocks in the field warehouses and the central distribution point in Atlanta. But so far her complaints and warnings had been essentially disregarded.

"We understand your concern," management told Marge. "But it just wouldn't pay us to keep a heavier stock of some of these items in our warehouses. We must consider the investment in inventory, you know."

"Well, if a major account is lost, maybe then they'll wise up to the situation," Marge thought.

One major customer was a trucking firm operating out of Birmingham, Alabama. According to the maintenance schedule, a half-dozen trucks had been taken off the road for an overhaul. The customer needed parts and dutifully sent the order to the Mobile warehouse. Mobile had been out-of-stock for several of the key parts needed; it had routinely filled the customer's order for available items and sent them out, backordering the missing parts. When a field warehouse was out-of-stock the Atlanta distribution point customarily was notified immediately. The backordered items usually could be sent directly to the customer from Atlanta, sometimes arriving at the customer's premises a day or so after the original order had been received. Next-day or 2-day-later delivery of backordered items was usually acceptable to customers. Although some grumbled to Marge's salespeople, most recognized that no warehouse could maintain a 100-percent in-stock situation for thousands of items. But more serious delays often occurred.

Sometimes the field warehouse was slow to notify Atlanta of out-of-stocks; sometimes it did not notify them, through carelessness. And sometimes Atlanta was also out of the particular items and would not have them until another shipment was received from a manufacturer, which might take a week or even more. All of these delays and mix-ups occurred without the sales department's knowledge—that is, until customers complained about the unreliable deliveries. An increasing amount of the sales representatives' time was involved with tracking down backorders and unfilled customer needs.

"Part of the trouble is that in sales we have no control and no communication with the warehousing and order-filling departments. I blame poor supervision in this part of the operation at least as much as keeping warehouse stocks too lean," Marge confided to Lois Brinkman, director of personnel.

Lois admitted that hiring practices for some of the warehouse staff and order clerks had not been satisfactory. "This last year, Marge, has seen a tight labor market, both in Mobile and Jacksonville. A few years ago we probably wouldn't have hired some of the people we've been forced to take. So I'm afraid this could well lead to the carelessness and lack of concern that you're talking about."

"But do our customers have to bear the brunt of our own physical distribution inefficiencies?" Marge then asked.

1. What, if anything, can Marge do about a situation that is becoming almost intolerable from the standpoint of the sales department and its customer relations?
2. Can you justify the top management's thinking regarding inventory levels at the warehouses?
3. How can the sales department's relations with physical distribution operations be improved?

15.4 Valcor, Inc.: Improving Customer Service

"Steve, the situation is just intolerable," Jennifer Reed, stereo buyer for the Emporium Stores, said. "It seems that customers return every other one of your components because of defects. What on earth is wrong with your manufacturing and quality control?"

Steve Wellman nodded sympathetically. This was not the first complaint he had heard in the last 6 weeks. The problem was that demand for stereo components that his employer, Valcor, manufactured was increasing by leaps and bounds. "The only explanation I can give, is that demand has been so heavy that we must not be using enough care on the assembly. I'll certainly carry your comments and problems back to my boss and see if we can improve the situation shortly. I'm so very sorry to cause you and your customers all this inconvenience."

Jennifer nodded sadly. "I know you're not to blame, Steve. And your company has had good products in the past. So I'll continue to do business with you for a while longer. But I hope you get this mess straightened out soon." She frowned at Steve. "Meanwhile, what are you going to do about all the defectives I have in the back room?"

"Of course, we'll take them back. Just have your stockroom people box them up, note the quantity and style numbers of the items you are sending back, and describe the problem. You do have that information, don't you?"

"I'm not sure we have that in all cases, but I'll see what we can do." Steve got up to leave. Hurriedly, Jennifer concluded: "You realize that having to send back all these defectives is a real pain. My people are busy, the stockroom people are busy, and we have to put other things aside to send these back. Otherwise, we're stuck here with money tied up in unsalable inventories. Steve, express my real displeasure about this situation to your manage-

ment and tell them that you've got to get it straightened out quickly or you've lost a customer."

All Steve could do was to apologize again for the company and ensure the customer that he would convey her complaints to his management. Looking over his past sales records that night, he noted that Jennifer Reed and the Emporium Stores had been good customers. They had placed orders amounting to more than $155,000 in the last year. If there was anything he could do, he must prevent the loss of this customer.

Steve called his sales manager in Louisville, Kentucky, the next morning, explained what had taken place in the Emporium offices, and expressed his fears that a major customer might be lost. Later in the day he received an urgent message from his sales manager asking him to fly to Chicago the next day. At company headquarters they would talk with the general sales manager, Patricia Monahan, and the production vice president, Al Russo.

At the headquarters meeting Steve was a little nonplussed to see a half-dozen other executives and staff people also in attendance. He was asked to report on his experiences at Emporium Stores and elsewhere in the last several months, during which a big increase in customer complaints had been encountered.

Al Russo, the production man, then explained the quality problems that were being encountered. "We are having serious problems in getting sufficient, trained production workers to handle the increase in demand. As you know we had a 2-month strike last year. We lost about 25 percent of our experienced people during that time. We have had to replace them as well as add other workers, and they are just not as good yet as they should be."

"When is this situation going to improve?" asked the executive vice president.

"I'm afraid it will be 4 to 6 months before we can be assured that output will be up to past standards of excellence and free from defects. It takes time before these new people can be brought up to a sufficient level of capability." Al paused and surveyed the group. "The only alternative, as I see it, is to cut production back drastically, operate with only our experienced and proven capable people, and gradually expand production as we have well-trained workers ready to step in."

Patricia Monahan, the general sales manager, cautioned, "If we cancel all the outstanding orders and refuse to accept others, or if we take them on allotment, we're simply inviting competitors to take over our business. The long-term effects . . . we may never regain the lost ground."

"What other alternatives do we have?" the executive vice president boomed.

Patricia broke the silence. "There are two things we can do. They may be stopgap measures, but they may keep us from losing business to competitors." She hesitated, then continued. "First, we need to beef up our quality control, try to catch more of the obvious defects before our customers do."

Several people, including Al and his quality control man, interrupted. But Patricia continued,

"Please let me finish. I realize that quality control is not likely to catch all the defects unless we're willing to spend a lot more for it than we really can afford to. So, what I'm saying is, let's tighten up where we can, but accept the situation that there still will be a lot of defects going out into the stores. Now, what can we do about this situation to avoid losing our reputation and our customers because of poor quality? I think we have one feasible alternative. Our customer service can be improved to be the best in the industry! We can bend over backward to accommodate our customers who have problems. We can make it easy for them to get refunds or replacement goods. We can do everything in our power to assure that they will not be inconvenienced, that they will not be put out, will not have to commit their time and effort to handling problems that are our fault."

Patricia paused again. Steve noted a number of people nodding their heads affirmatively. Then Patricia resumed, "I believe that our sales force can be the key to excellence in customer service. If you all agree with me, I will ask my sales managers and some senior and capable salespeople, such as Steve Wellman here, to develop specific proposals and recommendations to build excellence in customer service."

QUESTIONS

1. Do you think Patricia's ideas should be approved? Why or why not?

2. What specifics can you come up with for implementing Patricia's general plan? Combine these to develop a service strategy for the Valcor Company.

3. Do you really think excellent customer service can compensate for poor quality and defective products?

PART V
CONTROLLING SALES EFFORTS

CHAPTER 16
Controlling Through Analyzing Overall Sales Performance

CHAPTER 17
Controlling Through Analyzing Marketing Costs and by the Marketing Audit

CHAPTER 18
Controlling Through Evaluating Individual Performance

CHAPTER 19
Handling Legal and Ethical Considerations

CHAPTER 16
Controlling Through Analyzing Overall Sales Performance

CHAPTER PERSPECTIVE

As you recall, the management functions are planning, organizing and staffing, directing, and controlling. Controlling is the vital final step in the sequence of managerial activities. Its purpose is to ensure that performance conforms to plans.

Controlling implies evaluating performance. It provides feedback on how well a task is being done. Without this feedback, a manager cannot judge whether improvement is possible, where it should occur, how much is needed, and how quickly it must be accomplished. A vital part of controlling is to detect emerging problems before they become too serious for corrective action. The control or measurement tools that provide the feedback must furnish relevant information promptly or their usefulness is seriously jeopardized. For example if a particular sales territory encounters difficulty in

meeting sales goals (which may be due to the sales representative's "letting down" or, more likely, competitive changes), feedback must be prompt.

Chapters 16 and 17 examine important tools for evaluating overall sales performance that help higher management to monitor field performance. The sales manager also has a major stake in this and in particular is vitally concerned with her district's performance relative to the other sales districts. Chapter 18 discusses measures of performance for the individual salesperson that are important in enabling the field sales manager to appraise the sales force's performance.

As you read Chapter 16, consider whether the size of each salesperson's commission check would be a sufficient indicator of sales performance, obviating a sales analysis.

CHAPTER OBJECTIVES

□ Understand the steps involved in the process of controlling and the necessary conditions for effective control.

□ Become aware of situations—marketing mistakes—where better controls would have helped detect emerging problems or opportunities before they became serious or were pounced on by competitors.

□ Know the four major tools used to evaluate overall marketing performance.

□ Become thoroughly familiar with the sales analysis and the associated iceberg principle.

□ Become aware of the problems involved in analyzing sales.

□ Understand the market share analysis, the implications, and the sources of market share data.

□ Understand the cautions in relying on market share data.

NATURE OF CONTROL

Three steps are involved in the process of controlling:

1. Sales performance standards or planned operating results must be established.
2. Actual performance must be compared with planned.
3. Where variations occur, either corrective action or revision of plans is indicated.

The control function clearly is intimately related to planning and budgeting. However, for control to be effective, two conditions should be met. (1) Control standards should be tied to individual responsibility. (2) Strategic control points should be established. In sales management control these two conditions usually present no particular problems.

Individual Responsibility

The designation of sales territories and sales districts and their assignation to individuals makes individual responsibility readily ascertainable. The *profit-center concept* is operative here, because each territory's and each salesperson's sales and contribution to overhead are identifiable and measurable, as are the performance statistics for the territories that comprise the districts.

Strategic Control Points

Measurable areas of performance that are important to the total operation are strategic control points. When these can be identified, deviations from planned expectations warrant close management attention to determine why exceptions are occurring and what corrective action should be taken. If all deviations were control points, management might be deluged with too much data to assimilate. Hence, only the more important exceptions must be considered control points. For example no sales manager can monitor all sales force activities. Territorial deviations from quota and planned sales, however, indicate that something is amiss and, if serious, may deserve further investigation into the causes and the possible solutions. Consequently, certain points in the operation, or composite figures, must suffice for control purposes. If control points are either not established or are ill defined, the manager must stipulate and closely monitor those key operational areas that she considers most representative of general activity.

Management by Exception

For busy executives, whether high-level or field sales managers, a surfeit of daily problems, correspondence, and reports is the rule. Executives are better

444

off receiving reports on performance or operational results only when exceptions or deviations occur. They can then assume that unless they receive a report, matters are proceeding on schedule and as planned. An exception requiring notification of sales executives might be a significant drop in a product's sales in one territory to a particular customer. More positive exceptions from plan might be unusually large orders from a certain customer or for a specific product, unusually numerous backlog orders, or an unusual number of new customers.

To effectively compare actual with planned performance so that corrective action can be taken, performance reports must be prompt. To discover at the end of March that sales in a particular category fell well under plan in February may make it difficult both to identify the real source of the trouble and to take corrective action in time.

Personnel Implications of Control

Not all managers and employees welcome performance standards and control points. Control most often deals with mistakes, because most deviations occur in not achieving expectations and plans. Failures tend to result in someone's being blamed, and excuses and buck-passing may be fostered. Controls are better accepted and less destructive to morale when the objective is clear. The objective is not to fix blame or find criticisms but rather to find solutions to problems or changing situations. The salesperson and the sales manager, however, cannot escape accountability for results in their areas of responsibility. Capable and ambitious people welcome visible accountability, because superior performance is readily evident and often quickly rewarded. But the salesperson or manager cannot always be blamed or praised for deviations from plan, because exogenous factors may be major contributors. For example a new or more aggressive competitor, or energy shortages that may force customers into curtailments, or other major shifts in market patterns may affect results far more than individual performance, whether exceptional or mediocre.

Marketing Mistakes: Would Better Controls Have Helped?

Marketing mistakes are probably inevitable, given the state of marketing knowledge and the dynamic environment in which uncontrollable and sometimes unpredictable factors are often introduced. Multifaceted competition, both intra- and inter-industry, increasingly add to marketing worries (and challenges). Foreign firms, as you know, also have invaded the domestic market and have carved surprising niches with a variety of products—from motorcycles and automobiles to electronic equipment and steel. Even firms entrenched in stable industries are vulnerable to innovative competition.

Mistakes fall into two categories: (1) *mistakes of commission,* in which wrong decisions were made and/or bad actions taken, and (2) *mistakes of omission,* in which no action was taken and the status quo was contentedly embraced amid a changing environment. Alert and aggressive management is characterized by certain actions or reactions to mistakes. Three stages can be identified for most effectively reacting to mistakes. (1) Looming problems or present mistakes and their causes should be quickly recognized. (2) Corrective action should be taken quickly; sometimes this action may require ruthlessly axing the product or the promotional approach. (3) Mistakes should be treated as learning experiences; mistakes should not be repeated; and the total operation should be improved as a result.

When a long-established company finds itself in a deteriorating situation for a number of years, and the response is late in coming and ill conceived, criticism is in order. Controls were either inadequate or ignored; marketing evaluation was superficial or biased; actions were finally taken without careful diagnosis of the problems and the causes. Sometimes a company permits itself to bask in the luxury of complacency a little too long. Reactions and adjustments may then come quickly, although not before substantial competitive inroads are made. A classic example of complacency is that of the Gillette Company in the early 1960s. It withheld its introduction of the stainless steel razor blade because it thought this could cannibalize (i.e., take business away from) its own very profitable Super Blue Blade. Competitors did not miss the opportunity to get the jump on Gillette. They rushed their own stainless steel blades to market and took market share from Gillette that was never fully regained.

More recently, the mighty Procter & Gamble took its time in testing refastenable tabs on Pampers diapers. Kimberly-Clark rushed to introduce its refastenable Huggies brand, and quickly captured a large market share.

The balance of this chapter and the next two chapters explore using the various analytical tools available to sales managers to detect emerging problems and opportunities before they become serious or captured by competitors, and how sales managers can focus on operational aspects that most need corrective action.

MEASURES OF OVERALL MARKETING PERFORMANCE

Four major tools are used to evaluate overall marketing performance: (1) sales analysis, (2) market share analysis, (3) marketing cost analysis, and (4) the marketing audit. Figure 16.1 depicts these tools and their major data sources. These tools are examined in greater detail later in this chapter and in Chapter 17.

In evaluating sales and marketing performance, a key point that you should recognize is that these tools should be used on a current and continuing

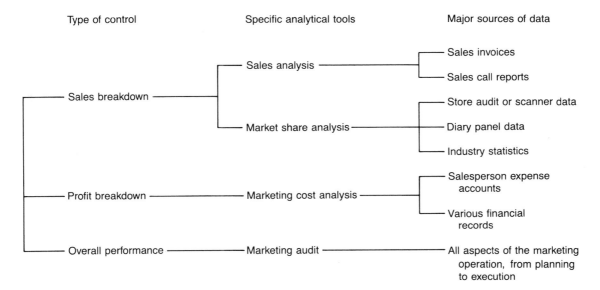

FIGURE 16.1 Types of overall marketing performance controls.

basis to provide feedback on business activities and early warnings of worsening situations. A one-time analysis, perhaps of sales and market share coverage in various territories, may do almost more harm than good. Without comparative figures for determining if performance is improving or worsening, problem areas may go undetected and fears may be allayed. Consequently, many firms make sales and market share analyses monthly or at least quarterly. In today's competitive milieu, conditions can change very quickly. Unless a firm's sensors (its feedback sources on performance) are tuned to provide prompt and continuing information, competitive inroads or changing customer requirements or such insidious problems as deteriorating quality control or delivery scheduling could go undetected for too long.

SALES ANALYSIS

Almost every company has wide variations in sales performances between territories, products, salespeople, and customers, as well as certain other inputs in conducting the business. These differences tend to balance each other out or are disguised in analyses of gross sales performance and/or gross market share performance. This phenomenon of highs and lows of performance balancing out is commonly known as the *iceberg principle*, and a sales analysis or a detailed breakdown of sales is required to expose problem areas.

The Iceberg Principle

As everyone knows, most of the mass—and danger—of an iceberg is submerged beneath the surface. For a business enterprise most emerging problems are hidden when only gross sales figures are considered. For example a poor sales performance with one customer may be completely disguised or overlooked because of stronger sales than expected from other customers. The imminent danger is that one customer may be moving toward other suppliers for numerous reasons, of which the following are most common:

□ Poor rapport with the salesperson (and is this symptomatic of poor rapport with other customers?)

□ Worsening quality control (and is this likely in the near future to result in other customers' also switching to competitors?)

□ A noncompetitive price (and if this is true in one market, is it not also likely to become the situation in other markets?)

□ Certain customers' increasing vulnerability to competition (and should the company consider changing its channel of distribution to include more aggressive dealers, even if some old customers must be antagonized or even lost in so doing?)

Consequently, by identifying deeper likely problems, the iceberg principle can raise a number of alternatives for management consideration. But without the detailed sales analysis, the hidden performance aspects may not be studied soon enough to pursue or at least consider the more advantageous courses of action.

Now complete Exercise 16.1.

EXERCISE 16.1

1. If a noncompetitive price is found to be the root cause of diminished performance in one market area, should prices be reduced only in that area (resulting in nonuniform pricing practices), or should this be done throughout the company?

2. Are there any drawbacks to management preoccupation with poorly performing territories, products, and customers?

Sales Breakdowns

The sales manager faces an important decision regarding the detail required for sales breakdowns to provide adequate information for evaluating various performance aspects. The more common subdivisions for reporting and analyzing sales follow:

1. Geographical regions—states, cities, or sales territories

2. Salespeople if each representative does not have a separate territory; otherwise, analyze territories

3. Customers—size, type or class of trade, and perhaps key or major customers
4. Products—dollars and/or physical units for various sizes, colors, styles, or categories

Additional information may sometimes be desired, such as analysis by sale methods (i.e., mail order, telephone, or direct sale), order size, sale terms, and date sold. The type and extent of data gathered should be tailored to the firm's needs and any perceived problem areas. The following focuses on the three most common bases for analysis: geographical area, customers, and products. Also briefly considered are circumstances when other bases might be preferred, such as sale method.

Analysis by Geographical Area

A firm can analyze its sales performance geographically using several approaches. If a quota system has been developed for each salesperson and each territory, this is simply extended to quotas for each sales district and region. Then any deviations of sales from quotas can provide important feedback for further analysis and possible corrective action. Of course, the assumption is that the quotas accurately reflect the sales potential in the various geographical areas.

Deviations of sales from quota.   Table 16.1 shows the sales performance for a home furnishings manufacturer for the last 6 months of 1988. Obviously, the Knoxville district had serious difficulties. In fact the difficulties were more serious than first indicated by the under-quota attainment of the southern region. The entire region was $120,000 under plan, whereas the Knoxville district was $220,000 under. After obtaining these results, the sales manager called for a closer investigation of the Knoxville district, and Table 16.2 shows the deviations from quotas of the four territories comprising the Knoxville district. This further analysis showed only one trouble spot, but a serious one, more serious than the 99.3 percent of quota attained by the southern region

TABLE 16.1   Sales performance, southern region, July to December 1988.

Region	Sales ($ Hundreds)			Actual as a Percentage of Quota
	Quota	Actual	Difference	
Atlanta	5,300	5,380	+ 80	101.5
Richmond	4,600	4,650	+ 50	101.1
New Orleans	3,900	3,870	− 30	99.2
Knoxville	3,800	3,580	− 220	94.2
Total southern region	17,600	17,480	− 120	99.3

TABLE 16.2   Sales performance, Knoxville territories, July to December 1988.

Territories	Sales ($ Hundreds) Quota	Actual	Difference	Actual as a Percentage of Quota
A	900	940	+ 40	104.4
B	1,100	1,110	+ 10	100.9
C	1,000	740	− 260	74.0
D	800	790	− 10	98.8
Total Knoxville district	3,800	3,580	− 220	94.2

and the 94.2 percent of quota achieved in the Knoxville district would have led one to suspect. Territory C was a whopping $260,000 under quota, having reached only 74 percent of its quota for the period. The more detailed analysis of sales does not explain why sales results were under plan, but it does identify the problem area. A sales manager would want to quickly investigate further to ascertain the causes. This not-unusual situation illustrates the iceberg principle and shows how gross figures may not indicate more serious problems.

Complete Exercise 16.2.

EXERCISE 16.2

1. What are possible explanations for territory C's performance in Table 16.2?
2. What would you do as sales manager?

Deviation of sales from a specific index of sales potential.   When a quota system has not been developed (or when it is felt that quotas do not accurately reflect sales potentials), then some other determination of sales potentials must be developed. (It might be helpful to review Chapter 5 on measuring market potential at this point.)

As an example of developing a sales potential index, a statistical study of market factors affecting the sales of a Chicago-based men's apparel manufacturer found that an index consisting of population (weighted .333) and effective buying income (weighted .667) had a correlation coefficient of .92, a rather high relationship, when compared to sales over the preceding 5 years.[1] Company sales for the past year follow:

Illinois	$11,040,000
Indiana	$ 2,780,000
Iowa	$ 2,120,000
Missouri	$ 4,060,000
Total	$20,000,000

Tables 16.3 and 16.4 show the analysis of the sales performance.

TABLE 16.3 Determination of composite index of sales potential.

	Population (Hundreds)	Percentage of Four-State Total	Effective Buying Income ($ Hundreds)	Percentage of Four-State Total	Index of Potential
Illinois	11,084	46.8	40,342,360	51.3	49.8
Indiana	5,138	21.5	16,047,793	20.5	20.8
Iowa	2,814	11.8	8,523,775	10.3	10.8
Missouri	4,642	19.9	13,677,773	17.9	18.6
Total	23,678	100.0	78,591,701	100.0	100.0

Note: Calculation of weighted index, with population weighted .333 and income weighted .667:
  .333(46.8) + .667(51.3) = 49.8 for Illinois
  .333(21.5) + .667(20.5) = 20.8 for Indiana
  .333(11.8) + .667(10.3) = 10.8 for Iowa
  .333(19.9) + .667(17.9) = 18.6 for Missouri

Source: Sales & Marketing Management's Survey of Buying Power.

TABLE 16.4 Deviations of sales performance from potential.

	Index of Potential	Sales ($ Hundreds) Actual	Sales ($ Hundreds) Par	Sales ($ Hundreds) Difference	Actual as a Percentage of Par
Illinois	49.8	11,040	9,960	+ 1,080	110.8
Indiana	20.8	2,780	4,160	− 1,380	66.8
Iowa	10.8	2,120	2,160	− 40	98.1
Missouri	18.6	4,060	3,720	+ 340	109.1
Total		20,000	20,000		

Note: Par is computed by multiplying total sales achieved, $20 million, by the index of potential for each state.

Now complete Exercise 16.3.

---

1. What interpretation and action does the preceding analysis suggest?
2. Are there other factors that might be related to this company's sales?
3. If population were weighted .75 and effective buying income only .25, how would this effect performance efficiency?

**EXERCISE
16.3**

Analysis by Salesperson and by Method of Sale

Analyzing sales by territories in most firms essentially is synonymous with analyzing by salesperson, because usually only one sales representative is assigned to a territory. This can vary, of course, if one or more apprentice salespeople are helping in a territory or if a salesperson is introducing a successor to a particular territory.

Occasionally, analyzing sales by mail order, telephone, and direct sale may be preferred. As Chapter 17 shows, a firm may find that the economics of direct contacts are impractical for many of its smaller customers, and rather than lose such accounts, it will attempt to convert them to telephone or mail order sales. Analyzing sales in this way may indicate the effectiveness of sale methods, reveal emerging problems that may require strategy reevaluations, or illustrate the need for increased emphasis on the more economically efficient sale methods.

For example if a firm finds that mail order and telephone order sales have decreased from 24 to 19 percent of its total business within 1 year, it should institute greater incentives for customers to use these indirect order-placement methods. The decrease may also suggest that the sales force should be strongly encouraged to make greater use of the telephone. A firm may find, however, that although its indirect sales methods are rising relative to direct sales efforts, the total sales volume is decreasing in some territories. This suggests that drastic action may be needed (perhaps a reversal of the policy to push indirect sales methods) unless profitability constraints preclude using direct selling methods with many smaller accounts.

Analysis by Customers

Sales also can be analyzed by customers and products to uncover performance deviations. Returning to territory C of the Knoxville district shown in Table 16.2 and analyzing this weak territory more extensively, shows that both a customer and a product analysis seem warranted to clarify the problem, its causes, and possible solutions. Table 16.5 shows an analysis of sales performance by customers.

Table 16.5 shows a marked change in the mix of customer business over the previous years, on which the sales quota was primarily based. In

TABLE 16.5 Sales performance by customer, territory C of Knoxville district, July to December 1988.

Customer	Sales ($ Hundreds)			Actual as a Percentage of Quota
	Quota	Actual	Difference	
Department store A	150	40	− 110	26.6
Department store B	100	30	− 70	30.0
Discount store A	200	230	+ 30	115.0
Catalog showroom A	150	180	+ 30	120.0
Wholesaler A	100	80	− 20	80.0
Independent retailers	300	180	− 120	60.0
Total	1,000	740	− 260	74.0

TABLE 16.6 Sales performance by product, territory C of Knoxville district, July to December 1988.

Product	Sales ($ Hundreds)			Actual as a Percentage of Quota
	Quota	Actual	Difference	
Regular blankets	300	280	− 20	93.3
Electric blankets	100	140	+ 40	140.0
Tailored bedspreads	150	70	− 80	46.7
Heirloom bedspreads	100	50	− 50	50.0
Regular towel ensembles	200	180	− 20	90.0
Higher-priced towel ensembles	150	20	− 130	13.3
Total	1,000	740	− 260	74.0

territory C, the more traditional retailers (the two department stores, the wholesaler, and the smaller independents) have cut their orders drastically from the expected level. The two discount firms, however, have increased their purchases substantially over that expected, but by no means enough to compensate for the loss of the other business.

Analysis by Products

Table 16.6 shows a further examination of the effect on product sales by the shift of customers in territory C. The only product category showing an increase in sales over quota was electric blankets (further investigation revealed that these had been used as a loss leader by discount stores during the period, with severe price cutting). The higher-priced and higher-profit categories in the line (particularly the bedspreads and the higher-priced towel ensembles) had taken a severe beating, reflecting the decrease in business with the department stores and the small independent retailers.

These examples demonstrate that serious problems may be disguised or hidden under global sales figures, with strengths in certain areas covering up weaknesses in others. Only sales analysis using more detailed breakdowns will reveal hidden problems so that corrective action can be taken before the situation becomes too serious.

Now do Exercise 16.4.

1. As sales manager, what would you do now regarding territory C? What further investigations would you make? What action would you take?
2. Do you think the problem uncovered in territory C indicates similar problems in other territories?

EXERCISE 16.4

Problems Involved in Analyzing Sales

To perform sales analyses like those previously described, accounting records must be designed to yield more than simply gross sales and sales returns and allowances. A system must be established to collect and group sales into the various desired categories, such as sales by territories and other geographical units, customers, products, and so on. With today's electronic data-processing equipment, data gathering is less formidable than in the past. But special arrangements usually must be made to process this information from sales invoices and other sources; otherwise, it tends to be buried in files after the normal accounting and billing are performed. A caveat is suggested, however: The data gathered and analyzed are worthless unless they are used. Busy executives may disregard overabundant sales reports and analyses unless provision is made to flag significant deviations from plans or quotas or other standards.

Although informative, sales analysis alone usually is not sufficient as a measure of sales and marketing performance. Two important considerations needed for an evaluation are missing. (1) How does the company's performance compare with that of competitors? Is it improving or worsening? (2) What is the sales performance profitability? Should the firm change product or customer emphasis to produce more profitable sales? As an example of the profitability issue, one product may show healthy sales increases. Perhaps the increases are due to strong customer approval, which can generate contagious enthusiasm among the sales force. Or the item may experience widespread popularity because it is a real ''value'': the manufacturer's profit on it may be far less than on other items in the line that are being neglected. The answer to the first of these questions, regarding performance compared with the competition, is found in market share analysis, which is discussed in more detail in the balance of this chapter. The second consideration, profitability, involves a distribution or marketing cost analysis and is described in Chapter 17.

MARKET SHARE ANALYSIS

A sales analysis alone has a significant deficiency, because it does not indicate how the firm and its products are faring vis-à-vis competition. The desire to surpass the competition is a common human tendency whether in sports or in business. A measurement of performance relative to competitors encourages this urge and can be a highly motivating device for management and salespeople alike. Furthermore, market share performance should be a key indicator on how well a firm is doing and is of particular value in spotting emerging problems. Market share data usually avoid the contaminating effects of noncontrollable exogenous factors. For example declining sales over the preceding year with a constant or improving market share suggests that the firm is doing a good job; and although certain factors adversely affected the industry for that particular period, weakness in the company's selling efforts cannot be blamed.

Changes in market share from preceding periods, especially when these changes show a worsening competitive position, should induce strenuous efforts to ascertain the cause and take corrective actions. To disregard or treat these events lightly may even jeopardize the firm's viability. Differences in market share among different sales territories and districts also deserve follow-up efforts to determine the cause. Where does the fault lie? Is it in the district sales manager, the sales force, or conditions that the firm can control? Or is the erratic market share performance due to exogenous (probably competitive) factors over which the firm has little or no control? Market share changes are not always the firm's fault and may not necessarily reflect operational inadequacies.

An Example of Market Share Disparities

Table 16.7 shows an example of market share differences in various markets. Notice that Boston and Detroit show a particularly poor relative performance, falling far behind the company's national 15-percent market share average. New York and St. Louis, although not as bad as Boston and Detroit, still are considerably under the company average. Cleveland and Kansas City, however, are star producers. This erratic market share performance in the various districts should certainly be investigated to ascertain why and what, if anything, can be done to bring the weak areas up to the company average. Furthermore, the strengths in Cleveland and Kansas City also deserve further evaluation to determine if successful practices there can be applied to other areas.

TABLE 16.7 Industry sales and ABC Company sales by ABC sales districts ($ millions).

District	Total Industry Sales	ABC Sales	ABC's Percentage of Market
Boston	68	5	7.4
New York	66	8	12.1
Chicago	62	12	19.4
Detroit	53	4	7.5
Philadelphia	48	8	16.7
St. Louis	39	4	10.3
Cleveland	36	12	33.3
Kansas City	32	8	25.0
Total	404	61	15.1

TABLE 16.8   Trend in market share by ABC Company sales districts, 1980 to 1988.

	ABC Company Percentage of Market Share		
District	*1980*	*1985*	*1988*
Boston	10.1	8.7	7.4
New York	11.6	12.2	12.1
Chicago	12.0	16.9	19.4
Detroit	9.1	8.4	7.5
Philadelphia	14.1	16.8	16.7
St. Louis	11.3	11.1	10.3
Cleveland	27.5	30.0	33.3
Kansas City	26.0	24.7	25.0
Total	14.8	15.2	15.1

Absent from Table 16.7 and from this market share analysis is the trend in market share. These data are vital to an in-depth analysis of the competitive situation and the performance evaluation. Table 16.8 supplies the missing trend data for the years 1980 to 1988. Table 16.8 shows that although total market share has remained fairly constant during these 8 years, the various sales districts have been notably inconsistent. Some have lost significant market share, while others (notably Cleveland and Chicago) made major gains, and still others showed little change.

Now perform Exercise 16.5.

EXERCISE 16.5

1. As a new general manager (hired after a successful stint with another firm), what would you do after receiving the data in Tables 16.7 and 16.8?
2. Would you accept the explanation that competition is much tougher in the Boston and Detroit markets? Why or why not?
3. What other information or statistics would you like to have before making a decision regarding possible corrective action?

Computing Market Share

Market share can be measured by (1) share of overall industry sales, (2) share relative to certain competitors (usually the top firm or several top firms in the industry), and (3) served-market share.

Overall market share.   Most often one thinks of market share as a company's sales as a percentage of total industry sales. Thus, if industry sales for a particular period are $350 million, and our company, Universal Products Company, has sales of $70 million, then the market share is the following:

$$\frac{\$70,000,000}{\$350,000,000} = 20\%$$

Sometimes rising sales can disguise problems. If in the next period Universal Products experiences sales of $80 million (supposedly a nice increase of over 14 percent), but industry sales rise to $440 million, the market share would indicate a worsening situation:

$$\frac{\$80,000,000}{\$440,000,000} = 14.3\%$$

Although calculating market share is relatively easy, industry sales must be obtained or accurately estimated. But in most industries this information is not difficult to obtain (sources of market share information will be examined shortly). Defining the total industry sometimes is more difficult then calculating market share, and management can misjudge it. The classic example of misjudged total industry market share involves Harley-Davidson, the motorcycle maker.

In the early 1960s Harley-Davidson dominated the U.S. motorcycle market. In 60 years this firm had destroyed all its U.S. competitors and controlled 70 percent of the market. Yet, almost inconceivably, in half a decade, Harley-Davidson's market share fell to 5 percent, and the total market expanded many times over what it had been for decades. Honda, an unknown Japanese firm, bearded the tiger, and won. Although one can severely criticize Harley-Davidson's complacency in its lack of aggressive reaction to the Honda threat, there was an additional explanation. Harley-Davidson defines its industry as standard-sized motorcycles, which it still dominated. It did not perceive that the motorcycle market was vastly changing, with the introduction of the lightweights by Honda and other foreign manufacturers.

More recently, Adidas misread the potential for running shoes in the United States, and allowed Nike, an upstart, to gain dominance. Still more recently, Nike passed the baton to Reebok, by failing to recognize other dimensions of the running and fitness market.

Relative market share to leading competitors. A firm may be particularly concerned with changes in its sales relative to those of its major competitor or competitors. For example if Universal Products Company has two major competitors whereas the rest of the industry is composed of small firms, it might compare its market share as follows:

	Sales
Universal	$70,000,000
Competitor A	$90,000,000
Competitor B	$60,000,000
Total	$200,000,000

Relative market share of Universal:

$$\frac{\$70,000,000}{\$200,000,000} = 35\%$$

Tracking sales as a percentage of the leading competitor's sales might be useful. The J. C. Penney Company long tracked its sales relative to Sears'. Table 16.9 shows the ebb and flow of J. C. Penney's performance from 1942 to 1974. You can readily see how J. C. Penney lost substantial ground after World War II, as its policies were far more conservative than the more aggressive Sears. By the late 1960s, under new management and a drastic overhaul of traditional merchandising policies, J. C. Penney began to recapture some lost ground, but by no means all that was lost.

Served market share.   The served market can be defined as the market that would be interested in the company's offerings and that can be reached by the company's marketing efforts.[2] A firm's served market share will always be larger than its share of the total industry sales and will reflect its dominance of the particular customer segments or sectors it is attempting to attract. For

TABLE 16.9   Relative market shares, J. C. Penney and Sears, 1942 to 1974.

Year	J. C. Penney ($ Hundreds)	Sears ($ Hundreds)	Market Share (Sales as a Percentage of Total Penney's and Sears' sales)	
			J. C. Penney	Sears
1942	490,295	915,058	35	65
1944	535,363	851,535	38	62
1946	676,570	1,045,259	39	61
1948	885,195	1,981,536	32	68
1950	949,712	2,168,928	31	69
1952	1,079,257	2,932,338	28	72
1954	1,107,157	2,981,925	27	73
1956	1,290,867	3,306,826	28	72
1958	1,409,973	3,600,882	28	72
1960	1,437,489	4,036,153	26	74
1962	1,553,503	4,267,678	27	73
1964	1,834,318	5,115,767	26	74
1966	2,289,209	6,390,000	26	74
1968	2,745,998	7,330,090	27	73
1970	3,756,092	8,862,971	30	70
1972	4,812,239	10,006,146	32	68
1974	6,243,677	12,306,229	33	67

Source: Adapted from respective annual reports.

example, Kohler seeks to attract the upscale consumer with its plumbing equipment. Its success in maintaining and enhancing its share of this higher-priced market is of more concern to it than its share of the total plumbing supply market, although it will still be interested in whether this part of the total market is showing growth.

Estimating served market share is usually more difficult than making comparisons of company sales against either total industry sales or sales of major competitors. However, estimates usually can be made that are sufficiently useful. Some marketing research may be required, and trade association and trade journal estimates also may be employed.

Sources of Market Share Data

To make market share analyses, external data must be obtained about sales of competing brands and firms in the various markets. Fortunately, external data are not difficult to obtain in most industries, although some costs may be involved. Trade associations or trade publications provide reasonably accurate sales figures for many industries. Although this information usually does not include brand breakdowns, marketers can determine their own share of the total market, as well as the trends. Government agencies provide data for other industries, such as automotive, liquor, and insurance, from compulsory reports (e.g., new car registrations), as well as from excise and other tax data.

For certain consumer goods manufacturers, several syndicated services measure competitive brand positions, a basis for projecting total market size, and other helpful statistics. The two major services are the A. C. Nielsen Company, which conducts store audits in grocery, drug, and certain other fields, and the Market Research Corporation of America (MRCA), which gathers information on expenditures through a panel of consumers maintaining a record of their purchases in diaries. Burgoyne Index, Ehrhart-Rabic Associates, and Store Audits also provide retail store audit services. Many companies are now provided consumer samples from National Family Opinion, the best known after MRCA. Speedata provides an intermediate step in measuring product flow by recording shipments of grocery products through one hundred major warehouses, servicing 31,404 retail outlets in twenty-two market areas. Figure 16.2 shows the point of data collection by the Nielsen, MRCA, and Speedata services:

FIGURE 16.2 Point of data collection.

TABLE 16.10   Information furnished by Nielsen and MRCA services.

Offered by Both

Total U.S. consumer sales by brand
Consumer sales by regions or districts
Sales by type of grocery and drug outlet
Sales by size of package

Offered by Nielsen	*Offered by MRCA*
Dealer mark up	Characteristics of families buying
Average order size by dealers	products and specific brands
Local advertising	Repeat buying
Shelf price	Rate of addition of new customers
Stock condition and inventory	Source of new customers ·
Store displays	Lost customers
	Frequency of purchase
	Volume moving at various price
	levels
	Volume accounted for by coupon
	redemptions

MRCA, Market Research Corporation of America

These services are expensive, frequently costing in the six figures annually, but some manufacturers subscribe to several because they furnish somewhat different information, as shown in Table 16.10.

These services can be faulted as being based on sampling outlets and consumers of questionable representativeness. They also are limited to consumer goods moving through grocery and drug stores. Despite some limitations, however, their use for several decades reflects their value in providing information badly needed in a competitive environment. Another major reason for using these services is the time lag between sale by the manufacturer and purchase by the consumer. Because the manufacturer does not sell directly to consumers, but rather through distributors and dealers, its current sales invoices may not reveal the latest information on consumer purchases. For example sales to wholesalers and retailers may merely indicate building up or replacing inventories due to past sales. With conditions changing rapidly, past sales may not adequately illustrate the present situation.

Cautions in Relying on Market Share Data

Although market share information is a valuable management tool, it should not be used as the primary or sole measure of marketing performance. Its major flaw is that it ignores profitability. An overcommitment to increasing market share can lead to rash sales growth at the expense of profits. However, some executives are motivated in this direction because their prestige depends on company size and growth relative to other firms in the industry. Heavy doses of advertising, or concern for short-term sales results at the expense of more satisfied customers and dealers, will undoubtedly increase market share. But a firm more concerned with profitable business, and with the necessary weeding out of unprofitable products and customers, may find market share declining while profits are rising.

Market share conclusions may need qualification by numerous considerations. Outside environmental forces, for example, may not affect all firms equally. Foreign competition on a low-price basis, will affect the higher-cost domestic producers more severely than those with more modern plants. If a new firm enters the industry, every existing firm likely will experience a decrease in market share. Such a decrease does not indicate the management is deficient but simply that more firms are now competing for the same market potential. A firm may deliberately sacrifice market share to improve profits. Unprofitable customers and products may be dropped, resulting in some loss of business but profit enhancement. And finally, market share may fluctuate, reflecting large sales made at the beginning or end of the reporting period and no fundamental changes in the market position.[3]

An important thing to remember about market share measurements is that they should signal areas needing further research and investigation. Perhaps there is a satisfactory explanation for an initial decline in market share, as described earlier. A declining market share, however, may indicate a serious lapse of performance that must be quickly rectified.

Another important consideration regarding market share, as well as the other evaluation tools, bears repeating here. *Trend information* is vitally important. A firm must know if the situation is improving or worsening. Only a comparison with past periods gives the insight needed to truly target problem areas.

SUMMARY

At the beginning of the chapter I asked you to consider whether the size of commission check going to each salesperson would be a sufficient indicator of performance, obviating a sales analysis. I hope that by now you have a solid understanding of the role of a sales analysis. To some extent, the size of each salesperson's commission check indicates relative sales performance, with the better performers presumably receiving higher commission checks. But there are several drawbacks in using commission checks as the sole indicator of performance. For the salesperson on straight commission, the commission size, although reflecting total sales, may not reflect sales relative to potential. When the commission check is given only for sales over quota, this drawback is minimized, provided that the quota adequately reflects past performance and future potential. When no commission check is forthcoming, however, because the salesperson did not achieve quota, one cannot differentiate those who almost reached their quota from those who were far under quota. Commission checks do not reveal other performance aspects. In particular sales of various products and sales to various customers are not identified unless a sales analysis is made, and this information may be highly desired to identify weak customers and weak products for possible corrective action and weeding out.

Control involves planning operating results, comparing actual against planned results, and taking corrective action where deviations occur. For effective control, however, two conditions should be met: Performance must be tied to individual responsibility and strategic control points established.

The four major tools used in evaluating overall marketing performance are sales analysis, market share analysis, marketing cost analysis, and the marketing audit.

The sales analysis is based on the iceberg principle, which recognizes that serious problems may lie beneath the surface of an operation and may not be uncovered without a detailed sales breakdown. These breakdowns most commonly are by geographical region, salesperson, customer, and product.

A market share analysis compares a firm's performance with its competitors. Trend information is important to the analysis; is performance improving or worsening? Industry market share data sources are necessary for the analysis and are usually available. For consumer goods manufacturers, various syndicated services (e.g., Nielsen and MRCA) provide needed data on relative market performance. In evaluating market share data, certain cautions should be noted. For example market share can be bought, with heavy doses of advertising, or emphasis on short-term sales results, but this is not always compatible with maximizing profitability.

QUESTIONS

1. Discuss strategic control points, their identification, and their importance.

2. Do you think a salesperson should be furnished data not only on her own performance but also on that of fellow workers?

3. What is the iceberg principle? What is its importance to the sales manager?

4. Market share analysis requires data on total industry sales or, at least, the sales of major competitors. How is this information to be obtained? Is there a lag in getting such information that may prevent timely action?

5. Should a fall in market share always trigger corrective action?

6. How should a sales manager handle deviations from plans or expectations?

7. The Santee Company is a small firm manufacturing and selling novelties in the New York City area. Because of its limited geographical area and

the large base of potential customers, it has not needed to designate either territories or quotas for its eleven salespeople. Discuss the effectiveness of control in this situation.

Please evaluate the alternatives.

    In the last few months, several large customers have drastically reduced their orders in your district. Information from the several salespeople involved has yielded nothing significant. What would you do at this point?

1. Visit the customers along with the salespeople to ascertain the reason for switching or reduced purchasing.

2. Visit the customers and talk with the purchasing agents by yourself.

3. Before making any dramatic personal visits, check on the frequency and caliber of customer complaints for the last 6 months to determine why customers might be moving to new suppliers.

4. Investigate any changes in competition in these market areas, both in person and with a quick investigation conducted by the marketing research department.

5. Don't panic. Wait a few more months and see if the situation doesn't right itself. Two months is just too short a time to establish any meaningful trend needing corrective action.

PEOPLE PROBLEM: REDUCED ORDERS FROM LARGE CUSTOMERS

NOTES

1. Adapted from "Sturdi-Wear Clothing Company," case 9–571–706, Intercollegiate Case Clearing House, Harvard University Graduate School of Business Administration. By permission of the author, Professor Donald W. Scotton, Cleveland State University.

2. Philip Kotler, *Marketing Management,* 5th ed. (Englewood Cliffs, N.J.: Prentice-Hall, 1984), 747.

3. Alfred R. Oxenfeldt, "How to Use Market-Share Measurement," *Harvard Business Review* (January-February 1969): 59–68.

cases

16.1 Complaints About a Sales Representative

One of your top producers is Elaine Miller. She graduated from college with a major in computer science and had been working in your firm's research department until her repeated requests to enter direct sales were agreed to.

Despite the fact that her territorial sales have exceeded plan by as much as 10 percent for the last three quarters, several customer complaints have come to your attention. These complaints focused on two aspects of her performance. She was overly aggressive and used high pressure, and her product knowledge regarding specific performance expectations was faulty at best—one customer even maintained that he was purposely misled.

QUESTION

How would you handle this situation?

16.2 Erratic Product Sales

Shirley De Lorenzo was baffled after the latest sales analysis data were developed. The relative sales of certain products among her various territories demonstrated no uniformity. For example product A accounted for about 20 percent of all sales in several territories, but only 5 percent in some others; products D and E likewise presented a very erratic picture. Shirley had the nagging suspicion that major opportunities were being missed in the below-average territories. Yet a sales analysis by territories showed all producing up to and beyond plan. Only the product mix varied.

QUESTIONS

1. What might explain these erratic product sales among the various territories?

2. What, if anything, should Shirley consider doing about this?

16.3 United Foods, Dog Food Division: Appropriate Action for a Decrease in Market Share

Norman Markham, general manager of the dog food division of United Foods, a diversified manufacturer of food and related products, frowned as he looked at the latest market share data that had just crossed his desk. Table 16.11 presents the market share information compiled by the Nielsen service for Spot, United's major brand of dry dog food.

The Milwaukee area was a continuing problem. Not only was market share one of the lowest of any major market area, but it appeared to be decreasing, contrary to the recent experiences in most other markets. Norman decided to call in Fred Ratzsche for an explanation. Norman mused that the Milwaukee district had been a continual problem for him. And Fred always had the same excuse and the same solution for the situation. Increasingly, Norman thought that Fred's excuses and recommendations were designed to hide his own incompetence as a sales manager.

"What explanation do you have this time?" Norman asked Fred a few days later.

"It's the same one, Norman. As I've told you

TABLE 16.11 Market share data for Spot dog food.

	Percentage Market Share for Dry Dog Food	Percentage Change Over Previous Year
Los Angeles	16	+ 1.5
Phoenix	12	+ 0.6
Denver	18	+ 0.3
Houston	21	+ 0.5
Kansas City	20	− 0.1
Minneapolis–St. Paul	22	+ 0.3
Milwaukee	12	− 0.4
Chicago	18	+ 0.2
St. Louis	11	+ 0.2
Detroit	17	+ 0.5
Cleveland	18	+ 0.6
Atlanta	24	+ 1.3
Miami	19	− 0.3
Washington	17	− 0.1
New York	15	—
Boston	11	+ 0.4

before, we have heavy local competition. It's only a small firm, and they only distribute in eastern Wisconsin. But their prices are less than ours, they're well-known, and they have a lot of customer acceptance. The only way we're going to make a bigger dent in this market is to advertise heavier, give more free goods to the grocers, and maybe use a little couponing."

Fred was earnest, there was no doubt about that, Norman thought. But, then, he always had been a good salesman; that was why he was tapped for the management job in Milwaukee 4 years ago. Maybe that had been a mistake, Norman thought.

"Other districts have local competition, too," Norman reminded Fred. "Yet they seem to be able to handle it and get a decent market share, and most are still increasing their penetration."

"It's not the same, Norman. Our local firm is widely accepted, deeply entrenched, and, incidentally, has a very good product."

Norman sorted out some papers on his desk. "Here, Fred, are the promotional expenditures in each market [see Table 16.12]. As you can see, each district is budgeted with the same percentage/sales ratio, 3 percent. This means, of course, that the

districts with the higher sales get more promotional dollars. It's as simple as that. Get your salespeople out there with a little more hustle, and you'll have more money to spend."

"But, Norman, we still need more money initially to blast our way into this market. We have been trying to do this for 7 years. Can't you make a special exception and give us a 5-percent promotional budget for 1 year? I think I can almost guarantee you that this will raise our market share 2 or 3 percentage points and give us some momentum."

"Fred, I don't believe in buying market share. Sure, we can spend more money. Sure, this is bound to increase market share somewhat. But where are the profits in doing this? Increase sales, but decrease profits? You know that profits are the name of the game. We can make a reasonable profit with a 3-percent promotional effort and still have a good impact on the market—most markets, that is." Norman looked at Fred appraisingly. "I'm afraid, Fred, I have to lay it on the line. In the next 6 months, if we don't see some improvement in market share, you'd better start looking for another job."

TABLE 16.12 Promotional expenditures for Spot dog food ($ hundreds).

	1987 Sales	Promotional Expenses (at 3%)
Los Angeles	2,260	67.8
Phoenix	480	14.4
Denver	620	18.6
Houston	1,470	44.1
Kansas City	1,250	37.5
Minneapolis–St. Paul	1,360	40.8
Milwaukee	430	12.9
Chicago	2,410	72.3
St. Louis	590	17.7
Detroit	960	28.8
Cleveland	840	25.2
Atlanta	860	25.8
Miami	770	23.1
Washington	920	27.6
New York	2,450	73.5
Boston	600	18.0

QUESTIONS

1. Evaluate this situation and conversation: the criticism, the defense, the final threat.

2. What other sources of analysis would have been useful in this case?

3. Discuss the pros and cons of increasing the promotional budget by two-thirds, as Fred wanted.

4. Should market share be such a major indicator of performance?

5. Do you think budgeting promotional efforts as a fixed and uniform percentage of sales is best? Why or why not?

CHAPTER 17

Controlling Through Analyzing Marketing Costs and by the Marketing Audit

CHAPTER PERSPECTIVE

Sales analysis examines variations from plans or quotas. Market share analysis compares performance with the competition. But a firm also must determine the relative profitability of present business methods, and this is accomplished through a marketing (or distribution) cost analysis.

The importance of the marketing cost analysis has increased in recent years, because many firms encountered rapidly rising costs, softening demand, and resistance to higher prices, and even inability to charge higher prices. Firms accordingly needed to shift their emphasis from sales volume to cost control to increase profits. Although production costs long have received concerted management attention, better cost control of marketing operations today may represent the most fruitful avenue to realizing higher profits.

The ultimate tool for evaluating performance is the marketing audit. The most comprehensive assessment of total performance, it is used more often in extreme situations, when a firm's marketing performance is suffering so badly that drastic action seems required to maintain viability. But the marketing audit is better used as a periodic tool to compare marketing efforts against marketing opportunity.

As you read this chapter, consider the results of a marketing cost analysis. Develop a set of guidelines for a policy statement regarding unprofitable customers. Would you permit any exceptions to your policies? Why or why not?

CHAPTER OBJECTIVES

□ Understand the nature of a marketing cost analysis and the related 80/20 principle.

□ Be able to differentiate the types of costs used in this analysis with ordinary accounting costs.

□ Become familiar with the procedure for analyzing marketing costs.

□ Understand the problems involved in analyzing marketing costs.

□ Become aware of the various alternatives for corrective actions regarding misdirected marketing efforts uncovered by a marketing cost analysis.

□ Understand the marketing audit, the various kinds, the procedure for doing an audit, and the best use of a marketing audit.

NATURE OF A MARKETING COST ANALYSIS

A marketing cost analysis assigns or apportions the various costs of doing business to the different marketing categories, such as territories, customers, products, size of orders, and types of sale (cash or credit). It often reveals that a substantial part of a firm's efforts do not yield commensurate profits. Efforts then could better be directed to areas that can make larger contributions to profit. The term applied to misdirected marketing efforts is the 80/20 principle.

The 80/20 Principle

As mentioned in previous chapters, the 80/20 principle means that 80 percent of the profits comes from 20 percent of the customers. The same principle also typically characterizes products and salespeople. For example 20 percent of a company's products and 20 percent of its salespeople may contribute most of the profits. Of course, exact percentages will vary, but even well-managed firms have imbalances. Table 17.1 gives an example of a firm whose imbalance is even more extreme: 13 percent of the customers generate 81 percent of the total shipments, whereas 63 percent of the customers account for only 2.3 percent of total business.

A certain unevenness of profit contribution is inevitable. Some products are easier to sell and can take a higher markup; some salespeople are star producers; some customers buy in bigger quantities and require less push and less service. Unfortunately, the emphasis on sales in most firms (as commissions are usually paid on sales volume, not on profit contribution) creates reluctance to eliminate unprofitable smaller customers and a natural inclination to push the easier-to-sell products, rather than those that might yield the most profit. Weeding out weak products seems to be inherently difficult, so some remain in the line far longer than they should. Sales force turnover usually results in a sales force that consists of salespeople with varying degrees

TABLE 17.1 Example of one firm's imbalance: Shipments by account size.

Total per Year's Volume (Pounds)	Number of Accounts	Percentage of All Accounts	Percentage of Total Sales
Under 1,000	302	44	0.3
1,000–1,999	129	19	2
2,000–9,999	44	6	2
10,000–19,999	48	7	3
20,000–49,999	68	10	11.5
50,000–99,999	42	6	14
Over 100,000	47	7	67

of training, experience, and motivation. But even without turnover, sales-people would differ in motivation, effective energy, and competence. Some disparity cannot be prevented, but when it becomes excessive, efficiency is diminished and marketing costs soar. This disparity in profit contribution tends to grow unless periodic analyses are made of the profitability of territories and salespeople, products, customers, and similar units of measurement.

Relationship with the Accounting System

A marketing cost analysis is not part of a business's regular accounting system, which routinely records transactions for financial and tax purposes but does not analyze costs of these transactions. If the account classification system is highly detailed, the cost analysis is easier, although it must still be developed as a separate study conducted periodically or sporadically. The difficulty of restructuring natural accounts into functional accounts is not slight. Commonly, detail received from salespeople is combined into natural accounts and not kept in a disaggregated state in the computer. Hence, to restructure the natural accounts into functional accounts requires the analyst to return to the original detail and redo the entire posting operation. If the data had been kept in a data bank with several identification codes, the restructuring process would be only a matter of writing an appropriate program to recapture the data in the desired format, but this seldom occurs.

Types of Costs

The types of costs relevant for the marketing cost analysis are (1) natural, (2) functional, (3) direct, and (4) indirect.

Natural costs are typically found in accounting records and refer to the nature of the expenditure (i.e., salaries, rent, advertising, telephone, and auto expenses). Although these accounts are in the form in which costs are usually invoiced, they do not indicate the purpose of the cost-incurring activity.

Functional costs, on the other hand, are classified by the purpose behind the activity. For example salaries would encompass portions attributable to contacting various customers, completing administrative tasks, processing orders and billing, filling and packaging orders, performing research, and so forth. Similarly, the natural costs of rent, telephone, and auto expenses would be apportioned to various selling and nonselling aspects of the operation. When costs are classified by function, they may include part of a number of natural cost accounts.

Direct costs are directly attributable and chargeable to a particular territory or segment of business. Sales salaries, commissions earned, and travel and other sales force expenses can be charged directly to the territories and sales-people involved. Any local advertising and display costs in a particular territory can be identified as direct costs.

Indirect costs are incurred for more than one territory or sales entity. Examples of indirect costs are sales office expenses, warehouse expenses, supplies, billing, and the like. As discussed later, the allocation of indirect costs may present difficult decisions about the most equitable method.

Costs sometimes can be both direct and indirect. For example sales salaries and expenses usually will be direct when charged to a territory, because the salesperson presumably is making efforts only in his own territory. But when apportioned to customers and to products, costs will be indirect, because these efforts and costs are spread over a number of customers and product entities.

PROCEDURE FOR ANALYZING MARKETING COSTS

Step 1: Converting Natural Accounts into Functional Cost Accounts

To make a marketing cost analysis, the first step is to convert the natural expenses into their functional costs, that is, the purpose for which they were incurred. Determining the correct distribution sometimes is not easy. However, time studies, observation, and management estimates can provide sufficient basis for allocations. Table 17.2 shows the reassignment of natural accounts to functional accounts for a few representative items.

Step 2: Allocating the Functional Costs to the Marketing Entities

After the natural accounting costs have been assigned to functional accounts, the next step is to reallocate these functional costs to territories, products, and customers or to any other entities to be analyzed. The total costs will be the same as those in the natural accounts, but now the costs are organized

TABLE 17.2   Separation of natural accounts into selected functional accounts.

Natural Accounts	Functional Accounts ($)				
	Total	Packing	Selling	Sales Administration	Order Processing
Salaries	18,000	2,000	12,500	2,000	1,500
Office supplies	2,500	250	500	1,100	650
Telephone	1,600	150	700	600	150
Auto expense	2,600	—	1,500	1,100	—
Total	24,700	2,400	15,200	4,800	2,300

differently. However, just as some difficulty may be encountered in equitably assigning the natural costs to functional costs, so the bases for allocating the various functional costs are seldom clear-cut and noncontroversial. Table 17.3 shows recommended bases for allocating selected direct and indirect costs.

How are the bases determined? An analysis should be made to establish whether particular functional costs relate to some measures of activity. For example Table 17.3 suggests that number of order lines (i.e., the number of different items ordered on each purchase order) should be the basis for allocating order-processing costs to territories, products, and customers. The validity of this allocation could be determined by observing the amount of clerical time and other costs (such as expenditures on order forms) incurred in handling a sample of orders having various numbers of order lines. Validity would be established if the costs of processing increased directly in relation to the number of order lines.

Although this is a simplified version of a marketing cost analysis, because we are using only a few accounts and allocations, the procedures and rationale do not differ for a detailed analysis. Table 17.4 shows the allocation of the selected functional accounts to territories; Table 17.5, to customers; and Table 17.6, to products. If you follow the calculations through each of these tables, you should better grasp the mechanics of marketing cost analysis.

TABLE 17.3   Bases for allocating selected functional costs to sales territories, products, and customers.

	Bases of Allocation		
Functional Cost Groups	*Territories*	*Products*	*Customers*
Selling—Direct costs (salaries, commissions, travel, etc.)	Direct cost	Time studies	Number of sales calls
Selling—Indirect costs (field office expense, training, etc.)	Equal charge for each salesperson	Charge in proportion to direct selling time	Number of sales calls
Advertising	Direct cost; or analysis of media circulation	Cost of space for specific products	Cost of space of specific customer advertising
Transportation, storage, and shipping	Weight	Weight	Weight
Order processing	Number of order lines	Number of order lines	Number of order lines
Accounts receivable	Number of invoices posted	Number of invoices posted	Number of invoices posted

Source: Adapted from Charles H. Sevin, *Marketing Productivity Analysis* (New York: McGraw-Hill, 1965): 13–15; Charles H. Sevin, "Analyzing Your Cost of Marketing," in *Management Aids for Small Manufacturers* (Washington, D.C.: Small Business Administration, June 1957): 3.

TABLE 17.4 Allocating selected functional costs to territories.

Functional Accounts	Costs to Be Allocated ($)	Basis of Allocation	Allocation to Territories ($)			
			A	B	C	D
Packing	2,400	Weight*	498	702	732	468
Field selling	15,200	Direct	3,200	4,800	4,200	3,000
Sales administration	4,800	Equal	1,200	1,200	1,200	1,200
Order processing	2,300	Number of order lines†	548	613	701	438
Total	24,700		5,446	7,315	6,833	5,106

*Calculation of packing costs allocation: Weight of orders by territories (in 100 lbs.)

A 1,700 $\frac{1,700}{8,200} \times \$2,400 = \$ 498$

B 2,400 $\frac{2,400}{8,200} \times \$2,400 = \$ 702$

C 2,500 $\frac{2,500}{8,200} \times \$2,400 = \$ 732$

D 1,600 $\frac{1,600}{8,200} \times \$2,400 = \$ 468$

8,200 $2,400

†Calculation of order-processing allocation: Number of order lines by territories

A 50 $\frac{50}{210} \times \$2,300 = \$ 548$

B 56 $\frac{56}{210} \times \$2,300 = \$ 613$

C 64 $\frac{64}{210} \times \$2,300 = \$ 701$

D 40 $\frac{40}{210} \times \$2,300 = \$ 438$

210   $2,300

TABLE 17.5 Allocating selected functional costs to customers.

Functional Accounts	Costs to Be Allocated ($)	Basis of Allocation	Allocation to Customers ($)		
			X	Y	Z
Packing	2,400	Weight*	1,405	615	380
Field selling	15,200	Number of calls†	8,290	4,145	2,765
Sales administration	4,800	Number of calls‡	2,618	1,309	873
Order processing	2,300	Number of order lines§	876	767	657
Total	24,700		13,189	6,836	4,675

*Calculation of packing costs allocation: Weight of orders by customer (in 100 lbs.)

X 4,800 $\frac{4,800}{8,200} \times \$2,400 = \$1,405$

Y 2,100 $\frac{2,100}{8,200} \times \$2,400 = \$ 615$

Z 1,300 $\frac{1,300}{8,200} \times \$2,400 = \$ 380$

8,200 $2,400

†Calculation of field selling costs allocation: Number of calls per customer

X 60 $\frac{60}{110} \times \$15,200 = \$ 8,290$

Y 30 $\frac{30}{110} \times \$15,200 = \$ 4,145$

Z 20 $\frac{20}{110} \times \$15,200 = \$ 2,765$

110   $15,200

‡Calculation of sales administration costs allocation: Number of calls per customer

X 60 $\frac{60}{110} \times \$4,800 = \$2,618$

Y 30 $\frac{30}{110} \times \$4,800 = \$1,309$

Z 20 $\frac{20}{110} \times \$4,800 = \$ 873$

110   $4,800

§Calculation of order processing costs allocation: Orders processed per customer (number of order lines)

X 80 $\frac{80}{210} \times \$2,300 = \$ 876$

Y 70 $\frac{70}{210} \times \$2,300 = \$ 767$

Z 60 $\frac{60}{210} \times \$2,300 = \$ 657$

210   $2,300

TABLE 17.6 Allocating selected functional costs to products.

Functional Accounts	Costs to Be Allocated ($)	Basis of Allocation	Allocation to Products ($) R	S
Packing	2,400	Weight*	1,551	849
Field selling	15,200	Time studies†	8,444	6,756
Sales administration	4,800	Charge in proportion to direct selling time‡	2,667	2,133
Order processing	2,300	Number of order lines§	1,205	1,095
Total	24,700		13,867	10,833

*Calculation of packing costs allocation: Weight of orders by product (in 100 lbs.)

R   5,300 $\dfrac{5,300}{8,200} \times \$2,400 = \$1,551$

S   2,900 $\dfrac{2,900}{8,200} \times \$2,400 = \$\ \ 849$

    8,200 $2,400

†Calculation of field selling costs allocation: Total hours devoted to each product, as obtained from time studies

R   600 $\dfrac{600}{1,080} \times \$15,200 = \$\ 8,444$

S   480 $\dfrac{480}{1,080} \times \$15,200 = \$\ 6,756$

    1,080 $15,200

‡Calculation of sales administration costs allocation: Charge in proportion to direct selling time, as obtained from time studies (therefore, same percentage allocation as field selling costs)

R   600 $\dfrac{600}{1,080} \times \$4,800 = \$2,667$

S   480 $\dfrac{480}{1,080} \times \$4,800 = \$2,133$

    1,080 $4,800

§Calculation of order processing costs allocation: Number of order lines per product

R   110 $\dfrac{110}{210} \times \$2,300 = \$1,205$

S   100 $\dfrac{100}{210} \times \$2,300 = \$1,095$

    210                               $2,300

Step 3: Determining the Profit and Loss for Each Marketing Entity

By placing the functional cost allocations into a profit and loss statement, one can determine the ultimate profitability of the various marketing entities analyzed. Table 17.7 shows a profitability analysis by customers, using the cost figures from Table 17.5. Table 17.7 shows the profit and loss from dealing with customers X, Y, and Z.

TABLE 17.7   Profitability by customer ($).

	X	Y	Z	Total
Sales	73,000	28,000	14,600	115,600
Costs of goods sold	51,100	19,600	10,220	80,920
Gross margin*	21,900	8,400	4,380	34,680
Expenses (from Table 17.5)	13,189	6,836	4,675	24,700
Net profit (loss)	8,711	1,564	(295)	9,980

*It is assumed here that a gross margin of 30 percent of sales is achieved with each customer. In reality gross margin tends to vary among customers due to quantity discounts and purchases of products with varying markups.

Table 17.7 demonstrates considerable disparity in the profitability of the three customers, as X contributes most of the total profits of the business. Although higher expenses were incurred in doing business with X, they remained a smaller percentage of sales, relative to the other two customers. Because the costs of doing business with Z are higher than the gross margin on this business, management should make a decision. Are there compelling reasons for continuing to do business with Z, or should this customer be dropped? Possible corrective actions for unprofitable customers are explored later in this chapter.

PROBLEMS INVOLVED IN ANALYZING MARKETING COSTS

Despite the ability to compute cost allocations as shown in the preceding analysis, certain problems are involved in conducting a marketing cost analysis. These problems primarily concern (1) the difficulty in allocating the indirect costs and (2) the time and expense involved in developing and analyzing the various detailed records and other data that must be gathered.

Difficulty in Allocating Marketing Costs

Business firms long have recognized the importance of production cost analysis (cost accounting) and have devoted large staffs to seek more efficient production. As a result, material, factory wages, equipment maintenance, and the like can be apportioned fairly accurately to the various products and processes. Most companies have not devoted the same attention to marketing costs. Consequently, marketing costs, which admittedly are difficult to measure and apportion (and therefore to control) often are allocated somewhat arbitrarily. The effect of various marketing efforts on the final order, therefore, usually cannot be determined as precisely as the effect of material and labor inputs on production outputs.

Several simplistic approaches to allocating indirect costs sometimes are used. Costs such as administrative overhead can be divided up equally among all territories, products, and customers. You can see, however, how inequitable this tends to be, because there are wide variations in sales volume, and presumably, expenses have some correlation with sales achieved.

Another approach—with a better rationale on superficial examination—is to allocate these costs in proportion to the sales volume achieved. This method, however, almost negates the objective of the marketing cost analysis, because it does not probe deeply enough to uncover high-cost segments of the marketing operation. Furthermore, this method of allocating disregards the very real probability that the problem territories, products, and customers require disproportionately more time (and expense) than those that function smoothly.

An offshoot of allocating indirect costs on the basis of sales is to assign them in proportion to direct expenses, so that the territory with the highest direct selling costs also would receive the highest allocation of indirect expenses. But, again, these allocations tend to mask profit-draining segments of the business.

Consequently, one is left with bases for allocating certain expenses such as shown in Table 17.3. These should give a more equitable distribution. But do they? Is it any more equitable to allocate sales administration, training, and office expense to territories on the bases of an equal charge for each salesperson, or to customers on the basis of number of sales calls, as the table recommends? Not all salespeople require the same amount of management time, nor do all customers require, or want, the same level of service.

Because of the allocation difficulties, particularly with indirect costs, controversy arises over whether all costs should indeed be allocated. So far in this chapter, the discussion has concerned the *full-cost method,* in which all expenses, including the indirect, are distributed. Thus, a net profit or loss figure can be derived for each customer, as in Table 17.7, or for each territory or product.

Contribution-to-margin approach. Because of the previously described allocation difficulties, some advocate a contribution-to-margin approach. This method considers only those measurable costs definitely related to the marketing segment analyzed and focuses attention and responsibility on direct costs rather than on a total of direct and indirect costs. Accordingly, only marketing costs that would be incurred whether or not the particular segment or subdivision were present (e.g., administrative and warehousing costs) would not be allocated. The controversies that can accompany arbitrary assignment of indirect costs that favorably or unfavorably affect certain measures of relative performance are then avoided. The contribution-to-margin method purports to show only the amount that is actually contributed to the general overhead and profits.

As an example of the contribution-to-margin approach, let us take the data in Table 17.7, profitability by customers, and see how the three customers would fare. Table 17.8 presents this analysis. For the sake of simplicity we will consider that half of the packaging and order-processing costs and all of the field selling costs would be eliminated if the particular customer were dropped. Sales administration would continue in full even though a customer were lost. Table 17.8 shows that now all the customers are making some contribution to margin, even Z, who was unprofitable under the full-cost method of Table 17.8.

Even the contribution-to-margin approach, however, poses some allocation problems. For example consider a salesperson's direct expenses to the firm—base salary and travel expenses. Breaking these expenses down and distributing them to products and customers may not always be equitable. The common allocation in proportion to volume sold disregards the fact that all products and customers are not equally easy to sell.

Time and Expense Involved

As noted before, most companies' accounting systems do not permit pulling marketing cost information directly from ledger accounts. Most accounting records are maintained in so-called natural accounts, and the first step in developing the marketing costs analysis is to restructure these expenses into functional accounts, which is costly and time-consuming. Then the problem remains to reallocate these expenses to the various segments of the marketing operation. Although these allocations may be arbitrary and not particularly equitable, the analysis still is complex. If more equitable bases are desired, additional studies may be required, such as exhaustive time-and-motion studies of how salespeople spend their time on products, customers, and other

TABLE 17.8   Contribution to margin by customers ($).

	X	Y	Z
Gross margin (from Table 17.7)	21,900	8,400	4,380
Direct operating expenses (from Table 17.5)			
Sales salaries	8,290	4,145	2,765
Half of packing	703	308	190
Half of order processing	438	384	329
Total expenses	9,431	4,837	3,284
Contribution to margin	12,469	3,563	1,096

activities and how sales managers allot their time. The results still may be inequitable.

As a consequence of the time and expense in making marketing cost analyses, many firms do not develop them regularly but wait until a problem occurs. Firefighting is not the best use of the marketing cost analysis, because problems usually are rather far advanced before they become clearly visible. If the cost analyses are not continual, they are best repeated at least every few years or sooner when marketing costs appear problematic. On balance, despite the difficulties in equitably allocating costs, and despite the time and expense involved, the benefits of systematically analyzing marketing costs are significant.

AREAS FOR CORRECTIVE ACTION

The payoff of conducting a somewhat tedious and relatively expensive marketing cost analyses comes in the corrective actions that should follow. Flagging of unprofitable segments of business normally should result in efforts to improve the profitability of these segments or perhaps to eliminate them entirely. Because the complete analysis covers territories, customers (or customer categories), products, and possibly other entities (perhaps method of distribution or methods of sale), these will be the target of any corrective action. The marketing cost analysis, however, like the sales analysis, seldom determines the needed corrective action. The analysis only identifies relative problem areas that deserve further attention and investigation.

Unprofitable Territories

A number of alternatives can be considered for an unprofitable territory. The temptation is to blame the sales representative or the field sales manager. But often a restructuring of the territory is needed. The territory may be too small, so the volume obtained is insufficient to cover selling expenses. Or the territory may be so large that it cannot be adequately serviced. A different combination of marketing efforts may be necessary, such as more advertising or a lowered price, to surpass aggressive competitors.

Perhaps the mix of customers and competitors has changed, so that little can be done without incurring exorbitant costs, and the best course of action is to abandon the territory or incorporate it with neighboring territories. An alternative to abandoning a weak territory (which, though weak, probably still contributes to overhead beyond its direct expenses) is to limit it to mail and telephone selling rather than allowing direct sales visits. A weak or unprofitable territory often is found in sparsely populated areas where great distances must be covered to reach small customers, which also may require terminating direct sales visits. Of course, the sales representative may be to blame for poor territorial performance; if so, improved support for the sales representative, better training, or perhaps replacement would be indicated.

Unprofitable Customers

A firm may analyze its customers in several ways. It may want to determine the profitability of its business with different Standard Industrial Classification (SIC) groups. For example a firm may find that its business with #3537, the industrial trucks and tractors industry, is profitable, while that with #3533, farm machinery, is not. It may want to analyze profitability by distribution channel, such as wholesalers, national chains, regional chains, and large local retailers. Most often a manufacturer finds that an analysis by annual purchases is instructive. The usual assumption is that the smaller accounts are the least profitable and the biggest customers are the most profitable, but this is not always true, as shown in the following section.

An example of profitability by customer-volume groups.   Although large customers generally are thought to be the most profitable business, sometimes the higher gross margin that can be realized with a small customer more than compensates for the higher costs of doing business with such a customer (see Table 17.9). Table 17.9 shows marketing cost-analysis results by customer-volume categories and contains several profitability indicators. First, gross margin does not indicate profitability, because the unprofitable customers in the under $3,000-volume category have the highest gross margin percentage—that is, the manufacturer can charge them a high unit price relative to other customers. Second, the largest customers are not the most profitable because of their high-quantity discounts, which more than coun-

TABLE 17.9   One firm's analysis of profitability by customer-volume groups.

Customer-Volume Groups—Volume of Purchases ($)	Number of Customers— Percentage of Total	Sales Volume— Percentage of Total	Gross Margin— Percentage of Sales	Marketing Costs— Percentage of Sales	Relative Profits— Percentage of Sales
1–2,999	87.3	17.8	45.9	54.1	−8.2
3,000–9,999	8.0	13.6	45.4	34.4	11.0
10,000–19,999	1.2	6.7	39.9	22.4	17.5
20,000–49,999	2.2	19.4	34.3	11.3	23.0
50,000–99,999	0.9	20.8	27.4	7.2	20.2
100,000 and up	0.4	21.7	17.2	5.0	12.2
Total	100.0	100.0			
Average performance			35.0	24.4	12.6

Note: Gross margin variations are due to quantity discounts.

teract the lower marketing costs. The customers in the middle-volume categories, particularly the $20,000 to $49,999 group provide this firm with the most profitable business.

Now complete Exercise 17.1.

Using the data in Table 17.9, what would you as sales manager do? Evaluate the various alternatives and defend your choice.

EXERCISE 17.1

Alternatives in dealing with unprofitable customers. The most obvious alternative in handling a markedly unprofitable customer is simply to discontinue doing business with this account. Two other alternatives should be considered, however: (1) increasing the average order size and (2) decreasing the marketing costs of dealing with such a customer. If the manufacturer can accomplish either or both of these alternatives without much loss of total business, then an unprofitable segment of the operation can probably be turned around. More likely, some business will be lost, but the remainder will be most preferred.

The average order size can be increased very simply by establishing a minimum order quantity or instituting a service charge for small orders. A somewhat more complicated move would be to switch packaging to larger containers, such as three dozen instead of one dozen. These arbitrary moves may arouse resentment in smaller customers, although this may be reduced by explaining the company's position and reason for the change. The sales force can help with explanations, but they can also serve an important role in persuading their customers to buy in larger amounts, to concentrate their purchases with fewer vendors, or to stop buying on a hand-to-mouth basis and thereby minimize merchandise out-of-stocks (which lead to lost sales) and handling expenses. A bonus can even be used to reward salespeople who obtain large orders.

The two principal ways to decrease the marketing costs of dealing with small customers are reducing the number of sales calls to them and eliminating sales calls entirely. The firm can rely on direct mail and telephone selling for most of the customer contacts. Again, the arbitrary decision to limit direct customer contacts and servicing calls likely will cause customer dissatisfaction and even resentment, and some customers may switch to other suppliers. But explaining the company's position and the reason for the change should help to hold others; further, business lost was unprofitable and should hardly be missed. (Although these customers may be unprofitable on a full-cost allocation, at least some of this business may still contribute to margin. Still, it is not the most productive use of company resources.)

The other alternative for reducing the marketing costs is to shift these customer accounts to a wholesaler and to discontinue direct sales. The company may have to search for a suitable wholesaler who is willing to take on the manufacturer's line and who is not already handling competing products, but this should not be a serious problem in most market areas. Although some customers may resent paying the higher prices that a wholesaler's margin requires and no longer having direct contact with the manufacturer, usually the better servicing and quicker delivery afforded by local wholesalers offers small customers advantages that are not possible when dealing directly with distant manufacturers.

Unprofitable Products

The 80/20 rule holds for products just as it does for customers. When a firm makes a marketing cost analysis, many products may show up poorly, based on a strict profitability appraisal. The obvious answer is to weed out the unprofitable products, thereby freeing up management and salespeople to concentrate their efforts on the more profitable products. A weak product carries hidden costs:

- ☐ The weak product tends to consume a disproportionate amount of management's time.
- ☐ It often requires frequent price and inventory adjustments.
- ☐ It generally involves short production runs in spite of expensive setup times.
- ☐ It requires both advertising and sales force attention that might better be diverted to making the healthy products more profitable.
- ☐ Its unfitness can cause customer misgivings and adversely affect the company's image.
- ☐ It may delay the aggressive search for replacement products.[1]

Not all weak products should be pruned, however; rationale for keeping them may be strong. In particular, the weak products may be necessary to complete a line to benefit sales of other products. They may be essential for customer goodwill. When needed by customers despite the low volume of use, some weak products may enhance the company's image or prestige. Although the weak products make no money in themselves, still their intrinsic value to the firm may be substantial. Other weak products may merely be unproven, too new in their product life cycle to have become profitable; in their growth and maturity stage they may contribute profits.

Analyzing the marketing costs of a new product.   A new product sometimes may seem an attractive addition to the line because of a higher-than-average gross margin. An analysis of marketing costs, however, may call for a reevaluation. A common misconception is that a new addition to the line costs nothing to distribute because it may be sold and delivered along with the other products. If such a new product carries a high markup (gross margin), its attractiveness is considered to be proved. But a detailed analysis of its costs of distribution may indicate otherwise. Table 17.10 shows the cost breakdown for the various products groups of one company along with such a new product, E.

The volume of E, together with the fact that the company could sell it only to small dealers despite the effort to obtain new customers, very nearly offset the per-unit gross margin, which was more than double the average of all products in the line. The firm reevaluated marketing efforts, particularly for E and for C, the highest-volume product in the line that was actually incurring a loss. The firm decided to deemphasize the sales promotion of E, to direct more salesperson time to promoting products with a larger net profit, such as A, B, and D. Table 17.11 shows the results 1 year later. Thus, overall

TABLE 17.10   Analysis of product marketing costs.

Product Groups	Gross Margin per Unit of Product ($)	Volume per Item, Percentage of Average	Distribution Cost per Unit of Product ($)	Profit or Loss per Unit of Product ($)
A	0.56	168	0.51	0.05
B	0.45	98	0.40	0.05
C	0.24	197	0.26	−0.02
D	0.81	52	0.68	0.13
E (new)	1.41	14	1.38	0.03
Average	0.69	106	0.65	0.04

TABLE 17.11   Analysis of product marketing costs 1 year later.

Product Groups	Gross Margin per Unit of Product ($)	Volume per Item, Percentage of Average	Distribution Cost per Unit of Product ($)	Profit or Loss per Unit of Product ($)
A	0.58	171	0.51	0.07
B	0.46	102	0.40	0.06
C	0.26	180	0.26	0
D	0.83	56	0.69	0.14
E	1.41	12	1.28	0.13
Average	0.71	104	0.63	0.08

distribution costs were reduced from 65 cents per unit to 63 cents, whereas the average net profit per unit of product increased from 4 cents to 8 cents. Complete Exercise 17.2.

1. The firm in Tables 17.10 and 17.11 decided to reduce the marketing efforts for new product E somewhat, an action that succeeded in bringing E well into the black, although volume was disappointing. Are there other alternatives you would recommend for product E? What action would you take?
2. What rationale can you offer for keeping product C, which earns no profit, in the line?

A managerial approach to dealing with weak products. Some weak products deserve a fresh examination of their marketing strategy. Perhaps the price is out of line; maybe more advertising is needed to communicate the availability and particular benefits to an unknowing market. The distribution choice may be faulty, and success may yet come with a change, for example, from department stores to mass merchandisers. Despite the rationale for keeping some poorly performing products, many others undoubtedly should be eliminated. The firm's productive efficiency, warehousing, and selling efforts thereby would be freed for more profitable ventures. But product termination frequently meets with resistance, "the sadness of a final parting with old and tried friends."[2] The product slated for termination often has a supporter in the organization, possibly the one who developed it and brought it into the product line, so the decision to discontinue a product frequently is political as much as economic.

Perhaps the best way to handle the problem of weak products comes in the aftermath of a marketing cost analysis by which they are identified. At this point, unless their continuation can be definitely supported by the responsible managers, they should be eliminated. The key to a product elimination program is periodic evaluation and positive support for continuation contingent on probable future promise or intrinsic need.

THE MARKETING AUDIT

Any audit implies objectivity and a critical review. A *marketing audit* is an objective total evaluation of marketing efforts. Accounting audits are best known. These are periodically conducted by outsiders, usually public accountants, to protect stockholders and creditors. The marketing audit is not legally prescribed but is rather a top-management tool for examining the marketing program.

Marketing audits are of two basic types—general and functional. The *general audit* examines all aspects of the marketing mix and their effective relationships. It is concerned with the overall marketing operation, from objectives, policies, and organization, to methods and personnel.

A *functional audit* focuses on one aspect of the total marketing effort, such as the personal selling aspect or distribution. Although functional audits seem more relevant to sales management, when used alone they can be seriously flawed because they tend to neglect the coordination and relationship aspects. For example selling effectiveness, as discussed in earlier chapters, is affected by other marketing and operational activities such as advertising, quality control, and inventory control. The causes of poor selling effectiveness and excessive sales force turnover may therefore lie in deficiencies in other parts of the operation that make the selling job overly difficult against more aggressive and efficient competitors. Consequently, the more comprehensive general audit tends to be more effective in locating problem areas as well as opportunities.

Procedure for a Marketing Audit

To ensure objectivity a separate department in the firm or outside consultants should conduct the audit. Although self-audits, in which managers use a checklist to rate their own operations, are better than nothing, generally these lack the desired objectivity as well as a broad perspective. Sometimes a corporate auditing office, such as used by the 3M Company, will provide marketing audit services to the various divisions.[3] This is preferred to the self-audit, although the use of outside consultants who have broad experience in a number of industries may be preferred.

The procedure for conducting a marketing audit is generally fourfold. (1) Establish a clear understanding with company management of the scope and time frame of the investigation, as well as its purpose and events that led to its being commissioned. (2) Collect the necessary data, from both internal and external sources, not relying solely on company records and executive opinions but also contacting customers, dealers, and any other relevant outsiders. (3) Develop the necessary analyses and recommendations. (4) Present the conclusions to management for their use in planning any needed actions.

A marketing audit usually results in some changes, even in firms that supposedly are in good health. Improvements are always possible and desired, because the status quo can be a deadly trap for any firm.

Components of the marketing audit. Marketing executives use the sales analysis, marketing cost analysis, and the various measures of advertising and sales force effectiveness as tools to improve the marketing operation, according to established policies and practices. The marketing audit exceeds these tools and is used to evaluate the marketing objectives and policies and even management itself. Kotler has suggested that a marketing audit should examine six major components of the company's marketing situation:

☐ Marketing environment audit—Analyzing major macroeconomic forces and trends that affect the firm (e.g., its markets, customers, competitors, distributors and dealers, suppliers, and facilitators)

☐ Marketing strategy audit—Reviewing objectives and strategy as to how well they mesh with the present and forecasted marketing environment

☐ Marketing organization audit—Evaluating the capability of the marketing organization, both executives and personnel

☐ Marketing systems audit—Examining the quality of the company's systems for planning and control

☐ Marketing productivity audit—Examining the profitability and cost-effectiveness of the various marketing entities and expenditures

☐ Marketing function audits—Evaluating major marketing mix components, such as products, price, distribution, sales force, advertising and other promotions[4]

Using the marketing audit to fullest advantage. To gain the benefits possible from a comprehensive audit, management must face the possibility that their efforts could be improved and that performance is not as good as it might be. No one likes to be exposed to criticism and to have others learn of it. Perhaps for this reason more than any other, marketing audits are performed infrequently, and then usually when marketing, and even the entire firm, is faltering, and the audit then amounts to fire fighting (a last desperate device to save a company or a division). This is not the best way to use an audit. An audit is intended for "prognosis as well as diagnosis. . . . It is the practice of preventive as well as curative marketing medicine."[5] The audit can be used to aid decision making, such as evaluating various alternatives before a decision is reached. It can be used to identify strong points so that these can be exploited. If certain parts of the operation are weak, an informed management is better able to take corrective action. If used to its fullest potential, a marketing audit can lead to new perspectives and innovative thinking.

Despite several decades of attention given to the marketing audit, its use is still limited. To be a viable part of the evaluation process, to be more than simply a desperation measure when company life is in jeopardy and time and money are too short to do more than take short-term remedial action, the marketing audit should be made more palatable to marketing executives. Its use as a tool for grading performance should be changed. The potential value of periodic audits will not be realized until these become tools of operating management rather than criticisms of management. Despite the growing number of experts who advocate the comprehensive approach of a marketing audit, it must be better sold to top management as well as to operating executives. Marketing efficiency thereby may be improved.

SUMMARY

At the beginning of the chapter I asked you to think about the aftermath of a marketing cost analysis and to develop a policy statement regarding unprofitable customers. The policy statement should spell out recommended courses of action regarding various categories of unprofitable customers. You perhaps mentioned minimum order sizes and reduction or elimination of sales force calls. One of the things I hope you considered was the trend of customer business. If the trend of orders has been increasing over the last several years, in contrast to other customers whose orders have remained stable or declined, would you make some exceptions to your policies? Another factor that you may not have recognized as worth considering is the duration of a customer's business with the firm. For example do you eliminate an old and faithful customer, because its order level is unprofitable? Some flexibility or exceptions should be built into the policy statement. Of course, you may argue that any exceptions smack of favoritism and unfair dealings; however, a company has the right to view the merits of each customer in the realm of present and potential profitability and past relations and to act accordingly.

The marketing cost analysis apportions the various costs of doing business to market entities such as territories, customers, and products. After conducting a marketing analysis, a firm often finds that a minority of territories, customers, and products contribute most of the profitable business, hence the 80/20 principle (80 percent of the profits come from 20 percent of the accounts, products, etc.). Such a severe imbalance of business is not preferred. Corrective action may be needed to lessen the imbalance and misdirected marketing efforts, and a firm may exercise numerous options in doing so.

To perform a marketing cost analysis, the natural accounts must be converted into their functional costs, that is, the purpose for which they were incurred. Then these functional costs are allocated to the marketing entities. From this the profit or loss of each marketing entity can be determined.

The equitable allocation of indirect marketing costs can be problematic in a full-cost method. Some firms therefore use a contribution-to-margin approach in which only those measurable costs directly related to the entity (the customer, product, etc.) are allocated.

A marketing audit is an objective total evaluation of marketing efforts. It is the most thorough and costly measure of overall performance. It is more often used when an operation is having difficulties, but periodic audits can benefit healthy operations as well by leading to new perspectives and innovative thinking.

QUESTIONS

1. What is the 80/20 principle? What is its importance in performance appraisal?
2. Differentiate between the full-cost and the contribution-to-margin approach to analyzing marketing costs.
3. What should be done with an unprofitable territory?
4. When should a firm keep weak or unprofitable products in the product line?
5. Are large customers necessarily profitable accounts? Discuss.
6. Are there any drawbacks to making a marketing cost analysis?
7. If a sales representative's business continues to show up as unprofitable, is this conclusive grounds for dismissal?

PEOPLE PROBLEM: WHAT TO DO ABOUT A WEAK TERRITORY

Please evaluate the alternatives.

You are concerned with the findings of the latest marketing cost analysis. It shows that Harriet Robinsky of the Little Rock territory continues to have the weakest territory in the entire central region. Profits do not justify continuing to do business in this territory. The situation was only slightly better a year ago, at the time of the last analysis, but you had hoped that your pressure on Harriet would have resulted in significantly improved performance. It has not. What should you do?

1. Two consecutive years of low or no profits is ample cause for abandoning this territory.

2. Although last year you had thought that the cause of the poor showing was Harriet's fault, maybe that is not really fair to her. You decide to investigate the situation further. In particular, you want to examine Harriet's call reports before taking further action.

3. You note that advertising and display support has not been very high in Harriet's territory, partly because of the low sales volume but also because Harriet has not pushed for this as much as some of the other sales representatives. You decide to increase support before writing off the territory.

4. You cannot help but conclude that Harriet is just not the person for this job. She is not aggressive enough, and you cannot resist the nagging thought that she is not giving full effort to the job. The warning last year seems to have made no impression. You must seriously consider her discharge.

NOTES

1. Philip Kotler, *Marketing Management: Analysis, Planning, and Control,* 3rd ed. (Englewood Cliffs, N.J.: Prentice-Hall, 1976), 242.
2. R. S. Alexander, ''The Death and Burial of 'Sick' Products,'' *Journal of Marketing* (April 1964): 1.
3. Philip Kotler, William Gregor, and William Rodgers, ''The Marketing Audit Comes of Age,'' *Sloan Management Review* (Winter 1977): 31.
4. Philip Kotler, *Marketing Management,* 5th ed. (Englewood Cliffs, N.J.: Prentice-Hall, 1984), 766.
5. Abe Shuchman, ''The Marketing Audit: Its Nature, Purposes, and Problems,'' *Analyzing and Improving Marketing Performance,* Report No. 32 (New York: American Management Association, 1959), 14.

cases

17.1   The Fairness of Allocating Costs

Ron Crenshaw has stormed into your office. You know, even before he starts talking, what the trouble is. The latest marketing cost analysis has shown his to be a high-cost territory. A good sales performance has been wiped out after costs have been allocated.

"It's not fair," he almost shouts. "My territory is subsidizing the rest of this blasted operation!"

You must agree—sort of. Indirect costs such as warehousing, order processing, administrative overhead, advertising, and point-of-purchase display materials are allocated to the various territo-

ries on the basis of sales. Ron's territory has a disproportionate number of large accounts in relation to most of the other territories, so his sales are considerably larger. Thus, his territory has also been allocated the largest proportion of these indirect expenses.

"This makes me look bad," he says. "You know perfectly well that my territory is not incurring larger expenses than the other territories. Indeed, we're probably costing the company less because we have more large orders as well as fewer complaints and adjustments."

QUESTION

What would you do?

17.2   Coping with a Cost-Cutting Campaign

A decree has come down from top management. A crash cost-cutting campaign is in effect. All unprofitable business will be eliminated; all products that are not carrying their load will be scrapped; any salespeople who are not producing enough to cover their compensation and expenses also will be terminated. Blanche White, sales manager, is concerned about such an arbitrary and uncompromising decree. Fortunately, no salespeople in her district qualify for termination; she can put up with any product elimination.

One customer in Blanche's district, however,

who would be affected and apparently would be dropped, troubles her. This is the O'Neill Company, a firm that is only 2 years old, but in Blanche's estimation, is bound to make it big. It also is small now, but the experience and ability of the two partners and the innovative and aggressive approach they have manifested so far make their future bright. Blanche has established an excellent rapport with the two entrepreneurs and is most upset about abandoning this customer account. Yet, in the past her top management has been adamant in policy statements: No exceptions allowed.

QUESTION

What advice do you have for Blanche White in her dilemma?

17.3   Oswego Industries: What to Do with Unprofitable Distributors?

The consumer paper products division of Oswego Industries markets paper products such as toilet

paper, paper towels, napkins, and, in recent experiments, disposable diapers, through fifteen dis-

490

tributors nationwide. The paper products market is extremely competitive, dominated by the likes of Procter & Gamble and Scott Paper. However, Oswego has captured a secure niche within the market, although its market share is much smaller than that of the industry behemoths, by offering off-branded goods at attractive prices. Lacking the advertising thrust of its major competitors, it has competed on a price basis.

Jess Willard, general sales manager of the division, has become concerned about the apparent unevenness of distributors' effectiveness. Table 17.12 shows a breakdown of sales of Oswego's paper products by location of the various distributors. Five of the distributors appear to be very weak in sales productivity compared to the other ten. This disparity of sales led Jess to request a profit analysis of the distributors, and the result is shown in Table 17.13.

Jess was the first to admit that the methods chosen for the allocation of the various indirect expenses could be questioned and was probably not an exact and definitive cost breakdown; still, the results of the marketing cost analysis raised

TABLE 17.12 Oswego Paper Products, sales by distributor ($ hundreds).

Boston	4,200	Chicago	6,300
Baltimore	1,600	Kansas City	1,500
Richmond	2,400	Houston	3,450
Tampa	2,000	Los Angeles	6,400
New Orleans	4,500	Minneapolis–St. Paul	4,500
Memphis	1,200	Denver	2,100
St. Louis	3,800	Seattle	3,500
Cleveland	3,700		

TABLE 17.13 Oswego Paper Products, profit analysis ($ hundreds).

Location	Sales	Gross Profit on Sales	Direct Sales Cost*	Indirect Overhead†	Gain or (Loss)
Boston	4,200	1,260	300	360	600
Baltimore	1,600	480	360	320	(200)
Richmond	2,400	720	290	280	150
Tampa	2,000	600	275	275	50
New Orleans	4,500	1,350	495	555	300
Memphis	1,200	360	360	400	(400)
St. Louis	3,800	1,140	320	320	500
Cleveland	3,700	1,110	280	380	450
Chicago	6,300	1,890	480	460	950
Kansas City	1,500	450	270	280	(100)
Houston	3,450	1,040	210	230	600
Los Angeles	6,400	1,920	380	440	1,100
Minneapolis–St. Paul	4,500	1,350	220	330	800
Denver	2,100	630	310	420	(100)
Seattle	3,500	1,140	280	260	600

*Cost of visits, shipments, local promotion, and order placing
†Sales office expenses, credit, warehousing, etc.

some serious questions in his mind. Two issues in particular seemed important: (1) Should Oswego continue to do business with these unprofitable accounts? (2) Can these unprofitable accounts somehow be converted to profitable customers?

In attempting to reach a decision on these issues, Jess discussed the situation with Irene Jericho, divisional marketing research director, who had worked with the controller's office in developing the marketing cost analysis.

"In looking at these figures, Irene, it clearly seems as though we should drop these distributors and either find some others to replace them or at least temporarily drop out of those markets. It is essentially costing us money to do business in those four markets. Is that the way you read it?"

"The evidence is pretty convincing," she said. "I see two problems, though, in arbitrarily dropping these distributors. First, are others available that can be persuaded to take on our line and do a better job with it? We need to check this out, but I suspect that availability of good substitute distributors may be a problem in several of these markets. The other thing that bothers me is that we don't have any trend information. As you know, this is the first time we have attempted a marketing cost analysis, at least in the paper products division. So we don't know if these distributors are getting stronger or weaker. If they are improving, then maybe the situation will become profitable in another year or so."

"I can look up the sales volume we have done with them in the last several years," offered Jess.

"That should help, although we still don't know whether the same or less sales effort was exerted in those years—in other words, whether the costs of doing business with them was about the same percentage as today."

"The other possibility is that we could reduce some of our contacts and other efforts with these weak distributors and in that way incur less costs in doing business with them."

Irene nodded. "The problem with this, Jess, is that we have no research telling us the relationship of sales to effort. It may be that with less contacts, these distributors will do a much poorer job for us."

Jess smiled wryly. "Next you'll say that there may be a direct relationship between number of salesperson visits and efforts, on one hand, and sales by these distributors, on the other."

Irene nodded, "Doesn't that seem likely?"

"In that case, then, the answer might be to increase our costs of doing business with these unprofitable accounts in the expectation that resulting sales increases will more than offset these increased costs."

Irene laughed, "We don't seem to be getting very far in the decision, do we!"

QUESTIONS

1. Do you think these unprofitable distributors should be dropped? Why or why not?

2. What other information, if any, do you think would be helpful in making this decision?

3. Does Oswego have any other alternatives regarding this unprofitable business that might be more desirable?

4. Do you think these distributors can be induced to accept less direct sales contacts and assistance and still maintain their present sales volume?

5. Do you think the decision should be made now? Why or why not?

CHAPTER 18

Controlling Through Evaluating Individual Performance

CHAPTER PERSPECTIVE

Chapters 16 and 17 were concerned with evaluating and controlling overall sales performance and marketing costs by territory, customer, product, and other marketing entities. This chapter is concerned with evaluating the performance of the salespeople themselves. Measures of an individual's performance are both a part of the control process and also a vital aspect of supervising and directing sales efforts.

Despite the crucial benefits in formally evaluating individual performance, if poorly done, performance evaluations can create substantial problems and inequitable treatment. This chapter examines the most constructive uses of performance evaluation.

As you study this chapter, consider how you would determine whether any salespeople are using high-pressure techniques or other undesirable methods.

CHAPTER OBJECTIVES

☐ Become aware of the specific benefits of evaluating individual performance.
☐ Become familiar with the major problems that can arise from performance evaluations.
☐ Consider how detailed or complex the evaluation procedure should be.
☐ Become familiar with supervisory guidelines for evaluating performance.
☐ Know the best procedures for evaluating performance and the various bases for doing so.
☐ Know the various information sources about performance.
☐ Know the extenuating circumstances that should be considered in perhaps modifying or tempering the initial appraisal.
☐ Consider the issue of the amount and type of corrective action that may be desired when performance does not meet expectations.
☐ Understand the process of management by objectives and its benefits and drawbacks in performance evaluation.

BENEFITS OF INDIVIDUAL PERFORMANCE EVALUATION

Although salespeople may espouse the independence and relative freedom from close supervision that typifies many selling jobs, they cannot escape being measured for their relative effectiveness—nor should they want to. Any evaluation procedure tends to work to the advantage of the able, though it should pinpoint the weak, who may be strengthened by better guidance. And this is made possible through determining those areas where improvement is needed.

In general, if an evaluation process is systematic, objective, and well defined, it should help improve salesforce performance. This is achieved as follows:

1. Weak performances (and performers) can be corrected or eliminated.
2. Actions of sales personnel can be guided in the desired directions.
3. Performance evaluation can improve motivation.
4. Feedback on the acceptability and effectiveness of past performance is provided.
5. Persons with potential for management positions can be identified.
6. Emerging problems, both in the territory and in the salesperson's training and application of efforts, can be uncovered in time for corrective action.

Correcting Weak Areas of Performance

A carefully constructed evaluation program—using objective criteria, perhaps supplemented by subjective judgments—should enable a firm readily to identify the poorer performers, as well as their weak areas. The sales manager then can work with these personnel in correcting their deficiencies and improving their performances. When deficiencies persist or the person is unwilling or unable to improve performance to an acceptable level, transfer or termination may be necessary.

Guiding Actions in Desired Directions

Performance appraisal should be accompanied by an evaluation interview in which the sales manager discusses with each salesperson the strengths and weaknesses of her performance. In organizations where the sales force is spread widely, this is the best chance for the manager to communicate on a face-to-face basis. Here is an ideal time to stress the desired directions for future selling efforts, for example, emphasis on more profitable products, better servicing, customer prospecting, the practice of varying sales efforts and calls according to customer size and importance.

In addition to personal communication as a means of directing sales efforts in desired directions, the bases used for evaluation should be designed to encourage this. For example, if a particular company-wide emphasis is on improving the profitability of sales, then the appraisal instruments should give special emphasis to the gross margin or sales profitability. The evaluation interview also is a good time to discuss the goals and objectives that salespeople should have for the following year. This is the first step toward *management by objectives*, which we will discuss more thoroughly later in this chapter. Further evaluation then can be structured around how well the planned and agreed-on objectives have been met.

Improving Motivation

Motivation can be improved by performance evaluation. Knowing that one's performance will be reviewed and comparisons (both favorable and unfavorable) made with fellow salespeople stimulates most individuals to their best efforts. As shown in the next section, however, the evaluation procedure can have the opposite effect on morale and motivation if not handled carefully.

Providing Feedback on Performance Acceptability

Not the least of the benefits of formal performance evaluation is that feedback is thereby provided on achievements, whether these efforts are acceptable or superior, or whether improvement definitely is needed. Without feedback, any employee may think job performance is entirely satisfactory, only finding, on receipt of a termination notice, that management considered the work unsatisfactory. The commission check alone seldom adequately indicates effective job performance (of course, if sales are so poor that the commission is negligible, the implications are more obvious), because it does not provide feedback on performance relative to other salespeople and to management expectations.

Identifying Managerial Potential

By evaluating performance against prescribed standards and other employees, managerial potential can more easily be identified. Thoroughness and promptness in filling out required reports can be one indicator of such potential. Other valuable clues are initiative in developing customers and a territory, attitude toward coaching trainees, and reaction in handling unexpected problems. But these clues may go undetected without a systematic and thorough evaluation procedure.

Uncovering Emerging Problems

Finally, the performance evaluation can uncover emerging problems in time for effective corrective action. For example the cause of an unexpectedly poor sales performance may be found to be a new competitor or more aggressive competitive promotional and pricing practices in a given territory; these may need to be countered quickly to avoid permanent erosion of business. Perhaps the salesperson is in a rut or has developed negative traits (e.g., lack of enthusiasm, too much high pressure or not enough closing push, or perhaps lack of sufficient knowledge about an important new product in the line) so that performance suffers. Family or personal problems can also develop suddenly, to the detriment of job performance. Some of the problems detected can be quickly solved with additional training or coaching; other problems, of course, require more drastic action.

PROBLEMS IN EVALUATING PERFORMANCE

Effect on Morale

No one likes to be critically evaluated, to have performance or personality deficiencies identified, perhaps scrutinized closely and unsympathetically, and then to be directed by a superior to correct the deficiencies before the next evaluation. When evaluations affect promotions and pay increases, as they usually do, the superior's judgment is crucial to job satisfaction, career advancement, and even continuing employment. Of course, the poorer performers are singled out for criticism more often than the better ones. But the performance evaluation and the accompanying interview often focus almost exclusively on employees' faults that need improvement rather than on their strong points and solid accomplishments.

In a typical critical atmosphere (and management will maintain that this is constructive criticism, not destructive, although that is not always perceived by the employee), it is not surprising that morale and motivation can be diminished, far from being improved by recognition and feedback about one's performance. In some firms the morale of the entire work force not uncommonly dips sharply for several weeks after the round of evaluation interviews. This should not happen. A proper balance between support and acknowledgment of good performance and a constructive exploration by both parties of ways to improve areas of weak performance can mitigate the destructive potential of performance evaluation. Furthermore, the procedure is more likely to be beneficial and constructive if mostly objective criteria can be used rather than subjective ratings.

Drawbacks of Subjective Judgments

Although objective standards are preferred in evaluating performance, some firms rely more on subjective judgments of experienced sales managers. Unfortunately, when subjectivity is used exclusively, the judgments' validity may be suspect, and the potential always exists for the problems discussed in the following paragraphs.[1]

Irrelevant personality traits. Initiative, aggressiveness, personal appearance, and resourcefulness are often considered to be important, and even essential, to selling competence, but their actual relationship is suspect.[2]

Halo effect. Chapter 9 discussed how the halo effect can impede the effectiveness of the selection interview; it also can color the performance evaluation. With a halo effect, a rating assigned to one or a few characteristics, whether good or bad, significantly influences the ratings assigned to all others.

Leniency or harshness. Supervisors tend to differ considerably in their overall ratings, either rating most subordinates as high in most attributes, or the opposite. This results in a serious lack of uniformity in overall company appraisals.

Central tendency. Some managers never rate subordinates at the extremes of the scale but rather rate everyone as average. These evaluations tend to be meaningless because they do not differentiate between the better and worse performers.

Bias. Some managers are biased positively or negatively toward certain subordinates, perhaps based on some subtleties of their personalities, appearances, or social or racial backgrounds. The degree to which these managers personally like or dislike the subordinate will affect the evaluation.

Organizational use of evaluation. If performance evaluations are tied in with promotions and raises, some managers tend to be more lenient. Where ratings may be used to compare sales groups, a manager may have a strong incentive to pad the evaluation reports to create a better picture of the employee's effectiveness.

Role of isolated instances. A few isolated instances of effectiveness or ineffectiveness tend to color the manager's judgment of the total spectrum of performance. These instances can be especially influential when they occur close to the evaluation time.[3]

Subjective judgments are also harder to defend in the evaluation interview than are performance deviations from specified objective standards or goals. The result is greater likelihood of subordinate bewilderment and resentment regarding an unfavorable performance rating. Why, then, are subjective evaluations used? Some firms have not developed the controls and records necessary for objective standards. Furthermore, some firms have difficulty convincing experienced managers that their judgment and shrewd appraisal of personnel can be improved.

Time and Effort

A systematic procedure of performance evaluation takes time and effort. Some argue that the gains are illusory. The greater reliance on objective standards, the more time generally required to compile and analyze records. Evaluation interviews take time away from productive selling activities, but the evaluation interview must be conducted for constructive and goal-directed performance appraisal.

Role of Outside Factors

A problem confronting any attempt to evaluate performance equitably is assessing the effect and importance of exogenous and uncontrollable factors. Generally, outside influences do not affect all territories and salespeople equally. But differing degrees of competition, local economic conditions, and even weather can affect performance and should be considered in the total performance evaluation.

HOW COMPLEX SHOULD THE EVALUATION PROCEDURE BE?

Firms differ greatly in the extent and sophistication of their sales force evaluations. At one extreme no system exists for evaluating performance. Does this imply that there is no evaluation, however? No, because people still are promoted, fired, and disciplined. In the absence of a systematic approach, subjective judgments, with all the inherent drawbacks previously described, are relied on. The result may be an inequitable and erroneous assessment. At the other extreme a highly complex system employs extensive numerical ratings and judgments on all aspects of the selling job. Figure 18.1 shows the different approaches on a continuum.

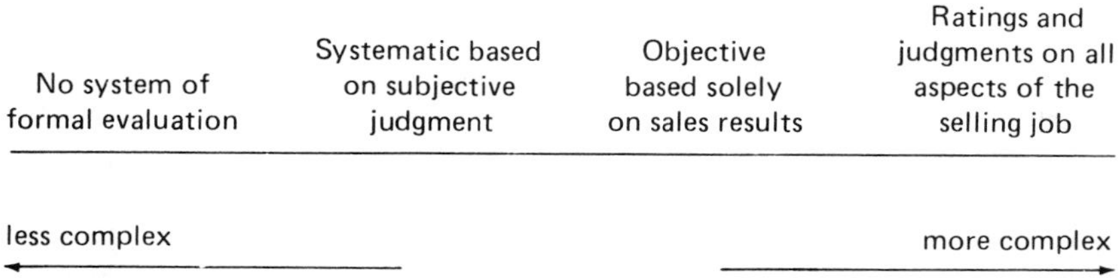

No system of formal evaluation	Systematic based on subjective judgment	Objective based solely on sales results	Ratings and judgments on all aspects of the selling job

less complex ←——————————————→ more complex

FIGURE 18.1   Complexity of procedures for individual performance evaluations.

Although it appears that the more complex the procedure, the more equitable and effective the evaluation, that is not necessarily the case. The time and expense involved in detailed objective ratings that cover many facets of the job have been noted. More important is the temptation, to which some managers give in, to fill out the evaluation forms carelessly to finish a distasteful job as quickly as possible. Often the use of complex ratings leads to most employee's being rated "above average," thereby resulting in performance inflation, which does not clearly differentiate the various individuals or identify areas needing improvement.

Some flexibility is desired in evaluating performance. A combination of objective and subjective standards may be used, with the subjective, or qualitative, used for job dimensions that the objective standards do not clearly reveal, as well as for adjustments in performance expectations because of exogenous or noncontrollable factors. Later, this chapter examines the various quantitative and qualitative bases that can be used for evaluation. Theoretically, the more bases used, the more complete the evaluation of an individual's total performance. But if the bases are ill used and are not wholly accepted by management as of sufficient value beyond the time and effort involved, then a simplified evaluation is preferred. At the very least, however, the procedure should be conducted regularly in a standardized format.

SUPERVISORY GUIDELINES FOR EVALUATING PERSONNEL

Certain principles or recommended procedures apply to evaluation of both salespeople and other employees, including managers. The advantages of the appraisal process itself were discussed earlier. But further guidelines are needed for the appraisal's operational effectiveness. One must consider who should do the evaluation? How often should it be done? Is an evaluation interview desired and necessary?

Who Should Do the Evaluation?

The immediate supervisor should conduct the appraisal, because she should know more about the employee's performance than anyone else in the organization. Some firms include other participants in the appraisal process, particularly people from the personnel department or perhaps supervisors who are somewhat removed from the immediate superior but have had some contact with the employee. Occasionally, firms may ask important customers for input. Other staff departments, such as sales promotion, may also evaluate certain aspects of a salesperson's performance, such as effectiveness in setting up point-of-purchase displays. Some firms also ask the employee to make a self-evaluation. More rarely, firms may ask co-workers or peers to make evaluations.

Self-appraisal is an interesting approach to performance evaluation, although it probably should not be used alone. Some persons tend to denigrate their efforts; others tend to assess themselves too optimistically. Such divergences from reality are probably to be expected, since no one can view herself and her efforts objectively. Objectivity is best achieved by an unbiased third party.

How Often Should an Evaluation Be Done?

Conducting the evaluation procedure on some regular basis is important; it should not be sporadic or haphazard, so that benefits can be gained. Generally all employees should be appraised at least once a year. For new employees appraisal after 3 or 6 months has considerable merit to correct any deficiencies, as well as to assure them that their performance is being observed and to determine that progress is being made on schedule. Some firms regularly review employees more often than once a year, possibly every 6 months. Although prompt feedback is good, the time and effort involved in frequent evaluations may not be worthwhile. If the evaluation process results in improved morale and performance, then more frequent evaluations are justified. But as noted before, sometimes the opposite effect occurs, and morale and performance may suffer temporarily after the performance appraisal.

Is an Evaluation Interview Necessary?

The person being appraised should be informed of the rating, the reasons for it, and the future efforts that should be undertaken to improve any deficiencies. Most managers find that this discussion is the hardest part of the appraisal process, because they must defend their judgment of various aspects of a subordinate's worth before a skeptical, unconvinced, and even resentful audience. However, few would argue for eliminating this step; the subordinate has the chance to explain unsatisfactory performance. Furthermore, the manager has the chance to direct the subordinate's attention to areas needing improvement. Mutually understood and accepted performance goals then can be set for the succeeding periods.

The success of the evaluation interview as a motivational and directional tool depends a great deal on the skill of the manager doing the interviewing. Reference to the employee's progress and appropriate praise generally should start the interview. One of the worst sins managers commit in the performance interview is conducting the entire affair in an overall critical atmosphere. Certainly, criticisms and suggestions for improvement should not be smothered under effusive and even unmerited praise. To enhance motivation and produce willingness to improve, however, criticism should not dominate the interview to the exclusion of good points.

Evaluation model

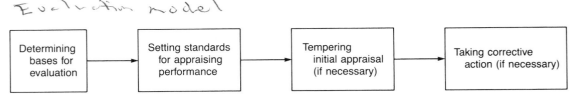

FIGURE 18.2   Four steps in the development of an effective performance appraisal program.

PROCEDURE FOR EVALUATING PERFORMANCE

An effective performance evaluation procedure consists of the four steps shown in Figure 18.2. A major difference between the evaluation process for sales and sales management jobs and the process for many other positions is that the evaluation of sales jobs can rely more on objective, quantitative, performance measures.

Bases for Evaluation

Evaluating sales performance on as many different bases as possible is preferred. Because the sales job is multidimensional, these bases are best used in combination to appraise the overall job performance. Evaluating an individual with only one or a few of these measures might well disregard some important performance aspects.

Quantitative bases.   Table 18.1 shows the more common objective bases or ratios used to evaluate salespeople.

all outcomes quan.

Another quantitative measure of performance is to evaluate by either efforts or results, as shown in Table 18.2. Of course, a combination of the two can be used. Efforts-oriented measures are more appropriate for relatively new salespeople or for those whose job entails a substantial amount of missionary or nonselling servicing activities. Bottom-line sales and profit effectiveness is more readily and concretely ascertained by the various results-oriented measures. The more common specific measures, listed in Table 18.1, are discussed next in greater detail.

The most common objective measure is also the simplest—sales volume produced. The salesperson who consistently makes the most sales thereby is the best. This yardstick alone, however, is seldom a sufficient measure except for certain jobs in which salespeople must find their own customers without territorial restraint, as in insurance, mutual funds, and real estate sales.* In

---

*As noted earlier some ''sales'' personnel, such as missionaries and drug detail people, are not expected to produce sales directly. Hence, the sales-connected measures do not apply to all sales jobs.

TABLE 18.1 Objective bases commonly used to evaluate salespeople.

Measures	Explanation
General	
Sales volume alone or in relation to quota	Most commonly used measure, but does not indicate profitability of business generated
Gross margin on goods sold	Measures contribution to profits
Call activity	
Call rate, i.e., no. calls per day = no. calls ÷ no. days worked	Generally, the more calls made, the more sales; a measure of hustle, not necessarily of effectiveness
Batting average, i.e., order/call ratio = no. orders ÷ total no. calls	A measure of effectiveness, especially in dealing with certain customer groups
Calls/account ratio = no. calls ÷ no. accounts	A measure of account coverage and servicing, but does not measure servicing efforts toward different-sized accounts
Average no. orders per day = no. orders ÷ no. workdays	Does not indicate order size
Account development	
Account penetration ratio = accounts sold ÷ total accounts available	A measure of territory coverage; whether it is only "skimmed," or is well penetrated
Sales/account ratio = sales dollar volume ÷ total no. accounts	Another measure of market penetration, but does not indicate account size
Average order size = sales dollar volume ÷ total no. orders	Best used in conjunction with the average no. orders per workday
Order/cancellation ratio = no. cancelled orders ÷ total no. orders	To some extent a measure of high pressure and lack of customer trust
New account ratio = no. new accounts ÷ total no. accounts	A measure of new business generation
Lost account ratio = previous accounts not sold ÷ total no. accounts	A measure of customer dissatisfaction perhaps due to inadequate servicing
Expense ratios	
Sales/expense ratio = expenses ÷ sales	A measure of the profligacy in producing sales
Cost/call ratio = total costs ÷ no. sales calls	Another measure of profligacy in producing sales

TABLE 18.2 Efforts- and results-oriented measures for evaluating salespersons.

Effort-Oriented Measures	*Results-Oriented Measures*
1. Number of sales calls made	1. Sales volume (total or by product or model)
2. Number of complaints handled	
3. Number of checks on reseller stocks	2. Sales volume as a percentage of quota
4. Uncontrollable lost job time	
5. Number of inquiries followed up	3. Sales profitability (dollar gross margin or contribution)
6. Number of demonstrations completed	4. Number of new accounts
	5. Number of stockouts
	6. Number of distributors participating in programs
	7. Number of lost accounts
	8. Percentage volume increase in key accounts
	9. Number of customer complaints
	10. Distributor sales/inventory ratios

Source: Reprinted from Joseph P. Guiltinan and Gordon Paul, *Marketing Management* (New York: McGraw-Hill, 1985), 341.

more common selling situations, in which territories are assigned, the lack of complete equity in territorial assignment often makes gross sales comparisons unfair. One territory may have more potential—more population, more stores, larger accounts. As previously observed, in greater metropolitan New York, a salesperson might produce in a day as much business as another in North or South Dakota might produce in a month.

Measures of relative sales performance (i.e., the sales/quota ratio) therefore often are necessary, but even these may prove inadequate. For example the sales/quota ratio does not indicate the salesperson's contribution to profit, because she may concentrate on the lowest-profit items that often are the easiest to sell. It also fails to recognize customer relations; for example pressure tactics may generate large sales but will have a long-term detrimental effect.

Gross profit on sales made is a better measure of effectiveness, especially when diverse products with differing gross margins are sold. However, even this method has some flaws, because territorial potential may differ and intensity of competition in certain territories may prevent peak sales in some product categories.

To comment on just a few of the other measures, the *call rate* may vary according to customer density, but compared to other salespeople in similar territories can be quite revealing. A rate below the norm may indicate that a representative is not putting in a full day, is spending too much time with each customer, or is losing too much time waiting to see prospects. On the other hand, a large number of calls per day may indicate that the representative is giving inadequate time and attention to each customer.

The *batting average*, which is the number of orders received compared with the number of calls made, can be an important indicator of a salesperson's ability to locate good prospects and to close a sale. When used with the call rate, it can pinpoint problem areas that might deserve further training or attention.

The *average number of orders* per workday should be closely compared with the *average order size*. This comparison may reveal that a person has too many small, possibly unprofitable orders although total volume may be satisfactory. Although this may be due to smaller-than-average customers in a territory, more likely it is due to failure to sell all the items in the product lines or to suggest sufficiently large quantities to customers.

The importance of gaining new customers, and keeping old customers, is obvious. Indeed, some sales managers consider good showings here to be the most important performance measure.

A salesperson's true worth to a firm is not always easily determined; gross figures are seldom a sufficient measure. A balanced picture with a number of quantitative measures, including cost per call and new accounts generated, generally is preferred to a strong showing by certain yardsticks and weakness by others. Application 18.1 illustrates how a salesperson can look strong if only certain aspects of the selling situation are considered, but in reality may be weak in overall performance.

APPLICATION 18.1   Evaluating Various Objective Dimensions of Performance

The T. J. Thomas Company was experimenting with increasing the basis used for evaluating its salespeople. It had been considering sales performance solely on gross sales. But this method proved to be unfair to representatives in territories with less potential. Also, the type of corrective action or improvement in individual selling performance was not easily determined by looking at gross sales figures. Thus, several other measures were being examined. The following figures show how four salespeople compared using three additional bases:

	Number of Calls per Day	Average Number of Orders per Day	Batting Average (%)
Roger	6.0	2.2	37
Bill	7.0	2.1	30
Linda	6.5	1.8	28
Joseph	9.0	2.2	24

Examination of these relative performances clearly identified Roger as the most effective. Although his number of calls made per day was low, the much higher batting average suggested that more time per call was resulting in a higher rate of closing. Joseph, with the lowest batting average, clearly appeared to need help in

APPLICATION 18.1 *continued*

becoming a better closer. Furthermore, he was probably making too many calls and not spending enough time with each customer. Linda, with the fewest number of orders per day, needed to be encouraged both to make more calls and to concentrate on improving her closing.

The sales manager, however, was troubled by Roger's supposed superior performance, and requested the accounting department to provide data on each salesperson's average order size. The sales manager then calculated the average productivity per day (by multiplying the average number of orders by the average order size). This was the result:

	Average Order Size ($)	Average Productivity per Day($)
Roger	210	462
Bill	305	641
Linda	280	504
Joseph	260	572

Now, instead of appearing to be the best sales representative, Roger clearly was the weakest. Bill showed the most balanced performance. Armed with these data, the sales manager was in a position to work with the salespeople to improve specific weaknesses.

After reading Application 18.1, do Exercise 18.1.

EXERCISE 18.1

1. What explanation can you give for Joseph's having made so many more calls per day? As sales manager, would you strongly urge the other salespeople to make more calls, or Joseph to make less?
2. What kind of corrective action would you take with Roger?
3. Are there additional factors that you think are important to consider? (Assume that all the territories are reasonably equivalent in effort required and sales potential.)

Qualitative bases. As Figure 18.1 showed, some firms use a performance evaluation based solely on subjective, qualitative judgments by the evaluator. Despite a conscious effort to be objective and impartial, this is difficult to achieve in the absence of objective measures and standards. Many firms use a combination of the objective and the subjective. A typical rating form for evaluating qualitative factors requires rating each salesperson from poor to outstanding for such personal factors as the following:

Cooperation

Enthusiasm

Aggressiveness

Judgment

Willingness to take responsibility

Industriousness

Emotional stability

Leadership

Other rated factors may relate more closely to various aspects of the sales presentation:

Knowledge of company and products

Ability to close a sale

Ability to handle objections

Servicing customers

Concern with profitability

Desire to sell

When the personality traits on the rating form are ill defined, different evaluators may rate the same person very differently. As mentioned earlier, some sales managers tend to rate most of their subordinates on the high side, whereas others are more critical, and this hinders the rating comparability. Differences in ratings may not reflect valid differences in performance, on which promotions and raises should depend, but may reflect only differences in the persons doing the rating.

When factors relating closely to the sales presentations are rated, the supervisor may be asked to make subjective judgments that can be more objectively and thoroughly determined by quantitative input. For example ability to close a sale can be determined more conclusively by an individual's batting average than by the sales manager's sporadic observation of the person. Similarly, concern with profitability is best established by the relative gross margin on sales of individual salespeople. Even one's knowledge of company and products and the ability to handle objections can be inferred from actual sales performance.

Table 18.3 shows the percentage of sales managers using various objective and subjective performance measures in a survey of 213 sales executives. The small percentage, 14 percent, measuring performance on profitability of sales suggests that a major evaluation tool is being neglected. Interestingly, none of the sales managers reported using personality traits such as judgment, honesty, emotional stability, self-discipline, and responsibility. However, personality may have influenced evaluations of public relations activities, personal appearance, time management, market intelligence effectiveness, and problem solving.

Quantitative inputs generally provide better measures of sales performance. But some qualitative inputs are desired, such as the supervisor's eval-

TABLE 18.3 Current practices in evaluating sales representatives.

Measure	Percentage of Sales Managers Using
Selling Activities	
Dollar or unit sales volume	81
New accounts opened	71
Calls made	57
Sales against quota or sales budget	54
Number of active accounts	43
Sales versus territory potential	34
Ratio of orders to calls (batting average)	26
Expenses	22
Average order size	15
Gross margin on orders	14
Nonselling Measures	
Nonselling activities such as public relations	90
Personal appearance	82
Time management	73
Effectiveness as market "intelligence agent"	72
Problem-solving ideas	69
Product and policy knowledge	59
Customer service calls or assignments	24

Note: The data are based on a survey of 213 sales executives.

Source: Adapted from Donald W. Jackson, Jr., Janet E. Keith, and John L. Schlacter, "Evaluation of Selling Performance: A Study of Current Practices," *Journal of Personal Selling and Sales Management* (November 1983): 46–47.

uation of cooperation, willingness to accept responsibility, and desire for advancement and self-improvement. These are best used as supplementary input for material that cannot readily be measured quantitatively.

Behaviorally Anchored Rating Scales. Since the early 1980s, firms have focused considerable attention on a somewhat different approach, subjective evaluation. Proponents of the behaviorally anchored rating scales (BARS) contend that identification of achievement-associated behaviors permits a more powerful evaluation. The BARS essentially identifies certain behaviors that appear related to desired performance. Specific critical incidents of behavior are crucial to this procedure. These incidents of both effective and ineffective performance behavior must be identified and agreed on, and they are rated on a scale, usually from 1 to 10. The result is a rating scale, as shown in Figure 18.3, which shows the specifics of evaluating one aspect of sales performance, in this case, promptness in meeting deadlines.[4]

The verdict is still out regarding the contribution of the BARS to the evaluation process. When performed according to recommended procedure, the BARS involves both managers and subordinates in considering in detail

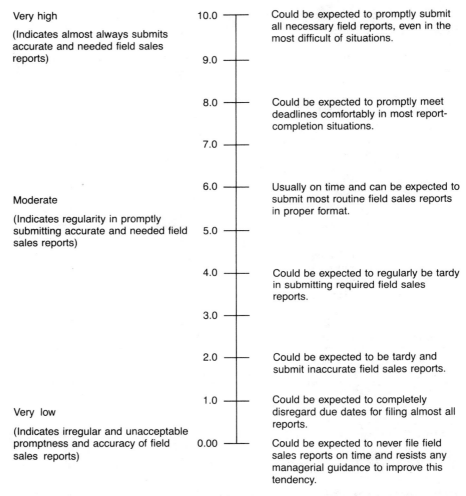

Very high

(Indicates almost always submits accurate and needed field sales reports)

10.0 — Could be expected to promptly submit all necessary field reports, even in the most difficult of situations.

9.0 —

8.0 — Could be expected to promptly meet deadlines comfortably in most report-completion situations.

7.0 —

6.0 — Usually on time and can be expected to submit most routine field sales reports in proper format.

Moderate

(Indicates regularity in promptly submitting accurate and needed field sales reports)

5.0 —

4.0 — Could be expected to regularly be tardy in submitting required field sales reports.

3.0 —

2.0 — Could be expected to be tardy and submit inaccurate field sales reports.

1.0 — Could be expected to completely disregard due dates for filing almost all reports.

Very low

(Indicates irregular and unacceptable promptness and accuracy of field sales reports)

0.00 — Could be expected to never file field sales reports on time and resists any managerial guidance to improve this tendency.

FIGURE 18.3 A BARS scale for the attribute ''promptness in meeting deadlines.'' (*Source*: Reprinted from A. Benton Cocanougher and John M. Ivancevich. ''BARS Performance Rating for Sales Force Personnel,'' *Journal of Marketing,* July 1978, 92.)

the components of effective job performance. However, whether the BARS is superior to more traditional rating systems is still unproven.[5] And this posits additional confirmation of the basic weaknesses inherent in subjective rating systems. Although one can increase the instrument's sophistication, one cannot eliminate the judgment factors that may bias or distort the conclusions.

Setting Performance Standards and/or Comparisons

To evaluate performance on the various bases, some notion of what is par, or reasonably acceptable, is needed. Otherwise, the manager does not have a good idea whether particular performance is good or is poor and should be improved. And the employees also do not know what specifically is expected of them. Two approaches are used in setting standards for the quantitative factors: (1) developing specific standards for each factor (e.g., how many sales calls are to be made) and (2) comparing an individual's performance against the average or median for the rest of the sales force.

Developing specific standards is not easy if they are to be equitable and not destructive to morale. Earlier chapters discussed the difficulties in equitably assigning territories and in deriving fair quotas. Standards for factors such as sales volume per call, gross margin of sales, number of calls, number of displays set up, and cost per call are difficult to develop because of differences in territories, customer mix, and the like. A careful study of how salespeople spend their time may provide data for establishing more realistic goals or standards, but it may be expensive. Executive judgment, by executives who have recent field experience, and some sampling of field patterns may have to suffice.

An alternative to setting specific standards is using performance relative to other members of the sales force. Accordingly, an individual is compared to other salespeople on the bases that have been selected for performance evaluation. (Application 18.1 illustrates comparative performances.) Two alleged drawbacks can occur with this type of rating. First, comparability is a recurring problem, with inequality of territories, conditions in the field, experience, and so forth. However, inequality is a drawback to all comparisons, whether between fellow workers or against predetermined standards. The other flaw is that the overall performance of the group may be mediocre or worse. In rebuttal to these arguments, the quality of the entire sales force probably reflects conditions in the labor market, which are unlikely to change in the short run, and accordingly, a firm has to adapt to them. Comparing individual performance against the average or median for the group therefore is easiest, and the alleged drawbacks are not all that persuasive. Furthermore, most salespeople thrive on competition, and intrafirm and intradistrict competition can stimulate individual improvement.

Most sales organizations widely publicize comparisons. An individual then can readily see how she compares with the rest of the sales force, which acts both as a reward and a spur, and often can be self-motivating without any further efforts by management.

Sources of Performance Information

Information used for performance evaluations principally has three sources: company records, salespersons' reports, and managers. Unfortunately, constraints of time and expense may limit the number of quantitative bases that can be used. A firm may then have to decide whether the advantages of having additional inputs of performance information are cost- and time-effective.

Company records.   As discussed in Chapter 17, a marketing cost analysis necessitates revising the regular accounting classifications (the so-called natural accounts) into functional accounts. Similarly, company records such as invoices and customers' orders are not usually developed to provide a continuous tally of, for example, gross margin on sales by individual salespeople or average order size. Consequently, a separate tabulation may be required to provide such information, which time and expense may prohibit. However, the increasing use of computers, which of course can be programmed to provide almost any desired data combination and analysis, greatly adds to the ready availability of such management tools.

Salespersons' reports.   The reports most widely required of salespeople are sales call, or activity, reports, and expense reports. Some firms also require periodic reports on territorial business conditions and competitive activities. Other reports occasionally used are lost sale reports, reports on customer complaints and/or adjustments, and reports on new or potential new business.

Call or *activity reports* provide information on each call made to a customer. Although required data will vary with firms and with the nature of the selling or servicing situation, the following information frequently is specified:

Customer name

Individual who was contacted

Type of call—selling, servicing, routine, or prospecting

Objective of visit

Results of visit—sales made, promises, etc.

Time spent

Miscellaneous, such as customer comments regarding compensation, complaints, servicing requirements

Call reports may be turned in daily; more commonly, they are summarized in weekly activity reports. Figure 18.4 shows a representative call report format.

The sales call report furnishes the data for a number of quantitative bases by which sales performance can be evaluated. As noted in Chapter 14, salespeople tend to view reports impatiently (because they are time-consuming and often completed at night after a full day of selling) and even with hostility (because management can use reports to criticize and urge better performance). The negative feelings toward reports are further fostered in those firms that make little use of the information that the salesperson supplies. When salespeople's reports are used as a basis for corrective action and as one important source for performance evaluation, there is a temptation to fake or pad them, as examined a little later in this section.

Salesperson _____ Date _____

1. Customer _____ Nature of business _____

   Address _____

   Talked to _____ Title _____

   Status of customer (Amount of LY business, if any) _____

   Objective of call _____

What product(s) was demonstrated?	What service was performed?	What did you sell?	Order Value?
_____	_____	_____	_____
_____	_____	_____	_____

   Time spent _____ Expect to call again on _____

   Request for office action _____

   Comments _____

   _____

2. Customer _____ Nature of business _____.

   Address _____

FIGURE 18.4 Representative call report (LY, last year).

Expense reports are necessary, not only because the firm wishes to maintain some control over expenses but also because the records must be kept for tax purposes. Reports generally vary according to the plan used for reimbursing expenses, as described in Chapter 13. In many firms, however, these expense reports are unnecessarily detailed and even complicated, having been prepared by accountants with little or no perception of actual field conditions. An analysis of expenses can enable the sales manager to uncover inefficiencies, perhaps in routing or in entertaining clients, that can be improved to do a more effective selling job and also to keep the sales costs within a more desirable range.

The sales force can furnish valuable information about changes and activities, competitive and otherwise, in the marketplace. The feedback comes from personal contacts with customers in which information can be gathered about the company's products, its methods of doing business, and any present or potential areas of problems or opportunity. Some firms overlook this valuable source of market information or establish no systematic procedure to encourage it. Some information that should be faithfully reported and used to understand the firm's sales experiences in individual markets follows:

> . . . information about changes in the company's own prices, special offers that were made and the responses to those offers; reports on changes in competitors' prices; statements by customers and by noncustomers to the salesperson; and information on the amount and form of competitors' sales efforts, including copies of their advertisements, indications of additions to their sales forces, and any concerted sales programs initiated by them.[6]

Faking and padding reports.   Some salespeople are always tempted to falsify the information supplied in their reports, especially if they think the likelihood of being caught is remote. The reports most likely to be falsified are the sales call or activity reports. The expense report can be padded somewhat, but the requirement of receipts for major expenditures curbs the worst abuses. Consequently, management must stress the importance of the sales call report and periodically conduct spot checks to verify a sampling of entries.

Rather than faking or falsifying a report (which may result in severe reprimand or even dismissal, if detected), sales personnel are more tempted to "manage" their activities to present a better report. For example a salesperson can easily pad the number of calls made per day by calling with frequency on a small number of "friendly" accounts. Similarly, a salesperson may judiciously call on accounts likely to need more stock and may produce a fairly good average number of orders per day. Or a friendly account might be induced to hold back some orders for the next visit, thus also helping the statistic on average number of orders. This padding readily can be detected, however, if a number of bases are used for evaluation. By comparing the number of calls against the batting average, or order/call ratio (which will probably be abnormally low), a sales manager will easily spot the deficient performance in the first example. And for the other two practices, comparing average number of orders per day with the average order size would single out an area of performance needing improvement.

Now perform Exercise 18.2.

EXERCISE 18.2

1. Can you think of other ways a salesperson might pad performance to look better?
2. How might these other ways of padding be detected?

Company executives.   The third major source of information for evaluation purposes consists of the sales managers and other company executives. Most of this information is qualitative and suffers from the potential drawbacks discussed previously. The question can well be raised whether behavior under the direct observation of a superior, who generally is not in very close contact with the subordinate, represents actual behavior and performance in the field. For some salespeople, observed behavior may be less effective because of the tension or presumed pressure; for others, the observed performance may be optimum and far better than customary. Certain personality attributes, however, such as cooperation and leadership ability, cannot be determined from quantitative records.

Tempering the Initial Appraisal

Both exogenous and endogenous factors can affect a salesperson's relative performance. Although alluded to before, they are worth repeating and summarizing. Exogenous (external) factors include the following:

- Differences in sales territory potential, ease of geographical coverage, and company support
- Differences in competitive activity and economic conditions in the various territories
- Extraordinary occurrences, such as floods, strikes, fire in a major customer

Endogenous (internal) factors include the following:

- Differences in acclimation to and familiarity with a territory
- Differences in time spent in new business development and other non-productive and indirect sales activities
- Extraordinary occurrences, such as windfall sales
- Extraordinary personal difficulties, such as illness and family problems

Some of these factors, such as differences in territorial potential and ease of coverage, should be reflected in differences in sales quotas. Others may have developed after the quota derivation, as could be the case with changes in competitive activities and extraordinary occurrences, such as floods and strikes.

In fairness the personal factors should also be considered in the total performance evaluation. The new person in a territory requires some time before peak performance is likely, because it takes time to meet and become accepted by various customers and to know their needs on a personal basis. And how should one evaluate the sales representative who spends a great amount of time on a major potential customer, only to lose the sale eventually to a competitor, largely not through her own fault? Should the individual be penalized for an effort that proved fruitless, though it had sufficient promise to risk a heavy commitment of sales efforts? Most would agree that some tempering of the performance appraisal should be made in this case and also when a good salesperson had a serious illness or family problems that affect sales performance during an evaluation period. A windfall sale can make one salesperson appear outstanding and the others compare unfavorably. Some modification of the performance evaluation would seem indicated here also. Although objective quantitative bases for evaluation are designed to evaluate total performance, perhaps supplemented with qualitative ratings, the final appraisal often must be adjusted somewhat to be fair.

Taking Corrective Action

When performance deficiencies occur, corrective action is needed to fully realize control. But should every deviation from standard or plan and every salesperson who falls below the median be faced with some kind of corrective action? A general rule of thumb is to take corrective action whenever it is likely to improve performance effectiveness. This recommendation suggests that some aspect of almost every person's performance needs corrective action, because something could be improved in everyone. Certain supervisors accept this rule and closely direct and supervise their subordinates. A few managers, on the other hand, take virtually a laissez-faire, or "hands-off," position, abdicating the responsibility for taking corrective action to the individual salespeople, who are presumably interested in their own self-development. Figure 18.5 shows this relationship along a continuum. There is a direct correlation in most management situations between closeness of supervision and extent of control and corrective action. See Chapter 14 for the discussion of how closely one should supervise and the conditions favoring closer or looser supervision.

Management by exception.   The middle or moderate position on the continuum in Figure 18.5 can be more strongly supported than either extreme. In the control technique called management by exception, the sales manager is apprised only of deviations that occur in selected areas where standards exist. Other less significant deviations can be handled by subordinates; in the sales organization these are usually the salespeople themselves. With this approach to control, the sales manager is not overburdened by a host of

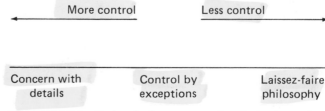

FIGURE 18.5   Scale of sales managers' attitudes toward corrective action.

details so that other important parts of the job, such as planning, are neglected. But subordinates must be relied on to have the motivation and wisdom for self-correction of many performance deficiencies.

Major advantages of management by exception are, first, that management efficiency can be improved by freeing time and attention for the more important areas and, second, that subordinates are permitted more self-management. The latter should improve morale, should help develop a higher-caliber sales force, and may improve overall performance from what it would be with overcontrol or undercontrol. (Later in the chapter the dangers of overcontrol are examined.)

Management by exception has two major disadvantages. Selecting the strategic control points at which any exceptions should be promptly passed on to management is not always easy. If only deviations from sales quotas are reported to the sales manager, many other aspects of performance, where significant improvements could occur, are hidden. Focusing attention on every minor expense item that exceeds median figures, however, is unproductive unless the firm has serious problems keeping expenses in line and therefore temporarily must concentrate on expenses. Management by exception presupposes an effective information system that provides prompt feedback of deviations at strategic control points.

The sales manager should not only be alerted to negative deviations (i.e., performance below standards, goals, or median figures). Deviations that exceed expectancies may highlight significant opportunities that are just emerging, so that plans and expectations should be adjusted upward. For example if a product's sales volume in one territory far exceeds that of other territories, a possible new use or new market is suggested and should be explored and might well be developed in other territories.

The focus of corrective actions.   The manager has a limited amount of time to devote to corrective actions even if a firm policy of concentrating on strategic control points and management by exception is in force. Another question then arises: Should management spend time primarily on improving below-average performers or in helping the top producers become even better?

Focusing attention on top producers.   Although extra management and training time may further improve top producers, giving them a disproportionate amount of attention can entail dangers. The implications of close supervision can be anathema to many successful salespeople who relish their independence and self-management. Most sales managers therefore work more closely with the below-average people to help them to improve. An exception to this might occur with new and inexperienced salespeople who show outstanding promise and above-average early performance. An investment in additional supervision and training may advance these individuals much faster than would be possible if left on their own.

Focusing attention on below-average producers. Giving greater attention to the poorly performing salespeople contrasts with the general rule of thumb that a far greater payoff will result from concentrating efforts on the better customers and the better products than on the smaller, less important customers and the weaker products. Unlike weak products (which usually are weak because of circumstances largely beyond the firm's control, such as limited demand or intense competition, or because the product is nearing the end of its life cycle) weak salespeople usually can be improved with proper coaching, direction, and training. Better-performing salespeople tend to operate near the limit of their efficiency. If the sales manager can help weaker people to attain just average or standard performance, much more selling efficiency likely will result. The following discussion illustrates this more specifically.

The mathematical advantages of concentrating attention on below-average salespeople. Table 18.4 shows the relative increase in production that could result from the sales management time expended with a top producer and a low producer. You can see that extra attention given to salesman A, who is already operating near the peak of his efficiency, still results in a 5-percent increase in performance. Salesman B, on the other hand, can be improved by some 30 percent with the same amount of managerial time and effort, even though, in this example, B has still not reached the sales force median. The gain in sales through increasing the efficiency of B would be considerably greater than that obtained by working with A. Why did B show such an increase in productivity? Poor salespeople usually exhibit glaring faults. They may not be forceful enough or smooth enough in closing; they may not have sufficient product knowledge; they may have abrasive personalities; they may prospect poorly or plan their sales calls poorly. The sales manager who carefully evaluates a subordinate's performance will notice the obvious deficiencies. Many of these faults can be improved quickly with proper guidance; complete Exercise 18.3.

TABLE 18.4 Increase in sales with additional management time.

	Sales in 6 Months ($)	Efficiency as a Percentage of Median	Percentage of Improvement with Additional Management Time	New Efficiency Percentage	Sales Gain ($)
Salesman A	125,000	129	5	134	6,250
Salesman B	55,000	61	30	91	16,500
Median of entire sales force	90,000	100			

Would you recommend that a sales manager concentrate her attention on the very poorest producers? Why or why not?

EXERCISE 18.3

Types of action. The corrective action that should be taken on finding serious deviations from standards or from median performance falls into the following categories:

☐ Working environment

☐ Selection and training

☐ Motivation

☐ Discipline

☐ Standards and goals

Adjusting the working environment. Below-standard or below-average performance sometimes is not so much the fault of the salesperson as of the territory definition and/or the company efforts in that territory. Inequities may become too pronounced, and territorial or quota adjustment would seem indicated. Sometimes, despite the sales representative's best efforts, deliveries, quality control, and other aspects of a particular transaction become fouled up. This can cause serious problems regarding the salesperson's promises and the company's reputation. The sales manager should make every effort to ensure that the sales environment is conducive to achieving goals, and if, for some reason, the environment is at fault, the salesperson involved should be exonerated from any direct blame for performance below expectations.

Reviewing the selecting and training procedures. Most often the corrective action involves working with the problem salespeople directly or assigning them to senior salespeople, or perhaps the staff training department, to correct the deficiencies and improve the sales performance. If a salesperson has trouble closing sales, this perhaps can be improved by example, by training tips, or sometimes by a more formal training session. The cause of poor performance sometimes is the selection process itself. Perhaps not enough effort was made to recruit qualified people; perhaps the selection tools were poorly applied or must be reevaluated. For example a firm may find that hiring salespeople who are inexperienced with its particular industry and products and expecting them to acquire competence rapidly is asking too much. On the other hand a firm may find that eager and highly motivated people, regardless of experience, work out best. The answer, however, is to identify weaknesses in the selection process and adjust it accordingly. If the labor market is tight, though, a firm may have to hire less than fully qualified people and rely more heavily on training and supervision to develop them into reasonably effective producers.

Assessing motivation. Lack of sufficient motivation may cause individual poor performance. Perhaps something in the job situation, some annoyance, causes less than conscientious efforts. Corrective action involves tracing the cause of the lack of motivation and then either removing a source of friction (perhaps by transfer in the more extreme cases) or encouraging a more positive attitude. The latter may involve disciplinary action, although this is seldom as effective as management would like, or environmental changes to stimulate improved motivation. Often poor motivation is related to a perceived inequitable territory or quota or training that is insufficient to generate self-confidence. In these cases the resolution of these other problems may improve motivation. Usually, when insufficient motivation is a serious problem, one should determine whether this condition pervades the entire sales force or is unique to one or a few individuals. Widespread poor motivation suggests a need to reevaluate many operational aspects, ranging from the compensation plan to managerial direction and supervision. See Chapters 13 and 14 for more details on handling motivation and morale problems.

Disciplining.   Chapter 14 also discussed guidelines for disciplining in some detail. The higher the level of the sales force, the less discipline one would expect to use. But few supervisors escape occasionally needing to discipline to improve individual performance and also to prevent a general deterioration of goal-directed behavior.

Modifying standards and goals, where necessary.   Standards and goals sometimes are too high, at least for certain individuals and territories. Being unrealistic, they can only result in frustration over poor showing and lead to job dissatisfaction. When plans are unrealistic (which is due often to external factors but sometimes to factors such as erratic deliveries, tight credit authorizations, and inadequate quality control) adjustments must be made. As noted before, not all deviations from standards or from median sales performances are the individual's fault. Conditions can change, and plans should be adjusted accordingly.

Danger of Overcontrol

Reasonably successful salespeople tend to view close supervision and control with disdain. Too much control, especially of high-level people who are strongly motivated toward independence and self-reliance, may alienate them. The following are specific symptoms of problems within the sales organization:

- ☐ Increased turnover of salespeople
- ☐ Increased turnover of customer accounts
- ☐ Increased customer complaints
- ☐ Increased mail or phone orders for no apparent reason
- ☐ Low morale, which may be indicated by negative attitudes toward the company, lack of enthusiasm, signs of restlessness, and job hunting

□ General decrease in quality of performance as shown by less sales calls, lower order/call ratios, smaller orders, and increasing costs/sales ratios

To be sure, these symptoms can indicate a number of problem areas, ranging from recruiting and training to supervision and control. When other factors can be eliminated, such as compensation below that offered in similar firms, and when there is a relatively high-level sales force, then these symptoms suggest overcontrol and increasing dissatisfaction. Some adjustment of the control mechanisms may be overdue.

MANAGEMENT BY OBJECTIVES

Management by objectives (MBO) is a well-known management planning and control procedure (see Figure 18.6). It involves joint objective setting by a supervisor and a subordinate, and it also is known by the terms *management*

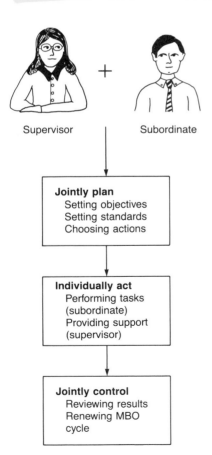

Supervisor + Subordinate

Jointly plan
Setting objectives
Setting standards
Choosing actions

Individually act
Performing tasks
(subordinate)
Providing support
(supervisor)

Jointly control
Reviewing results
Renewing MBO
cycle

FIGURE 18.6   The management by objectives (MBO) process. (*Source*: Reprinted from John R. Schermerhorn, Jr., *Management for Productivity.* New York: John Wiley & Sons, 1984, 464.)

by results, management by goals, and *work planning and review.* In its simplest terms, MBO involves a formal agreement between a supervisor and subordinate concerning the following:

1. The subordinate's performance objectives for a given time period
2. The plan(s) through which the objectives will be accomplished
3. Standards for measuring whether or not the objectives have been accomplished
4. Procedures for reviewing results[7]

Although the most common objectives involve sales growth, profitability, new accounts, and other positive performance achievements, the MBO can also be effectively used as a "personal development plan" for sales representatives to correct weaknesses. The format would then be as follows:

Weakness	*Action to Take*	*Follow-up*
Lack of customer knowledge		
Expense overspending		
Overaggressive selling		
Turnover of customers		
Delayed reports		

With the preceding format, performance weaknesses are identified and jointly agreed on; they are specific and not general or vague. Usually with such specific identification, the action to take is obvious. For example lack of customer knowledge requires homework; customer turnover suggests better servicing and efforts to please; delayed reports should induce efforts to be more prompt. The follow-up at the next evaluation period will be simple, given these identified areas needing improvement. At follow-up the weakness either has been or is being corrected, or the reason why it is not must be valid and acceptable (Application 18.2).

APPLICATION 18.2   Performance Evaluation Using a Management by Objectives Format

Figure 18.7 shows the form that one major firm uses in its evaluation procedure. The goals of the performance evaluation follow:

☐ Foster a continuing communication between superior and subordinate concerning job objectives, progress toward meeting job objectives, training and development needs, and career expectations.

☐ Identify, clarify, and prioritize the key parts of the job, using the job description as a starting point.

☐ Mutually establish objectives that will motivate the employee toward expected performance.

Performance Planning and Employee Development — Part 1

D-1373-1B

Name	Date Employed	Division/Department-Location	Position Title	Time on this job	Date of Last Review

No.	Key Parts of Job	Actual Performance (What has been accomplished?)

No.	Past Objectives (What has been accomplished?)

Overall Performance (Circle Number)

1 2	3 4 5 6	7 8
Needs Improvement	Good	Outstanding

Comments

Employee Signature	Date	Immediate Supervisor (Signature)	Date	Reviewed by (Signature)	Date

Distribution: White—Supervisor   Canary—Division/Department   Green—Employee

FIGURE 18.7 Performance planning and employee development form.

Performance Planning and Employee Development — Part 2

D-1372-2B

| Name | Division/Department - Location | | Position Title | | | |

Future Objectives

| No. | State and Define | Target Date | Date Achieved | Initials | |
| | | | | Employee | Superv. |

Training Needed for this Position and Action Planned

Performance Planning and Employee Development — Part 3

D-1373-3

| Name | Division/Department - Location | Position Title |

Personal and Career Goals as stated by Employee (What, Where, When, How?)

Employee Potential as stated by Supervisor and Means to Achieve Potential (Indicate training, management development, job rotation, eduction needs to realize potential)

Comments from Manager of Function/Facility

FIGURE 18.7 *continued*

APPLICATION 18.2 *continued*

- ☐ Mutually evaluate progress toward meeting previously established objectives, and develop plans to improve performance as necessary.
- ☐ Mutually gain a better understanding of the subordinate's career aspirations, and offer counsel as necessary concerning these aspirations.
- ☐ Mutually discuss and identify the employee's training and development needs.

Note the continual use of the word *mutual*, thus aiming for a mutual understanding and agreement. In this firm the employee first completes the relevant sections of the form in Figure 18.7 as a self-review. Then she discusses it with her supervisor, and officially completes the form. Note the major categories on the form:

- ☐ Key parts of the job (from the job description)
- ☐ Actual performance in meeting these key parts
- ☐ Past objectives (from the previous evaluation form) and the extent of their achievement
- ☐ Overall performance, this being the only "scorecard" section on the form
- ☐ Future objectives, with target dates for reaching
- ☐ Training needed for this position and action planned
- ☐ Personal and career goals; the employee completes this section
- ☐ Employee potential; the supervisor completes this section, commenting on concurrence or lack of agreement with employee's stated goals
- ☐ Comments from the supervisor's boss responding to the employee's personal and career goals and the individual development plan

Benefits and Drawbacks of Management by Objectives

As the preceding description of the MBO procedure shows, the employee participates in the evaluation process almost as much as the supervisor. Employee involvement usually produces better acceptance and more realistic appraisals, with a focus on mutually agreed-on, specific performance goals. Better motivation should result, with a real focus on improvement and personal development.

Critics point out that the MBO concept is expensive and time-consuming. Some also complain that the joint goal setting, which is espoused as one of the key benefits of MBO, does not always occur; instead, the supervisor may dominate the goal-setting process. Some managers complain that identifying objectives in sufficient detail to cover all aspects of the job is difficult. And if management wants an employee to do something that was not covered in the original agreement, how is this to be handled?[8]

Perhaps the major limitation of a result- or outcome-oriented approach, which essentially describes the MBO, is that a considerable amount of time may elapse between behavior and outcome. For example up to a year may be involved in completing a sale of a computer system or expensive equipment. This kind of selling requires a more timely evaluation of job-related behavior to identify strengths and weaknesses so that any improvement needed can be made in time.[9]

To overcome the limitations of the MBO and to give the most comprehensive performance appraisal, Muczyk and Gable recommend combining the MBO with a BARS-type of subjective behavior analysis and also with a forced choice rating of personality factors. Figure 18.8 shows excerpts of the

FIGURE 18.8 Comprehensive performance appraisal for a salesperson.

		Progress Measured in Absolute Numbers and Percentage of Completion	
Objective for Next 12 Months	*Means by Which Objective Will Be Measured (ROI, Quantity, Quality, Cost, Profit, etc.)*	*Number*	*Percentage*
Sell 2000 units of product "A"	units	2000	100
Obtain new customers who will generate $200,000 of business	dollars	100,000	50
Do missionary work in a new territory by calling on 200 potential customers	number of calls and completion of questionnaire on each call	250	125

Part A
Management by Objectives

Part B
Behavioral Observations Scale for Evaluating a Salesperson

I. Customer Relationships:

(1) Asks customers for their ideas for promoting business
Almost Never   1   2   3   4   5   Almost Always   NA

(2) Offers customers help in solving their problems
Almost Never   1   2   3   4   5   Almost Always   NA

(3) Is constantly smiling when interacting with customers
Almost Never   1   2   3   4   5   Almost Always   NA

(4) Admits when he doesn't know the answer, but promises to find out
Almost Never   1   2   3   4   5   Almost Always   NA

(5) Generates new ways of tackling new or ongoing problems
Almost Never   1   2   3   4   5   Almost Always   NA

(6) Returns customers' calls the same day
Almost Never   1   2   3   4   5   Almost Always   NA

FIGURE 18.8 *continued*

(7) Retains his composure in front of customers
Almost Never   1   2   3   4   5   Almost Always   NA

(8) Delivers what he promises on time
Almost Never   1   2   3   4   5   Almost Always   NA

(9) Remains positive about company in front of customers
Almost Never   1   2   3   4   5   Almost Always   NA

Part C
Forced Choice Performance Appraisal of Achievement Motivation

In each of the pairs of words below, check the one you think most or least describes the subordinate being evaluated.

	Most Descriptive	Least Descriptive			Most Descriptive	Least Descriptive
1. Capable	___		6. Thoughtful		___	
Discreet	___		Fair-minded		___	
Conceited		___	Rattle-brained			___
Infantile		___	Disorderly			___
2. Understanding	___		7. Responsible		___	
Thorough	___		Reliable		___	
Changeable		___	Hard-hearted			___
Prudish		___	Self-pitying			___
3. Cooperative	___		8. Dignified		___	
Inventive	___		Civilized		___	
Careless		___	Dissatisifed			___
Foolish		___	Outspoken			___
4. Persevering	___		9. Imaginative		___	
Independent	___		Self-controlled		___	
Apathetic		___	Sly			___
Egotistical		___	Excitable			___
5. Loyal	___		10. Honest		___	
Dependable	___		Generous		___	
Weak		___	Irresponsible			___
Selfish		___	Impatient			___

A "5" indicates that the employee engages in the specified behavior 95–100 percent of the time it is appropriate.
A "4" indicates that the employee engages in the specified behavior 85–94 percent of the time it is appropriate.
A "3" indicates that the employee engages in the specified behavior 75–84 percent of the time it is appropriate.
A "2" indicates that the employee engages in the specified behavior 65–74 percent of the time it is appropriate.
A "1" indicates that the employee engages in the specified behavior 0–64 percent of the time it is appropriate.
An "NA" represents not applicable. The rater circles "NA" when he/she has not had an opportunity to observe the behavior.

Below Adequate	Adequate	Good	Excellent	Superior*
9–15	16–22	23–29	30–37	38–45

*Scores are set by management.

ROI, return on investment.

Source: Reprinted from Jan P. Muczyk and Myron Gable, "Managing Sales Performance Through a Comprehensive Performance Appraisal System," *Journal of Personal Selling and Sales Management,* May 1987, 46–47.

three components of a comprehensive system. Muczyk and Gable admit, however, that a combined procedure is not needed for all kinds of selling:

> Some sales jobs, such as sales clerks, call for the BOS [BARS-type] component only. Other sales positions, such as manufacturers' representatives, need only the MBO component. Individuals engaged in missionary sales could be evaluated on a combination of BOS and Forced Choice.[10]

The authors recommend using all three components for sales managers and for salespeople being considered for jobs very different from their current position.

SUMMARY   At the beginning of this chapter I asked you to consider how you would determine whether any of your salespeople are using high-pressure techniques or other undesirable selling methods. Detecting the use of high-pressure techniques and/or deceptive sales statements often is difficult until considerable damage has been done to customer relations. A particularly high batting average or order/call ratio may indicate very effective sales performance or may provide a clue that high pressure is being used. A larger order size than most other salespeople have achieved again may indicate very effective performance or may also indicate that this salesperson is loading up customers (selling them more than they can use in a reasonable time) and that customer relations may soon be adversely affected. Judicious inquiries to customers usually can elicit information about possible problems in the customer–salesperson interaction. If the truthfulness of a salesperson's report is in question, some spot-checking with customers may be necessary to verify calls and services. Padding of expenses is more difficult to check on, but because most major expenditures require receipts (for all purchases greater than $25 for tax purposes, at least), the problem is seldom substantial. Stated expenses that vary considerably from those of other salespeople in similar territories may highlight extravagances. In general when various aspects of a salesperson's performance are compared with those of other salespeople and of earlier periods, discrepancies become obvious.

The process of evaluating individual performance should help improve future performance. This is not always achieved, however, perhaps because of invalid subjective judgments by the supervisor or an overly critical atmosphere that is destructive to employee morale.

The evaluation procedure can range from informal subjective judgments to highly complex systems. The immediate supervisor should conduct the appraisal regularly, at least once a year, and the employee must be informed of the rating and its rationale.

The steps involved in effective appraisal are determining bases, setting standards, adjusting standards if necessary, and taking corrective action if needed. For evaluating sales performance numerous quantitative, result-oriented bases can be used. Qualitative ratings are also commonly used, although these subjective judgments can cause problems. Behaviorally anchored rating scales (BARS) offer a more systematic qualitative approach to evaluating behavior. Setting performance standards and/or comparisons is particularly important with quantitative bases. Sources of performance information are company records, salespersons' reports, and observation by company executives.

Both exogenous and endogenous factors can affect a salesperson's relative performance, and to be fair some adjustment of the final appraisal may be needed. When performance deficiencies occur, corrective action should be taken whenever future performance likely will be improved. Corrective action may focus on the working environment, selection and training, motivation, discipline, and revised standards and goals.

Management by objectives (MBO) is a well-known procedure for performance evaluation. It involves a formal agreement between a supervisor and subordinate concerning performance objectives and is results oriented. A more comprehensive appraisal system combines MBO with behavior-oriented measures.

QUESTIONS

1. Discuss the pros and cons of an evaluation interview.

2. What is management by objectives? What is the significance of the sales performance evaluation?

3. Are there any disadvantages or limitations to performance appraisals?

4. What arguments can be given for having someone more objective—such as the personnel department or a higher-level executive than the immediate supervisor—make the performance appraisal? On balance, how strong do you think these arguments are?

5. Should the person being evaluated be informed of the ratings? Why or why not?

6. What does the order/call ratio purport to measure? To be useful, what other performance measures should be combined with the order/call ratio?

7. What are the limitations of evaluating on qualitative bases?

8. Discuss the advantages and limitations of management by exception.

9. Sales volume is an easy standard to use. Discuss its deficiencies in performance evaluation.

10. How can the effectiveness of a new salesperson be compared with that of older, more experienced salespeople?

PEOPLE PROBLEM: COMPLAINTS REGARDING PRIORITIZING SALES MANAGEMENT TIME

Please evaluate the alternatives.

You are angry. Several of your senior salespeople have gone over your head to complain to the vice president of sales that you are ignoring them and their problems and spending all of your time on the newer salespeople and the poor performers. Your boss has asked you to justify your actions.

1. You admit the charge, but point out that you must prioritize your limited time. You believe that more ultimate advantage to the company will result from your time spent bringing the poorer producers up to par than would time spent with the already successful people.

2. You defend your actions in #1, and you vow inwardly to get some retribution from those salespeople who went over your head with their unjustified complaints.

3. You admit to a question in your own mind about whether your limited time should be spent mostly with the poorer or the better producers. You and your boss agree that your time should be apportioned differently.

4. After your chat with the vice president, you begin to consider whether the overall performance might be better if you let the poorer performers sink or swim on their own efforts—discharging rather promptly those unable to meet the performance standards—and concentrate your efforts on helping the better performers become even more effective.

5. You request an assistant sales manager who can work with the poorer performers, while you will concentrate your time on the top producers as well as on some of the major accounts.

NOTES

1. A. Benton Cocanougher and John M. Ivancevich, " 'BARS' Performance Rating for Sales Force Personnel," *Journal of Marketing* (July 1978): 87–95.

2. Most studies have found little relationships between personality factors and sales performance. For example, see Lawrence M. Lamont and William J. Lundstrom, "Identifying Successful Industrial Salesmen by Personality and Personal Characteristics," *Journal of Marketing Research* (November 1977): 517–529.

3. The list of limitations in traditional, subjective evaluation systems is adapted from John P. Campbell, Marvin D. Dunnette, Edward E. Lawler, III, and Karl E. Weick, Jr.: *Managerial Behavior, Performance, and Effectiveness.* (New York: McGraw-Hill, 1970), 119–120.

4. A. Benton Cocanougher and John M. Ivancevich, "BARS Performance Rating for Sales Force Personnel," *Journal of Marketing* (July 1978): 87–95. See also John F. Rockart, "Chief Executives Define Their Own Data Needs," *Harvard Business Review* (March–April 1979): 81–93; H. John Bernardin and Richard W. Beatty, *Performance Appraisal: Assessing Human Behavior at Work* (Boston, Mass.: Kent Publishing, 1984).

5. Cocanougher and Ivancevich, "BARS Performance," 84.

6. Alfred R. Oxenfeldt, *Pricing for Marketing Executives* (San Francisco: Wadsworth, 1961), 64.

7. John R. Schermerhorn, Jr., *Management for Productivity* (New York: John Wiley & Sons, 1984), 464.

8. For more discussion of management by objectives (MBO), see Donald W. Jackson, Jr., and Ramon J. Aldag, "Managing the Sales Force by Objectives," *MSU Business Topics* (Spring 1974): 53–54; Harry Levinson, "Management by Whose Objectives," *Harvard Business Review* (July–August 1976): 30. Charles M. Futrell, John E. Swan, and Charles W. Lamb, "Benefits and Problems in a Sales Force MBO System," *Industrial Marketing Management* (June 1977): 279–283.

9. Jan P. Muczyk and Myron Gable, "Managing Sales Performance Through a Comprehensive Performance Appraisal System," *Journal of Personal Selling & Sales Management* (May 1987): 41–52.

10. *Ibid.*, 50.

cases

18.1   A Puzzling Appraisal

As the general sales manager, you must review the appraisal reports of the sales force. The appraisals are completed entirely by the immediate supervisor of each salesperson, the district sales manager. Your company, like many companies, uses a combination of quantitative and qualitative factors for evaluations. However, the quantitative is limited to how well each person is achieving her quota. These evaluations rest heavily on the sales managers' subjective judgments of various personal qualities and of potential for further growth and advancement in the company.

You are somewhat puzzled about Joseph Spies, salesman in the Dallas territory. He has consistently met his sales quota in the last several years, but his immediate supervisor, on whom you must depend as knowing his people best, is strongly critical. The evaluations state "Lacks aggressiveness; is not a self-starter; am suspicious that he falsifies his sales call reports; lacks ambition; is not enthusiastic."

"Rather condemning," you must admit. "And yet, he always seems to make his sales quotas."

QUESTION

What, if anything, would you do?

18.2   A Negative Sales Evaluation

Michelle Hammerstein feels embarrassed and decidedly ill at ease. "Darn these evaluation reports," she mutters. "Not only do we have to devote a lot of time to making them out for every employee, but we also must discuss them with the employee. This is not so bad when we have good things to say to the person, but when we don't. . . ."

Michelle is a young sales manager who graduated 2 years ago from a well-known business school. Although not the best salesperson in those 2 years, her sheer dedication to learning the business and alertness to sales opportunities for the company, not only in her own territory but elsewhere, placed her on a fast track. Now she must discuss a rather poor evaluation report with Max Rudelius, an old-timer with 20 years in the company.

Although Michelle continues attempts to gain rapport with the older man, it is a hopeless task. Max becomes more defensive and hostile as Michelle reviews the mediocre sales performance, the below-average call ratio, the lack of cooperation in report writing, the refusal to help in the training of new people, and so on.

Max finally terminates the discussion abruptly by standing up and growling: "If you don't like the way I'm doing things, I'll quit and take all my customers to a competitor!"

QUESTION

What should Michelle do?

18.3   Andrews Publishing: Evaluating Salesperson Effectiveness in the Absence of Objective Measures

Roberta Edwards is a fairly new field representative of the Andrews Publishing Company, a publisher of college textbooks. Roberta is determined to make her way in a field dominated by men. "Is there any reason why a woman can't sell textbooks to a professor just as well as a man?" she had demanded of the skeptical sales manager recruiting on the campus of the University of Missouri.

Her forcefulness and refusal to accept the traditional business pattern in this field had led to her being hired over a number of highly qualified men. But now Roberta was feeling frustrated. She felt she was doing a superior job of contacting professors and persuading them to try Andrews' books in their classes. Yet, the company lacked specific quantitative measures of performance by sales representatives. Comparison with the company's other salesmen was impossible. In the absence of any objective measures of performance, she felt she was underestimated by the sales manager. She knew that he had hired her reluctantly, and suspected that he had been under pressure from higher management to bring a few women on board. Now it seemed to Roberta that his prejudices were surfacing, coloring his recognition of her performance and worth.

"How do you like your work?" he had asked her at a counseling session a few weeks earlier. She had given an affirmative answer. "As far as I hear, you are doing an adequate job. With more experience, I believe you should do a fairly good job for us."

Roberta chafed at these remarks. "How do you know who is doing an excellent job and who is barely adequate?" she confronted the sales manager.

"We have our ways, Miss Edwards," he said stiffly.

She had to be content with that vague statement, although the feeling that her good performance was not recognized persisted.

Textbook salespeople face a particularly frustrating task, whether with Andrews or with any other publisher. Their objective is to persuade professors to adopt their firms' books for their classes. The university bookstores order according to the dictates of the academic staff, and the actual sales to students occur a few months after the professors have made their decisions. The task of selling to the academic community consists of reminding them of the availability of particular books and ensuring that each professor has received samples of the relevant books for her classes. Because the professors are experts in their subjects and often are biased and highly opinionated, each publisher's salespeople must use a "soft sell" approach; a "hard sell" effort would probably eliminate any chances for a sale. And because a salesperson's visit seldom results in an immediate sale, the effectiveness of the visit is difficult to assess.

A second objective of the textbook salespeople is to uncover professors who are interested in writing textbooks and perhaps already have a manuscript in process. The task then is to persuade the writer to send the material and/or ideas to an editor in the publisher's home office. From here on, events generally are beyond the salesperson's control.

The salespeople are paid a straight salary with a moderate expense account that permits some entertaining of prospective authors and book adopters. Occasionally, a dean or a department head might be entertained to foster a general feeling of goodwill toward the publisher. If the company or a particular sales district has an especially good year, the salespeople involved might receive a year-end bonus. Thus far, Roberta had not received a bonus.

Roberta knew she had been instrumental in inducing four or five professors to send queries to Andrews editors about writing projects, although the home office maintained no record of this by salesperson or territory. She also was fairly certain that several of Andrews' books probably would not have been adopted without her efforts. She had been informed that sales in her territory had increased by 15 percent over the previous year. But her superiors seemed reluctant to credit the increase to her efforts. Rather, they implied that the book list was particularly attractive this year and that prices were a bit higher, and these factors accounted for the favorable showing perhaps more than any sales force actions.

QUESTIONS

1. Evaluate how Andrews measures salesperson effectiveness.
2. What changes, if any, would you recommend in performance measures, in compensation plan, or in other aspects of the sales force operation and management?
3. Do you think Roberta has a justifiable complaint?

CHAPTER 19
Handling Legal and Ethical Considerations

CHAPTER PERSPECTIVE

This last chapter strictly concerns the qualitative and judgmental—determining right and wrong. Although a sales manager may choose not to concern himself with ethical and moral issues, he must know the definitions of legal and illegal conduct.

Consider the following situation.

Jill Marko has received her first territorial assignment. She will take over the territory of Sid Wasserman, who unexpectedly passed away.

Jill came to the firm with good credentials; she graduated in marketing from a top business school, near the top of her class, and was vice president of the marketing club. She seems destined for a fast track, and she realizes the firm's regard for her in assigning her this territory. It is one of the best, having several large department store accounts in a fairly concentrated area. Her sales manager had strongly hinted that a good job here would set her up for the first available district sales management position.

Jill was rather shocked, however, her second week on the job. During lunch, Herb Morris, the buyer for the biggest account in the territory, told her, "I expect you to take care of me, the same as Sid did. That is, if we are to continue doing business."

"What do you mean?" Jill tensely asked.

"Sid gave me a little bonus each season."

"Oh . . . ?"

"Yes. $2,000, cash of course."

Jill gulped, then felt herself sweat as she realized that her sales manager would be out of the country for the next several weeks.[1]

Consider what would you do if you were Jill. As the example shows, problems dealing with ethics and even legality can crop up unexpectedly. And their resolution may be far from clear-cut, with many implications resulting from each course of action.

CHAPTER OBJECTIVES

□ Become familiar with the laws and regulations that can affect sales management.
□ Be able to discuss the relationship between ethics and the law.
□ Become aware of marketing practices that can fall into the "gray area," not clearly unethical but perhaps not entirely ethical.
□ Become aware of the incentives for questionable practices.
□ Understand the relationship of ethics to profits.
□ Understand the major ethical concerns that sales managers face.

GOVERNMENT REGULATION

Sales executives today cannot ignore the influence and constraints of federal, state, and local governments. The complexities of laws and regulations are such that no business should operate without expert legal advice. The following discussion can present only an overview of an intricate and multidimensional subject as it is relevant to sales management.

Types of Governmental Laws and Regulations

Governmental regulation of business can be discussed in three main categories. (1) Federal laws and regulations enacted to maintain competition and to protect consumers, (2) state and local laws and regulations designed to protect local interests and consumers, and (3) quasi-legal practices, including commercial bribery and reciprocity. A few of these laws, which are of major importance to the salesperson–customer interaction, are singled out for greater discussion in the following sections. Although other laws also exist that affect a salesperson's actions, these illustrate the general constraints faced in selling.

Federal laws affecting competition.   Several major pieces of legislation have been enacted through the years aimed at prohibiting certain acts "in restraint of trade" or competition:

Sherman Antitrust Act (1890)—Prohibits monopolies, contracts, and conspiracies in restraint of trade.

Clayton Act (1914)—Prohibits specified acts, the effect of which may be to lessen competition or create a monopoly.

Federal Trade Commission Act (1914)—Created an organization with broad powers to investigate unfair methods of competition and issue cease and desist orders.

Robinson-Patman Act (1936)—Defines price discrimination and prohibits certain types of price discrimination as well as discrimination in advertising allowances, brokerage fees, and special services.

Wheeler-Lea Act (1938)—Broadened the powers of the Federal Trade Commission (FTC) to protect the consumer from deceptive advertising.

Foreign Corrupt Practices Act (1977)—Makes it illegal to pay foreign officials commissions or bribes to obtain business.

Price fixing, in which prices are set in collaboration with competitors, has been particularly singled out as illegal per se. Price fixing sometimes has evolved out of efforts to stabilize or to increase industry prices that have eroded, perhaps due to severe price competition accompanying a supply and demand imbalance. Middle-management people, such as sales managers, are involved in price fixing more often than are top company executives. The

---

APPLICATION 19.1   The Classic Example of Price Fixing: The Electrical
Equipment Conspiracy of 1960

In 1960 practically the entire electrical equipment industry was indicted for price
fixing. Twenty-nine firms, including General Electric, Westinghouse, and Allis-
Chalmers, and fifty-three of their executives were involved. The price fixing resulted from sealed bids (one firm submitted the lowest bid on each contract; the
other firms by agreement would bid higher) so that the contracts were rotated
among the participants on a fixed percentage.

Fines totaling about $2 million were imposed on the companies and on forty-
five individuals. And for the first time, seven corporate officials received 30-day jail
sentences, while twenty-three others were placed on probation. In addition the
companies faced more than 1,800 suits brought by their customers for triple
damages.

Source: For a detailed account of the electrical equipment conspiracy and the factors leading
up to it, see Richard Austin Smith, ''The Incredible Electrical Conspiracy,'' *Fortune*, April, May
1961.

most celebrated violation of the Sherman Act and its prohibition of price
fixing was the electrical conspiracy of 1960. For the first time in the history
of the Act, prison sentences were imposed on corporate officials for conspiring
to fix prices (see Application 19.1).

After reading Application 19.1 complete Exercise 19.1.

---

1. All of the executives indicted were from middle-management ranks. How
   do you account for top management's being unaware of such a widespread
   conspiracy?
2. Can you suggest some factors that might have led to such a conspiracy?

**EXERCISE
19.1**

The Robinson–Patman Act was spawned in the Depression of the 1930s to
protect smaller firms against the vastly superior bargaining power of larger
competitors. It has some of the most important implications of all federal laws
for salespeople and sales managers. Specifically, it prohibits price discrimination as well as discrimination in promotional allowances and display aids.
The Act reads in part:

> It shall be unlawful . . . to discriminate in price between different purchasers of
> commodities of like grade and quality . . . where the effect . . . may be to sub-
> stantially lessen competition or tend to create a monopoly, or to injure, destroy,
> or prevent competition.

The inclusion of the phrase ''to injure, destroy, or prevent competition''
meant that the FTC (which is the enforcing body for the Act) no longer had
to prove that competition was substantially lessened, but only that it was

injured. This quickly was interpreted by courts to mean "injury to competitors," and greatly increased the ease of prosecution.

The Act stipulates that a manufacturer must offer merchandise at the same price to every customer it sells to in a given market, unless a price difference can be justified by savings in production or distribution costs or is necessary to meet the lower price of a competitor. Although quantity discounts can be offered, they must be based strictly on cost savings to the manufacturer, which implies that savings in processing large orders must be definitive and provable if large customers are given any price breaks.

Advertising allowances or any special services, such as demonstrators and display materials, must also be provided to all buyers on proportionately equal terms. (The Robinson-Patman Act has nothing to do with the prices that a retailer sets. Retailers may discriminate if they wish. It is concerned only with the prices charged by a manufacturer or wholesaler to dealers.)

Both buyers and sellers can be guilty of a crime. The purchasing agent may try to coerce the seller to offer a better price, possibly leading the salesperson and the sales manager into a dangerous legal trap to avoid losing an important customer. The seller must be certain that anything offered to one customer is offered in proportionately equal amounts to all customers. In the face of aggressive enforcement, the sales manager must take care to ensure that promotion and pricing policies and efforts to use different strategies in reaching different segments of the market do not result in violations of the Act.

Federal laws aimed at consumer protection. A plethora of federal laws has been enacted, most since the 1950s, concerned with consumer protection and elimination of deceptive practices. Table 19.1 lists the more im-

TABLE 19.1 Important federal consumer legislation.

1872	Mail Fraud Act
1906	Food and Drug Act
1938	Federal Food, Drug, and Cosmetic Act
1951	Fur Product Labeling Act
1953	Flammable Fabrics Act
1959	Textile Fiber Products Identification Act
1960	Federal Hazardous Substances Labeling Act
1965	Fair Packaging and Labeling Act
1966	Cigarette Labeling Act
1968	Consumer Credit Protection Act
1969	Child Protection and Toy Safety Act
1970	Fair Credit Reporting Act
1972	Consumer Product Safety Act
1975	Magnuson-Moss Warranty Act

portant laws, and describing them is beyond the scope of this book. Managers should recognize, however, that these laws make the business environment increasingly complex, subject to scrutiny, and vulnerable to possible legal action.

In addition to new consumer protection legislation, more than one hundred federal agencies exercise some measure of control over private business. Many of these, such as the FTC and the Food and Drug Administration, became more aggressive as consumerism and public pressure demanded action. The FTC is particularly concerned with false or deceptive practices and unfair methods of competition that may hurt both the public and other business firms.

State and local laws affecting marketing. In addition to federal laws aimed to protect consumers, many states and local communities have also passed laws ostensibly aimed at consumer protection. Almost all states have enacted so-called "cooling-off" legislation aimed at preventing the worst abuses of high-pressure door-to-door selling.

Cooling-off laws. Door-to-door selling has been susceptible to some of the worst selling abuses. Of course, there are many reputable door-to-door sellers, such as Avon, and the Fuller Brush man, who is almost part of our national heritage. But flagrant abuses have occurred in sales of sewing machines, encyclopedias, aluminum siding, home fire-alarm systems, freezers, correspondence courses, and a variety of get-rich-quick schemes. Many of the consumers victimized by high pressure and trickery have been the poor, uneducated, and unsophisticated—in short, the most vulnerable.

To blunt the impact of abusive selling practices, in the early 1970s many states began enacting cooling-off-period legislation, and now almost all states have these statutes. On July 7, 1974, a federal 3-day cooling-off law was passed, which provided that in all door-to-door sales transactions of over $25, the customer had three business days in which to cancel the contract and to receive a full refund of all money paid. Thus, the customer who succumbs to high pressure and/or misleading statements is permitted to review the transaction at leisure, perhaps listen to the advice of friends and neighbors, and have the option of changing his mind after the salesperson has left.

Complete Exercise 19.2.

---

1. Do you see any drawbacks in the federal cooling-off law?
2. What would you expect to be the impact of the federal cool-off law on an encyclopedia company?
3. Do you think this legislation should prevent all deceptive and abusive practices in door-to-door selling?

**EXERCISE
19.2**

Restrictive laws and regulations.   Many state and local laws are restrictive in some way and reflect entrenched special interest groups in state and local communities who want to keep out or restrict competitors. This tendency contrasts with federal laws, aimed primarily at protecting competition. Frequently, the large corporation or the chain or discounter owned by out-of-state interests is the object of local restrictions. Many of these laws date from the 1930s, when small merchants' fear of big firms and especially of the chains was at its peak. The influence of these laws is waning today in most states. The various types of state and local laws and restrictions are as follows:

- ☐ Zoning—Types of stores and other businesses are restricted to a given area.
- ☐ Licenses—Certain types of stores, such as liquor stores, and certain occupations, such as accounting, law, and medicine, require licenses. Certain standards are thereby enforced, but competition is also limited.
- ☐ Blue laws—Store hours and Sunday selling are restricted.
- ☐ Green River ordinances—Activities of salespeople representing firms located outside the city are banned.
- ☐ Unfair trade practices acts—Retailers are prohibited from using loss leaders and offering goods at or near cost.

Quasi-legal practices.   Certain practices are condemned at the extreme, but may be tolerated in moderation. Ethical as well as legal considerations may be involved, especially in matters such as gift giving, which at the extreme becomes commercial bribery. The attempt to influence an employee by a gift of some sort can be considered an unfair method of competition under the Federal Trade Commission Act. Various state and federal laws specifically prohibit bribing of governmental employees. And the Foreign Corrupt Practices Act of 1977 makes it a criminal offense to offer a payment to a foreign official to obtain foreign business. No other industrialized nation has imposed this restriction on its business executives. And this is making it more difficult for American firms to compete in those foreign environments where bribery is a way of life.

What constitutes *commercial bribery?* The free lunch,[2] the football tickets, the bottle of Scotch or the fruit basket at Christmas time—is this commercial bribery? Probably not; these are traditional gifts and are commonly accepted industry practices. But where does one draw the line? It is merely one step further to the cash gift, the paid "business" vacation, or the expensive gift, such as a fur coat or a car. Because "modest" hospitality or gifts can escalate into a semblance of bribery and can affect objective business judgment, some firms have a policy that purchasing agents and other executives may not accept even token gifts or free meals.

Reciprocity is another area where abuses can occur. Essentially, reciprocity means, "If you buy from me, I'll buy from you." This has long been common in the oil, steel, and chemical industries. Large firms, of course, have the advantage here, because they are both large buyers and large suppliers. For reciprocity to be operative, a firm's customers must supply products that it can use; sales are traded, though probably not in equal proportions. Reciprocity may take precedence over the lowest prices consistent with quality and dependability. Yet, this practice may be forced on purchasing departments. When prices and quality are competitive, a reciprocal arrangement is difficult to overcome by an outside supplier. The federal government, however, is increasingly critical of reciprocity because it restricts competition.

ETHICAL CONSIDERATIONS

Ethics and the Law

The relationship between ethical conduct and the law sometimes is confusing. Some would rationalize that actions within the law are therefore ethical and perfectly justifiable. But an "if it's legal, it's ethical" attitude disregards the fact that the law "codifies only that part of ethics which society feels so strongly about that it is willing to support it with physical force."[3] Many practices are within the law, such as firing an employee just before retirement benefits become vested, or charging a naive customer more than a fair price; yet many people would see these as unethical practices.

Can actions be ethical but illegal? Violating the fair trade laws, which at one time prohibited retailers from offering certain brands below a designated price, is a case in point. If a firm engages in illegal price cutting, is this unethical? Or is the violation of blue laws (local laws prohibiting doing business on Sundays) unethical? Many people see these acts as ethical, even though they are against the law.

Ethics and Marketing Behavior

Ethics concerns standards for decision making and right conduct. Unfortunately, there is little agreement as to what constitutes ethical behavior. At the extremes, of course, there is not much dispute. For example most observers would consider representing used goods as new as unethical and a "no questions asked" refund policy as ethical. But other practices fall into a "gray area," which is not clearly unethical and not illegal, yet perhaps not entirely ethical:

□ Using handicapped or poor people to sell products through emotional appeals

☐ Using high-pressure tactics in persuading people to buy

☐ Misleading customers into thinking they are getting a bargain

☐ Entertaining clients with call girls

☐ Disclosing confidential information about one customer to another customer

☐ Cheating on expense accounts

☐ Making false or disparaging remarks about a competitor*

Disagreement about ethical conduct arises particularly regarding the amount and veracity of information that should be supplied potential customers in making their buying decisions. This is, of course, less of a problem with industrial buyers and professionals than with consumers. In recent years increasing pressure has been applied for direct legislation for tire standards, unit prices, truth in packaging, and the like, and has resulted in some legislation. The conviction is even growing that anything less than full disclosure is unethical. Yet many sellers still see nothing unethical in extolling their products' virtues (perhaps with enthusiastic exaggeration commonly known as "puffing"), while maintaining complete silence on any known inadequacies. This is simply part of selling, they claim.

Figure 19.1 represents the perspective of ethical and legal behavior, reflecting some of the issues presented in the last few sections. Although most people would consider certain actions as ethical or unethical, legal or illegal, other behavior falls in the gray area. In Figure 19.1 plot the examples of questionable practices from the preceding list. Several points are already established in this figure. Representing used goods as new is equal to point 1.1 and would be both unethical and illegal. Doing business on Sunday despite blue laws is plotted as point 1.4 and is illegal but ethical. Firing an old employee shortly before retirement benefits become vested might best be plotted as 4.1, being legal but likely unethical. And a "no questions asked" refund policy certainly would be both legal and ethical and would be plotted as 4.4. Now, where would you plot using handicapped people to sell through emotional appeals, using high-pressure tactics, misleading customers, using call girls, violating confidentiality, expense-account cheating, and disparaging a competitor?

Ethics and Profits

Many business people assume that the more strictly one interprets ethical behavior, the more profits suffer. Certainly, the muted sales efforts that may

---

*Although some of these practices are not specifically prohibited by law, the FTC may consider some to be "unfair trade practices" that can injure a competitor or a customer.

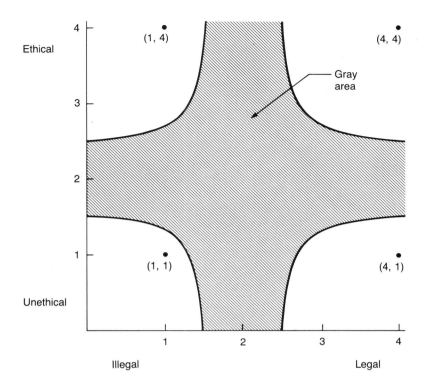

1, 4 = Doing business on Sunday despite "Blue Laws"

1, 1 = Representing used goods as new

4, 1 = Firing an old employee just before retirement benefits become vested

4, 4 = A "no questions asked" refund policy

FIGURE 19.1 Perspective of ethical and legal behavior.

result from toning down product claims or resisting customer hints and even demands (especially in some foreign countries) for bribes or kickbacks may hurt profits. Yet, a strong argument can also be made that scrupulously honest and ethical behavior is better for business and for profits. Well-satisfied customers tend to bring repeat business. An unbending disavowal of the unethical practices of bribery and kickbacks may help to restore a healthier business environment for an entire industry. The firm's reputation for honest dealings can be a powerful competitive advantage. Ethical conduct is compatible with maximizing profits in the *long run,* although in the very short run, disregard of high moral principles may yield more profits.

INCENTIVES FOR QUESTIONABLE PRACTICES

The perception that unethical and shady practices will yield more sales and profits (or are necessary even for reasonable profits) still prevails. Given this attitude, several factors or conditions can be identified that tend to motivate less than desirable practices, whether illegal or merely ethically questionable, such as (1) overemphasis on performance measurement (both individual and firm); (2) intensity of competition; (3) expediency and/or indifference; and (4) custom.

Overemphasis on performance.   In most firms performance is measured by sales and profits. Job promotion and higher pay depend on achieving greater sales and profits. This is true not only for individual employees and executives, but for departments, divisions, and the entire firm. The value that stockholders and investors, creditors, and suppliers place on a firm depends to a large extent on growth. And the evidence of growth is increasing sales and profits. The better the growth rate, the more money available for further expansion by investors and creditors at attractive rates. Suppliers and often customers are more eager to do business. Top-quality personnel and executives are also more easily attracted. This emphasis on quantitative measures of performance, however, has some negative potential consequences.

> Men are not measured on the basis of their moral contribution to the business enterprise. Hence, they become caught up in a system which is characterized by an ethic foreign to and often lower than the ethics of man. There is always the temptation for the business man to push harder even though there are infractions of the "rules of the game."[4]

Top management cannot always be blamed for motivating employees toward questionable actions. An ambitious sales manager, or perhaps a salesperson interested in substantially increasing immediate income, can be tempted to make a strong short-term showing.

Intensity of competition.   An intensely competitive environment, especially if coupled with an inability to differentiate products substantially or to cement segments of the market, can motivate unethical behavior. The actions of one or a few firms in such an industry may generate a follow-the-leader situation, requiring the more ethical competitors to choose lower profits or lower ethics.

Expediency and/or indifference.   The attitude of expediency and indifference to customers' best interests accounts for some questionable practices. These attitudes, whether permeating an entire firm or affecting only a few individuals, are hardly conducive to repeat business and customer loyalty. They are more prevalent in firms with many small customers and when repeat business is relatively unimportant, such as in certain areas of consumer goods and services marketing including used cars, home repairs, and recreational land. Here, unfortunately, deceptive practices and even fraud are not uncommon.

Custom. The adage caveat emptor, let the buyer beware, applied to many business dealings until the last few decades, but today generally does not. Now customers are more knowledgeable and demanding, competition is more intense, and the government often is intrusive. Yet the tradition of considering the marketplace as an arena of psychological combat between buyer and seller persists among some salespeople, sales managers, and also customers.

ETHICAL ISSUES FACING SALES MANAGERS

Potential ethical problems or issues that should concern the sales manager cover numerous dimensions. At the very least, the sales manager has potential ethical concerns in dealing with subordinates, his own company, customers, competitors, and dealers and suppliers. Other relations, such as those with the local community, the government, stockholders, and unions, are less often within the sales manager's purview, although they should be of concern to the firm.

The following discussion does not cover all ethical issues but only some of the more common. Prescriptions or formulas for moral conduct are not offered because morality is, essentially, a matter of degree, and opinions differ considerably about where to draw the line. The main intent here is to raise questions and point out areas of potential ethical violations.

Relations with Subordinates

Fair and equitable. The sales manager should be fair and equitable in treatment of employees, but complete equity will likely never be achieved. As noted in previous chapters, even in designing and assigning territories, it is practically impossible to achieve both relative uniformity of sales potential and ease of coverage; some territories will invariably be choicer than others. Also, the issue of seniority usually must be considered. Does the older, more senior employee deserve some preferential treatment, perhaps in vacation scheduling, special assignments, and certain other matters? However, every effort should be made to distribute rewards and punishments as fairly and objectively as possible.

No false promises. One would expect that no false promises would be made regarding career advancement potential, compensation, company benefits, and the like. Furthermore, withholding justified promotions or transfers to better positions either because of a desire to keep a star performer or because of revenge or retaliation for perceived insolence smacks of unethical behavior.

Cheating. Cheating salespeople on commissions (perhaps through not crediting them for all sales, exaggerating customer returns, or incorrectly computing the value) obviously would be unethical and even illegal. Even if the intent is not to cheat the employee, but rather is the result of a sloppy accounting system or carelessness, the question of ethics can be raised.

Relations with the Company

Padding expense accounts.   Both sales managers and salespeople may be guilty of padding expenses. Expenses may be overstated by quite a bit (if controls are rather loose) or only by a little (such as fudging on mileage or on tips). Some managers rationalize that any padding by themselves or their sales force is justified, because it compensates for niggardly expense maximums on food or lodging or because it provides the needed extra inducement to attract good people. The trouble with dishonesty in small things, such as expense claims, is that it fosters an atmosphere and a practice that can lead to more serious dishonesties and loss of integrity.

Not giving fair effort.   Not giving fair effort can be a greater problem with salespeople than with any other type of employee. Salespeople typically operate independently, on their own, without close supervision, with no constraints such as time clocks, four walls, and nearby associates. Hence, if a sales representative spends an afternoon at the matinee, he may escape detection unless this occurs frequently. What constitutes an honest day's work? There can probably be no agreement here; the extremes, however, are readily apparent as an ethical issue.

Relations with Customers

Commercial bribery.   Commercial bribery, or "payola," was discussed earlier in this chapter. Admittedly, purchasing agents sometimes solicit bribes or "kickbacks," perhaps covertly, but sometimes more obviously. Payola has reached its apex in international dealings, as bribery is accepted practice and even required to do business in some countries. In the early 1970s disclosure of foreign bribery caused a strong public reaction, illustrating that most people feel that gift giving beyond a nominal value has serious moral and legal implications. Reciprocity was also discussed earlier in the chapter and may be of questionable legal and ethical significance.

Confidentiality. The sales manager and salespeople, while servicing various customers, may be exposed to information that might be valuable to competitors (e.g., present sales and profits, new products being developed, imminent marketing strategy changes). Is the customer entitled to have this information kept confidential and not disclosed to competitors or anyone who might benefit or take advantage of it?

Deception and fraud. Moral standards may be compromised in the actual selling situation. The temptation in selling to "puff" the product, exaggerating merits and ignoring any limitations has been noted previously. Puffery can easily become deception, when accompanied by unrealistic promises and unfounded claims. The extreme situation is outright fraud. Fraud is more likely to occur in sales to unsophisticated customers and with products and services that have no repeat business and therefore no need for customer loyalty. Fraudulent practices can range from misrepresenting a used product as new to taking a down payment or complete payment for a product and never delivering.

Relations with Competitors

A competitor generally should not be viewed as an enemy but rather as a rival. Fair play and not "jungle warfare" should prevail. Often unethical practices toward consumers are related to those toward competitors. For example fraudulent advertising that bilks consumers also is unfair to competitors because it takes business from the competitor.

Maligning a competitor. Can a salesperson or company executive denigrate a competitor to a customer? Opinions differ regarding the ethics of this practice, and most would consider it a matter of degree. The temptation is to criticize a competitor and its products, executives, salespeople, and even service facilities. Disparagement is not always discouraged if it is truthful. Since the late 1970s the FTC has encouraged *comparative advertising,* in which the advertiser names the competitors and tells why the advertised product is better than the competitions.

Competitive espionage. More hostile actions toward competitors may involve "espionage" aimed at getting trade secrets. "Spies" may be planted in the competitor's organization for the purpose of getting important information. More commonly, firms hire competitors' executives, researchers, and salespeople and expect, and even demand, that the hirees supply information and perhaps customers. Firms may pirate competitors' key employees, both as a means of weakening their operations and strengthening one's own. The judgment as to what is unethical in these circumstances usually depends on the degree of espionage and pirating. A more clearly unethical practice is helping to foment labor disputes and work stoppages in competitors' facilities.

Aggressive anticompetitive activities. Aggressive actions such as price cutting to drive out smaller firms, discriminatory advertising or promotional allowances, and extortion, generally are illegal as well as unethical. Competitive activity that involves cooperation leading to conspiracy or collusion also is illegal.

Relations with Dealers and Suppliers

Exercise of clout. When a manufacturer is in a powerful position regarding its dealers, perhaps because of size, strong brand acceptance, or absence of other suitable suppliers, the matter of ethics can arise in its use of clout. The distribution channel for a large, well-financed manufacturer with wide brand recognition and customer appeal may not be comfortable for smaller dealers and suppliers, who may be vulnerable to unreasonable dictates and requirements. Although one would expect a *symbiotic relationship* in a distribution channel, with all members cooperating and benefiting from the success of the product(s) and brand(s), the manufacturer dominance may lead to the following (review Chapter 15 for more discussion of channel conflict):

> Manufacturers may create conflict and upset the channel balance by such actions as selling to a middleman's customers, thus competing directly with him; by making heavy demands on middlemen, such as requiring large and varied inventories, special promotional support, extensive service facilities, burdensome payment terms, etc.; by refusing to protect middlemen against model changes and price changes; by making goods available to a middleman's competitors, perhaps to firms of a different type.[5]

Coercion, which may have ethical overtones, also may occur in relations with suppliers, especially when a supplier depends heavily on one customer; that is, when one customer buys most of the output, so that losing this customer would jeopardize the supplier's viability. Force can then be used to obtain special prices, concessions, and advantages over other customers. Although sales managers often are not directly involved with their firm's suppliers, they can make unreasonable demands for services and prices bordering on extortion.

A SALES MANAGER'S CODE OF CONDUCT

The following sentiments of a practicing sales manager nicely summarize standards of good conduct for that position. The theme is "management by responsible example."

You're a leader. That's your responsibility, but more than that, it's your opportunity to influence people and events in selling and the wider world it thrives in.

When you're a manager, a leader, your subordinates look to you for direction, help, and example. It's in your power to set the responsible example. You're on display every day, in your business and far beyond your business.

The manager who starts the day late and ends it early can expect even less work from his subordinates. But the manager who sets the responsible example of starting early and working a fair full day will get the same from his salesmen. More than that, his subordinates will get in the habit of "giving a fair shake" to all others.

The manager who knocks his company can't expect loyalty from his subordinates. But the manager who sets the responsible example of honestly analyzing the strengths and limitations of his company will gain the respect of his men. More than that, his subordinates will get in the habit of examining both sides of a question.

The manager who shortchanges a customer can expect to be shortchanged himself in times to come. But the manager who sets the responsible example of seeing to it that the customer gets his "full measure" regardless of *caveat emptor* will win the respect of customer and salesmen alike. More than that, his subordinates get in the habit of being fair to those people they sell to.

The manager who reneges on a promise can't expect subordinates to have confidence in his words, nor should he believe theirs. But the manager who sets the responsible example of living up to his word can expect his subordinates to weigh their commitments carefully because they will want to meet them. More than that, they'll get into the habit of demonstrating integrity to all those around them.

It can start with one manager setting a responsible example. Others will follow suit. Ultimately each manager must take a leadership role and teach his subordinates the ethics of selling and living: a full day's work and pride in achievement; an honest loyalty to employer and satisfaction in being at work; a concern that the customer get full value because he has paid for it; and living up to commitments because it's the honorable thing to do.

Morality in business can lead to a revitalized climate in the nation, for America is the Reflection of its business community. It starts with you.[6]

This philosophy of management by responsible example expressed by a sales manager over a decade ago is just as valid today. Go out and supervise "by responsible example"!

In the beginning of this chapter, you read a description of Jill Marko's problem with a big customer who demanded a payoff. How would you handle this? By now you probably have identified and weighed Jill's various alternatives. Most boil down to either paying or not paying the bribe; and if the bribe is not paid, how best to communicate this to Herb Morris, the buyer. You can

SUMMARY

readily see some possible consequences of either paying or not paying. If you pay, this is commission money out of your pocket and is illegal, which might have serious repercussions. If you don't pay, you risk losing the major account on your second week on the job. Jill cannot ascertain that her predecessor actually paid off Herb; maybe the buyer is trying to take advantage of a green sales representative. But how would you find out if your deceased predecessor was actually paying off Herb? And how much help will Jill's company be in this gut-wrenching decision? Her sales manager is out of the country and obviously is unavailable for counsel. What would higher company executives tell Jill if she approached them? Can't you see them saying, "Don't do anything illegal." And in the next breath, "You better not lose the account." What would you advise Jill? It is easy to moralize and condemn unethical practices in the classroom but vastly more difficult when your job is on the line. Thus, we can see how acceptance of unethical and even illegal activities can occur.

Sales executives today are constrained by federal, state, and local laws and regulations. Major federal legislation affecting marketing concerns price fixing, price discrimination, deceptive practices, unfair methods of competition, bribery, and consumer protection. Most state and local laws also are aimed ostensibly at consumer protection, but many of these also are geared to protecting local interests and restricting competition. Certain quasi-legal practices, such as commercial bribery and reciprocity, may be condemned when extreme, although tolerated when practiced in moderation.

The relationship between ethical conduct and the law is confusing. At the extreme certain acts are both unethical and illegal, but there are numerous exceptions. The relationship between ethics and profits is less murky; unethical behavior may be more profitable in the short run but by no means in the long run. The major incentives for unethical behavior are overemphasis on performance, intense competition, expediency and/or indifference, and industry custom.

In sales management ethics involve relations with subordinates, the company, customers, competitors, and dealers and suppliers. Each of these relations provides the temptation and opportunity for behavior that cannot be condoned as moral and forthright.

QUESTIONS

1. Can a seller offer a big customer a special price inducement to buy? Why or why not?

2. Why is reciprocity frowned on by the federal government?

3. Discuss puffing regarding its ethical and legal considerations.

4. Discuss the relationship between illegal acts and unethical acts. Are the two the same? If not, how and when might they differ? Give examples.

5. What is the rationale for such laws as Green River ordinances and blue laws?

6. In industries and countries of the world where commercial bribery is prevalent, what recourse is there for a firm that wishes to do business with these firms and these countries?

7. What are two conditions that particularly encourage unethical and even fraudulent practices?

8. What is a symbiotic relationship? Why is it not always operable?

NOTES

1. This example concerning ethics and legality is adapted from personal experience. It is not entirely unusual, as indicated by a similar scenario presented in Benson P. Shapiro, *Sales Program Management* (New York: McGraw-Hill, 1977), 546–548.

2. For an interesting assessment of the luncheon meeting between sales representatives and buyers, see Paul J. Halvorson and William Rudelius, "Is There a Free Lunch?" *Journal of Marketing* (January 1977): 44–49.

3. John H. Westing, "Some Thoughts on the Nature of Ethics in Marketing," in Reed Moyer, ed., *Changing Marketing Systems*, 1967 Winter Conference Proceedings (Chicago: American Marketing Association, 1968), 162.

4. Robert J. Holloway and Robert S. Hancock, *Marketing in a Changing Environment* (New York: Wiley, 1968), 212.

5. Edwin H. Lewis, *Marketing Channels: Structure and Strategy* (New York: McGraw-Hill, 1968), 64–65. For a summary of interorganizational conflict and channel power, see Louis W. Stern and Adel I. El-Ansary, *Marketing Channels*, 2nd ed. (Englewood Cliffs, N.J.: Prentice-Hall, 1982).

6. Jacob Weisberg, eastern regional sales manager, West Chemical Products, as presented in *Sales Management* (14 Oct. 1974): 28. Reprinted by permission from *Sales & Marketing Management* magazine. Copyright © 1974.

19.1   Dealing with Falsified Call Reports

Several reliable sources have informed you that Simon LaPorte had been seen at a movie theater on weekday afternoons. Simon is one of your better salesmen—not the best, but above average. After hearing this information, you immediately checked his call reports. His reported number of calls was slightly below average for the total sales force, but not enough to arouse any suspicion. You were reluctant to take the next step and check on whether some of the calls had been falsified. Checking up on a salesman did not seem conducive to good customer relations, because it implied that the salesman involved was cheating or not performing satisfactorily. But finally you decide to check and to verify all the reported afternoon calls for the preceding 2 weeks. One afternoon each week was found to be falsified. You confront Simon with this information.

He immediately becomes heated. "I give you a fair week's work. Don't my sales prove it? Furthermore, I have to work several evenings a week, and sometimes even on Sunday to make out the blasted reports and handle paperwork and correspondence. So I take one afternoon a week off. So what? Lawyers and doctors do this, so why shouldn't I, as long as I'm giving you an honest week's work?"

QUESTIONS

1. How would you respond?
2. What action, if any, would you take?

19.2   Pirating Employees from the Competition

Marie Hauck believed she had a successful philosophy for building up a sales force. Instead of using other available sources for recruiting, she preferred to get her new people from her three major competitors. She had, over the years, even developed spies in these organizations—usually office people and receptionists who were good information sources about the sales staff and who, for an occasional "gift" or token of appreciation, would forward to Marie the names of promising salespeople in their organization.

Many of these competitors' salespeople were most flattered when Marie approached them out of the blue with a job offer of more money, with a special bonus for every customer they could bring with them.

At a national convention, when one of her fellow sales managers jokingly accused Marie of pirating, she replied: "Call it what you like. It works. And anything's fair in competition. That's the name of the game."

QUESTION

Discuss Marie's attitude from the standpoint of law and ethics.

19.3   Denison-Adler Company: Influencing Customers

Denison-Adler manufactured drapery hardware. Its products, which ranged from traverse rods to drapery hooks, were sold through both department stores and discount stores. To avoid direct competition between its customers, a different brand was offered to each, although the products were essentially the same. A wide variety of goods had to be carried for a full line of drapery hardware, so Denison-Adler, like its competitors, supplied retailers with free displays for merchandising the line. These displays ranged from 6 to 24 feet for large stores carrying the complete line. The displays showed every item and its use and, in general, were a good information source for customers as well as a promotional vehicle. Because of the hundred or so different drapery hardware items that might be carried, as well as the space required to display and merchandise them adequately, few stores carried more than one brand. If the drapery hardware manufacturer could once gain entry into a store, it was virtually ensured continuous business unless exceedingly poor customer relations and servicing problems should ensue.

Diane Horning was the drapery and hardware buyer for the Bi-Rite Stores, a successful and rapidly growing discount chain. Bi-Rite had nine stores in Texas and Oklahoma, but was planning to double within 2 years and quadruple in another 2 years. The large and growing sales volume of these stores made them especially attractive to many manufacturers, including Denison-Adler. Presently, Diane carried another brand of drapery hardware in the nine stores.

Lou Sibley, southwestern sales manager of Denison-Adler, was by no means unaware of Bi-Rite Stores. What made the company even more attractive in his estimation was that they were a subsidiary of a highly successful department store firm headquartered in Houston. This ensured the subsidiary adequate financial backing and competent management people. Lou called Bill Scarpino, salesman for the Houston territory into his office. "Bill, what gives with Bi-Rite Stores? I've

seen no orders come through, and they probably represent the best potential of any account in your territory."

Bill grimaced. "Diane Horning, their drapery buyer, is happy with the brand she has. I've been in to see her half a dozen times in the last 3 months. But she's convinced that her brand is as good as any, and their service has been excellent. I just can't persuade her to change. Our prices are as good as theirs. I think our display is nicer, but try to convince her of that. . . . "

Lou quietly asked, "What do you think it would take to get her to put our display and merchandise into her next two stores?"

"I don't think anything is going to change her mind at this point."

"Would it help if I came along to help you out on your next call to her office?"

"I don't see how. But come if you think it best."

Lou mused as he looked over Bill's call reports. "I see you've taken her out to lunch each time you made a call. Maybe that's not enough, Bill. Did you ever think about that? Maybe you should entertain her in better fashion. Tell you what. Next time you're in Houston, take her out to dinner in some fancy restaurant and then to the theater or whatever afterward."

"I don't think that will work. I'm sure she's been entertained like that before, and I doubt if she'll be so easily swayed."

"Um," the sales manager filled and lit his pipe. "Maybe we need to go a bit further. Remember, you're only asking her to try our products in her next two stores. If she's not happy with them or with the servicing, we'll jerk them out whenever she wants." He paused and gazed steadily at his salesman. "How do you think she'd react if you offered to buy her a new coat if she'd just let us test our brand in her next two stores?"

QUESTIONS

1. What do you think likely will be the result of this commercial bribery?

2. Should the buyer have any qualms about accepting the bribe, as long as the prices and quality are similar to that of competing brands? Would your answer change if the prices and quality are not as attractive as those of similar brands?

3. What do you think would be the attitude of higher executives of the Bi-Rite Company regarding bribery?

4. How prevalent do you think payola is in business and industry?

5. Is there some point at which entertaining and gift giving becomes unethical and unacceptable behavior?

19.4 Dowd Company: Should All Customers Be Treated Equally?

"I've got two complaints about your prices and terms," the buyer of Mathia Stores, a large regional chain of drug stores, told Wendy Casey, sales representative of the Dowd Company, a hosiery manufacturer. "Your markup at the suggested retail price is only 40.5 percent. That just isn't enough for us to try out a new brand."

"Don't you think this new packaging idea is exciting and should be highly attractive to customers?" Wendy quietly asked.

"It may be. But then, again, one never knows. It's just not worth it to find out when the markup is so unattractive."

"What else bothers you about the deal?" Wendy asked. "You said you had two complaints."

"The other problem is your minimum order quantity, 500 dozen. Your firm must be kidding. Nobody's going to order such a big quantity to try it out."

"Well, Dowd realizes that a small retailer probably will not be able to order that quantity. But then, we're not after small retail accounts. We want to place this merchandise in big chains such as yourself. And with 200 stores, what's 500 dozen?"

The buyer snorted. "Friend, I never place a new and untried item in all stores. I want to test it out first, see if it sells sufficiently to be worth wide distribution. And 500 dozen is just too big a quantity for me to test. So unless you folks can be a little more flexible, then no business today."

Wendy consulted her notes. She frowned and then shrugged. "You drive a hard bargain. But I've been given some flexibility, according to the latest letter from our general sales manager. It states that where necessary to get a new account, we can drop the cost low enough to give you a 46 percent markup. Would you be interested now at this special price?"

The buyer smiled. "That's a little more like it. But what about your unreasonable minimum order requirement? I'm not going to commit myself to 500 dozen without testing this out first."

Wendy looked up from her notes. "Our sales manager also notes that although the stated requirements are a 500-dozen minimum, we will accept smaller orders. So I guess this means you can order whatever quantity you want to at this time." She cleared her throat. "Doesn't this make the deal attractive to you now?"

"Now your company is showing good sense. Sure. I'll place an initial order under these conditions. I'll give you an order now for 100 dozen. If sales look fairly good, maybe we can jack up the reorder."

Wendy Casey had been with Dowd for over 2 years. She had been hired after graduating from college with a degree in marketing and was doing well financially, although she aspired to enter management eventually. Something she learned in school came to mind, and made her wonder about this particular sale. When she visited the general sales manager, Marvin Keogh, a few weeks later, she queried him about the possible danger of not offering the same prices and terms to all customers. "Aren't we in danger of violating the Robinson-Patman Act if we don't offer the same prices and terms to all customers?"

"Nonsense," Marvin replied. "We are making these lower prices and smaller minimum-order quantities available to all customers if they just ask for them. How can this be a violation of the Robinson-Patman Act?"

"As I remember from my marketing courses, illegal price discrimination can be perceived if the same goods are sold at different prices to different customers, unless there is a demonstrated cost savings in doing business with certain larger customers, or unless you are forced to do this to meet competition in certain isolated locations."

"There is no intent at discrimination here, Wendy. Besides, we must have some flexibility in our marketing efforts."

QUESTIONS

1. Do you think this practice is in violation of the Robinson-Patman Act?
2. Could this situation with the customer have been better handled? If so, how?
3. What kind of constraints does the Robinson-Patman Act impose on the selling situation?

Index

Activity reports. *See* Reports
Advertisements, recruiting, 225
Advertising allowances, 538
Allocating sales efforts, 262–263
Analysis of sales volume. *See* Sales analysis
Application blanks, 230–231
  weighted, 231–234
Approach, 49
Aptitude tests. *See* Testing
Attitude surveys, 430
Autocratic direction, 375–376
Automobiles. *See* Transportation

Bad debts, 358
Batting average, in performance evaluation, 52, 506
Behaviorally anchored rating scales, 509–510
Benefits, of good customer service, 421–422
Blue laws, 540–541
Boomerang method of handling objections, 52
Bonuses, 347, 353–354

Branch organization, 199–200
Bribes. *See* Commercial bribery
Budgeting
  benefits of, 158–159
  methods for controllable costs, 164–167
  procedure for, 162
  relationship to planning, 80
  requirements, 168–171
  special problems in, 171
Budgets
  alternative, 169
  flexible, 169
  rolling, 169–171
  types, 160–161

Call patterns, 257–258
Call rate, in performance evaluation, 505–506
Call reports. *See* Reports
Canned presentations, 51
Career paths, 402
Caveat emptor, 545
Centralized organization, 212
Centralized staffing, 212

Channel, 410–411, 415–416
Civil Rights Act, Title VII, 17, 220, 236
Clayton Act, 536
Closing, 52
Code of conduct, 548–549
Commercial bribery, 540
Comparative advertising, 547
Compensation
    characteristics, 340–341
    fringe benefits, 355–356
    level of earnings, 344–346
    payment method, 346–347
    problems, 356–359
    types, 350–355
Computers, 32–33
    customer service, 427–428
    forecasting and planning, 129, 137–138
Conferences. *See* Meetings
Contests, 397–400
Controlling. *See also* Evaluation of
        performance
    danger of overcontrol, 520–521
    nature of, 444–445
    role in planning, 69, 73
Conventions. *See* Meetings
Cooling-off laws, 539
Cooperative advertising, 417
Correlation analysis in forecasting,
        135–137
Customer analysis, 112–113
Customer expectations, use in
        forecasting, 130
Customer orientation, 5, 11
Customer, 55–57
    screening, 45–46, 419–420
Customer service
    abuses, 431–432
    benefits, 421–422
    costs, 422
    definition, 421
    handling complaints, 426–427
    improving delivery, 424
    intangible, 427–428
    measures of customer satisfaction,
        429–431
    types of, 422–424
Customer specialization, 197–198

Deadly parallel, 183–184
Decentralized organization, 187–188
Decentralized staffing, 212
Delegation, 182, 387–389
Delphi method of forecasting, 131
Departmentalization, 183–184
Detail men, 24
Directing. *See* Supervision
Disciplining, 390–393
Discrimination, 17, 220
Displays, 418–419
Distribution cost analysis. *See*
        Marketing cost analysis
Door-to-door selling, 24
Dual contribution to a sale, 356–357
Dun and Bradstreet, 48
Dyadic relationship, 54

Ego drive, 218
Eighty-Twenty (80-20) rule, 112, 415,
        470, 482
Empathy, 382
Entertainment, 360, 542
Equal Employment Opportunity
        Commission (EEOC), 220–230
Espionage, competitive, 547–548
Ethical problems, 541–548
Ethics, 541
Evaluation of performance
    individual
        bases for, evaluation, 503–509
        behaviorally anchored rating
            scales, 509–510
        corrective action, 516–520
        guidelines, 501–502
        problems, 498–500
        setting standards, 510–514
        sources of information, 511–515
    overall performance, 446–447
        marketing cost analysis, 470–
            484
        problems, 455–456
        sales analysis, 447–454
        sources of market share data,
            459–460. *See also* Controlling
Executive opinion, in forecasting,
        128–129
Expense reports. *See* Reports

Expenses
    controlling, 359–360, 362
    importance in total operation, 359
    Internal Revenue Service
        regulations, 361
    objectives of expense plan, 360–361
    padding, 514
    types of expense plans, 361–363
    types of expenses, 359–360
Expert opinion, in forecasting, 130
Exponential smoothing, as method of
        forecasting, 134–135

Fair trade laws, 541
Federal Trade Commission (FTC), 426,
        536–539
Following up, 53
Food brokers, 194
Forecasting. *See* Sales forecasting
Foreign Corrupt Practices Act, 536,
        540
Fraud, 547
Fringe benefits, 355–356

Gifts, 361
Girard, Joe, 26
Goals. *See* Objectives
Government. *See also* Cooling-off laws;
        Equal Employment Opportunity
        Commission; Fair trade laws;
        Federal Trade Commission;
        Internal Revenue Service; Legal
        problems; Office of Federal
        Contract Compliance;
        Robinson-Patman Act; Uniform
        Sales Act; Unfair trade practices
        acts; U.S. Censuses
    as customer, 31
    as regulator, 31, 536
Green River ordinances, 540
Grievances, handling, 389–390
Guarantees, 423

Herzberg's theory, 378
Honor awards, 401
House accounts, 357
Human factor in organization, 200–202
Human relations. *See* Morale

Iacocca, Lee, 14
Iceberg principle, 448–449
Informal organization, 201
Intangible customer service, 427–428
Intelligence tests. *See* Testing
Intensity of distribution, 420–421
Internal Revenue Service, 361
Interview. *See* Selection

Job analysis, 215–216

Leading indicators, 136
Legal problems, 536–540

Mail order sales, 357
Major accounts, 31–32
Management, general functions, 8–9
Management by exception, 516–517
Management by objectives, 521–528
Marketing audit, 484–487
Market factor, 96–97
Market index, 96–98
Market information, 84–87
Marketing concept, 5
Marketing cost analysis
    accounting system, 471
    areas for corrective action, 479–483
    contribution to margin method,
        477–488
    full-cost method, 472–477
    nature of, 470–472
    new product, 482–484
    problems, 476–479
    procedure, 472–476
    types of costs, 471–472
    use of findings, 473–476
Marketing mix, 4
Marketing research, 85–86
Market intelligence. *See* Market
        information
Market log, 85–86
Market potential. *See* Potentials
Market Research Corporation of
        America (MRCA), 459–460
Market share analysis, 454–460
Maslow's theory, 377–378
Meetings, 322–324, 385–386, 394–
        395, 459–460

Merchandise returns, 357–358
Metropolitan areas, 266
Missionary salespeople, 24, 418–419
Models, mathematical, 166
Moody's Industrial Manual, 48
Morale, 338
Motivation, 339–342, 376–379
Moving averages, method of
    forecasting, 131–133

Nielsen, A. C., Company, 459–460
Nonselling assignments, 359

Objections, meeting, 51–52
Objectives, 74–76, 82
Office of Federal Contract Compliance
    (OFCC), 220
On-the-job training, 319
Opinion surveys, 128–131
Organization, 185–197
    branch, 199–200
    departmentalization, 183–184
    essentials of, 182–183
    of field sales, 199
    informal, 201

Padding expenses, 362, 514
Participatory direction, 375–376
Payola. *See* Commercial bribery
Performance. *See* Evaluation of
    performance
Personal interviews. *See* Selection
Personality tests. *See* Selection
Pirating, 547–548
Planning. *See also* Strategic planning
    computer use in, 11
    reasons for, 68
    sales manager's role in, 80–84
    sources of information for, 85–87
    steps in, 72–73
    types of, 70–71
Portfolio analysis, 76–77
Potentials. *See also* Sales forecasts
    data, 100–104
    definitions, 94–95
    limitations, 116

measuring, 99–100
need for determining, 94
new products, 98–99
steps in determining, 96–100
uses of, 109–115, 449–451
Price cutting, 548
Price fixing, 536
Production function, 75–76
Product manager, 196–197
Product-opportunity matrix, 77
Product specialization, 196–197
Profit Impact of Market Study
    (P.I.M.S.), 76
Promotion mix, 4–5
Prospecting and qualifying, 45
Puffing, 547
Pull techniques, 417–418
Push techniques 417–418

Quality control, 424
Quantity discounts, 538
Quotas. *See* Sales quotas

Reciprocity, 541
Recognition awards, 401
Recruiting, 222–227
References, 234–235
Regression analysis. *See* Correlation
    analysis in forecasting
Reports, sales force, 386–387, 513–
    514
Response function, 262–263
Robinson-Patman Act, 414, 536–538
Role playing, 294
Routing, 273–275. *See also* Territories

Salary plans. *See* Compensation
Sales analysis, 447–453
Sales executive. *See* Sales management
Sales force, use in forecasting, 129–
    130
Sales forecasts. *See also* Potentials
    accuracy, 78–79
    computer use in, 137
    criteria, 146–148

Sales forecasts *continued*
  factors affecting, 124
  importance of, 125–126
  limitations, 142–145
  procedure, 127–128
Sales forecasting
  evaluation of, 140–142
  qualitative, 128–131
  quantitative, 131–140
Sales jobs
  activities besides selling, 25–26
  career opportunities, 11–15
  classification of, 23–25
  importance of, 5–7
  success, 27–30
Sales management
  compensation, 12–13
  drawbacks, 15
  levels of, 10, 11
  relationship to marketing, 4–5
  women in, 17
Salesmanship. *See* Selling process
Sales meetings. *See* Meetings
Salesperson performance. *See*
      Evaluation of performance
Sales potentials. *See* Potentials
Sales promotion, 4
Sales quotas
  adjusting base, 294–297
  administering, 297–299
  attributes of good quota, 290–291
  cautions, 298
  determining base, 292–294
  developing, 291–297
  setting, 110–111
  types, 288–290
  uses, 449, 452–453
Sales territories. *See* Territories;
      Routing
Scheduling. *See* Routing
Selection
  application blank, 230–234
  evaluation of process, 241
  interview, 235–241
  preliminary screening, 228–229
  references, 234–235
  testing, 236–237

Self-development, 320
Selling
  classified, 23–24
  costs, 6
  transition from, 34–36
  trends, 30–34
  types of jobs, 22–23
Selling expenses. *See* Expenses
Selling process, 44–54
  closing, 52
  follow-up, 53
  prospecting, 45–46
  sales presentation, 50–52
Service. *See* Customer service
Sherman Antitrust Act, 536–537
Simulation, 166–167
Small order problems, 415
Social responsibilities. *See* Ethical
      problems
Sources of salespeople, 224–226
Span of supervision, 186–187
Speedata services, 459
Staffing, 212–222. *See also* Recruiting;
      Selection
Standard Industrial Classification
      System (SIC), 102–103, 112–
      115, 480
Standard and Poor's Register of
      Corporations, Directors and
      Executives, 48
Statistical Abstract of U.S., 103
Strategic planning, 71–73
  business unit goals, 75–76
  steps, 72
Strategic window, 77–78
Supervision
  degree of, 383–384
  directing, 374–375
  following-up, 383
  motivating, 376–379
  planning, 314
  incentives, using, 394–402
  methods, 384–387
  problems, 389–393
  span, 186–187
Survey of Buying Power, 104
Survey of Current Business, 103

Survey of Industrial Purchasing Power, 104, 108, 114–115
Survey of Selling Costs, 6, 104, 363
Symbiotic relationship, 408, 411–412, 548
Systems selling, 31

Technical specialists, 24, 212–218
Telemarketing, 32
Telephone sales, 357
Territories. *See also* Routing
  administering, 272–273
  assigning salespeople, 268–270
  defining, 109
  designing, 266–267
  dividing, 256–263
  establishing, 252–253
  revising, 270–272
  setting up, 253–256
Testing
  evaluation, 237
  types of tests, 236–237
Test markets, 101
Thomas Register of American
    Manufacturers, 48
Time management, 57–59
Trade associations, 104
Trading areas, 266–267
Training
  benefits, 308–309
  categories, 308
  centralized, 322–323
  content, 314–317
  costs, 324–325
  decentralized, 323–324
  duration, 312–313
  evaluating, 327–328
  location, 322–324
  methods, 318–320
  responsibility for, 320–322
  scope, 311–313
  timing, 322
Transportation, 356, 361
Travel expenses. *See* Expenses
Trend analysis, in forecasting, 131–133

Unfair trade practices acts, 540
Uniform Sales Act, 423
U.S. Censuses, 102–103

Visual aids, 51

Warranties, 423
Weighted application blank, 231–234
Wheeler-Lea Act, 536
Windfalls, 358
Women in sales, 220–221
Women in sales management, 17

WE VALUE YOUR OPINION—PLEASE SHARE IT WITH US

Merrill Publishing and our authors are most interested in your reactions to this textbook. Did it serve you well in the course? If it did, what aspects of the text were most helpful? If not, what didn't you like about it? Your comments will help us to write and develop better textbooks. We value your opinions and thank you for your help.

Text Title _____ Edition _____

Author(s) _____

Your Name (optional) _____

Address _____

City _____ State _____ Zip _____

School _____

Course Title _____

Instructor's Name _____

Your Major _____

Your Class Rank _____ Freshman _____ Sophomore _____ Junior _____ Senior

_____ Graduate Student

Were you required to take this course? _____ Required _____ Elective

Length of Course? _____ Quarter _____ Semester

1. Overall, how does this text compare to other texts you've used?

_____ Superior _____ Better Than Most _____ Average _____ Poor

2. Please rate the text in the following areas:

	Superior	Better Than Most	Average	Poor
Author's Writing Style	_____	_____	_____	_____
Readability	_____	_____	_____	_____
Organization	_____	_____	_____	_____
Accuracy	_____	_____	_____	_____
Layout and Design	_____	_____	_____	_____
Illustrations/Photos/Tables	_____	_____	_____	_____
Examples	_____	_____	_____	_____
Problems/Exercises	_____	_____	_____	_____
Topic Selection	_____	_____	_____	_____
Currentness of Coverage	_____	_____	_____	_____
Explanation of Difficult Concepts	_____	_____	_____	_____
Match-up with Course Coverage	_____	_____	_____	_____
Applications to Real Life	_____	_____	_____	_____

3. Circle those chapters you especially liked:
   1   2   3   4   5   6   7   8   9   10   11   12   13   14   15   16   17   18   19   20
   What was your favorite chapter? _____
   Comments:

4. Circle those chapters you liked least:
   1   2   3   4   5   6   7   8   9   10   11   12   13   14   15   16   17   18   19   20
   What was your least favorite chapter? _____
   Comments:

5. List any chapters your instructor did not assign. _____

6. What topics did your instructor discuss that were not covered in the text? _____

   _____

7. Were you required to buy this book? _____ Yes _____ No

   Did you buy this book new or used? _____ New _____ Used

   If used, how much did you pay? _____

   Do you plan to keep or sell this book? _____ Keep _____ Sell

   If you plan to sell the book, how much do you expect to receive? _____

   Should the instructor continue to assign this book? _____ Yes _____ No

8. Please list any other learning materials you purchased to help you in this course (e.g., study guide, lab manual).

   _____

9. What did you like most about this text? _____

   _____

10. What did you like least about this text? _____

   _____

11. General comments:

   May we quote you in our advertising? _____ Yes _____ No

   Please mail to: Boyd Lane
                     College Division, Research Department
                     Box 508
                     1300 Alum Creek Drive
                     Columbus, Ohio 43216

   Thank you!